I0822109

Old Testament Introduction

Robin Routledge has now produced an invaluable companion volume to his highly successful *Old Testament Theology*. He gives a comprehensive orientation to all the dimensions of the study of the Old Testament, including canon, text, criticism and forms of interpretation, as well as an in-depth treatment of each individual book, and extensive bibliographical resources. Scholarly and lucid, it is designed especially for those who want to understand how to read the Old Testament as Christian Scripture, while doing justice to its nuances and enormous diversity. I commend it warmly.
Gordon McConville, Professor of Old Testament Theology, University of Gloucestershire

Robin Routledge

Old Testament Introduction

Text, Interpretation, Structure, Themes

APOLLOS (an imprint of Inter-Varsity Press)
36 Causton Street, London SW1P 4ST, England
Email: ivp@ivpbooks.com
Website: www.ivpbooks.com

First published 2016

British Library Cataloguing-in-Publication Data
A catalogue record for this book is available from the British Library.

ISBN: 978–1–78359–429–0
ebook ISBN: 978–1–78359–488–7

Set in Monotype Garamond 11/13pt
Typeset in Great Britain by CRB Associates, Potterhanworth, Lincolnshire
Printed and bound in Great Britain by Jellyfish Print Solutions

Inter-Varsity Press publishes Christian books that are true to the Bible and that communicate the gospel, develop discipleship and strengthen the church for its mission in the world.

IVP originated within the Inter-Varsity Fellowship, now the Universities and Colleges Christian Fellowship, a student movement connecting Christian Unions in universities and colleges throughout Great Britain, and a member movement of the International Fellowship of Evangelical Students. Website: www.uccf.org.uk. That historic association is maintained, and all senior IVP staff and committee members subscribe to the UCCF Basis of Faith.

CONTENTS

PREFACE

The OT is part of the canon of Christian Scripture, and as such has continuing significance for the church. However, the writings are set within a different historical era, a different culture and a different religious context that often incorporates unfamiliar worship practices. As a result, in order to understand the OT in a meaningful way, it must be read against its historical, cultural and theological background. My aim here is to provide readers with the relevant information to enable them to engage with the text. This will include discussion of date, authorship, the writers' intention and purpose, as well as significant textual issues. It will include, too, discussion of key scholarly approaches to the text, including historical-critical and literary approaches. And, because a key aim in facilitating understanding of the OT is that Christian believers are better able to interpret the text in order to apply it to current belief and praxis, it will also include substantial discussion of exegetical and hermeneutical approaches to the OT. There has been an increase in discussions in these areas in recent years, and it is easy for readers to become overwhelmed with the volume of material available. Part of the intention of this OT introduction is to provide an overview of relevant approaches, and to offer some guidance through what can appear to be a maze of new treatments and terminology. There will also be some discussion of key theological themes; though this will be kept to a minimum. For a more detailed treatment of theological issues, the reader is referred to commentaries and OT theologies, including my own.

Of course, it is impossible to look at the OT without considering the books that make it up, and there will also be some discussion of individual books, but because of the constraints of space, that must, necessarily, be limited. There will, however, be substantial footnotes, which point to more detailed discussion, and references to key texts for further reading, including lists of commentaries on individual books.

Following the discussion in the opening chapter of the significance of the OT, which seems a necessary starting point in that it is what justifies and motivates the study of the text, it seems logical, next, to enquire in more detail into what constitutes the OT. That, too, seems determinative for all that follows, and so chapter 2 focuses on the canon and text of the OT. Because of the significance of context, chapter 3 goes on to consider the world in which the OT came to be written: primarily its geographical, historical and literary background. This is followed by discussion of different genres present in the OT and the significance of genre for interpretation (ch. 4). Then, with much of the groundwork set out, chapter 5 will look, more particularly, at exegetical and hermeneutical approaches to the text, including what has become an important area of recent discussion: the location of a text's meaning, and the significance of the author's intention. The rest of the volume will then offer more specific introductions to the sections of the OT and of individual OT books; noting key distinctive issues and pointing to sources for further study. For convenience, particularly in the grouping of similar material, this follows the canonical order of the Hebrew text.

Like my previous volume, this book has grown out of a teaching context, and it is my hope that it will be of value to students. It has also grown out of many years of experience as a Christian minister, and I hope, too, that the emphasis on interpretation will be helpful to those teaching and preaching on OT texts.

As before, I refer to BC and AD, rather than the more widespread BCE and CE, reflecting my conviction that the coming of Jesus Christ marks a turning point in history, and that, while it has significance in its own right, the OT also points forward to, and finds its fulfilment in, him.

ACKNOWLEDGMENTS

This book is the result of several years' work, and I want to express my thanks to those who have helped me reach this point with it. I continue to be indebted to Martin Selman, who nurtured my love for the OT, and to John Rogerson, who encouraged me throughout my PhD studies. I am grateful, too, for friends and colleagues at Mattersey Hall, and to several cohorts of students, at Mattersey and elsewhere around the world, who have helped me 'try out' and develop the material that has found its way into this volume. Their comments and challenging questions have been very valuable in keeping me on my toes, and helping me to produce a volume that, I trust, will be useful to them and others.

My thanks, too, to Philip Duce, Eldo Barkhuizen and the team at IVP and SPCK, for their support, encouragement, hard work and considerable patience, especially during the recent period of significant transition.

Finally, my thanks to my family. To my wife and best friend, Ailsa, who has patiently borne with me when I have kept disappearing into the study to 'do just a little bit more'. I am glad that I can now answer her frequent, and quite understandable, question 'Isn't it finished yet?!' in the affirmative. Thanks, too, to my children and especially the grandchildren, Darcey, Rex, Lucas and Leo, who have seen much less of me over the last year or two than they might have liked. Whenever they come round they are now accustomed to go straight to the study to look for Granda. I am sure they think I live there! They seem to be of the opinion that playing with them should be my first priority. Darcey (6) recently asked me 'Are you being an author?' When I rather proudly said that I was, she replied 'Well stop it.' Now that this book is finished, I hope to be able to give them a little more attention. My apologies to them, though, that there are not more pictures!

ABBREVIATIONS

1QIsa[a]	1QIsaiah[a] (1QIsaiah) (Dead Sea Scrolls)
1QpHab	Habakkuk commentary (Dead Sea Scrolls)
4QDan[c]	4QDaniel[c] (Dead Sea Scrolls)
4QJer[a]	4QJeremiah[a] (Dead Sea Scrolls)
4QJer[b]	4QJeremiah[b] (Dead Sea Scrolls)
4QJer[c]	4QJeremiah[c] (Dead Sea Scrolls)
4QMMT	4Q Miqṣat Ma'aśe Ha-Torah (Dead Sea Scrolls)
11QTgJob	11Q Job Targum (Dead Sea Scrolls)
AB	Anchor Bible
ABD	*Anchor Bible Dictionary*, ed. D. N. Freedman, 6 vols. (New York: Doubleday, 1992)
AbOTC	Abingdon Old Testament Commentary
ABRL	Anchor Bible Reference Library
Ag. Ap.	*Against Apion* (Josephus)
ANE	ancient Near East, ancient Near Eastern
AOTC	Apollos Old Testament Commentary
AS	Assyriological Studies
ATJ	*Ashland Theological Journal*
AUSS	*Andrews University Seminary Studies*
AV	Authorized (King James) Version
BA	*Biblical Archaeologist*
BAR	*Biblical Archaeology Review*
BASOR	*Bulletin of the American Schools of Oriental Research*

b. B. Bat.	*Babylonian Talmud Baba Batra*
BBR	*Bulletin for Biblical Research*
BCOTWP	Baker Commentary on the Old Testament Wisdom and Psalms
b. Ḥag.	*Babylonian Talmud Ḥagigah*
Bib	*Biblica*
BLS	Bible and Literature Series
b. Meg.	*Babylonian Talmud Megillah*
b. Menaḥ.	*Babylonian Talmud Menaḥot*
b. Šabb.	*Babylonian Talmud Šabbat*
BSac	*Bibliotheca sacra*
BSL	Biblical Studies Library
BST	The Bible Speaks Today
BT	*Bible Translator*
BTB	*Biblical Theology Bulletin*
b. Yebam.	*Babylonian Talmud Yebamot*
BZAW	Beihefte zur Zeitschrift für die alttestamentliche Wissenschaft
CBC	Cambridge Bible Commentary
CBQ	*Catholic Biblical Quarterly*
CBR	*Currents in Biblical Research*
CC	Continental Commentary
ChrCent	*Christian Century*
COS	*The Context of a Scripture: Canonical Compositions, Monumental Inscriptions and Archival Documents from the Biblical World*, ed. William W. Hallo and K. Lawson Younger Jr., 3 vols. (Leiden: Brill, 2003)
CTJ	*Calvin Theological Journal*
CTM	*Concordia Theological Monthly*
CurBR	*Currents in Biblical Research*
DBI	*Dictionary of Biblical Imagery*, ed. L. Ryken, J. C. Wilhoit and T. Longman III (Downers Grove: InterVarsity Press; Leicester: Inter-Varsity Press, 1998)
DH	Deuteronomistic History
DOTHB	*Dictionary of the Old Testament: Historical Books*, ed. Bill T. Arnold and H. G. M. Williamson (Downers Grove: InterVarsity Press; Leicester: Inter-Varsity Press, 2005)
DOTP	*Dictionary of the Old Testament: Pentateuch*, ed. T. Desmond Alexander and David W. Baker (Downers Grove: InterVarsity Press; Leicester: Inter-Varsity Press, 2003)

DOTPr	*Dictionary of the Old Testament: Prophets*, ed. Mark J. Boda and J. Gordon McConville (Downers Grove: InterVarsity Press; Nottingham: Inter-Varsity Press, 2012)
DOTWPW	*Dictionary of the Old Testament: Wisdom, Poetry and Writings*, ed. Tremper Longman III and Peter Enns (Downers Grove: InterVarsity Press; Nottingham: Inter-Varsity Press, 2008)
DSB	Daily Study Bible
DTIB	*Dictionary for Theological Interpretation of the Bible*, ed. Kevin J. Vanhoozer (Grand Rapids: Baker Academic, 2005)
EA	El-Amarna tablets, numbered according to J. A. Knudtzon, *Die El-Amarna Tafeln: mit einleitung und erläuterungen herausgegeben*, 2 vols. (Leipzig: Hinrichs, 1915), and A. F. Rainey, *El-Amarna Tablets 359–379: Supplement to J. A. Knudtzon, Die El-Amarna Tafeln*, 2nd ed., Alter Orient und Altes Testament 8 (Neukirchen-Vluyn: Neukirchener Verlag, 1978)
ECC	Eerdmans Critical Commentary
EJT	*European Journal of Theology*
Enc	*Encounter*
EvQ	*Evangelical Quarterly*
EVV	English versions
ExAud	*Ex auditu*
FAT	Forschungen zum Alten Testament
FCB	Feminist Companion to the Bible
FOTL	Forms of Old Testament Literature
GBS	Guides to Biblical Scholarship
Ger.	German
Gk	Greek
GTJ	*Grace Theological Journal*
HAR	*Hebrew Annual Review*
HBM	Hebrew Bible Monographs
Heb.	Hebrew
HSM	Harvard Semitic Monographs
HTR	*Harvard Theological Review*
HTS	Harvard Theological Studies
HTS	*Hervormde Teologiese Studies*
HUCA	*Hebrew Union College Annual*
IBC	Interpretation: A Bible Commentary for Teaching and Preaching
IBD	*The Illustrated Bible Dictionary*, ed. J. D. Douglas, N. Hillyer et al., 3 vols. (Leicester: Inter-Varsity Press, 1980)

ICC	International Critical Commentary
IDB	*Interpreter's Dictionary of the Bible*, 4 vols., ed. G. A. Buttrick, T. S. Kepler, J. Knox, H. G. May, S. Terrien and E. S. Bucke (New York: Abingdon, 1962)
Int	*Interpretation*
IRT	Issues in Religion and Theology
ISBE	*The International Standard Bible Encyclopedia*, ed. G. W. Bromiley et al., 4 vols. (Grand Rapids: Eerdmans, 1979–86)
JANER	*Journal of Ancient Near Eastern Religions*
JANES	*Journal of the Ancient Near Eastern Society*
JAOS	*Journal of the American Oriental Society*
JBL	*Journal of Biblical Literature*
JEBS	*Journal of European Baptist Studies*
JESOT	*Journal for the Evangelical Study of the Old Testament*
JETS	*Journal of the Evangelical Theological Society*
JHS	*Journal of Hebrew Scriptures*
JNES	*Journal of Near Eastern Studies*
JPSBC	Jewish Publication Society Bible Commentary
JPSTC	Jewish Publication Society Torah Commentary
JPT	*Journal of Pentecostal Theology*
JSNT	*Journal for the Study of the New Testament*
JSNTSup	Journal for the Study of the New Testament, Supplement Series
JSOT	*Journal for the Study of the Old Testament*
JSOTSup	Journal for the Study of the Old Testament, Supplement Series
JTS	*Journal of Theological Studies*
LAI	Library of Ancient Israel
LBS	Library of Biblical Studies
LXX	Septuagint
mg.	margin
MT	Masoretic Text
m. Yad.	*Mishnah Yadayim*
NAC	New American Commentary
NCB	New Century Bible
NCBC	New Cambridge Bible Commentary
NDBT	*New Dictionary of Biblical Theology*, ed. T. D. Alexander, B. S. Rosner, D. A. Carson and G. Goldsworthy (Leicester: Inter-Varsity Press; Downers Grove: InterVarsity Press, 2000)

NIBCOT/UBC	New International Biblical Commentary on the Old Testament
NICNT	New International Commentary on the New Testament
NICOT	New International Commentary on the Old Testament
NIDOTTE	*New International Dictionary of Old Testament Theology and Exegesis*, ed. Willem A. VanGemeren, 5 vols. (Carlisle: Paternoster; Grand Rapids: Zondervan, 1996)
NIV	New International Version (1984)
NIVAC	New International Version Application Commentary
NovT	*Novum Testamentum*
NRSV	New Revised Standard Version (1995)
NS	new series
NSBT	New Studies in Biblical Theology
NT	New Testament
OBT	Overtures to Biblical Theology
OT	Old Testament
OTE	*Old Testament Essays*
OTG	Old Testament Guides
OTL	Old Testament Library
OTS	Old Testament Studies
PEQ	*Palestine Exploration Quarterly*
Presb.	*Presbyterion*
Proof	*Prooftexts: A Journal of Jewish Literary History*
RSR	*Recherches de science religieuse*
RTR	*Reformed Theological Review*
SBJT	*Southern Baptist Journal of Theology*
SBLDS	Society of Biblical Literature Dissertation Series
SBLMS	Society of Biblical Literature Monograph Series
SBLSBL	Society of Biblical Literature Studies in Biblical Literature
SBLSP	*Society of Biblical Literature Seminar Papers*
SBT	Studies in Biblical Theology
SBTS	Sources for Biblical and Theological Study
SemeiaSt	Semeia Studies
SHBC	Smyth & Helwys Bible Commentary
SJT	*Scottish Journal of Theology*
SOTBT	Studies in Old Testament Biblical Theology
Sound	*Soundings*
SP	Samaritan Pentateuch
SSN	Studia semitica neerlandica
STR	*Southeastern Theological Review*

SwJT	*South Western Journal of Theology*
TBC	Torch Bible Commentaries
TDNT	*Theological Dictionary of the New Testament*, ed. G. Kittel and G. Friedrich; trans. G. W. Bromiley, 10 vols. (Grand Rapids: Eerdmans, 1964–76)
TDOT	*Theological Dictionary of the Old Testament*, ed. G. Johannes Botterweck, Helmer Ringgren and Heinz-Josef Fabry, trans. John T. Willis, Geoffrey W. Bromiley, David E. Green and Douglas W. Stott, 15 vols. (Grand Rapids: Eerdmans, 1974–2006)
Tg. Lam.	*Targum Lamentations*
Them	*Themelios*
THOTC	Two Horizons Old Testament Commentaries
ThTo	*Theology Today*
TMSJ	*The Master's Seminary Journal*
TOTC	Tyndale Old Testament Commentaries
TS	*Theological Studies*
TynBul	*Tyndale Bulletin*
UBC	Understanding the Bible Commentary (formerly New International Biblical Commentary on the Old/New Testament)
VE	*Verbum et Ecclesia*
VT	*Vetus Testamentum*
VTSup	Supplements to Vetus Testamentum
WBC	Word Bible Commentary
WMANT	Wissenschaftliche Monographien zum Alten und Neuen Testament
WTJ	*Westminster Theological Journal*
WUNT	Wissenschaftliche Untersuchungen zum Neuen Testament
WW	*Word and World*
ZAW	*Zeitschrift für die alttestamentliche Wissenschaft*

1. THE SIGNIFICANCE OF THE OLD TESTAMENT

What's in a name?

The Christian Bible is traditionally divided into the Old and New testaments.[1] 'Testament' comes from the Latin *testamentum*, which, in Latin versions of the Bible frequently translates the Hebrew and Greek terms for 'covenant'.[2] This terminology indicates that a key point of distinction between these two sections

1. Another section, the Apocrypha, is often placed between the Old and New testaments; though specifically Catholic texts, including the *Clementine Vulgate* (1592), the *Jerusalem Bible* (1966) and the *New Jerusalem Bible* (1985), include many of these books within the OT. The relationship between apocryphal texts and the OT will be discussed at length below.
2. In the Latin Vulgate *testamentum* translates the Hebrew *bĕrît* (covenant), predominantly in the Psalms (e.g. Pss 25:10 [24:10]; 44:17 [43:18]; 74:20 [73:20]; 78:10 [77:10]; 89:3, 28 [88:4, 29]; 103:18 [102:18]; 105:10 [104:10]), though see also Exod. 30:26; Num. 14:44; 2 Sam. 6:15; Zech. 9:11; Mal. 3:1. *Bĕrît* is also translated by the Latin *foedus* (including in Jer. 31:31, though not in in its quotation in Heb. 8:8) and, most commonly, by *pactum*. In the NT *testamentum* usually translates the Greek *diathēkē* (e.g. Matt. 26:28; Mark 14:24; Luke 1:72; 22:20; 2 Cor. 3:6, 14; Heb. 7:22; 8:6; 12:24; Rev. 11:19).

of the Bible is the new covenant relationship between God and his people, which is promised in the OT (Jer. 31:31) and inaugurated through the death and resurrection of Jesus (e.g. Luke 22:20), and the earlier covenant relationship embodied, primarily, in the covenant between God and Israel at Sinai.[3] This contrast is evident in passages such as 2 Corinthians 3:4–18, which contains one of several references to the 'new covenant' (Gk *kainē diathēkē*, v. 6),[4] and the only specific biblical reference to the 'old covenant' (Gk *palaia diathēkē*, v. 14). The parallel here with the reading of 'Moses' (v. 15) suggests that 'old covenant' here refers to the books of the Law (the Torah or Pentateuch).[5] Similar language appears in Hebrews 8:7–13, where the 'new covenant' (vv. 8, 13) is contrasted with the earlier covenant that is 'obsolete' (v. 13, from the Gk *palaiō*, 'to grow old').[6] This gives some biblical warrant for the term 'Old Testament', though in a limited and fairly negative context. The use of the expression to refer to a wider collection of biblical texts appears to have been coined later, during the patristic period; one of the earliest references to 'Old Testament' is by Melito of Sardis, in the second century AD.[7]

---

3. Divine covenants in the OT include those with Noah, Abraham and David. The 'new covenant', though, is generally contrasted with the Sinaitic covenant.
4. See also Luke 22:20; 1 Cor. 11:25; Heb. 8:8; 9:15; 12:24; cf. Jer. 31:31.
5. Martin suggests that this refers to the public reading of the Law (cf. Acts 13:15), though notes that the term 'old covenant' is exceptional; see Ralph P. Martin, *2 Corinthians*, WBC 40 (Waco: Word, 1986), pp. 68–69; cf. Heinrich Seesmann, '*palaios*', in *TDNT* 5:720, n. 13. Barnett argues that this terminology may not be unprecedented; he notes that Paul's 'new covenant' language comes directly from Jesus (1 Cor. 11:25; cf. Luke 22:20), and suggests a link with Mark 2:21, where the same 'old'/'new' contrast appears; see Paul Barnett, *The Second Epistle to the Corinthians*, NICNT (Grand Rapids: Eerdmans, 1997), p. 194, n. 25.
6. Barnett, *Second Epistle to the Corinthians*, p. 194, n. 25. Note that I have generally translated Greek and Hebrew verbs using the infinitive, as the more common way to express this in English, rather than the first or third person singular as in Greek and Hebrew respectively.
7. Trobisch notes that Eusebius records a reference by Melito of Sardis to 'the books of the Old Testament' (David Trobisch, *The First Edition of the New Testament* [Oxford: Oxford University Press, 2000], p. 44). Martin suggests that this is the next occurrence of the term 'Old Testament' after 2 Cor. 3:14 (*2 Corinthians*, p. 69); see also Lee Martin McDonald, *The Biblical Canon: Its Origin, Transmission and Authority* (Grand Rapids: Baker Academic, 2007), pp. 14–17.

The designation 'Old Testament' may indicate that it is no longer relevant or has been superseded by what follows, and to emphasize its continuing significance as part of the 'canon' of Christian Scripture,[8] it has been suggested that 'first testament' is a more appropriate term.[9] However, 'Old Testament' has persisted in common usage.

The expressions 'Old Testament' and 'first testament' are distinctively Christian. They suggest that this collection of texts is incomplete on its own, and points forward to the 'New Testament' and the fulfilment of all that has gone before in and through Jesus Christ. In recent years the term 'Hebrew Bible' has become increasingly popular.[10] This description is not strictly accurate, since parts of the text are in Aramaic (Ezra 4:8 – 6:18; 7:12–26; Jer. 10:11; Dan. 2:4 – 7:28), however, it does emphasize that before it became part of the Christian Bible it was, and continues to be part of the canon of Jewish Scripture. And its pre-Christian origin needs to be taken into account in interpretation.[11] This designation is more acceptable to Jews, and promotes discussion between Christian and Jewish interpreters of what is, essentially, the same text. Another term, 'Tanak', is an acronym based on the three sections of the text of the Hebrew Bible: Torah (Law), comprising Genesis–Deuteronomy (the Pentateuch);

---

8. Here the term 'canon' refers to the collection of texts that have been accepted by the believing community as having authority for faith and practice. See below, pp. 22–40.
9. E.g. John Goldingay, *Old Testament Theology 1: Israel's Gospel* (Downers Grove: InterVarsity Press; Milton Keynes: Paternoster, 2003), p. 15; Rolf Rendtorff, *The Canonical Hebrew Bible: A Theology of the Old Testament* (Leiden: Deo, 2005), pp. 747–748.
10. See further Bill T. Arnold, *Introduction to the Old Testament* (Cambridge: Cambridge University Press, 2014), pp. 4–5; Roger Brooks and John J. Collins, *Hebrew Bible or Old Testament: Studying the Bible in Judaism and Christianity*, Christianity and Judaism in Antiquity 5 (Notre Dame: University of Notre Dame Press, 1990); Brevard S. Childs, *Introduction to the Old Testament as Scripture* (London: SCM Press; Minneapolis: Fortress, 1979), pp. 659–671; Rendtorff, *Canonical Hebrew Bible*, pp. 746–749; Robin Routledge, *Old Testament Theology: A Thematic Approach* (Nottingham: Apollos; Downers Grove: IVP Academic, 2008), pp. 18–22.
11. Some suggest that the OT (and NT) is best understood from within a Jewish religious and cultural context; see e.g. David H. Stern, *The Complete Jewish Bible* (Clarksville: Messianic Jewish Resources International, 1998). In my view that is not necessarily so; Judaism, like Christianity, represents a development of the faith of the OT.

nĕbî'îm (Prophets), which is further divided into the *former prophets* (Joshua, Judges, Samuel and Kings – which, in the Hebrew text appear as single books), and the *latter* (or *writing*) *prophets* (Isaiah, Jeremiah, Ezekiel and the twelve minor prophets); and *kĕtûbîm* (Writings or Hagiographa), comprising Psalms, Job, Proverbs, Ruth, Song of Songs, Ecclesiastes, Lamentations, Esther, Daniel, Ezra-Nehemiah and Chronicles.[12] However, as with the term 'Old Testament', 'Tanak' also has a confessional aspect: the Hebrew text of both is the same, but its readers reflect the faith communities to which they belong. This confessional stance may not have a direct impact on the exegesis of individual passages within their historical context, where some degree of objectivity is important. It is significant, though, for the way those texts are understood within their wider biblical context, and particularly in the area of biblical theology.[13] It is argued that by referring to the text as the 'Hebrew Bible', those confessional elements that may be less acceptable to other groups are minimized, thus giving greater scope for scholars from different faith communities to work more closely together.

Differences between Christian and Jewish approaches to the text are evident in two important ways. First, as noted already, although the text is essentially the same, the ordering of their respective canons is different (see Table 1.1). The Tanak ends with Chronicles, which has as one of its key emphases the planning and building of the Jerusalem temple, under David and Solomon. Following a relatively brief review of the history of Judah to the exile and a description of the destruction of the temple by the Babylonians, the book closes with the edict

12. Another term used to refer to the Jewish Scriptures is *miqrā* (sometimes written *mikrā*). This, literally, means 'reading' (from the Heb. *qārā'*, 'to read'), and points to the significance of the public reading of Scripture.

13. E.g. Rolf Rendtorff, 'Old Testament Theology, Tanakh Theology, or Biblical Theology. Reflections in an Ecumenical Context', *Bib* 73.2 (1992), pp. 441–451 (448–449); see also Brevard S. Childs, *Old Testament Theology in a Canonical Context* (London: SCM Press, 1985), pp. 7–8; *Biblical Theology of the Old and New Testaments: Theological Reflection on the Christian Bible* (London: SCM Press, 1992), pp. 63–68; Gerhard Hasel, *Old Testament Theology: Basic Issues in the Current Debate*, 4th ed. (Grand Rapids: Eerdmans, 1991), p. 36; Jon Levenson, *The Old Testament, the Hebrew Bible, and Historical Criticism* (Louisville: Westminster John Knox, 1993), pp. 80–81; cf. Walter Brueggemann, *Old Testament Theology: Testimony, Dispute, Advocacy* (Minneapolis: Augsburg Fortress, 1997), pp. 89–95; *An Introduction to the Old Testament: The Canon and Christian Imagination*, 2nd ed. (Louisville: Westminster John Knox, 2012), pp. 1–3.

Table 1.1

Hebrew Bible/Tanak (24 books)		*Old Testament, excluding Apocrypha (39 books)*	
Torah	*Writings (Hagiographa)*	*Pentateuch*	*Major Prophets*
Genesis, Exodus,	Psalms, Job, Proverbs,	Genesis, Exodus,	Isaiah, Jeremiah,
Leviticus, Numbers,	Ruth, Song of Songs,	Leviticus, Numbers,	Lamentations,
Deuteronomy	Ecclesiastes,	Deuteronomy	Ezekiel,
Former Prophets	Lamentations,	*History*	Daniel
Joshua, Judges,	Esther, Daniel,	Joshua, Judges, Ruth,	*Minor Prophets*
Samuel, Kings	Ezra-Nehemiah,	1 Samuel, 2 Samuel,	Hosea, Joel, Amos,
Latter Prophets	Chronicles	1 Kings, 2 Kings,	Obadiah, Jonah, Micah,
Isaiah, Jeremiah,		1 Chronicles,	Nahum, Habakkuk,
Ezekiel,		2 Chronicles,	Zephaniah, Haggai,
Book of the Twelve,		Ezra, Nehemiah,	Zechariah, Malachi
Hosea, Joel, Amos,		Esther	
Obadiah, Jonah,		*Poetry*	
Micah, Nahum,		Job, Psalms, Proverbs,	
Habakkuk,		Ecclesiastes,	
Zephaniah, Haggai,		Song of Songs	
Zechariah, Malachi			

of Cyrus that the temple will be rebuilt (2 Chr. 36:22–23), and in the final sentence the people are urged to 'go up' (v. 23). In this way the Hebrew Bible points to a new beginning for God's people after the exile, linked with the restoration of the religious life of the nation (including the birth of Judaism, which is primarily associated with Ezra). The OT ends with the prophetic books, suggesting a link between the future hope of the people of God and the second part of the Christian Bible.[14] In particular the last book, Malachi, points to the coming of the day of the Lord, which will be preceded by the return of Elijah. This opens the way for the NT focus on John the Baptist and his announcement that the kingdom of God has come in the person of Jesus Christ. These are the same Scriptures, but the different canonical ordering means that they prepare their respective readers for different historical fulfilments. These different expectations are seen, too, in the second important distinction: the ways in which the text is read forward into other religious literature. Clearly, Christians read the OT forward into the NT. As noted already, the OT is incomplete without the NT (just as, we could argue, the NT is incomplete without the OT). The Tanak, similarly, is incomplete without later writings, in particular the Mishnah and the Talmud.[15]

---

14. See e.g. Rendtorff, 'OT Theology', p. 442.
15. See e.g. W. Brueggemann, *Introduction*, p. 4; Rendtorff, 'OT Theology', p. 442; Levenson, *Hebrew Bible*, p. 38; Routledge, *OT Theology*, p. 20.

Rendtorff's observation that 'we read the same text as the Jews when studying the first part of our Bible in its original language, but we do not have the same canon'[16] is significant. It is important not to lose sight of the historical and cultural roots of the OT; it is important, too, to be open to the insights of those who are studying the same texts from a Jewish perspective. It is equally important, though, particularly when looking at the way texts function within the wider biblical canon, to recognize the importance of the confessional context in which the text is being studied. For that reason, I will refer to this part of Scripture, which I read as a Christian, as the 'Old Testament', though without the suggestion that it may be considered to be outdated or irrelevant to the life of the church.

The Christian significance of the Old Testament

The first Christians were Jews who viewed the OT as authoritative Scripture. Indeed, for a time this would have been their only sacred text. They recognized the significance of the new relationship with God that was made possible through the death and resurrection of Jesus, and of the new revelation they had received, but they did not discard the OT, which was to them already an important document of faith. On the contrary, a key concern of NT writers was to present the coming of Christ as the fulfilment of OT hope, and to demonstrate continuity both between the faith of the OT and that of Christian believers, and between the people of God in the OT and the community of those who put their trust in Jesus Christ.[17] The NT writers were convinced that what God had promised to his people in the past was now being fulfilled in and through the person and work of Jesus, and this gave continuing significance to the OT.

However, as the Christian church moved beyond its Jewish roots it came to comprise, predominantly, Gentiles, who had little or no cultural interest in the OT; and, other than the fact that it was already in circulation as a Christian text, they had no reason to attach religious significance to it. The question for these non-Jewish believers was not how to read what was already an important document of faith in the light of the coming of Jesus but, more fundamentally,

16. Rendtorff, 'OT Theology', p. 442.

17. See e.g. Childs, *Introduction*, pp. 41–43. For discussion of the reapplication of OT texts to the Christian community, see Robin Routledge, 'Replacement or Fulfillment: Re-applying Old Testament Designations of Israel to the Church', *STR* 4.2 (2013), pp. 137–154.

why bother with the OT at all? One solution, set out, for example, in the *Epistle of Barnabas*, was to claim the OT as a distinctively Christian text, which had been misunderstood by the Jews, who interpreted things like the sacrificial and food laws literally rather than spiritually.[18] A more extreme solution, put forward by Marcion in the second century, was to remove the OT from the Christian canon altogether.[19] Marcion reflected Gnostic thought in presenting a contrast between the inferior God of the OT and the loving Father proclaimed by Jesus. He claimed that the attempt by the early Christian community to emphasize continuity between the Old and New testaments was mistaken. For Marcion, only Paul properly understood the gospel of grace and, as a result, Marcion suggested a canon that excluded not only the OT, but also much of the NT.[20] The response to Marcion included an affirmation of the importance of the OT, though still as an essentially Christian document that could be properly understood only in the light of the coming of Christ.[21]

These two extremes, one that regards the OT, or a substantial part of it, as irrelevant to the life of the church, and the other that seeks to 'Christianize' it,

---

18. Based on a mistaken reading of Jer. 7:22, *Barnabas* 2 claims that sacrifices were not required by God; see *Early Christian Writings*, trans. Maxwell Staniforth (London: Penguin, 1987), pp. 159–160. *Barnabas* 10 contains an allegorical interpretation of the dietary laws of Lev. 11 and Deut. 14. In the prohibition '*You are not to eat of swine; nor yet of eagle, hawk, or crow; nor of any fish that has not got scales* . . . Moses was taking three moral maxims and expounding them spiritually; though the Jews with their carnal instincts, took him to be referring literally to foodstuffs' (Staniforth, *Early Christian Writings*, pp. 171–172 [italics his]).
19. On Marcion see e.g. John Barton, 'Marcion Revisited', in *The Old Testament: Canon, Literature and Theology: Collected Essays* (Aldershot: Ashgate, 2007), pp. 67–81; Adolf von Harnack, *Marcion: The Gospel of the Alien God*, trans. John E. Steely and Lyle D. Bierma (Eugene: Wipf & Stock, 2007). See also Peter Head, 'The Foreign God and the Sudden Christ: Theology and Christology in Marcion's Gospel Redaction', *TynBul* 44.2 (1993), pp. 307–321; MacDonald, *Biblical Canon*, pp. 324–333; Bruce M. Metzger, *The Canon of the New Testament: Its Origin, Development and Significance* (Oxford: Oxford University Press, 1987), pp. 90–99.
20. The Marcionite canon comprised Luke's Gospel and Paul's letters (excluding the Pastoral Epistles).
21. According to Tertullian, one of Marcion's main critics, 'Christ is present in the Old Testament . . . everything points to him and only through him can it be understood' (Eric Osborn, *Tertullian: First Theologian of the West* [Cambridge: Cambridge University Press, 1997], p. 152).

are represented in the modern debate. There are those, such as Adolf von Harnack, who have argued for rejecting the OT entirely as a document of the Christian church;[22] though the more common approach is to subordinate the message of the OT to the teaching of the NT and to other perceived sources of moral authority, so that any value depends on the OT's agreement with them. Thus the OT has no authority of its own, and its retention as part of the canon seems more out of historical interest or as a concession to Christian tradition than out of a sense of its own intrinsic worth. In an attempt to give the OT greater value as part of the Christian canon another approach is to interpret it primarily as a witness to Christ and to find direct links between the OT text and the life, ministry, death and resurrection of Christ.[23] While of some value, this approach means that the OT is of value only in so far as it can be linked to aspects of NT teaching about Christ. Some OT texts may be open to such a reading, though there is considerable debate about which ones. But does that mean that a text has value only if it can be given such a 'Christian' interpretation? A consequence of this may be that commentators and preachers either ignore the large sections of the OT that cannot easily be related to Christ directly, or engage in imaginative and speculatory interpretations in an endeavour to make the link.

One further consequence of recognizing the significance of the OT only in so far as it can be related directly to the NT is that the text may be spiritualized to such an extent that important aspects of its meaning are not developed. So, for example, the Song of Songs (Song of Solomon) is frequently taken to refer to the relationship between God and his people or between Christ and the church. However, it also includes the sexual expression of the love between a man and a woman, and that aspect of the text is rarely expounded. Another example may be the approach to OT sacrifices. Instructions regarding animal sacrifices in the OT are not relevant to the practice of the church today: Christ's sacrifice makes them no longer necessary. Consequently, OT texts referring to sacrifices may be taken simply to point to their fulfilment in the death of Christ. They do that, of course; but they also contain important

---

22. According to von Harnack, 'To reject the Old Testament in the second century was a mistake which the Church rightly repudiated; to retain it in the sixteenth century was a fate which the Reformation could not yet avoid; but to keep it as a canonical document after the nineteenth century is the result of religious and ecclesiastical paralysis' (Barton, 'Marcion Revisited', in *Collected Essays*, pp. 67–68).

23. Cf. Luke 24:27. See e.g. Sidney Greidanus, *Preaching Christ from the Old Testament: A Contemporary Hermeneutical Method* (Grand Rapids: Eerdmans, 1999), p. 8.

spiritual principles, including recognizing the seriousness of sin, the importance of confession, the nature of sacrifice as something meaningful and costly, and so on. These principles need to be recontextualized, but they remain relevant to the life of the church.[24]

A key problem associated with both of these approaches is that they fail to recognize the significance of the OT as Scripture in its own right. Certainly, the OT cannot be fully understood in isolation from the NT; but nor should it be subordinated to the NT, or derive its authority solely from its agreement with the NT. The OT is the Word of God, and as such has its own inherent worth.[25] Reasons for reading the OT as authoritative Christian Scripture include the following.

The Old Testament is part of the biblical canon

As noted already, both Christian and Jewish faith communities have accepted the OT as part of the canon of Scripture. That gives the text a particular status and authority in matters of faith and practice. Just how the OT operates in this way presents a challenge; but because it has been widely recognized as canonical Scripture we must not overlook or neglect it.

The Old Testament reveals truths about God, and his dealings with his people and his world

We recognize that it is the same God who is revealed in the OT and the NT, and that there is, therefore, a consistency and coherence in the nature of God and in the way he acts in relation to his people, the nations and the world.[26] That allows us to draw correspondences between the OT context and our own, and to apply the theological principles that underlie his dealings with his people and his world in the OT to the life of the church today, and to the world today.

---

24. See Robin Routledge, 'Sacrifice, Prayer and Forgiveness', *EJT* 18.1 (2009), pp. 17–28.
25. See Routledge, *OT Theology*, pp. 71–80; see also e.g. John Bright, *The Authority of the Old Testament* (London: SCM Press, 1967; repr. Biblical and Theological Classics Library; Carlisle: Paternoster, 1998); John Goldingay, *Approaches to Old Testament Interpretation* (Leicester: Apollos, 1990); Greidanus, *Preaching Christ*; William Sanford LaSor, David Allan Hubbard and Frederic William Bush, *Old Testament Survey: The Message, Form, and Background of the Old Testament*, 2nd ed. (Grand Rapids: Eerdmans, 1996), pp. 585–590.
26. In the OT God appears, sometimes, to act in ways that Christians find questionable; see e.g. Routledge, *OT Theology*, pp. 250–260. However, despite difficulties, the portrayal of God in the OT is generally compatible with that in the NT.

Jesus and the writers of the New Testament accepted the Old Testament as Scripture

Jesus made frequent reference to the OT. He used it to support his claims and as a basis for his teaching, and, significantly, he maintained that the OT pointed towards him (e.g. Luke 4:21; 24:27; John 5:39). The NT writers were also rooted in the OT. They saw faith in Christ and the emergence of the church as continuous with OT expectation, and they frequently refer back to the OT to give authority and credibility to their own message. As Wolff observes, 'no New Testament writer felt he was in a position to witness to Jesus Christ without constantly opening and quoting the OT. Both the proclamation of Jesus and the preaching of the early Christians are unthinkable without the Old Testament'.[27]

The Old Testament helps us to understand the New Testament

Because the NT writers are so dependent on the OT, any proper understanding of the NT needs to be grounded in an understanding of the OT. This is all the more necessary because when NT writers develop OT concepts, they may not offer much explanation, on the assumption that these things were already well known. Examples include references to 'covenant', to the 'kingdom of God', to the 'Passover' and to links between Jesus and the 'Passover Lamb', to the role and function of 'temple' and to the description of the church as 'the people of God'.[28] References to the 'Law' in the NT are best understood in the light of the use of the term in the OT.[29] There is also a growing body of literature on the use of 'new exodus' or 'second exodus' imagery in the NT;[30] and this,

27. Hans Walter Wolff, 'The Hermeneutics of the Old Testament', in Claus Westermann (ed.), *Essays on Old Testament Interpretation* (London: SCM Press, 1963), pp. 160–199 (188).
28. See Greidanus, *Preaching Christ*, p. 29.
29. See e.g. Routledge, *OT Theology*, pp. 173–174.
30. See e.g. David W. Pao, *Acts and the Isaianic New Exodus*, BSL (Grand Rapids: Baker Academic, 2002); Rikki E. Watts, *Isaiah's New Exodus in Mark*, BSL (Grand Rapids: Baker Academic, 1997); Richard J. Clifford, 'The Exodus in the Christian Bible: The Case For "Figural" Reading', *TS* 63 (2002), pp. 345–361; Fred L. Fisher, 'The New and Greater Exodus: The Exodus Pattern in the New Testament', *SwJT* 20.1 (1977), pp. 69–79; Matthew Thiessen, 'Hebrews and the End of the Exodus', *NovT* 49 (2007), pp. 353–369; see also Robin Routledge, 'The Exodus and Biblical Theology', in Mike Fox (ed.), *Reverberations of the Exodus in Scripture* (Eugene: Pickwick, 2014), pp. 187–209.

too, assumes a, sometimes detailed, knowledge of the OT. Permeating these things, we see, too, the developing drama of redemption history, which runs through the OT and reaches its climax in the sacrifice of Christ. Individual scenes of that drama may be viewed separately; but each one is properly understood only in the light of the biblical whole. Thus, Wolff comments, 'the proposition that the OT can be properly understood only in the light of the New . . . stands in need of its converse: The New Testament Christ-event can be fully understood only in the light of the OT'.[31] John Goldingay makes a similar comment: 'the Old Testament's insights must be seen in light of those of the New, but only as we immediately add that it is necessary to see the New Testament's insights in light of those of the Old'.[32]

The Old Testament is the primary source of some biblical teaching

There are some things that may be assumed by the NT writers, but about which they say little because the primary discussion is in the OT.[33] So, for example, while NT writers refer to God as the Creator (e.g. Rom. 1:25; 1 Pet. 4:19), and emphasize Christ's role in creation (e.g. John 1:3; Col. 1:16–17; Heb. 1:2–3), that teaching builds on the more developed view of creation found in the OT.[34] An important element in the creation story is the creation of human beings in God's 'image' (Gen. 1:26–27; cf. 1 Cor. 11:7), with the task of exercising responsible stewardship over creation.[35] This is relevant to the current ecological debate and, again, is found, predominantly, in the OT.[36] It is in the OT, too, that we are given details of human beings' fall into sin; a fall that has, in traditional theological understanding, brought all of the created order under a divine curse, and

31. Wolff, 'Hermeneutics of the OT', in Westermann, *Essays*, p. 187.
32. Goldingay, *Israel's Gospel*, p. 21.
33. See Greidanus, *Preaching Christ*, pp. 27–28.
34. E.g. Gen. 1 – 2; Job 26:7–14; 38 – 39; Ps. 104; Isa. 40:21–26; 42:5; 45:18.
35. The divine imperative to 'rule' or 'have dominion' over the created order (Gen. 1:26; cf. Ps. 8:6) is commonly taken in that way. See e.g. James Limburg, 'The Responsibility of Royalty: Genesis 1–11 and the Care of the Earth', *WW* 11.2 (1991), pp. 124–130 (125–126); David L. Baker, '"In the Beginning . . . It Was Very Good": Genesis 1 – 2 and the Environment', in Jonathan Moo and Robin Routledge (eds.), *As Long as the Earth Endures: Biblical and Theological Perspectives on Creation and the Environment* (Nottingham: Apollos, 2014), pp. 50–69 (54–57).
36. This is not to suggest that the NT does not provide any basis for environmental ethics; see e.g. Jonathan Moo, 'Christian Hope and a New Testament Environmental Ethos', in Moo and Routledge, *Earth Endures*, pp. 146–168.

that necessitates God's plan of redemption, fulfilled in Christ.[37] There are some NT allusions to this 'fall' (e.g. Rom. 3:23; 8:19–22; 1 Cor. 15:21–22), and the NT sets out God's response to it, but in general it and its effects are assumed. In these, and other areas, the NT writers build on what has gone before, and the primary source of the teaching is found in the OT.

The Old Testament as revelation

The nature of revelation

As we have seen, the OT has been accepted as Scripture, an acceptance underpinned by the conviction that its human writers were moved to set out divinely inspired revelation. There is not the opportunity here to discuss this in detail;[38] though some aspects will be considered at relevant points in what follows. But it is appropriate to say something of how this volume approaches the issue of the OT as revelation.

It is a common article of faith that God reveals himself in a variety of ways, including through the created order (e.g. Ps. 19:1–4; Rom. 1:19–20). In general, though, primacy is given to the written, biblical text. It is frequently noted that, particularly in the OT, God is made known through what he does, and God's activity in history plays an important part in revelation.[39] But we are made aware

37. Some argue that the OT does not contain the idea of a 'universal fall' that affects all creation, and explains the presence of sin in the world; see e.g. John J. Bimson, 'Reconsidering a "Cosmic Fall"', *Science & Christian Belief* 18.1 (2006), pp. 63–81. However, see Robin Routledge, 'Cursing and Chaos: The Impact of Human Sin on Creation and the Environment', in Moo and Routledge, *Earth Endures*, pp. 70–91; *OT Theology*, pp. 154–156.
38. For further discussion, see e.g. Paul J. Achtemeier, *Inspiration and Authority: The Nature and Function of Christian Scripture* (Peabody: Hendrickson, 1999; Grand Rapids: Baker Academic, 2010); John J. Collins, *Introduction to the Hebrew Bible*, 2nd ed. (Minneapolis: Fortress, 2014), pp. 612–616; David R. Law, *Inspiration of the Scriptures* (London: Continuum, 2001); LaSor, Hubbard and Bush, *OT Survey*, pp. 591–597; I. Howard Marshall, *Biblical Inspiration* (London: Hodder & Stoughton, 1982; Vancouver: Regent College Publishing, 2004).
39. Revelation through divine acts in history was important in the 'biblical theology movement'; see e.g. G. Ernest Wright, *The God Who Acts: Biblical Theology as Recital* (London: SCM Press, 1964). Aspects of this have been questioned (see e.g. Routledge, *OT Theology*, pp. 38–41), particularly in regard to how to understand

of that divine activity through the biblical account. According to the NT, God is revealed, supremely, through Jesus Christ (e.g. John 1:18; 14:9; Col. 1:15; Heb. 1:1–3); but there, too, our access to that revelation is, primarily, through the written text. The text, then, is central, and the text that has been accepted as the source of that revelation is, as noted already, the canon of Scripture.[40] There is debate about the precise content of that canon and when it might have been formalized.[41] It seems clear, though, that from an early stage within Judaism there was a reverence for those written texts that were believed to have been inspired by God, and which might be designated 'Scripture'.[42] And this was carried over into the church.

There are several views relating to how God reveals himself through Scripture. At one end of the spectrum it may be argued that the Bible contains the testimony of those who are simply bearing witness to their experiences of God. Understood in this way Scripture may be helpful in guiding our own reflections, but has no real authority. At the other extreme is the view that God dictated the text of Scripture to its human writers, putting his words into their mouths, and overruling their personalities and agendas, so that what we read is precisely what God has said. If that were the case, though, we would not expect to see the variety of styles and different theological emphases that are clearly present within the Bible. The best way to view the divine inspiration of Scripture would appear to lie somewhere between those extremes. On the one hand, the OT is the work of human writers and editors, who may indeed be reflecting on their own, and the nation's, experiences of God – recalling what God has said to them, or seeking to apply their understanding of God to their own context.

'history' (see below, pp. 167–169). Nevertheless, the relationship between revelation and history is still viewed as important. Goldingay notes that 'the nature of the First Testament's narrative theology is to define Yhwh in terms of acts' (*Israel's Gospel*, p. 869); cf. Millard J. Erickson, *Christian Theology*, 3rd ed. (Grand Rapids: Baker, 2013), pp. 149–154.

40. Significant sections of the church accept that God continues to speak through charismatic gifts, including prophecy. However, it is widely acknowledged that this must be tested against Scripture, which thus retains its priority.

41. See below, pp. 22–40.

42. The importance of written, authoritative texts is evident in the response to the discovery of the 'Book of the Law' (probably all, or part, of the book of Deuteronomy) during Josiah's reforms (2 Kgs 22:11–13). Similarly, after the return from exile, Ezra's reading of the Law led to the people's renewed consecration (Neh. 8 – 10).

And what is written, including content, style and language, reflects their agenda and is set within the cultural and theological world view, of the writers and of their first audience. That is why context and background are important for a proper understanding of the text. However, while in one sense this is a 'human book', there is also a divine element: God has 'breathed into' the human writers in such a way as to ensure that what has been written down is, indeed, divine revelation.

The precise mechanism of what we generally call 'divine inspiration' is unclear. Sometimes we are told that God spoke directly to, or through, individuals and groups. Sometimes, particularly in the case of OT prophets, that revelation is linked with the agency of God's Spirit;[43] and Jewish and Christian tradition has further linked the Spirit of God with the inspiration of the Scriptures as a whole.[44] Often, though, while readers may, rightly, hold to that general view of divine inspiration, individual texts themselves make no such claims, even implicitly. The OT writers penned, we may assume, what they considered to be important messages; but relatively rarely do they attribute that writing directly to divine inspiration. And yet God was working in them in such a way that what they wrote may, legitimately, be described as God's Word. Some see a link between the human and divine elements present in this written 'word', with the human and divine natures perfectly united in Jesus Christ – the true Word of God.[45] We may also see an analogy with the way OT writers understood

---

43. E.g. Isa. 61:1–2; Ezek. 3:24; 11:5; Mic. 3:8; Zech. 7:12; cf. 2 Pet. 1:21. For more on the role of the Spirit in relation to prophetic inspiration, see e.g. David G. Firth and Paul D. Wegner (eds.), *Presence, Power and Promise: The Role of the Spirit of God in the Old Testament* (Nottingham: Apollos; Downers Grove: InterVarsity Press, 2011), pp. 174–256; see also Routledge, *OT Theology*, pp. 114–115.
44. See e.g. Kaufmann Kohler, 'Inspiration', in *The Jewish Encyclopaedia*, 12 vols. (New York: Funk & Wagnalls, 1901–6), 6:607–609; 'Bible Canon', in ibid., 3:140–154 (147). In discussion of Esther as authoritative Scripture a key consideration by the rabbis was whether or not it was written under the inspiration of the Holy Spirit; see e.g. *b. Meg.* 1.4, II.2–II.3; J. Neusner, *The Babylonian Talmud: A Translation and Commentary*, 22 vols. (Peabody: Hendrickson, 2005), 7b:31–32. P. J. Achtemeier suggests that 'the prophet became the model for an understanding of the inspiration of Scripture' (*Inspiration*, p. 17; see also LaSor, Hubbard and Bush, *OT Survey*, p. 595); and the Spirit's role in inspiring prophets is thus extended to all of the OT. This view appears to have been taken over by the NT writers (e.g. 2 Tim. 3:16; 2 Pet. 1:20–21).
45. See e.g. Peter Enns, *Inspiration and Incarnation: Evangelicals and the Problem of the Old Testament* (Grand Rapids: Baker, 2005), pp. 17–21.

God's activity in history.[46] There are occasions where God appears to intervene directly in the history of his people, for example in the events of the exodus. Often, though, that is not the case. When Joseph, now a ruler in Egypt, confronts the brothers who had sold him into slavery, he acknowledges God's hand in it all (Gen. 50:20). Von Rad comments on this,

> only at the very end, when God has resolved everything for good, does one learn that God has held the reins in his hand all along and has directed everything . . . But how? No miracle ever occurred. Rather, God's leading was worked in secret, in the plans and thoughts of men's hearts.[47]

The result is, nevertheless, that God's purposes were fulfilled. Similarly, God may be seen to work within and through the agendas, reflections and decisions of human agencies to ensure that what is recorded in Scripture may be considered to be his inspired word. This includes any editing of the text into its final canonical form.[48] This is of particular importance when it comes to the discussion of narrative approaches to the OT text.

Inerrancy?

One of the points of, sometimes heated, discussion when it comes to viewing Scripture as inspired divine revelation is the issue of 'inerrancy'.[49] This

---

46. See Routledge, *OT Theology*, pp. 311–315.
47. Gerhard von Rad, *God at Work in Israel* (Nashville: Abingdon, 1980), pp. 143–144.
48. According to Childs, the final canonical form of the text 'alone bears witness to the full history of revelation' (*Introduction*, pp. 75–76). See also below, pp. 208–211. Grisanti also allows for 'inspired editorial activity' in the production of the final form of the text (Michael A. Grisanti, 'Inspiration, Inerrancy, and the OT Canon: The Place of Textual Updating in an Inerrant View of Scripture', *JETS* 44.4 [2001], pp. 577–598).
49. See e.g. Erickson, *Christian Theology*, pp. 188–209; Norman L. Geisler (ed.), *Inerrancy* (Grand Rapids: Zondervan, 1980), especially Paul D. Feinberg, 'The Meaning of Inerrancy' (pp. 267–304); Wayne Grudem, *Systematic Theology: An Introduction to Biblical Doctrine* (Grand Rapids: Zondervan; Leicester: Inter-Varsity Press, 1994), pp. 90–104; see also John Warwick Montgomery (ed.), *God's Inerrant Word: An International Symposium on the Trustworthiness of Scripture* (Minneapolis: Bethany Fellowship, 1974). For more recent defences of inerrancy, see e.g. G. K. Beale, *The Erosion of Inerrancy in Evangelicalism: Responding to New Challenges to Biblical Authority* (Wheaton: Crossway, 2008); Norman L. Geisler and William C. Roach, *Defending Inerrancy: Affirming the Accuracy of Scripture for a New Generation* (Grand Rapids: Baker, 2011).

represents an attempt to maintain the integrity of divine revelation and the authority of Scripture in the face of modern biblical criticism;[50] and asserts that, because God cannot lie, and because every word in Scripture comes from him, every word in Scripture must therefore be free from error. However, a difficulty arises over what constitutes 'error'. Current approaches to inerrancy generally allow that the Bible writers wrote within a particular context, which must be taken into account in interpretation.[51] However, that does not go far enough for many evangelicals.[52] A significant problem is that the point at which accommodation to ancient cultural, historical and theological ideas crosses the boundary into error can appear arbitrary. Some things, including non-chronological history writing, imprecise quotations and describing the world in phenomenological terms (i.e. as it appears to the writer rather than using exact scientific language, for example 'the sun rises'), are deemed acceptable on the grounds that they conform to the literary conventions of the day. On the other hand, the suggestion that OT writers describe creation and the created order using the kind of mythological language and imagery that is found elsewhere in the ANE is often seen as crossing the line into error;[53]

---

50. The seriousness with which this issue was regarded is reflected in the title of an early, influential publication: Harold Lindsell, *The Battle for the Bible* (Grand Rapids: Zondervan, 1976); cf. Donald W. Dayton, 'The Battle for the Bible: Renewing the Inerrancy Debate', *ChrCent*, 10 Nov. (1976), pp. 976–980. See also John Warwick Montgomery, 'Biblical Inerrancy: What Is at Stake', in Montgomery, *God's Inerrant Word*, pp. 15–42. The depth of feeling over this is expressed by Lewis: 'at stake here is no minor detail of Scripture but *the very essence of Christianity*' (Gordon R. Lewis, 'The Human Authorship of Inspired Scripture', in Geisler, *Inerrancy*, pp. 229–264 [263] [italics his]).
51. 'The Chicago Statement on Biblical Inerrancy', produced by the International Council on Biblical Inerrancy (1978) allows that 'in inspiration, God utilized the culture and conventions of his penman's milieu'; this is reproduced e.g. in Beale, *Erosion*, pp. 267–279 (276). See also e.g. Erickson, *Christian Theology*, pp. 201–204; Grudem, *Systematic Theology*, pp. 91–92.
52. See e.g. Enns, *Inspiration*; Clark H. Pinnock, *The Scripture Principle: Reclaiming the Full Authority of the Bible*, 2nd ed. (Grand Rapids: Baker Academic, 2006). For a brief but balanced comment, see Leslie C. Allen, 'Revelation and Inspiration', in LaSor, Hubbard and Bush, *OT Survey*, pp. 591–597 (596–597).
53. The terms 'myth' and 'mythological' are sometimes taken to imply 'untrue', and are rejected by advocates of inerrancy (cf. Beale, *Erosion*, pp. 25–37). Others argue that myths express a view of the world and an understanding of reality in pre-scientific terms; see e.g. Brevard S. Childs, *Myth and Reality in the Old Testament* (London: SCM

even though it can be argued that that, too, is likely to have been normal practice at the time.[54]

This issue is a complex one. On the one hand, it is important to affirm a commitment, not only to the authority, but also to the integrity, truthfulness and reliability of Scripture. On the other hand, that commitment must be accompanied by the recognition that the message of the OT writers is set within a particular historical, cultural and theological milieu, which will, necessarily, be reflected in the language and imagery of the text. As Christian readers of the OT we believe that its message has universal significance: it is for all people for all time. However, it was also written for a particular audience at a particular point in history, and for its message to be communicated effectively its writers needed to present it in a form that would make sense then. That includes writing in the light of their own and their contemporaries' world view. The OT writers were people of their time, sharing many of the ideas of those around them;[55] and the process by which they were inspired to write Scripture, unless specifically required to do so by the nature of the revelation, did not override those characteristics, even if that meant some accommodation to their limited understanding in the way key theological ideas were communicated. In my view such an accommodation does not constitute error, and it should not be seen as undermining the integrity and reliability of the biblical account.

Progressive revelation

God did not reveal everything that human beings need to know about himself and his purposes at once. Theological understanding was gradual and progressive. This progression is particularly evident between the OT and the NT, and

---

Press, 1960); Enns, *Inspiration*, p. 40; Goldingay, *Israel's Gospel*, pp. 878–881, though, because of confusion over the term 'myth', Goldingay prefers 'imaginative parables' (p. 878); cf. John H. Walton, *Ancient Near Eastern Thought: Introducing the Conceptual World of the Hebrew Bible* (Grand Rapids: Baker Academic, 2006). OT writers appear to use contemporary mythological language, though they did not embrace the related religious systems; see Routledge, *OT Theology*, pp. 124–136 (126–127).

54. For further discussion, see e.g. Enns, *Inspiration*; see also Routledge, *OT Theology*, pp. 124–136 (126–127); Walton, *ANE Thought*; Davis A. Young and Ralph Stearley, *The Bible, Rocks and Time: Geological Evidence for the Age of the Earth* (Downers Grove: InterVarsity Press, 2008), pp. 165–210.

55. So Walton suggests that similarities between OT and ANE stories 'could exist because Israel adapted something from ancient Near Eastern culture or literature, or . . . because they simply resonated with the culture' (Walton, *ANE Thought*, p. 24).

the complete revelation found in Christ; but it is also seen within the OT. This may take the form of new truth that is directly revealed. So, for example, Exodus 6:3 indicates that the name of God revealed to Moses had not hitherto been known.[56] Similarly, Jeremiah 31:31–34 points to a new covenant, which, though continuous with the earlier Sinaitic covenant, will also be substantially different from it;[57] and passages that indicate a move from corporate to individual responsibility (e.g. Jer. 31:29–30; Ezek. 18:2–3) present that, too, as an innovation. And, though not stated directly, there may be evidence of a growing theological understanding within the text itself. While there continues to be debate about when much of the OT material came to be written down in the form that we now have it, there is wide agreement that the traditions that lie behind the text cover many centuries. And during that time there appears to have been some development in the perception of God and his relationship with his people and his world. I am not suggesting that God himself is changing.[58] In my view he remains constant! The issue here is how he is perceived and portrayed by writers who do not have the whole picture set out for them from the beginning. That said, where there is development it builds on rather than contradicts earlier perceptions.

Examples of this latter kind of progression include the move towards a more strictly defined monotheism. The patriarchs are portrayed as worshipping one God; but their attitude to those who worshipped other gods was fairly easy going. The exclusivity of Israel's relationship with its one God was formalized in connection with the exodus, the covenant at Sinai and the Law. Even at this point, though, there is not the outright denial of the existence of other gods,

---

56. On references to the name 'Yahweh' in the book of Genesis see below, p. 54; see also Routledge, *OT Theology*, pp. 92–94.
57. On the 'new covenant' see ibid., pp. 269–272.
58. Some argue that because God is relational, and interacts with people and a world that are changeable, he, too, must be subject to change. According to Brueggemann, the God of the OT 'is always emerging in new ways in response to the relationship at hand. This God is fully engaged in interaction with several partners and is variously impinged upon and evoked to new responses and . . . to new dimensions of awareness and resolve' (Walter Brueggemann, *An Unsettling God: The Heart of the Hebrew Bible* [Minneapolis: Fortress, 2009], pp. 4–5). This relational aspect of God is a feature of 'process theology'; see e.g. Bruce G. Epperly, *Process Theology: A Guide for the Perplexed* (London: T&T Clark International, 2011); Robert Mesle, *Process Theology: A Basic Introduction* (St. Louis: Chalice, 1993); see also Terence E. Fretheim, *The Suffering of God: An Old Testament Perspective* (Minneapolis: Fortress, 1984).

which full monotheism requires. The view that other gods exist as no more than worthless idols seems to come later, particularly in the prophetic texts of Isaiah 40 – 55 and Jeremiah.[59]

Another example is the OT understanding of afterlife. This is an important element of Christian faith, and it is tempting to assume that it formed an important part of the faith of the OT writers, too; but that does not seem to be the case. For much of the OT period, the idea is not prominent and there is no clearly articulated theology of an afterlife; not one, at least, that was sufficient to have a substantial impact on life here and now.[60] That is significant when it comes to interpreting and applying OT texts. The OT, as the rest of the Bible, does hold to the principle of divine vindication, reward and punishment. However, if there is no strong expectation of an afterlife, then the focus for these things shifts to the present. Thus Job receives his vindication within his lifetime; and, conversely, there is a sense of injustice because the wicked do not appear to be punished in this life, but instead prosper (e.g. Ps. 73:3; Jer. 12:1).

The view of supernatural spiritual agencies in the OT, and particularly the idea of Satan, also seems to undergo some development. In the earlier part of the OT, perhaps in the light of the constant temptation towards polytheism, everything, good or bad, is attributed to God. There is little emphasis on demons and evil spirits, and where they appear, they remain under God's control (e.g. 1 Sam. 16:14; 1 Kgs 22:19–23).[61] Even (the) Satan in the book of Job can act only with God's permission, and within clearly prescribed limits (e.g. Job 1:12; 2:6). This development is evident in the parallel accounts of the census carried out by David. In 2 Samuel 24:1 we are told that God incited David to number the people. This reflects the view, emphasized in the earlier period, that God is responsible for everything. By contrast, in 1 Chronicles 21:1, which is generally thought to have been written later, perhaps in the fifth

---

59. For further discussion of the development of monotheism, see e.g. Routledge, *OT Theology*, pp. 85–101.

60. See further e.g. Philip Johnston, *Shades of Sheol: Death and Afterlife in the Old Testament* (Leicester: Apollos; Downers Grove: InterVarsity Press, 2002); 'Afterlife', in *DOTP*, pp. 1–5; R. L. Routledge, 'Death and Afterlife in the Old Testament', *JEBS* 9.1 (2008), pp. 22–39; *OT Theology*, pp. 302–310.

61. For further discussion, see Robin Routledge, 'An Evil Spirit from the Lord – Demonic Influence or Divine Instrument', *EvQ* 70.1 (1998), pp. 3–22; *OT Theology*, pp. 117–123; Andrew E. Hill and John H. Walton, *A Survey of the Old Testament*, 3rd ed. (Grand Rapids: Zondervan, 2009), p. 316.

or fourth century BC,[62] the census is taken at the behest of Satan. By this time spiritual agencies appear to have come to be viewed as operating independently of, and in opposition to, God.

A fourth, important area of theological development is in relation to the non-Israelite nations. In the early days of Israel's settlement in Canaan the surrounding nations posed a threat to their life as the people of God, and that is reflected in instructions to remain distinct from them. For much of the rest of their history, the people of Israel were oppressed by the nations and, understandably, saw their future vindication in terms of the defeat and subjugation of oppressive enemies. However, alongside what seems to be an exclusive, nationalist agenda, there is a developing universalistic view that sees the future people of God made up of those from all nations, who come on the basis of their faith, and who will share equally in the blessings of salvation.[63] I have argued that aspects of this are present within the OT from the beginning;[64] however, its theological articulation develops over time.

One of the significant events in the development of the theology of the OT was the Babylonian exile. The destruction of Jerusalem and the temple, and expulsion from the land, led to a serious evaluation of the nation's relationship with God. A major issue was the question of how a faithful God could allow such a thing to happen.[65] Another was how to maintain that relationship in a hostile, polytheistic culture, and that is reflected both in the focus on monotheism, and also in a clearer articulation of the view of God as the Creator, which distinguishes him from the worthless gods of Babylon. Linked to that, a third important issue related to the nation's future hope: the God who has created order out of chaos is able to transform the exile, which is viewed as a return to the disorder of Genesis 1:2 (e.g. Jer. 4:23), and bring about a new creation.[66] It is important to emphasize that this is still divine *revelation*; it is not

---

62. On the date of Chronicles see below, p. 382.
63. See e.g. Robin Routledge, 'Is There a Narrative Substructure Underlying the Book of Isaiah?', *TynBul* 55.2 (2004), pp. 183–204; *OT Theology*, pp. 315–334.
64. Robin Routledge, 'Mission and Covenant in the Old Testament', in Rollin G. Grams, I. Howard Marshall, Peter F. Penner and Robin Routledge (eds.), *Bible and Mission: A Conversation Between Biblical Studies and Missiology* (Schwarzenfeld: Neufeld, 2008), pp. 8–41.
65. This is an important element in the so-called Deuteronomistic History; see below pp. 253–257.
66. See e.g. Robin Routledge, 'Did God Create Chaos? Unresolved Tension in Genesis 1:1–2', *TynBul* 61.1 (2010), pp. 69–88 (86–87).

merely a human response to a particular crisis. There may be an element of discovery, as God's people reflect on what they already know of him and apply that to their current situation. Nevertheless, that needs to be seen as part of the continuing divine–human interaction within the process of inspiration. And by the same token these are not theological innovations. Rather, they build on an earlier understanding of God; though within that new historical context they take on a fresh importance and as a result find clearer articulation.

In the study of the OT it is important to be aware of progressive revelation, and to read texts, not only against their historical and cultural background, but also against the theological background of what was understood and believed by the writers and their audiences at the time. For Christian readers, this includes being careful not to read ideas from the NT or from Christian theology back into the OT.

2. WHAT IS THE OLD TESTAMENT? CANON AND TEXT

The Old Testament canon[1]

The term 'canon' comes from the Greek term *kanōn* (measuring rod),[2] and refers to the standard by which other things are judged. When related to Scripture, 'canon' is generally taken to refer to the definitive collection of texts that have been accepted by the believing community as authoritative and normative for faith.

---

1. See e.g. Bernard W. Anderson, *The Living World of the Old Testament*, 4th ed. (Harlow: Longman, 1988), pp. 636–643; Roger Beckwith, *The Old Testament Canon of the New Testament Church and Its Background in Early Judaism* (London: SPCK, 1985); F. F. Bruce, *The Canon of Scripture* (Glasgow: Chapter House, 1988); Stephen B. Chapman, *The Law and the Prophets: A Study in Old Testament Canon Formation* (Tübingen: Mohr Siebeck, 2000); 'The Old Testament Canon and Its Authority for the Christian Church', *ExAud* 19 (2003), pp. 125–148; 'What Are We Reading? Canonicity and the Old Testament', *WW* 24.4 (2009), pp. 334–347; Childs, *Biblical Theology*, pp. 55–69; Collins, *Introduction*, pp. 2–7; Stephen Dempster, 'Canons on the Right and Canons on the Left: Finding a Resolution in the Canon Debate', *JETS* 52.1 (2009), pp. 47–77; E. Earle Ellis, *The Old Testament in Early Christianity: Canon and Interpretation in the Light of Modern Research*, WUNT 54 (Tübingen: Mohr Siebeck, 1991); Norman K. Gottwald, *The Hebrew Bible: A Sociological Introduction* (Philadelphia: Fortress, 1987), pp. 102–114; R. K. Harrison, *Introduction to the Old Testament* (London: Inter-Varsity Press, 1977), pp. 260–288; LaSor, Hubbard and Bush, *OT Survey*, pp. 598–605; Lee Martin McDonald, *Biblical Canon*, pp. 73–242. See also Further reading, p. 386.
2. See e.g. McDonald, *Biblical Canon*, p. 38; cf. P. J. Achtemeier, *Inspiration*, pp. 104–109; Hermann Wolfgang Beyer, '*kanōn*', in *TDNT* 3:596; LaSor, Hubbard and Bush, *OT Survey*, p. 598.

We have already noted that one of the main reasons to continue to value the OT is that it has been accepted as part of this biblical canon. However, there is disagreement between Protestants and Catholics as to which texts should make up the OT canon; with the latter including seven additional books, as well as extra material in Esther and Daniel.[3] Since designating a text as canonical invests it with significant authority, it is important to consider the formation of the OT canon and why Christians accept some texts as authoritative Scripture, and not others. And there is a further important consideration: where did the Christian OT canon come from? Was it inherited from Israel as a collection of texts that were already accepted as divinely inspired Scripture? Or was it something created by the church? The answers have significant implications for the way we understand the OT as Scripture.

The formation of the Hebrew canon

The Hebrew Bible comprises twenty-four books, divided into three sections: Law, Prophets and Writings. The apocryphal text, 2 Esdras 14.45, dating from the end of the first century AD, refers to twenty-four books that were given by God to Ezra for public reading; however the books are not listed, and it cannot automatically be assumed that this is the same collection.[4] The first text to set out what became the full canonical listing of the Prophets and Writings is *Baba Batra*, dated in the second century AD;[5] though it is not certain that this list was widely accepted at that time. This leads some to conclude that the formalization of the structure of the Hebrew canon was a relatively late development, post-dating the NT and the separation between Christians and Jews. That then raises the question of what were the Scriptures of the NT writers, and what was their relationship to *Baba Batra*'s list? We begin this discussion by noting that there is some evidence to support the view of a tripartite Hebrew canon before or around the time of the NT.

---

3. These additional books are included in the *Apocrypha*, which some bibles insert between the testaments. In Catholic bibles they are included within the OT. Greek and Russian Orthodox Churches include these and some further material in their OT canon.
4. See e.g. McDonald, *Biblical Canon*, pp. 160–163. 2 Esd. 14.42–46 refers to seventy other books that appear to have equal status with the twenty-four, but which are restricted to 'the wise'.
5. 'This is the correct order of the prophets: Joshua, Judges, Samuel, Kings, Jeremiah, Ezekiel, Isaiah, the twelve prophets . . . This is the correct order of the writings: Ruth, Psalms, Job, Proverbs, Qohelet [Ecclesiastes], Song of Songs, Lamentations, Daniel, the scroll of Esther, Ezra, and Chronicles' (*b. B. Bat.* 14b).

A tripartite canon?

One significant source is the prologue to *The Wisdom of Ben Sirach* (*Ecclesiasticus*).[6] The book itself is generally dated around 180 BC, and the prologue, which purports to have been written by Ben Sirach's grandson, is dated around 120 BC.[7] This prologue mentions the threefold division of the books of the Hebrew Bible three times: 'the Law and the Prophets and the others [or "other books"] that followed them', 'the Law and the Prophets and the others [or other books] that followed them' and 'the Law . . . the Prophets and the other books of our ancestors' (NRSV). This is often taken as evidence that at least the first two sections of the Hebrew Bible (the Law and the Prophets) were well established as canonical Scripture at least by the latter part of the first century BC, and maybe much earlier.[8] There seems little doubt that the Law, here, is the Pentateuch. With regard to the Prophets, in Sirach's list of 'famous men' (Sir. 44 – 50) he appears to be aware of the books of Joshua, Samuel, Kings, Isaiah, Jeremiah and also the 'Twelve Prophets', suggesting that this section, too, was relatively stable.[9] However, there is considerable debate about whether the third division, which is referred to in generalized terms, had also been fixed by that time.

---

6. See e.g. Chapman, *Law and Prophets*, pp. 258–259; Dempster, 'Canons to the Right', pp. 59–61; Ellis, *OT in Early Christianity*, pp. 9–10; LaSor, Hubbard and Bush, *OT Survey*, p. 599; Timothy H. Lim, *The Formation of the Jewish Canon* (New Haven: Yale University Press, 2013), pp. 94–106; McDonald, *Biblical Canon*, pp. 80–84; Eugene Ulrich, 'The Non-Attestation of a Tripartite Canon in 4QMMT', *CBQ* 65 (2003), pp. 202–214 (212–213).
7. Chapman suggests a date of 120 BC ('Old Testament Canon', p. 137); McDonald notes a range from 130 to 110 BC, and prefers 116–110 BC (*Biblical Canon*, p. 82).
8. See also Alon Goshen-Gottstein, 'Ben Sira's Praise of the Fathers: A Canon Conscious Reading', in Renate Egger-Wenzel (ed.), *Ben Sira's God*, BZAW 321 (Berlin: de Gruyter, 2002), pp. 235–266. Goshen-Gottstein argues that the arrangement of the hymn reflects a bipartite canonical division, with Sir. 45:26 providing a clear break at the point of transition from Law to Prophets (pp. 240–241).
9. However, see John Barton, '"The Law and the Prophets". Who Are the Prophets?', in *Canon, Literature and Theology*, pp. 5–18. Barton argues that even towards the end of the first century AD there was only a bipartite division: Law and everything else; and that the prophetic books did not emerge as a distinct category until later. This argument is developed and expanded in John Barton, *Oracles of God: Perceptions of Ancient Prophecy in Israel After the Exile* (London: Darton, Longman & Todd, 2007), esp. pp. 13–95.

The process of 'canonization' is sometimes linked with the reference in 2 Maccabees 2.13–15 to the collection by Judas Maccabeus of texts lost during the war, which ended in 164 BC and which secured a brief period of independence for Judea (the Greek and Roman name for the province that corresponded, broadly, to Judah).[10] The verses also refer to an earlier collection, by Nehemiah, of 'books about the kings and prophets, and the writings of David, and letters of kings about votive offerings' (NRSV). Since the significance of the Law at the time of Nehemiah may be assumed, the reference to 'books about kings and prophets, and the writings of David' (the Psalms?) may suggest two further sections, indicating a tripartite division, though the details are uncertain. It is not certain that Judas Maccabeus' collection included the same tripartite elements as Nehemiah's; though if there was no intended correlation it seems odd that Nehemiah's collection is mentioned in such detail.

Another suggested reference to a tripartite canon before the NT period has been discovered at Qumran. A line in the text 4QMMT, which scholars date variously from the mid-second to the late first century BC,[11] has been partly reconstructed to read, 'the book of Moses and the books of the Prophets and (the writings of) David'.[12] This suggests the division of Law and Prophets, and the last category may refer to the Psalms, which as the first book of the Writings may stand for the whole section. Ulrich questions this reconstruction, which seems to be influenced by the assumption that a tripartite canon was in existence at the time.[13] Lim accepts the general reconstruction, though challenges the view that it refers to David's *writings*.[14] He argues that this does not indicate a tripartite canon, but may reinforce the idea of a 'broadly bipartite' collection of Scriptures.[15]

---

10. See e.g. Sid Z. Leiman, *The Canonization of Hebrew Scripture: The Talmudic and Midrashic Evidence* (Hamden: Archon, 1976), pp. 29–30; cf. McDonald, *Biblical Canon*, pp. 84–86.
11. See e.g. Hanna von Weissenberg, *4QMMT: Reevaluating the Text, the Function, and the Meaning of the Epilogue* (Leiden: Brill, 2009), pp. 15–17, 48.
12. See Ulrich, 'Non-Attestation', p. 202; see also Chapman, *Law and Prophets*, pp. 256–257; Dempster, 'Canons to the Right', pp. 61–62; Lim, *Formation*, pp. 127–131; McDonald, *Biblical Canon*, pp. 89–92. The 'writings of David' here is an interpretation of *be-David* in the reconstructed text.
13. Ulrich, 'Non-Attestation', pp. 209–212; see also von Weissenberg, *4QMMT*, pp. 48–53.
14. Lim, *Formation*, pp. 127–128 (128).
15. Ibid., p. 128.

The NT generally refers to this same bipartite division of Law and Prophets (e.g. Matt. 7:12; Luke 16:16; 24:27; Acts 13:15); though Luke 24:44 appears to indicate a threefold division: 'the Law of Moses, the Prophets and the Psalms'.[16] Here, as with the reference to David in 4QMMT, 'Psalms' may be seen to stand for the 'Writings' as a whole. However, that is not certain, and McDonald sees the reference to the Psalms alone as a further indication that, while maybe suggesting movement towards a tripartite division, the third section of the canon was not yet complete.[17] Luke 11:51 (Matt. 23:35) reports Jesus challenging the Pharisees over their treatment of prophets, from Abel to Zechariah (whose death is recorded in 2 Chr. 24:20–22). This is consistent with the view that a text extending from Genesis to Chronicles (as in *Baba Batra*'s list) was already known during the NT period. Bruce notes that while, chronologically, there may have been other martyred prophets (e.g. Uriah in Jer. 26:20–23), Zechariah was the last such, canonically.[18] Jesus does not confine the range to the Law and Prophets, suggesting that at least part of the third section of the Hebrew Bible was also regarded as Scripture. The evidence is not conclusive; but it does support the argument for a threefold canonical text that may have been in roughly the same form as that outlined later in *Baba Batra*.

A further, important piece of evidence for a tripartite canon is found in Josephus' tract *Against Apion*, written in the closing years of the first century AD. In it he refers to 'twenty-two books, which contain the records of all the past times; which are justly believed to be divine'; and he further subdivides the collection, 'five belong to Moses, which contain his laws and the traditions of the origin of mankind till his death', and then 'the prophets, who were after Moses, wrote down what was done in their times in thirteen books. The remaining four books contain hymns to God, and precepts for the conduct of human life'.[19] Josephus then goes on to note the significance of these books:

> How firmly we have given credit to those books of our own nation, is evident by what we do; for during so many ages as have already passed, no one has been so bold as either to add anything to them, to take anything from them, or to make any change

16. Dempster, 'Canons to the Right', p. 65; Lim, *Formation*, pp. 156–166; McDonald, *Biblical Canon*, pp. 93–95.
17. E.g. McDonald, *Biblical Canon*, pp. 93–94; see also Lim, *Formation*, p. 164.
18. Bruce, *Canon*, p. 31; however, cf. McDonald, *Biblical Canon*, pp. 95–100.
19. Josephus, *Ag. Ap.* 1.38–40, taken from William Whiston (trans.), *The Works of Josephus*, new updated ed. (Peabody: Hendrickson, 1980).

> in them; but it becomes natural to all Jews, immediately and from their very birth, to esteem those books to contain divine doctrines, and to persist in them, and, if occasion be, willingly to die for them.[20]

This suggests the existence of a fixed, tripartite list of books that have authoritative status for the Jewish faith.[21] Josephus may exaggerate the fixedness and the authority of this collection, though in an apologetic work it would not have been in his interests to make statements that might easily be refuted by opponents.[22] This evidence, though, is not without problems. The content of this 'canon' is not clear; Josephus mentions only twenty-two books, not twenty-four as in the formalized Hebrew canon; and though he indicates a threefold division, the second and third sections (including thirteen books in 'the prophets') do not correspond to the later canon. One suggested explanation of the different order is that Josephus deliberately rearranged the collection to include all of the history books alongside the 'former prophets' in the second section.[23] It is possible, too, that 'hymns to God' may be a reference to the Psalms; although the rest of the third section is unclear.[24]

These texts indicate that by the end of the first century AD, and maybe for some time before that, there was movement towards a definitive collection of authoritative books. And Josephus' evidence, the prologue to Sirach, Luke 24:44 and, possibly, 4QMMT, may further indicate a tripartite division of texts, comprising (1) the Law, (2) a collection of prophetic books, which contains most or all of what became the later canonical collection, but that may not yet be definitive, and (3) a third section, which is less clearly defined but appears to contain the Psalms,[25]

---

20. Ibid. 1.42.
21. Though see Barton, 'Who Are the Prophets?', pp. 7–9.
22. So e.g. McDonald raises doubts about Josephus' reliability (*Biblical Canon*, pp. 153–155); however, cf. Chapman, *Law and Prophets*, p. 273.
23. See e.g. Chapman, *Law and Prophets*, p. 274; Dempster, 'Canons to the Right', p. 63; see below, n. 27.
24. See further Duane L. Christensen, 'Josephus and the Twenty-Two-Book Canon of Sacred Scripture', *JETS* 29.1 (1986), pp. 37–46; Leiman, *Canonization*, pp. 31–34.
25. Philo of Alexandria, early in the first century AD, appears to indicate a similar threefold collection. He notes that a Jewish sect, the Therapeutae, held sacred 'laws and oracles delivered through the prophets, and psalms and the other books' (Philo of Alexandria, *The Contemplative Life*, p. 25; David Winston [trans.], *The Contemplative Life, Giants and Selections* [Mahwah: Paulist Press, 1981], p. 46); cf. also McDonald, *Biblical Canon*, pp. 87–89.

and (on the evidence of Luke 11:51 and Matt. 23:35) may end with the book of Chronicles.

The number of books in the Hebrew canon

The number of books in the final, formalized Hebrew canon is twenty-four. That is also the number referred to in 2 Esdras 14.45. As we have seen, Josephus refers to twenty-two books, and it has been claimed that a version of the book of *Jubilees*, which dates from the first century AD, also refers to twenty-two books (though that version of the text has not survived, and some question whether it ever existed).[26] It has been suggested that Josephus' twenty-two books are the same as the traditional list of twenty-four, with Ruth added to Judges and Lamentations to Jeremiah.[27] These numbers are probably related to the twenty-two and twenty-four letters in the Hebrew and Greek alphabets, respectively.[28] Freedman's suggestion of an early canon made up of twenty-three books (excluding Daniel, which was added later) is also based on the number of letters in the Hebrew alphabet, and dates to the Persian period when, he argues, *śin* and *šin* (the two forms of the twenty-first Hebrew character) were treated as separate letters.[29]

Views of the emergence of the Hebrew canon

A classic work seen, in the past, as a standard treatment of the development of

---

26. Charles claimed that *Jubilees* 2.23, which refers to 22 works of creation and 22 leaders of humankind, also included mention of 22 letters of the alphabet and 22 sacred books; see R. H. Charles, *Book of Jubilees or the Little Genesis* (San Diego: Book Tree, 2003), p. 44, n. 10; see also Beckwith, *OT Canon*, pp. 235–239; however, cf. James C. VanderKam, *From Revelation to Canon: Studies in the Hebrew Bible and Second Temple Literature* (Leiden: Brill, 2000), pp. 18–19; McDonald, *Biblical Canon*, pp. 158–161.
27. See e.g. Beckwith, *OT Canon*, pp. 118–119; Bruce, *Canon*, p. 33; Ellis, *OT in Early Christianity*, p. 7, n. 25; LaSor, Hubbard and Bush, *OT Survey*, pp. 602–603. The suggested list is the 5 books of the Law, the 8 books usually included within the Prophets plus Job, Esther, Chronicles and Ezra-Nehemiah (and Ruth and Lamentations, which are not named separately), making 13, and Psalms, Proverbs, Ecclesiastes and Song of Songs making up the final 4. This reconstruction, though, remains somewhat speculative.
28. See e.g. McDonald, *Biblical Canon*, p. 41.
29. Cf. ibid., pp. 165–167; see D. N. Freedman, 'The Symmetry of the Hebrew Bible', *Studia Theologica*, 46(2), 1992, pp. 83–108.

the OT canon is H. E. Ryle's *The Canon of the Old Testament.*[30] This argues for a linear, three-stage development. The *Law* appears always to have been regarded as the most significant section of the OT, and its public reading by Ezra (Neh. 8) is seen as an indication of its acceptance as canonical scripture. Ryle also notes that the Pentateuch was the only text accepted by Jews and Samaritans, and concludes that it must have been regarded as canonical before the schism between Jews and Samaritans (which he dates around 432 BC). The Law appears in all of the suggested canonical listings and there is general agreement about its early acceptance as authoritative scripture. According to Ryle, the second canonical section, the *Prophets*, must have been closed before Daniel, which is generally viewed as a prophetic book, was recognized as having canonical status, otherwise it would have been included. It is widely held that Daniel was not in its final canonical form until after 165 BC,[31] and this gives the latest date for the completion of the second section of the canon. The references in Sirach to what appears to be a distinct collection of prophetic books, including the book of the Twelve Minor Prophets, going back at least to 180 BC led Ryle to set a date of around 200 BC for the closure of the second section of the canon. According to Ryle, the third section of the canon, which is not so clearly defined in the early literature, was not closed until the Council of Jamnia (or Jabneh) in around 90 AD.[32] This 'Council' is alleged to have discussed and determined the content of the Hebrew canon, which thus reached its final, fixed form by the end of the first century AD.

Ryle's view remained the standard theory for the best part of a century; though it has, more recently, been challenged. With most recent scholars on all sides of the canon debate, Beckwith questions the view that the Hebrew canon was closed at the 'Council of Jamnia'. It appears that Jewish scholars did gather at Jamnia, particularly in the period following AD 70, to discuss how the Jewish faith might respond to the loss of the temple and, with it, the sacrificial system. As part of those discussions, there was debate about the value of some OT texts. However, this was not a 'council' as such; that language seems to have

---

30. H. E. Ryle, *The Canon of the Old Testament: An Essay on the Gradual Growth and Formation of the Hebrew Canon of Scripture* (London: Macmillan, 1892). For a more detailed statement and discussion of Ryle's view see e.g. Beckwith, *OT Canon*, pp. 4–7 and *passim*; Chapman, *Law and Prophets*, pp. 3–7 and *passim*; 'OT Canon', pp. 127–128; 'What Are We Reading?', pp. 335–340.
31. For discussion of the date of Daniel, see below, pp. 371–373.
32. Ryle's view of a Council of Jamnia follows Graetz, who put forward the idea in 1871; see Heinrich Graetz, *Kohelet oder der Salomonische Prediger* (Leipzig: Winter, 1871).

been borrowed from later Christian practice, where councils, which were generally representative of the church at large, were called to make formal decisions on a variety of important issues. Jamnia was not like that, and it seems unlikely that any final decisions regarding the canon were made there.[33] As we have noted, some maintain that those decisions were not made until very much later, in the second or even as late as the fourth century AD. Beckwith, however, argues that the canon was closed much earlier. In his view the prologue to Sirach indicates a closed, tripartite canon by the last third of the second century BC:

> for this writer there are three groups of books which have a unique authority . . . and not only does he state that in his own day there was this three-fold canon, distinguished from all other writings, in which even the Hagiographa formed a closed collection of old books, but he implies that such was the case in his grandfather's time also.[34]

This suggests that the canon may have been in existence by 180 BC;[35] though the formal distinction between Prophets and Writings was not made until Judas Maccabeus' collection of traditional Jewish literature around 164 BC.[36]

McDonald represents those who continue to argue in favour of the late closure of the Hebrew canon. He allows that there might have been the beginnings of a tripartite canon during the first century BC and the first century AD, though its make-up is not clear.[37] This, he suggests, was a loose collection that was generally accepted within Judaism and taken over by the early church, and it was only much later that it was narrowed down to a fixed list. He argues that

---

33. For further discussion of the 'Council of Jamnia', see e.g. Anderson, *Living World*, pp. 639–640; Beckwith, *OT Canon*, pp. 276–277; Bruce, *Canon*, pp. 34–36; Gottwald, *Hebrew Bible*, pp. 113–114; McDonald, *Biblical Canon*, pp. 174–175; Robert C. Newman, 'The Council of Jamnia and the Old Testament Canon', *WTJ* 38.4 (1976), pp. 319–348; Albert C. Sundberg, *The Old Testament of the Early Church*, HTS 20 (Cambridge, Mass.: Harvard University Press; London: Oxford University Press, 1964), pp. 113–128.
34. Beckwith, *OT Canon*, p. 111.
35. Beckwith acknowledges that Daniel might be as late as 165 BC, and might not have been part of this earlier collection, though it was included in Judas Maccabeus' collection. He suggests, though, that it might have been written earlier than the Maccabean period (ibid., pp. 356–357).
36. As noted above (n. 25) this is also the date for the completed Hebrew canon suggested by Leiman.
37. McDonald, *Biblical Canon*, p. 99.

the reference in *Baba Batra* should not be taken to suggest a widely recognized, fixed collection; and in the light of evidence of a continuing debate within Judaism until well after that time, he maintains that the Hebrew canon was not closed before the middle of the fourth century AD.[38]

Variations in the Hebrew texts of OT books discovered at Qumran are also taken to argue against the existence of an early fixed canon,[39] though those differences may not be as significant as the opponents of a fixed canon have claimed.[40] Textual variations are only to be expected, particularly in texts that were widely circulated. Nevertheless, lack of agreement over its precise content does not rule out the possibility that a book may be accepted as authoritative Scripture. Indeed, there are significant variations in Pentateuchal texts,[41] and these were regarded as Scripture from an early stage.

Dempster takes a different approach to the development of the OT canon, noting, in particular, internal evidence that reinforces its canonical structure.[42]

---

38. See e.g. Lee Martin McDonald, 'The Integrity of the Biblical Canon in the Light of Its Historical Development', *BBR* 6 (1996), pp. 95–132; *Biblical Canon*, pp. 173–174, 230.
39. See e.g. R. Timothy McLay, 'The Use of the Septuagint in the New Testament', in McDonald, *Biblical Canon*, pp. 224–242 (229); Eugene Ulrich, 'Our Sharper Focus on the Bible and Theology Thanks to the Dead Sea Scrolls', *CBQ* 66 (2004), pp. 1–24. Ulrich claims that 'over half of the books of the Hebrew Bible circulated in variant literary editions at the time of the origins of Christianity and rabbinic Judaism' ('Sharper Focus', p. 9); James C. VanderKam, 'Questions of Canon Viewed Through the Dead Sea Scrolls', *BBR* 11.2 (2001), pp. 269–292.
40. So e.g. Ulrich highlights differences between two Qumran texts of Isaiah (1QIsa[a], 1QIsa[b]); see Ulrich, 'Sharper Focus', pp. 2–4. Oswalt, commenting on the same scrolls, also notes variants, but sees general consistency between them; see John Oswalt, *The Book of Isaiah 1–39*, NICOT (Grand Rapids: Eerdmans, 1986), pp. 29–31. Swanson, too, suggests that the evidence from Qumran points to a relatively stable text in the first century BC; see Dwight Swanson, 'The Text of Isaiah at Qumran', in David G. Firth and H. G. M. Williamson (eds.), *Interpreting Isaiah: Issues and Approaches* (Nottingham: Apollos; Downers Grove: IVP Academic, 2009), pp. 191–212.
41. See VanderKam, 'Questions of Canon'.
42. Stephen Dempster, 'An "Extraordinary Fact": Torah and Temple and the Contours of the Hebrew Canon, Part 1', *TynBul* 48.1 (1997), pp. 23–56; 'An "Extraordinary Fact": Torah and Temple and the Contours of the Hebrew Canon, Part 2', *TynBul* 48.2 (1997), pp. 191–218; 'Canons to the Right', pp. 69–76; see also Chapman, 'What Are We Reading?', pp. 343–344.

He points out that the ending of Deuteronomy, which indicates Moses' pre-eminence as a prophet (Deut. 34:10–12), assumes other prophets since Moses, and thus anticipates the Prophets. At the end of the book of Malachi there is a reference to Moses and the Law (4:4), as well as to Elijah, who may be taken as representative of the Prophets (4:5–6); 'thus at the end of the prophetic books, there is a call to consider the Torah and Prophets together'.[43] There is also continuity between the Law and the beginning of the Prophets, with a further reference to Moses, and the challenge to Joshua to meditate (*hāgâ*) on the Law (*tôrâ*) day and night (Josh. 1:8). Psalms, which is frequently listed as the first book in the Writings, uses the same language to issue the same call: to meditate (*hāgâ*) on the Law (*tôrâ*) day and night (Ps. 1:2).[44] In Dempster's view these texts, which occur at the boundaries of the divisions of the Hebrew Bible, are the result of deliberate editing, by those who were aware of its overall canonical shape. This implies a relatively early 'closure' for the threefold canonical division, which, according to Dempster, took place in the Maccabean period.

A criticism of some approaches to the discussion of the emergence of the Hebrew canon is the undue emphasis placed on the incorporation of texts into a *closed canonical collection*. While it is important to recognize authoritative collections of books, it is also important to note that for books to be included in a final collection, they must have already acquired a certain level of acceptance. Thus the people of God viewed the Law as authoritative before it acquired formal canonical status. It appears that, during the exile with the loss of the land and the temple, which were closely linked to national identity and of God's presence with his people, focus shifted to the Law, as the key element of continuity. The exile, too, was seen as punishment for sin, and the way to guard against the same kind of tragedy recurring was renewed obedience to the Law. Both of these things put a renewed emphasis on the Law after the return from exile and especially during the reforms of Ezra and Nehemiah. Nevertheless, that was only confirming an authority and status that were already present. The book of Joshua may have been separated from the Pentateuch because it does not share a direct link with Moses.[45] On the other

43. Dempster, 'Canons to the Right', p. 71.

44. As Dempster points out *hāgâ* (to meditate) is linked to *tôrâ* (law) only in Josh. 1:8 and Ps. 1:2. The further reference to 'day and night' also occurs only in these two references.

45. E.g. Beckwith, *OT Canon*, pp. 154–166. Gottwald offers the sociological explanation, that the book of Joshua might have stirred up a nationalism that would have been inappropriate at the time of the return from exile while the people were still under Persian rule (*Hebrew Bible*, pp. 102–106).

hand, because of the close personal association of Joshua with Moses, that book and the history books that also make up the 'former prophets' are also likely to have had a special status from an early period. That status would also have been accorded to the 'latter prophets', who were regarded as delivering oracles from God. And, whatever date we ascribe to the closure of the second section of the canon, some of those prophetic texts would by then have been in circulation for centuries, and to retain their significance they too must have been viewed as authoritative well before they were formally canonized.

In the light of this, recent discussions of the development of the Hebrew Bible note the need to clarify the use of the term 'canon'. Although usually taken to refer to a final closed authoritative collection of books, the term may also denote texts that are authoritative, but have not yet been incorporated into a fixed list. A common way of clarifying this distinction is to refer to the fixed collection of authoritative texts as 'canon 2', and the more open set of texts, still viewed as authoritative but not yet forming a fixed collection, as 'canon 1'.[46] It seems reasonable to suppose that even where a collection of books was not yet formally closed in the sense of 'canon 2', and where there was the theoretical possibility of other books being added, at least in some circles that collection might have formed a standard set of authoritative texts, which in practice was unlikely to be altered significantly. It may be that there was no formalized 'canon 2' until very much later; however, it does seem possible that a standard set of texts, corresponding broadly to the list in *Baba Batra*, was recognized by the first century AD, and maybe considerably earlier.

Problem texts

The development of the Hebrew canon was not entirely straightforward, and there was debate among rabbis over some books.[47] In that debate, rather than using the term 'canon', rabbinic Judaism referred to its authoritative texts as things that 'impart uncleanness to (or defile) the hands', a somewhat counter-intuitive expression that appears to be related to their

46. This terminology is attributed to Graham Sheppard, 'Canon', in *The Encyclopedia of Religion*, 15 vols. (New York: Macmillan, 1987), 3:62–69; see e.g. Chapman, 'OT Canon', pp. 135–136; Dempster, 'Canons on the Right', pp. 50–51; McDonald, *Biblical Canon*, pp. 55–58.

47. See e.g. Beckwith, *OT Canon*, pp. 283–337; Gottwald, *Hebrew Bible*, pp. 113–114; Newman, 'Council of Jamnia'.

value.[48] The Mishnah indicates that, within the first and second centuries AD, concern was expressed as to whether Ecclesiastes and the Song of Songs came into this category.[49] Ecclesiastes takes a somewhat negative view of life,[50] and also appears to contain contradictions.[51] The problem with the Song of Songs may have been its somewhat risqué content,[52] or the fact that it makes no mention of God. The Babylonian Talmud notes that there was some debate over whether or not Ruth and Esther also defile the hands.[53] In the case of Ruth there might have been a perceived conflict between the acceptance of Ruth, a Moabitess, and Deuteronomy 23:3, which excludes Moabites from the assembly of the Lord. Esther, like the Song of Songs, does not mention God, and there may be an issue with its introduction of a non-Mosaic festival (Purim). There appear, too, to have been questions about Proverbs, which was also thought to contain contradictions,[54] and Ezekiel, whose content, probably in relation to offerings presented in the new temple (chs. 40 – 44), was thought to be at variance with the teachings of the Law.[55]

There is an indication that some of these issues were discussed among rabbis at Jamnia, towards the end of the first century BC,[56] and that some were still being debated afterwards. However, apparent tensions and contradictions appear finally to have been resolved, and even the Song of Songs was retained, by being

48. The Mishnah explains that, with regard to the 'Holy Scriptures . . . according to their preciousness is their uncleanness' (*m. Yad.* 4.6; see Jacob Neusner, *The Mishnah: A New Translation* [New Haven: Yale University Press, 1988]). See Beckwith, *OT Canon*, pp. 278–280; Bruce, *Canon*, p. 35; McDonald, *Biblical Canon*, pp. 58–61.
49. *m. Yad.* 3.5.
50. E.g. Gottwald, *Hebrew Bible*, p. 113.
51. *b. Šabb.* 30b. Contradictions include Eccl. 4:2 ('the dead . . . are happier than the living') and 9:4 ('a live dog is better off than a dead lion!').
52. There is some emphasis in *m. Yad.* 3.5 on the 'holiness' of the Song of Songs, maybe because its content might suggest otherwise.
53. *b. Meg.* 7a.
54. *b. Šabb.* 30b. The texts noted are Prov. 26:4 ('Do not answer a fool according to his folly') and 26:5 ('Answer a fool according to his folly').
55. *b. Šabb.* 13b; *b. Ḥag.* 13a; *b. Menaḥ.* 45a. See also Marvin A. Sweeney, 'The Problem of Ezekiel in Talmudic Literature', in Andrew Mein and Paul M. Joyce (eds.), *After Ezekiel: Essays on the Reception of a Difficult Prophet*, LBS (New York: T&T Clark International, 2011), pp. 11–23.
56. So e.g. the Talmud refers to rabbis known to have been prominent at Jamnia at this time.

interpreted as an allegory of the relationship between God and Israel. As noted already, though, the issue here seems to have been not primarily whether these texts should be added to an authoritative list that they would not otherwise be part of, but rather to recognize and ratify the authoritative status they had already acquired.

The Septuagint and the Alexandrian canon

Following the fall of Jerusalem, many Jews were taken into exile in Babylon; others sought refuge, particularly in Egypt. When Cyrus gave permission for exiled Jews to return to their homeland, some remained in Babylon, and others settled elsewhere. As a result, by the fourth century BC Jews were scattered around the Greco-Roman world. It was a deliberate policy of Alexander the Great to spread Greek culture and language across his empire, and that had an impact on the 'Diaspora' Jews, many of whom were no longer able to speak and read Hebrew. It thus became necessary to provide for them a version of their sacred writings in Greek. This work was largely undertaken within the substantial Jewish community in Alexandria from around 250 to 150 BC. The *Letter of Aristeas*, written in the latter part of the second century BC, links the translation of the Law into Greek with the expansion of the library at Alexandria under Ptolemy II. That seems plausible, though other parts of the account are more dubious. According to legend, seventy-two translators were appointed, and that gives the translation its name, Septuagint, from the Latin *septuaginta* (seventy), sometimes represented by the Roman numerals LXX. These men worked independently, but even so their translations were identical, and this affirmed the accuracy and divine authority of the finished text. In subsequent years other Hebrew texts were translated, though with somewhat uneven quality, and some texts written originally in Greek were also added to them, and this larger body of literature also became known, collectively, as the Septuagint.[57]

---

57. For further discussion of the development and significance of the LXX, see e.g. Jennifer Dines, *The Septuagint* (New York: Continuum, 2004); Timothy Michael Law, *When God Spoke Greek: The Septuagint and the Making of the Hebrew Bible* (New York: Oxford University Press, 2013); Karen H. Jobes and Moisés Silva, *Invitation to the Septuagint* (Grand Rapids: Baker Academic, 2000); Emmanuel Tov, *Textual Criticism of the Hebrew Bible*, 3rd ed. (Minneapolis: Fortress, 2012), pp. 127–146; Ernst Würthwein, *The Text of the Old Testament: An Introduction to the Biblia Hebraica*, 2nd ed. (Grand Rapids: Eerdmans, 1995), pp. 59–78; see also Bruce, *Canon*, pp. 43–44; Collins, *Introduction*, pp. 6–7; Martin Goodman, 'Introduction to the Apocrypha', in Martin Goodman (ed.), *The Apocrypha*, Oxford Bible Commentaries (Oxford:

In time Palestinian Judaism became unhappy with the LXX, possibly because its variance from the Hebrew Bible called its accuracy into question and made aspects of it theologically doubtful, and rejected it in favour of what became the Hebrew canon.

Some, in the past, have argued that the LXX, which includes the apocryphal books, corresponds to an 'Alexandrian Canon', which was accepted as authoritative Scripture among Greek-speaking Jews. And since the LXX was the main text used by the NT writers, this was, in effect, the canon adopted by the Christian church. This view assumes that the Hebrew canon was fixed at an early stage, and attempts to account for the continued significance of texts that lay outside that canon. The idea of the existence of an Alexandrian Canon has, though, been called into question, not least by Albert Sundberg,[58] and these days is widely regarded as unsustainable.[59]

The constitution of the Old Testament canon

At the beginning of this chapter I posed two key questions in relation to the OT canon: (1) Which books make up the OT canon and should therefore be considered authoritative by the church for faith and praxis? And (2) did the church inherit or create its OT canon? The second question has, largely, been answered. There appears to have been a body of sacred literature that was generally recognized as inspired, authoritative Scripture (in the sense of 'canon 1') in the first century AD, and these texts were 'inherited' by the church. Even McDonald, who argues that the collection of Hebrew texts was not finally accepted as canonical, in the sense of 'canon 2', until the fourth century AD, agrees that the church did inherit a set of authoritative texts, in the sense of

---

(*Footnote 57 cont.*) Oxford University Press, 2001), pp. 1–13 (1–2); Bruce M. Metzger, 'Important Early Translations of the Bible', *BSac* 150 (1993), pp. 35–49 (36–40); Gottwald, *Hebrew Bible*, pp. 121–122; LaSor, Hubbard and Bush, *OT Survey*, p. 616; McDonald, *Biblical Canon*, pp. 115–124.

58. See e.g. Sundberg, *OT of the Early Church*; Albert C. Sundberg, 'The Old Testament of the Early Church (A Study in Canon)', *HTR* 51.4 (1958), pp. 205–216; 'The Protestant Old Testament Canon: Should It Be Re-examined', *CBQ* 28 (1966), pp. 194–203; 'The "Old Testament": A Christian Canon', *CBQ* 30 (1968), pp. 145–155; '"The Old Testament of the Early Church" Revisited', in Thomas J. Sienkewicz and James E. Betts (eds.), *Festschrift in Honor of Charles Speel* (Monmouth: Monmouth College Press, 1997), pp. 88–110.

59. See e.g. Bruce, *Canon*, pp. 44–45; McDonald, *Biblical Canon*, pp. 100–103; cf. Dines, *Septuagint*, p. 12.

'canon 1'.[60] The answer to the question of which books make up the OT canon is less clear.

There seems little doubt that the five books of the Law were regarded as sacred Scripture from an early period in Israel's history. On the basis of its prologue, and of Sirach 44 – 50, the Prophets appears to have been accepted before 180 BC; though there are those who question whether the content of that collection was fixed even by the NT period.[61] There is more doubt over the third section, which the prologue to Sirach describes as 'the other books'. It seems likely that, by the NT period, those books that appear in *Baba Batra*'s list were regarded as Scripture, even those over which the rabbis raised concerns. All of them, for example, are included in the LXX. But were there others? If the Hebrew canon was fixed in AD 90 at the Council of Jamnia, then a good case could be made for its widespread acceptance in that form decades earlier. However, that scenario now seems very unlikely, and the final content of that canon might not have been agreed until much later. It is thus possible for the inclusion of other texts in the collection inherited by the church.

As already noted, the LXX was the version of the OT most commonly used by the early church and the writers of the NT. Most OT quotations in the NT are from this translation, and that accounts for many of the differences between these and what appears in the OT, which have generally been translated from the Hebrew Masoretic Text (MT).[62] And, because the LXX includes the books and additions found in the Apocrypha it has been argued that these, too, were among the texts inherited by the church as Scripture.

NT writers quote or allude to texts outside the Hebrew Bible, suggesting at least familiarity with other writings. McDonald gives an extensive list,[63] though accepts that this does not necessarily imply they were regarded as Scripture.[64] Childs goes further and asserts that 'the New Testament does not *cite as scripture* any book of the Apocrypha and Pseudepigrapha'.[65] In fact, McDonald's list includes only two texts where the language suggests that they are being viewed as Scripture. The formula 'it is written' appears in 1 Corinthians 2:9. Here, though, the NT passage seems much closer to the biblical text of Isaiah 64:4 than any of

60. See e.g. McDonald, *Biblical Canon*, pp. 29, 104.

61. See e.g. Barton, *Oracles of God.*

62. On the MT see below, pp. 40–43.

63. McDonald, *Biblical Canon*, pp. 452–464; cf. p. 195; see also Sundberg, *OT of the Early Church*, pp. 54–55; cf. Dempster, 'Canons to the Right', pp. 65–66.

64. McDonald, *Biblical Canon*, p. 195.

65. Childs, *Biblical Theology*, p. 62 (italics his).

the alleged extra-canonical alternatives. The remaining example is the reference in Jude 14–15 to what Enoch 'prophesied' (*1 Enoch* 1.9). Childs insists that this is not an exception to the general rule.[66] McDonald argues, however, that to describe the text as prophetic implies that it is inspired by the Spirit, and therefore has the status of Scripture.[67] The NT writers, though, with their experience of prophetic gifts being exercised in the course of worship, would not always have made the same connection between what is prophesied, even though inspired by the Spirit, and authoritative Scripture. Dempster, following VanderKam, suggests that Jude 14–15 may be a case of special pleading for the value of this one passage in one particular context, rather than the recognition of the whole book as Scripture.[68]

The lack of clear citations in the NT of material outside what became the Hebrew canon is not definitive; the NT does not contain, for example, any citations of some books that did come to be viewed as canonical (including Judges, Ruth and Esther). However, it does indicate that, even when using the LXX translations of OT books, NT writers had a relatively narrow view of what constituted Scripture.[69]

In the early Christian centuries there does not seem to be formal agreement on the precise content of the OT canon, though the areas of disagreement appear relatively limited.[70] Melito of Sardis describes a journey to the east to discover the content of what he terms the 'old testament', and his list, probably dating from the late second century AD, is very similar to the later Hebrew canon, with the omission of Esther.[71] Origen, in the first half of the third century AD,

66. Ibid.
67. McDonald, *Biblical Canon*, p. 106.
68. Dempster, 'Canons to the Right', p. 66.
69. A criticism of both sides of the debate is that they make assumptions about the canon, possibly reflecting a confessional position, and then accept or dismiss evidence on the basis of those assumptions. McLay notes that with a different set of assumptions Beckwith may have used the description of the words from *1 Enoch* as 'prophecy' to emphasize its canonicity; see McLay, 'Use of the Septuagint', in McDonald, *Biblical Canon*, p. 231.
70. See e.g. Bruce, *Canon*, pp. 68–82; Collins, *Introduction*, pp. 6–7; McDonald, *Biblical Canon*, pp. 200–206.
71. Melito refers to 'the Proverbs of Solomon and his wisdom', which may suggest inclusion of the apocryphal Wisdom of Solomon (McDonald, *Biblical Canon*, p. 200), though it may be a single description of Proverbs (Bruce, *Canon*, p. 71). Bruce's interpretation is reinforced by the view that the inclusion of Wisdom would give a list of twenty-three books rather than the more likely figure of twenty-two.

similarly, records the twenty-two books of the canonical Hebrew Bible, though his list includes Esther, and combines Judges and Ruth as a single book. However, this list also includes the apocryphal Letter of Jeremiah alongside Jeremiah and Lamentations.[72] Later in the third century AD Athanasius also gives a list of twenty-two books, corresponding to the number of letters of the Hebrew alphabet. Like Melito he excludes Esther, and separates Judges and Ruth. Lamentations is combined with Jeremiah, and Athanasius includes with them also the apocryphal texts of Baruch and the Letter of Jeremiah. The OT lists of Cyril of Jerusalem and Gregory of Nazianzus, in the fourth century AD, also include twenty-two books. Cyril includes Esther and combines Judges and Ruth, while Gregory has the same list as Athanasius. In his prologue to the books of Kings in the Latin Vulgate (written AD 390–405), Jerome also lists twenty-two books, the same list that appears in the Hebrew canon, or, if Ruth and Lamentations are included separately, twenty-four (corresponding to the twenty-four elders in Rev. 4:4). He goes on to emphasize the significance of texts originally written in Hebrew, which he considered to be canonical and acceptable for establishing doctrine, over against others that he describes as 'the apocrypha'.[73] Nevertheless, Jerome did include the apocryphal texts in the Vulgate and these additional books remained in wide use.[74] A challenge to their authority came from Martin Luther, who claimed that they were the source of some dubious theology. In response to that challenge, which was seen, too, as a challenge to the authority of the Roman Catholic Church, the Council of Trent (1546) declared that all of the apocryphal texts were included in the canon of Scripture.

The variations in lists, including different views about the value of the Apocrypha, suggest that there was continuing debate about the content of the OT canon. And the evidence is not sufficiently conclusive to resolve the

---

72. Bruce suggests that this may be an oversight (*Canon*, p. 75); Ellis views it as a later gloss (*OT in Early Christianity*, pp. 14–16). Origen did, however, attach significance to other books, both inside and outside the LXX; see e.g. Bruce, *Canon*, pp. 75–76; McDonald, *Biblical Canon*, p. 201. Sundberg notes that Origen is not trying to define the OT canon for Christians, but to set out the canon as accepted by Jews (*OT of the Early Church*, pp. 135–137).

73. The term 'apocrypha' had been used before to describe books that were of dubious value; however, Jerome appears to have been the first to link it with a specific collection of deuterocanonical books; see e.g. Goodman, 'Introduction to the Apocrypha', in Goodman, *Apocrypha*, p. 1.

74. One reason for the continued popularity of the apocryphal texts was the support given by Augustine.

issue definitively. However, while the Hebrew canon might not have been fixed, formally, until well into the Christian era, a good case can be made for the acceptance of a tripartite body of texts, corresponding to that later canon, as authoritative Scripture by the time the NT came to be written, and these are the texts the church inherited. The apparent lack of general recognition given to the apocryphal books by NT writers would also seem to support this view. It is possible, even likely, that the Christian use of the LXX led to the wider acceptance of additional Greek texts as Scripture. However, when the church fathers looked to clarify the content of the OT canon, they did so, primarily, by going back to the Hebrew Bible. And Luther's appeal to Hebrew Scripture follows a pattern that goes back to Melito, Athanasius and Jerome.

The debate will go on, influenced, no doubt, by ecclesiological tradition. In my view the weight of evidence is in favour of accepting as canonical only those books that have been included in the Hebrew Bible, and, as a result, that will be the primary focus of the following discussion.

The text of the Old Testament: textual criticism

Having considered which books make up the canon of the OT, a further, important introductory issue is to consider the correct text of those books.[75] In the past, particular versions of the text were regarded as 'inspired'. From the second century AD the LXX appears to have been viewed as the 'received text';

75. See e.g. Arnold, *Introduction*, pp. 25–28; Gottwald, *Hebrew Bible*, pp. 114–124; Harrison, *Introduction*, pp. 211–243; LaSor, Hubbard and Bush, *OT Survey*, pp. 606–618; David R. Law, *The Historical-Critical Method: A Guide for the Perplexed* (London: T&T Clark International, 2012), pp. 81–112; John Haralson Hayes and Carl R. Holladay, *Biblical Exegesis: A Beginner's Handbook*, 3rd ed. (Louisville: Westminster John Knox, 2007), pp. 34–52; Mark F. Rooker, 'The Transmission and Textual Criticism of the Old Testament', in Eugene H. Merrill, Mark F. Rooker and Michael A. Grisanti, *World and Word: An Introduction to the Old Testament* (Nashville: B&H, 2011), pp. 108–121; Al Wolters, 'The Text of the Old Testament', in David W. Baker and Bill T. Arnold (eds.), *The Face of Old Testament Studies: A Survey of Contemporary Approaches* (Grand Rapids: Baker; Leicester: Apollos, 1999), pp. 19–37. More specifically on the subject of textual criticism see also Ellis R. Brotzman, *Old Testament Textual Criticism: A Practical Introduction* (Grand Rapids: Baker Academic, 1994); Tov, *Textual Criticism*; Paul D. Wegner, *A Student's Guide to Textual Criticism of the Bible: Its History, Methods and Results* (Downers Grove: IVP Academic, 2006).

later the MT was regarded in that way. Nowadays the general view among evangelical scholars is that none of the versions available to us is, in itself, the primary, inspired text, which is usually thought of in terms of what was originally written. However, since we do not have those originals, and work only from much later copies and translations and copies of translations, recovering the original text is difficult, if not impossible. Consequently any investigation must generally be satisfied with determining the most accurate approximation to the original text. This issue is made more complicated because if, for example, a book has been edited, it is difficult to define what is meant by the 'original' version. In such cases it may be more helpful to look for the final canonical version of the text.[76] Nevertheless, while there may be debate over what is meant by 'original', it is reasonable to posit the existence of what Tov terms 'determinative texts', against which the relative accuracy of available texts may be judged. And though these original or determinative texts may be ultimately elusive, with a few exceptions, the textual evidence we have can take us close to them, and we can have confidence in the key theological ideas that depend on them.

Transmission of the text

It is not clear when the text of the various parts of the OT came to be written in the form that we now have them. A common view is that this happened relatively late, and not before the exile. Whether or not that is so, it is reasonable to suppose that traditions, either oral or written, were passed on from one generation to the next, thus ensuring the reliability of the final text.

The script of the earliest documents is likely to have been *paleo*-Hebrew (also known as Old Hebrew).[77] An example of this script is seen on the oft-reproduced seal of Jeroboam II;[78] and it is evident, too, in some of the texts at Qumran. Following the exile, Hebrew seems to have been written using Aramaic characters,[79] from which the more familiar Hebrew script is derived. The

76. For further discussion of the aims of textual criticism, see e.g. Ulrich, 'Sharper Focus', pp. 16–18; Tov, *Textual Criticism*, pp. 161–169; Bruce K. Waltke, 'Aims of Textual Criticism', *WTJ* 5.1 (1989), pp. 93–108; Wegner, *Textual Criticism*, pp. 29–37.

77. See e.g. Gottwald, *Hebrew Bible*, p. 115; LaSor, Hubbard and Bush, *OT Survey*, pp. 607–608; Wegner, *Textual Criticism*, pp. 59–60; Würthwein, *Text of the OT*, pp. 2–4.

78. The seal has the inscription 'Belonging to Shema, servant of Jeroboam', and it is usually dated to the reign of Jeroboam II in the eighth century BC.

79. Suggestions for the date of this transition vary. Wegner suggests between the fifth and third centuries BC (*Textual Criticism*, p. 60); LaSor, Hubbard and Bush suggest

Hebrew text would, at first, have been written in consonantal form, that is, without vowels; though to facilitate reading, some consonants may appear as vowels (known as *matres lectiones*).

Hebrew is one of a number of Semitic languages.[80] These are usually classified into groups: North-western Semitic, which includes Hebrew, Aramaic and Ugaritic; Eastern Semitic, which includes Akkadian; and South-western Semitic, which includes Arabic. In order to understand a particular language better, it is helpful to compare a number of different texts written in the same or related languages. There are very few Hebrew texts contemporary with the OT, and comparisons, primarily with texts in the same North-western Semitic group, are very valuable. Of particular significance was the discovery, in the late 1920s, of a large number of Ugaritic texts, dating back to the fourteenth century BC.[81] The further discovery, in the mid-1970s, of texts at Ebla, going back to before 2400 BC, and written in a hitherto unknown language, given the name 'Eblaite', is also important.[82] This language is thought to be close to Akkadian (and so part of the Eastern Semitic family), though it also displays North-western

---

(*Footnote 79 cont.*) 200 BC (*OT Survey*, p. 607); Würthwein argues that it is impossible to be more precise than 'between the fourth and second centuries BC' (*Text of the OT*, p. 3). During the first half of the first millennium BC the significance and influence of the Aramaic language had increased rapidly. As well as being spoken in Syria, its widespread use led to its becoming an official language in Mesopotamia, and well known all around the ANE; see e.g. Mario Liverani, *The Ancient Near East: History, Society and Economy* (Abingdon: Routledge, 2014), pp. 445–447.

80. The term 'Semitic' derives from the name of Noah's son Shem. It was first used in the eighteenth century in relation to a family of Western Asian languages, and then of the people groups that spoke those languages.

81. See e.g. Michael D. Coogan and Mark S. Smith, *Stories from Ancient Canaan*, 2nd ed. (Louisville: Westminster John Knox, 2012), esp. pp. 3–25; Peter C. Craigie, *Ugarit and the Old Testament: The Story of a Remarkable Discovery and Its Impact on Old Testament Studies* (Grand Rapids: Eerdmans, 1983).

82. See e.g. Robert Biggs, 'Eblaite Texts', in *ABD* 2:263–270; Cyrus H. Gordon, 'Eblaite', in Alan S. Kaye (ed.), *Semitic Studies: In Honor of Wolf Leslau on the Occasion of His Eighty-fifth Birthday* (Wiesbaden: Otto Harrassowitz, 1991), pp. 550–557; K. A. Kitchen, *The Bible in Its World: The Bible and Archaeology Today* (Exeter: Paternoster, 1977; Downers Grove: InterVarsity Press, 1979), pp. 37–55; Gary A. Rendsburg, 'Eblaite and Some Northwest Semitic Lexical Links', in Cyrus H. Gordon and Gary A. Rendsburg (eds.), *Eblaitica: Essays on the Ebla Tablets and the Eblaite Language*, vol. 4 (Winona Lake: Eisenbrauns, 2002), pp. 199–208.

Semitic characteristics,[83] making it significant, too, for the understanding of Hebrew.

The original Hebrew script is likely to have been continuous text, without divisions between words, though word spacing is referred to in the Babylonian Talmud and so must have been included before AD 500. The decision about where to divide words could result in problems with translation. Wegner notes Amos 6:12 as an example.[84] The literal translation of the first two lines is,

'Do horses run on rocky crags?
Does one plough with oxen [*babĕqārîm*]?'

It appears that the second line, like the first, should anticipate a negative answer, and one solution, as in the NIV, is to assume that both refer to the same location: 'does one plough *there* [i.e. on rocky crags]'.[85]

Alternatively, by separating the plural ending from 'oxen' and changing its vowels it can be read as 'sea' (*yām*), giving the more consistent translation 'Does one plough the sea [*yām*] with oxen [*babĕqār*]?' (as NRSV).

The lack of original versions of OT books is not surprising since the first texts were probably written on scrolls made from papyrus, which is perishable. No doubt over the course of time some writings will have been lost for ever, including some that are mentioned in the OT, such as the *Book of Jashar* (2 Sam. 1:18) and the annals of the Kings of Israel (e.g. 1 Kgs 14:19; 15:31; 16:5) and of Judah (e.g. 1 Kgs 14:29; 15:7; 22:45). Significant texts, though, were copied, and may have been transferred to leather (vellum or parchment), which would have lasted longer. To be manageable, scrolls were limited to 8 or 9 metres (26 or 30 feet) in length, enough to accommodate the longer biblical books. The Twelve Minor Prophets would have been put together on a single scroll.[86] All copying would have been done by hand, and in the course of what would have been a very lengthy process mistakes would almost certainly have

83. Liverani describes Eblaite as 'a western language influenced by Akkadian scribal tradition' (*ANE*, p. 177).

84. Wegner, *Textual Criticism*, pp. 61–62; cf. Würthwein, *Text of the OT*, p. 110; see also Hans Walter Wolff, *Joel and Amos*, Hermeneia (Philadelphia: Fortress, 1977), p. 284.

85. Cf. NRSV mg.: 'does one plough *them* with oxen'.

86. See e.g. Brotzman, *OT Textual Criticism*, pp. 39–40; Gottwald, *Hebrew Bible*, p. 115; Würthwein, *Text of the OT*, pp. 5–7. Brotzman notes that the Hebrew text of Samuel, Kings and Chronicles fitted on to single scrolls, but the Greek translations, which occupied more space, necessitated spreading them over two scrolls.

been made, and, over time, this would have led to several variant readings of the texts.

The history of the transmission of the Hebrew text up to early in the first millennium AD is not clear. As we have seen, in the period 250–150 BC books were translated from Hebrew into Greek, and became the LXX. A different version of the text, the Samaritan Pentateuch (SP),[87] was preserved in paleo-Hebrew by the Samaritans, following their separation from the Jews. Depending on when that schism occurred, some date the current SP as early as the fifth century BC, or as late as the Hasmonean period, in the second century BC.[88] The most influential Hebrew text is the MT,[89] which reached its final, definitive form around the tenth century AD, though it is generally thought to preserve a much earlier, *proto*-MT text, which some date back to the third century BC.[90]

The Dead Sea Scrolls, discovered at Qumran between 1947 and 1956, provide valuable information about how the OT text might have developed. These texts are written, predominantly, in Hebrew (some in paleo-Hebrew), and are dated between around 200 BC and AD 70 – several centuries earlier than any other available Hebrew manuscripts. The Qumran texts have added to the debate about the relationship between the three main text families (LXX, SP and proto-MT).[91]

---

87. See e.g. McDonald, *Biblical Canon*, pp. 136–138; Tov, *Textual Criticism*, pp. 74–92; Wegner, *Textual Criticism*, pp. 168–172; Wolters, 'Text of the OT', in Baker and Arnold, *Face of OT Studies*, pp. 27–28; Würthwein, *Text of the OT*, pp. 45–47; see further Robert T. Anderson and Terry Giles, *The Samaritan Pentateuch: An Introduction to Its Origin, History, and Significance for Biblical Studies* (Atlanta: Society of Biblical Literature, 2012).
88. The split between Jews and Samaritans, which had become a serious problem by the NT period, is variously dated to shortly after the return from exile, when Samaritans were among those who opposed rebuilding work (cf. Neh. 4:1–2), or the second century BC, when John Hyrcanus destroyed the Samaritan temple. See e.g. Gary N. Knoppers, *Jews and Samaritans: The Origins and History of Their Early Relations* (Oxford: Oxford University Press, 2013), pp. 169–216; Würthwein, *Text of the OT*, p. 45.
89. See e.g. Gottwald, *Hebrew Bible*, pp. 117–121; Tov, *Textual Criticism*, pp. 24–73; Würthwein, *Text of the OT*, pp. 10–44.
90. See e.g. Wegner, *Textual Criticism*, p. 65.
91. For further discussion on the Dead Sea Scrolls and their significance, see e.g. John J. Collins, *The Dead Sea Scrolls: A Biography* (Princeton: Princeton University Press, 2013); Frank Moore Cross and Shemaryahu Talmon (eds.), *Qumran and the History of the Biblical Text* (Cambridge, Mass.: Harvard University Press, 1975); Joseph A. Fitzmyer, *A Guide to the Dead Sea Scrolls and Related Literature* (Grand Rapids:

Tov notes that around 45% of the Qumran texts reflect the proto-MT.[92] However, of the remaining texts there are also some that support variant readings of the LXX, suggesting that differences between the LXX and MT are not due only to variations in translation, as had sometimes been assumed, but that a different Hebrew text lies behind the LXX. There are also texts that support the SP,[93] against the proto-MT, suggesting that it, too, belongs to a separate Hebrew tradition. This indicates that before the third century BC at least three Hebrew versions of the OT text were in circulation, and each was of sufficient significance to continue to be recorded.

One view of the relationship between these main texts, advocated by Cross, is that they are local versions of an original text, maybe going back to the fifth century BC, which circulated, and were copied in different geographical locations: the SP in Palestine, the proto-MT in Babylon and the pre-LXX in Egypt.[94] Talmon, however, suggests that there was originally much greater diversity in Hebrew texts, and those reflected in the LXX, MT and SP are only three of several, which were preserved because of their significance for the early Christian community, rabbinic Judaism and the Samaritans respectively.[95] Tov also notes that a significant proportion of the Qumran texts are not aligned with any of these three main families, indicating a more complicated situation, with greater fluidity of texts even as late as the first century AD.[96]

The close relationship between a substantial proportion of the texts discovered at Qumran and the MT helps to confirm the latter's accuracy; that is significant, because the earliest available MT manuscripts date from the eleventh

Eerdmans, 2008); James C. VanderKam, *The Dead Sea Scrolls and the Bible* (Grand Rapids: Eerdmans, 2012); *The Dead Sea Scrolls Today*, 2nd ed. (Grand Rapids: Eerdmans, 2010).

92. See Tov, *Textual Criticism*, pp. 108–110.
93. According to Tov, 11% of the Torah texts at Qumran 'exclusively reflect' the SP (ibid., p. 108).
94. See e.g. F. M. Cross, 'The Contribution of the Qumran Discoveries to the Study of the Biblical Text', in Cross and Talmon, *Qumran*, pp. 278–292; 'The Evolution of a Theory of Local Texts', in ibid., pp. 306–320; see also e.g. Gottwald, *Hebrew Bible*, pp. 116–117; Tov, *Textual Criticism*, pp. 185–187; VanderKam, *Dead Sea Scrolls*, pp. 15–16; Wegner, *Textual Criticism*, pp. 66–68.
95. See e.g. Shemaryahu Talmon, 'The Textual Study of the Bible – a New Outlook', in Cross and Talmon, *Qumran*, pp. 321–400.
96. Tov, *Textual Criticism*, pp. 109–110, 174; see also Talmon, 'Textual Study', in Cross and Talmon, *Qumran*, p. 325.

century AD. As already noted, it appears that the (proto-) MT came to be regarded as the standard Hebrew text early in the first millennium AD, and maybe by late in the first century AD. Traditionally that has been taken to indicate its priority over other texts.[97] Tov notes that the MT might have been accepted as standard in temple circles, though he suggests that its more widespread acceptance might have been more by historical accident than by design.[98] Ulrich argues that even by the end of the first century AD the texts relating to the OT were 'pluriform and still developing'.[99] He rejects the view that the MT was regarded more highly than other versions in that period, and insists that it should not have priority today. Others continue to argue in favour of the priority of the MT. Würthwein, for example, points out that the MT includes fewer *matres lectiones* compared with other Hebrew texts,[100] and goes on to note that the MT 'gives the impression of greater age and reliability'.[101]

As with the development of the canon, there is little here that is certain. There is some evidence to suggest that the proto-MT may be older and more

---

97. So e.g. Cross suggests that Greek texts were being revised in line with the proto-MT by the beginning of the first century AD ('Contribution of Qumran Discoveries', in Cross and Talmon, *Qumran*, pp. 281–282).
98. Tov suggests that following the destruction of the temple and the separation of the synagogue and church, the MT was the only one of the three main texts remaining to have an influence on Judaism (*Textual Criticism*, p. 179). Albrektson suggests that this was the text used by the Pharisees, and so survived the defeat by the Romans in AD 70 (Bertil Albrektson, 'Reflections on the Emergence of a Standard Text of the Hebrew Bible', in J. A. Emerton [ed.], *Congress Volume: Göttingen 1977*, VTSup 29 [Leiden: Brill, 1978], pp. 49–65). This implies that there was a measure of acceptance of the proto-MT by the Pharisees prior to this, and also that by then the LXX had already been largely discounted (see e.g. Wegner, *Textual Criticism*, p. 72).
99. Ulrich, 'Sharper Focus', p. 17.
100. Würthwein, *Text of the OT*, p. 15; see also David Noel Freedman, 'The Massoretic Text and the Qumran Scrolls: A Study in Orthography', in Cross and Talmon, *Qumran*, pp. 196–211; Wegner, *Textual Criticism*, p. 65; Wolters, 'Text of the OT', in Baker and Arnold, *Face of OT Studies*, pp. 28–31.
101. Würthwein, *Text of the OT*, p. 15. See also Bruce, *Canon*, p. 284; Childs, *Introduction*, pp. 100–106. In his *Hexapla*, a six-column comparison of the LXX, other Greek texts and a Hebrew text, Origen notes where the LXX differs from the Hebrew text, suggesting that he may be seeking to correct the LXX in line with the Hebrew; see e.g. Bruce, *Canon*, p. 73; McDonald, *Biblical Canon*, p. 119; Wegner, *Textual Criticism*, p. 95; Würthwein, *Text of the OT*, pp. 55, 57–59.

reliable than other texts, though there is also evidence to indicate that even into the first century AD there was some fluidity in the biblical text. In the light of that it may be that the role of the MT as the standard Hebrew text has been emphasized too much, and that more account needs to be taken of other witnesses to the text of the OT.[102] However, as noted already, the differences are not as great as has sometimes been suggested, and reducing, or at least re-evaluating, the value of the MT will not result in a substantially different text or in significant changes to the theological ideas that derive from it.

Whether or not it was regarded as a standard text earlier, the proto-MT became the standard Hebrew text during the first millennium AD.[103] In the early centuries it was preserved through meticulous copying by Sopherim (scribes). From around the sixth century AD accents and vowel markings ('pointing') were added to what was at that time still a consonantal text, and to this the Masoretes added marginal notes (*masora*).[104] There appear to have been several schools of copyists, each with their own textual traditions, though by the tenth century AD the Masoretic schools of ben Asher and a rival ben Naphtali, based at Tiberias, had become dominant. What we generally refer to as the MT is largely based on ben Asher's version of the Hebrew text; this includes the earliest complete text of the OT that we have, the *Codex Leningradensis*, which was written in around AD 1010 and forms the basis of current standard Hebrew texts.[105] The Masoretes indicated the division into verses, though verses were not numbered, and there were no chapter divisions. Breaking the Hebrew text into chapters appears to

102. See e.g. Tov's discussion of the importance of the LXX in the literary analysis of the OT (Emmanuel Tov, 'The Septuagint as a Source for the Literary Analysis of Hebrew Scripture', in Craig A. Evans and Emmanuel Tov (eds.), *Origins of the Bible: Canon Formation in Historical, Literary, and Theological Perspective* (Grand Rapids: Baker Academic, 2008), pp. 31–56.

103. For discussion of the development of the MT, see e.g. Russell Fuller, 'The Texts of the Tanak', in Alan J. Hauser and Duane F. Watson (eds.), *A History of Biblical Interpretation*, vol. 2: *The Medieval Through the Reformation Periods* (Grand Rapids: Eerdmans, 2009), pp. 201–226.

104. Traditionally the functions of copying, pointing and adding marginal notes is associated with three groups: Sopherim, Nakdanim (pointers) and Masoretes, whose name implies that they preserved traditions. There may have been overlap, particularly between the second and third groups, and both may be referred to, collectively, as Masoretes.

105. The current full standard text is the *Biblia Hebraica Stuttgartensia* (*BHS*), 4th ed. The fifth edition, the *Biblia Hebraica Quinta* (*BHQ*), is expected to be complete in 2017. It, too, is based on the Leningrad Codex.

have taken place after Stephen Langton, who later became Archbishop of Canterbury, had first done it for a version of the Vulgate, in 1205, to facilitate referencing. Numbering of verses does not seem to have been widespread until around the fifteenth century.

The Targums, Peshitta and Latin versions of the Old Testament[106]

In addition to the texts already noted, there are other texts that may give further information about the OT text, and enable us to build up a more accurate picture.

One group of texts are Targums, versions of parts of the OT written in Aramaic. Jews spoke Aramaic from the time of the exile, and we have noted that some parts of the OT are written in Aramaic. As Jews became less familiar with Hebrew, Aramaic commentaries may have accompanied the reading of the Hebrew text. These were originally oral, and while they may have included straightforward translation, they appear, more usually, as paraphrased interpretations. The earliest versions circulated in Palestine, maybe towards the end of the first millennium BC, though texts were not standardized then. The most significant texts, the *Targum Onkelos* (Law) and the *Targum Jonathan* (Prophets), were revised versions of Palestinian texts, and were given official approval only in the fifth century AD. Because of their relatively late date, and because they are not true translations, the value of Targums for textual study is limited. However, they have a pre-history and may reflect earlier Hebrew sources, and so help to corroborate other texts. Their usefulness has also been enhanced by the discovery of Targum fragments among the Qumran texts.

Another version, the Peshitta (or Peshitto), meaning 'simple', possibly in the sense of 'plain meaning', is a translation of the Bible into Syriac, an eastern Aramaic language. The Syriac OT was produced in the early Christian centuries. However, it shows signs of having been influenced by the Palestinian Targum and by the LXX, and so is of limited value as an independent source.

From the end of the second century AD Latin versions of the text began to appear, culminating in Jerome's Vulgate, or 'common' version of the text, at the end of the fourth century AD. Earlier Latin versions relied heavily on the LXX, though Jerome also worked with the Hebrew text.

---

106. See e.g. Brotzman, *OT Textual Criticism*, pp. 63–86; Craig A. Evans, 'Introduction', in Evans and Tov, *Origins of the Bible*, pp. 15–29 (18–21); Gottwald, *Hebrew Bible*, pp. 122–124; LaSor, Hubbard and Bush, *OT Survey*, pp. 614–618; Metzger, 'Important Early Translations of the Bible', pp. 40–49; Tov, *Textual Criticism*, pp. 147–154; Wegner, *Textual Criticism*, pp. 172–176, 271–276, 287–292; Würthwein, *Text of the OT*, pp. 79–99.

Comparing versions

Because Scripture is authoritative divine revelation it is important to work with the version of the text that seems best to reflect the original or determinative text. This involves comparing available texts and noting points of agreement and disagreement in order to trace them back to earlier sources. As we have seen, traditionally, the MT has been regarded as the primary text, and its readings are generally preferred unless two or more of the LXX, SP and Dead Sea Scrolls agree against it, suggesting that they may be working from an earlier Hebrew original. The Targums, Peshitta and Latin texts may also provide additional support.

Variations in the text may occur during copying. Sometimes those changes are made deliberately by well-meaning scribes. There are two key rules when comparing variants. One is that the shorter reading (*lectio brevis*) is generally preferred on the grounds that an editor or copyist is more likely to add words of explanation than to remove text. The second is that the more difficult reading (*lectio difficilior*) is more likely to be correct because it is more probable that a scribe will try to simplify a difficult text, and possibly try to harmonize it with other texts, than to make a relatively straightforward text more difficult to understand. An example of the latter is Deuteronomy 32:8. The text as set out in the NIV (whose main text follows the MT) and in the NRSV (whose main text follows a variant reading) is indicated in Table 2.1.

Table 2.1

Deuteronomy 32:8 (NIV)	*Deuteronomy 32:8 (NRSV)*
When the Most High gave the nations their inheritance, when he divided all mankind, he set up boundaries for the peoples according to the number of the sons of Israel.[c]	When the Most High apportioned the nations, when he divided humankind, he fixed the boundaries of the peoples according to the number of the gods.[c]
[c]Masoretic Text; Dead Sea Scrolls (see also Septuagint) *sons of God*	[c]Q Ms (Qumran maunuscript, i.e. Dead Sea Scrolls) Compare Gk (LXX) Tg (Targum): MT *the Israelites*

The text as it appears in the MT, is that God apportioned land to the non-Israelite nations while ensuring that there was sufficient room for the Israelites. The text preserved in the LXX and Dead Sea Scrolls refers to the number of 'gods' or 'sons of god', an expression that occurs on several occasions in the OT referring to heavenly beings.[107] This suggests that God assigned heavenly guardians over the nations.[108] This latter reading is the more difficult of the two. And, while it is relatively easy to see how a scribe who considered Israel to be the 'sons of God' might have changed this to 'sons of Israel', for the sake of clarity, a change in the other direction is more difficult to explain. The idea of apportioning heavenly guardians is also supported by the following verse which refers to Israel being 'Yahweh's portion'.

These 'rules' need to be balanced, too, with the possibility of copying errors.[109] For example, the text of 1 Samuel 14:41 is longer in the LXX than in the MT, reflected in the NRSV and NIV respectively[110] (see Table 2.2).

Table 2.2

1 Samuel 14:41 (NIV)	*1 Samuel 14:41 (NRSV)*
Then Saul prayed to the LORD, the God of Israel, 'Give me the right answer.'[g] And Jonathan and Saul were taken by lot and the men were cleared. [g]*41* Hebrew (MT); Septuagint: *'Why have you not answered your servant today? If the fault is in me or my son Jonathan, respond with Urim, but if the men of Israel are at fault, respond with Thummim.'*	Then Saul said, 'O LORD God of Israel, why have you not answered your servant today? If this guilt is in me or in my son Jonathan, O LORD God of Israel, give Urim; but if this guilt is in your people Israel,[u] give Thummim.' And Jonathan and Saul were indicated by the lot, but the people were cleared. [u]Vg (Vulgate) Compare Gk (LXX): Heb (MT) [41]*Saul said to the LORD, the God of Israel*

107. The expression in the LXX is *angelōn theou* (angels of God); other Greek manuscripts have *huioi theou* (sons of God) corresponding to the Hebrew *bĕnē ha'ĕlohîm* (sons of [the] god[s]), which refers to heavenly beings in e.g. Gen. 6:2; Job 1:6; 2:1. See further Michael S. Heiser, 'Deuteronomy 32:8 and the Sons of God', *BSac* 158 (2001), pp. 52–74.
108. See e.g. Routledge, *OT Theology*, pp. 120–122.
109. For further discussion, see e.g. Brotzman, *OT Textual Criticism*, pp. 107–122; Tov, *Textual Criticism*, pp. 219–262; Wegner, *Textual Criticism*, pp. 44–57; Würthwein, *Text of the OT*, pp. 107–112.
110. See e.g. Tremper Longman III and Raymond B. Dillard, *An Introduction to the Old Testament*, 2nd ed. (Nottingham: Apollos, 2007), p. 162; David G. Firth, *1 & 2 Samuel*, AOTC (Nottingham: Apollos; Downers Grove: InterVarsity Press, 2009), p. 161.

The longer version refers to two answers indicated by Urim and Thummim (cf. Deut. 33:8). Only the second of these is preserved in the MT, and it is pointed differently (*tāmîm* rather than *tummîm*) to give the meaning 'whole, sound' (hence the translation 'the right answer' in the NIV). Though it may be tempting to prefer the shorter reading, in this case it is more likely that this is a scribal error. This appears to be an example of *homoioteleuton*, where a scribe's eye jumps in the text from one word that has just been copied to a later occurrence of the same word, in this case from the first to the third reference to 'Israel', and continues copying from there.[111] Here it seems that the LXX preserves the original text and the MT introduces or preserves the error.

There are a number of other possible copying errors. These include *haplography*, where letters or words are repeated in a sequence and one is accidentally omitted; *dittography*, where letters or words are repeated; mistakes due to incorrect word division;[112] and the mistaken copying of letters that appear similar, especially in texts written by hand. However, because it seems unlikely that several scribes will all make the same mistakes, these may often be detected by comparing texts that have come to us along different transmission streams. As noted in the examples above, variant readings and their sources will appear in footnotes, and should not be ignored in exegesis.

Historical criticism

For many scholars, another important factor, when looking at the biblical text, is how it came to be in the form in which we now have it. Looking at when, how, where and why it originated, and how it may have developed over its generally long period of transmission come under the heading of historical criticism.[113] Approaches that focus on the development of the text through time are described as *diachronic*, and provided the standard tools for looking at biblical texts from the nineteenth until the second half of the twentieth centuries. Significant among historical-critical approaches are source

111. *Homoioteleuton* (same ending) may also apply where the copyist's eye jumps from one word to another close to it with the same ending. Omitting text because the scribe jumps to a word with the same beginning is known as *homoioarcton*.

112. See above, p. 43.

113. In older discussions textual criticism, dealing with the transmission of the text, is sometimes referred to as 'lower criticism', and historical criticism, relating to the development of the text, as 'higher criticism'.

criticism, form criticism and redaction criticism, and it is to those that we now turn.

Source criticism[114]

The underlying assumption of source criticism is that the text that we now have is the result of a process of editing, in which material from various written sources was put together. The OT itself refers to documents that may have been used as sources: for example the *Book of Jashar* (Josh. 10:13; 2 Sam. 1:18), the annals of the Kings of Israel and Judah (e.g. 1 Kgs 14:19, 29; 15:7, 23, 31) and the annals of Solomon (1 Kgs 11:41). Source criticism goes further and seeks to identify sources that are not specifically noted in the text.

The Documentary Hypothesis[115]

Probably the best-known example of source criticism is the 'Documentary Hypothesis', which is set out by Julius Wellhausen in his book *Prolegomena to the History of Israel*, published in 1878. He argues that the Pentateuch was compiled

---

114. See e.g. John Barton, *Reading the Old Testament: Method in Biblical Study*, 2nd ed. (Louisville: Westminster John Knox, 1996), pp. 20–29; Norman C. Habel, *Literary Criticism of the Old Testament* (Philadelphia: Fortress, 1971); Law, *Historical-Critical Method*, pp. 113–139; Pauline A. Viviano, 'Source Criticism', in Steven L. McKenzie and Stephen R. Haynes (eds.), *To Each Its Own Meaning: An Introduction to Biblical Criticisms and Their Application*, rev. and enlarged ed. (Louisville: Westminster John Knox, 1999), pp. 35–57.

115. See e.g. Arnold, *Introduction*, pp. 55–57; D. W. Baker, 'Source Criticism', in *DOTP*, pp. 798–805; Lawrence Boadt, *Reading the Old Testament: An Introduction* (Mahwah: Paulist Press, 1984), pp. 81–83; Antony F. Campbell and Mark A. O'Brien, *Sources of the Pentateuch: Texts, Introductions, Annotations* (Minneapolis: Augsburg Fortress, 1993); *Rethinking the Pentateuch: Prolegomena to the Theology of Ancient Israel* (Louisville: Westminster John Knox, 2005); R. E. Clements, *A Century of Old Testament Study* (London: Lutterworth, 1976), pp. 7–30; Collins, *Introduction*, pp. 49–67; Gottwald, *Hebrew Bible*, pp. 136–141, 151–153, 310–314; Walter Houston, *The Pentateuch* (London: SCM Press, 2013), pp. 89–117; LaSor, Hubbard and Bush, *OT Survey*, pp. 6–13; Longman and Dillard, *Introduction*, pp. 42–45; Ernest Nicholson, *The Pentateuch in the Twentieth Century* (Oxford: Clarendon, 1998); Jean-Louis Ska, *Reading the Pentateuch*, trans. Pasquale Dominique (Winona Lake: Eisenbrauns, 2006), pp. 40–61; Gordon J. Wenham, 'Pondering the Pentateuch: The Search for a New Paradigm', in Baker and Arnold, *Face of OT Studies*, pp. 116–144; *Exploring the Old Testament*, vol. 1: *The Pentateuch* (London: SPCK, 2003), pp. 159–185.

from four written sources, J, E, D and P. Similar views had been expressed by others, including Graf, whose name is often linked with Wellhausen; though it was Wellhausen who provided its scholarly foundation. Despite challenges to this hypothesis, and some modifications to the original theory, this approach to the Pentateuch remained widely accepted among OT scholars until late into the twentieth century.[116]

Reasons for the hypothesis Barton rightly notes that exponents of the Documentary Hypothesis were led to their conclusions by discrepancies within the biblical text.[117] For example, the traditionally held view that the Pentateuch was written by Moses was challenged by sections of the text that must clearly have come from a later period. The note in Genesis 12:6 'at that time the Canaanites were in the land' suggests it was written when the Canaanites were no longer in the land, and therefore significantly later than the time of Moses. Genesis 36:31 refers to a time 'before any Israelite king reigned', suggesting that it was written after the inception of the monarchy. The account of Moses' death (Deut. 34:1–12) is also unlikely to have been written by him. The 'Law of the King' (Deut. 17:14–20) is regarded as anachronistic. The request for a king like surrounding nations (v. 14) seems to echo the language of 1 Samuel 8:5, and the subsequent warning against acquiring horses, particularly from Egypt, having many wives and accumulating great wealth (vv. 16–17) seems to be aimed at Solomon (cf. 1 Kgs 10:26–29; 11:1–8).[118]

There are also occasions where the same story seems to be told in different ways, suggesting that they are from different sources. For example, there appear to be two accounts of creation (Gen. 1:1 – 2:4a; 2:4b–25); and there are three accounts of a patriarch passing his wife off as his sister (Gen. 12:10–20; 20:1–18; 26:7–11). While the same thing might have happened three times, it seems implausible that Abraham would have been worried by possible designs on his 90-year old wife (Gen. 20:2; cf. 17:17; 18:11–12).

Sometimes a story appears to include inconsistent elements. So, for example, Exodus 24:1–18 seems to contain different accounts of Moses going up on to Mount Sinai. Verses 3–8 appear to continue from the end of the previous chapter. Verses 1–2 refer to Moses going on to the mountain with 'Aaron, Nadab

---

116. E.g. Wenham, 'Pondering the Pentateuch', in Baker and Arnold, *Face of OT Studies*, p. 11.

117. Barton, *Reading*, pp. 21–22 (22).

118. Bright suggests that this is a plea that any future king 'should be as little like Solomon as possible' (John Bright, *The Kingdom of God: The Biblical Concept and Its Meaning for the Church* [Nashville: Abingdon, 1985], p. 49).

and Abihu, and seventy of the elders of Israel'. That specific combination is mentioned again in verse 9. Verse 12 may be a command for Moses to go further up the mountain. However, in verses 13–14 the names of the principal elders are different: Joshua and Hur are now mentioned, but not Nadab and Abihu. This suggests that this is a separate account from a different source. Then, in verses 15–18, only Moses is mentioned, and it is not clear what has happened to Joshua. This, again, indicates another separate account. It is possible to reconcile these accounts, but they feel disjointed. However, though source critics are agreed about the number of accounts, there is disagreement about which account belongs to which source.

Two of the sources, J and E, are so called because of their respective use of God's name: Yahweh (Ger. Jahwe) and Elohim. According to Exodus 6:3, the divine name, Yahweh, was first revealed to Moses; but there are also indications in the narrative that it was used from earliest times (e.g. Gen. 4:26). It is argued that here, too, we have an indication of more than one source: the Yahwistic source (J) uses the name Yahweh throughout the narrative, while the Elohistic source (E) refers to Yahweh only after the name has been revealed to Moses.

The sources Perhaps the most readily identifiable source is D, which comprises most of Deuteronomy. This is widely identified with the 'Book of the Law', which was found during Josiah's renovation of the temple (2 Kgs 22:8) and which gave impetus to his religious reforms. It is a common view that this book was composed not long before its discovery, in the late seventh century BC. It condemns idolatry and gives instruction for worship at a single sanctuary, thus supporting Josiah's destruction of 'high places' and the centralization of worship in the Jerusalem temple (2 Kgs 23:1–23) – referred to in Deuteronomy as 'the place the LORD your God will choose from among all your tribes to put his Name there for his dwelling' (Deut. 12:5; cf. 1 Kgs 8:29; 2 Kgs 21:4).

Wellhausen argues that the regulations set out in Ezekiel 44:9–16, which criticize the Levites and allow only Zadokites to serve as priests, appear as an innovation. This suggests that the distinction between priests and Levites in Numbers 3:1–10 was not known, and so must post-date Ezekiel. In Wellhausen's view worship in ancient Israel was much less elaborate: the first Passover lambs were killed by heads of families, and the young Samuel slept beside the Ark at Shiloh (1 Sam. 3:3), contrary to the regulations in Leviticus 16. These later instructions are included in P (the *Priestly Code*), which is therefore post-exilic. Some of the other emphases, such as creation (Gen. 1:1 – 2:4a), holiness and law, are also important post-exilic themes. Collins suggests that P is one of the easiest sources to recognize: it has a formulaic style (e.g. Gen. 1), focuses on dates, genealogies (e.g. Gen. 5) and ritual observance, and emphasizes the significance of divine covenants.[119] The core of the P source is generally thought to be the legal material in Exodus 25 – Numbers 10.

The *Yahwistic source* is considered to be the oldest, dating from about the tenth century BC. It is thought to have been composed in the south, maybe during the reign of Solomon, when national prosperity and achievement were seen to be at their height. Apart from the divine name, this source is thought to have other literary distinctives: the mountain of God is referred to as Sinai (in E it is Horeb) and Moses' father-in-law is named Reuel (in E he is Jethro). Judah became the main southern tribe and this may be reflected, for example, in the J material in Genesis 37, which gives Judah prominence over Jacob's firstborn, Reuben.

The *Elohistic source* is usually dated in the ninth century BC. Some suggest it originated in the north, because it omits the stories of Abraham and Lot, which take place in the south, and points to the significance of northern sanctuaries, such as Bethel. There is also emphasis on Joseph, the father of Ephraim, which became one of the designations of the northern kingdom.

According to Wellhausen, these existed as separate literary sources, and were combined by redactors. J and E might have been combined after the fall of the northern kingdom. Other sections were added later, with the Pentateuch reaching its final form in the post-exilic period.

Criticism of the Documentary Hypothesis Although undergoing some modification, Wellhausen's view, in a recognizable form, persisted until the 1970s. Since then the Documentary Hypothesis has been challenged, particularly in the key areas of identifying and dating the sources.[120] Because D and P correspond to relatively clearly defined sections of the text they have given rise to fewer challenges, though it has been argued that Deuteronomy may be much earlier than the seventh century BC,[121] and there is a small group of scholars who

---

119. Collins, *Introduction*, pp. 59, 143–162; see also LaSor, Hubbard and Bush, *OT Survey*, pp. 18–19; Ska, *Reading the Pentateuch*, p. 146.

120. See e.g. Joseph Blenkinsopp, *The Pentateuch: An Introduction to the First Five Books of the Bible*, ABRL (New Haven: Yale University Press, 2000), pp. 19–30; Collins, *Introduction*, pp. 64–65; Ska, *Reading the Pentateuch*, pp. 127–164; Gordon Wenham, 'Pentateuchal Studies Today', *Them* 22.1 (1996), pp. 3–13; *Pentateuch*, pp. 171–183.

121. See below, pp. 121–123, 248–249; see also J. G. McConville, *Law and Theology in Deuteronomy*, JSOTSup 33 (Sheffield: JSOT Press, 1984); *Deuteronomy*, AOTC 5 (Leicester: Apollos; Downers Grove: InterVarsity Press, 2002), pp. 21–38; Gordon Wenham, 'The Date of Deuteronomy: Linch-pin of Old Testament Criticism. Part One', *Them* 10.3 (1985), pp. 15–20; 'The Date of Deuteronomy: Linch-pin of Old Testament Criticism. Part Two', *Them* 11.1 (1985), pp. 15–18.

buck the general trend and argue that P should be dated before the exile.[122] Much of the current debate, though, relates to the existence and/or dating of J and E.

Van Seters argues against the existence of E, and claims that the source is a unified narrative extending from creation to the death of Moses. In his view it has affinities with Greek historiography and Mesopotamian myth, and he concludes that it was written during the Babylonian exile.[123] Whybray argues for the unity of composition of the Pentateuch and, like Van Seters, dates this in the sixth century BC.[124] Blenkinsopp, beginning from the relatively solid ground of the existence of P, and moving from there to what is more speculative, questions the existence of J and E as literary sources,[125] and suggests that material that might correspond to J is later than P.[126]

Rendtorff has also questioned the existence of J as well as E, arguing that the Pentateuch is made up of blocks of tradition that arose independently, rather than material from continuous narrative sources.[127] Developing Rendtorff's view, Blum, too, rejects J and E, suggesting that the narrative section

---

122. This was proposed by Yehezkel Kaufmann, *Toledot ha-'Emunah ha-Yisre'elit*, 4 vols. (Tel Aviv: Dvir, 1937–56); trans. and abr. by Moshe Greenberg as *The Religion of Israel: From Its Beginnings to the Babylonian Exile* (Chicago: Chicago University Press, 1960); the view is supported by e.g. Jacob Milgrom, 'The Antiquity of the Priestly Source: A Reply to Joseph Blenkinsopp', *ZAW* 111 (1999), pp. 10–22; Moshe Weinfeld, *Deuteronomy and the Deuteronomic School* (Oxford: Oxford University Press, 1972), esp. pp. 179–189. However, cf. Joseph Blenkinsopp, 'An Assessment of the Alleged Pre-Exilic Date of the Priestly Material in the Pentateuch', *ZAW* 108 (1996), pp. 495–518; E. E. Meyer, 'Dating the Priestly Text in the Pre-Exilic Period: Some Remarks About Anachronistic Slips and Other Obstacles', *VE* 31.1 (2010), pp. 1–6. See also Wenham, 'Pentateuchal Studies Today', pp. 8–9.

123. John Van Seters, *Prologue to History: the Yahwist as Historian in Genesis* (Louisville: Westminster John Knox, 1992); *The Life of Moses: The Yahwist as Historian in Exodus–Numbers* (Louisville: Westminster John Knox, 1994).

124. R. Norman Whybray, *The Making of the Pentateuch: A Methodological Study*, JSOTSup 89 (Sheffield: JSOT Press, 1987); *Introduction to the Pentateuch* (Grand Rapids: Eerdmans, 1995).

125. Blenkinsopp, *Pentateuch*, esp. pp. 25–28.

126. Ibid. p. 93.

127. Rolf Rendtorff, *The Problem of the Process of Transmission in the Pentateuch*, JSOTSup (Sheffield: JSOT Press, 1990).

of Genesis–Numbers, was compiled by editors during the exile,[128] though using some earlier material. This was then subject to a subsequent redaction, and the addition of further material, by P.[129] This may appear to affirm the place of D and P in the process, though it raises the question of whether they are sources or compositional stages.

As may be expected, these criticisms have, themselves, been criticized by those who claim they do not deal, adequately, with all of the issues that the Documentary Hypothesis seeks to address. So, for example, Collins suggests that there is evidence of a distinction between J and E particularly in Genesis.[130] The current situation is, therefore, unclear, as competing views vye with one another. In the absence of any convincing, or widely accepted, alternative, some modified version of the Documentary Hypothesis may, still, be the best option.[131] Final form readings of the text have also become part of the debate,[132] though that may not necessarily rule out historical-critical issues.[133]

---

128. 'Deuteronomic editors' are so called because they belong to the theological school sometimes referred to as the Deuteronomic School that may also be responsible for the compilation of Deuteronomy. It is associated with the 'Deuteronomic movement', which is thought to have influenced Josiah's reforms; see e.g. Rainer Albertz, *A History of Israelite Religion in the Old Testament Period*, 2 vols. (London: SCM Press; Louisville: Westminster John Knox, 1994), 1:195–231; Anderson, *Living World*, pp. 373–376. See on the Deuteronomistic History below, pp. 253–257.
129. Erhard Blum, *Studien zur Komposition des Pentateuch*, BZAW 189 (Berlin: de Gruyter, 1990); see also Thomas B. Dozeman and Konrad Schmid (eds.), *Farewell to the Yahwist: The Composition of the Pentateuch in Recent European Interpretation* (Atlanta: Society of Biblical Literature, 2006). Collins suggests that P edited material in Genesis–Numbers; the addition of Deuteronomy, and any further (Deuteronomic) redaction came later (*Introduction*, p. 66).
130. Collins, *Introduction*, p. 66. For an extended discussion of the continued validity of a revised form of the Documentary Hypothesis, see Joel S. Baden, *The Composition of the Pentateuch: Renewing the Documentary Hypothesis* (New Haven: Yale University Press, 2012).
131. E.g. Arnold, *Introduction*, pp. 56, 296; Collins, *Introduction*.
132. E.g. David J. A. Clines, *The Theme of the Pentateuch*, 2nd ed. (Sheffield: Sheffield Academic Press, 1997); see also below, p. 159.
133. See e.g. Ska, *Reading the Pentateuch*, pp. 161–164.

Examples of multiple sources in other Old Testament narratives[134]

Multiple sources can also be identified elsewhere. In the account of the institution of the monarchy in Israel (1 Sam. 8 – 12) there appear to be two views expressed: one positive (e.g. 1 Sam. 9:1 – 10:16; 11:1–11) and one negative (1 Sam. 8:1–22; 10:17–25). It has been suggested that these reflect pro- and anti-monarchic sources.[135]

There appear to be two introductions to David. In the first (1 Sam. 16:11–23) he is anointed by Samuel, and then enters Saul's service. In the following chapter he is taking food to his brothers who are fighting the Philistines, but is introduced again (1 Sam. 17:12–15). Again he is described as the youngest son of Jesse who tends the sheep, but there is no mention of the events of the previous chapter. In his conversation with Saul there is no suggestion of recognition (1 Sam. 17:32–37) and after David has killed Goliath, Saul asks to know his name (1 Sam. 17:55–58), implying that he does not know who he is. This suggests that two separate sources, which describe David's appearance at court in different ways and probably circulated independently, have been combined.[136]

Other approaches suggest that earlier collections of stories have been incorporated into the books of Samuel and Kings. These include the Ark narrative

---

134. See e.g. Gottwald, *Hebrew Bible*, pp. 310–314; Longman and Dillard, *Introduction*, pp. 153–156.

135. Wellhausen's attempt to link these with J and E respectively is largely discredited; nevertheless, at least two sources appear to be deliberately held in tension. For further discussion of the institution of monarchy and possible explanations of the different attitudes reflected in the text, see e.g. Lyle Eslinger, 'Viewpoints and Points of View in 1 Samuel 8–12', *JSOT* 26 (1983), pp. 61–76; Israel Finkelstein, 'The Emergence of the Monarchy in Israel: The Environmental and Socio-Economic Aspects', *JSOT* 44 (1989), pp. 43–74; J. Maxwell Miller, 'Saul's Rise to Power: Some Observations Concerning 1 Sam 9:1–10; 10:26–11:15 and 13:2–14:46', *CBQ* 26.2 (1974), pp. 157–174; Dennis J. McCarthy, 'The Inauguration of the Monarchy in Israel: A Form-Critical Study of 1 Samuel 8–12', *Int* 20.4 (1973), pp. 401–412; J. Robert Vannoy, *Covenant Renewal at Gilgal: A Study of 1 Samuel 11:14–12:25* (Eugene: Wipf & Stock, 2008), pp. 197–239. See also the discussion below, p. 171.

136. Cf. below, p. 160. See also e.g. Collins, *Introduction*, pp. 237–239. David's encounter with Goliath might have occurred before his anointing and the narrator has changed the order to suit a narrative purpose (e.g. Firth, *1 & 2 Samuel*, pp. 180–181). That helps explain some anomalies in the accounts, though such a reordering is more likely in the process of compiling accounts from different sources.

(1 Sam. 4 –7; 2 Sam. 6), the story of David's rise (1 Sam. 16 – 2 Sam. 5) and the succession narrative (2 Sam. 9 – 20; 1 Kgs 1 – 2).[137]

Form criticism[138]

Source criticism looks, primarily, for the written traditions that lie behind a text. Form criticism goes back further and seeks to discover its pre-literary history. It assumes that the written text contains smaller units that once circulated in spoken form, and those units are better understood in their earlier, oral, context. These oral units can be classified according to their 'form' (Ger. *Gattung*), a recognizable pattern seen, for example, in their content, structure or style, or in repeating formulae. Each of these types of speech is thought to have originated and been transmitted within a particular context, or 'setting in life' (Ger. *Sitz im Leben*), before it was incorporated into a written text. Hermann Gunkel is credited with first applying this approach, in a commentary on Genesis, published in 1901.[139] He suggested, for example, that some of the stories in the patriarchal narratives appear to be designed to explain why certain places had become sanctuaries, and maybe why some sanctuaries were more important than others. Stories about a particular sanctuary would then have been passed on as part of the oral tradition associated with that sanctuary before it came to be written down.[140]

Gunkel is perhaps best known for applying this approach to the study of the Psalms. He claimed that the Psalms could be classified into a relatively small

---

137. This follows a significant work by Leonhard Rost, *The Succession to the Throne of David* (Sheffield: Almond, 1982), originally published in German in 1926. For further discussion, see below, pp. 268–269.

138. See e.g. Arnold, *Introduction*, pp. 296–298; Barton, *Reading*, pp. 30–44; Boadt, *Reading the OT*, pp. 84–85; Martin J. Buss, 'Form Criticism', in Steven L. McKenzie and Stephen R. Haynes (eds.), *To Each Its Own Meaning: An Introduction to Biblical Criticisms and Their Application* (London: Geoffrey Chapman, 1993), pp. 69–85; Gottwald, *Hebrew Bible*, pp. 95–102; Hayes and Holladay, *Biblical Exegesis*, pp. 104–114; Law, *Historical-Critical Method*, pp. 140–180; Longman and Dillard, *Introduction*, pp. 46–47, 94–95; Marvin A. Sweeney, 'Form Criticism', in *DOTWPW*, pp. 227–241; 'Form Criticism', in McKenzie and Haynes, *To Each Its Own Meaning* (1999), pp. 58–89; R. A. Taylor, 'Form Criticism', in *DOTP*, pp. 336–343; Gene M. Tucker, *Form Criticism of the Old Testament* (Philadelphia: Fortress, 1971).

139. Clements, *Century*, pp. 14–15.

140. This kind of story is included in Gunkel's category of saga; other categories relating to the Pentateuch include myths, folktales, history, legend and novelette; see e.g. Taylor, 'Form Criticism', in *DOTP*, pp. 337–340; Tucker, *Form Criticism*, pp. 22–54.

number of categories, with the psalms in each category following a particular, clearly defined, pattern, and that the most likely *Sitz im Leben* was the context of public worship. Psalm types will be discussed in more detail later.[141]

Redaction criticism[142]

Both source and form criticism look at elements of the text that have been brought together. That compilation is the work of an editor, or redactor, and redaction criticism focuses on how the pieces have been used to produce the final canonical form of the text. Editors adapt the text available to them by rearranging and splicing together material, and by adding their own. They approach the text with their own agenda, and edit it in order to produce a message that meets the needs of their community. Redaction criticism begins with that final form of the text, and to that extent it is close to more recent literary approaches. It is different, though, in so far as it seeks to analyse the text's composition: to note the editorial layers and to understand the processes by which the text has been created, including the background, agenda and motivation of its creators. In that it belongs with other diachronic approaches.

For example, there is a body of opinion that Isaiah 1 – 39 went through a major redaction during the reign of Josiah.[143] It is argued that references to the imminent demise of Assyria were much more credible during that period. And with the loosening of Assyrian control, which allowed Josiah to make significant territorial gains, there was a greater optimism about the future of the nation and of Jerusalem. In Isaiah 31:4–9 this approach may be applied as follows:

---

141. See below, pp. 152–156.

142. Arnold, *Introduction*, pp. 297; Barton, *Reading*, pp. 45–60; Gottwald, *Hebrew Bible*, pp. 93–95; Hayes and Holladay, *Biblical Exegesis*, pp. 127–138; Law, *Historical-Critical Method*, pp. 181–215; Reinhard Müller, Juha Pakkala and Bas ter Haar Romeny, *Evidence of Editing: Growth and Change of Texts in the Hebrew Bible* (Atlanta: Society of Biblical Literature, 2014); Norman Perrin, *What Is Redaction Criticism?* (Philadelphia: Fortress, 1969); Lawson G. Stone, 'Redaction Criticism: Whence, Whither and Why? Or, Going Beyond Form and Source Criticism Without Leaving Them Behind', in Eugene E. Carpenter (ed.), *A Biblical Itinerary: In Search of Method, Form and Content. Essays in Honor of George W. Coates*, JSOTSup 240 (Sheffield: Sheffield Academic Press, 1997), pp. 77–90; Gail P. C. Sweete, 'Redaction Criticism', in McKenzie and Hayes, *To Each Its Own Meaning* (1999), pp. 105–121.

143. As a representative of this view see e.g. R. E. Clements, *Isaiah 1–39*, NCB (London: Marshall, Morgan & Scott; Grand Rapids: Eerdmans, 1980), pp. 5–6; *Isaiah and the Deliverance of Jerusalem*, JSOTSup 13 (Sheffield: JSOT Press, 1984).

verse 4, which is generally taken to include the negative image of Yahweh as a lion (and Judah as his prey), who will come down 'to fight against' (*liṣbō' 'al*) Mount Zion,[144] is a continuation of the judgment announced in verses 1–3, and these form part of the prophet's original message; verses 5, 8–9, which express hope of deliverance, including the fall of Assyria, are from the Josianic redaction, while verses 6–7 may be from a later redaction.[145]

Limitations of historical criticism

Our primary reason for studying Scripture is with a view to interpretation: what does the text say and mean, both in its original context and for the church today? In so far as historical-critical approaches contribute to that goal, they have value. And we have noted already the importance of historical background and context.

The idea of multiple sources, even where there may be minor inconsistences reflecting different versions of the story,[146] or even that text has been redacted, does not necessarily undermine the idea of the inspiration of Scripture. Although, where stories are dismissed as wholly unhistorical, such as at least two of the accounts of the 'endangered ancestress', we need to exercise more caution.

One key issue is how much a diachronic approach, whose result is to fragment the text, can contribute to our understanding of the meaning of the text in front of us. There is a danger of focusing on the origin, content and purposes of the sources or oral units, or on the content and agenda of particular editorial layers, rather than on the way the various elements function within the final version of the text. This will be considered further when we look at narrative and canonical criticism.[147]

---

144. In v. 4 *liṣbō' 'al* may be translated, 'fight upon', allowing a more positive interpretation, e.g. of a lion guarding and protecting its prey; see Otto Kaiser, *Isaiah 13–39*, OTL (London: SCM Press, 1974), pp. 316–317. Clements, however, argues that the expression should be taken negatively, and it is only taken positively because of the influence of the Josianic redactor (*Isaiah 1–39*, p. 257). Childs, too, insists that v. 4 portrays divine hostility, though disagrees with the fragmentary approach; see Brevard S. Childs, *Isaiah*, OTL (Louisville: Westminster John Knox, 2001), pp. 232–233. Seitz's interpretation, that Yahweh fights upon Mount Zion against those who do not put their trust in Yahweh (cf. vv. 1–3) and thereby defends Jerusalem, gives greater unity to the passage; see Christopher R. Seitz, *Isaiah 1–39*, IBC (Louisville: John Knox, 1993), pp. 222–227 (225–226).

145. Clements, *Isaiah 1–39*, pp. 256–259.

146. See below, p. 168.

147. See below, pp. 159–160.

Another problem is epistemological: How much can we really know about the literary and oral units that may lie behind the text, or about the editorial processes at work? Much is speculation, and as one speculative theory rests on another the conclusions become increasingly uncertain. We have no access, for example, to most of the documents that form the basis of the Documentary Hypothesis, and cannot say with any certainty that they even existed. When these approaches developed, there was a much greater confidence about how much could be known. In more recent times there has been a greater degree of realism about the limits of historical knowledge.

A third, related, issue is that following historical-critical approaches the meaning of a text becomes bound up with our ability to discover what lies behind the text. But if our knowledge of that prehistory is limited, how certain can we be about a particular interpretation? What happens if something that has hitherto been regarded as key to a text's interpretation is challenged, or even shown to be false? That may not be a serious problem if all that is affected is an academic theory. However, if we regard Scripture as authoritative and normative for faith, we need a more substantial foundation. One proposed solution is to look at the text as we now have it as a piece of literature. As literature, the meaning is inherent within the text. It does not depend on anything external to the text, and is not subject to historical or scientific verifiability; and by the same token, the meaning does not change if something that has been assumed proves to be incorrect. This approach will be explored later.

3. THE OLD TESTAMENT IN ITS CONTEXT

The stories contained within the OT cover the whole of history: from creation to consummation; from the beginnings of the world and of human life on earth, to the coming of God's kingdom and the renewal of the created order. And that wider perspective, which reflects God's interest in the whole of the created order, remains vitally important. However, within that broad sweep of history the OT focuses primarily on God's dealings with one particular people, the nation of Israel, and is set and written within a particular historical and geographical context. That context is, as we have noted, significant when it comes to understanding and interpreting the OT.

Important, too, is the literary, cultural and theological context of the OT. This volume is committed to the view that the text of the OT was and is divine revelation. However it was not delivered in a vacuum. It comes to us through human authors who were real people living in the real world, and as such they were not blank canvasses, without presuppositions, on which God could simply set out the lines and shapes of a new and distinctive faith. Rather, as has been noted already, the writers of the OT, and those who first received their message, were children of their time, who heard and responded to God's word within a particular cultural and religious milieu. And, as we have also seen, in order to speak in terms that people can understand, God takes that context into account. It is important to stress that in this God's revelation is in no way compromised: his word remains true. However, the way that truth is presented, including the language and imagery used, is accommodated to the particular world view and understanding of those who first received it. And that, too, is significant for OT interpretation.

This chapter will focus on three key areas: the geographical and historical backgrounds to the OT, and also the backdrop of other ANE literature.

The geographical background[1]

Israel's geographical location

The region of primary interest so far as the OT is concerned is referred to, variously, as Israel, Judah (or Judea), Canaan and Palestine. The OT writers refer to the land occupied by the Israelites after the exodus as 'the land of Canaan' (e.g. Exod. 6:4; Num. 13:2; Deut. 32:49; Josh. 24:3), and subsequently as 'the land of Israel'.[2] After the division of the kingdom after the death of Solomon, the southern kingdom was referred to as Judah, while the northern kingdom retained the name Israel (e.g. 2 Kgs 5:2; 6:23) until its destruction by the Assyrians in 722/721 BC. The southern kingdom continued to be referred to as Judah, before and also after the Babylonian exile (e.g. 2 Chr. 15:8; Neh. 5:14; Jer. 31:23; 40:12; Amos 7:12), and with political expansion under the Hasmoneans, Judea (the Greek form of Judah) covered much of the area formerly designated 'Israel'. The name Palestine comes from the same root as 'Philistine',[3] and was

1. See e.g. Yohanan Aharoni, *The Land of the Bible: A Historical Geography*, rev. and enlarged ed. (Philadelphia: Westminster, 1979), pp. 3–80; Gottwald, *Hebrew Bible*, pp. 36–49; Hill and Walton, *Survey*, pp. 33–54; LaSor, Hubbard and Bush, *OT Survey*, pp. 619–631; Victor H. Matthews and James C. Moyer, *The Old Testament: Text and Context*, 3rd ed. (Grand Rapids: Baker Academic, 2012), pp. 5–14; J. Maxwell Miller and John H. Hayes, *A History of Ancient Israel and Judah* (London: SCM Press, 1986), pp. 30–52; K. L. Noll, *Canaan and Israel in Antiquity: A Textbook on History and Religion*, 2nd ed. (London: T&T Clark, 2013), pp. 10–15; John Rogerson and Philip Davies, *The Old Testament World*, rev. and expanded ed. (London: T&T Clark, 2005), pp. 3–23; Jonathan M. Golden, *Ancient Canaan and Israel: An Introduction* (Oxford: Oxford University Press, 2004), pp. 15–27; John Rogerson, *Chronicles of the Bible Lands: A History of the Holy Land* (London: Angus, 2003).
2. The name 'Israel' is more often applied to the people rather than the region; nevertheless, there are several references to the 'land of Israel' (e.g. 1 Sam. 13:19; Ezek. 7:2; 11:17; cf. Matt. 2:20–21).
3. The term *Palashtu* occurs in Assyrian texts referring to Philistia; see e.g. *COS* 2:114G; Aharoni, *Land of the Bible*, p. 79.

first used by the Greeks in the fifth century BC,[4] though was not adopted as a designation for the whole area until after Bar Kochba's revolt in AD 135, possibly because the Romans wanted to avoid reference to the former name, Judea. At first Palestine covered a larger area, including land on both sides of the Jordan, but the term was later used to refer, primarily, to the land west of the Jordan.[5] Although Christians have referred to the region as Palestine for many years, more recently it may be taken to suggest anti-Jewish sentiment, and so it may be better to go back to the biblical names: Canaan, before the conquest, and Israel and Judah as appropriate after the conquest.[6]

The land of Israel is strategically located, forming a bridge between Africa and Asia. To the east is Mesopotamia, the centre of significant empires including the Sumerian, Akkadian, Babylonian, Assyrian and Persian. Also significant, between the sixteenth and thirteenth centuries BC, were the Hittites, located to the north and west. To the south is Israel's oldest and archetypal protagonist, Egypt (see Figure 3.1).

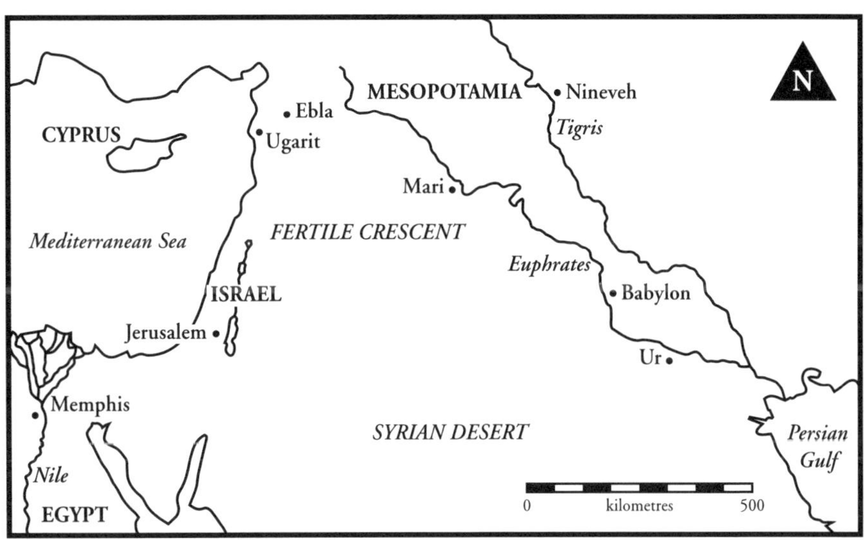

Figure 3.1

4. Herodotus (*The Histories*, 1.105.1) refers to the Scythians being *en tē Palaistinē Syriē* (in the part of Syria called Palestine).
5. For discussion of the name of the region, see e.g. Aharoni, *Land of the Bible*, pp. 64–80; LaSor, Hubbard and Bush, *OT Survey*, p. 620.
6. However, the areas denoted by these terms are not always precise.

One of the reasons for Israel's strategic importance was its location on the 'Fertile Crescent', a belt of land that followed the rivers, primarily the Tigris and Euphrates, from the Persian Gulf around to northern Syria and then down towards Egypt. Egypt was frequently looking to expand its influence northwards. Similarly, empires based in Mesopotamia wanted to push down into Egypt, which was seen as a rich prize. And, because troops could not easily move through the desert, and generally followed the more accessible route around the Fertile Crescent, movement between Mesopotamia and Egypt led through Israel. Following this route a Mesopotamian army would approach Israel from the north, and this explains the references to Cyrus, king of Persia, coming from both the east and the north (Isa. 41:2, 25; 46:11).

As well as its strategic position between Mesopotamia and Egypt, what was to become the nation of Israel also had cultural links with both of those areas. According to the biblical account, Abraham, the nation's ancestor, came from Ur, which was the centre of a Mesopotamian dynasty,[7] and the nation spent several centuries in Egypt, first as guests, then as slaves. Joshua's challenge to the people to 'throw away the gods your forefathers worshipped beyond the River and in Egypt, and serve the LORD' (Josh. 24:14) suggests that even when beginning a new life in the Promised Land some of the cultural and religious influences of those two geographical regions remained.

The geography of Israel (Canaan)

A classical way of describing the physical geography of the land of Canaan/Israel was set out by George Adam Smith in 1931.[8] He divided the land into six

7. The location of Abraham's Ur is debated. Cities with similar names include Urfa, in northern Mesopotamia, and Ur(a) in Haran; and several scholars argue in favour of a northern location; see e.g. Cyrus Gordon, 'Abraham and the Merchants of Ura', *JNES* 17 (1958), pp. 28–31; 'Where Is Abraham's Ur?', *BAR* 3.2 (1977), pp. 20–21; Victor P. Hamilton, *The Book of Genesis: Chapters 1–17*, NICOT (Grand Rapids: Eerdmans, 1990), pp. 363–365; Hershel Shanks, 'Abraham's Ur: Is the Pope Going to the Wrong Place?', *BAR* 26.1 (2000), pp. 16–19, 66–67. Evidence is inconclusive, but there seems to be no compelling reason to question the more widely accepted location in southern Mesopotamia; see e.g. Alan R. Millard, 'Where Was Abraham's Ur? The Case for the Babylonian City', *BAR* 27.3 (2001), pp. 52–53, 57; see also K. A. Kitchen, *On the Reliability of the Old Testament* (Grand Rapids: Eerdmans, 2003), p. 316.
8. George Adam Smith, *The Historical Geography of the Holy Land*, 25th ed. (London: Hodder & Stoughton, 1931), p. 48. For a more detailed discussion of these areas, see e.g. Aharoni, *Land of the Bible*, pp. 21–42; Gottwald, *Hebrew Bible*, pp. 40–49; Hill and

'strips' running from north to south, though not all of the strips are continuous, and 'areas' may be a better term. These areas have distinctive geographical and climatic features. The most easterly was the Transjordanian desert, about which there is little to say in this context, and so comment will be restricted to the other five.

Next to the Mediterranean Sea, is the coastal plain, which, apart from an interruption by Mount Carmel, extends to south of Tyre. In the south it includes the lands of the Philistines. In ancient times this was an important trade route, the Way of the Sea (Isa. 9:1; cf. Exod. 13:17),[9] and was usually under the control of one of the world empires.

The Shephelah (lowlands) is a small fertile area comprising the foothills between the coastal plain and the hill country of Judah, to the north and east. It provided a route eastwards from the coast into Judah, and was the scene of fighting with the Philistines (e.g. Judg. 14 – 15; 1 Sam. 17; 2 Chr. 28:18). The region was fortified against the Philistines and others who might seek to attack Judah from the coast. The capital of this region, from the fourteenth century BC, was the city of Lachish. Stone reliefs, currently on display at the British Museum, depict the siege and capture of Lachish by Sennacherib, when he invaded Judah at the end of the eighth century BC (2 Kgs 18:13–14).

To the east of the coastal plain and the Shephelah is the hill country. This is a mountain range that runs for most of the length of the land, broken by the plain (or 'valley') of Jezreel, and extending west to the coast, at Mount Carmel. In the south this region is made up of the hill country of Judah (e.g. Josh. 14:12; 21:11) and of Ephraim (Judg. 2:9; 3:27; 1 Sam. 1:1). In the north the hill country includes upper and lower Galilee (Josh. 21:32; 1 Kgs 9:11; 2 Kgs 15:29; Isa. 9:1). Following the conquest of Canaan, the hill country was the principal area of Israelite settlement (cf. Josh. 11:21; Judg. 1:19), and it is the scene of many of the important events in biblical history. Major cities in the northern hills include Shechem, which became the first capital of the northern kingdom under Jeroboam (1 Kgs 12:25), and Samaria, built by Omri as his capital (1 Kgs 16:24). On the border of the hill country of Judah and Ephraim was Jerusalem. This was part of the territory allocated to the tribe of Benjamin (Josh. 18:28), though, perhaps because of its strategic importance, particularly on the north–south road through the hill country, it was also attacked by Judah (Josh. 15:63; Judg. 1:8), which lay directly to the south (Josh. 15:8). Jerusalem (or *Jebus*) was a

---

Walton, *Survey*, pp. 44–48; LaSor, Hubbard and Bush, *OT Survey*, pp. 620–629; Rogerson and Davies, *OT World*, pp. 4–11; Rogerson, *Chronicles*, pp. 73–213.

9. See Aharoni, *Land of the Bible*, pp. 45–54.

Jebusite city which does not appear to have been brought under control during the conquest either by Judah or Benjamin (Josh. 15:63; Judg. 1:21; cf. 19:10–12),[10] and was still occupied by the Jebusites at the time of its capture by David (2 Sam. 5:6–10). Under David it was the capital of the whole nation of Israel; after the division of the kingdom it remained the capital of Judah. The 'valley' of Jezreel was the scene of victories by Barak and Deborah over the Canaanites (Judg. 4), and by Gideon over the Midianites (Judg. 6 – 7).

Further east is the Jordan Valley, stretching from Dan, in the north, to the Dead Sea, the lowest natural point in the world. It is part of a rift valley that extends from Turkey to East Africa. South of Dan is Lake Hulah, and south of that is the Sea of Galilee. Beyond the Dead Sea, is the Arabah, a dry valley running south to the Gulf of Aqaba, though in the OT the term may also refer to the Jordan Valley.[11] The Dead Sea has no outlet, and the evaporation of water from its surface results in a very high concentration of mineral salts. This, in turn, means it cannot support life; hence its name. This is reversed in Ezekiel's vision of a river flowing from the temple, which purifies the waters of the Dead Sea and allows life to flourish there (Ezek. 47:1–12).[12]

To the east of the Jordan are the Transjordanian hills. These rise steeply out of the Jordan Valley, and then slope eastwards towards the desert. In the north was Bashan, a fertile region known for the quality of pasture for cattle (cf. Ezek. 39:18; Amos 4:1). South of Bashan was Gilead, another fertile region. From the conquest onwards there were Israelites living in Gilead. This was part of the region allocated to the tribes of Reuben, Gad and the half-tribe of Manasseh (Josh. 12:5–6; 13:8–13), and people from Ephraim might also have settled there (Judg. 12:4). Probably as a result of pressure from the Ammonites (e.g. Judg.

---

10. According to Josh. 15:63, Judah could not 'dislodge the Jebusites'. However, Judg. 1:8 suggests that Judah did capture and burn the city. Any success, though, does not seem to have been decisive. See e.g. Rogerson, *Chronicles*, pp. 164–165; see also Aharoni, *Land of the Bible*, p. 30; Arthur E. Cundall, 'Judges', in Arthur E. Cundall and Leon Morris, *Judges and Ruth*, TOTC (Leicester: Inter-Varsity Press, 1968), pp. 7–215 (53–54).

11. E.g. Deut. 1:1, 7; Josh. 11:16; 2 Sam. 2:29; Ezek. 47:8. The Hebrew term *'ărābâ* may also refer to 'plain' or 'desert' (e.g. Num. 22:1; Josh. 5:10; Isa. 35:1; 40:3; Jer. 2:6; 50:12).

12. Here the Dead Sea is referred to simply as 'the sea'. Elsewhere in the OT it is described as 'the Salt Sea' (*yām hammelaḥ*) (e.g. Gen. 14:3; Num. 34:3, 12; Josh. 15:2, 5). It is also referred to as the 'eastern sea' (Zech. 14:8), and the 'sea of the Arabah' (e.g. Deut. 3:17; 4:49; Josh. 3:16; 12:3; 2 Kgs 14:25).

11:4–33; 1 Sam. 11:1–11), whose land lay to the south, the ongoing Israelite presence east of the Jordan appears to have been limited largely to Gilead. Further south was Moab. This, too, was a fertile region, and the book of Ruth describes Naomi and her family travelling to Moab during a time of famine in Israel (Ruth 1:1). According to the book of Numbers, Moses addressed the people of Israel as they camped on the 'plains of Moab', just before crossing the Jordan to enter the Promised Land (e.g. Num. 22:1; 33:48; 36:13). Below Moab was Edom, which extended south from the Dead Sea to the Gulf of Aqaba. The Edomites were viewed, traditionally, as descendants of Esau (Gen. 36:1; Obad. 8–9), and so were related to the Israelites (Num. 20:14; Deut. 23:7; Obad. 10).

The distinctive physical geography of the land of Israel, a relatively long, thin region with hills, plains and deep valleys, made travel from one part to another difficult. Roads running north–south were relatively few; those running east–west often involved a significant climb. The Hebrew language contains verbs meaning, specifically, 'to go up' (*'ālâ*) and 'to go down' (*yārad*), and Rogerson suggests that these 'were used advisedly' in the light of the terrain.[13] And, while this topography was possibly helpful when faced with attacks from outside, it made communication between different parts of the region, and with it any real sense of unity and national identity, difficult to establish and maintain.[14] This was particularly true in the early days of the settlement, and it played a part in the division of the kingdom following the death of Solomon.

The historical background

The biblical account includes narrative that goes back to the creation. It is common, though, to refer to the events described in Genesis 1 – 11 as 'pre-history',[15] and to focus historical discussion on Genesis 12 or, more accurately, the end of chapter 11, which begins the Abraham narrative. There is debate about whether the stories of Abraham and the other patriarchs are historical. The approach adopted here is that the narratives have the look and feel of history writing, and there is enough corroborating external evidence to justify

---

13. Rogerson and Davies, *OT World*, p. 11.
14. LaSor, Hubbard and Bush note that 'physical features also contributed to frequent Israelite disunity. The land was designed more for tribal possessions or city states than for a strongly unified nation' (*OT Survey*, p. 631).
15. See below, p. 237.

the view that, subject to the norms of biblical storytelling,[16] they are, broadly, historical.[17] The suggested date for the beginning of the patriarchal period is around 2000 BC, which coincided with a general upheaval in Lower Mesopotamia.[18] The world of the patriarchs, and much of the history that follows, was, though, shaped by events going back at least another millennium.[19]

We have already noted the significance of the geographical location of the land of Israel, lying on the Fertile Crescent between Mesopotamia and Egypt, and also its cultural links with those regions, through Abraham (Mesopotamia) and Joseph and the events that gave rise to the exodus (Egypt). Israel's history

---

16. See below, pp. 156–176.
17. See further e.g. John Bright, *History of Israel*, 4th ed. (Louisville: Westminster John Knox, 2000); V. Philips Long, *The Art of Biblical History* (Grand Rapids: Zondervan, 1994); 'Historiography of the Old Testament', in Baker and Arnold, *Face of OT Studies*, pp. 145–175; V. Philips Long, David W. Baker and Gordon J. Wenham (eds.), *Windows into Old Testament History: Evidence, Argument, and the Crisis of 'Biblical Israel'* (Grand Rapids: Eerdmans, 2002); V. Philips Long (ed.), *Israel's Past in Present Research: Essays on Ancient Israelite Historiography*, SBTS 7 (Winona Lake: Eisenbrauns, 1999); Victor H. Matthews, *A Brief History of Ancient Israel* (Grand Rapids: Eerdmans, 2002); Iain Provan, V. Philips Long and Tremper Longman III, *A Biblical History of Israel* (Louisville: Westminster John Knox, 2003). For other views (of varying degrees of scepticism about the historicity of the OT), see Further reading, p. 386. For discussion of recent approaches to the study of Israel's history, see e.g. Megan Bishop Moore and Brad E. Kelle, *Biblical History and Israel's Past: The Changing Study of the Bible and History* (Grand Rapids: Eerdmans, 2011).
18. Mesopotamia, whose name links it with the rivers Tigris and Euphrates, is usually divided into Lower Mesopotamia, which includes the land from the Persian Gulf to north of Babylon, and Upper Mesopotamia, which stretches to northern Syria; see e.g. Liverani, *ANE*, pp. 94, 221; Susan Pollock, *Ancient Mesopotamia* (Cambridge: Cambridge University Press, 1999), p. 30. Van De Mieroop refers to Lower Mesopotamia as Babylonia (Marc Van De Mieroop, *A History of the Ancient Near East: Ca. 3000–323 BC*, 2nd ed. [Oxford: Blackwell, 2007], p. 7).
19. Van De Mieroop notes that history has traditionally relied on written sources, and since writing is generally thought to date back to around 3000 BC, that is seen as the start of the historical period (Van De Mieroop, *History*, p. 2); see also e.g. Bright, *History*, p. 33; LaSor, Hubbard and Bush, *OT Survey*, p. 33; William W. Hallo and William Kelly Simpson, *The Ancient Near East: A History*, 2nd ed. (Orlando: Harcourt Brace, 1991), p. 25.

during the OT period is, therefore, closely related to the history of those two regions.[20]

Significant, when looking at the historical context of the OT, are archaelogical artefacts and, particularly, texts and inscriptions. Key to our understanding of these are two important discoveries: the Rosetta Stone and the Behistun Inscription. The Rosetta Stone,[21] dated around 196 BC, was discovered in 1799 during Napoleon's Egyptian campaign. It includes the same text written in three different scripts: Egyptian hieroglyphics (the script used in important documents), demotic (the script used more generally in Egypt) and Greek, the language of the rulers of Egypt at that time. Having the same text in all three scripts resulted in a breakthrough in deciphering Egyptian hieroglyphics, by Champollion, in 1922. The Behistun Inscription,[22] which dates to the reign of the Persian king Darius (522–486 BC), was discovered on a rock face in Behistun, Iran. It was examined and copied by Henry Rawlinson between 1835 and 1845. Like the Rosetta Stone it also shows the same text, written in different scripts, including Old Persian and Akkadian, a Semitic script used in many Mesopotamian texts. As a result of earlier work, Rawlinson was able to translate the Old Persian text, and by comparing it with its Akkadian counterpart opened the way to deciphering Akkadian cuneiform.

To the exodus and settlement

Mesopotamia[23]

In Lower Mesopotamia the latter half of the fourth century BC was characterized by what is sometimes referred to as the 'Urban Revolution':[24] a relatively

20. The view adopted in the following discussion is that the OT records are broadly historical.
21. See e.g. T. C. Mitchell, *The Bible in the British Museum: Interpreting the Evidence*, new ed. (Mahwah: Paulist Press, 2004), pp. 101–102; William H. Stiebing Jr., *Uncovering the Past: A History of Archaeology* (Oxford: Oxford University Press, 1993), pp. 57–58, 69–74.
22. See e.g. Stiebing, *Uncovering the Past*, pp. 92–96.
23. See e.g. Anderson, *Living World*, pp. 27–41; Bill T. Arnold, *Who Were the Babylonians?* (Atlanta: Society of Biblical Literature, 2004), pp. 1–86; Hallo and Simpson, *ANE*, pp. 25–80; Liverani, *ANE*, pp. 59–170; Van De Mieroop, *History of the ANE*, pp. 19–84; Hans J. Nissen, *The Early History of the Ancient Near East: 9000–2000 B. C.* (Chicago: University of Chicago Press, 1988).
24. Liverani, *ANE*, pp. 61–81; Hallo and Simpson, *ANE*, pp. 25–31; Van De Mieroop, *History of the ANE*, pp. 19–40. This expression, though debated, reflects the

rapid transition from family and tribal groups into cities, with fortifications and an increasingly shared economy. This urbanization included the concentration of wealth, the specialization of labour and the development of social organization. This led to stability and economic prosperity, which also allowed for the growth of civic structures, including monuments and temples. It also made possible increased trade, and the need for record keeping was influential in the development of writing.[25] Early writing seems to have been, generally, in cuneiform, which began as a kind of pictorial script, which, over the centuries became more stylized and developed into symbols, which were easier to impress into clay, the common medium for writing.

The Sumerians were dominant in Lower Mesopotamia in the third millennium BC, during what is usually referred to as the Early Dynastic Period (*c.*2900–2350 BC),[26] until the rise of the Akkadian Empire. This was founded by Sargon, and named after the city Akkad, which he established as his capital. Akkadians were a Semitic people, who had long been present in the region. Sargon appears to have risen to power in the city of Kish and quickly asserted control over the whole of Mesopotamia. The empire faltered under Sargon's sons; it was revived under his grandson, Naram-Sin, though fell into terminal decline around 2200 BC as a result of internal pressures and external threats. At its height the Akkadian Empire stretched from the Persian Gulf to northern Syria, and included victories over the significant cities of Mari and Ebla.[27]

(*Footnote 24 cont.*) significant change brought about by urbanization during this period. Because of the importance of the city of Uruk, this period is also referred to as the 'Uruk Period'; see also e.g. Nissen, *Early History of the ANE*, p. 5; Pollock, *Ancient Mesopotamia*, pp. 5–6.

25. See e.g. Liverani, *ANE*, pp. 73–79; Van De Mieroop, *History of the ANE*, pp. 28–35.

26. This period is further subdivided into Early Dynastic (ED) I (2900–2750 BC), ED II (2750–2600 BC) and ED III (2600–2350 BC); see e.g. Liverani, *ANE*, p. 93; Van De Mieroop, *History of the ANE*, pp. 41–42; Nissen, *Early History of the ANE*; Pollock, *Ancient Mesopotamia*, p. 2; cf. Hallo, who lists the dates as 2900–2700 BC, 2700–2500 BC and 2500–2300 BC respectively (*ANE*, p. 34, n. 25). Dates in other reference works have additional differences; though when dealing with such ancient events minor variations are to be expected.

27. Ebla appears to have been subdued by Sargon; it became prominent again during the reign of his sons, before being destroyed by Naram-Sin in the twenty-third century BC. In the following centuries it did not regain its earlier significance. See e.g. Liverani, *ANE*, pp. 115–129; Donald J. Wiseman, 'Ebla', in *IBD* 1:405–407.

During this period, Akkadian became the common language in Mesopotamia, and remained so, in varying forms, until the first millennium BC.[28] As already noted, this is generally classified as an Eastern Semitic language, which has links with Hebrew.[29] It was different from Sumerian, though it had points of contact with it, and still used cuneiform script.

With the decline of the Akkadian Empire, Lower Mesopotamia reverted to independent city states. This was followed, in around 2100 BC,[30] by a Sumerian revival under Ur-Nammu, the founder of the Ur III dynasty. Its centre was the city of Ur, though it exercised control over the wider region. Ur-Nammu is linked with building projects, including the Great Ziggurat at Ur,[31] and with the formulation of the earliest known law code. The Ur-Nammu Stele,[32] which notes some of his achievements, depicts the king pouring out a water libation

---

28. Akkadian developed two principal variants: Assyrian and Babylonian. These developed over time. Old Babylonian was dominant until around 1595 BC, though there is also evidence of Old Assyrian texts in that same period. With the end of Babylonian power in Mesopotamia there was a gradual transition to Middle Babylonian, which retained some dominance as an international language until the end of the second millennium BC. The rise of Assyria led to the more widespread use of Middle Assyrian. In the early first millennium BC there is evidence of Neo-Assyrian and Neo-Babylonian, as well as Standard Babylonian, which was used particularly for literature. See further Andrew George, 'Babylonian and Assyrian: A History of Akkadian', in J. N. Postgate (ed.), *Languages of Iraq, Ancient and Modern* (London: British School of Archaeology in Iraq, 2007), pp. 31–71; see also e.g. Liverani, *ANE*, pp. 370–371.
29. See above, pp. 42–43.
30. This is widely regarded as marking the transition between Early Bronze Age (EBA) to Middle Bronze Age (MBA) in Mesopotamia.
31. Ziggurats were high, stepped temple towers. Their purpose appears to have been either to bring worshippers closer to the heavenly abode of the gods or, more likely, to provide a gateway for the gods to descend and have greater contact with human beings. See e.g. Harriet Crawford, *Sumer and the Sumerians*, 2nd ed. (Cambridge: Cambridge University Press, 2004), pp. 34–35; Walton, *ANE Thought*, pp. 119–123. It has been suggested that the Tower of Babel (Gen. 11:1–9) was such a construction; see further e.g. John Walton, 'The Mesopotamian Background of the Tower of Babel Accounts and Its Implications', *BBR* 5 (1995), pp. 155–175.
32. There is debate about whether this stele should be attributed to Ur-Nammu, or to his son Shulgi; see e.g. William W. Hallo, *The World's Oldest Literature: Studies in Sumerian Belle-Lettres* (Leiden: Brill, 2010), pp. 471–491.

to the moon god, Nanna,[33] the chief god of Ur. Ur-Nammu's dynasty, though, was relatively short-lived, and by the end of the third millennium BC, partly as a result of attacks from Elamites in the east and Amorites in the north, it too fell into decline.[34] Ishbi-Irra, a former general of the Ur III dynasty's last king, Ibbi-Sin, established a dynasty based in the city of Isin, but was not able to exert authority over the wider region. After a century of relative peace, he was defeated by a rival dynasty based in Larsa, which took control of much of the south, including Ur. Journeys of nomads around the Fertile Crescent were not unusual at that time, though the upheaval and uncertainty following the fall of Ur III may have led to a more general migration. And the movement of Abraham's family from Ur to Haran (Gen. 11:31) might have been part of that.[35]

There are a number of texts giving information about the third millennium BC. These include discoveries at Ur, dating to around 2800 BC. We have noted, too, discoveries at Ebla, a northern Syrian city whose significance in the twenty-third and twenty-fourth centuries BC had not been appreciated before the mid-1970s. That city's extensive archives shed light on the history of this period and, as we have seen, play a part in understanding the development of the Hebrew language. Information about rulers in Mesopotamia is provided, too, by the Sumerian King List, which gives a list of kings from a time before a flood swept over the earth down to the Isin dynasty.[36] In line with its claim that kingship is a gift from the gods the Sumerian King List presents the different

---

33. Nanna is the Sumerian name; the Akkadian equivalent is Sin.
34. The end of the Ur III Dynasty is generally thought to mark the transition from the Neo-Sumerian to the Old Babylonian Period (2000–1600 BC). The first part of this period is sometimes designated 'Early Old Babylonian'.
35. See e.g. Bright, *History*, pp. 44, 82.
36. Hallo suggests that the Sumerian King List was composed during the Isin Dynasty to present that dynasty as a legitimate successor to those that preceded it (Hallo and Simpson, *ANE*, p. 83; Hallo, *World's Oldest Literature*, pp. 386–387). Others suggest that the original composition may date to the Ur III Dynasty, and that references to later dynasties are editorial; see e.g. Thorkild Jacobsen, *The Sumerian King List*, AS 11 (Chicago: Chicago University Press, 1939), pp. 128–141; Michael B. Rowton, 'The Date of the Sumerian King List', *JNES* 19.2 (1960), pp. 156–162. See also e.g. Mark Chavalas, 'Genealogical History as "Charter": A Study of Old Babylonian Period Historiography and the Old Testament', in A. R. Millard, J. K. Hoffmeier and D. W. Baker (eds.), *Faith, Tradition and History* (Winona Lake: Eisenbrauns, 1994), pp. 103–118 (110–113); R. K. Harrison, 'Reinvestigating the Antediluvian Sumerian King List', *JETS* 36.1 (1993), pp. 3–8; Van De Mieroop, *History of the ANE*, pp. 43–44.

dynasties, based around various city states, including Kish, Uruk, Ur, Mari and Akkad, as consecutive, with hegemony over the region passing from one to the other. Other sources suggest, however, that in several cases dynasties ruled concurrently. This, and the mythological and legendary data included, particularly in the early part of the Sumerian King List, limits its value as historiography; nevertheless, it remains an important source of information.

During the early Old Babylonian Period, several dynasties vied for power in Lower Mesopotamia. Eventually, Larsa in the south, and Babylon in the north became dominant. In the same period, under Shamshi-Adad, Assyria rose to prominence in Upper Mesopotamia, though with the Assyrian king's death the region was again broken up into smaller states, with Mari the most powerful. This gave Hammurabi, who became king early in the eighteenth century BC, the opportunity to increase his power, and by the middle of the century he had established dominance over most of Mesopotamia.

Hammurabi claims to have been of Amorite descent. Amorites were Western Semitic (semi-) nomads, possibly from the Syro-Arabian desert. They were present in Mesopotamia during the third millennium BC, though appeared in greater numbers following the fall of Akkad. Amorites seem, also, to have moved into Canaan. In the Ur III period they were presented as hostile invaders, and a wall was constructed to keep them out. They appear, nevertheless, to have become prominent within Mesopotamian society, and the fall of Ur III opened the way for the establishment of Amorite dynasties in several Mesopotamian cities.

Literature appears to have flourished under Hammurabi and his successors. Hammurabi is noted for his 'Law Code'. The text appears on the Hammurabi Stele, which also shows the king receiving symbols of authority from Shamash, the sun god, who was also the god of justice. This reinforces the idea, common in the ANE, that earthly order was a reflection of the heavenly order. Hammurabi's collection of laws includes some things that are similar to the Mosaic Law, including 'an eye for an eye' and 'a tooth for a tooth'.[37] Versions of the *Gilgamesh Epic*, which tells the story of Gilgamesh, a legendary king of Uruk who reigned, probably, early in the third millennium BC, and the *Atrahasis Epic*, which tells the story of a flood, may also date to this time.[38] Texts found at Mari give substantial information about the politics, as well as social customs, of this period.[39]

---

37. For further discussion of Hammurabi's law code, see below, pp. 118–120.
38. See below, pp. 106–109.
39. See e.g. Van De Mieroop, *History of the ANE*, p. 87; Donald J. Wiseman, 'Mari', in *IBD* 2:945–948.

The wider power of Babylon waned after Hammurabi's death, though his successors remained in control of the northern part of Lower Mesopotamia. That ended in around 1595 BC when a Hittite army under their king, Mursili, advanced along the Euphrates and sacked the city.

The defeat of Babylon appears to have triggered a century-long 'dark age', so called because there are few written records to give information about what took place. Two groups in particular emerged during this period: the Hurrian kingdom of Mitanni in north Syria and Upper Mesopotamia, and the Kassites in Lower Mesopotamia. Mitanni remained dominant until the fourteenth century BC, when it was defeated by the Hittites. This then gave opportunity for the re-emergence of Assyria as a power that would have an impact on the region, including the land of Israel, over the next seven hundred years.

Important sources of information about this period are texts discovered at Nuzi,[40] which, in particular, describe social customs in the fifteenth century BC. These, and other Mesopotamian texts, such as those found at Mari, reveal several points of contact with the biblical patriarchal narratives.[41] Some of the parallels have been exaggerated, and more recent studies suggest a more cautious approach.[42] Nevertheless, it is reasonable to conclude that, while the historicity

---

40. See e.g. Martin J. Selman, 'Nuzi', in *IBD* 2:1103–1104.

41. See e.g. Bright, *History*, pp. 77–87; Enns, *Inspiration*, pp. 29–31; Tikva Frymer-Kensky, 'Patriarchal Family Relationships and Near Eastern Law', *BA* 44.4 (1980), pp. 209–214; Kitchen, *Reliability*, pp. 313–343; Provan, Long and Longman, *Biblical History*, pp. 112–114; Victor H. Matthews and Don C. Benjamin, *Old Testament Parallels: Laws and Stories from the Ancient Near East*, 3rd ed. (Mahwah: Paulist Press, 2006), pp. 47–53; John H. Walton, *Ancient Israelite Literature in Its Cultural Context: A Survey of Parallels Between Biblical and Ancient Near East Texts* (Grand Rapids: Zondervan, 1989), pp. 45–58.

42. See e.g. Martin J. Selman, 'Comparative Customs and the Patriarchal Age', in A. R. Millard and D. J. Wiseman (eds.), *Essays on the Patriarchal Narratives* (Leicester: Inter-Varsity Press, 1980), pp. 93–138. Enthusiasm over discoveries at Nuzi, Mari, etc., led to confident claims about the historicity and dating of the patriarchal narratives; see e.g. Cyrus Gordon, 'Biblical Customs and the Nuzi Tablets', *BA* 3 (1940), pp. 1–12; E. A. Speiser, *Genesis*, AB 1 (New York: Doubleday, 1964). This elicited a response from opponents; see e.g. Thomas L. Thompson, *The Historicity of the Patriarchal Narratives: The Quest for the Historical Abraham* (Berlin: de Gruyter, 1974; Harrisburg: Trinity, 2002); John Van Seters, *Abraham in History and Tradition* (New York: Yale University Press, 1975); see also P. Kyle McCarter Jr., 'The Patriarchal Age: Abraham, Isaac and Jacob', in H. Shanks (ed.), *Ancient Israel: A Short History*

of the patriarchal narratives cannot be proven, what we see there is in accord with what we know of the practices and customs of the second millennium BC.

Egypt[43]

By the start of the third millennium BC Egypt was already an advanced civilization. Information about the kings and dynasties that ruled over Egypt comes from several sources. The Palermo Stone, a stele dating from around 2400 BC, lists kings going back to prehistoric times. The *Turin Royal Canon* dates from the thirteenth century BC; it, too, includes rulers from Egypt's very distant past, as well as more reliable details of kings from 3000 BC.[44]

Egypt was made up of two regions: Upper Egypt, in the south, and Lower Egypt, in the north, and Pharaoh was known as the 'Lord of the two lands'.[45] The unification of these 'two lands' appears to have taken place around the end of the fourth millennium BC.[46] Central to Egypt's prosperity was the river Nile, and the country was stretched along its banks. This created an administrative problem, since the capital city was always distant from other regional centres, with only the river as the primary means of communication. As a result, Pharaoh was very dependent on local governors. The nation also relied on a sophisticated irrigation system, which collected and distributed water following the regular

---

from Abraham to the Destruction of the Temple (Washington: BAS, 1989), pp. 1–29. Selman's approach is more measured. He notes important points of contact, while emphasizing the importance of not claiming too much from archaeological evidence; cf. Kenneth A. Kitchen, 'The Patriarchal Age: Myth or History?', *BAR* 21.2 (1995), pp. 48–57, 88–95.

43. See e.g. Hallo and Simpson, *ANE*, pp. 183–296; Marc Van De Mieroop, *A History of Ancient Egypt* (Chichester: Wiley-Blackwell, 2011); Ian Shaw (ed.), *The Oxford History of Ancient Egypt*, new ed. (Oxford: Oxford University Press, 2003); Toby Wilkinson, *The Rise and Fall of Ancient Egypt: The History of a Civilisation from 3000 BC to Cleopatra* (London: Bloomsbury, 2010). For the early period of Egypt's history, see also John Romer, *A History of Ancient Egypt: From the First Farmers to the Great Pyramid* (London: Penguin, 2013).
44. Kings are also listed in burial lists from Abydos, Sakkara and Karnak; see e.g. *COS* 1:37A–D.
45. See e.g. Wilkinson, *Ancient Egypt*, pp. 30–37; cf. Van De Mieroop, *Ancient Egypt*, p. 27.
46. Bard sets this at around 3200 BC; see e.g. Kathryn A. Bard, 'The Emergence of the Egyptian State (*c.* 3200–2686 BC)', in Shaw, *Ancient Egypt*, pp. 57–82. Van De Mieroop gives a date of 3000 BC (*Ancient Egypt*, p. 27).

flooding of the Nile. When all was well, this was a great strength of the Egyptian economy. When there were difficulties between local regions, the irrigation system was not maintained, and its failure could lead to serious food shortages. The potential lack of unity in Egypt, and the problems associated with it, meant that there were significant fluctuations in the fortunes of the land: with periods of prosperity interspersed with periods of weakness and decline.

The Old Kingdom (twenty-seventh to twenty-second centuries BC),[47] also known as the 'Pyramid Age', was a golden age in Egypt's history, both culturally and in terms of international influence. The pyramids reflect Egypt's obsession with death, and 'pyramid texts', inscribed on their walls, contain spells, prayers and incantations that are intended to assist the ruler's safe passage into the realm of the dead.[48] Some of these texts include a brief description of the origin of the world.[49] The form of writing developed in Egypt was hieroglyphics, which, like cuneiform, was a pictorial language. Egyptians also used papyrus, which could be written on with ink. This was much easier than making indentations in clay, but was also very expensive.

Towards the end of the third millennium, maybe due to rivalry between local governors and the collapse of central authority, the Old Kingdom fell into decline, leading to the 'First Intermediate Period'. This may have marked the beginnings of 'coffin texts'.[50] These are similar to 'pyramid texts', but appear,

---

47. See e.g. Hallo and Simpson, *ANE*, p. 213; Ian Shaw, 'Introduction: Chronologies and Cultural Change in Egypt', in Shaw, *Ancient Egypt*, pp. 1–15 (4); Jaromir Malek, 'The Old Kingdom (*c.* 2686–2160 BC)', in ibid., pp. 83–107. As with the chronology of the ANE in general, there are differences in the dates suggested for these early periods of Egyptian history (cf. Wilkinson, *Ancient Egypt*, p. xv).
48. See e.g. Van De Mieroop, *Ancient Egypt*, pp. 70–71; Wilkinson, *Ancient Egypt*, p. 103.
49. See below pp. 112–114.
50. Numbers of coffin texts appear to have increased, particularly, in the Middle Kingdom, though this move might have begun in the First Intermediate Period; see e.g. Stephan Seidlmayer, 'The First Intermediate Period (2160–2055 BC), in Shaw, *Ancient Egypt*, pp. 108–136 (115–116). The appearance of coffin texts is taken to suggest that the afterlife had become 'democratized', and was now available not just to royals; cf. Gae Callender, 'The Middle Kingdom Renaissance (*c.* 2055–1650 BC)', in ibid., pp. 137–171 (168–169); Van De Mieroop, *Ancient Egypt*, pp. 81–83; Wilkinson, *Ancient Egypt*, pp. 143–145. This view, though, has been challenged; see e.g. Harold M. Hays, 'The Death of Democratisation of the Afterlife', in Nigel Strudwick and Helen Strudwick (eds.), *Old Kingdom, New Perspectives: Egyptian Art and Archaeology 2750–2150 BC* (Oxford: Oxbow, 2011), pp. 115–130.

now, on the coffins of non-royals. It seems possible that this may be linked with the pessimism and hardship associated with this period, resulting in a more widespread focus on the soul's safe journey to the afterlife.

The First Intermediate Period was followed by recovery, reunification and renewed prosperity in the Middle Kingdom (twenty-first to seventeenth centuries BC). The extent of Egyptian influence is evident from *Execration Texts* (*c.*1900 BC). These were part of a ritual that involved cursing enemies by writing their names on clay statues or pots, which were then smashed and buried. These indicate Egypt's traditional enemies as well as particular threats, and refer to the Canaanite cities of Jerusalem and Ashkelon.[51] There are further insights into life in Canaan, including marriage and burial customs, in *The Tale of Sinuhe*, which tells the story of an Egyptian who spent years in exile in the region. Other literature from the Middle Kingdom includes *The Eloquent Peasant*, a quest for justice that is sometimes compared with the book of Job, and *The Dialogue of a Man with His Soul*, which includes discussion of the meaning and value of life on earth, and has points of contact with the book of Ecclesiastes.[52]

The Middle Kingdom gave way to a Second Intermediate Period, which began in the first part of the seventeenth century BC and continued until around 1550 BC. During this period, people of Western Semitic origin, known as the Hyksos, which appears to derive from a term meaning 'foreign-chiefs', became dominant in Egypt.[53] The Egyptian historian Manetho,[54] writing in the third century BC, describes them as ruthless invaders, who burned cities and destroyed temples, and the general view of early scholarship was of a fairly rapid incursion. It is now recognized that this was a more gradual process of infiltration. Western Semites had become established in the Nile Delta towards the end of the Middle Kingdom. They eventually gained political control of Lower Egypt, and established their capital at Avaris, in the north-east of the Nile Delta, and later claimed authority over the whole country. The traditional line of Egyptian kings fled to

---

51. E.g. *COS* 1:32.
52. See e.g. R. B. Parkinson, *The Tale of Sinuhe and Other Ancient Egyptian Poems 1940–1640 BC*, Oxford World's Classics (Oxford: Oxford University Press, 2009). For further discussion of possible links with OT texts, see below, pp. 126–128.
53. See e.g. Janine Bourriau, 'The Second Intermediate Period (*c.* 1650–1550 BC)', in Shaw, *Ancient Egypt*, pp. 172–206; Bright, *History*, pp. 59–65; Hallo and Simpson, *ANE*, pp. 248–251; Liverani, *ANE*, pp. 235–239; Van De Mieroop, *Ancient Egypt*, pp. 131–136, 144–149; Wilkinson, *Ancient Egypt*, pp. 188–192.
54. Manetho's work *Aegyptiaca* has not survived, though fragments have been preserved in the writings of other historians, including Josephus.

Thebes, from where they appear to have exercised some control over Upper Egypt, though maybe as vassals of the Hyksos.[55] At first the Hyksos may have retained their own distinctive culture, though in time they embraced aspects of Egyptian culture, which included adopting Egyptian throne names and claiming sanction for their rule from Egyptian gods.[56] It is possible that Joseph, and later the whole of Jacob's family, came to Egypt during the Hyksos period. It seems more likely that another Western Semite, like Joseph, might rise to a position of significant power under Hyksos rule than under a native Egyptian Pharaoh.

Hyksos rule ended in the middle of the sixteenth century BC, when they were defeated and expelled by Ahmose (*c.*1550–1525 BC), who established the New Kingdom, which lasted until around 1070 BC. During this period, Egypt recovered its strength. It regained control of Canaan and made conquests into Asia. Military campaigns reduced under Amenhotep III (*c.*1390–1352 BC),[57] who consolidated the empire won by his predecessors, by diplomacy.

Amenhotep III's son Amenhotep IV (*c.*1352–1336 BC) appears to have taken little interest in international affairs. His main claim to fame was in advocating the sole worship of a single god, the Aten or Sun Disk. He changed his name to Akhenaten, and established a new capital, which he named Akhetaten (the modern-day El-Amarna).[58] Akhenaten's form of 'monotheism' has been compared with the call to Israel, under Moses, to worship God alone.[59] However, while it may indicate that worship of a single deity does not need to be a late

55. See e.g. Bright, *History*, p. 61; Wilkinson, *Ancient Egypt*, p. 191. However, Van De Mieroop notes that there is little evidence of Hyksos control throughout Upper Egypt (*Ancient Egypt*, p. 135).
56. Bourriau notes that the Hyksos were 'peculiarly Egyptian', displaying a 'mixture of Egyptian and Syro-Palestinian cultural traits' ('Second Intermediate Period', in Shaw, *Ancient Egypt*, p. 182); see also Van De Mieroop, *Ancient Egypt*, p. 132; Wilkinson, *Ancient Egypt*, p. 191.
57. The Greek form of Amenhotep is Amenophis.
58. See e.g. Hallo and Simpson, *ANE*, pp. 265–273; Jacobus van Dijk, 'The Amarna Period and the Later New Kingdom (*c.* 1532–1069 BC)', in Shaw, *Ancient Egypt*, pp. 265–307 (269–270); Van De Mieroop, *Ancient Egypt*, pp. 279–298.
59. A celebrated example is Sigmund Freud, *Moses and Monotheism* (London: Hogarth, 1939). Freud speculates that Moses was an Egyptian who learned his monotheism from Akhenaten; cf. Jan Assmann, *Moses the Egyptian: The Memory of Egypt in Western Monotheism* (Cambridge, Mass.: Harvard University Press, 1997); *The Price of Monotheism* (Stamford: Stamford University Press, 2009), pp. 35–39; Van De Mieroop, *Ancient Egypt*, pp. 210–211.

idea, as some scholars have suggested, there are no other points of contact.[60] There are several similarities between the *Hymn to Aten*, which appears to originate from this period, and Psalm 104, though the precise relationship between them is debated.[61]

Correspondence from vassal rulers in Canaan and Syria to Amenhotep III and Akhenaten is preserved in the so-called 'Amarna Letters'.[62] These are written, primarily, in Akkadian cuneiform,[63] which was recognized as an international language. The letters give insights into the rivalries between local city rulers and the threats they felt themselves to be under from larger powers, from other rulers and from the 'Apiru (or Habiru).[64] It is tempting to identify these

---

60. See e.g. Alan R. Millard, 'Abraham, Akhenaten, Moses and Monotheism', in Richard S. Hess, Philip E. Satterthwaite and Gordon J. Wenham (eds.), *He Swore an Oath* (Cambridge: Tyndale House, 1993), pp. 119–129. For discussion of the development of monotheism in the OT, see Routledge, *OT Theology*, pp. 94–99.
61. See below, pp. 128–129.
62. See William L. Moran, *The Amarna Letters* (Baltimore: Johns Hopkins University Press, 1992); *COS* 3:92A–G; Eva von Dassow and Kyle Greenwood, 'Correspondence from El-Amarna in Egypt', in Mark W. Chavalas (ed.), *The Ancient Near East: Historical Sources in Translation* (Oxford: Blackwell, 2006), pp. 182–214; Matthews and Benjamin, *OT Parallels*, pp. 146–150; see also e.g. Hallo and Simpson, *ANE*, pp. 271–272; Van De Mieroop, *History of the ANE*, pp. 134–137; *Ancient Egypt*, pp. 156, 187–191; Carol A. Redmount, 'Bitter Lives: Israel in and out of Egypt', in Michael Coogan (ed.), *The Oxford History of the Biblical World* (Oxford: Oxford University Press, 1998), pp. 58–89 (83–84); Martin J. Selman, 'Amarna', in *IBD* 1:37–39; Wilkinson, *Ancient Egypt*, pp. 266–270. Although primarily from vassals, the Amarna tablets contain other international correspondence; see Moran, *Amarna Letters*, pp. xxii–xxxiii.
63. E.g. Moran, *Amarna Letters*, pp. xviii–xxii. Moran notes that there are also a few letters in Assyrian, Hurrian and Hittite languages. He also notes that while letters from Babylonia are in 'good' Middle Babylonian (see above, p. 73, n. 28), those from Canaan display significant localized variations (p. xix).
64. As a sample of what is a very extensive literature on the 'Apiru/Habiru see B. J. Beizel, 'Habiru', in *ISBE* 2:586–590; Meredith G. Kline, 'The Ha-bi-ru – Kin or Foe of Israel?', *WTJ* 19.1 (1956), pp. 1–24; *WTJ* 19.2 (1957), pp. 170–184; *WTJ* 20.1 (1957), pp. 46–70; N. P. Lemche, 'Habiru, Hapiru', in *ABD* 3:6–10. See also e.g. Anderson, *Living World*, pp. 39–40; Bright, *History*, pp. 93–95; Tony W. Cartledge, *Vows in the Hebrew Bible and the Ancient Near East*, JSOTSup 141 (Sheffield: JSOT Press, 1993), pp. 200–221; Collins, *Introduction*, pp. 88, 196; K. A. Kitchen, *Ancient*

'Apiru, who presented a threat to Canaanite cities, with the Hebrews under Joshua.[65] 'Apiru are also referred to in other texts across the ANE from the end of the second millennium BC, and it has been suggested that Abraham belonged to this group, and that the name 'Hebrew' derives from *habiru*;[66] though that seems unlikely.[67] It is widely agreed that the designation 'Apiru does not indicate a particular ethnic group, but those from various nationalities who live on the margins of society. In the Amarna Letters the 'Apiru appear to represent the rejection of (Egyptian) authority,[68] and are presented as bands of mercenaries,[69] who support some cities against others,[70] things that do not fit with the biblical account of the conquest. Thus, while the identity of the 'Apiru is not clear, direct identification with the Hebrews seems improbable.

Links are also suggested between the early Israelites and another group referred to in Egyptian texts from the fifteenth century BC, the Shasu.[71] They

---

(*Footnote 64 cont.*) *Orient and Old Testament* (Downers Grove: InterVarsity Press, 1966), pp. 69–70; Marc Van De Mieroop, *The Eastern Mediterranean in the Age of Ramesses II* (Oxford: Blackwell, 2007), pp. 48–50; *History of the ANE*, pp. 198–200; Miller and Hayes, *History*, pp. 65–67; Provan, Long and Longman, *Biblical History*, pp. 170–172; Redmount, 'Bitter Lives', in Coogan, *Biblical World*, p. 72.

65. E.g. Gleason L. Archer, *A Survey of Old Testament Introduction*, rev. and expanded ed. (Chicago: Moody, 1994), pp. 288–295. Brueggemann uses the identification to point to Hebrews as outsiders, and emphasizes the importance of welcoming strangers; see Walter Brueggemann, *Interpretation and Obedience: From Faithful Reading to Faithful Living* (Minneapolis: Augsburg Fortress, 1991), pp. 290–298.
66. See e.g. William F. Albright, 'Abram the Hebrew: A New Archaeological Interpretation', *BASOR* 163 (1961), pp. 36–54; 'From the Patriarchs to Moses: I. From Abraham to Joseph', *BA* 36.1 (1973), pp. 5–33; Gottwald, *Hebrew Bible*, pp. 172–173.
67. See e.g. Hamilton, *Genesis 1–17*, pp. 404–405; Anson Rainey, 'Shasu or Habiru: Who Were the Early Israelites?', *BAR* 34.6 (2008), pp. 51–55; Manfred Weippert, *The Settlement of the Israelite Tribes in Palestine*, SBT 2.21 (London: SCM Press, 1971), pp. 63–102; Donald J. Wiseman, 'Abraham in History and Tradition: Part 1. Abraham the Hebrew', *BSac* 134 (1977), pp. 123–130 (128–129).
68. *EA* 197 and *EA* 286 contrast the 'Apiru with those who represent Egyptian authority; cf. *COS* 3:237.
69. The price of hire is noted in *EA* 112 (cf. *EA* 246).
70. E.g. *EA* 276; cf. *EA* 79; *EA* 82.
71. See e.g. Arnold, *Introduction*, pp. 162–163; Joseph Blenkinsopp, 'The Midianite–Kenite Hypothesis Revisited and the Origins of Judah', *JSOT* 33.2 (2008), pp. 131–153; Anthony J. Frendo, 'Back to Basics: A Holistic Approach to the

appear to be pastoral nomads or semi-nomads, and are associated with several locations, though are most commonly connected with Edom.[72] A text dating from the reign of Amenhotep III, early in the fourteenth century BC, associates the Shasu with 'Yhw', a term widely linked with the divine name Yahweh.[73] This has reinforced the view that Yahweh was first worshipped among people in north-east Sinai,[74] and that Moses was introduced to Yahweh during his time

---

Problem of the Emergence of Israel', in John Day (ed.), *In Search of Pre-Exilic Israel* (London: T&T Clark International, 2004), pp. 41–64 (50–52); Israel Finkelstein, Amihai Mazar and Brian B. Schmidt, *The Quest for the Historical Israel: Debating Archaeology and the History of Early Israel* (Atlanta: Society of Biblical Literature, 2007), pp. 94–95; James K. Hoffmeier, *Ancient Israel in Sinai: The Evidence for the Authenticity of the Wilderness Traditions* (Oxford: Oxford University Press, 2005), pp. 241–245; Nadav Na'aman, 'The Exodus Story: Between Historical Memory and Historiographical Composition', *JANER* 11 (2011), pp. 39–69; Noll, *Canaan and Israel*, pp. 121–123; Rainey, 'Shasu or Habiru?'; Donald B. Redford, *Egypt, Canaan, and Israel in Ancient Times* (Princeton: Princeton University Press, 1992), pp. 269–280; Redmount, 'Bitter Lives', in Coogan, *Biblical World*, p. 100; Gary S. Rendsburg, 'Israel Without the Bible', in Frederick E. Greenspahn (ed.), *The Hebrew Bible: New Insights and Scholarship* (New York: New York University Press, 2008), pp. 3–23; William A. Ward, 'Shasu', in *ABD* 5:1165–1167.

72. An Egyptian text refers to 'the Shasu tribes of Edom' being given permission to pass an Egyptian border post in order to water their flocks (*COS* 3:5); elsewhere they are linked with Mount Seir. See e.g. Frendo, 'Back to Basics', in Day, *In Search of Pre-Exilic Israel*, pp. 50–51; Noll, *Canaan and Israel*, p. 121; Redford, *Egypt, Canaan, and Israel*, p. 272.
73. Redford regards the identification as clear (*Egypt, Canaan, and Israel*, pp. 272–273); others are more circumspect; see e.g. Hoffmeier, *Ancient Israel in Sinai*, pp. 242–243; Na'aman, 'Exodus Story', p. 67; Noll, *Canaan and Israel*, p. 123. References to the Shasu usually link them with places, suggesting that *Yhw* is also a place name. If it is linked with 'Yahweh', that suggests either that the deity was named after the place or the place was named after the deity (Blenkinsopp, 'Midianite-Kenite Hypothesis', p. 140).
74. See e.g. Arnold, *Introduction*, p. 162; Rainer Albertz, *A History of Israelite Religion in the Old Testament Period*, 2 vols. (London: SCM Press; Louisville: Westminster John Knox, 1994), 1:52–53; William G. Dever, *Who Were the Early Israelites and Where Did They Come From?* (Grand Rapids: Eerdmans, 2003), pp. 150–151, 236–237; Frendo, 'Back to Basics', in Day, *In Search of Pre-Exilic Israel*, p. 43; Redford, *Egypt, Canaan, and Israel*, pp. 273–274. OT texts also link Yahweh with this region; see e.g. Deut. 33:2; Judg. 5:4; Isa. 63:1; Hab. 3:3, 7. The narrative surrounding the tabernacle suggests that Yahweh 'moves' with Israel from Sinai to the Promised Land.

in Midian, maybe by his father-in-law, Jethro.[75] This may appear to undermine the uniqueness of Israel's faith. However, Moses' own encounter with Yahweh at the burning bush was certainly unique, and it seems possible that Israelite Yahwism, which grew out of that encounter, represented a distinctive development, rather than a copy, of earlier religious ideas.[76] Another view is that the Shasu, or some of them, are to be identified with the early Israelites.[77] This, though, raises questions about the exodus, since there is no indication that the Shasu came from Egypt.[78] Ultimately, as with the 'Apiru, there is no clear evidence to link the Shasu directly with Israel.

---

75. This is in line with an older view that the worship of Yahweh originated with the Kenites; see Blenkinsopp, 'Midianite-Kenite Hypothesis'; see also e.g. Arnold, *Introduction*, pp. 162–163.
76. Exod. 18:9–12 portrays Jethro's offering sacrifices to Yahweh; however, his statement 'Now I know that the LORD is greater than all other gods' (v. 11) suggests, at the very least, that he is being introduced to an aspect of Yahweh with which he was previously unfamiliar.
77. See e.g. Redford, *Egypt, Canaan, and Israel*, pp. 269–280. In Redford's view the people who became Israel were from the region round about Canaan. Some conservative scholars link these Shasu with the Israelites following the exodus (which must, therefore, have taken place in the fifteenth century BC); see e.g. Charles Aling and Clyde Billington, 'The Name Yahweh in Egyptian Hieroglyphic Texts', *Artifax* 24.4 (2009). Further evidence for a link between the Shasu and Israel has been claimed from reliefs in the Temple of Karnak, which depict battle scenes involving Egypt and various other peoples. It has been argued that these scenes correspond to the victories listed in the Merneptah Stele; see Frank J. Yurco, '3,200-Year-Old Picture of Israelites Found in Egypt', *BAR* 16.5 (1990), pp. 20–38; cf. Anson F. Rainey, 'Scholars Disagree: Can You Name the Panel with the Israelites?', *BAR* 17.6 (1991), pp. 56–60; see also e.g. Dever, *Who Were the Early Israelites?*, pp. 207–208; Richard S. Hess, 'Early Israel in Canaan, a Survey of Recent Evidence and Interpretations', in Long, *Israel's Past*, pp. 492–518 (504); Hoffmeier, *Ancient Israel in Sinai*, pp. 244–245. Israel is referred to on the Merneptah Stele but not in the reliefs, while the Shasu, who are not mentioned on the Merneptah Stele, do appear on the reliefs. Since other references correspond, the conclusion is that the Shasu and Israel must be the same. Others, however, argue that the specific reference to Israel on the Merneptah Stele indicates that it is distinct from the Shasu (e.g. Hoffmeier, *Ancient Israel in Sinai*, p. 243).
78. See e.g. Noll, *Canaan and Israel*, p. 123.

Akhenaten's death ended Egypt's brief flirtation with 'monotheism'. He was followed by his son,[79] whose name was changed from Tutankhaten to the more traditional Tutankhamun, and as a further act of rejection of Akhenaten's 'heresy' the religious centre of the country was moved back to Thebes. Tutankhamun was a child when he came to the throne, and reigned for ten years. After Tutankhamun's death, Ay, a military commander, became king, and he was followed by Horemheb, another general. Horemheb restored the significance of the army, and sought to enhance Egypt's tarnished reputation on the international scene. Horemheb was succeeded by Rameses I, the founder of the Ramesside dynasty, which held power for a little over a century. Rameses I reigned only briefly and was succeeded by Seti I, who was followed, in turn, by one of Egypt's more notable Pharaohs, Rameses II, also known as Rameses the Great (*c.*1279–1213 BC).[80] It is widely held that the exodus took place during the reign of Rameses II.[81]

Rameses II sought to renew control over Canaan and to push northwards into Syria. Those plans, though, were frustrated by the Hittites. Following the indecisive battle of Kadesh, and further incursions that resulted in no permanent gains, Rameses signed a peace treaty with the Hittites. In the following years he appears to have turned to major building projects at home, and this may have left Canaan relatively free from direct Egyptian interference. Control over Canaan appears to have weakened sufficiently to necessitate a campaign by Rameses' successor, Merneptah (1213–1203 BC), around 1209 BC.

The date of the exodus

Opinion is divided between two dates for the exodus: an earlier date in the mid-fifteenth century BC, and a later date in the thirteenth century BC.[82]

---

79. The details of the succession after Akhenaten are unclear. Tutankhamun appears to have acceded to the throne a few years after Akhenaten's death.
80. These appear to be widely agreed dates; see e.g. Kitchen, *Reliability*, p. 255; Van De Mieroop, *Ancient Egypt*, p. 214; though other dating systems show a discrepancy of up to eleven years (i.e. 1290–1224 BC).
81. However, see the discussion below.
82. For more detail, including arguments and counter-arguments, see e.g. John J. Bimson, *Redating the Exodus and Conquest*, JSOTSup 5 (Sheffield: Sheffield Academic Press, 1978); John J. Bimson and David Livingston, 'Redating the Exodus', *BAR* 13.5 (1987), pp. 40–48, 51–53, 66–68; Charles C. Dyer, 'The Date of the Exodus Reexamined', *BSac* 140 (1983), pp. 225–243; Gottwald, *Hebrew Bible*, pp. 190–192; James K. Hoffmeier, *Israel in Egypt: The Evidence for the Authenticity of the Exodus*

The earlier date is based on 1 Kings 6:1, which notes that work on Solomon's temple began 480 years after the exodus. The temple took seven years to build and is thought to have been dedicated around 960 BC. This suggests that the exodus took place in around 1447 BC, with the conquest forty years later. Judges 11:26 appears to indicate a similar date. Jephthah, in around 1100 BC,[83] claims that by then Israel had been in the land 300 years. According to this dating, the long oppression of Israelites by 'a new king, who did not know about Joseph' (Exod. 1:8) might have begun during the Hyksos period, and then continued into the New Kingdom, and the Pharaoh of the exodus would have been Thutmose III (*c.*1479–1425 BC).

The later date is based on references to the store cities of Pithom and Rameses (Exod. 1:11). These are now thought to have been built during the reigns of Seti I and Rameses II, suggesting that Rameses II was the pharaoh of the exodus. Exodus 2:23 is sometimes taken to imply that only one pharaoh had died in the 'long period' since Moses' flight from Egypt. But that is not necessarily so. Moses was settled in Midian, and was not looking for the first opportunity to return to Egypt. This text simply prepares the way for the next

---

(*Footnote 82 cont.*) *Tradition* (Oxford: Oxford University Press, 1996), pp. 107–134; 'What Is the Biblical Date for the Exodus? A Response to Bryant Wood', *JETS* 50.2 (2007), pp. 225–247; Kitchen, *Ancient Orient*, pp. 57–75; *Reliability*, pp. 307–310; Tremper Longman III, *How to Read Exodus* (Downers Grove: InterVarsity Press, 2009), pp. 68–82; Merrill, Rooker and Grisanti, *World and Word*, pp. 194–207; Provan, Long and Longman, *Biblical History*, pp. 131–132; Nahum M. Sarna, 'Israel in Egypt: The Egyptian Sojourn and the Exodus', in Shanks, *Ancient Israel*, pp. 31–52 (33–40, 51–52); J. H. Walton, 'Exodus, Date of', in *DOTP*, pp. 258–272; Bryant G. Wood, 'The Rise and Fall of the 13th-Century Exodus-Conquest Theory', *JETS* 48.3 (2005), pp. 475–489; Leon J. Wood, *A Survey of Israel's History*, rev. ed. (Grand Rapids: Zondervan, 1986), pp. 69–86; for a different date see Gary A. Rendsburg, 'The Date of the Exodus and Conquest/Settlement: The Case for the 1100s', *VT* 42.4 (1992), pp. 510–527. For a more sceptical view of the exodus narrative as historical, see e.g. William G. Dever, *What Did the Biblical Writers Know and When Did They Know It? What Archaeology Can Tell Us About the Reality of Ancient Israel* (Grand Rapids: Eerdmans, 2001), pp. 62–63, 98–99, 121; *Who Were the Early Israelites?*; Noll, *Canaan and Israel*, pp. 95–103; Redford, *Egypt, Canaan, and Israel*, pp. 257–281; see also below, p. 92, n. 104.

83. Wood suggests that there were 50 years between Jephthah and Saul (*Survey of Israel's History*, pp. 69–70); according to Kitchen, Jephthah was later, around 1073 BC (*Reliability*, p. 207).

phase in the story (cf. Exod. 4:19). Thus Moses may have fled during Horemheb's reign, and returned when Rameses II was Pharaoh, suggesting a date for the exodus of around 1270–1250 BC. If Joseph came to Egypt during the Hyksos period, the 'new king' might then be a Pharaoh of the New Kingdom, who, after the experience with the Hyksos, might well have seen the growing number of Israelites as a serious threat.

Those who support the late view and want, too, to support the integrity of the biblical record, suggest that the 480 years in 1 Kings 6:1 is symbolic: twelve generations, each reckoned as forty years.[84] The 300 years mentioned in Judges 11:26 cannot be explained in this way; however, there is a question about the date of Jephthah.[85] It may be noted, too, that 300 years is Jephthah's own assessment, and his accuracy may be questioned without calling into question the inspiration and authority of the text as a whole.

Both views claim some support from extrabiblical sources, though the evidence is inconclusive. Geopolitically, either is possible. Although Egypt controlled Canaan and might have been expected to step in to prevent a wholesale conquest, the Amarna Letters point to Egypt's inaction in Canaan during the earlier period, even in the face of threats to its cities. And there also seems to have been little direct involvement in the region in the later years of Rameses II. Links between emergent Israel and the 'Apiru or Shasu, which have sometimes been taken to suggest an earlier date, are inconclusive.[86] Garstang appeared to have discovered Joshua's Jericho, which he dated in the fourteenth century BC, though Kenyon subsequently showed that what Garstang had discovered were the walls of two cities, both dating to well before the time of Joshua.[87] However,

---

84. If a 'generation' is closer to 25 years, 12 generations (300 years) would take us back to the time of Rameses II. However, if the figures are symbolic it is not certain that 12 is a literal figure, and attempts to fix a precise date are questionable. The LXX version of 1 Kgs 6:1 has 440 (rather than 480) years; though not significant for dating, this may suggest that counting was in 40-year blocks.

85. After Jephthah, three judges led Israel for a total of 25 years (Judg. 12:8–15), though their periods may have overlapped. It is not clear where Samson's 20 years (Judg. 16:31), the 40 years that Eli led Israel (1 Sam. 4:18) and Samuel's period of office, which was in excess of 20 years (1 Sam. 7:2), fit in. See the discussion on the chronology of the settlement, below, pp. 93–94.

86. See above, pp. 81–84.

87. John Garstang and J. B. E. Garstang, *The Story of Jericho* (London: Marshall, Morgan & Scott, 1948); Kathleen Kenyon, *Digging up Jericho: The Results of the Jericho Excavations, 1952–1956* (New York: Praeger, 1957). These results have been widely

she found no evidence, either, of a major city in the thirteenth century BC. There is some indication of the destruction of Canaanite cities in the late thirteenth century BC, but no proof that they were the result of an Israelite invasion, and there is no similar evidence of the destruction of other cities.

A key source is the Stele of Merneptah, dated around 1209 BC, which includes the earliest extrabiblical reference to Israel. The stele celebrates the Pharaoh's victories in Canaan and includes the claim 'Israel lies desolate; its seed is no more'. This gives a *terminus ad quem* for Israel's presence in Canaan, and suggests that the exodus cannot have taken place after 1250 BC. It has been suggested that the hieroglyph relating to Israel indicates a people rather than a territory,[88] thus indicating that the conquest might still have been underway at that time. However, while 'seed' here may refer to Israel's progeny and so indicate, metaphorically, an overwhelming Egyptian victory, the expression often refers, literally, to the destruction of an enemy's grain store, and that may indicate that Israel was a more settled nation.[89] In the end, here, as with the other biblical and extrabiblical evidence relating to the date of the exodus, the matter remains unclear.

The route of the exodus[90]

The exact route of the exodus is difficult to determine, not least because it is impossible to be sure of the locations of places named in the various accounts.

(*Footnote 87 cont.*) discussed as part of the debate about the date of the exodus (see above, pp. 85–86, n. 82); see also Pekka M. A. Pitkänen, *Joshua*, AOTC 6 (Nottingham: Apollos; Downers Grove: InterVarsity Press, 2010), pp. 162–169.

88. Redmount suggests that the hieroglyph may indicate a nomadic people ('Bitter Lives', in Coogan, *Biblical World*, pp. 71–72); however, see Michael G. Hasel, 'Merneptah's Reference to Israel: Critical Issues for the Origin of Israel', in Richard S. Hess, Gerald A. Klingbeil and Paul J. Ray Jr., *Critical Issues in Early Israelite History* (Winona Lake: Eisenbrauns, 2008), pp. 47–59 (53).

89. Ann E. Killebrew, *Biblical Peoples and Ethnicity: An Archaeological Study of Egyptians, Canaanites, Philistines, and Early Israelites, 1300–1100 B.C.E.* (Atlanta: Society of Biblical Literature, 2005), pp. 154–155.

90. See e.g. Aharoni, *Land of the Bible*, pp. 195–200; G. I. Davies, *The Way of the Wilderness: A Geographical Study of the Wilderness Itineraries in the Old Testament* (Cambridge: Cambridge University Press, 1979); P. Enns, 'Exodus Route and Wilderness Itinerary', in *DOTP*, pp. 272–280; Kitchen, *Reliability*, pp. 254–274, 628–631; LaSor, Hubbard and Bush, *OT Survey*, pp. 60–62; Gordon J. Wenham, *Numbers*, TOTC (Leicester: Inter-Varsity Press; Downers Grove: InterVarsity Press, 1981), pp. 220–230.

Two key issues are the subjects of continuing debate: the locations of the Red Sea and of Mount Sinai, and these will be discussed here, briefly.

The name 'Red Sea' (*yam sûp*; literally, 'sea of reeds') is applied to the Gulf of Aqaba (e.g. 1 Kgs 9:26; cf. Num. 14:25; 21:4), and, probably, also to the Gulf of Suez (e.g. Exod. 10:19; Num. 33:10). It may also refer to the lakes between the Gulf of Suez and the Mediterranean, including Lake Menzaleh, Lake Timsah or the Bitter Lakes.[91] According to Exodus 14:2, the Israelites 'turned back' before they reached the Sea. This suggests that they travelled north and then south-east to cross Lake Menzaleh, or that they travelled south and then north-east to cross Lake Timsah or the Bitter Lakes.[92]

Mount Sinai is traditionally identified with Jebel Musa (mountain of Moses), at the southern end of the Sinai peninsula. However, if Mount Sinai was a three-day journey from Egypt (Exod. 5:3; 8:27), Jebel Musa is too far away, and Jebel Sin Bisher, lying east of the Gulf of Suez, but much further north, may be a better candidate.[93] The evidence, though, is scant, and suggestions are speculative.[94] Significantly, the location of Mount Sinai does not seem to have been of great interest to OT writers outside the Pentateuch. Only Elijah is recorded as having visited it (1 Kgs 19:8–18), and, theologically, traditions associated with Sinai appear to have been transferred to Zion.[95]

Israel in Canaan

Merneptah's 'Israel' stele gives evidence of Israel's presence in Canaan at the

---

91. See e.g. Kitchen, *Reliability*, pp. 261–263; Wenham, *Numbers*, p. 224.
92. Other suggestions include Lake Sirbonis; see e.g. Aharoni, *Land of the Bible*, pp. 196–197.
93. See e.g. Wenham, *Numbers*, pp. 225–227. Exod. 4:27 may also indicate a location closer to Egypt.
94. Another suggestion, Jebel Helal, further east, seems too close to Kadesh Barnea (Deut. 1:2). A popular view, but with little scholarly support (though see Gal. 4:25) identifies Mount Sinai with Jebel Al Lawz, in Midian, and the Red Sea as the Gulf of Aqaba. However, the Red Sea crossing is much earlier in the narrative than this allows, and it seems unlikely that Aaron would travel so far to meet Moses (Exod. 4:27).
95. See e.g. J. Gordon McConville, 'Jerusalem in the Old Testament', in P. W. L. Walker (ed.), *Jerusalem Past and Present in the Purposes of God* (Cambridge: Tyndale House, 1992), pp. 21–51 (25); Routledge, *OT Theology*, pp. 276, 329.

end of the thirteenth century BC. The nature of that people and how they came to be there is, though, the subject of considerable debate.[96]

The biblical account describes Israel's conquest of Canaan, under Joshua. That conquest, though, was not rapid and complete. There are indications of significant victories (e.g. Josh. 11:16–20), but also of setbacks (e.g. Josh. 15:63; 16:10; 17:12; 19:47). Many years later it is clear that there is still much to do (Josh. 13:1), and the book of Judges also indicates a continuing struggle.

In the 1920s Albrecht Alt put forward another view of Israel's emergence. He suggested that semi-nomadic groups gradually infiltrated the hill country of Canaan, and eventually challenged the city states in the lower-lying areas.[97]

---

96. See e.g. Albertz, *History*, 1:40–94; Anderson, *Living World*, pp. 137–147; Arnold, *Introduction*, pp. 195–201; John J. Bimson, 'The Origins of Israel in Canaan: An Examination of Recent Theories', *Them* 15.1 (1989), pp. 4–15; Bright, *History*, pp. 133–143; Joseph A. Callaway, 'The Settlement in Canaan: The Period of the Judges', in Shanks, *Ancient Israel*, pp. 53–84; Collins, *Introduction*, pp. 189–198; Dever, *Who Were the Early Israelites?*; Israel Finkelstein and Neil Asher Silberman, *The Bible Unearthed: Archaeology's New Vision of Ancient Israel and the History of Its Ancient Texts* (New York: Touchstone, 2001), pp. 72–96; Norman K. Gottwald, *The Tribes of Yahweh: A Sociology of the Religion of Liberated Israel, 1220–1050 BCE* (Maryknoll: Orbis, 1979; Sheffield: Sheffield Academic Press, 1999), esp. pp. 191–233; *Hebrew Bible*, pp. 261–288; Hess, 'Early Israel in Canaan', in Long, *Israel's Past*; Longman and Dillard, *Introduction*, pp. 125–127; Yehezkel Kaufmann, *The Biblical Account of the Conquest of Canaan*, 2nd ed. (Jerusalem: Magnes, 1985); Eugene H. Merrill, 'The Late Bronze/Early Iron Age Transition and the Emergence of Israel', *BSac* 152 (1995), pp. 145–162; Moore and Kelle, *Biblical History*, pp. 77–144; Provan, Long and Longman, *Biblical History*, pp. 139–147; Redford, *Egypt, Canaan, and Israel*, pp. 263–269; Eveline J. van der Steen, *Tribes and Territories in Transition* (Leuven: Peeters, 2004), pp. 252–272; K. Lawson Younger Jr., 'Early Israel in Recent Biblical Scholarship', in Baker and Arnold, *Face of OT Studies*, pp. 176–206. See also Albrecht Alt, *Essays on Old Testament History and Religion* (Oxford: Blackwell, 1966), pp. 133–169; George E. Mendenhall, 'The Hebrew Conquest of Palestine', *BA* 25 (1962), pp. 66–87; Manfred Weippert, *The Settlement of the Israelite Tribes in Palestine*, SBT 2.21 (London: SCM Press, 1971).
97. See also Martin Noth, *The History of Israel* (London: SCM Press, 1983), pp. 68–74. Noth linked the tribal league with Greek amphictyonies, where a group of tribes united around a central sanctuary (pp. 87–88); see also e.g. John H. Hayes, *Interpreting Israelite History, Prophecy, and Law* (Eugene: Cascade, 2013), pp. 111–133; A. D. H. Mayes, *Israel in the Period of the Judges*, SBT 2.29 (London: SCM Press, 1974).

In Alt's view these tribal groups worshipped gods linked with their ancestors, including Abraham, Isaac and Jacob.[98] Over time these settlers, who originally had nothing to do with each other, united and constructed a genealogy to link their ancestors. These tribes came from the desert, where they might have come into contact with the worship of Yahweh. However, this 'peaceful infiltration' model does not allow for the exodus. More recent versions of this view suggest that these early settlers may have been 'Apiru or Shasu.[99]

Another series of suggestions argues that Israel emerged, primarily, from among people already in Canaan. In Mendenhall's view those from lower echelons of society came together in the common worship of Yahweh, which appeared to envisage a more egalitarian community. Gottwald developed Mendenhall's view of a 'peasant's revolt' in line with a Marxist understanding of society.[100] He argued that these lower classes rose up against their masters, and the ensuing violence might have led to the idea of a 'conquest'. This process might have been catalysed by the arrival from Egypt of a relatively small group of escaped slaves,[101] and thus allows for the exodus, though on a significantly reduced scale. There was, however, no invasion and conquest.[102] Albertz suggests a similar model. Canaan was experiencing social and political change, including rebellion against Egyptian power. The 'exodus group', whose God was associated with liberation, helped effect that change. It is suggested that the experience of this group gave rise to the traditions associated with the exodus, and that this became part of the collective memory of all Israel.[103]

---

98. Albrecht Alt, 'The God of the Fathers', in *Essays*, pp. 3–77.
99. See above, pp. 81–84; see also e.g. Moore and Kelle, *Biblical History*, p. 102; K. L. Sparks, 'Religion, Identity and the Origins of Ancient Israel', *Religion Compass* 1.6 (2007), pp. 587–614.
100. Though Mendenhall may not have agreed with Gottwald's political rather than ideological emphasis; cf. Moore and Kelle, *Biblical History*, p. 103.
101. Mendenhall, 'Hebrew Conquest', pp. 73, 79; Gottwald, *Hebrew Bible*, pp. 272–273.
102. E.g. Mendenhall, 'Hebrew Conquest', p. 73.
103. One view is that only the 'Joseph tribes' (Ephraim, Manasseh and Benjamin) were in Egypt; see e.g. Dever, *Who Were the Early Israelites?*, pp. 229–230. Gottwald notes this possibility (*Tribes*, pp. 206–207). Bright also suggests that not all of those who became Israel were in Egypt, but also notes that certainty is impossible (*History*, pp. 133–143). For further discussion of the relationship between collective memory and historiography, see e.g. Collins, *Introduction*, pp. 110–113; Dever, *Who Were the Early Israelites?*, pp. 229–234; Ronald Hendel, 'The Exodus in Biblical Memory', *JBL* 120.4 (2001), pp. 601–622; Na'aman, 'Exodus Story'. Bright comments, 'since the

Those who argue that what became 'Israel' was made up primarily of people from within the land, suggest that the number of people who came out of Egypt was probably in the thousands,[104] whereas the number that took part in the occupation appears to have been much larger. The fact that Shechem, which is not listed among the cities captured, had become an important Israelite centre before Joshua's death (Josh. 24:1), suggests that, even within the biblical account, not all of the land was taken by conquest. We see, too, that Israel was made up of people from mixed origins (e.g. Exod. 12:38). Caleb, for example, was a Kenizzite (Num. 32:12; cf. Gen. 15:19), maybe an Edomite clan, which seems to have been incorporated into Judah.[105]

Another view sees the 'conquest' as wholly from within. According to Finkelstein, the collapse of Canaanite culture on the plains led to a shortage of grain. As a result, nomadic groups, which could no longer buy excess grain, established new villages in the hills.[106] Dever agrees with Finkelstein that archaeological evidence does not support the conquest or gradual infiltration models, and that the expansion of hill villages was due to the resettlement of people from within Canaan. However he argues that the numbers who settled in the hill country cannot be accounted for only by nomadic settlement, and argues, too, for movement from within Canaan by 'agrarian reformers with a new social

---

(*Footnote 103 cont.*) group that experienced exodus and Sinai was the true nucleus of Israel, and constitutive of Israel, the Bible is in a profound sense correct in insisting that all Israel was there' (*History*, p. 140).

104. See e.g. Albertz, *History*, 1:44–45; Bright, *History*, pp. 133–134; Philip J. Budd, *Numbers*, WBC 5 (Waco: Word, 1984), pp. 6–9; Eryl W. Davies, *Numbers*, NCB (London: Marshall Pickering; Grand Rapids: Eerdmans, 1995), pp. 14–18; Wenham, *Numbers*, pp. 60–66. According to Num. 1:46 (cf. 26:51) Israel could muster over 600,000 fighting men, which suggests a population in excess of two million. However, these were served by just two midwives (Exod. 1:15–22), were terrified by the Egyptian army and crossed the Red Sea in a single night (Exod. 14:21–25). Wenham also notes the indication that the Israelites were, initially, too few to effect an immediate occupation (e.g. Exod. 23:29–30; Deut. 7:21), and that the number of fighting men from Dan noted in Judg. 18:16 (600) contrasts with the very much higher figures in Num. 1:38–39 (62,700) (*Numbers*, p. 61).

105. The Kenizzites were an Edomite tribe descended from Kenaz (Gen. 36:42–43); however, according to Num. 34:19, Caleb represented Judah.

106. Finkelstein and Silberman, *Bible Unearthed*, pp. 105–120; see also Dever, *Who Were the Early Israelites?*, pp. 153–166.

vision'.[107] In both cases, though, the exodus is a myth. For Finkelstein, it was a reading back from the seventh century of Josiah's expansionist policies and his conflict with Pharaoh Neco.[108] For Dever, the exodus stands simply as a 'metaphor for liberation'.[109]

The biblical picture clearly points to a conquest, and the evidence for alternative views is not compelling. In particular it is difficult to set aside the exodus, which played such an important part in the nation's self-understanding, and features so prominently in the people's collective memory.[110] However, the number of people leaving Egypt remains a problem. It may be noted, too, that the religion of Israel did have an egalitarian emphasis that might have been attractive to oppressed Canaanites.[111] Some cities, like Shechem, seem to have been incorporated into Israel by peaceful means, and there might have been people, like Rahab (Josh. 2:11–12; 6:25), who chose to join Israel in Canaan.[112] If so, the covenant at Shechem (Josh. 24:1–27) might have been intended to unite disparate elements into one religious and political entity.[113]

The chronology of the settlement As already indicated, there are difficulties fitting the events described between the exodus and settlement and the establishment of the monarchy into the time frame available. The impression given by the book of Judges is that judges presided over the whole nation and their periods of office, and the periods of oppression, ran consecutively, giving a total of 410 years.[114] Adding to that the additional 40 years in the desert, the time from the occupation to the death of Joshua and the elders who outlived him, 40 years for Eli (1 Sam. 4:18), time for Samuel's period of office and for Saul's reign, 40 years for David (1 Kgs 2:11) and 4 years for Solomon, that gives a figure far in excess of the 480 years referred to in 1 Kings 6:1. If the later

107. Dever, *Who Were the Early Israelites?*, p. 191.
108. Finkelstein and Silberman, *Bible Unearthed*, pp. 92–96.
109. Dever, *Who Were the Early Israelites?*, p. 233.
110. See e.g. Routledge, 'Exodus', in Fox, *Reverberations*, pp. 187–192.
111. See e.g. below, p. 120.
112. Others joining themselves to Israel and accepting the worship of Israel's God would not necessarily violate the command not to make alliances with the people of the land (e.g. Exod. 34:12; Deut. 7:2; 23:6; cf. Josh. 11:19). See below, pp. 261–262.
113. See e.g. Anderson, *Living World*, pp. 142–145; Bright, *History*, pp. 143, 164–165.
114. 8 + 40 (Othniel), 18 + 80 (Ehud), 20 + 40 (Deborah and Barak), 7 + 40 (Gideon), 3 (Abimelech), 23 (Tola), 22 (Jair), 18 + 6 (Jephthah), 7 (Ibzan), 10 (Elon), 8 (Abdon), 40 + 20 (Samson) – a total of 410.

date for the exodus is accepted, the timescale is reduced by a further two centuries.[115]

One way of reducing the problem is to note the frequent references to 40-year periods.[116] As noted already, these periods may be figurative rather than literal. It is noticeable, too, that, rather than being national figures, Israel's judges were usually linked with only a few tribes, and their areas of operation were localized. This suggests that they might have operated in different areas, and that their periods in office might have overlapped. It has been suggested, further, that the 40 years of Philistine oppression (Judg. 13:1), which includes Samson (Judg. 15:20; 16:31), also includes Eli and Samuel.[117] That seems unlikely. There were attacks by the Philistines during the time of Eli and Samuel, but those attacks continued into the reign of Saul and were part of an ongoing conflict rather than the continuation of a period of oppression.

Given the lack of detail and frequent references to what may be figurative periods of time, it seems impossible to set out a chronology of this period that brings together the biblical account and dating from external evidence.

The 'Sea Peoples'[118] It is widely held that there was a significant upheaval in the ANE and the Aegean around 1200 BC, marking the transition between the

---

115. For further discussion of the chronological difficulties, see e.g. Miller and Hayes, *History*, pp. 87–91; Provan, Long and Longman, *Biblical History*, pp. 161–166.

116. The periods of peace of *40* (or in the case of Ehud *80*) years in Judg. 3:11, 30; 5:31 and 8:28 are described using the same expression *tišqōṭ hā'āreṣ* (the land had peace), suggesting that this is formulaic. The wilderness wanderings (e.g. Josh. 5:6), the Philistine oppression (Judg. 13:1), Eli's leadership (1 Sam. 4:18) and the reigns of David (1 Kgs 2:11) and Solomon (1 Kgs 11:42) also lasted 40 years (see also 1 Sam. 13:1; cf. Acts 13:21).

117. See e.g. Provan, Long and Longman, *Biblical History*, p. 164; Wood, *Survey of Israel's History*, pp. 69–70.

118. For further discussion, see LaSor, Hubbard and Bush, *OT Survey*, pp. 55–56, 156–157; Van De Mieroop, *Ancient Egypt*, pp. 250–254, 258–259; Redford, *Egypt, Canaan, and Israel*, pp. 241–246; Ian Shaw, 'Egypt and the Outside World', in Shaw, *Ancient Egypt*, pp. 308–323 (321–322); Itamar Singer, 'Sea Peoples', in *ABD* 5:1059–1061. See also Robert Drews, *The End of the Bronze Age: Changes in Warfare and the Catastrophe CA. 1200 B.C.* (Princeton: Princeton University Press, 1993), pp. 48–72; Ann E. Killebrew and Gunnar Lehmann (eds.), *The Philistines and Other 'Sea Peoples' in Text and Archaeology* (Atlanta: Society of Biblical Literature, 2013); Othniel Margalith, *The Sea Peoples in the Bible* (Wiesbaden: Harrassowitz, 1994); N. K. Sandars, *The Sea Peoples: Warriors of the Ancient Mediterranean*, rev. ed. (London: Thames & Hudson, 1985).

Bronze and Iron Ages in the Mediterranean.[119] This is commonly linked with a large-scale movement of sea-faring peoples around the eastern Mediterranean coast, which appears to have contributed to the end of the Hittite kingdom and the de-urbanization of parts of Canaan and Syria, including the destruction of Ugarit. A number of Egyptian texts also note battles with invaders, described as 'sea peoples', during the reigns of Merneptah and Rameses III.[120] The origin of these groups and the reason for their migration is, however, unclear.[121] The lists of people mentioned in Egyptian texts include the Peleset.[122] These are often identified with the Philistines, who settled on the coastal plain of Canaan and who feature prominently in the stories of Israel's settlement.

The need for a king As already noted, in the early period of the settlement Israel was presided over by judges, who were probably local leaders. During that time, there appears to have been a decline in the spiritual and moral values of the nation. This might have been halted, temporarily, during the lifetime of particular leaders (e.g. Judg. 2:18–19), but remained a significant problem. The book of Judges associates it, repeatedly, with the absence of a king (Judg. 17:6; 21:25; cf. 18:1; 19:1). At the same time, threats from other nations, especially the Philistines, made it increasingly necessary to think about having a central authority to coordinate national defence. The appointment of a king seemed to offer a solution to both concerns.

Following the people's request for a king, Saul was the first to be chosen,[123] though he disappointed, leading to the accession of David. Until that time there

---

119. See e.g. Drews, *End of the Bronze Age*; Liverani, *ANE*, pp. 381–400; Killebrew, *Biblical Peoples*, pp. 21–49; Van De Mieroop, *History of the ANE*, pp. 190–206.

120. The designation 'Sea Peoples' comes from their description in texts relating to these two kings; however, the same names occur in other texts. For a list of texts, see Matthew J. Adams and Margaret E. Cohen, 'The "Sea Peoples" in Primary Sources', in Killebrew and Lehmann, *Philistines*, pp. 645–664; see also Anne E. Killebrew and Gunnar Lehmann, 'Introduction: The World of the Philistines and other "Sea Peoples"', in Killebrew and Lehmann, *Philistines*, pp. 1–17 (2–5).

121. Shaw suggests the reason was 'major crop failures in the northern and eastern Mediterranean' ('Egypt and the Outside World', in Shaw, *Ancient Egypt*, p. 321). The movement of people following the Trojan War and the collapse of Mycenaean Greece may also have been factors.

122. The earliest reference to the Peleset appears to be in the list of peoples defeated by Rameses III.

123. 1 Sam. 8 – 12. For further discussion of the institution of the monarchy and OT attitudes towards it, see below, p. 171.

seems to have been the implicit understanding that a son would succeed his father: thus Abimelech assumed that one of Gideon's sons would rule after Gideon's death (Judg. 9:1–2); one of the reasons the people asked Samuel for a king was concern about the unsuitability of his sons to take over from him (1 Sam. 8:5), and after Saul's death his son, Ishbosheth, continued to reign, at least over the northern tribes (2 Sam. 2:8–9). However, this was not automatic. With the appointment of David, succession became dynastic (2 Sam. 7:11b–16), and this opened the way for the understanding of the Messiah as a descendant of David.

To the end of the Old Testament period

David's empire

After Saul's death, David was appointed as king by Judah (2 Sam. 2:4). After several years of fighting between Judah and the northern tribes, who continued to support Saul's heirs, David was anointed as king over all Israel (2 Sam. 5:1–3).

According to the biblical account, Israel reached its height during the reigns of David and his successor, Solomon, with an empire that stretched from the Gulf of Aqaba, in the south, to the Euphrates in the north. However, there is surprisingly little extrabiblical evidence relating to this period, raising questions about its historicity. There are three extrabiblical texts that may refer to David.[124] First, a stele discovered at Tel Dan dating to around 841 BC, which celebrates a Syrian victory over Joram of Israel and Ahaziah of Judah, probably by Hazael (cf. 2 Kgs 8:25–29), includes the text *bytdwd* in relation to Ahaziah. This is generally translated 'the house of David',[125] and is almost

124. See e.g. Israel Finkelstein, 'Digging for the Truth', in Finkelstein, Mazar and Schmidt, *Quest for Historical Israel*, pp. 9–20 (14–15); K. A. Kitchen, 'A Possible Mention of David in the Late Tenth Century BCE, and Deity Dod As Dead as the Dodo?', *JSOT* 76 (1997), pp. 29–44; *Reliability*, pp. 92–93; Steven L. McKenzie, *King David: A Biography* (Oxford: Oxford University Press, 2000), pp. 9–24; Provan, Long and Longman, *Biblical History*, pp. 216–217; P. E. Satterthwaite, 'David', in *DOTHB*, pp. 198–206 (202–205).

125. Some dispute the significance of the discovery; see e.g. Philip R. Davies, '"House of David" Built on Sand: The Sins of the Biblical Maximizers', *BAR* 20.4 (1994), pp. 54–55; Niels Peter Lemche, '"House of David": The Tel Dan Inscription(s)', in Thomas L. Thompson (ed.), *Jerusalem in Ancient History and Tradition*, JSOTSup 381 (London: T&T Clark, 2003), pp. 46–67. The Tel Dan inscription is, though, widely regarded as an authentic reference to David; see above, n. 124; see also e.g. Arnold,

certainly a reference to Judah. Although this gives no information about David himself, it does point to him as the founder of the dynasty. Second, the Mesha Stele (or Moabite Stone), again dating to the second half of the ninth century BC, describes how Mesha, king of Moab, rebelled against Israel (cf. 2 Kgs 3:4–5). It contains a similar expression (*bt[d]wd*), which Lemaire also took to refer to the 'house of David'.[126] Third, a relief by Pharaoh Shoshenq I, who invaded Israel towards the end of the tenth century BC,[127] gives a list of place names, including the 'heights of *Dwt*', a further, possible, reference to David. While not overwhelming, these texts provide extra-biblical evidence in support of the view that David was a real historical figure.[128]

David was succeeded by his son Solomon, who was responsible for building the temple (1 Kgs 6:1–38). He consolidated the kingdom and is noted for his wisdom and great wealth (e.g. 1 Kgs 10:14–25). Sometimes his reign is viewed as a golden age of Israelite prosperity, in which the promises to Abraham were

---

Introduction, p. 219; Baruch Halpern, 'Erasing History: The Minimalist Assault on Ancient Israel', in Long, *Israel's Past*, pp. 415–426; A. Lemaire, 'The Tel Dan Stela as a Piece of Royal Historiography', *JSOT* 81 (1998), pp. 3–14; Brian B. Schmidt, 'Tel Dan Stele', in Chavalas, *ANE*, pp. 305–307. In the Tel Dan Stele the Syrian ruler claims credit for the deaths of Joram and Ahaziah, which in 2 Kgs 9:21–29 is attributed to Jehu. Exaggeration, though, is not uncommon on such monuments, which are intended to enhance the king's reputation. It has also been suggested that this may indicate Syrian support for Jehu's rebellion; see William M. Schniedewind, 'Tel Dan Stela: New Light on Aramaic and Jehu's Revolt', *BASOR* 302 (1996), pp. 75–90.

126. See A. Lemaire, '"House of David" Restored in Moabite Inscription', *BAR* 20.3 (1994), pp. 30–37. It was while studying the occurrence of *bytdwd* in the Tel Dan inscription that Lemaire noticed a similar expression on the Mesha Stele. See also Arnold, *Introduction*, p. 251; Brian B. Schmidt, 'Moabite Stone', in Chavalas, *ANE*, pp. 311–316.

127. Shoshenq is generally identified with Shishak (1 Kgs 11:40; 14:25–26).

128. There remains debate about the importance of David and Solomon in the early first millennium BC. Some see them as relatively minor rulers, whose significance was exaggerated by later writers, and assert, instead, the relative importance of Israel. See e.g. Finkelstein and Silberman, *Bible Unearthed*, pp. 123–147; Israel Finkelstein and Neil Asher Silberman, *David and Solomon: In Search of the Bible's Sacred Kings and the Roots of the Western Tradition* (New York: Simon & Schuster, 2007); Liverani, *ANE*, pp. 405–406.

fulfilled (1 Kgs 4:20). However, in order to maintain his building projects, his personal wealth, and an increasing government bureaucracy, Solomon imposed taxes. He also gave twenty towns to Hiram of Tyre (1 Kgs 9:11), maybe to pay off debts incurred during his extravagant building programmes. All of this put a great burden on the people (1 Kgs 12:4), and caused discontent that resulted in large-scale rebellion, a rebellion that led, during the reign of Solomon's son, Rehoboam, to the division of the kingdom.

The chief opposition to Rehoboam was Jeroboam, who had been one of Solomon's officials. After being anointed as a future king, he was forced to flee to Egypt (1 Kgs 11:29–40). After Solomon's death, Jeroboam returned and was received as leader by the northern tribes. After unsuccessful negotiations with Rehoboam to reduce the burden on the people, the northern tribes rejected the Davidic succession, and appointed Jeroboam as king. The southern kingdom of Judah, though, remained loyal to David.

The Neo-Assyrian period (900–612 BC)

By the end of the second millennium BC Assyria was becoming dominant.[129] Its influence, though, was spasmodic, and there was no involvement in Israel during the time of David and Solomon. The beginning of the ninth century BC, however, saw an Assyrian resurgence, under Ashurnasirpal II (883–859 BC) and especially Shalmaneser III (858–824 BC). Having become established in Mesopotamia, they looked westward.

Shalmaneser faced a coalition led by Syria and which included Ahab, king of Israel.[130] This is not specifically mentioned in the OT, though 1 Kings describes a period of peace in the fighting between Ahab and Ben-Hadad of Syria (1 Kgs 20:34; 22:1), maybe prompted by the common threat of Assyria. Shalmaneser claimed a victory at Qarqar (853 BC), though the evidence is not conclusive. Over the next decade several more battles were fought, though none appears to have been decisive. In a further campaign, around 841 BC, Shalmaneser defeated Jehu of Israel. The 'Black Obelisk', which celebrates Shalmaneser's victories, shows Jehu (or his representative) bowing to the Assyrian

---

129. See e.g. Bright, *History*, pp. 269–309; Hallo and Simpson, *ANE*, pp. 119–143; Liverani, *ANE*, pp. 475–553; Van De Mieroop, *History of the ANE*, pp. 230–269; Miller and Hayes, *History*, pp. 314–376; see also Andrew G. Vaughn and Ann E. Killebrew (eds.), *Jerusalem in Bible and Archaeology: The First Temple Period* (Atlanta: Society of Biblical Literature, 2003).

130. This is referred to on the Kurkh Stele, erected to celebrate Shalmaneser's victory at the battle of Qarqar; see Mitchell, *Bible in the British Museum*, pp. 49–50.

king.[131] Shalmaneser also defeated the Syrian army but did not capture Damascus. And after his departure the Syrians, under Hazael, were free to resume attacks on Israel and Judah (2 Kgs 12:17–18; 13:3). A few years later Shalmaneser did turn his attention on Damascus, and may be the 'deliverer' referred to in 2 Kings 13:5. After Shalmaneser's death, Assyria faced an internal crisis. There was, however, a fresh Assyrian resurgence under Tiglath-Pileser III (744–727 BC), which continued under Shalmaneser V (726–722 BC), Sargon II (721–705 BC) and Sennacherib (704–681 BC).

Following the defeat of Syria, and while Assyria was relatively weak, Israel, under Jehoash and Jeroboam II, expanded its territory (2 Kgs 13:25; 14:25–28). Judah, too, grew in strength under Uzziah (Azariah). Jeroboam's death, around 750 BC,[132] brought instability, and a series of kings, representing pro- and anti-Assyrian factions, vied for power. The Israelite king Pekah, an anti-Assyrian, allied with Syria and tried to draw Judah, under Ahaz, into the coalition. Ahaz refused and turned to Assyria for help (see Isa. 7 – 8). In 735/734 BC Tiglath-Pileser destroyed Damascus, subjugated Israel and made Judah a vassal state. Some years later, Israel's last king, Hoshea, rebelled against Assyria, probably with Egypt's encouragement. This led to a further invasion (721 BC) by Sargon. Samaria was destroyed and many Israelites were deported, bringing the northern kingdom to an end.

During this period, Egypt was going through its Third Intermediate Period, and was relatively quiet on the international stage.[133] A Libyan dynasty, beginning with Sheshonq I (Shishak) (945–925 BC) was more aggressive. According to the biblical account, he harboured Jeroboam when the latter fled from Solomon (1 Kgs 11:40), and after the division of the kingdom invaded Judah (1 Kgs

---

131. E.g. ibid., pp. 51–54. The tribute is also recorded: 'I received tribute from Jehu of the house of Omri: silver, gold, a golden bowl, a gold tureen, gold vessels, gold pails, tin, the staffs of the king's hands, and spears' (Bill T. Arnold and Bryan E. Beyer [eds.], *Readings from the Ancient Near East: Primary Sources for Old Testament Study* [Grand Rapids: Baker Academic, 2002], p. 144; cf. *COS* 2:113F; Brent A. Strawn, 'Black Obelisk', in Chavalas, *ANE*, pp. 291–293). In the OT account Jehu usurped the throne and so was not from 'the house of Omri'; that, though, may have been an Assyrian name for Israel. The reference may also be intended to legitimize Jehu's reign; see Nadav Na'aman, *Ancient Israel and Its Neighbors: Interaction and Counteraction* (Winona Lake: Eisenbrauns, 2005), pp. 13–15.

132. For suggested dates of kings of Israel and Judah, see below, p. 278.

133. See e.g. Van De Mieroop, *Ancient Egypt*, pp. 260–282; John Taylor, 'The Third Intermediate Period (1069–664 BC)', in Shaw, *Ancient Egypt*, pp. 324–363; Wilkinson, *Ancient Egypt*, pp. 383–421.

14:25–26).[134] Egypt then, attempting to influence events but with no real power, returned to a more modest foreign policy. Thus when Hoshea turned to So (probably Osorkon IV) for help (2 Kgs 17:4), none was forthcoming.

In 705 BC, after the death of Sargon, Hezekiah, king of Judah, with Egyptian support joined a rebellion against Assyria.[135] This prompted an invasion of Judah by the new Assyrian ruler Sennacherib,[136] who destroyed many of its cities, including Lachish.[137] According to the biblical account, Hezekiah tried to buy him off with a large tribute (2 Kgs 18:13–16), but that appears not to have been enough. The Assyrian army laid siege to Jerusalem, though was forced to withdraw (2 Kgs 18:17 – 19:36). One suggestion for the failure to capture the city is that, though Assyria claimed victory at the key battle of Eltekeh (701 BC) over the Egyptians under Tirhakah, who had come to support Hezekiah (cf. 2 Kgs 19:9), the coalition was still able to protect Jerusalem.[138] Others affirm that the Assyrians were overwhelming victors at Eltekeh,[139] which would have left Jerusalem at Sennacherib's mercy.[140] If so, he might have been expected to

---

134. We have already noted the inscription referring to his conquests; see above, p. 97.

135. Egypt had, by this time, regained some of its former strength under a Nubian dynasty, which under Piankhi (747–716 BC) and Shabaqo (716–702 BC) gained control of all Egypt; see e.g. Van De Mieroop, *Ancient Egypt*, pp. 290–295; Taylor, 'Third Intermediate Period', in Shaw, *Ancient Egypt*, pp. 345–353; Wilkinson, *Ancient Egypt*, pp. 414–430.

136. See e.g. Anderson, *Living World*, pp. 347–355; Bright, *History*, pp. 284–288; Clements, *Isaiah and the Deliverance of Jerusalem*; Brevard S. Childs, *Isaiah and the Assyrian Crisis*, SBT 2.3 (London: SCM Press, 1967); Collins, *Introduction*, pp. 291–294; LaSor, Hubbard and Bush, *OT Survey*, pp. 214–215; see also Paul S. Evans, *The Invasion of Sennacherib in the Book of Kings*, VTSup 125 (Leiden: Koninklijke Brill, 2009).

137. Reliefs of the siege of Lachish are in the British Museum; see e.g. Mitchell, *Bible in the British Museum*, pp. 67–71.

138. See e.g. Van De Mieroop, *Ancient Egypt*, p. 291.

139. Wilkinson suggests that Egypt's defeat at Eltekeh heralded the end of the Egyptian revival (*Ancient Egypt*, p. 431); see also Taylor, 'Third Intermediate Period', in Shaw, *Ancient Egypt*, p. 352.

140. This reflects Sennacherib's own account: '[Hezekiah] himself I shut up like a caged bird within Jerusalem, his royal city . . . the awful splendour of my lordship overwhelmed him . . .'; he then mentions tribute of both troops and large amounts of gold and silver; and he goes on, 'He sent a personal messenger to deliver the tribute and make a slavish obedience' (Arnold and Beyer, *Readings*, p. 147); cf. Sarah C. Melville, 'Sennacherib', in Chavalas, *ANE*, pp. 342–350 (345–349, esp. 346); *COS* 2:119B; see also Mitchell, *Bible in the British Museum*, p. 66.

take the city, and why he did not is unclear. It is not implausible that it was attributable to some catastrophe that overtook his army, as indicated in the biblical account.[141]

Assyria's power, though, continued to grow, reaching its zenith under Esarhaddon (680–669 BC), with the conquest of Egypt.[142] After Esarhaddon's death, there was civil war. This was eventually won by Assurbanipal (668–631 BC) but led to a decline in Assyrian power, which allowed Josiah to assert Judah's independence and extend its territory. The Egyptians also had a brief revival and, because of the growth of Babylon, decided to ally with Assyria against this new threat. Assyria, though, was in terminal decline. After Assurbanipal's death, there was further civil war, and rebellion by the Babylonians and Medes, who captured the Assyrian capital, Nineveh, in 612 BC. The Egyptian king Neco II went to help Assyria (2 Kgs 23:29–30). Josiah tried to stop him, but was killed at Megiddo (609 BC), though this might have delayed Neco long enough to prevent his offering Assyria any effective assistance. On his return he took control of Judah, deposed Jehoahaz, Josiah's son, and put Jehoahaz's brother, Eliakim (Jehoiakim), on the throne instead (2 Kgs 23:31–35).

Babylonians, Persians, Greeks and Romans (626–63 BC)

As Assyria declined, Babylon's power grew.[143] In 605 BC, under Nebuchadnezzar, they defeated the Egyptians at Carchemish (Jer. 46:2), and Judah came under Babylonian control (2 Kgs 24:1). There might have been some deportations

141. One suggestion is that Sennacherib heard a 'rumour' (cf. 2 Kgs 19:7) necessitating his return home (see e.g. Anderson, *Living World*, p. 353; Bright, *History*, p. 288; Collins, *Introduction*, p. 293), and Hezekiah's prompt capitulation meant that the city was spared. Clements suggests that later generations attributed Jerusalem's survival to the non-historical miracle recorded in 2 Kgs 19:35–36; see Clements, *Isaiah and the Deliverance of Jerusalem*; see also Miller and Hayes, *History*, pp. 358–363 (363). Bright suggests that 2 Kgs 18:17 – 19:37 relates to a second campaign around 686 BC (*History*, pp. 287–288, 298–309); see also William H. Shea, 'Sennacherib's Second Palestinian Campaign', *JBL* 104.3 (1985), pp. 401–418; 'The New Tirhakah Text and Sennacherib's Second Palestinian Campaign', *AUSS* 35.2 (1997), pp. 181–187. Cf. Robin L. Routledge, 'The Siege and Deliverance of the City of David in Isaiah 29:1–8', *TynBul* 43.1 (1992), pp. 181–190.

142. See e.g. Wilkinson, *Ancient Egypt*, pp. 430–435.

143. See e.g. Arnold, *Who Were the Babylonians?*, pp. 87–106; Bright, *History*, pp. 310–339; Gottwald, *Hebrew Bible*, pp. 425–428; Liverani, *ANE*, pp. 537–570; Van De Mieroop, *History of the ANE*, pp. 266–285; Miller and Hayes, *History*, pp. 406–436.

around that time (Dan. 1:1), though they are not mentioned in Kings or in extrabiblical sources.[144] Some see this as a historical error,[145] but an attack on Jerusalem on that occasion is not impossible.[146] A few years later, maybe prompted by an indecisive battle between Babylon and Egypt, Jehoiakim transferred his allegiance back to Egypt (2 Kgs 24:1b). This led to a further Babylonian invasion, and during the ensuing siege of Jerusalem Jehoiakim died; he was probably assassinated. The city was captured in 597 BC and some of the population, including Jehoiakim's successor, Jehoiachin, and the prophet Ezekiel (Ezek. 1:1–3) were deported. Zedekiah, Jehoiachin's uncle, was made king. Ten years later, Zedekiah rebelled against Babylon (Ezek. 17:11–21; cf. Jer. 37:5). Egypt was expected to help, but withdrew in the face of the Babylonian army. The Babylonians destroyed Jerusalem in 587 BC,[147] and many more of the people were taken into exile.

After the death of Nebuchadnezzar in 562 BC, there was political instability in Babylon, before Nabonidus took the throne in 555 BC. He spent much of his time in Arabia, and left Babylon in the charge of his son, Belshazzar. Meanwhile, further east, the Persian, Cyrus, established control over Media and turned towards Lydia, Babylon and Egypt. Nabonidus offered little resistance and, in 539 BC, Cyrus entered Babylon without a fight. The Cyrus Cylinder includes Cyrus' account of his victory over Babylon, and also expresses his intention to allow exiled peoples

---

144. However, 2 Chr. 36:6–7 suggests that the Babylonians took some action against Jehoiakim.

145. See e.g. Carol A. Newsom, with Brennan W. Breed, *Daniel*, OTL (Louisville: Westminster John Knox, 2014), pp. 39–40; Norman W. Porteous, *Daniel*, OTL (London: SCM Press; Philadelphia: Westminster, 1965), pp. 25–27.

146. See e.g. Joyce G. Baldwin, *Daniel*, TOTC (Leicester: Inter-Varsity Press, 1978), pp. 19–20; Ernest C. Lucas, *Daniel*, AOTC 20 (Leicester: Apollos; Downers Grove: InterVarsity Press, 2002), pp. 50–52; D. J. Wiseman, 'Some Historical Problems in the Book of Daniel', in D. J. Wiseman (ed.), *Notes on Some Problems in the Book of Daniel* (London: Tyndale, 1965), pp. 9–18 (16–18).

147. This takes Zedekiah's first regnal year as 597 BC and his eleventh year, when Jerusalem fell (2 Kgs 25:2), as 587 BC. Another view counts Zedekiah's first year from New Year 596 BC, and so dates the fall of Jerusalem in 586 BC (cf. Ezek. 40:1). For further discussion, see Jeremy Hughes, *Secrets of the Times: Myth and History in Biblical Chronology*, JSOTSup 66 (Sheffield: JSOT Press, 1990), pp. 229–232; though cf. Edwin R. Thiele, *Mysterious Numbers of the Hebrew Kings*, 3rd ed. (Grand Rapids: Zondervan, 1983), pp. 186–192. The difference of a single year is probably not significant.

to return to their homeland.[148] The Jews are not specifically mentioned, but would have been included (cf. 2 Chr. 36:23; Ezra 1:1–4). That return, and the problems associated with rebuilding the temple and the city walls are recorded in Ezra-Nehemiah, and in the prophetic books Haggai, Zechariah and Malachi.

After the fall of Babylon, the Persian Empire dominated the ANE for two hundred years,[149] until it was defeated by Alexander the Great, and gave way to the Greek, or Macedonian, empire.[150] The book of Daniel, dated by many scholars around 165 BC,[151] describes some of these events, though using symbolic imagery and language. Alexander defeated the Persians at the battle of Issus in 333 BC and again, decisively, at Gaugamela in 331 BC, to take control of the ANE, including Judah (cf. Dan. 8:3–7). When Alexander died without an heir, in 323 BC, his kingdom divided among four of his generals (cf. Dan. 8:8; 11:2–4). The two whose areas included Judea were Ptolemy, in Egypt,[152] and Seleucus, in Syria.[153]

Judea was first ruled over by the Ptolemies; then, in 198 BC, it came under the control of the Seleucids. Daniel 11 appears to describe the war between the

---

148. '[Marduk] got [Cyrus] into Babylon without hardship or battle . . . He put an end to Nabonidus the king who did not show him reverence . . . to the cities of Ashur and Susa, Agade, Eshunna, the cities of Zamban, Meternu, Der, as far as the region of the land of Gutium, the holy cities beyond the Tigris whose sanctuaries had been in ruins for a long period, the gods whose abode is in the midst of them, I returned to their places . . . I gathered together all their inhabitants and restored to them their dwellings' (Arnold and Beyer, *Readings*, pp. 148–149); cf. *COS* 2:123B; see also Mitchell, *Bible in the British Museum*, p. 92.
149. See e.g. Pierre Briant, *From Cyrus to Alexander: A History of the Persian Empire* (Winona Lake: Eisenbrauns, 2002); Bright, *History*, pp. 360–362, 405–412; Gottwald, *Hebrew Bible*, pp. 428–439; Liverani, *ANE*, pp. 554–570; Van De Mieroop, *History of the ANE*, pp. 286–301; Miller and Hayes, *History*, pp. 437–474.
150. See e.g. Anderson, *Living World*, pp. 610–615; Bright, *History*, pp. 412–413; Lester L. Grabbe, *A History of the Jews and Judaism in the Second Temple Period: 2. The Early Hellenistic Period (335–175 BCE)* (London: T&T Clark, 2008), pp. 267–329; Lee I. A. Levine, 'The Age of Hellenism: Alexander the Great and the Rise and Fall of the Hasmonean Kingdom', in Shanks, *Ancient Israel*, pp. 177–204; D. S. Russell, *The Jews from Alexander to Herod*, new ed. (Oxford: Oxford University Press, 1973), pp. 1–59.
151. See below, pp. 371–373.
152. See Wilkinson, *Ancient Egypt*, pp. 470–490.
153. See e.g. Bright, *History*, pp. 414–422. Alexander's four 'successors' are referred to collectively as the Diadochi. The other two were Antigonus, in Macedon, and Lysimachus, in Pergamon (Pergamum).

Ptolemies (the king of the South) and the Seleucids (the king of the North), and the rise of Antiochus IV Epiphanes (175–164 BC),[154] who is portrayed in the book of Daniel as the epitome of evil. He launched several successful attacks on Egypt, but in so doing attracted the attention of Rome, which was emerging as a significant power. During a further campaign in Egypt (167 BC), Antiochus was instructed by a Roman embassy to withdraw, and had no choice but to comply. This abortive attack may be indicated in Daniel 11:29–30, and 'the ships of Kittim' (v. 30) is generally taken to refer to the Roman intervention.[155] Antiochus then appears to have turned his attention against the Jews (cf. Dan. 11:30–35).[156] He issued an edict that effectively proscribed the Jewish faith (cf. 1 Macc. 1.41–64; 2 Macc. 6.1–11); he stopped the regular temple sacrifices and set up an altar dedicated to Zeus, where, as a further act of desecration, he sacrificed pig's flesh (cf. Dan. 9:27; 11:31). He also established a citadel in Jerusalem, which housed a garrison against further Jewish rebellion.

There were various outbreaks of resistance against both the proscription of the Jewish faith, and the 'Hellenization' of Judea, as Greek culture spread.[157] The most effective opposition came through Judas Maccabaeus, who won a series of victories, and in 164 BC rededicated the temple: an event celebrated annually in the Jewish festival of Hanukkah. Eventually the resistance movement became a fight for full independence, which was granted, finally, in 142 BC and continued until Roman occupation under Pompey in 63 BC.

The Old Testament and ancient Near Eastern literature

Although the OT expresses the unique faith of the people of God, which was made known to them by divine revelation, it also has points of contact with

154. See e.g. Baldwin, *Daniel*, pp. 185–201; John Goldingay, *Daniel*, WBC 30 (Dallas: Word, 1987), pp. 293–305; Lucas, *Daniel*, pp. 278–293; Porteous, *Daniel*, pp. 156–169.

155. E.g. Baldwin, *Daniel*, p. 194; Goldingay, *Daniel*, p. 301; Lucas, *Daniel*, p. 286; Porteous, *Daniel*, p. 167.

156. According to 2 Macc. 5.1–16, Jason, an ousted high priest (2 Macc. 4.7–9, 23–26), following rumours that Antiochus had been killed in Egypt, attacked Jerusalem; this gave Antiochus an excuse for his actions.

157. See e.g. Anderson, *Living World*, pp. 610–618; Bright, *History*, pp. 416–422; Gottwald, *Hebrew Bible*, pp. 439–456; Grabbe, *Early Hellenistic Period*, pp. 125–165; Russell, *Alexander to Herod*, pp. 23–30, 35–39.

other ANE texts.[158] That is not unexpected. The OT was first written for those who viewed the world in a similar way to their ANE neighbours, and even distinctive truths needed to be communicated in a way that was understandable. This section looks at the literary context of some key OT texts.

Flood and creation stories

The flood[159]

Some versions of the Sumerian King List refer to a universal deluge, and to eight kings from the antediluvian period, who lived to much greater ages than

---

158. For the most significant texts, see Arnold and Beyer, *Readings*; for a more complete set of ANE texts see *COS*. See also e.g. Matthews and Benjamin, *OT Parallels*; Kenton L. Sparks, *Ancient Texts for the Study of the Hebrew Bible* (Peabody: Hendrickson, 2005); Walton, *Ancient Israelite Literature*; *ANE Thought*, pp. 43–83. Additional bibliography is included in the discussion of particular texts.

159. See e.g. W. Brueggemann, *Introduction*, pp. 60–64; *COS* 1:158 (Eridu); 1:130 (Atrahasis); 1:132 (Gilgamesh); Alan Dundes (ed.), *The Flood Myth* (Berkeley: University of California Press, 1988); Stephanie Dalley, *Myths from Mesopotamia: Creation, The Flood, Gilgamesh, and Others*, rev. ed. (Oxford: Oxford University Press, 2000); Tikva Frymer-Kensky, 'The Atrahasis Epic and Its Significance for Our Understanding of Genesis 1–9', *BA* 40.4 (1977), pp. 147–155; Robert Gnuse, *Misunderstood Stories: Theological Commentary on Genesis 1–11* (Eugene: Cascade, 2014), pp. 180–192; Alexander Heidel, *The Gilgamesh Epic and Old Testament Parallels: A Translation and Interpretation of the Gilgamesh Epic and Related Babylonian and Assyrian Documents* (Chicago: University of Chicago Press, 1949); Thorkild Jacobsen, 'The Eridu Genesis', *JBL* 100.4 (1981), pp. 513–529; Helge Kvanig, *Primeval History: Babylonian, Biblical, and Enochic: An Intertextual Reading*, Journal for the Study of Judaism Supplement Series 149 (Leiden: Brill, 2011), pp. 13–82; Tremper Longman III, *How to Read Genesis* (Downers Grove: InterVarsity Press; Milton Keynes: Paternoster, 2005), pp. 81–87; W. G. Lambert and A. R. Millard, *Atrahasis: The Babylonian Story of the Flood* (Oxford: Clarendon, 1969; repr. Winona Lake: Eisenbrauns, 1999); John R. Maier (ed.), *Gilgamesh: A Reader* (Wauconda: Bolchazy-Carducci, 1997); Mitchell, *Bible in the British Museum*, pp. 26–27 (Atrahasis), pp. 80–81 (Gilgamesh); Matthews and Benjamin, *OT Parallels*, pp. 21–42; Arnold and Beyer, *Readings*, pp. 13–15 (Eridu Genesis), pp. 21–31 (Atrahasis), pp. 66–70 (Gilgamesh); William H. Shea, 'A Comparison of Narrative Elements in Ancient Mesopotamian Flood-Creation Stories with Genesis 1–9', *Origins* 11.1 (1984), pp. 9–29; Van Seters, *Prologue*, pp. 47–77; John H. Walton, 'Flood', in *DOTP*, pp. 315–326; *Ancient Israelite Literature*, pp. 19–44; *Genesis 1 as Ancient Cosmology* (Eisenbrauns: Winona Lake, 2011).

those afterwards.[160] These eight generations before the flood are sometimes compared with the genealogy in Genesis 5 (excluding Adam and Noah).[161] In the biblical account ages also decrease dramatically after the flood, though the scale is very different.[162]

The Mesopotamian *Atrahasis Epic* probably dates from the early second millennium BC.[163] It begins with an account of the creation of human beings. A lesser class of gods, the Igigi, who were responsible for work on earth, went on strike, set fire to their tools and complained to the chief god, Enlil. One of the gods was killed, and from his blood, mixed with clay, seven pairs of human beings were created to do the work instead. However, as the population increased the noise became so great that it disturbed Enlil's rest: 'Enlil heard their noise and addressed the great gods. The noise of humankind has become too intense for me, with their uproar I am deprived of sleep.'[164] This 'noise' may have a moral dimension: Finkelstein sees it as a metaphor for human wickedness.[165] After trying, unsuccessfully, to deal with the increase in population through plagues, Enlil decided to send a flood to destroy the human race. Another god, Enki, warned Atrahasis to escape and gave him instructions to build a boat. With his family, Atrahasis took on board birds, cattle and other creatures. The rain fell for seven days and seven nights, after which Atrahasis emerged and offered a sacrifice to the gods, providing them with welcome food. Atrahasis was then spared, and other means were introduced to limit population growth.[166]

---

160. According to the Weld-Blundell Prism, eight kings before the flood reigned for a total of 241,200 years. After the flood, the combined reign of twelve kings is a more modest 2,130 years! See Arnold and Beyer, *Readings*, pp. 150–151; see also Piotr Michalowski, 'Sumerian King List', in Chavalas, *ANE*, pp. 81–85. For further discussion of the Sumerian King List, see above, p. 74, n. 36.
161. See Walton, *Ancient Israelite Literature*, pp. 127–131.
162. Jacobsen notes that in the Lagash King List, kings who reigned immediately after the flood also lived to great ages, but grew up very slowly ('Eridu Genesis', pp. 520–521). He suggests that something similar may be reflected in the great ages of biblical figures, who appear to be quite old before having children.
163. See e.g. Arnold and Beyer, *Readings*, p. 21; Mitchell, *Bible in the British Museum*, p. 26.
164. Arnold and Beyer, *Readings*, p. 26.
165. Jacob J. Finkelstein, 'Bible and Babel: A Comparative Study of the Hebrew and Babylonian Religious Spirit', *Commentary* 26 (1958), pp. 431–444 (437); see also Walton, *Ancient Israelite Literature*, p. 31.
166. Arnold and Beyer, *Readings*, p. 31; *COS* 1:130.

The *Gilgamesh Epic* is written on eleven tablets, with a twelfth added later. It dates, probably, from the first half of the second millennium BC, though some suggest that it includes traditions that may date from the third millennium BC.[167] It tells of the quest of the eponymous hero Gilgamesh, a legendary king of Uruk in the third millennium BC, for immortality. His quest led him to Utnapishtim, the survivor of the flood, who had been rewarded with eternal life. Tablet XI records Utnapishtim's account of the flood. It is similar to the story in the *Atrahasis Epic*, and is generally thought to be dependent on it, even to the extent, at one point, of referring to the flood hero as 'Atrahasis'.[168] In this account, following the decision to send the flood, the god Ea told Utnapishtim to build a ship and 'take the seed of all living things aboard' (cf. Gen. 7:2–3).[169] As in the *Atrahasis Epic*, instructions were given for building the ship, and when it was finished Utnapishtim and his family and the craftsmen who had worked on it, and all the living creatures, went on board. After raging for six days and nights, the storm abated and the boat came to rest on Mount Nisir. On the seventh day Utnapishtim sent out a dove, which found nowhere to settle and returned (cf. Gen. 8:8–9). Next he sent out a swallow, which also came back. Finally, he sent out a raven, which did not return (cf. Gen. 8:7). Those in the boat then emerged; Utnapishtim offered sacrifices, and was given divine status and immortality. Although there is not a direct link in this account between the flood and human sin, Ea's words to Enlil 'On the sinner impose his sin, on the transgressor impose his transgression! Yet be lenient lest he be cut off'[170] suggest that it might have been a factor.

A fragmentary Sumerian account of the flood, dating to the seventeenth century BC, contains similar elements.[171] Enlil decided to send a flood to wipe out the human race because, as in the *Atrahasis Epic*, their noise was disturbing the gods' sleep. In this account, Enki warned Ziusudra, the king of Shruppak, who built a boat, though the specific instructions are missing. Following the flood, the people and animals on the boat disembarked. Ziusudra offered sacrifices, which were well received by the gods, and Enlil gave Ziusudra godlike immortality.

---

167. See e.g. Arnold and Beyer, *Readings*, p. 66; Mitchell, *Bible in the British Museum*, p. 80.

168. Arnold and Beyer, *Readings*, p. 70; *COS* 1:132.

169. Arnold and Beyer, *Readings*, p. 66; *COS* 1:132.

170. Arnold and Beyer, *Readings*, p. 69; *COS* 1:132.

171. This text, which relates to the flood, has been combined with two others, found in different locations, but which some consider to be part of a single original text, the *Eridu Genesis*, which relates to creation, the building of cities and temples, kingship and the flood; see Jacobsen, 'Eridu Genesis'.

There are clearly similarities between ANE flood stories and the account in Genesis 6 – 9. Both begin with the divine decision, possibly linked with the moral decay of humankind, to send a flood to wipe out the human race. One man is chosen to save himself, his family and other living creatures, by building a boat. He follows the divine instructions, and is spared. The rains come and a flood destroys the rest of the world. The boat eventually comes to rest on a mountain, and birds (including a dove and a raven) are sent out. The hero emerges from the boat and offers sacrifices to the gods, the gods smell and welcome the sacrifices, and the hero receives divine blessing. Finally, following the deluge, human beings are renewed on the earth. Several of those elements are hardly surprising. The most obvious way to escape a flood is by building a boat. And if the flood is widespread, it seems reasonable to suppose that provision must be made for the survival of wild animals, alongside the flood hero, since they are clearly in evidence afterwards, and so need to be preserved somehow. There are elements, however, including the release of particular birds, that may suggest a closer relationship.[172]

Alongside the similarities are also significant differences. Mesopotamian flood stories are set against the background of polytheism, with a clear disagreement between Enlil, who is primarily responsible for the flood, and Enki/Ea, who warns the flood hero and thus undermines Enlil's authority. Ea questions Enlil's wisdom when he asks, 'How could you, unreasoning, bring on the deluge?'[173] This contrasts with the monotheism of the biblical account. The reason for the flood is also different. In the Mesopotamian accounts the flood is prompted by Enlil's irrational anger, whereas in Genesis 6:5–6 it is presented as God's judgment on unrelenting and all-pervasive human sin.[174] While divine wrath does feature prominently in the OT, it is never the arbitrary pique that we see in the other flood literature, and Genesis 6:6 suggests that God is filled more with grief and pain than with anger. The purpose of the flood is also different. In the Mesopotamian accounts it is to limit the population, whereas in the biblical account that is explicitly not the goal, and after the flood Noah and his

---

172. See e.g. Walton, 'Flood', in *DOTP*, p. 324.

173. Arnold and Beyer, *Readings*, p. 69; cf. *COS* 1:130. A similar charge appears in the *Atrahasis Epic*, 'he who did not consider but brought about a flood' (Arnold and Beyer, *Readings*, p. 30).

174. Hendel suggests that the ethical explanation of the flood in Gen. 6:5–8 was a later addition; see Ronald S. Hendel, 'Of Demigods and the Deluge: Towards an Interpretation of Genesis 6:1–4', *JBL* 106.1 (1987), pp. 13–26 (16–17); cf. Robin Routledge, '"My Spirit" in Genesis 6:1–4', *JPT* 20 (2011), pp. 232–251 (233–234).

family are told to 'be fruitful and increase in number and fill the earth' (Gen. 9:1).[175] Following the flood, in Utnapishtim's account, the gods gather around his sacrifice 'like flies', probably because during the flood no sacrifices were being offered and the gods went hungry. There is no such significance attached to sacrifice in the OT.[176]

Superficially, the accounts are similar; theologically they are very far apart. What accounts for the similarities? It seems unlikely, in view of their respective dating, that the Mesopotamian accounts are dependent on the biblical account. Though, if the general historicity of the flood is accepted, it is not impossible that the Genesis account preserved an accurate tradition that was then adapted by other cultures. The view more often put forward is that the OT writers were aware of other accounts and converted them to a form more compatible with their understanding of God and his relationship with humanity. However, while it seems likely that the OT writers were familiar with the content of those earlier flood stories, Walton is right to challenge the idea of borrowing, and to point to a more sophisticated use of ancient literature by the OT writers.[177] The use of similar language and imagery should, perhaps, not be surprising. First, as noted already, although based on a unique divine revelation, the OT is written within the same conceptual world as other ANE texts, and in that context some mythological language and imagery may be appropriate. Second, there is also the likelihood that the biblical account includes polemic: it tells the story in a way that not only recalls stories that were well known in the ANE, but also, in the light of the writers' unique faith in Yahweh, criticizes and challenges those stories, and draws a clear distinction between Yahweh and other gods.

Creation[178]

Mesopotamian texts As we have seen, the *Atrahasis Epic* describes the creation of

---

175. See e.g. Frymer-Kensky, 'Atrahasis Epic', pp. 150–152.
176. See e.g. Routledge, *OT Theology*, pp. 188–189.
177. Walton, 'Flood', in *DOTP*, p. 324.
178. See e.g. W. Brueggemann, *Introduction*, pp. 54–60; Dalley, *Myths from Mesopotamia*, pp. 228–277; Gnuse, *Misunderstood Stories*, pp. 13–31; Gerhard F. Hasel, 'The Significance of the Cosmology in Genesis I in Relation to Ancient Near Eastern Parallels', *AUSS* 10 (1972), pp. 1–20; Longman, *How to Read Genesis*, pp. 71–80; Gordon H. Johnston, 'Genesis 1 and the Ancient Egyptian Creation Myths', *BSac* 165 (2008), pp. 178–194; David Adams Leeming, *Creation Myths of the World: An Encyclopedia*, 2nd ed. (Santa Barbara: ABC-CLIO, 2010), pp. 56–60 (Babylonian),

human beings, from the blood of a god, and maybe his spirit,[179] mixed with clay. This combination of earthly and divine elements is also seen in the OT, where human beings are made from the dust of the earth and animated by divine breath (Gen. 2:7).[180] However, here, too, the differences are greater than the similarities. A significant distinction is the reason for the creation of human beings. In the *Atrahasis Epic* they are created to serve the gods. Following the revolt of the Igigi, the request is made to 'create humanity that he may . . . carry the toil of the gods'.[181] By contrast, in the OT, human beings are made in God's image to reflect his glory,[182] and are thus conferred with a wholly different dignity and status.

The text most often compared to the Genesis account of creation is *Enuma Elish*, which takes its name from its opening words 'when on high'. This is usually dated to the end of the second millennium BC. Here Tiamat and Apsu, who represent the primeval waters, are the first to emerge from primordial chaos, and go on to produce other gods. Woken by the noise of the younger gods, Apsu plans to kill them, but is himself killed by Ea, the father of Marduk. Tiamat, with Kingu, then leads an army against the other gods. Ea and Anu (earth and sky) attack Tiamat, but are forced back, and in desperation turn to Marduk for help. Marduk agrees, on the condition that the other gods accept him as king. He then defeats and kills Tiamat, and divides her body to make heaven and earth, establishing a solid dome to ensure her waters did not escape.

(*Footnote 178 cont.*) pp. 102–106 (Egyptian), pp. 247–249 (Sumerian); E. C. Lucas, 'Cosmology', in *DOTP*, pp. 130–139; A. R. Millard 'New Babylonian "Genesis" Story', *TynBul* 18 (1967), pp. 3–18; Mitchell, *Bible in the British Museum*, p. 79; Matthews and Benjamin, *OT Parallels*, pp. 11–20; Arnold and Beyer, *Readings*, pp. 31–66; Rogerson and Davies, *OT World*, pp. 111–123; Routledge, 'Did God Create Chaos?'; *OT Theology*, pp. 124–138; Mark S. Smith and Wayne T. Pitard (eds.), *The Ugaritic Baal Cycle*, VTSup 114 (Leiden: Brill, 2009); John H. Walton, 'Creation', in *DOTP*, pp. 155–168; *Ancient Israelite Literature*, pp. 19–44; *The Lost World of Genesis One: Ancient Cosmology and the Origins Debate* (Downers Grove: InterVarsity Press, 2009), pp. 38–107; Ellen Van Wolde, *Stories of the Beginning: Genesis 1–11 and Other Creation Stories* (London: SCM Press, 1996).

179. 'Let there be a spirit from the god's flesh . . . let it proclaim living man as its sign . . . so that this may not be forgotten let there be a spirit' (Arnold and Beyer, *Readings*, p. 24); cf. *COS* 1:130.

180. See e.g. Routledge, *OT Theology*, pp. 138–142.

181. Arnold and Beyer, *Readings*, p. 24; cf. *COS* 1:130.

182. Routledge, *OT Theology*, pp. 138–142.

Marduk then places the stars and divides the months and seasons. He entrusts the night to the moon and sets in place a thirty-day lunar cycle (cf. Gen. 1:14–16). Then from Kingu's blood he creates human beings, to serve the gods. In the final scene Marduk is affirmed as king.

Enuma Elish has been called 'the Babylonian Genesis'. Gunkel argued that Genesis was simply a Judaized version of it, written during the exile, which was when, in his view, the people of Judah came into contact with Mesopotamian myths.[183] That, in turn, implies a late date for the OT concept of God as the Creator. However, while the exile was probably an important catalyst for the *articulation* of key theological themes,[184] those ideas were probably present much earlier. There are enough points of contact to suggest that the OT writers were aware of *Enuma Elish*. However, discoveries at Ugarit indicate that Mesopotamian stories were in wide circulation, and might well have been known to the OT writers long before the exile.

One point of contact is the reference in Genesis 1:2 to the 'deep', which translates the Hebrew *tĕhôm*. Gunkel sees this as a reference to Tiamat, though Tsumura has convincingly refuted any suggestion of dependence.[185] Nevertheless, *tĕhôm* and Tiamat are probably from the same root, and the text may make an intentional allusion to the Mesopotamian deity. Significantly, though, *tĕhôm* is not personified or given divine status, and the conflict motif in general is missing from the creation account in Genesis 1. The separation of the waters in Genesis 1:7 further parallels Marduk's division of the body of Tiamat. The expression *tōhû wābōhû* (formless and empty), which is associated with the deep, may also allude to the primeval chaos evident at the start of *Enuma Elish*. However, while the term suggests something negative and undesirable,[186] there is no indication that this is in active opposition to the Creator. There may also

183. Hermann Gunkel, 'The Influence of Babylonian Mythology upon the Biblical Creation Story', in Bernard W. Anderson (ed.), *Creation in the Old Testament*, IRT 6 (London: SPCK, 1984), pp. 25–52; *Schöpfung und Chaos in Urzeit und Endzeit* (Göttingen: Vandenhoeck & Ruprecht, 1895), trans. K. William Whitney Jr., as *Creation and Chaos in the Primeval Era and the Eschaton: A Religio-Historical Study of Genesis 1 and Revelation 12* (Grand Rapids: Eerdmans, 2006).

184. See above, pp. 20–21.

185. David T. Tsumura, *The Earth and the Waters in Genesis 1 and 2: A Linguistic Investigation*, JSOTSup 83 (Sheffield: Sheffield Academic Press, 1989), rev. and expanded in David T. Tsumura, *Creation and Destruction: A Reappraisal of the Chaoskampf Theory in the Old Testament* (Winona Lake: Eisenbrauns, 2005).

186. See Routledge, 'Did God Create Chaos?', pp. 73–75.

be a point of contact between the *rûaḥ 'ĕlōhîm*,[187] which is described as 'hovering over the waters' (Gen. 1:2), and possibly, thereby, exercising some control over the primeval chaos,[188] and the wind created by Anu, in *Enuma Elish*, to trouble Tiamat.[189]

As with the flood accounts, differences between Genesis 1 and *Enuma Elish* (and other Mesopotamian creation stories)[190] far outweigh similarities. The latter is set against the background of polytheism, and natural forces and elements in the physical world are identified with deities who emerge from the primordial chaos. Marduk, along with the other gods, owes his existence to Apsu and Tiamat, and his act of 'creation' involves making one thing from something else. In contrast, the Bible depicts only one God, who exists independently of the world and who calls everything into being.[191] The Genesis account may allude to *Enuma Elish* and other Mesopotamian creation myths, though this is partly as polemic: to emphasize the truth that it was Israel's God, and not the Babylonian chaos monsters, who existed first and created the universe. And, particularly during the difficult period of the exile, this would serve to reassure the Israelites that their God has final authority in the history of his people.

Egyptian texts According to the OT accounts, the people of Israel spent several centuries in Egypt. Even so, we see fewer points of contact between the OT and Egyptian theological ideas than we might expect. There are, though, some notable similarities.[192] As in the Mesopotamian accounts, the primeval state is represented by water and darkness.[193] One Egyptian cosmogony, from Hermapolis, also includes infinity and invisibility, with each of the four elements

---

187. Because *rûaḥ* may be translated 'wind' as well as 'spirit', this expression is variously translated 'Spirit of God', 'wind from God', 'mighty wind'. Walton rightly notes that the semantic range of the term includes both ideas, and we should not distinguish too sharply between them ('Flood', in *DOTP*, p. 157). How the text is nuanced, though, is important for its interpretation, and in my view the translation 'Spirit of God' is preferable here.
188. See e.g. Routledge, 'My Spirit', pp. 246–249; cf. Job 26:12–13; Ps. 33:6–7.
189. Arnold and Beyer, *Readings*, p. 34; *COS* 1:111.
190. For a brief summary of these and other Mesopotamian texts, see Walton, *ANE Thought*, pp. 44–48.
191. See e.g. Raymond C. Van Leeuwen, '*br*",' in *NIDOTTE* 1:728–735 (732); Routledge, 'Did God Create Chaos?', pp. 78–79.
192. See also Johnston, 'Egyptian Creation Myths'.
193. Cf. *COS* 1:8.

represented by two deities (the 'Ogdoad'),[194] and some have suggested links with the deep, darkness, the formless void and the Spirit of God, in Genesis 1,[195] though this is somewhat speculative.[196] Walton notes possible links between the *rûaḥ 'ĕlōhîm* in Genesis 1:2 and the role of the 'wind' in creation in some Egyptian texts.[197] The *Instructions of Merikare*, dated around the close of the third millennium BC,[198] further links the creation of earth and sky with subduing 'the water monster'.[199] It also refers to the creator god giving breath to human beings (cf. Gen. 2:7), and refers to them as 'his images' (cf. Gen. 1:26–27). In other texts human beings are formed from the tears of Atum, shed over his offspring, Shu and Tefnut.[200] Another significant Egyptian text is the *Memphite Creation Theology*. This is included on a stele dating to around 700 BC, though may reflect traditions going back to the Old Kingdom.[201] Creation, here, is attributed to Ptah, the god particularly associated with Memphis, and, like the Genesis account, it indicates that creation took place through the divine word: 'all the divine order . . . came into being through what the heart thought and the tongue commanded'.[202] Another point of contact is that after his work of creation, Ptah 'was satisfied' (cf. Gen. 1:31).[203]

---

194. See e.g. Ulrich H. Luft, 'Religion', in Donald B. Redford (ed.), *The Oxford Encyclopedia of Ancient Egypt*, vol. 3 (Oxford: Oxford University Press, 2001), pp. 139–145 (141).
195. E.g. James K. Hoffmeier, 'Some Thoughts on Genesis 1 & 2 and Egyptian Cosmology', *JANES* 15 (1983), pp. 39–49 (43–45).
196. Cf. Walton, *Ancient Israelite Literature*, p. 33.
197. John H. Walton, 'The Ancient Near Eastern Background of the Spirit of the Lord in the Old Testament', in Firth and Wegner, *Presence*, pp. 38–67 (44–48).
198. See e.g. Walton, *Ancient Israelite Literature*, pp. 172–173; Leo G. Perdue, 'The Testament of David and Ancient Royal Instructions', in William C. Hallo, James Moyer and Leo G. Perdue (eds.), *Scripture in Context II: More Essays on the Comparative Method* (Winona Lake: Eisenbrauns, 1983), pp. 79–96 (85–87).
199. Arnold and Beyer, *Readings*, p. 65; *COS* 1:35.
200. *COS* 1:9.
201. Walton, *ANE Thought*, p. 48.
202. Arnold and Beyer, *Readings*, p. 64; cf. *COS* 1:15.
203. Arnold and Beyer, *Readings*, p. 22. This could be translated, 'and Ptah rested'; e.g. *COS* 1:15. Matthews and Benjamin combine these elements: 'And so Ptah rested and was content with his work' (Matthews and Benjamin, *OT Parallels*, p. 6). Cf. Gen. 2:1–4.

Hoffmeier may be right when he suggests a past tendency to overlook comparisons between Egyptian cosmogonies and Genesis 1 in favour of comparisons with Mesopotamian texts.[204] However, while there are points of contact, including the idea of creation by divine speech, which is not found elsewhere, these appear in very different contexts, and there does not seem to be the same conscious allusion to Egyptian creation accounts. Similarities are, however, a further indication that ANE creation stories have some common conceptual aspects.

The Ugaritic Baal cycle The motif in *Enuma Elish*, of the creator god defeating the primeval waters, sometimes referred to as *Chaoskampf* (battle with chaos), is also apparent in the *Baal Cycle*. This Ugaritic text, from around 1400 BC, depicts a battle between Baal and Yam, representing the Sea. Yam claims authority over the assembly of gods, led by El, and demands that Baal be handed over. Baal refuses and, instead, fights and kills Yam. Baal's pride then leads him to challenge Mot (Death). He dies, but is revived, and as well as possibly reflecting the creation myth, the death and revival of Baal (the storm or weather god) also reflects the cycle in nature.

The *Baal Cycle* does not describe a formal act of creation, and some do not regard it as a creation story.[205] However, there is the suggestion that Baal's victory over Yam, and later over Mot, results in order being brought to the cosmos, including pouring 'well-being out into the earth, calmness into the fields',[206] and sending rain in its season.[207] This, together with the acknowledgment of Baal's kingship and the building of a temple,[208] which may also have cosmological

204. Hoffmeier, 'Some Thoughts', pp. 40–41.

205. E.g. D. J. McCarthy, '"Creation" Motifs in Ancient Hebrew Poetry', *CBQ* 29 (1967), pp. 393–406; John H. Walton, 'Creation in Genesis 1:1–2:3 and the Ancient Near East: Order out of Disorder after Chaoskampf', *CTJ* 43 (2008), pp. 48–63. In contrast, Day argues that Gen. 1 is dependent on the language of Ps. 104, which reflects Ugaritic mythology; see John Day, *God's Conflict with the Dragon and the Sea: Echoes of a Canaanite Myth in the Old Testament*, University of Cambridge Oriental Publications 35 (Cambridge: Cambridge University Press, 1985), pp. 51–53. Levenson also notes similarities between Gen. 1 and Ps. 104; see Jon D. Levenson, *Creation and the Persistence of Evil: The Jewish Drama of Divine Omnipotence* (Princeton: Princeton University Press, 1988), pp. 53–59.

206. *COS* 1:86; cf. Arnold and Beyer, *Readings*, p. 53.

207. Ibid., p. 56.

208. Ibid., pp. 56–57.

significance,[209] has led to the view that there may be creation of sorts in the text.[210]

The Ugaritic text has several parallels in the OT.[211] Baal is given the title 'Rider on the Clouds',[212] and in the OT similar language is used to describe God (e.g. Deut. 33:26; Pss 68:4; 104:3; Isa. 19:1; see also Dan. 7:13). A number of OT passages refer to Leviathan (Job 3:8; 41:1; Pss 74:14; 104:26; Isa. 27:1), the equivalent of Lotan,[213] who is probably to be identified with Yam. In particular, the description of Leviathan in Isaiah 27:1 as 'the gliding serpent . . . the coiling serpent' is very like the description of Lotan in the Baal myth.[214] Rahab (Job 26:12; Ps. 89:9–10; Isa. 51:9) may be another name for Leviathan,[215] though the term does not appear outside the OT. The OT also refers to *tannîn*, a more

---

209. G. K. Beale, *The Temple and the Church's Mission: A Biblical Theology of the Dwelling Place of God* (Leicester: Apollos; Downers Grove: InterVarsity Press, 2004); R. E. Clements, *God and Temple* (Oxford: Basil Blackwell, 1965); Levenson, *Creation*, pp. 78–99; Walton, *Lost World*, pp. 38–107; see also Loren R. Fisher, 'From Chaos to Cosmos', *Enc* 26.2 (1965), pp. 183–197; 'Creation at Ugarit and in the Old Testament', *VT* 15.3 (1965), pp. 313–324.

210. See e.g. Fisher, 'Chaos to Cosmos'; Jakob Grønbæk, 'Baal's Battle with Yam – A Canaanite Creation Fight', *JSOT* 33 (1985), pp. 27–44; see also Day, *God's Conflict*, pp. 7–18; John N. Day, 'God and Leviathan in Isaiah 27:1', *BSac* 155 (1998), pp. 423–436. Walton argues, generally, against the view that the theomachy in the *Baal Cycle* is linked with cosmogony, though allows that the text may contain creation material (*Lost World*, p. 29).

211. See e.g. B. W. Anderson, *Creation Versus Chaos: The Reinterpretation of Mythical Symbolism in the Bible* (New York: Association, 1967); *From Creation to New Creation: Old Testament Perspectives*, OBT (Minneapolis: Fortress, 1994); T. E. Fretheim, *God and World in the Old Testament: A Relational Theology of Creation* (Nashville: Abingdon, 2005); Routledge, 'Did God Create Chaos?', pp. 69–75. For an alternative view, see Tsumura, *Creation and Destruction*; Rebecca S. Watson, *Chaos Uncreated: A Reassessment of the Theme of 'Chaos' in the Hebrew Bible*, BZAW 341 (Berlin: de Gruyter, 2005).

212. Arnold and Beyer, *Readings*, pp. 51–59; cf. *COS* 1:86.

213. See e.g. J. A. Emerton, 'Leviathan and *ltn*: The Vocalization of the Ugaritic Word for the Dragon', *VT* 32.3 (1982), pp. 327–331.

214. 'Lotan, the Fleeing Serpent . . . the Twisting Serpent, the Seven-Headed Monster', see Arnold and Beyer, *Readings*, p. 58; cf. *COS* 1:86. That Leviathan is many-headed is reflected in e.g. Ps. 74:14 – 'you who crushed the *heads* of Leviathan'.

215. Like Leviathan, Rahab is described as 'the fleeing serpent' (Job 26:12–13, NRSV); see further 'Monsters', in *DBI*, pp. 562–565 (562).

general term sometimes translated 'sea monster' or 'dragon' (e.g. Gen. 1:21; Ps. 74:13; Isa. 27:1; Ezek. 32:2), and this, too, is associated with Yam in the Baal myth.

Creation accounts and the Old Testament As noted already, a comparison of ANE creation accounts and the OT does not in any way indicate dependence. There are allusions, particularly to Mesopotamian creation texts, probably against the background of the exile and primarily for polemic purposes. Other similarities place the OT within a more general ANE conceptual context. This includes a common view of pre-creation chaos, represented by primeval waters, and of cosmology, in which waters surround the world, and where the waters above the earth are held back by a solid dome, the sky.[216] In the biblical account God remains in control of the waters of chaos. As noted, Genesis 1 contains no suggestion of divine conflict, and, though there are elements of the *Chaoskampf* motif elsewhere in the OT,[217] chaos is nowhere depicted as a challenge to God.[218] It may return, but only as God allows.

This last point demonstrates that while OT writers may use language and imagery that was common in the ANE, they retain a distinct theological perspective. A further important aspect of this is the reapplication of mythological imagery to the events of Israel's history. For example, the waters of the deep associated with creation are taken to symbolize the waters of the Red Sea (e.g. Pss 74:12–17; 77:16–19; Isa. 51:9–10), which may thus be viewed as a creative act marking the birth of God's people. The nations that threaten Israel are sometimes depicted as chaos monsters (e.g. Ps. 74:14; Isa. 51:9; Ezek. 29:3–5; 32:2–8), and in Psalm 46 the roaring waters (v. 3) are paralleled with the uproarious nations (v. 6). Isaiah 27:1 may refer to a historical enemy, though it may be better to see this as eschatological: God's victory over chaos at creation will be repeated in a final battle, resulting in a new creation. There is the possibility that human sin may allow chaos and disorder to return, as in the flood, where

216. The Hebrew term *rāqia'* (Gen. 1:6–8), which the NRSV translates 'dome', suggests something solid or 'hammered out' that holds back the waters; see e.g. Paul H. Seely, 'The Firmament and the Water Above Part 1: The Meaning of *rāqia'* in Gen. 1:6–8', *WTJ* 53 (1991), pp. 227–240; David Toshio Tsumura, '*rāqia'*', in *NIDOTTE* 3:1198; Walton, 'Creation', pp. 158–159; Young and Stearley, *Bible, Rocks and Time*, pp. 182, 206–207. See also Routledge, *OT Theology*, pp. 130, 131; cf. Beale, *Erosion of Inerrancy*, pp. 198–206.

217. See e.g. Routledge, *OT Theology*, pp. 127–131; 'Did God Create Chaos?', pp. 70–72. Cf. Tsumura, *Creation and Destruction*; R. S. Watson, *Chaos Uncreated.*

218. However, cf. Levenson, *Creation*, pp. 15–25.

the waters again cover the earth.[219] Jeremiah uses the expression *tōhû wābōhû* to refer to the impact of the Babylonian exile (Jer. 4:23; cf. Gen. 1:2), suggesting that this was viewed as a kind of 'uncreation';[220] and the same terms, *tōhû* and *bōhû* occur in Isaiah 34:11, again in the context of 'uncreation' (cf. Isa. 34:4). Zephaniah 1:2–3, which also has links to the flood, appears, further, to depict divine judgment on sin as a reversal of creation.[221] Though the positive corollary of these parallels is that the God who brought order out of chaos in the beginning can transform this chaos, too, and bring about a new creation for his people.

Recognizing these points of contact, it is important to read the OT in the light of its ANE context if we are to have a better grasp of what the OT writers meant and how their message would have been understood by those to whom it was first addressed. Berlin makes a further important observation. Commenting on Psalm 104, and its view of creation, which appears to draw on ANE cosmological ideas, she notes that these ideas would have become an established part of Israelite thinking well before the OT text was written down, and we should not, therefore, overemphasize their 'foreignness'.[222] Nonetheless, such comparative readings need also to be undertaken cautiously, because of the unique nature of the OT as divine revelation.

---

219. See e.g. Anderson, *Creation to New Creation*, pp. 34–36; Joseph Blenkinsopp, *Creation, Uncreation, Re-Creation: A Discursive Commentary on Genesis 1–11* (London: T&T Clark International, 2011); Clines, *Theme*, p. 80–83; Fretheim, *God and World*, pp. 79–83; Routledge, 'Cursing and Chaos', in Moo and Routledge, *Earth Endures*, pp. 83–84.
220. Walter Brueggemann, *Jeremiah: Exile and Homecoming* (Grand Rapids: Eerdmans, 1998), pp. 59–60; Michael Fishbane, 'Jeremiah IV 23–26 and Job III 3–13: A Recovered Use of the Creation Pattern', *VT* 21.2 (1971), pp. 151–167; Hetty Lalleman, 'Jeremiah, Judgement and Creation', *TynBul* 60.1 (2009), pp. 15–24 (18–20).
221. See e.g. O. Palmer Robertson, *The Books of Nahum, Habakkuk and Zephaniah*, NICOT (Grand Rapids: Eerdmans, 1991), pp. 257–260; Michael DeRoche, 'Zephaniah i 2–3: The "Sweeping of Creation"', *VT* 30.1 (1980), pp. 104–109; 'The Reversal of Creation in Hosea', *VT* 31.4 (1981), pp. 400–409; see also Routledge, *OT Theology*, pp. 133–136.
222. Adele Berlin, 'The Wisdom of Creation in Psalm 104', in Ronald L. Troxel, Kelvin G. Friebel and Dennis R. Magary (eds.), *Seeking out the Wisdom of the Ancients: Essays Offered to Honor Michael V. Fox on the Occasion of His Sixty-Fifth Birthday* (Winona Lake: Eisenbrauns, 2005), pp. 71–83 (75).

Law, covenant and conquest

Legal traditions

The OT contains a number of legal codes.[223] At the heart of OT law are the Ten Commandments (Exod. 20:1–17). These offer a summary statement, which sets out moral and ethical absolutes, and brings together a right relationship with God and a right relationship with others. It is elaborated on by the 'Book of the Covenant' or 'Covenant Code' (Exod. 21:2 – 23:33). The first section (21:2 – 22:27) consists mainly of *case law*, noting hypothetical situations and prescribing appropriate penalties. Case law has parallels in the law codes of other ancient civilizations. *Apodictic law*, often characterized by 'do' or 'do not', sets out absolute principles of behaviour. Another important OT legal text is the 'Holiness Code' (Lev. 17 – 26). As its name suggests, this emphasizes the need for holiness, and contains the key principle for God's people: 'Be holy because I, the LORD your God, am holy' (Lev. 19:2). Another important legal text is Deuteronomy 12 – 26, which appears to expand on earlier legal traditions, and includes regulations found nowhere else, such as the conduct of wars, regulations about courts and judges, and divorce and remarriage.

Several fragmentary texts from the ANE have been discovered, which have points of contact with OT law. We have already noted laws associated with Ur-Nammu and Hammurabi. Others include laws of Lipit-Ishtar, ruler of Isin, and laws from Eshunna, both from early in the second millennium BC, Hittite and Middle Assyrian laws from later in the second millennium BC, and Neo-Babylonian laws from the seventh century BC. Hammurabi's 'Law Code' is the longest, and the most interesting from the point of view of comparison with the OT. Some question whether this is a 'law code',[224] in the sense of a

---

223. See further e.g. Richard E. Averbeck, 'Law', in D. Brent Sandy and Ronald L. Giese (eds.), *Cracking Old Testament Codes: A Guide to Interpreting the Literary Genres of the Old Testament* (Nashville: B&H, 1995), pp. 113–138; Arnold, *Introduction*, pp. 125–129; Rogerson and Davies, *OT World*, pp. 137–150; Routledge, *OT Theology*, pp. 243–245; Gordon Wenham, 'Law and the Legal System in the Old Testament', in B. N. Kaye and G. J. Wenham (eds.), *Law, Morality and the Bible* (Downers Grove: InterVarsity Press, 1978), pp. 24–52.

224. See e.g. Arnold, *Introduction*, p. 128; Collins, *Introduction*, pp. 101–110, 124–128, 140–148; *COS* 2:19, 130–133, 153–154; Matthews and Benjamin, *OT Parallels*, pp. 101–130; Arnold and Beyer, *Readings*, pp. 104–117; Martha T. Roth, *Law Collections from Mesopotamia and Asia Minor*, 2nd ed. (Atlanta: Scholars Press, 1995); Walton, *Ancient Israelite Literature*, pp. 69–92.

comprehensive set of laws devised and enforced specifically as a legal document.[225] Walton prefers to use the term 'treatise'.[226] Its purpose seems to be primarily religious and political: to commend Hammurabi to both gods and people as the upholder of justice, which includes helping the weak in society.[227] However, while it may not be a comprehensive 'code', this collection does represent an early attempt to set out a number of case laws that could be applied in a wide variety of situations. Several of the instructions overlap with OT laws, including the well-known 'eye for eye, tooth for tooth': 'If an AWILU should blind the eye of another AWILU, they shall blind his eye . . . If an AWILU should knock out the tooth of another AWILU . . . they shall knock out his tooth' (cf. Exod. 21:24).[228]

It has been suggested that OT legal codes are dependent on ANE laws.[229] It seems more likely, though, that they shared a common legal tradition.[230] And similarities are not surprising since these codes attempt to deal with similar, commonly occurring, situations. There are also differences. Some are understandable, as the regulations are applied to their respective contexts. There are

---

225. Rogerson and Davies, *OT World*, p. 137; Ronald A. Veenker, 'Syro-Mesopotamia: The Old Babylonian Period', in Mark W. Chavalas and K. Lawson Younger Jr. (eds.), *Mesopotamia and the Bible* (London: T&T Clark, 2003), pp. 149–168 (157–158); Walton, *ANE Thought*, pp. 287–288.

226. Walton, *ANE Thought*, p. 288.

227. Hammurabi sets out the goal 'to make justice prevail in the land, to abolish wicked and evil, to prevent the strong from oppressing the weak, to rise like the sun-god Shamash over all humankind, to illuminate the land' (Arnold and Beyer, *Readings*, p. 112; *COS* 2:131).

228. Arnold and Beyer, *Readings*, p. 113; *COS* 2:131, §§196, 200. Another oft-quoted example is what to do in the case of an ox that gores (Exod. 21:28–32). Very similar instructions appear in the Eshunna laws (Arnold and Beyer, *Readings*, p. 111; *COS* 2:130, §§53–55) and the Hammurabi law code (Arnold and Beyer, *Readings*, p. 114; *COS* 2:131, §§250–252).

229. E.g. David P. Wright, 'The Laws of Hammurabi as a Source for the Covenant Collection (Exodus 20:23 – 23:19)', *Maarav* 10 (2003), pp. 11–87; *Inventing God's Law: How the Covenant Code of the Bible Used and Revised the Laws of Hammurabi* (Oxford: Oxford University Press, 2009); cf. Bruce Wells, 'The Covenant Code and Near Eastern Legal Traditions: A Response to David P. Wright', *Maarav* 13.1 (2006), pp. 85–118; David P. Wright, 'The Laws of Hammurabi and the Covenant Code: A Response to Bruce Wells', *Maarav* 13.2 (2006), pp. 211–260.

230. Arnold, *Introduction*, p. 128.

also more fundamental distinctions.[231] For example, in the Hammurabi collection, while all people are included in the regulations, and accorded rights, the higher, citizen class (the Awilu) receive greater compensation than commoners, and if an Awilu injures a commoner, the penalty is a fine, not an equivalent injury.[232] This contrasts with the laws of the OT, which make no class distinctions, and which accord even foreigners a high degree of legal protection. Law codes of Mesopotamia have a clear divine dimension, and the Hammurabi Stele depicts the king standing before the god, Shamash. It is not clear, though, whether Hammurabi is given the law itself, or the divine authority to make law.[233] In my view the latter seems more likely. The law code nowhere suggests that it has come directly from heaven. Instead, it points to Hammurabi's credentials as one appointed by the gods to establish ways of justice for the people.[234] The laws are, therefore, primarily to ensure the smooth and equitable running of society, and offences are against society, and against the authority of the ruler. By contrast, law in the OT is viewed as coming directly from God, and is closely related to the people's covenant relationship with God. Law breaking is an offence against others, and appropriate recompense must be made; but it is also an offence against God, and even where compensation is stipulated, sacrifices are also required.

Covenant and ancient Near Eastern treaties

The relationship between God and his people is expressed in the form of a covenant (Heb. *bĕrît*).[235] Covenants were a common feature of life in the ANE

---

231. See e.g. Walther Eichrodt, *Theology of the Old Testament*, 2 vols. (London: SCM Press, 1961–7), 1:74–82.

232. Arnold and Beyer, *Readings*, p. 113; *COS* 2:131, §§198–199, 201.

233. Cf. Roth, *Law Collections*, p. 73.

234. Hammurabi sets out his commission, 'When the god Marduk commanded me to provide just ways for the people of the land . . . I established truth and justice' (Arnold and Beyer, *Readings*, p. 113; cf. *COS* 2:131).

235. See e.g. Arnold, *Introduction*, pp. 110–112; Scott J. Hafemann, 'The Covenant Relationship', in Scott J. Hafemann and Paul R. House (eds.), *Central Themes in Biblical Theology: Mapping Unity in Diversity* (Nottingham: Apollos; Grand Rapids: Baker, 2007), pp. 20–65; Hayes, *Interpreting Israelite History*, pp. 269–281; J. Gordon McConville, '*bĕrît*', in *NIDOTTE* 1:747–755; Meredith G. Kline, *Treaty of the Great King* (Grand Rapids: Eerdmans, 1963); Dennis J. McCarthy, *Treaty and Covenant* (Rome: Pontifical Biblical Institute, 1963); *Old Testament Covenant* (Oxford: Blackwell, 1972); Ernest C. Lucas, 'Covenant, Treaty and Prophecy', *Them* 8.1 (1982), pp. 19–23;

and played an important part in business, politics and family life, as well as in religion. A covenant was a solemn bond established between two or more parties, usually on the basis of a promise or pledge, and involved a firm commitment to the relationship established by the covenant and to its obligations. The derivation of *bĕrît* is not certain, though one possibility, which reinforces the idea of covenant as a binding agreement, is a suggested link with the Akkadian *biritu* (fetter).

Some scholars claim that the idea of covenant developed late in Israel's history. It is often associated with the 'Deuteronomic movement',[236] in the seventh century BC. However, covenants, in the form of international treaties, were well known in the fourteenth and thirteenth centuries BC. In an article published in 1954[237] Mendenhall pointed out significant parallels between the structure of the Sinaitic covenant, as it is set out in the Pentateuch,[238] and late second millennium BC Hittite suzerain–vassal treaties, where a king made a treaty with a subject power, offering protection in return for loyalty and obedience. The Sinaitic covenant appears to have a similar form, with God and Israel as suzerain and vassal. Israel received God's help and in return accepted him as their Lord.

Mendenhall argued that this type of covenant structure was not known during the first millennium BC, and this strengthened the arguments in favour of an early dating of Deuteronomy.[239] However, Weinfeld has suggested that Assyrian treaties dating from the seventh century BC, and in particular the Esarhaddon Succession Treaty, have a similar structure, as well as significant affinities with

---

George E. Mendenhall, 'Covenant', in *IDB* 1:714–723; E. W. Nicholson, *God and His People: Covenant and Theology in the Old Testament* (Oxford: Oxford University Press, 1986); Routledge, *OT Theology*, pp. 159–175; Moshe Weinfeld, '*bĕrît*', in *TDOT* 2:253–279; 'The Covenant of Grant in the Ancient Near East', *JAOS* 90 (1970), pp. 184–203; P. R. Williamson, 'Covenant', in *NDBT*, pp. 419–429; *Sealed with an Oath: Covenant in God's Unfolding Purpose*, NSBT 23 (Nottingham: Apollos; Downers Grove: IVP Academic, 2007).

236. See above, p. 57, n. 128.

237. George E. Mendenhall, 'Covenant Forms in Israelite Tradition', *BA* 17 (1954), pp. 50–76.

238. Josh. 24 follows a similar structure.

239. See e.g. Peter C. Craigie, *The Book of Deuteronomy*, NICOT (Grand Rapids: Eerdmans; London: Hodder & Stoughton, 1976), pp. 22–24; LaSor, Hubbard and Bush, *OT Survey*, pp. 144–146; Lucas, 'Covenant'; John A. Thompson, *Deuteronomy*, TOTC (Leicester: Inter-Varsity Press, 1974), pp. 14–21.

Deuteronomy. He thus argues that the Hittite forms are not unique, and might not have been the only, or even the best model for the Sinaitic covenant.[240] Kitchen has produced a very detailed analysis of ANE treaties.[241] He points to significant differences between second and first millennium BC treaties and concludes that the only context for the Sinaitic covenant is the late second millennium BC. Hittite treaties from this period include the following elements:[242]

- *Title*: an introduction or preamble that identifies the speaker (cf. Exod. 20:1; Deut. 1:1–5; Josh. 24:2).
- *Historical prologue*: describing the events leading up to the treaty and noting what the suzerain has already done for the vassal (cf. Exod. 20:2; Deut. 1:6 – 3:29; Josh. 24:2–13).
- *Stipulations*: the requirements and obligations placed upon the vassal (cf. Exod. 20:3–17; 21 – 23; Deut. 4 – 26; Josh. 24:14–25).
- *Document clause*: instructions for depositing a copy of the covenant in the vassal's sanctuary and, maybe, for its public reading or renewal (cf. Deut. 27:1–26; Josh. 24:26).
- *Witnesses*: usually the gods of the participating nations who were called to act as guarantors of the treaty (cf. Exod. 24:4; Deut. 30:19; 31:19; cf. 32:1–43; Josh. 24:26–27).
- *Curses and blessings*: the result of non-compliance or compliance with the terms of the treaty (cf. Deut. 28 – 30).[243]

---

240. Weinfeld, *Deuteronomy*, pp. 59–81. For a more recent critique of Weinfeld's position, see Alexander Rofé, *Deuteronomy: Issues and Interpretation* (Edinburgh: T&T Clark, 2002), pp. 221–230. See also e.g. Bernard M. Levinson, 'Esarhaddon's Succession Treaty as the Source for the Canon Formula in Deuteronomy 13:1', *JAOS* 130.3 (2010), pp. 337–347; Bernard M. Levinson and Jeffery Stackert, 'Between the Covenant Code and Esarhaddon's Succession Treaty: Deuteronomy 13 and the Composition of Deuteronomy', *Journal of Ancient Judaism* 3 (2012), pp. 123–140; see also Collins, *Introduction*, pp. 163–166.

241. Kenneth A. Kitchen and Paul J. N. Lawrence, *Treaty, Law and Covenant in the Ancient Near East*, 3 vols. (Wiesbaden: Harrassowitz, 2012); see also Kitchen, *Reliability*, pp. 286–288; Walton, *Ancient Israelite Literature*, pp. 95–107.

242. See e.g. *COS* 2:17A–C.

243. Some of these features are also evident in Hammurabi's 'Law Code', including the historical prologue, laws, document clause, and blessings and curses (see e.g. Thompson, *Deuteronomy*, pp. 18–19; Wenham, *Pentateuch*, pp. 143–144).

In the case of the Sinaitic covenant 'heaven and earth' rather than gods are invoked as witnesses (Deut. 30:19), together with other permanent reminders, such as pillars of stones (Exod. 24:4; cf. Josh. 24:26–27), and songs are composed that will become part of the nation's heritage (Deut. 31:19; 32:1–47). Also, in the OT, blessings precede curses. In general, though, the similarity with second millennium BC treaties is striking, whereas in later ANE treaties some of the elements are absent.[244] This lends substantial support to the view that covenant was a key way of describing the relationship between God and his people from the beginning.[245]

Conquest texts

In a significant study Younger compares Joshua 9 – 12 with Hittite, Assyrian and Egyptian conquest texts.[246] He concludes that while there are differences, not least between the characters of the gods of the respective nations, there are also important similarities. These include the use of hyperbole when describing successes. So it is common in ANE texts to talk in terms of a conquest being 'complete', and to exaggerate the number of enemy dead (cf. Josh. 10:40–42).[247] Modern history writing is uncomfortable with such claims, and as a result has tended to treat the historicity of the biblical conquest narratives with caution. However, this appears to be a normal part of ancient historiography: emphasizing the power of the victor and of the victor's god. In this context, too, the idea of 'conquest' may mean different things. Sometimes it may indicate subjugation, but it may also refer to a temporary victory.

---

244. Kitchen notes that Assyrian treaties include only title, witnesses, stipulations and curses (*Reliability*, p. 288).

245. On the early dating of the idea of covenant see also e.g. John Bright, *Covenant and Promise: The Prophetic Understanding of the Future in Ancient Israel* (Philadelphia: Westminster, 1976), pp. 28–43; Stephen L. Cook, *The Social Roots of Biblical Yahwism*, SBLSBL 8 (Leiden: Brill, 2004), pp. 23–24, 158–159; Eichrodt, *Theology of the OT*, 1:37; Routledge, *OT Theology*, pp. 160–163.

246. K. Lawson Younger Jr., *Ancient Conquest Accounts: A Study in Ancient Near Eastern and Biblical History Writing*, JSOTSup 98 (Sheffield: JSOT Press, 1990); see also e.g. Jeffrey J. Niehaus, 'Joshua and Ancient Near Eastern Warfare', *JETS* 31.1 (1988), pp. 37–50; Pitkänen, *Joshua*, pp. 47–51.

247. Younger, *Ancient Conquest Accounts*, pp. 241–247; see also Richard S. Hess, *Joshua*, TOTC (Leicester: Inter-Varsity Press, 1996), pp. 37–38; Kitchen, *Reliability*, pp. 173–174. However, see T. A. Clark, 'Complete v. Incomplete Conquest: An Examination of Three Passages in Joshua', *TynBul* 61.1 (2010), pp. 89–104.

These comparisons give a context to the impression given by the book of Joshua of a rapid and complete conquest. As we have noted, this is often seen to be at odds with the picture at the start of Judges. However, the description of the conquest in Joshua is in line with comparable ANE accounts, and as such it may be viewed as historiography rather than simply as an idealized, and therefore largely unhistorical, narrative.

Wisdom and poetry

The main texts associated with wisdom teaching in the OT are the books of Proverbs, Job and Ecclesiastes.[248] A key aspect of wisdom is practical advice for successful living. The world is ordered by divine wisdom (Prov. 8:22–31),[249] and the outworking of divine order and justice imply that actions have inevitable consequences: a law of cause and effect in the moral realm. Those who are wise seek to understand that law, to conduct their own lives in accordance with it, and to teach others to do the same. This insight into the way the world works comes largely through observation, and is therefore based on general rather than special revelation. Nevertheless, in the OT it also has an important theological dimension (Job 28:28; Ps. 111:10; Prov. 1:7; 9:10; 15:33; cf. Ps. 14:1). Wisdom may also include more speculative or contemplative thinking about difficult issues, particularly those that touch on the execution of divine justice, such as the problem of why the innocent suffer (Job) and the apparent meaninglessness of life (Ecclesiastes).

There are examples of this kind of teaching among Israel's neighbours in Egypt and Mesopotamia going back to the third millennium BC. Egyptians associated order in the universe with the idea of *ma'at*.[250] In order to ensure the stability of the state and individual prosperity it was necessary to live in harmony with *ma'at*, and this underlies instructions passed on from one generation to the next. Similar kinds of instructions are found in Mesopotamian texts. And in texts from both Egypt and Mesopotamia there is also evidence of the more contemplative reflections on problem issues.[251]

---

248. For more general discussion of wisdom teaching in the OT, see Further reading, p. 387. See also below, pp. 187–194.
249. See also Roland E. Murphy, 'Wisdom and Creation', *JBL* 104 (1985), pp. 3–11.
250. Sometimes Ma'at is portrayed as a goddess.
251. For lists of comparative texts, see e.g. Richard J. Clifford (ed.), *Wisdom Literature in Mesopotamia and Israel* (Atlanta: Society of Biblical Literature, 2007), pp. xii–xiii; James L. Crenshaw, *Old Testament Wisdom: An Introduction*, 3rd ed. (Philadelphia:

Several ANE texts contain instructions similar to Proverbs.[252] The Mesopotamian *Counsels of Wisdom*[253] and the Egyptian *Instructions of Ptahotep*[254] include sustained teaching discourses, comparable with the early chapters of Proverbs.[255] Other texts contain short pithy maxims like those found elsewhere in the book.[256] Of particular significance is the Egyptian *Wisdom of Amenemope*.[257] This is generally thought to date from the twelfth century BC.[258] It comprises thirty chapters, giving instructions for prosperous living, which it views more in terms of moral character than in outward indications of success. There appear to be close links between this and Proverbs 22:17 – 24:22, suggesting that the latter might have known and used the Egyptian collection, though, as Kidner notes, it 'sits loose to it: choosing its own order, its own emphases and its own range of subjects'.[259]

Westminster John Knox, 2010), pp. 7, 251–272; Matthews and Benjamin, *OT Parallels*, pp. 223–245, 293–302; Arnold and Beyer, *Readings*, pp. 175–191; Walton, *ANE Thought*, pp. 74–78.

252. See also K. A. Kitchen, 'Proverbs 2: Ancient Near Eastern Background', in *DOTWPW*, pp. 552–566.
253. W. G. Lambert, *Babylonian Wisdom Literature* (Oxford: Oxford University Press, 1960), pp. 96–107.
254. Arnold and Beyer, *Readings*, pp. 182–184; Matthews and Benjamin, *OT Parallels*, pp. 283–288.
255. See e.g. LaSor, Hubbard and Bush, *OT Survey*, pp. 448–449.
256. For a list of Mesopotamian texts, see Lambert, *Babylonian Wisdom Literature*, pp. 222–282. Egyptian texts include the *Instructions of Merikare* (*COS* 1:35; Arnold and Beyer, *Readings*, pp. 184–185) and *Instruction of Any* (*COS* 1:46; Arnold and Beyer, *Readings*, pp. 185–186).
257. *COS* 1:47; Matthews and Benjamin, *OT Parallels*, pp. 293–302; Arnold and Beyer, *Readings*, pp. 187–189.
258. See e.g. Arnold and Beyer, *Readings*, p. 187; Walton, *ANE Thought*, p. 77; *Ancient Israelite Literature*, pp. 174–175.
259. Derek Kidner, *An Introduction to Wisdom Literature: The Wisdom of Proverbs, Job and Ecclesiastes* (Leicester: Inter-Varsity Press; Downers Grove: InterVarsity Press, 1985), pp. 44–45 (45); see also e.g. Michael V. Fox, *Proverbs*, 2 vols., AB 18A–B (New Haven: Yale University Press, 2000, 2009), 2:754–767; Tremper Longman III, *How to Read Proverbs* (Downers Grove: InterVarsity Press, 2002), pp. 67–68, 70–72; Roland Murphy, *Proverbs*, WBC 22 (Nashville: Nelson, 1998), pp. 319–322; Bruce K. Waltke, *The Book of Proverbs*, 2 vols., NICOT (Grand Rapids: Eerdmans, 2004, 2005), 1:21–24; Walton, *ANE Thought*, p. 304.

A number of Mesopotamian texts have parallels with Job.[260] A Sumerian text, *Man and His God*, from the beginning of the second millennium BC, tells of a righteous young man who, in the face of his trials and suffering wonders whether he has been abandoned by his god. Nevertheless, he remains faithful, and is eventually restored.[261] Like Job, this addresses the question of innocent suffering. The same theme is addressed in a Babylonian text, *Ludlul bel Nemeqi* (I will praise the Lord of Wisdom), from the third quarter of the second millennium BC.[262] This has been called the 'Babylonian Job'. It describes how a man is forsaken by his gods and faces ostracism and illness, but is finally restored by Marduk. *The Babylonian Theodicy* (*c.*1000 BC) is a dialogue between a man who is suffering and a friend who, like Job's 'comforters', offers orthodox replies to his questions about divine justice.[263] It includes complaints about the success of the wicked and the suffering of the righteous. It is possible that Job might have been influenced by such texts, though there are no direct links with the biblical account, which stands out as unique. The comparison does show that the issues addressed were common throughout the ANE.[264]

Ecclesiastes ponders the brevity of life and the transience of human achievements, which are brought to an end by death. The advice offered is to accept that there is injustice in the world and that human existence may appear meaningless, and to make the most of the life God has given.[265] This theme is reflected in texts from Egypt and Mesopotamia.[266] In the Egyptian text *The Dialogue of a Man with*

---

260. Kidner, *Wisdom*, pp. 132–138; see also e.g. David J. A. Clines, *Job*, 3 vols., WBC 17–18B (Dallas: Word, 1989; Nashville: Nelson, 2006, 2011), 1:lix–lx; John E. Hartley, *The Book of Job*, NICOT (Grand Rapids: Eerdmans, 1988), pp. 6–11.
261. *COS* 1:179; Arnold and Beyer, *Readings*, pp. 175–176.
262. *COS* 1:153; Lambert, *Babylonian Wisdom Literature*, pp. 21–63; Arnold and Beyer, *Readings*, pp. 177–179.
263. Matthews and Benjamin, *OT Parallels*, pp. 239–244; *COS* 1:154; Lambert, *Babylonian Wisdom Literature*, pp. 63–91.
264. Other ANE texts compared with Job include *The Dialogue of a Man with His Soul*, which also has links with Ecclesiastes (see below), *The Eloquent Peasant* (*COS* 1:43), which deals with a peasant's quest for justice after mistreatment by a local official, and *The Admonitions of Ipuwer* (*COS* 1:42; Arnold and Beyer, *Readings*, pp. 208–210), which bemoans injustice in society and looks for an ideal future ruler. In the latter cases the focus is more on injustice within society than on theodicy.
265. Cf. Routledge, *OT Theology*, p. 223.
266. See also e.g. Roland Murphy, *Ecclesiastes*, WBC 23A (Dallas: Word, 1992), pp. xli–xlv.

His Soul,[267] which also has affinities with Job, a man, weary of life, contemplates death. He notes injustice, disloyalty, the lack of righteous men and the prevalence of sin in the world, and concludes that it would be better to die. His soul (*ba*) appears to seek to dissuade him, though the language is ambiguous. He is urged to 'follow the happy day and forget care'.[268] Some see this as a dialogue, though it may be better to see it as an internal struggle.[269] The *Harper's Song* from the tomb of Pharaoh Intef is an Egyptian funeral lament.[270] Copies date from around 1300 BC, though it seems likely that these are from a much earlier original. It reflects on the transience of human achievement and the pointlessness of existence and, again, advises the reader to seek happiness and enjoy life while it lasts.[271] A similar exhortation appears in the *Gilgamesh Epic*, where Gilgamesh is given advice by Siduri. This again reflects on the futility of life, and urges Gilgamesh to

> fill your belly, make merry day and night! Let your clothes be sparkling fresh, your head washed, your body bathed. Give your thought to the child whose hand is in yours, and let your wife delight in your embrace! These things are the human lot.[272]

Kidner compares this with Ecclesiastes 9:7–9:

> Go, eat your food with gladness, and drink your wine with a joyful heart . . . Always be clothed in white, and always anoint your head with oil. Enjoy life with the wife, whom you love, all the days of this meaningless life . . . For this is your lot in life.[273]

The *Gilgamesh Epic* also refers to the brevity of life and the ephemeral nature of human achievement.[274] Disillusionment with life is also expressed in the

267. *COS* 3:146; Matthews and Benjamin, *OT Parallels*, pp. 223–229.
268. *COS* 3:146; cf. Eccl. 3:12.
269. See e.g. *COS* 3:146; Walton, *ANE Thought*, p. 76.
270. *COS* 1:130; Kidner, *Wisdom*, pp. 138–139.
271. 'Put myrrh on your head, dress in fine linen, anoint yourself with oils fit for a god. Heap up your joys, let your heart not sink! Follow your heart and your happiness' (*COS* 1:130); cf. Eccl. 3:12; 9:7–9.
272. Kidner, *Wisdom*, p. 139; Matthews and Benjamin, *OT Parallels*, p. 26.
273. Kidner, *Wisdom*, p. 139.
274. See e.g. W. G. Lambert, 'Some New Babylonian Wisdom Literature', in John Day, Robert P. Gordon and H. G. M. Williamson (eds.), *Wisdom in Ancient Israel* (Cambridge: Cambridge University Press, 1995), pp. 30–42 (37); Lambert notes other Mesopotamian texts with a similar theme.

Dialogue with Pessimism or *The Obliging Servant*.[275] This describes a conversation between a master and his slave, in which the master suggests a course of action, the servant agrees, the master then suggests the opposite, and the servant again agrees. Murphy notes that though links with ANE texts need to be recognized, the nature of the relationship is unclear.[276] It is probably best to see this as a further example of the common wisdom traditions of the ancient world. OT writers were a part of that world, though they also viewed wisdom through the eyes of their distinctive covenant faith, which gives these texts a unique perspective.

The Song of Songs is sometimes listed among wisdom texts. As a love song it is frequently compared with ANE literature.[277] Closest parallels are with Egyptian texts,[278] though there are also points of comparison with texts from Mesopotamia and Ugarit.

Another frequently noted text is the Egyptian *Hymn to Aten*,[279] which has parallels with Psalm 104. This *Hymn*, perhaps going back to Akhenaten, addresses Aten as the sole creator of the world and everything in it. He gives life to its creatures; he watches over all that he has made and supplies their needs; he gives life and appoints the time of death. It also describes the passage of day and night, pointing to the silence at night, and the emergence of creatures when light dawns. There seems to be general agreement that the parallels indicate some connection between the *Hymn to Aten* and Psalm 104,[280] though

275. *COS* 1:154; Kidner, *Wisdom*, pp. 139–141.
276. Murphy, *Ecclesiastes*, p. xlii.
277. See e.g. G. Lloyd Carr, 'The Love Poetry Genre in the Old Testament and the Ancient Near East: Another Look at Inspiration', *JETS* 25.4 (1982), pp. 489–498; Michael V. Fox, *The Song of Songs and the Ancient Egyptian Love Songs* (Madison: University of Wisconsin Press, 1985); G. A. Long, 'Song of Songs 2: Ancient Near Eastern Background', in *DOTWPW*, pp. 750–760; Tremper Longman III, *Song of Songs*, NICOT (Grand Rapids: Eerdmans, 2001), pp. 49–54; Ernest Lucas, *Exploring the Old Testament*, vol. 3: *The Psalms and Wisdom Literature* (London: SPCK, 2003), pp. 79–90, 180–184; Walton, *Ancient Israelite Literature*, pp. 189–191.
278. See e.g. *COS* 1:49–51.
279. Ibid. 28; Matthews and Benjamin, *OT Parallels*, pp. 275–279; Arnold and Beyer, *Readings*, pp. 196–197.
280. See e.g. Leslie C. Allen, *Psalms 101–150*, WBC 21 (Waco: Word, 1983), pp. 29–30; John Goldingay, *Psalms*, BCOTWP, 3 vols. (Grand Rapids: Baker Academic, 2006–8), 3:182; Hill and Walton, *Survey*, p. 377; Derek Kidner, *Psalms*, 2 vols., TOTC (London: Inter-Varsity Press, 1975), 2:367–368.

commentators are divided on whether or not the psalm is dependent on the Egyptian text. Day argues that there is dependence, but that this is limited to Psalm 104:10–20.[281] However, while there may be similarities, even in those verses there are also significant differences, which appear to rule out any sense of direct borrowing.[282] One key difference is that whereas the *Hymn to Aten* praises the sun, in Psalm 104 the sun is treated as part of the created order. It seems that here, as elsewhere, the OT writers might have been aware of ANE texts, and might have incorporated common ideas, and possible intentional allusions, but their view of God and their relationship with him retains its distinctiveness.

These parallels between the OT and poetic texts from Mesopotamia, Egypt and Ugarit place the OT within the literary world of the ANE. In addition, because of a common North-western Semitic heritage, and similarities in poetic style and structure, Ugaritic texts, in particular, have played a significant part in enhancing our understanding of the form and structure of Hebrew poetry.[283]

---

281. John Day, 'Psalm 104 and Akhenaten's Hymn to the Sun', in Susan Gillingham (ed.), *Jewish & Christian Approaches to the Psalms: Conflict & Convergence* (Oxford: Oxford University Press, 2013), pp. 211–228.

282. See e.g. P. C. Craigie, 'The Comparison of Hebrew Poetry: Psalm 104 in the Light of Egyptian and Ugaritic Poetry', *Semitics* 4 (1974), pp. 10–21; Kidner, *Psalms*, 2:368. Day notes a difference between the sun as a source of life in the *Hymn to Aten* and the role of God's Spirit as the source of life in Ps. 104:29–30 ('Psalm 104', in Gillingham, *Jewish & Christian Approaches*, p. 217).

283. See e.g. Hill and Walton, *Survey*, pp. 377–379; LaSor, Hubbard and Bush, *OT Survey*, pp. 236–237. See also P. C. Craigie, 'The Poetry of Ugarit and Israel', *TynBul* 22 (1971), pp. 3–31; Simon B. Parker, 'Ugaritic Literature and the Bible', *Near Eastern Archaeology* 63.4 (2000), pp. 228–231.

4. WHAT KIND OF TEXT?

Genre criticism[1]

Genre refers to the form or type of a text: what kind of writing it is. In our own day we are aware of a variety of different literary genres, including letters, emails, newspaper articles, poetry (some with rhyming couplets, some written as blank

---

1. See e.g. Barton, *Reading*, pp. 8–19; Roland Boer (ed.), *Bakhtin and Genre Theory in Old Testament Studies* (Atlanta: Society of Biblical Literature, 2007); Jeannine K. Brown, 'Genre Criticism and the Bible', in David G. Firth and Jamie A. Grant (eds.), *Words and the Word: Explorations in Biblical Interpretation and Literary Theory* (Nottingham: Apollos, 2008), pp. 111–150; *Scripture as Communication: Introducing Biblical Hermeneutics* (Grand Rapids: Baker Academic, 2007), pp. 139–165; Sandy and Giese, *Cracking OT Codes*; E. D. Hirsch, *Validity in Interpretation* (New Haven: Yale University Press, 1967), pp. 68–126; V. P. Long, *Art of Biblical History*, pp. 38–57; Tremper Longman III, 'Form Criticism, Recent Developments in Genre Theory and the Evangelical', *WTJ* 47 (1985), pp. 46–67; 'Israelite Genres in their Ancient Near Eastern Context', in Marvin A. Sweeney and Ehud Ben Zvi (eds.), *The Changing Face of Form Criticism for the Twenty-First Century* (Grand Rapids: Eerdmans, 2003), pp. 177–195; Longman and Dillard, *Introduction*, pp. 29–31; Grant R. Osborne, *The Hermeneutical Spiral: A Comprehensive Introduction to Biblical Interpretation*, 2nd ed. (Downers Grove: InterVarsity Press, 2006), pp. 181–344 (esp. 181–183); Kevin J. Vanhoozer, *Is There a Meaning in This Text? The Bible, the Reader, and the Morality of Literary Knowledge* (Leicester: Apollos, 1998), pp. 335–350.

verse), legal contracts, novels, and so on. These may frequently be identified by their structure: they are written in a particular way, often according to a generally recognizable pattern.[2] For example, a narrative that begins 'Once upon a time' and ends 'And they all lived happily ever after' may be identified as a fairy tale. These forms of writing also have a particular function, within their own context. Sometimes information about the function and context may be clear from the genre itself, as, for example, in the cases of legal contracts, minutes of meetings and newspaper articles. Sometimes it may be less clear. Letters and emails may be written in the setting of an intimate relationship, or may be more formal communication between associates or with strangers. In such cases the context and the way the text is intended to function may be made clearer by analysis of the content. And, because different genres function in different ways, they need to be interpreted differently. We would not, for example, read a piece of poetry in the same way as the minutes of a meeting, or a newspaper article in the same way as a novel. With regard to the OT, too, identifying both the genre of a text, and the way that genre is intended to function in its particular context, is widely regarded as playing a significant part in its interpretation.[3]

Nevertheless, questions have been raised about some aspects of genre criticism,[4] and about its application to OT texts.[5] Brown challenges a traditional way of viewing genre as a container into which the content of the writing is poured.[6] This suggests that writers choose which genre will best communicate their message and accommodate their writing to that particular form. Such a view seems to assume that genres, and the rules that accompany them, can be precisely defined and categorized, and that writers generally accept the rigid constraints

---

2. Categorizing texts by structure and pattern plays a key part in form criticism.
3. For discussion of the relationship between genre and meaning, see e.g. Barton, *Reading*, pp. 16–18; Hirsch, *Validity in Interpretation*, pp. 75–76; Longman, 'Form Criticism', pp. 61–63; Osborne, *Hermeneutical Spiral*, pp. 26, 181–183. See also below, pp. 134–135.
4. Cf. Osborne, *Hermeneutical Spiral*, pp. 181–182.
5. It was not until Plato and Aristotle that the idea of literary genre was explicitly recognized; see e.g. Brown, 'Genre Criticism', in Firth and Grant, *Words and the Word*, pp. 113–114; Longman, 'Form Criticism', p. 53; 'Israelite Genres', in Sweeny and Ben Zvi, *Changing Face*, p. 179. There seems to be little direct focus on genre in ANE texts, and this raises questions about the application of this approach to those texts; however, see Longman, 'Israelite Genres', in Sweeny and Ben Zvi, *Changing Face*, pp. 179–180.
6. Brown, 'Genre Criticism', in Firth and Grant, *Words and the Word*, pp. 117–118, 120.

and conventions imposed by their choice of genre. However, writers appear to use genre more flexibly. Texts only rarely reflect a single or 'pure' genre; most contain a mixture of literary forms, and so resist efforts to classify them precisely. That is not to say OT writers completely ignore conventions associated with genre.[7] Because text is, essentially, communication, there needs to be some common ground between writers and readers. Writers may be innovative, but they must also engage with the expectations of readers, and it seems reasonable to suppose that there is some level of constraint to conform, even if sometimes loosely, to the expectations associated with genre.[8] However, writers use a range of styles, and may even deliberately flout what appear to be accepted conventions for literary effect. This flexibility on the part of writers requires a corresponding flexibility of approach by interpreters when analysing genre.

A second issue is that the classification of genre is recognized to be historically, socially and culturally conditioned. Many of Shakespeare's plays are classed as 'comedies', which at the time distinguished them from tragedies; however, many would not fit with current understanding of what constitutes comedy.[9] And even today what is deemed comedic varies according to cultural context. Poetry in different cultural settings may take different literary forms. It may also be viewed differently even within the same cultural setting; so, for example, for younger children it may be expected to consist of rhyming couplets. For a post-Enlightenment Western world view, historical narrative would be expected to contain a large degree of reliable, and where possible verifiable, factual material. However, in history writing in the OT the meaning of an event is at least as important as the accurate recording of the event itself. Consequently, OT writers have some freedom in how they recount the story and may not write according to the conventions of modern history writers.[10] In applying genre criticism to the biblical text we must, therefore, be wary of reading back our own understanding.[11] There may be similarities between genres in the OT and current genres, but we cannot assume too much.

---

7. Ibid., p. 120.
8. Ibid., pp. 120, 130–132; Longman, 'Form Criticism', pp. 51–53; 'Israelite Genres', in Sweeny and Ben Zvi, *Changing Face*, pp. 177–178; Osborne, *Hermeneutical Spiral*, pp. 182–183; Vanhoozer, *Is There a Meaning?*, pp. 337–338, 343–350.
9. This has led to the further category of 'problem plays'.
10. For further discussion of the relationship between narrative and history, see below, pp. 167–169.
11. Longman notes two approaches to literary analysis. The 'emic' approach looks at the literary features of the text from within its contextual setting and seeks to use native

Another key question in genre criticism is what constitutes a genre classification. There are certain genres that deliberately impose certain constraints; examples include the sonnet (fourteen lines) and the Haiku (seventeen syllables). However, for most texts, and particularly OT texts, there are no fixed rules. In practice, genre is determined by analysing a range of similar texts and noting common features, sometimes described as 'family resemblances'.[12] These resemblances may include setting, structure and content,[13] as well as the way some of those features function within the text and contribute to its overall generic shape.[14] Of course, not all similar texts will exhibit the same features, and it is for the reader or researcher to decide which, and how many, shared aspects are necessary to justify comparisons and a common classification.[15] This leads to a

---

categories. This allows comparisons between similar biblical texts and with other ANE texts. The 'etic' approach uses external literary classifications. See Longman, 'Form Criticism', pp. 54–56; 'Israelite Genres', in Sweeny and Ben Zvi, *Changing Face*, pp. 180–181; see also Brown, 'Genre Criticism', in Firth and Grant, *Words and the Word*, pp. 128–130.

12. Several scholars follow Wittgenstein and Fowler in the use of this expression; see e.g. Brown, 'Genre Criticism', in Firth and Grant, *Words and the Word*, p. 120; Hirsch, *Validity in Interpretation*, p. 71; cf. Carol A. Newsom, 'Spying out the Land: A Report from Genology', in Boer, *Bakhtin and Genre Theory*, pp. 19–30 (22–23). See Ludwig Wittgenstein, *Philosophical Investigations*, 4th ed. (Oxford: Blackwell, 2009), §67; A. Fowler, 'The Future of Genre Theory: Functions and Constructional Types', in R. Cohen (ed.), *The Future of Literary Theory* (New York: Routledge, 1989), pp. 291–303.
13. In his key contribution to the study of the Psalms Gunkel identified several psalm genres, determined by their (1) setting within Israel's worship, (2) common thought and mood, and (3) linguistic form, including grammar, vocabulary and structure; see e.g. Hermann Gunkel, *An Introduction to the Psalms*, trans. James D. Nogalski (Macon: Mercer, 1998), pp. 1–21 (15–17). Longman criticizes Gunkel because his categories are too limited, and argues for a wider approach (Longman, 'Form Criticism', pp. 48–50); see also Brown, 'Genre Criticism', in Firth and Grant, *Words and the Word*, pp. 123–125.
14. Brown, 'Genre Criticism', pp. 122–123, 130–131; Longman, 'Form Criticism', pp. 59–60; 'Israelite Genres', in Sweeny and Ben Zvi, *Changing Face*, p. 183.
15. Longman notes that genre categories can be larger, with a smaller number of similarities, or smaller, with a larger number of similarities ('Form Criticism', p. 57; 'Israelite Genres', in Sweeny and Ben Zvi, *Changing Face*, p. 183; cf. Brown, 'Genre Criticism', in Firth and Grant, *Words and the Word*, pp. 131–132).

more fluid approach to genre. And by looking at the function of generic features within the text as a whole, it also means that genre is not determined only by the presence of certain key elements, and conversely, that the absence of some of those elements does not necessarily exclude a text from a particular genre classification.[16]

This view of genre moves it away from the idea of rigid categorization.[17] As Longman notes, it is possible to observe patterns within ANE texts, including the OT, which make them 'conducive to a generic approach'.[18] However, genre categories are flexible, and may be considered at more than one level. Thus, at a general level, a psalm may be considered as poetry, but it may also be viewed within the more narrowly defined genre determined by its form. Similarly, a prophetic text may be considered generally as prophecy, or as a more narrowly defined oracle type. Some texts display characteristics of more than one genre. Many parts of the prophetic books are written in the form of poetry, and have characteristics in common with other poetic texts. Job and Ecclesiastes are generally considered as wisdom literature, but they also have a number of poetic features. And, as already mentioned, there may be occasions, too, where a writer's creativity results in generic innovation.

When it comes to the interpretation of a text, generic characteristics need to be considered. Genre provides a framework for approaching the text, and plays an important part in the process of determining meaning. Where genre is not properly understood it can result in inadequate or even misleading interpretations. However, because genre can be determined only by looking at the text as a whole, and therefore will, to some extent, also depend on the meaning of the text, it may be necessary to view the initial categorization of genre as provisional, and open to be revised in the light of more detailed analysis.[19] Such circularity is a necessary part of the hermeneutical process; however, as Barton notes, it is not a vicious circle.[20] A text may be analysed on the basis of certain generic assumptions, which are then refined in the light of further study,

---

16. Brown, 'Genre Criticism', p. 123.
17. See also Branson L. Woodward Jr. and Michael E. Travers, 'Literary Forms and Interpretation', in Sandy and Giese, *Cracking OT Codes*, pp. 29–43 (42–43).
18. Longman, 'Form Criticism', p. 55; 'Israelite Genres', in Sweeny and Ben Zvi, *Changing Face*, pp. 179–180.
19. See e.g. Brown, 'Genre Criticism', in Firth and Grant, *Words and the Word*, pp. 133–135; Hirsch, *Validity in Interpretation*, pp. 78–89; Longman, 'Form Criticism', pp. 61–62; Osborne, *Hermeneutical Spiral*, p. 181.
20. Barton, *Reading*, pp. 5–6.

in order to arrive at a clearer understanding of its genre,[21] and therefore of its meaning.

Within the OT there is broad agreement about genre categories, though with minor variations. Giese identifies three main genres – prose, poetry and prophecy – which he then subdivides into ten main forms. Prose is divided into narrative, history and law; poetry is divided into psalms and wisdom; and these two categories are further divided into psalms of lament, psalms of praise, proverbs and non-proverbial wisdom; prophecy is subdivided into oracles of salvation, announcements of judgment and apocalyptic.[22] In relation to the OT, Osborne identifies six main genres: law, narrative, poetry, wisdom, prophecy and apocalyptic, again with subdivisions in each category.[23] Giese's main divisions may be a little narrow; while his subdivisions, though valid, seem a little arbitrary. There are other distinct forms of prophetic literature, and maybe of psalm types that might also have been included. It may be better to start with more general categories, such as those highlighted by Osborne. Of these, law and legal texts have already been considered in some detail.[24] The other five categories, and their impact on interpretation, will be considered further below. The broader categories of poetry and narrative, which have a significant bearing on the others, will be the subject of more detailed discussion.

Poetry[25]

What is biblical poetry?

Although not clearly distinguished as poetry in the Hebrew text, most recent translations of the OT are set out in a way that indicates which sections are

---

21. Hirsch describes this as a text's 'intrinsic genre' (*Validity in Interpretation*, pp. 78–89); cf. Longman, 'Form Criticism', pp. 61–62.
22. Giese, 'Literary Forms', in Sandy and Giese, *Cracking OT Codes*, pp. 5–27 (17–23).
23. Osborne, *Hermeneutical Spiral*, pp. 185–290.
24. See above, pp. 118–123.
25. See e.g. Robert Alter, *The Art of Biblical Poetry*, rev. ed. (New York: Basic, 2011); 'Characteristics of Ancient Hebrew Poetry', in Robert Alter and Frank Kermode (eds.), *The Literary Guide to the Bible* (Cambridge, Mass.: Harvard University Press, 1987), pp. 611–624; Barry Bandstra, *Reading the Old Testament: An Introduction to the Hebrew Bible*, 4th ed. (Belmont: Wadsworth Cengage, 2009), pp. 377–381; Adele Berlin, 'On Reading Biblical Poetry: The Role of Metaphor', in J. A. Emerton (ed.), *Congress Volume Cambridge 1995* (Leiden: Brill, 1997), pp. 25–36; Lawrence Boadt,

intended to be read as poetry; generally, shorter lines and the presence of more white space. The main poetic sections of the OT are Psalms, Proverbs, Song of Songs, Lamentations, substantial parts of Job and Ecclesiastes, and large sections of the prophetic books.

Poetry is often contrasted with prose narrative. The latter is frequently used to convey information or to tell a story. Poetry may also tell a story, though it tends to appeal to its readers or hearers on a different level. It often uses pictorial language, and may use devices and techniques that make it attractive to read, especially out loud. Longman compares the two descriptions of what happened at the Red Sea: Exodus 14:21–31, which is written as prose narrative, and Exodus 15:1–12, which is written as poetry.[26] The first account describes the events in more detail and gives more historical information. The second appears to give a greater sense of excitement and better captures the feelings of the Israelites.

(*Footnote 25 cont.*) 'Reflections on the Study of Hebrew Poetry Today', *Concordia* 24.2 (1998), pp. 156–163; W. Brueggemann, *Introduction*, pp. 26–32; David Noel Freedman, 'Pottery, Poetry, and Prophecy: An Essay on Biblical Poetry', *JBL* 96.1 (1977), pp. 5–26; 'Another Look at Hebrew Poetry', in Elaine R. Follis (ed.), *Directions in Hebrew Biblical Poetry* (Sheffield: Sheffield Academic Press, 1987), pp. 11–28; Susan E. Gillingham, *The Poems and Psalms of the Hebrew Bible* (Oxford: Oxford University Press, 1994); Hill and Walton, *Survey*, pp. 373–389; William L. Holladay, 'Hebrew Verse Structure Revisited (I): Which Words Count?', *JBL* 118.1 (1999), pp. 19–32; 'Hebrew Verse Structure Revisited (II): Conjoint Cola and Other Considerations', *JBL* 118.3 (1999), pp. 401–416; David M. Howard Jr., 'Recent Trends in Psalms Study', in Baker and Arnold, *Face of OT Studies*, pp. 329–368 (344–355); 'The Psalms and Current Study', in Philip S. Johnston and David G. Firth, *Interpreting the Psalms: Issues and Approaches* (Leicester: Apollos; Downers Grove: IVP Academic, 2005), pp. 23–40 (29–33); Tremper Longman III, *How to Read the Psalms* (Downers Grove: InterVarsity Press, 1988), pp. 89–122; E. C. Lucas, 'Poetics, Terminology of', in *DOTWPW*, pp. 520–525; *Psalms and Wisdom*, pp. 67–77; M. O'Connor, *Hebrew Verse Structure* (Winona Lake: Eisenbrauns, 1980); Osborne, *Hermeneutical Spiral*, pp. 222–236; David L. Petersen and Kent Harold Richards, *Interpreting Hebrew Poetry*, GBS: OT Series (Philadelphia: Fortress, 1992); W. D. Tucker Jr., 'Psalms 1: Book of', in *DOTWPW*, pp. 578–593 (585–589); Wilfred G. E. Watson, *Classical Hebrew Poetry: A Guide to Its Techniques*, JSOTSup 26 (Sheffield: Sheffield Academic Press, 1984); Beat Weber, 'Towards a Theory of the Poetry of the Hebrew Bible: The Poetry of the Psalms as a Test Case', *BBR* 22.2 (2012), pp. 158–188.

26. Longman, *How to Read the Psalms*, pp. 90–93.

It also uses more dramatic language to convey the intensity of the event. So, for example, while the first account describes the waters returning and covering the Egyptians (Exod. 14:27–28), the second replaces 'water' with 'floods' (v. 5, NRSV), the plural of *tĕhôm* (see also v. 8), thus possibly evoking the imagery of Genesis 1:2, and it refers to the Egyptians being 'hurled into the sea' (Exod. 15:1) and sinking 'like a stone' (v. 5). Earlier, in the prose account, the sea is driven back by a 'strong east wind' (Exod. 14:21); in the poetic version it is by the 'blast of [Yahweh's] nostrils' (Exod. 15:8).

There is some debate as to the characteristics of poetry in the OT. In a classic series of lectures in the mid-eighteenth century Robert Lowth identified parallelism, which he categorized as synonymous, antithetic or synthetic, as the defining element in biblical poetry.[27] That view, with modifications, particularly to the categories of parallelism, featured prominently in discussions of Hebrew poetry until late in the twentieth century. In more recent years the centrality of parallelism has been questioned,[28] though there remains widespread agreement about its significance.[29] Several recent scholars take a linguistic approach to Hebrew poetry. One significant exponent of this approach,

---

27. Robert Lowth, *Lectures on the Sacred Poetry of the Hebrews* (Boston: Crocker & Brewster, 1829).
28. See James L. Kugel, *The Idea of Biblical Poetry: Parallelism and Its History* (New York: Yale University Press, 1981).
29. See also e.g. Alter, *Art of Biblical Poetry*; Adele Berlin, *The Dynamics of Biblical Parallelism*, rev. and expanded ed. (Grand Rapids: Eerdmans, 2008); 'Parallelism', in *ABD* 5:155–162; D. J. A. Clines, 'The Parallelism of Greater Precision', in Follis, *Directions*, pp. 77–100; J. P. Fokkelmann, *Reading Biblical Poetry: An Introductory Guide* (Philadelphia: Westminster John Knox, 2001), pp. 25–35, 61–86; Jamie A. Grant, 'Poetics', in Firth and Grant, *Words and the Word*, pp. 187–225 (212–221); Francis Landy, 'Poetics and Parallelism: Some Comments on James Kugel's *The Idea of Biblical Poetry*', *JSOT* 28 (1984), pp. 61–87; J. M. LeMon and B. A. Strawn, 'Parallelism', in *DOTWPW*, pp. 502–515 (503–512); Longman, *How to Read the Psalms*, pp. 95–110; Petersen and Richards, *Interpreting Hebrew Poetry*, pp. 21–36; Longman and Dillard, *Introduction*, pp. 27–29; W. G. E. Watson, *Classical Hebrew Poetry*, pp. 114–159. For discussion of more specific areas, see e.g. Richard Abbott, 'Forked Parallelism in Egyptian, Ugaritic and Hebrew Poetry', *TynBul* 62.1 (2011), pp. 41–64; David Toshio Tsumura, 'Vertical Grammar of Parallelism in Hebrew Poetry', *JBL* 128.1 (2009), pp. 167–181; Wilfred E. Watson, 'Gender-Matched Synonymous Parallelism in the Old Testament', *JBL* 99.3 (1980), pp. 321–341.

Michael O'Connor,[30] focuses on the syntactical patterns observed in lines of poetry and suggests a set of rules, or 'syntactic constraints',[31] that govern Hebrew poetry, and give it its distinctive identity. O'Connor's arguments and conclusions are complex. Nevertheless, he has helpfully highlighted the importance of syntax in analysing poetry, and others have followed aspects of his approach, particularly in relation to parallelism. In the past, probably because of their importance in Greek and Roman poetry, metre and rhythm were viewed as key features of biblical poetry. However, they are no longer considered central, and some question whether they have a role at all.[32] Another important feature of biblical poetry is what has become known as 'terseness':[33] expressing meaning through concise statements.[34] A third key element of biblical poetry is the use of imagery.[35] There are several other techniques, including inclusio, acrostics and assonance that may also be part of poetic texts. Some of these features are also found in prose, and, conversely, not all poetry contains all of them. However, by looking at the way the elements combine, and their concentration in particular texts, it is generally possible to distinguish poetry from other literary genres.

Before discussing biblical poetry in a little more detail, it is necessary to define some terms. As noted already, most recent translations of the OT set out poetry in (usually) short lines. Each of these printed lines is generally

---

30. O'Connor, *Hebrew Verse Structure*; see also Holladay, 'Which Words Count?'; 'Conjoint Cola'; Lucas, *Psalms and Wisdom*, pp. 68–70; Howard, 'Psalms and Current Study', in Johnston and Firth, *Interpreting the Psalms*, pp. 29–30.
31. O'Connor, *Hebrew Verse Structure*, p. 69.
32. On the significance of metre see e.g. Alter, *Art of Biblical Poetry*, pp. 5–8; W. McConnell, 'Meter', in *DOTWPW*, pp. 472–476; Kugel, *Idea*, pp. 69–76; Tremper Longman III, 'A Critique of Two Recent Metrical Systems', *Bib* 63 (1982), pp. 230–254; *How to Read the Psalms*, pp. 94, 108; Petersen and Richards, *Interpreting Hebrew Poetry*, pp. 37–48; W. G. E. Watson, *Classical Hebrew Poetry*, pp. 87–113.
33. See e.g. Tremper Longman III, 'Terseness', in *DOTWPW*, pp. 791–794; see also Kugel, *Idea*, pp. 87–92.
34. In *Specimens of the Table Talk of the Late Samuel Taylor Coleridge*, Coleridge distinguishes prose, 'words in their best order', from poetry, 'the best words in their best order'.
35. Longman and Lucas note parallelism, terseness and imagery as significant features in poetry features (Longman, 'Terseness', in *DOTWPW*, pp. 791–792; *How to Read the Psalms*, pp. 111–122; Lucas, 'Poetics', in *DOTWPW*, pp. 520–522); see also B. A. Strawn, 'Imagery', in *DOTWPW*, pp. 306–314 (306–309); Longman and Dillard, *Introduction*, pp. 27–29.

equivalent to what is usually referred to as a 'colon' (plural 'cola').[36] In OT poetry it is common for a pair of cola to be linked together, often through a parallelistic structure, to form a 'bicolon' or 'couplet', though combinations of three or four cola ('tricolon' and 'tetracolon' respectively) are not unusual.[37] These units, which make up two or more of the printed lines of text, are frequently referred to as poetic 'lines', though that terminology is not consistent among scholars.[38] A 'strophe' refers, generally, to a unit made up of two or more complete lines of poetry, and a 'stanza' may then indicate a larger unit, made up of strophes.[39] Though here, again, there is some variation in the use of terms.[40]

Metre

The significance of metre and rhythm for exegesis is limited. There may, though, be some form of metre based on accented syllables in the text (usually the last syllable of each Hebrew word).[41] Common metres in biblical poetry count two or three accents in each cola (denoted as 2 + 2 or 3 + 3). The 3 + 2 metre

---

36. Alter prefers 'verset' to colon (*Art of Biblical Poetry*, p. 8). Sometimes translations combine short cola into a single printed line (e.g. Ps. 23:1).
37. Tricola occur relatively frequently, especially in the Psalms (including Ps. 1:1). Tetracola are less frequent, and are not always easy to distinguish from two bicola (e.g. Isa. 34:10; 42:8; Jer. 2:13); see further W. G. E. Watson, *Classical Hebrew Poetry*, pp. 185–187; Petersen and Richards, *Interpreting Hebrew Poetry*, p. 23.
38. See e.g. Alter, *Art of Biblical Poetry*, p. 9; Fokkelmann, *Reading Biblical Poetry*, pp. 3–5, 87–140; Kugel, *Idea*, p. 1; Longman, *Introducing the Psalms*, p. 96 (Longman also refers to 'poetic phrases' rather than cola). Others identify 'line' with 'colon'; see e.g. Bandstra, *Reading the OT*, pp. 377–379; Petersen and Richards, *Interpreting Hebrew Poetry*, pp. 22–24; W. G. E. Watson, *Classical Hebrew Poetry*, pp. 11–14; see also Lucas, 'Poetics', in *DOTWPW*, p. 520.
39. See e.g. Fokkelmann, *Reading Biblical Poetry*, p. 6; Lucas, 'Poetics', in *DOTWPW*, pp. 523–524; W. G. E. Watson, *Classical Hebrew Poetry*, p. 13 (though see n. 40, below).
40. Watson uses 'strophe' for what others call a 'line' (*Classical Hebrew Poetry*, p. 13). Others do not distinguish between 'strophe' and 'stanza'; see e.g. Tremper Longman III, 'Stanza, Strophe', in *DOTWPW*, pp. 772–775. Petersen and Richards question the usefulness of the terms at all (*Interpreting Hebrew Poetry*, pp. 60–64).
41. See e.g. Fokkelmann, *Reading Biblical Poetry*, pp. 22–24; Longman, 'Two Recent Metrical Systems'; McConnell, 'Meter', in *DOTWPW*, pp. 473–476; W. G. E. Watson, *Classical Hebrew Poetry*, pp. 97–103.

has been observed in some laments;[42] this suggests a falling away, or limping, reflecting reducing strength or unfulfilled hopes. We see this, for example, in Lamentations 1:13b:

/ / /	
Pāraś rišet lĕraglay	He spread a net for my feet;
/ /	
hĕśîbanî 'āḥōr	and turned me back

Within OT poetry more generally, however, there does not appear to be any overall metrical structure, and even where patterns can be observed, there is no indication that writers observed particular conventions. Consequently, while in the past, irregular or broken metre might have been taken to suggest issues with the transmission of the text, such as missing words or phrases, conclusions based on metre are no longer justified.

Parallelism[43]

As already noted, parallelism, understood as the correspondence between cola in a line of poetry,[44] remains an important feature of biblical poetry,[45] though the nature of that correspondence is the subject of continuing discussion. Lowth's threefold categorization continues to feature in the ongoing debate. However, his third category, *synthetic parallelism*, has been challenged, and in the search for a new approach that better accounts for the examples in this last category there has been a more detailed analysis of parallelism within the other categories, resulting in new terminology. The recent focus on linguistic approaches to poetry, for example by Berlin,[46] refers to *semantic*

---

42. This is known as *qînâ* (lament) metre; see e.g. McConnell, 'Meter', in *DOTWPW*, pp. 475–476.

43. See above, p. 137, n. 29.

44. According to Berlin, parallelism 'is a *correspondence of one thing with another*' that 'involves repetition or the substitution of things which are equivalent on one or more linguistic levels' (*Dynamics*, p. 2 [italics hers]; see also Petersen and Richards, *Interpreting Hebrew Poetry*, p. 34).

45. It also plays a part in Ugaritic poetry; see LeMon and Strawn, 'Parallelism', in *DOTWPW*, pp. 505–506. As noted above, there is a close link between Ugaritic and ancient Hebrew poetry; see above, p. 129.

46. Berlin, *Dynamics*. For an overview, see Berlin, 'Parallelism', in *ABD* 5:157–160; Howard, 'Recent Trends', in Baker and Arnold, *Face of OT Studies*, pp. 344–350;

parallelism,[47] where the parallel elements correspond in meaning; *grammatical* (or sometimes *syntactical*) *parallelism*,[48] where the elements are grammatically related, and *phonological* or *phonetic parallelism*,[49] which is based on similar word sounds. Recent treatments have brought important insights to the understanding of parallelism in OT poetry, though there is considerable overlap between these and the more traditional approach. The following discussion offers a synthesis. Lowth's three categories will serve as a point of departure.

In *synonymous parallelism* the second colon repeats the idea of the first using different, but broadly equivalent, terms:[50]

> O Lord, do not rebuke me in your anger
>   or discipline me in your wrath.
> (Ps. 6:1)

Here there is a clear link between 'rebuke' and 'discipline', and between 'anger' and 'wrath', and a clear semantic correspondence between the cola.[51] A variation of this is *chiasm*, where synonymous elements again appear, but in reverse order:

> From his temple he heard my voice;
>   my cry came before him, into his ears.
> (Ps. 18:6b)

Here 'he heard' parallels 'came . . . into his ears' and 'my voice' parallels 'my cry', and once again there is a semantic correspondence. Sometimes chiasm may be

---

LeMon and Strawn, 'Parallelism', in *DOTWPW*, pp. 507–509; Petersen and Richards, *Interpreting Hebrew Poetry*, pp. 31–34.

47. See e.g. Berlin, *Dynamics*, pp. 64–102.
48. See e.g. ibid., pp. 18–63; Longman, *How to Read the Psalms*, pp. 105–106; Petersen and Richards, *Interpreting Hebrew Poetry*, pp. 29–35. Lowth also considered grammatical correspondences.
49. See e.g. Berlin, *Dynamics*, pp. 103–126; Petersen and Richards, *Interpreting Hebrew Poetry*, pp. 33–34.
50. Their occurrence in synonymous parallel couplets suggests a semantic link between terms. This helps to determine the semantic range, particularly of difficult terms.
51. Synonymous and antithetic parallelism fit into the more recent category of semantic parallelism. Lowth appears to have regarded synthetic parallelism as also having a semantic correspondence; though that was not always clear, leading to criticism of his approach; see Kugel, *Idea*, p. 4.

used aesthetically; the ordering of the elements may also provide a particular emphasis.

A feature of synonymous parallelism is the emphasis on equivalent expressions. One common pairing is 'thousand(s)' / 'ten thousand(s)':

A thousand may fall at your side,
    ten thousand at your right hand.
(Ps. 91:7; see also Ps. 144:13b)

This emphasizes the largeness of the number, and with it the degree of divine protection. A similar pairing occurs in the song of the women in 1 Samuel 18:7:

Saul has slain his thousands,
    and David his tens of thousands.

Here what may appear to be an innocent poetic device is used subversively. At face value it may be taken to emphasize the scale of Israel's victory over the Philistines. However, by associating the greater number with David, he is given prominence over Saul; thus arousing the latter's jealousy.

Another frequently occurring pairing is of the form x / x + 1:

One thing God has spoken,
    two things have I heard
(Ps. 62:11)

There are three things that are never satisfied;
    four that never say, 'Enough!'
(Prov. 30:15b)

This construction may build up the significance of the things listed. A similar expression occurs in Amos 1:3 – 2:16, where God denounces the sins of the nations, including Israel and Judah. In each of the oracles God says:

For three sins of ——,
    even for four.
(Amos 1:3, 6, 9, 11, 13; 2:1, 4, 6)

Here, though, only one sin is mentioned. It may be that in this formula the last mentioned element is most significant, and it is to this final sin, which brings divine judgment, that Amos refers.[52]

52. See Wolff, *Joel and Amos*, p. 138. Wolff notes occurrences of the formula in Sirach (23.16–21; 26.5–6, 28), where the last sin is the one most seriously condemned.

In *merismus* two extremes are paired to represent totality:

In his hand are the depths of the earth,
  and the mountain peaks belong to him.
(Ps. 95:4)

Here the corresponding expressions 'depths of the earth' and 'the mountain peaks' together refer to the whole world. The next verse continues the theme:

The sea is his, for he made it,
  and his hands formed the dry land.
(Ps. 95:5)

In this verse, again, the extremes 'sea' and 'dry land' point to God as maker of everything. Taken together, these verses point to God's creation of, and authority over, the whole of the created order.

The second of Lowth's categories of parallelism is *antithetic parallelism*. In this case the meaning of the second colon is, again, broadly equivalent to that of the first, but is written using opposing terms:

A wise son brings joy to his father,
  but a foolish son grief to his mother.
(Prov. 10:1)

Each colon expresses the same general idea, but here 'wise son' corresponds to 'foolish son', and 'make glad' corresponds to 'grief'.

Lowth's third category, *synthetic parallelism*, recognizes that cola may be related, even though there is no formal synonymous or antithetical correspondence between the elements. These include simile and metaphor, as well as lines where the second and subsequent cola extend the meaning of the first. At one level this category may be viewed as a depository for all poetic lines that are not synonymous or antithetic.[53] One response to that has been to suggest new categories of parallelism. These include *emblematic parallelism*, where the correspondence between the cola is figurative:

As the deer pants for streams of water,
  so my soul pants for you, O God.
(Ps. 42:1)

---

53. See e.g. Fokkelman, *Reading Biblical Poetry*, p. 26; LeMon and Strawn, 'Parallelism', in *DOTWPW*, p. 504; Longman, *How to Read the Psalms*, p. 100; Petersen and Richards, *Interpreting Hebrew Poetry*, p. 26.

Like cold water to a weary soul
is good news from a distant land.
(Prov. 25:25)

Another suggested category is *repetitive* (or *staircase*) parallelism, where one or more elements are repeated in successive cola, but with new elements also being added:

Ascribe to the LORD, O mighty ones,
ascribe to the LORD glory and strength.
(Ps. 29:1)

The seas have lifted up, O LORD,
the seas have lifted up their voice;
the seas have lifted up their pounding waves.
(Ps. 93:3)

In *grammatical parallelism* corresponding elements are syntactically similar. In most such cases there is also semantic parallelism, though there are a few instances where the syntax is parallel, but there is no obvious direct relationship in meaning:

He provides food for those who fear him;
he remembers his covenant for ever.
(Ps. 111:5)

However, the syntactical parallelism also invites a closer look at a possible relationship at a semantic level.[54] And it seems reasonable to conclude that the second colon extends the first: God's provision of food is a particular example of his wider covenant faithfulness.

As has been noted, linguistic approaches to parallelism also identify phonological or phonetic parallelism, based on similar word sounds. This is not generally evident in translation, though if words have been chosen primarily because of their sound, this will have some relevance to interpretation. Sometimes phonological parallelism will involve word pairs:

May there be peace [*šālôm*] within your walls
and security [*šalâ*] within your citadels.
(Ps. 122:7)

---

54. See e.g. Berlin, *Dynamics*, pp. 22–23; Petersen and Richards, *Interpreting Hebrew Poetry*, p. 31.

This is synonymous parallelism, and the cola are semantically equivalent. However, the terms 'peace' (*šālôm*) and 'security' (*šalâ*) also sound very similar, giving the parallelism a phonological dimension. Another form of phonological correspondence is alliteration; for example, Psalm 127:1:

> Unless the LORD builds the house [*'im YHWH lō' yibneh bayit*],
> its builders labour in vain [*šāw' 'āmlû bônāyw bô*].
> Unless the LORD watches over the city [*'im YHWH lō' yišmār 'îr*],
> the watchmen stand guard in vain [*šāw' šāqad šômēr*].

There is a clear correspondence between the two complete lines, with both using a similar grammatical structure to emphasize the need to depend on God. Within the individual lines the correspondence between cola is alliterative. Gillingham notes that the *b*-alliteration in the first line (*yibneh bayit / bônāyw bô*) and the *š*-alliteration in the second (*yišmār / šāw' šāqad šômēr*) pick out the key words *bānâ* (to build) and *šāmar* (to watch over, guard, keep). The continued emphasis of those sounds point to the central themes of the verse: the need for God's involvement if human enterprise is to be worthwhile.[55]

In these examples it is possible to identify a parallel structure. In some cases, though, it is hard to identify any such structure.[56] Sometimes the second colon is simply a continuation of the previous clause:

> Because your love is better than life,
> my lips will glorify you.
> (Ps. 63:3)

> But their idols are silver and gold,
> made by the hands of men.
> (Ps. 115:4)

There is still here a relationship between the cola, and, in order to retain the term 'parallelism', recent studies have considered new ways of understanding such relationships. In her discussion of lexical and semantic aspects of parallelism[57] Berlin refers to paradigmatic and syntagmatic equivalences.[58] A paradigmatic equivalence is where one idea is substituted for another, and this covers, broadly, what is generally understood as synonymous and antithetic parallelism.

55. Gillingham, *Poems and Psalms*, pp. 193–194.
56. See e.g. Kugel, *Idea*, pp. 3–4.
57. Berlin, *Dynamics*, pp. 64–102.
58. Ibid., pp. 90–91.

Syntagmatic equivalence is one where, as in the examples above, the second (or subsequent) colon continues or advances the thought of the first;[59] and this, too, may thus be properly referred to as parallelism. Thus Berlin can suggest that 'in a certain sense parallelism *is* the essence of poetry'.[60]

An important question in relation, particularly, to synonymous parallelism, is the way the parallel expressions contribute to the text's overall meaning. Does the second merely repeat the first? Or is there something more? The rabbinic view was that each part of the line had a separate meaning.[61] This, though, seems unlikely. The view advocated by Lowth, and which became the standard approach, is that the parallel sections mean the same thing. That raises the question, though, of why it is repeated. Another possibility, advocated by Kugel, is that there is progression in the repetition: 'A is so, and what's more B'.[62] Longman also argues that the second colon takes forward and intensifies the first.[63] In Berlin's view parallel statements have both equivalence and contrast; they offer two different views of the same thing, and their combination 'produces a sense of depth'.[64] Clines suggests that in many parallel couplets the second adds precision to the first. This also indicates progression, though for Clines that does not reduce to Kugel's limited description.[65] In my view there are cases where there appears to be intensification, and that has implications for interpretation. And it may be possible to widen the idea of intensification to include Clines's examples. However, it seems possible that there may be occasions where repetition is primarily for emphasis; or where the statements complement one another so that, together, they afford a clearer perspective. It may, thus, be necessary to consider several possible relationships between the various elements.

Terseness

As we have seen, poetry in the OT is further distinguished by its concision. This is achieved in several ways. One is simply by a general economy of words: using the best words in the best way. Longman also notes that the use of imagery,

---

59. See also Petersen and Richards, *Interpreting Hebrew Poetry*, pp. 25–35.
60. Berlin, *Dynamics*, p. 4.
61. See e.g. Kugel, *Idea*, pp. 96–101.
62. See e.g. ibid, pp. 7–12.
63. Longman, *How to Read the Psalms*, pp. 97–98; see also Alter, *Art of Biblical Poetry*, pp. 10–12, 75–103; Fokkelmann, *Reading Biblical Poetry*, pp. 73–87 (75–76).
64. Berlin, *Dynamics*, p. 99.
65. Clines, 'Parallelism of Greater Precision', in Follis, *Directions*, p. 95.

and particularly metaphor, is also significant. For example, the statement 'the LORD is my shepherd' (Ps. 23:1) is brief; nevertheless, it invites a comparison between God and a range of roles and responsibilities of a shepherd, and thus that simple sentence contains a great deal of information.[66] The same can be true of the use of simile in emblematic parallelism. This compares a deeper truth with something that is already well known to the reader and so little further explanation is necessary.

Another factor is the occurrence of significantly fewer particles and conjunctions than in prose. According to Freedman, the definite article (*ha*), the sign of the direct object (*'et*) and the relative pronoun (*'ăšer*) occur, in general, 'six to eight times more frequently in prose passages than in poetry'.[67] While in prose, phrases and clauses tend to be linked together with conjunctions, that happens much less in poetry, maybe with the exception of *kî* (because).[68] This is sometimes obscured in translations, which may add the assumed conjunction; so in Psalm 122:7, noted above, the Hebrew text does not include 'and' in the second colon. The relationship between the cola is usually clear; thus in Psalm 23:1 – 'The LORD is my shepherd, I shall not be in want' – the reason for not being in want is that the Lord provides for the psalmist in the same way that a shepherd provides for sheep. However, while prose may make that explicit, maybe by including 'therefore' between the clauses, poetry is more economical with its words.

A further significant feature of OT poetry that contributes to terseness is *ellipsis*.[69] This is where a word or words from one colon, usually the first, are not repeated, but are assumed, in the another; for example:

Blessed is the man
   who does not walk in the counsel of the wicked

---

66. Longman, 'Terseness', in *DOTWPW*, p. 792.
67. Freedman, 'Pottery, Poetry, and Prophecy', p. 7; see also e.g. Freedman, 'Another Look', in Follis, *Directions*, pp. 11–18; Longman, 'Terseness', in *DOTWPW*, p. 792, W. G. E. Watson, *Classical Hebrew Poetry*, p. 54.
68. Longman, 'Terseness', in *DOTWPW*, p. 793.
69. See e.g. Alter, *Art of Biblical Poetry*, pp. 6, 25–28; Cynthia L. Miller, 'A Linguistic Approach to Ellipsis in Biblical Poetry (or, What to Do When Exegesis of What Is There Depends on What Isn't)', *BBR* 13.2 (2003), pp. 251–270; 'A Reconsideration of "Double-Duty" Prepositions in Biblical Poetry', *JANES* 31 (1980), pp. 99–110; 'Ellipsis', in *DOTWPW*, pp. 156–160; Petersen and Richards, *Interpreting Hebrew Poetry*, p. 33; W. G. E. Watson, *Classical Hebrew Poetry*, pp. 48, 174–176.

or stand in the way of sinners
  or sit in the seat of mockers.
(Ps. 1:1)

Here the first clause, 'blessed is the man', is linked with each of the following cola. Further examples include:

Is your love declared in the grave,
  your faithfulness in Destruction?
(Ps. 88:11)

Zion will be redeemed with justice,
  her penitent ones with righteousness.
(Isa. 1:27)

In these cases the verb in the first colon is understood in the second. Sometimes, though rarely, there is *reverse* or *backward* ellipsis, where the verb is omitted from the first colon:

Some [trust] in chariots and some in horses,
  But we trust in the name of the LORD our God.
(Ps. 20:7)

The NIV translators have included the verb in the first colon, though in the Hebrew text it appears only in the second.

One aspect of ellipsis is that occasionally another element is added to the second colon, so that the lengths of the cola are still similar:

He nourished him with honey from the rock,
  and with oil from the flinty crag.
(Deut. 32:13b)

This is sometimes known as *ballast variant parallelism*.[70] Alter objects to the term because it implies that what has been added is there simply to make up weight, rather than moving the parallelism of the line forward.[71]

---

70. See e.g. LeMon and Strawn, 'Parallelism', in *DOTWPW*, p. 511; W. G. E. Watson, *Classical Hebrew Poetry*, pp. 343–348.

71. Alter, *Art of Biblical Poetry*, pp. 25–28; see also Clines, 'Parallelism of Greater Precision', in Follis, *Directions*, pp. 91–92. W. G. E. Watson, though, does see this as a 'filler' (*Classical Hebrew Poetry*, p. 344).

It is not always clear, however, that the lack of a verb in one colon is a result of ellipsis. For example, in the NIV translation of Proverbs 13:1, backward ellipsis is assumed:

A wise son [heeds] his father's instruction,
but a mocker does not listen to rebuke.

By contrast, the NRSV attempts to make sense of the first colon as it stands:

A wise child loves discipline,
but a scoffer does not listen to rebuke.[72]

Another example is Psalm 49:3 (NRSV):

My mouth shall speak wisdom;
the meditation of my heart shall be understanding.

There is no verb in the second colon, and the translation above understands the verb 'to be'.[73] It seems more natural, though, to regard this as another example of ellipsis:[74]

My mouth shall speak wisdom;
the meditation of my heart [shall speak] understanding.

These examples demononstrate a consequence of terseness: ambiguity. Is the absence of a verb an indication of ellipsis, or should we understand the text in another way? The use of imagery, such as 'the LORD is my shepherd', enables a range of ideas to be expressed in a single expression. We might ask, though, in what ways is God a shepherd? The context implies provision and protection, but may the readers' imagination extend to other aspects of a shepherd's role? Ambiguity makes a definitive interpretation impossible, but, as Longman notes, 'it lends interest to the poem and requires the reader/interpreter to be deeply engaged with the material'.[75]

---

72. Here *'āb* (father) of the MT has been amended to *'ōhēb*, from *'āhēb* (to love); cf. Prov. 12:1. C. L. Miller argues that this text does not fit the pattern for backward ellipsis ('Linguistic Approach', pp. 267–268).

73. The NIV translates the verse in a similar way: 'My mouth will speak words of wisdom; the utterance from my heart will give understanding.'

74. See C. L. Miller, 'Linguistic Approach', pp. 256–257, 265–267.

75. Longman, 'Terseness', in *DOTWPW*, p. 794.

Imagery

As noted already, poetry contains a great deal of imagery or figurative language. In general, this involves representing one thing by another. It uses objects, situations and pictures that are familiar to the writers and their audience to convey important spiritual and theological truths. Key forms of imagery are metaphor and simile. Thus God is described as a shepherd (e.g. Ps. 23:1), and, correspondingly, his people are described as sheep (e.g. Ps. 100:3). The Lord 'roars' (Amos 1:2), depicting him, also, as a lion. The believer who seeks God is like a deer panting for water (Ps. 42:1). Human attributes are ascribed to the created order in celebration of God's presence and his deliverance of his people:[76] trees and rivers clap their hands, and mountains sing for joy (Ps. 98:8; Isa. 55:12). In the face of God's power the 'sea looked and fled' (Ps. 114:3), and in the same psalm, mountains, usually a symbol of permanence, are described as skipping like rams (Ps. 114:4, 6). The wind that drove back the waters of the Red Sea is described as 'the blast from [Yahweh's] nostrils' (Exod. 15:8); elsewhere God rides on the clouds and the storm (Pss 68:4; 104:3; Isa. 19:1). Such texts evoke powerful images and reflect important truth. Clearly, though, they are not intended to be taken literally, and when it comes to exegesis and interpretation the nature of the imagery and of its underlying significance need to be taken into consideration.

We have seen, too, that the OT writers also employ mythological imagery, which echoes some of the ideas found in other ANE texts. Thus Psalm 74:12–17, which offers hope to God's people in a time of crisis by emphasizing God's power as the Creator, refers to God's victory over the sea, and over the many-headed Leviathan (vv. 13–14), recalling the Ugaritic myth *Baal and the Sea*.[77] These allusions may include an element of polemic. But they also use familiar images that were part of a common ANE world view to highlight important theological truths.[78]

Modern readers face a significant challenge when it comes to interpreting poetic imagery in the OT. A key factor is how the imagery was understood by the poet and by those for whom it was written. We must be wary of reading back our understanding of a particular image, and seek to understand as best as we can the culture and background that gave rise to the imagery, and make that the basis for exegesis and interpretation.

---

76. See e.g. P. E. Koptak, 'Personification', in *DOTWPW*, pp. 516–519.

77. See above, p. 115.

78. See above, pp. 116–117.

Inclusio and acrostics

I want to conclude this section by referring to two further features of OT poetry: inclusio and acrostic. Inclusio involves the repetition (or near repetition) of an expression at the beginning and end of a section of text, which then act as brackets, enclosing the text, and holding it together in a literary 'envelope'.[79] This device serves to indicate the limits of a particular section of text,[80] and it may also point to the theme of the passage.[81] So, for example, Psalm 8 begins and ends with the line 'O LORD, our Lord, how majestic is your name in all the earth!' (vv. 1, 9), which draws attention to a key theme of the psalm. Ecclesiastes contains one of the longest inclusios in the OT. The book begins with the assertion '"Meaningless! Meaningless!" says the Teacher . . . "Everything is meaningless"' (Eccl. 1:2), and the same expression occurs near its end (Eccl. 12:8), thus setting the tone for much of the content in between.

In acrostic poems in the OT[82] the first letter of a line, or group of lines, of poetry follows the order of the twenty-two letters of the Hebrew alphabet.[83] Psalm 119 is a well-known example of this. It is made up of twenty-two groups of eight single-line verses, one group for each letter of the alphabet, and in each group each of the eight verses begins with the same letter. Four of the five chapters of Lamentations are also written as acrostics: chapters 1 and 2 comprise twenty-two verses, each made up of three lines of poetry, and each verse (though not each line) begins with a successive letter of the alphabet. Chapter 3 comprises sixty-six verses, each of one line. These are in twenty-two groups of three, with each of the three lines beginning with the same letter. Chapter 4 is also an acrostic, though its twenty-two verses each have two lines. The use of acrostics appears to be, primarily, an aesthetic literary device, though it may also have

---

79. Inclusio is also referred to as 'envelope figure' or 'envelope structure'. See e.g. Temper Longman III, 'Inclusio', in *DOTWPW*, pp. 323–325; *How to Read the Psalms*, p. 107; W. G. E. Watson, *Classical Hebrew Poetry*, pp. 282–286.

80. Inclusio may also be evident in non-poetic texts; so e.g. the repetition of the 'heavens and the earth' being 'created' in Gen. 1:1 and 2:4 sets limits around that section of the creation narrative.

81. See e.g. Longman, 'Inclusio', in *DOTWPW*, p. 323.

82. See e.g. C. J. Fantuzzo, 'Acrostic', in *DOTWPW*, pp. 1–4; D. N. Freedman, 'Acrostic Poems in the Hebrew Bible: Alphabetic and Otherwise', *CBQ* 48 (1986), pp. 408–431; Longman, *How to Read the Psalms*, pp. 107–108; W. G. E. Watson, *Classical Hebrew Poetry*, pp. 190–200.

83. In acrostic poems *ś* and *š*, both represented by the same Hebrew character, count as a single letter.

phonetic appeal.[84] It may also reflect a sense of divine order,[85] something that may be particularly significant following the disaster described in Lamentations, or completeness,[86] expressing, in the case of Lamentations, a sense of total grief and despair. The idea of completeness may also be evident in Proverbs 31:10–31, an acrostic describing the attributes of the perfect wife.

Psalm types

In his form-critical approach to the book of Psalms Gunkel suggested several main psalm types, broadly identified by their pattern:[87] hymns of praise, and corporate and individual laments and songs of thanksgiving. Other categories, which owe more to a psalm's content than to its form, include 'royal psalms', which focus on the king, and so-called 'wisdom psalms', which will be considered later alongside other wisdom literature. Gunkel's approach has been revised, and aspects of it have been questioned by more recent scholars.[88] His contribution to the study of the Psalms is, though, very significant, and his classification of psalms, albeit with some variation, is still widely followed.

---

84. See e.g. Petersen and Richards, *Interpreting Hebrew Poetry*, p. 94.
85. Longman, *How to Read the Psalms*, p. 108.
86. Fantuzzo, 'Acrostic', in *DOTWPW*, p. 104.
87. See above, p. 133, n. 13. On the categories of psalms see also e.g. Arnold, *Introduction*, pp. 296–302; Bandstra, *Reading the OT*, pp. 381–390; W. Brueggemann, *Introduction*, pp. 313–325; D. G. A. Clines, 'Psalm Study since 1955: II. The Literary Genres', *TynBul* 20 (1969), pp. 105–125; Collins, *Introduction*, pp. 485–491; John Day, *Psalms*, OTG (Sheffield: Sheffield Academic Press, 1992); Gunkel, *Introduction to the Psalms*; LaSor, Hubbard and Bush, *OT Survey*, pp. 432–439; Longman and Dillard, *Introduction*, pp. 247–250; Sigmund Mowinckel, *The Psalms in Israel's Worship*, 2 vols. (Oxford: Blackwell, 1962); Tucker, 'Psalms 1', in *DOTWPW*, pp. 581–585.
88. Westermann argues for a closer connection between hymns and songs of thanksgiving, which he calls 'descriptive praise' (focusing on God's being and his actions) and 'declarative praise' (focusing on specific acts of deliverance) respectively, and concludes that there are two basic psalm types: praise and lament; see Claus Westermann, *Praise and Lament in the Psalms* (Atlanta: John Knox, 1981). Brueggemann categorizes psalms according to function. He refers to psalms of *orientation*, which reflect a settled and ordered view of the world and include expressions of praise; psalms of *disorientation*, a category made up, primarily, of psalms of individual and corporate lament; and psalms of *new orientation*, which include thanksgiving and enthronement psalms; see Walter Brueggemann, *The Message of the Psalms: A Theological Commentary* (Minneapolis: Augsburg, 1984); *Introduction*, pp. 322–324.

Hymns of Praise are common in the psalter and give it its Hebrew name: *tĕhillîm* (praises).[89] Hymns often begin with a call to praise God, which is followed by the content of or cause for praise, or are often introduced with the Hebrew *kî* (for, because), and a conclusion, which may include a renewed call to praise God; as, for example, in Psalm 117:

Praise the LORD, all you nations;
extol him, all you peoples.
For great is his love towards us,
and the faithfulness of the LORD endures for ever.
Praise the LORD.

Psalm 33 also includes a call to praise (vv. 1–3), and the reason for praise (vv. 4–19), though, rather than a renewed call to praise God, the conclusion is an expression of trust, in the light of what God has done (vv. 20–22).[90] Reasons for praise include the acknowledgment of God as the Creator (e.g. Ps. 104), and his mighty acts in bringing deliverance (e.g. Ps. 105). Gunkel also includes in this category 'Songs of Zion' (Pss 46; 48; 76; 84; 87; 122), which focus on God's relationship with and presence in the city of Jerusalem, and 'Enthronement Psalms' (Pss 47; 93; 97; 99), which celebrate God's reign as king over the whole earth. A characteristic of many hymns is the verb *hālāl*, which in its piel form means 'to praise'. Particularly towards the end of the psalter this appears in the familiar form *halĕlû-yâ* (praise the Lord).[91] While hymns of praise are characteristic of the psalter, they occur, too, in many other parts of the OT.[92]

---

89. See also e.g. Kenneth L. Barker, 'Praise', in Sandy and Giese, *Cracking OT Codes*, pp. 217–232; M. D. Futato, 'Hymns', in *DOTWPW*, pp. 300–305; James Hely Hutchinson, 'The Psalms and Praise', in Johnston and Firth, *Interpreting the Psalms*, pp. 85–100; Gunkel's list of hymns of praise includes Pss 8; 19; 29; 33; 65; 67; 68; 96; 98; 100; 103; 104; 105; 111; 113; 114; 117; 135; 136; 145; 146; 147; 149; 149; 150; see Gunkel, *Introduction to the Psalms*, pp. 22–41 (23).

90. Barker suggests a more general structure: call to praise, causes for praise, conclusion to praise ('Praise', in Sandy and Giese, *Cracking OT Codes*, p. 221); cf. Futato, 'Hymns', in *DOTWPW*, pp. 301–304.

91. E.g. Pss 104:35; 105:45; 111:1; 113:1, 9; 117:2; 135:1, 3, 21; 146:1, 10; 147:1, 20; 148:1, 14; 149:1, 9; 150:1, 6. In this expression *yâ* is an abbreviated form of the divine name (Yahweh).

92. E.g. Exod. 15:1–18; Judg. 5:2–9; Job 5:8–16; 37:22 – 38:13; Isa. 26:1–6.

Laments or *complaints* include the prayers of individuals and of the community at a time of distress, and make up the largest section of the psalms.[93] Personal needs include illness (e.g. Pss 38; 41), persecution by enemies (e.g. Pss 17; 25; 56) and false accusation (e.g. Pss 7; 71; 109), as well as a sense of sin and the need for forgiveness (e.g. Pss 51; 130). Communal laments focus on national crisis, primarily defeat by enemies (e.g. Pss 44; 74; 79; 83), and there is also the complaint that God has brought this about, or at least not prevented it (e.g. Pss 44:9–12; 74:1; 79:5–7; 80:4–6).[94] Elements that occur most frequently in individual laments (though the order may vary) include[95] (1) a cry to God for help,[96] (2) the psalmist's complaint,[97] (3) an expression of confidence in God,[98] (4) an appeal for vengeance,[99] (5) a plea for help,[100] (6) confession of sin or protestation of innocence,[101]

---

93. See also e.g. C. C. Broyles, 'Lament, Psalms of', in *DOTWPW*, pp. 384–399; Tremper Longman III, 'Lament', in Sandy and Giese, *Cracking OT Codes*, pp. 197–215. Lists vary from scholar to scholar; however Pss 3; 5; 6; 7; 13; 17; 22; 25; 26; 27; 28; 31; 35; 38; 39; 41; 42; 43; 51; 54; 55; 56; 57; 59; 61; 63; 64; 69; 70; 71; 86; 88; 102; 109; 120; 130; 140; 141; 142; 143 appear to be individual laments, and Pss 12; 44; 60; 74; 79; 80; 83; 85; 90; 126 are generally classified as communal laments.
94. This element of complaint has led to the subclassification, particularly among Jewish scholars, of the 'law-court pattern', where petitioners appeal against their treatment by the divine judge. Jeremiah's 'confessions', as well as a number of psalms of complaint, fall into this category; see e.g. Joseph Heinemann, *Prayer in the Talmud: Forms and Patterns*, Studia Judaica 9 (Berlin: de Gruyter, 1977), pp. 193–217; Anston Laytner, *Arguing with God: A Jewish Tradition* (Oxford: Rowman & Littlefield, 1990).
95. See Lucas, *Psalms and Wisdom*, pp. 3–5; cf. Westermann, *Praise and Lament*, pp. 64, 66–67. There is general agreement on most points, but there are some differences. So Longman does not explicitly include the vow to praise God ('Lament', in Sandy and Giese, *Cracking OT Codes*, pp. 199–200); and Broyles does not include confession or assertion of innocence in his typical list ('Lament', in *DOTWPW*, pp. 387–388). The following list suggests how key elements appear in Pss 13; 17; 22; 54; 69; 109; 130.
96. E.g. 17:1–2; 22:1a; 54:1–2; 69:1; 109:1; 130:1–2.
97. E.g. 13:1–2; 17:9–12; 22:1b–2, 6–8, 12–18; 54:3; 69:2–4, 6–12, 19–21; 109:2–7; 130:3.
98. E.g. 13:5a; 17:6–7; 22:3–5, 9–10; 54:4, 7; 69:32–33; 109:26–29; 130:4–6.
99. E.g. 17:13–14; 54:5; 69:22–28; 109:6–20.
100. E.g. 13:3–4; 22:11, 19–21; 54:1–2; 69:13–18, 29; 109:21–25.
101. Confession: 69:5 (see also 51; 130:3–4); protestation of innocence: 17:3–5 (see also 5; 7:3–5, 8; 26).

(7) a vow to praise God in the future,[102] and (8) praise or thanksgiving to God.[103] Communal laments follow a comparable pattern,[104] though without the concluding expression of praise. Like hymns of praise, laments occur elsewhere in the OT, notably the book of Lamentations, which includes the *qînâ* lament and also contains elements of communal lament.[105]

Psalms of Thanksgiving offer thanks to God for a particular act of deliverance.[106] Westermann objects to this as a separate category, arguing that the Hebrew verb *yādâ* usually associated with giving thanks, may be better understood in the context of praise.[107] It may also be noted, too, that not all psalms usually placed in this category use the language of thanksgiving (e.g. Pss 34; 41; 124). However, the link with a specific answer to prayer, which Westermann also recognizes, does suggest that this kind of psalm may be considered as a separate category. As with laments, there appear to be both individual and (relatively few) communal thanksgiving psalms. There is, though, no general agreement as to which psalms fall into this category.[108] Thanksgiving psalms are related to laments. The latter frequently include a vow to praise God following his intervention, and psalms of thanksgiving may be seen to represent a fulfilment of that vow. There is no fixed structure for these psalms, though they may include (1) an introduction, in which the psalmist may express his intention to thank God, (2) a recollection of the need, the prayer for help and deliverance by God, and (3) a conclusion, which may be a further expression of praise.[109]

---

102. E.g. 13:5b–6a; 22:22; 54:6; 109:30.

103. E.g. 13:6b; 22:23–24; 54:7; 69:34–36; 109:31.

104. E.g. (1) 79:1; 83:1; (2) 79:1–4; 83:2–8; (3) 79:10–11, 13a; 83:9–12; this may also be linked with a recollection of God's past saving acts (44:1–8; 74:12–17; 80:8–11) (4) 79:6–7, 12; 83:9–18; (5) 79:5, 9; 83:1 (and *passim*); (6) Confession: 79:8–9; protestation of innocence: 44:17–22; (7) 79:13. See Westermann, *Praise and Lament*, pp. 52–54.

105. Adele Berlin, *Lamentations*, OTL (Louisville: Westminster John Knox, 2002), p. 24.

106. See also e.g. Barker, 'Praise', in *Cracking OT Codes*, pp. 221–223; R. P. Belcher Jr., 'Thanksgiving, Psalms of', in *DOTWPW*, pp. 805–808.

107. Westermann, *Praise and Lament*, pp. 25–32; cf. Day, *Psalms*, p. 44.

108. Day includes the following: (individual) 18; 30; 32; 34; 40; 41; 66; 107; 116; 118; 138, and (communal) 66; 67; 124; 129 (*Psalms*, pp. 45, 48–49); for variations see e.g. Barker, 'Praise', in *Cracking OT Codes*, p. 222; Belcher, 'Thanksgiving', in *DOTWPW*, p. 805; Collins, *Introduction*, p. 461; Lucas, *Psalms and Wisdom*, p. 11.

109. E.g. Ps. 116: (1) vv. 1–2; (2) vv. 3–11; (3) vv. 12–19. Day notes the pattern, but notes, too, that there is wide variation within this group of psalms (*Psalms*, pp. 46–47);

Psalms of Confidence are considered, by Gunkel, as a development of the lament, in which the expression of confidence in God has become the main theme.[110] Others see them closer to psalms of thanksgiving.[111] It may be better, though, to see them as a separate category. Generally written in the third person, this group includes Pss 11; 23; 62.[112]

Royal Psalms do not have a distinct literary form; they are classified by content, which focuses on Israel's king.[113] They note the king's role in the life of the nation and may emphasize his special relationship with God. Some may celebrate a coronation (Pss 2; 72; 101; 110); Psalm 45 appears to celebrate a royal wedding; Psalms 20 and 21 may be prayers before or after a battle; Psalm 72 points to the kinds of things that are expected of Israel's king: especially to uphold justice and to take care of the weak (vv. 2–4, 12–14). Over time some of these psalms may have been reapplied to the Davidic Messiah.[114]

Other kinds of poem

In addition to hymns, laments and songs of thanksgiving, there are other kinds of poem in the OT. These include love songs, characterized by the Song of Songs, proverbs and other forms of wisdom texts, as well as various kinds of prophetic speeches. Wisdom literature and prophetic oracles will be discussed further below.

Old Testament narrative[115]

Narrative plays an important part in the way we think about ourselves and who we are. Our lives are an unfolding story, where one thing leads to another, and

(*Footnote 109 cont.*) see also Barker, 'Praise', in *Cracking OT Codes*, pp. 222–223; Lucas, *Psalms and Wisdom*, pp. 5–6; Westermann, *Praise and Lament*, pp. 85–86, 103–104.

110. Something of that development may be evident in e.g. Pss 4; 16.
111. E.g. Mowinckel, *Psalms in Israel's Worship*, 1:219–220.
112. E.g. Day, *Psalms*, pp. 52–54. Others in this category may include Pss 91; 121; 125; 131.
113. See e.g. ibid., pp. 88–108; Jamie A. Grant, 'The Psalms and the King', in Johnston and Firth, *Interpreting the Psalms*, pp. 101–118; Tucker, 'Psalms 1', in *DOTWPW*, pp. 584–585.
114. E.g. Grant, 'Psalms and the King', in Johnston and Firth, *Interpreting the Psalms*, pp. 111–112.
115. See e.g. Robert Alter, *The Art of Biblical Narrative*, rev. ed. (New York: Basic, 2011); *The World of Biblical Literature* (New York: Basic; London: SPCK, 1992); Robert Alter

where we try to fit things together to make sense of what happens and try to discover meaning and purpose. More widely, sharing a common story gives us identity, and provides a link between us. At a national level we are aware of events in our history, and although we were not directly involved, we recognize that those things have a place in our self-understanding. When the people of Israel celebrated their deliverance from Egypt in the Passover, it was more than a memorial; each generation was to think of themselves as though they were there and had experienced the deliverance first hand. Similarly, when as Christians we celebrate Communion we are not simply remembering a past event: we are invited to participate in it (1 Cor. 10:16). It is part of the shared story that binds us together as God's people. Narrative, then, plays an important role, and that is certainly true when looking at the OT.

Around a third of the OT is narrative. One major narrative section is Genesis – 2 Kings, sometimes described as the 'Primary History'. This was composed over a long period of time; it contains many shorter narratives, and sometimes holds different political and theological views in tension. It is, nevertheless,

---

and Frank Kermode (eds.), *The Literary Guide to the Bible* (London: Fontana, 1989); Yairah Amit, *Reading Biblical Narrative: Literary Criticism and the Hebrew Bible* (Minneapolis: Fortress, 2001); 'Narrative Art of Israel's Historians', in *DOTHB*, pp. 708–715; Shimon Bar-Efrat, *Narrative Art in the Bible*, JSOTSup 70 (Sheffield: JSOT Press, 2000); Adele Berlin, *Poetics and Interpretation of Biblical Narrative* (Sheffield: Almond, 1983; Winona Lake: Eisenbrauns, 1994); W. Brueggemann, *Introduction*, pp. 17–26; J. P. Fokkelmann, *Reading Biblical Narrative: An Introductory Guide* (Louisville: Westminster John Knox; Leiderdorp: Deo, 1999; David M. Gunn, 'Narrative Criticism', in McKenzie and Haynes, *To Each Its Own Meaning* (1999), pp. 201–229; David M. Gunn and Danna Nolan Fewell, *Narrative in the Hebrew Bible*, Oxford Bible Series (Oxford: Oxford University Press, 1993); Tremper Longman III, *Literary Approaches to Biblical Interpretation* (Grand Rapids: Zondervan, 1987); L. D. Hawk, 'Literary/Narrative Criticism', in *DOTP*, pp. 536–544; Walter C. Kaiser Jr., 'Narrative', in Sandy and Giese, *Cracking OT Codes*, pp. 69–88; Peter D. Miscall, *The Workings of Old Testament Narrative*, SemeiaSt (Philadelphia: Fortress; Chico: Scholars Press, 1983); Robin Routledge, 'Guest or Gatecrasher: Questioning Assumptions in a Narrative Approach to the Old Testament', *JEBS* 3.3 (2003), pp. 17–28; Meir Sternberg, *The Poetics of Biblical Narrative: Ideological Literature and the Drama of Reading* (Bloomington: Indiana University Press, 1987); Francois Tolmie, *Narratology and Biblical Narratives: A Practical Guide* (Eugene: Wipf & Stock, 2012); Jerome T. Walsh, *Old Testament Narrative: A Guide to Interpretation* (Louisville: Westminster John Knox, 2010).

presented as a single narrative. Another major section is Chronicles and Ezra-Nehemiah – sometimes referred to as the 'Chronistic History'. The prophetic books also contain narrative: Jonah, for example, is substantially narrative, and Jeremiah includes narrative describing episodes in the life of the prophet. Esther and Daniel 1 – 6 are also narrative.

What is narrative?

In common usage, the terms 'narrative' and 'story' are used interchangeably. In more technical usage there is a subtle distinction. The *story* is, essentially, what happened. And a *narrative* is a particular retelling of that story.[116] Thus story is more abstract than narrative; however, in so far as without the story there would be no narrative and without the narrative there would be no knowledge of the story, the two cannot be separated. The distinction is helpful, though, particularly where the same story may be told in different ways. So, for example, a historical event may be recounted by an objective historian, by a subjective participant and by a tabloid newspaper with a particular agenda. The story will be the same, but the narratives may look very different. And interrogating those differences gives insight into the motives and intentions of those telling the story.

There are several things that distinguish narrative from other genres of text. A narrative involves *characters*, and, even in non-fiction, describes a world in which those characters live, think, feel, speak and interact with each other. Very significant for narrative, too, is the presence of a *narrator*, who tells the story and gives the reader necessary information about the characters and their world. Narrative also has a *plot* – a causally or temporally arranged, connected series of events, which unfold within *time*. Finally, narrative uses wordplay and other literary devices to maintain interest and to communicate the message. Despite its application to prose, this comes under the heading *poetics*. Some of these characteristics are shared with other genres: characters, plot and an internal time frame may be present in a drama; wordplay is also a feature of poetry. But, taken together, these things distinguish narrative from other literary forms.

Because a story can be narrated in a variety of ways, we may assume that the particular way chosen by the narrator has significance. A term associated with

---

116. See e.g. H. Porter Abbott, *The Cambridge Introduction to Narrative* (Cambridge: Cambridge University Press, 2002), p. 16; Gérard Genette, *Narrative Discourse: An Essay on Method* (New York: Cornell University Press, 1980), pp. 27–29; *Narrative Discourse Revisited* (New York: Cornell University Press, 1988), pp. 13–14; Hawk, 'Literary/Narrative Criticism', in *DOTP*, p. 538.

a narrative approach to the text is *close reading*. This is, as the name suggests, an in-depth analysis of the text, which involves analysing its structure: what is said, how it is said, and also what is not said. There may be deliberate gaps in the narrative that need to be filled by the reader. And there may, too, be an element of 'reading between the lines'.

Narrative and historical criticism

As we have seen, historical-critical approaches are diachronic. They assume a process of development, and look for what might have been the 'original' material, and what might have been changed or added.[117] Reading text as narrative does not necessarily rule out diachronic development; it is, though, essentially *synchronic*; that is, its focus is on the final form of the text. And there is an additional assumption: everything in the text has been included for a reason, and therefore we, as readers, may look for significance in all elements of the text.

As an example, Berlin refers to the narrative about Joseph and his brothers in Genesis 37.[118] Scholars often identify two separate sources here, J and E. In J, Joseph is defended by Judah,[119] and sold to the Ishmaelites (vv. 18–20, 25–27, 28b). In E, he is defended by Reuben and sold to the Midianites (vv. 21–24, 28a, 28c–30). It is possible that there were separate stories that circulated independently, and were then combined by an editor into a single account. That process has, though, according to Berlin, 'produced . . . a new work, a work worthy of serious consideration in its present form'.[120] And considering it in its present form will include, for example, looking at the relationship between Reuben and Judah in the narrative.[121]

---

117. See the discussion of historical criticism above, pp. 51–62.

118. Berlin, *Poetics*, pp. 114–121.

119. As already noted, J is thought to originate in the south and so attaches greater significance to Judah.

120. Berlin, *Poetics*, p. 121; see also e.g. Campbell and O'Brien, *Sources of the Pentateuch*, pp. 226–237.

121. Reuben was Jacob's firstborn and heir; however, Judah's tribe became prominent. Here the brothers are placed side by side, and the fact that it is Judah's plan that prevails may indicate his future primacy. There may be similar tension later in the Joseph story. So e.g. Jacob will not send Benjamin to Egypt despite Reuben's promise of protection (Gen. 42:37–38), but responds to a similar promise by Judah (Gen. 43:8–11).

Alter notes the narrative of Judah and Tamar in Genesis 38.[122] This has often been regarded as an interpolation. It appears to interrupt the story of Joseph, while having nothing to do with it. However, viewing the text as narrative, and so starting from the premise that this section has been included for a reason, links to its immediate context become more apparent. A significant point of contact is the occurrence of the Hebrew verb 'to recognize' (*nākar*) (e.g. Gen. 37:32–33; 38:25–26; cf. 42:7–8).[123]

Earlier we also noted that 1 Samuel 16 and 17 appear to contain two distinct introductions to David,[124] and a synchronic approach to the text asks why they have both been included. Alter suggests that they have been put together to reflect complementary aspects of David's rise to power: the first focuses, vertically, on God's anointing and enabling; while the second focuses, horizontally, on David's ability and resourcefulness.[125]

Characters[126]

In most novels we are given a substantial amount of detail about characters: height, build, eye and hair colour, facial features, distinguishing marks, clothes,

---

122. Alter, *Art of Biblical Narrative*, pp. 1–12; see also e.g. Esther Marie Menn, *Judah and Tamar (Genesis 38) in Ancient Jewish Exegesis* (Leiden: Brill, 1997), pp. 73–78.

123. Joseph's brothers took his blood-stained tunic to Jacob and asked him to recognize it (*haker-nā'*) (Gen. 37:32). The same term is used by Tamar when returning tokens given to her by Judah (Gen. 38:25). A kid also plays a part in both deceptions. This was recognized by the rabbis: 'The Holy One Praised be He said to Judah, "You deceived your father with a kid. By your life, Tamar will deceive you with a kid" . . . The Holy One Praised be He said to Judah, "You said to your father, *haker-na*. By your life, Tamar will say to you, *haker-na*"' (*Bereshit Rabbah* 84.11, 12; cf. Alter, *Art of Biblical Narrative*, p. 10); though note also John Barton, 'Intertextuality and the "Final Form" of the Text', in *The Old Testament: Canon, Literature and Theology: Collected Essays* (Aldershot: Ashgate, 2007), pp. 181–184 (182–183). A kid also features in Jacob's deception of Isaac (Gen. 27:16), where the verb *nākar* also appears (Gen. 27:23). See also Amit, *Reading Biblical Narratives*, pp. 143–147. Amit also points out the significance of Judah in the wider Joseph narrative (cf. n. 121, above).

124. Above, p. 58.

125. Robert Alter, *The David Story: A Translation with Commentary of 1 and 2 Samuel* (New York: Norton, 1999), pp. 110–111; *Art of Biblical Narrative*, pp. 147–148.

126. See e.g. Alter, *Art of Biblical Narrative*, pp. 143–162; Amit, *Reading Biblical Narratives*, pp. 69–93; Bar-Efrat, *Narrative Art*, pp. 47–92; Berlin, *Poetics*, pp. 23–42;

and so on. This enables us to build up a mental picture. In biblical narrative, though, even with important characters, the detail is minimal. There may be general descriptions of appearance,[127] or facial expressions,[128] or what a character is wearing.[129] But these are brief, and usually include only what is necessary for the plot.

We may be given information about a character's inner life, including thoughts, feelings and motives. Sometimes this is given directly by the narrator. Sometimes it comes through another character. Sometimes the reader is left to work out a character's motives from his or her words or actions, thus leaving room for different readers to come to different conclusions. The reliability of such characterization varies: the narrator's statements are generally regarded as trustworthy, while inferences drawn, indirectly, from a character's words or conduct are less reliable.[130] Characterization may also take place through comparisons. So David, the adulterer and murderer, may be contrasted with Uriah, the man of duty and integrity (2 Sam. 11:6–15),[131] characteristics that David should be demonstrating. Nabal is contrasted with his virtuous wife, Abigail (1 Sam. 25:2–3). There may be, also, an intended contrast between Abishag, who is described as 'very beautiful' (1 Kgs 1:4), and Bathsheba, who had been described in a similar way

---

Fokkelmann, *Reading Biblical Narrative*, pp. 55–72; Sternberg, *Poetics*, pp. 321–364; Tolmie, *Narratology*, pp. 39–62; Walsh, *OT Narrative*, pp. 33–52.

127. Jacob notes that 'my brother Esau is a hairy man, and I'm a man with smooth skin' (Gen. 27:11), explaining the need for subterfuge; David is 'ruddy and handsome' (1 Sam. 17:42), maybe explaining his popularity among women (cf. 1 Sam. 18:7); Bathsheba is 'very beautiful' (2 Sam. 11:2b), explaining David's lust and subsequent adultery; see also e.g. 1 Sam. 9:2; 2 Sam. 13:1; 1 Kgs 1:4.

128. After her conversation with Eli, Hannah's 'face was no longer downcast' (1 Sam. 1:18b); Amnon looked 'haggard morning after morning' (2 Sam. 13:4b) because of his unrequited love for Tamar; the king of Persia asked Nehemiah, 'Why does your face look so sad . . . ?' (Neh. 2:2).

129. Judah's daughter-in-law, Tamar, changed out of her widow's clothes to deceive Judah (Gen. 38:14); the men of Gibeon wore 'worn and patched sandals on their feet' and 'old clothes' (Josh. 9:5), also to perpetrate a deception; see also e.g. 2 Sam. 13:18–19; 14:2; Esth. 8:15.

130. Alter sets out a scale of reliability with regard to characterization (*Art of Biblical Narrative*, pp. 146–147).

131. So according to Berlin, David was at home, when he should have been at war (cf. 2 Sam. 11:1); Uriah would not go home. David had slept with Uriah's wife; Uriah refused to do the same (*Poetics*, p. 40).

(2 Sam. 11:2),[132] but is now old. It also highlights David's weakness: Bathsheba's beauty had enflamed lustful passion; now that earlier strength and vigour has passed![133]

There are a number of discernible character types. 'Round', or 'fully-fledged', characters are presented as real people, with complex, multidimensional personalities, and displaying a range of characteristics. In contrast, 'flat' characters are one-dimensional, usually displaying only a single characteristic. Thus the men of Gibeah are characterized as 'wicked' (Judg. 19:22); Nabal has the characterization implicit in his name, which means 'fool', confirmed by the additional description 'surly and mean' (1 Sam. 25:3). No further information about their characters is necessary for the plot, and none is given. Some characters are hardly characterized at all; they appear as 'agents' or 'functionaries'. This group may include messengers, whose role is only to bring a report (e.g. Gen. 14:13; Job 1:14–19). It may also include figures that occupy a more central position in the narrative, but still as little more than 'objects'. Berlin suggests that Bathsheba fills that role in 2 Samuel 11 – 12, where she appears as a 'non-person'. The central theme is David's adultery; this 'requires a married woman' and 'Bathsheba fills that function'.[134] The presence of such characters is necessary to move the plot forward, but they have little significance beyond that. In practice, characters may not fit precisely into one of these categories, and it is probably better to think in terms of a continuum between 'agent' and 'fully fledged' characters. And, as we see in the case of Bathsheba, characters may develop, and may be characterized differently in different narratives.

Significant, too, in biblical narrative is the presence of God as a character. And, as with human characters, we can build up a picture of God from what he does, says and thinks. There is, of course, no physical description of God. It might be argued, too, that the statements that allow us to infer other divine characteristics are all too brief, and do not always present a consistent picture. There are passages that point to God as faithful, compassionate, all-knowing, and so on. But there are others that suggest a different aspect. God needs to ask questions (e.g. Gen. 3:11) or make personal investigation (e.g. Gen. 11:5; 18:20–21) to find out what is happening. Sometimes there seems to be a more negative side. In the exodus narrative God gives Pharaoh

---

132. The expressions are not identical – 'beautiful' translates *tôb* and *yāpā* in 2 Sam. 11:2 and 1 Kgs 1:4 respectively – but the sense in each case is the same.

133. See e.g. Bar-Efrat, *Narrative Art*, pp. 49–50; Berlin, *Poetics*, pp. 27–30.

134. Berlin, *Poetics*, p. 27. Berlin also notes the contrast with Bathsheba's characterization in later narratives (pp. 27–30).

an opportunity to repent, but then hardens his heart, so making repentance impossible (Exod. 7:3; 10:20, 27).[135] This might be taken to suggest that God wants to push Egypt to the point of disaster. And in the meantime Israel also suffers. In the same narrative, while the reader knows that the divine intention is to bring the people of Israel out of Egypt and into their own land, God's message to Pharaoh suggests only a temporary leave of absence (Exod. 5:3), at best a half-truth. When David fled Jerusalem, he left ten concubines at the mercy of Absalom, who raped them in full sight of the people (2 Sam. 15:13–17; 16:21–22).[136] This is seen as divine judgment on David because of his adultery with Bathsheba (2 Sam. 12:11). David sinned, but the women suffered.

This raises questions about the character of God, as depicted in the narrative. In the light of what he regards as God's inconsistency Brueggemann concludes he is 'a conundrum of contradictions'.[137] Sternberg notes that the piecemeal portrayal of God across several narratives, and the fact that God is something of a special case when it comes to characterization, does result in anomalies. However, he also notes that, though there may be temporary ambiguity, there is a broad consistency in the overall presentation, with successive narratives serving to fill gaps and correct misunderstandings.[138] Others suggest a separation between God as he is portrayed in the narrative, and God as he is in reality.[139] It seems likely that, in the service of the narrative as a whole, there may be some 'poetic licence' in the depiction of characters. However, whether such licence extends to the portrayal of God is not certain, and there is also the question of where a 'real' picture of God comes from, if not from the text. In the OT in particular, God is known through what he does, and that action is seen, to a large extent, in narratives. That said, it is important to recognize that each narrative has a particular function, and characterization within each narrative (including the characterization of God) is often limited to what is necessary to

135. Gunn and Fewell, *Narrative*, pp. 85–87; see also David J. A. Clines, 'God in the Pentateuch: Reading Against the Grain', in *Interested Parties: The Ideology of Writers and Readers of the Hebrew Bible* (London: Bloomsbury, 1995), pp. 187–211 (195–197).

136. Gunn and Fewell, *Narrative*, pp. 85, 87–88.

137. W. Brueggemann, *OT Theology*, p. 362.

138. Sternberg, *Poetics*, pp. 322–325.

139. E.g. W. Lee Humphries, *The Character of God in the Book of Genesis: A Narrative Appraisal* (Louisville: Westminster John Knox, 2001), esp. pp. 1–6, 237–256; Walsh, *OT Narrative*, pp. 34–35.

serve that function. So, in the account of the exodus, God is characterized as Israel's deliverer, and his actions are linked primarily with that role. It may be that, reading against the grain of the narrative,[140] there is sympathy and concern about the treatment of the Egyptians or, later, the Canaanites, but that is not the purpose of this particular narrative. God's compassion, including for Israel's enemies, is emphasized elsewhere. Similarly, in Absalom's treatment of David's concubines, the emphasis is on divine retribution. For the purpose of the narrative, the concubines are characterized as agents, and Absalom's actions are viewed only in terms of their impact on David. Taken individually the depictions of these various aspects of God's character might be problematic, particularly if more is read into them than the narrative explicitly requires. However, as Sternberg suggests, comparing characteristics seen in a range of narratives, it is possible to build up a more coherent picture,[141] though one that is still not altogether without ambiguity and tension.

The narrator[142]

The narrator speaks directly to readers, and gives information about what is taking place. As noted already, this is one of the key things that distinguish narrative from drama. Within drama, information is conveyed through the dialogue and interaction of the characters. Within narrative we also hear the voice of the narrator. As in drama, there may be some things that we can discern from what the characters say and do. And, conversely, sometimes the narrator gives us less information than we might want, leaving us to make up our own mind about certain things. Nevertheless, the role of the narrator is important if we are to enter the world of the characters. The narrator describes the scene and gives information about the characters, including relevant descriptions, how they feel, what they are thinking and what motivates them. This may also include

140. See Clines, 'God in the Pentateuch', in *Interested Parties*, pp. 187–211.

141. For a critique of Sternberg's approach to the omniscience and reliability of the narrator, see e.g. David M. Gunn, 'Reading Right: Reliable and Omniscient Narrator, Omniscient God, and Foolproof Composition of the Hebrew Bible', in David J. A. Clines, Stephen E. Fowl and Stanley E. Porter (eds.), *The Bible in Three Dimensions: Essays in Celebration of Forty Years of Biblical Studies in the University of Sheffield* (Sheffield: JSOT Press, 1990), pp. 53–63.

142. See e.g. Amit, *Reading Biblical Narratives*, pp. 69–93; Bar-Efrat, *Narrative Art*, pp. 13–45; Berlin, *Poetics*, pp. 43–82; Fokkelmann, *Reading Biblical Narrative*, pp. 55–72; Sternberg, *Poetics*, pp. 84–152; Tolmie, *Narratology*, pp. 13–27; Walsh, *OT Narrative*, pp. 97–106.

opinions about whether a character's motives, or a particular outcome, were good or bad. And, as already noted, the narrator, within the context of the narrative, is regarded as reliable.[143]

Sometimes the narrator is a character within the narrative, in which case his knowledge and movement are limited.[144] More often there are few such restrictions, and the narrator is omniscient and omnipresent. He has access to the thoughts, feelings and motives of other characters, including God (e.g. Gen. 6:6), and listens in on intimate conversations. He is able, too, to move from one place to another at will; so, for example, when describing the conflict between the Israelites and Philistines in 1 Samuel 4:1–11, he can move from the battlefield (v. 2) to the Israelite camp (vv. 3–5) and then to the Philistine camp (vv. 6–9). Usually, the narrator simply tells the story, though sometimes he may reveal his presence, and expressions such as 'in those days' (e.g. Gen. 6:4; Judg. 17:6; 2 Sam. 16:23; 2 Kgs 10:32) and 'to this day' (e.g. Gen. 35:20; Josh. 8:28; Judg. 18:12; 2 Sam. 18:18; 1 Kgs 9:21) indicate his distance in time from the narrative.

Narrator and author

At a simple level, literary communication involves an *author* speaking to a *reader* through the *text*. In most cases, however, we have little or no external information about the author. All we know comes from the text itself. There may be emphases and nuances within the text suggesting that the author was a particular kind of person, from a particular background, with particular interests and a particular intention in writing. We cannot be sure, though, that those inferences are correct. So, instead of embarking on what might be a futile search for the actual author, we focus instead on the 'implied author': '*the author as he or she would be constructed, based on inference from the*

143. See e.g. Amit, *Reading OT Narratives*, pp. 93–102; Alter, *Art of Biblical Narrative*, pp. 146–147; Gunn and Fewell, *Narrative*, p. 53; Sternberg, *Poetics*, p. 51; Tolmie, *Narratology*, p. 21; Walsh, *OT Narrative*, p. 83. However, inconsistences in the wider narration may require limiting the narrator's reliability to a particular narrative; see e.g. Gunn and Fewell, *Narrative*, pp. 54–56; Gunn, 'Reading Right', in Clines, Fowl and Porter, *Bible in Three Dimensions*; see also Walsh, *OT Narrative*, p. 222, n. 4. Some also question the ideology of biblical narratives; the narrator tells the story within a particular cultural and ideological framework, which may include values that are different from those of the reader; see e.g. Clines, *Interested Parties*.

144. So e.g. much of the book of Nehemiah is narrated in the first person, and the narrator knows and sees only what Nehemiah knows and sees.

text'.[145] Corresponding to the implied author is the 'implied reader', the reader, or audience, implied by the text. The implied author then tells the story through the narrator. Corresponding to the narrator is the 'narratee', the one to whom the story is told, and who may or may not be the same as the implied reader. Theoretically the implied author and narrator are distinct, although in biblical narrative, where the narrator is not a character in the story, there appears to be little difference between them.[146]

Narrator and point of view

'Point of view' refers to 'the position or perspective from which a story is told'.[147] The reader does not have a direct view of the events set out in the narrative; he or she sees only what the narrator shows. And the impact of a narrative will be influenced by the way it is presented. Berlin uses the analogy of a film camera.[148] The camera may pull back to reveal a wide scene, or zoom in to focus on one small piece of action; or it may view a scene through the eyes of one of the characters. One way in which the narrator indicates a change in the point of view from which a scene is observed is by use of the word *hinnēh*, often translated 'behold'. After a scene inside Jael's tent, where she kills Sisera by hammering a tent peg through his head, *hinnēh* in Judges 4:22 turns attention to outside the tent, where we see Barak approaching. As Barak enters Jael's tent, a second *hinnēh* indicates that we are now seeing the scene from his point of view.[149] The narrator may also indicate different perceptions of the same event. In the account of the Amalekite attack on David's bases at Ziklag (1 Sam. 30:1–3), from the point of view of an observer, the narrator describes those taken captive as 'the women and all who were in [the city], both young and old' (v. 2); from the point of view of David and his men, however,

145. Longman, *Literary Approaches*, pp. 84–85 (84) (italics his). See also Gordon K. Oeste, *Legitimacy, Illegitimacy and the Right to Rule: Windows on Abimelech's Rise and Demise in Judges 9* (London: T&T Clark, 2011), pp. 5–9; Sternberg, *Poetics*, pp. 58–83; Tolmie, *Narratology*, pp. 5–10; Walsh, *OT Narrative*, pp. 6–9.

146. See e.g. Berlin, *Poetics*, p. 148, n. 24; Oeste, *Legitimacy*, p. 6; Sternberg, *Poetics*, pp. 74–75; cf. Walsh, *OT Narrative*, p. 9. The current discussion will not attempt to distinguish between implied author and narrator.

147. Berlin, *Poetics*, pp. 43–82 (42); see also e.g. Bar-Efrat, *Narrative Art*, pp. 34–41; Fokkelmann, *Reading Biblical Narrative*, pp. 123–155; Longman, *Literary Approaches*, pp. 87–88; Sternberg, *Poetics*, pp. 129–185; Tolmie, *Narratology*, pp. 29–38.

148. Berlin, *Poetics*, pp. 44–45; see also Walsh, *OT Narrative*, p. 44.

149. Berlin, *Poetics*, pp. 62–63; see also Walsh, *OT Narrative*, p. 49.

these are not just women and children: they are 'their wives and sons and daughters' (v. 3).

Reflecting the point of view of characters also allows *dramatic irony*.[150] This is where a character interprets a scene from his or her own limited viewpoint, while the reader knows that the true interpretation is very different. So when David hears Nathan's parable about the rich man and his action in taking the ewe lamb of his poor neighbour (2 Sam. 12:1–6), he is incensed, and pronounces judgment, not knowing (as we do) that he is the man (v. 7)! Dramatic irony is particularly prominent in the book of Esther, often at the expense of its chief protagonist, Haman. For example, when Haman is asked, 'What should be done for the man the king delights to honour' (Esth. 6:6), the reader knows that the king is speaking about rewarding Mordecai, a man Haman hates. Haman, though, thinks the king is referring to him, and so lists the things he would most like to receive. The result is double disappointment: Haman is not honoured and his chosen reward is given to his enemy!

The narrator's omniscience

As noted already, the narrator in biblical narrative is, in most cases, all-seeing and all-knowing. This raises the question of where that information comes from. How does the narrator know these things?

One view is that the stories are the product of imaginative writing. Alter describes biblical narrative as 'historicized prose fiction'.[151] His use of the term 'fiction' is intended to give storytellers room to use their artistry to present their characters as real people, by introducing facets of personality, thoughts, conversations and personal details. However, because these are things that the

---

150. See e.g. Bar-Efrat, *Narrative Art*, pp. 125–129; Berlin, *Poetics*, pp. 51–52; Gunn and Fewell, *Narrative*, pp. 73–74; Carolyn J. Sharp, *Irony and Meaning in the Hebrew Bible* (Bloomington: Indiana University Press, 2009). Irony may also be evident in the subversion of what appear to be straightforward statements. So descriptions of the reigns of David (1 Kgs 15:5) and Solomon (1 Kgs 3:3) appear positive; but are then subverted by the addition of the qualification 'except' (Heb. *raq*).

151. Alter, *Art of Biblical Narrative*, pp. 27–28. Alter follows Schneidau, who uses the term 'historicized fiction' to contrast the historical nature of biblical narratives with the mythological style found in other ancient writings; see Herbert Schneidau, *Sacred Discontent* (Baton Rouge: State University Press, 1976), p. 215. Frei also describes biblical narrative as 'history-like': it has the look and feel of being historical; see Hans Frei, *The Eclipse of Biblical Narrative: A Study in Eighteenth and Nineteenth Century Hermeneutics* (New Haven: Yale University Press, 1974), pp. 10–12.

narrator could not know, they can exist in the narrative only as the result of imaginative reconstruction; consequently, even passages that may appear to have a basis in history are not, strictly speaking, historiography. And narrative approaches to the text commonly view material as ahistorical, with no necessary link between narrative and history.[152]

Sternberg objects to the use of the term 'fiction'. He argues that what distinguishes historiography from fiction is the truth claim of the writer. Biblical narrative claims to be historical, and even when it is not accurate, that makes it only bad historiography, not fiction.[153] Certainly, there are difficulties when comparing characters and events in the narrative with those in the 'real' world, not least because, to a large extent, our only knowledge of these things comes through the text. However, the OT writers recognize history as an important medium of divine revelation, and it would be surprising if they did not take pains to ensure that what they recorded was broadly historical.

That is not to say that ancient history writing should be assumed to be the same as its modern counterpart. In the ancient world, including the world of the OT writers, historiography involved a merging of facts and more imaginative writing.[154] The events were important, but so was the meaning attached to those events. And the description of events might be adjusted to make the meaning clearer. This imaginative element might also give scope for elaboration on conversations and other aspects of characters' inner lives. It cannot, though, account for them completely.

A better explanation seems to be that these things were known through divine inspiration. Sternberg notes that this was the view of the rabbis, who attributed detailed information that the narrator could not have known to the inspiration of the Holy Spirit.[155] Sternberg goes on to argue that even those who may not

---

152. See above, p. 70, n. 17; see also Routledge, 'Guest or Gatecrasher', pp. 24–27.
153. Sternberg, *Poetics*, pp. 23–35. Halpern maintains that authors of historical works in the Bible 'had authentic antiquarian intentions. They meant to furnish fair and accurate representations of Israelite activity' (Baruch Halpern, *The First Historians: The Hebrew Bible and History* [University Park: Pennsylvania State University Press, 1996], p. 3; see also Amit, *Reading OT Narratives*, pp. 94–95).
154. Goldingay notes that 'God's inspiring the biblical historians did not make them write as if they were modern historians' (*Israel's Gospel*, p. 863). See also John Goldingay, *An Introduction to the Old Testament: Exploring Text, Approaches & Issues* (Downers Grove: IVP Academic, 2015), pp. 26–27, 70–71, 78–79, 162–163.
155. Sternberg, *Poetics*, pp. 58–59.

agree with the idea of inspiration must assume it as part of the convention of writing and reading biblical narrative.[156] This, of course, does not decide the matter. Nevertheless, it does provide an explanation of the narrator's privileged access to otherwise hidden information that will appeal to those who adopt a more conservative approach to Scripture. It also allows a more positive view of historiography in the OT.

Plot

A plot is a purposefully organized sequence of linked narrative units.[157] The smallest unit may be an event, where the character is the object, or an action, where the character is the subject. Relationships between the units vary. Sometimes units are linked sequentially: one thing follows another. In some cases there is also a causal connection: a second event or action is the consequence of the first. Sometimes the connection between units becomes clear only as the narrative unfolds.

Following Aristotle, a plot is generally taken to have a beginning, middle and end.[158] Most narratives begin with an *exposition*,[159] which introduces the situation and the characters, and provides other necessary background information. The plot of a narrative is driven by tension or conflict: something needs to be resolved, and the reader turns the page in order to see how it all works out. This conflict is then set out, and builds to a climax, whereupon the conflict begins to move, quite rapidly, towards a resolution, and the restabilization of the situation. This brings the action to an end, though there may also be a further conclusion. This broad structure is represented in Figure 4.1, overleaf.[160]

The beginning and ending of the narrative may be of particular significance. Turner notes that the way a plot is announced plays an important part in alerting

---

156. Ibid., p. 81.

157. See e.g. Amit, *Reading Biblical Narratives*, pp. 46–68; Bar-Efrat, *Narrative Art*, pp. 93–140; Fokkelmann, *Reading Biblical Narrative*, pp. 73–96; Gunn and Fewell, *Narrative*, pp. 148–155; Walsh, *OT Narrative*, pp. 13–22.

158. Aristotle, *Poetics* 7.26–27.

159. E.g. Amit, *Reading OT Narratives*, pp. 33–45; Bar-Efrat, *Narrative Art*, pp. 111–121. Berlin refers to this as the *orientation*, and also includes an *abstract*, which summarizes the story (*Poetics*, p. 102).

160. See e.g. Amit, *Reading OT Narratives*, p. 47; Longman, *Literary Approaches*, pp. 92–94. A very similar 'story mountain' also features in the current teaching of narrative in UK primary schools.

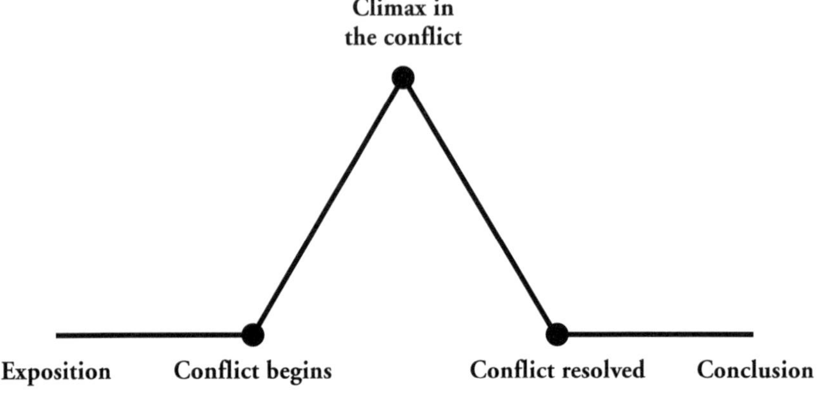

Figure 4.1

the reader to how the plot may develop, and which issues to look out for.[161] The ending may indicate closure, following the resolution of the conflict (e.g. Gen. 4:16); it may show how the narrative fits into a wider setting (e.g. Ruth 4:18–22); or it may prepare the reader for possible further repercussions (e.g. 2 Sam. 13:22).[162]

Within OT narrative there are also subplots. The testing of Abraham (Gen. 22:1–19) is a narrative unit, but it also is part of the larger story that deals with God's relationship with the patriarch (Gen. 11:27 – 25:11). And that may be seen, further, as part of the larger plot that focuses on the Promised Land and the growth of Israel as a nation. The story of Judah and Tamar (Gen. 38), too, is a distinct story, but it may also be seen as part of the larger Joseph narrative.

Poetics

Those responsible for giving biblical narrative its final shape were not only teachers and instructors, but also storytellers, skilful in their use of language and literary devices. So in order get the most out of the narrative we need to be aware of how the narrative is put together. In my view the writers of OT narrative, as well as being inspired by the Spirit, also worked with reliable

161. Lawrence A. Turner, *Announcements of Plot in Genesis*, JSOTSup 96 (Sheffield: Sheffield Academic Press, 1990).

162. For discussion of the significance of the endings of biblical narratives, particularly in the book of Genesis, see e.g. Susan Zeelander, *Closure in Biblical Narrative* (Leiden: Brill, 2012).

traditions, giving credibility to the text as historiography. However, as already suggested, they had some freedom in the way they used those traditions, including the way they ordered and structured the plot, their use of wordplay, their movement between viewpoints, and so on. This area of study assumes that narrative conforms to certain conventions; however, the only way to discover those conventions is by analysing texts and making comparisons between them.[163] This is necessarily subjective, and may lead to different conclusions, and so to different interpretations of the text.

Some of the wordplay is not visible in translation. One example is the play between the descriptions of Adam and Eve as 'naked' (*'ārôm*) (Gen. 2:25) and the serpent as 'crafty' (*'ārûm*) (Gen. 3:1), which provides a link between the two sections of narrative.

Close reading

We have noted that in the description of the appointment of Saul as Israel's first king (1 Sam. 8 – 12) the narrator appears to present positive and negative viewpoints. This probably reflects the reality of the situation. However, a close reading of the text may give some clues as to the narrator's own position.[164] One positive element is the anointing of Saul by Samuel (1 Sam. 9:15 – 10:13). This emphasizes that Saul is Yahweh's choice. However, in that passage Saul is referred to as a *nāgîd* (prince, ruler) and not as king (*melek*). In the context of the narrative that is significant. God is frequently referred to as *melek* (notably in 1 Sam. 8:7), but never as *nāgîd*, suggesting that Saul's role is intended to complement, not usurp, the divine role. When Saul is acknowledged by the people (1 Sam. 10:17–25), they proclaim him *melek*, but Samuel appears to avoid the term.[165] He does join the people in affirming Saul's kingship later (1 Sam. 11:14), though only after Saul has acknowledged his dependence on Yahweh (v. 13). And when he refers to Saul as *melek* in 1 Samuel 12 it is, again, to emphasize his proper place in relation to Yahweh (vv. 13–14). This suggests that the real issue is not the appointment of a king per se, but what kind of king, and in particular the relationship between the human king and Israel's divine king.

---

163. See e.g. Berlin, *Poetics*, p. 15.

164. See Lyle M. Eslinger, *The Kingship of God in Crisis: A Close Reading of 1 Samuel 1–12* (Sheffield: Almond, 1985); 'Viewpoints'.

165. He refers to *melek* in v. 19; but this is repeating the request of the people, and is understood negatively; see e.g. J. G. McConville, *God and the Earthly Power: An Old Testament Political Theology* (London: T&T Clark, 2006), pp. 137–138.

Repetition

An important poetic device in biblical narrative is *repetition.*[166] Narrative is, in general, concise, and includes only information necessary to progress the plot. However, there are several occasions where material is repeated: sometimes word for word; sometimes with subtle variations. The assumption that everything in the text is there for a reason prompts a closer look at text that may appear to be superfluous.

Repetition may serve a variety of purposes. It may provide an inclusio.[167] The repetition of a key word (Ger. *Leitwort*) may indicate a particular emphasis running through narratives and so have an impact on the way those narratives are understood.[168] We have noted the repetition of 'recognize' in the Joseph story. Bar-Efrat points out the repetition of the expression 'go forth' (*lek-lĕkā*) at Abraham's call (Gen. 12:1) and again when he is told to offer Isaac as a sacrifice (Gen. 22:2).[169] This is a rare expression, and its repetition appears to be significant, indicating two important movements in the narrative.[170]

Repetition may also indicate a change in point of view. So when Tamar visits Amnon, it is noted that he is 'lying down' (2 Sam. 13:8). The reader is already

---

166. See e.g. Alter, *Art of Biblical Narrative*, pp. 111–142; Bar-Efrat, *Narrative Art*, pp. 211–216; Berlin, *Poetics*, pp. 73–78; Fokkelmann, *Reading Biblical Narrative*, pp. 112–122; Gunn and Fewell, *Narrative*, pp. 148–155; Longman, *Literary Approaches*, pp. 95–96; Walsh, *OT Narrative*, pp. 81–96.
167. See above, p. 151.
168. The term *Leitwort* was coined by Buber; see Martin Buber, '*Leitwort* Style in Pentateuchal Narrative', in Martin Buber and Franz Rosenzweig (eds.), *Scripture and Translation* (Bloomington: Indiana University Press, 1994), pp. 114–128. See also e.g. Alter, *Art of Biblical Narrative*, pp. 116–122; Yairah Amit, 'The Multi-Purpose "Leading Word" and the Problems of Its Usage', *Proof* 9.2 (1989), pp. 99–114; Bar-Efrat, *Narrative Art*, pp. 212–214; Ronald Hendel, '*Leitwort* Style and Literary Structure in the J Primeval Narrative', in Shawna Dolansky (ed.), *Sacred History Sacred Literature: Essays on Ancient Israel, the Bible, and Religion in Honor of E. E. Freedman on His Sixtieth Birthday* (Winona Lake: Eisenbrauns, 2008), pp. 93–109; Longman, *Literary Approaches*, p. 96; Walsh, *OT Narrative*, p. 91.
169. Bar-Efrat, *Narrative Art*, pp. 212–213.
170. Both are associated with the promise of blessing for the nations (Gen. 12:3; 22:18), in the first, through Abraham, in the second, through his offspring. This suggests that Abraham's willingness to sacrifice his son opened the way for that son to become the channel for God's blessing to the world.

aware of that (2 Sam. 13:6); the repetition indicates that we are now viewing the scene from Tamar's perspective.

Repetition may also suggest links between characters. We have seen that already in relation to Bathsheba and Abishag. In Genesis 14:19 Melchizedek invokes 'God Most High, Creator of heaven and earth', and in verse 22 Abraham uses the same expression when addressing the king of Sodom. This suggests a deliberate indication that Melchizedek serves the same God as Abraham.[171]

Verbatim repetition may indicate obedience. In Genesis 6:18b God instructs Noah, 'you will enter the ark – you and your sons and your wife and your sons' wives with you'. The repetition in Genesis 7:7 – 'Noah and his sons and his wife and his sons' wives entered the ark' – indicates that Noah carried out God's instructions precisely.

If a character repeats something that the narrator has already stated, it may indicate the truthfulness of the character's perception. So, for example, Sarah's complaint to Abraham about Hagar's despising her because she is pregnant (Gen. 16:5) echoes the statement by the narrator in the previous verse. This confirms Sarah's judgment and gives some justification to her subsequent treatment of Hagar.[172]

Of particular interest is where a section of text is repeated, but with some changes. In Eve's response to the serpent (Gen. 3:2–3), she elaborates on God's original command (2:16–17) by adding the prohibition 'and you must not touch it'. This emphasizes the negative aspect of the command and suggests that Eve was already feeling dissatisfied, and thus was more open to the serpent's temptation. Some variation occurs because different people see the same thing in different ways. We have seen that in the case of those taken captive from Ziklag. When the people go to Samuel to ask for 'a king to lead us, such as all the other nations have', they preface their request with the observation 'You are old, and your sons do not walk in your ways' (1 Sam. 8:5), a concern endorsed by the narrator in the previous verses. In the subsequent narrative Samuel focuses only on the request for a king, and seems oblivious to the criticism of his sons. He also overlooks what appears to be a key phrase in the passage, 'such as all the other nations have'.[173] This suggests that his sense of personal rejection has blurred his perspective.

---

171. This identification could be seen as necessary since Melchizedek seems to be a Canaanite king, and the epithet 'God Most High' may apply to the Canaanite high god El.

172. Sternberg, *Poetics*, p. 389.

173. Ibid., p. 421.

There is also deliberate variation, both in the way the narrator describes characters and in the way characters relate events. The description of the way Cain and Abel offer sacrifices is similar (Gen. 4:3–5). However, by the subtle variation of language the narrator gives us a clue as to why Abel's offering is accepted and Cain's is rejected. Cain brought 'some of the fruits of the soil' (v. 3), whereas Abel brought 'fat portions from some of the firstborn of his flock' (v. 4). Abel brought the best of the best; Cain appears to have taken much less care.[174]

In the narrative of Samson and Delilah (Judg. 16:4–22) there are four occasions where Delilah, in the hope of being rewarded by the Philistines, asks him to reveal the secret of his strength (vv. 6–9, 10–12, 13–14, 15–20). The first two follow the same pattern: Delilah asks, and Samson lies; Delilah then does exactly what Samson has told her was necessary to remove his strength; men are hidden in the room; Delilah cries out, 'the Philistines are upon you', and Samson breaks free. The third is similar, though on this occasion there is no mention of men hidden in the room, maybe suggesting that the Philistines have lost interest. Significantly, Samson here mentions his hair. Is he is running out of excuses? Or is he overconfident, and pushes the boundaries of what is wise because he feels he has nothing to fear? In this account we also have mention of Samson sleeping (v. 14). We assume he also fell asleep on the previous occasions, but the narrator mentions it only here. Is this intended to suggest that Samson is lowering his guard? And, while he does break free from his bonds, it is not as decisive as in the other accounts. On the fourth occasion Delilah succeeds in wearing Samson down, and he tells her the truth. Here again we see Samson falling asleep, and Delilah has his hair cut off. Then again she shouts, 'the Philistines are upon you'. An important difference, though, is a glimpse of Samson's inner life: 'He . . . thought, "I'll go out as before and shake myself free"' (v. 20). This seems to indicate that, despite having revealed his secret to Delilah, he is not aware that his strength has gone. On each of the other occasions Delilah has followed his instructions to the letter; the repetition in the previous sections emphasizes her meticulous attention to detail. And it seems reasonable to suppose that Samson would have expected the same thing to happen again. And yet he also expected to be able to shake himself free. It seems possible that after performing feats of strength for so long, Samson had begun to take his great strength for granted. If so, a key theological emphasis in the narrative might be that the leaders of God's people must depend on him for their power (cf. v. 20).

---

174. See e.g. Bruce K. Waltke, 'Cain and His Offering', *WTJ* 48 (1986), pp. 363–372.

In Genesis 35:1 God commands Jacob, 'Go up to Bethel . . . build an altar there to God, who appeared to you when you were fleeing from your brother Esau'. When Jacob speaks to his household, he omits fleeing from Esau and refers instead to 'the day of my distress' (v. 3b).[175] Is he, thereby, trying to avoid a difficult and possibly embarrassing subject?

Another example of deliberate variation by a character is seen in the reports, given by Potiphar's wife,[176] of the alleged attempted rape by Joseph (Gen. 39:6b–18). The narrative includes three accounts: one by the narrator (vv. 7–12), and then two by Potiphar's wife: one to the servants (vv. 14–15), and one to Potiphar (vv. 17–18). Given the circumstances, we expect these last two accounts to differ from the account of the narrator, but they also differ from each other. Too much variation would arouse Potiphar's suspicion, but there are some differences. When speaking to the servants, Potiphar's wife refers to Joseph as a 'Hebrew', focusing on him as an outsider. She does not refer to him as a 'slave', because she wants to align herself with the servants against Joseph. And as part of that she claims that Joseph has been brought into the house to 'make sport of us'. The term *ṣāḥaq* may have sexual connotations, but it can also refer to insults more generally, and in her account to the servants Potiphar's wife seems to be implying that this latest action is one of many insults that have been endured by the whole household. She also implies that Potiphar, the one who brought Joseph into the house, shares the blame. That creates distance between the servants and Potiphar, maybe to ensure that any report the servants give is favourable to Potiphar's wife. In her report to Potiphar Joseph is now the 'Hebrew slave', one who has usurped his position. And the sexual nature of 'to make sport' is likely to be much more in view, and it is directed against Potiphar's wife, 'make sport of *me*'. Potiphar is again blamed for bringing Joseph on to the scene, but this time, probably to create a sense of guilt in order to manipulate him.

Gaps and ambiguity[177]

Narratives, of necessity, contain gaps; the narrator cannot include every detail. Some of those details may be of interest, but they are not directly relevant to the plot and their omission does not influence the narrative. In other cases, important information appears to have been omitted, and it is necessary for the

175. Sternberg, *Poetics*, p. 420.

176. For a more detailed narrative analysis, see e.g. Alter, *Art of Biblical Narrative*, pp. 134–139; Sternberg, *Poetics*, pp. 423–427.

177. See e.g. David G. Firth, 'Ambiguity', in Firth and Grant, *Words and the Word*, pp. 151–186; Sternberg, *Poetics*, pp. 186–320; Walsh, *OT Narrative*, pp. 65–80.

reader to fill in the gaps. In 1 Kings 1:13 Nathan tells Bathsheba to remind David of his promise that her son, Solomon, will succeed him. However, there is no record of that conversation, and the reader is left to ask if David actually made the promise, or were Nathan and Bathsheba taking advantage of the ageing king (1 Kgs 1:1)?[178] The reader must decide which direction the narrative takes.

Near the beginning of David's career, when he is about to confront Goliath (1 Sam. 17:20–40), the narrator's reticence allows ambiguity in the characterization of David. On the one hand, we see a naive young shepherd, going to fight Goliath because of his defiance of God; on the other, we see an ambitious young man who seems very much interested in 'What will be done for the man who kills this Philistine . . .' (1 Sam. 17:26).[179] The text appears to allow both possibilities; consequently, the view of David may vary from one reader to another.

Prophecy[180]

The role of the prophet

The principal role of the OT prophet appears to have been that of a mediator bringing direct communication from God to the people. Exodus 7:1–2 describes

178. See e.g. Alter, *Art of Biblical Narrative*, pp. 123–126; Walsh, *OT Narrative*, pp. 66–67.

179. See e.g. Miscall, *Workings of OT Narrative*, p. 1.

180. See e.g. B. W. Anderson, *Living World*, pp. 247–253; Arnold, *Introduction*, pp. 307–354; David E. Aune, *Prophecy in Early Christianity and the Ancient Mediterranean World* (Grand Rapids: Eerdmans, 1983); David W. Baker, 'Israelite Prophets and Prophecy', in Baker and Arnold, *Face of OT Studies*, pp. 266–294; Joseph Blenkinsopp, *A History of Prophecy in Israel*, rev. and enlarged ed. (Louisville: Westminster John Knox, 1996); C. Hassell Bullock, *An Introduction to the Old Testament Prophetic Books*, updated ed. (Chicago: Moody, 2007), pp. 13–44; Collins, *Introduction*, pp. 305–447; LaSor, Hubbard and Bush, *OT Survey*, pp. 221–230; Hill and Walton, *Survey*, pp. 502–517; Johannes Lindblom, *Prophecy in Ancient Israel* (Oxford: Blackwell, 1962); Jack R. Lundbom, *The Hebrew Prophets: An Introduction* (Minneapolis: Fortress, 2010); James Luther Mays and Paul J. Achtemeier (eds.), *Interpreting the Prophets* (Philadelphia: Fortress, 1987); David L. Petersen, *The Roles of Israel's Prophets*, JSOTSup 17 (Sheffield: JSOT Press, 1981); Paul L. Redditt, *Introduction to the Prophets* (Grand Rapids: Eerdmans, 2008), pp. 1–18; Rogerson and Davies, *OT World*, pp. 166–173; Routledge, *OT Theology*, pp. 209–215; Willem A. VanGemeren, *Interpreting the Prophetic Word: An Introduction to the Prophetic Literature of the Old Testament* (Grand Rapids: Zondervan, 1990); Pieter A. Verhoef, 'Prophecy', *NIDOTTE* 4:1067–1079; Robert R. Wilson, *Prophecy and Society in Ancient Israel* (Philadelphia: Fortress, 1980).

the prophetic office: 'the LORD said to Moses, "See, I have made you like God to Pharaoh, and your brother Aaron will be your prophet. You are to say everything I command you, and your brother Aaron is to tell Pharaoh to let the Israelites go out of his country"' (see also Exod. 4:16). Prophets received messages from God and proclaimed them to their intended recipients.

The usual Hebrew word for 'prophet' in the OT is *nābî'*. This is probably linked with the Akkadian verb 'to call', and it points to someone who is called by God or, possibly, one who calls to others on God's behalf.[181] The prophet's call was important: it validated his ministry and gave authority to his message (e.g. Isa. 6:8–9; Jer. 1:4–10; Amos 7:14–15; Jon. 1:1–2). Two further Hebrew words, *rō'eh* and *ḥōzeh*, come from verbs meaning 'to see' and are often translated 'seer'. Through divine revelation prophets could see what others could not. This might include glimpses of the future or spiritual truths. It might also be very practical: Saul went to Samuel for help to find his father's lost donkeys (1 Sam. 9:3–10, 20). Hebrew words translated 'visions' come from the same roots. 'Seer' seems to be an older term (1 Sam. 9:9), and at some time in Israel's history there might have been a difference between a 'seer' and a 'prophet', though there is no clear distinction in the OT.[182] Samuel is described as both a 'seer' (1 Sam. 9:19) and a 'prophet' (1 Sam. 3:20). Other titles used to describe OT prophets include 'man of God' (e.g. 1 Sam. 9:6–10; 1 Kgs 17:24; 20:28; 2 Kgs 1:9–13; 13:19) and 'inspired man', literally, 'man of the Spirit' (Hos. 9:7).

Several scholars suggest a difference between the earlier prophets in Israel, and the later 'classical' or 'writing' prophets,[183] from the eighth century BC

181. See e.g. H.-P. Müller, '*nābî'*', in *TDOT* 9:129–150 (130–135); Verhoef, 'Prophecy', in *NIDOTTE* 4:1067–1068; see also Eugene H. Merrill, 'Name Terms of the Old Testament Prophet of God', *JETS* 14.4 (1971), pp. 239–248. For a brief overview of the terms for 'prophet' in the OT, see Goldingay, *Introduction*, pp. 190–191.

182. In Isa. 30:10 *rō'eh* and *ḥōzeh* are parallel; and *nābî'* parallels *ḥōzeh* in Isa. 29:10. While there is no evident distinction in the OT, Samuel is consistently referred to as a *rō'eh*, and Gad as a *ḥōzeh* (e.g. 2 Sam. 24:11), and all three terms are used in 1 Chr. 29:29. This may suggest possible nuances of meaning, but it is unclear what they were. Some suggest that *nābî'* is mainly a northern term, while *ḥōzeh* is southern (Petersen, *Roles*, pp. 56–58; R. R. Wilson, *Prophecy and Society*, pp. 136–138, 254–256); this may account for the different terms used by Amaziah and Amos (Amos 7:12, 14).

183. This 'classical' period began with Amos and Hosea, and includes those whose books appear in the 'latter prophets'.

onwards.[184] In the earlier period prophets were involved in national affairs. Moses, the prophet par excellence (Num. 12:6–8; Deut. 18:15, 18; 34:10), led the nation, as did Samuel. During the period of the monarchy, a key prophetic role appears to have been to guide and counsel kings (e.g. 1 Kgs 22:6–7; 2 Kgs 3:11), and, where necessary, provide a corrective to the abuse of royal power. So Samuel challenged Saul (e.g. 1 Sam. 13:13), Nathan rebuked David (2 Sam. 12:1–14) and Elijah confronted Ahab and Jezebel (e.g. 1 Kgs 18:16–18; 21:20–24). From the eighth century BC onwards we still see some prophets, such as Isaiah and Jeremiah, advising kings; however, the prophetic ministry seems to be directed more towards the people and society as a whole. This might have been because of the worsening crisis facing Israel and Judah. Faced with impending judgment, a key prophetic task was to warn the people and call them to repentance. In that context the prophets were preachers, proclaiming God's Word to whoever would listen. This democratization of the prophetic message appears to have coincided with the increase in writing and the availability of written material. Some messages were intended to be delivered in writing (Isa. 8:1, 16; 30:8; Jer. 29:1; 36:1–10; Hab. 2:2); others that were initially proclaimed orally might also have been written down and arranged in collections.

Prophetic inspiration is linked with the activity of God's Spirit.[185] It has been suggested that the OT prophet received this inspiration and prophesied while in an ecstatic, uncontrolled or trance-like state;[186] and we see something of that with Saul (1 Sam. 19:23–24). However, while not uncommon elsewhere in the ANE (e.g. 1 Kgs 18:26–29),[187] and possibly more evident among earlier prophets

184. E.g. Arnold, *Introduction*, p. 319; Hill and Walton, *Survey*, pp. 504–507; LaSor, Hubbard and Bush, *OT Survey*, pp. 226–227; see also Robert R. Wilson, 'Early Israelite Prophecy', in Mays and Achtemeier, *Interpreting the Prophets*, pp. 1–13; Hans Walter Wolff, 'Prophecy from the Eighth Through the Fifth Century', in Mays and Achtemeier, *Interpreting the Prophets*, pp. 14–26.

185. E.g. Num. 11:25–29; 24:2–3; 1 Sam. 10:6, 10; 19:20, 23; 2 Sam. 23:2; Neh. 9:30; Isa. 48:16; Ezek. 2:2; 3:24; Zech. 7:12.

186. Lindblom argues that 'ecstasy', defined as a state where 'the normal current of thoughts and perceptions is broken off and the senses temporarily cease to function in a normal way' (*Prophecy*, pp. 105–108 [106]), was characteristic, too, of the classical prophets. See also e.g. Collins, *Introduction*, pp. 299–301; James D. Newsome, *The Hebrew Prophets* (Louisville: Westminster John Knox, 1984), pp. 1–11 (11).

187. Balaam may have been in a trance-like state (Num. 24:2–9), and his oracles were clearly at variance with what he intended to say. Collins notes that references to

in the OT, it seems rare among the classical prophets.[188] It may be that false prophets in Israel exhibited such behaviour to prove that they were inspired by God's Spirit.[189] In general, though, OT prophets appear to have been fully in control as they proclaimed their message. Their behaviour was sometimes very strange, and included prophetic symbolism, or sign acts;[190] and this, together with the frequently unacceptable content of their message, resulted in their sometimes being labelled 'mad' (Hos. 9:7; cf. 2 Kgs 9:11; Jer. 29:26); nevertheless, even then the classical prophets generally appear to have been in control of their actions and thought processes. Even where inspiration was through dreams and visions, which might suggest an ecstatic state, the message itself was often proclaimed later, after rational reflection.[191]

The precise means by which prophetic messages were received is not always clear. Sometimes 'the word of the Lord came to' the prophet.[192] On other occasions there is reference to the 'hand' of the Lord.[193] Prophets also received

---

prophets in texts from Mari and Assyrian archives includes 'ecstatics' (*Introduction*, pp. 300–301); see also Baker, 'Israelite Prophets', in Baker and Arnold, *Face of OT Studies*, pp. 271–275.

188. See e.g. LaSor, Hubbard and Bush, *OT Survey*, pp. 222–223.

189. See e.g. Daniel I. Block, 'The View from the Top: The Holy Spirit in the Prophets', in Firth and Wegner, *Presence*, pp. 175–207 (184). It has been suggested that this was one reason why some prophets, including Amos and Jeremiah, do not emphasize the role of the Spirit in prophetic inspiration; cf. James Robson, *Word and Spirit in Ezekiel*, LBS (London: T&T Clark International, 2006), pp. 100–103. Robson also refers to 'ecstasy', though does not appear to suggest the same lack of control as Lindblom's definition (p. 113). He emphasizes, though, that the presence of ecstatic or strange behaviour was not a determining factor for whether a prophet was considered true or false (p. 149).

190. E.g. Isa. 20:1–6; Jer. 13:1–11; 19:10–13; 27:1–7; Ezek. 4; 5:1–4; 12:1–17.

191. Ezekiel receives visions in the presence of others, but relays the content of those visions afterwards, not while in a visionary state (Ezek. 8:1; cf. 11:25). In a similar context (20:1) the word may be spoken directly to the assembled elders, but this is not in the form of a vision and is not necessarily delivered in a state of ecstasy.

192. E.g. 1 Sam. 15:10; 2 Sam. 7:4; 1 Kgs 16:1; 17:2, 8; 18:1; 19:9; 2 Kgs 20:4; Isa. 38:4; Jer. 1:2, 4, 11, 13; 2:1; 7:1; Ezek. 1:3; 3:16; 6:1; 7:1; Hos. 1:1; Joel 1:1; Jon. 1:1; Mic. 1:1; Hag. 2:10; Zech. 1:1.

193. E.g. Isa. 8:11; Jer. 15:17; Ezek. 1:3; 3:22; 8:1; 40:1. There is a close link in Ezekiel's prophecy between the 'hand of the Lord' and the Spirit (e.g. Ezek. 3:14; 37:1).

the divine word through dreams and visions (e.g. Num. 12:6).[194] In 1 Samuel 3:1 the absence of visions is linked with the absence of the prophetic voice (see also Lam. 2:9). Samuel (1 Sam. 3:15), Ezekiel (e.g. Ezek. 1:1; 8:3–4; 11:24; 40:2; 43:3), Daniel (e.g. Dan. 2:19; 7:1–2; 8:1; 10:1) and Zechariah (Zech. 1:8) received revelation in visions, and the books of Isaiah (2 Chr. 32:32; Isa. 1:1; 29:11), Obadiah (Obad. 1), Micah (Mic. 1:1) and Nahum (Nah. 1:1) are described as 'visions'. Dreams and visions are also linked with the more widespread prophecy which will accompany the pouring out of the Spirit described in Joel 2:28. Jeremiah claims to have been marked out as a true prophet by his access to the 'council of the LORD' (Jer. 23:18, 22). Several OT passages refer to this divine assembly,[195] where God presides over other heavenly beings (e.g. Job 1:6; 2:1; Ps. 82), and makes his will known. We see something similar in 1 Kings 22:19–23. Unlike the false prophets, Micaiah was given a vision of God sitting on his throne, surrounded by the heavenly host. He heard what was said and so was able to speak a true word from God.

There is also the question of the extent to which a prophet declared the exact words received from God. While that may have happened sometimes, it was probably more usual to interpret the message received, and present it using whatever rhetorical techniques would allow it to make most impact.

The message of the classical prophets[196]

A main theme of the prophetic literature is that the people have broken faith with God and failed to live up to the obligations of their covenant relationship with him. Their religious life has become syncretistic. They have continued

---

194. This distinguishes Moses, who spoke to God face to face, from other prophets, for whom the usual means of revelation was through dreams and visions.

195. See e.g. F. M. Cross, 'The Council of Yahweh in Second Isaiah', *JNES* 12 (1953), pp. 274–277; M. S. Heiser, 'Divine Council', in *DOTPr*, pp. 162–166; 'Divine Council', in *DOTWPW*, pp. 112–116; Min Suc Kee, 'The Heavenly Council and Its Type-Scene', *JSOT* 31.3 (2007), pp. 259–273; Patrick D. Miller, 'Cosmology and World Order in the Old Testament: The Divine Council as a Cosmic-Political Symbol', in *Israelite Religion and Biblical Theology: Collected Essays* (Sheffield: Sheffield Academic Press, 2000), pp. 422–444; Routledge, 'Evil Spirit', pp. 12–16; *OT Theology*, pp. 120–122; Walton, *ANE Thought*, pp. 92–97; Ellen White, *Yahweh's Council* (Tübingen: Mohr Siebeck, 2014).

196. See e.g. Donald E. Gowan, *Theology of the Prophetic Books: The Death and Resurrection of Israel* (Louisville: Westminster John Knox, 1998); Routledge, *OT Theology*, pp. 263–272.

with the official worship of Yahweh, but have added other things from the false religions around them. Practices condemned by the prophets include cult prostitution (e.g. Amos 2:7; Mic. 1:7) and the worship of other gods, such as Baal (Jer. 7:9; Hos. 2:13; 11:2; Zeph. 1:4), Molech (Isa. 57:9; Jer. 32:35; Zeph. 1:5) and Tammuz (Ezek. 8:14). References to Asherah poles (e.g. Isa. 17:8; Jer. 17:2; Mic. 5:14) and sacred trees (Isa. 1:29; Ezek. 6:13; Hos. 4:13) also reflect foreign religious customs. The prophets challenged, too, the mechanistic performance of ritual (e.g. Isa. 29:13; Jer. 12:2) that was not reflected in the way they lived their lives (e.g. Isa. 1:11–17; Jer. 6:19–20; Hos. 6:4–6; Amos 5:21–24). Micah summarizes the call for right living rather than insincere offerings:

> He has showed you, O man, what is good.
> And what does the LORD require of you?
> To act justly, and to love mercy
> and to walk humbly with your God.
> (Mic. 6:8; cf. vv. 6–7)

The prophets also challenge other religious leaders. Priests and prophets failed to lead the people in the ways of God. They were greedy for gain (Jer. 6:13; see also Isa. 56:11; Mic. 3:11), befuddled with wine (Isa. 28:7), godless (Jer. 23:11), idolatrous (Jer. 2:27–28) and faithless (Zeph. 3:4). They were called to be shepherds of God's people, but instead looked after their own interests (Isa. 56:11; Ezek. 34:2–6; cf. Jer. 10:21; 23:1; Zech. 10:2–3). With such corruption among the religious leaders it was not surprising that the religion of the nation as a whole was corrupt.

As part of their covenant relationship with God, the people were expected to behave in a right way towards one another. That included looking after weaker members of society, such as the poor, widows and orphans. However, with widespread corruption, that was not happening. Therefore the prophets often call for justice in society. They condemn oppression and exploitation of the poor and needy (e.g. Isa. 3:14–15; 10:2; Jer. 7:5–6; Amos 2:7; 4:1; 5:11), dishonest business practices (e.g. Hos. 12:7; Amos 8:5; Mic. 6:11), the failure of leaders to administer true justice (e.g. Isa. 1:23; 5:23; Jer. 5:27–28; Amos 5:12; Mic. 3:11; 7:3), the self-indulgence of the rich (Amos 6:4–6) and general drunkenness (e.g. Isa. 5:11; 28:1; Joel 1:5; Hab. 2:15). And they proclaim God's impending judgment, in the form of exile from the land.[197]

---

197. E.g. Isa. 5:13; 28:14–19; Jer. 4; 6; 22; Ezek. 4 – 7; 21; 39:21–24; Hos. 7 – 10; Amos 3:2; 5:2; 6:7; 8:2.

Another problem was complacency. The people had convinced themselves that, as God's elect, their future was secure. Amos reminds them that they, too, are sinful (9:8), and despite their special calling, and maybe even because of it, they, too, will be judged (3:2). The hoped for Day of the Lord, when God was expected to judge the non-Israelite nations and exalt his people,[198] would bring darkness and defeat to both alike (e.g. Joel 1:15; 2:1–2; Amos 5:18, 20; Zeph. 1:14–18).

Alongside the clear threat of judgment there is also a message of hope.[199] Out of the fire of exile will emerge a purified people, who will return to their land and be what God intended them to be. This hope includes both political restoration and spiritual renewal. Isaiah views the return from exile as a second exodus (e.g. Isa. 43:16–21; 48:20–21),[200] marking a new beginning. God will establish his kingdom of righteousness and peace (Isa. 11:6–9; 65:20–25), under a Davidic Messiah (Isa. 9:6–7; 11:1–5).[201] And God's redeemed and renewed people will reflect his glory to the rest of the world (Isa. 60:1–3). Jeremiah describes the new covenant that God will establish with his people (31:31–34).[202] The former covenant relationship failed because of the people's disobedience. But God remains committed to them and promises a new, everlasting covenant (see also Isa. 55:3; 61:8; Ezek. 16:60; 37:26). An important aspect of this new covenant is that God's laws will be written on the hearts of his people (Jer. 31:33; see also 24:7; 32:38–41). This suggests that not only will they know what to do, but they will also be transformed in such a way that they will also be enabled to do it. Ezekiel, too, talks about the promise of a new heart and with

---

198. See e.g. J. D. Barker, 'Day of the Lord', in *DOTPr*, pp. 132–143; Paul R. House, 'The Day of the Lord', in Hafemann and House, *Central Themes*, pp. 179–224; Routledge, *OT Theology*, pp. 274–275.

199. It has been claimed that the message of pre-exilic prophets such as Amos, Hosea, Isa. 1 – 39 and Micah was, primarily, of judgment, and that more hopeful sections (e.g. Hos. 14:4–9; Amos 9:11–15; Mic. 4 – 5) are editorial; see e.g. R. E. Clements, *Old Testament Theology: A Fresh Approach* (London: Marshall, Morgan & Scott, 1978), pp. 130–149; 'Patterns in the Prophetic Canon', in *Old Testament Prophecy: From Oracles to Canon* (Louisville: Westminster John Knox, 1996), pp. 191–202; Collins, *Introduction*, pp. 313, 341; however, see also H. G. M. Williamson, 'Hope Under Judgement: The Prophets of the Eighth Century BCE', *EvQ* 72.4 (2000), pp. 291–306.

200. See below, p. 287, n. 35.

201. See below, p. 290, n. 52.

202. For further discussion, see e.g. Routledge, *OT Theology*, pp. 269–272 (and bibliography); see also T. Rata, 'Covenant', in *DOTPr*, pp. 99–105 (103–104).

it a new desire and ability to obey God's laws, a transformation that will be brought about by God's Spirit (Ezek. 36:26–27).[203]

Different forms of prophecy[204]

Several formulae appear in connection with the delivery of prophetic speech.[205] By far the most frequent is the statement 'thus says the LORD',[206] often referred to as the 'messenger formula'. Serving a similar function, though stronger, is the 'oath formula' 'the Lord . . . has sworn' (Isa. 14:24; 62:8; Jer. 51:14; Amos 4:2; 6:8; 8:7). Other expressions, which may or may not be combined with these formulae include 'go and say to' or 'you shall say',[207] and 'hear the word of the LORD'.[208] The prophetic announcement may also simply be described as an 'oracle'.[209]

---

203. See further e.g. Robin Routledge, 'The Spirit and the Future in the Old Testament: Restoration and Renewal', in Firth and Wegner, *Presence*, pp. 346–367.
204. Bill T. Arnold, 'Forms of Prophetic Speech in the Old Testament: A Summary of Claus Westermann's Contributions', *ATJ* 27 (1995), pp. 3–40; Aune, *Prophecy*, pp. 92–101; Trent C. Butler, 'Announcements of Judgment', in Sandy and Giese, *Cracking OT Codes*, pp. 157–176; Katheryn Pfisterer Darr, 'Literary Perspectives on Prophetic Literature', in James Luther Mays, David L. Petersen and Kent Harold Richards (eds.), *Old Testament Interpretation Past, Present, and Future: Essays in Honour of Gene M. Tucker* (Nashville: Abingdon, 1995), pp. 127–146; Osborne, *Hermeneutical Spiral*, pp. 258–274; Antoon Schoors, *The Kingdoms of Israel and Judah in the Eighth and Seventh Centuries B.C.E.* (Atlanta: Society of Biblical Literature, 2013), pp. 121–132; Marvin A. Sweeney, 'Formation and Form in Prophetic Literature', in Mays, Petersen and Richards, *OT Interpretation*, pp. 113–126; Willem A. VanGemeren, 'Oracles of Salvation', in Sandy and Giese, *Cracking OT Codes*, pp. 139–155; Claus Westermann, *Prophetic Oracles of Salvation in the Old Testament* (Louisville: Westminster John Knox, 1991); *Basic Forms of Prophetic Speech* (Cambridge: Lutterworth; Louisville: Westminster John Knox, 1991).
205. See Aune, *Prophecy*, pp. 89–91.
206. 'Thus says the LORD' occurs over 40 times in the earlier prophetic period; this, and its near equivalent 'thus says the Lord GOD', occur more than 350 times in the classical prophets.
207. For the former, see e.g. Isa. 6:9; 38:5; Jer. 35:13; 39:16; cf. 2 Sam. 24:12; for the latter, which occurs predominantly in the book of Jeremiah, see e.g. 2 Sam. 7:8; 1 Kgs 14:5; 21:19; Jer. 7:28; 8:4; 11:3; 16:11; 21:4; 26:4; 36:29; Ezek. 2:4; 3:27.
208. This and the variant 'hear the word of the Lord GOD' occur around 30 times in the classical prophets; see e.g. Isa. 1:10; 28:14; 39:5; 66:5; Jer. 2:4; 19:3; 29:20; 42:15; Ezek. 6:3; 20:47; 37:4; Hos. 4:1; see also 1 Kgs 22:19; 2 Kgs 7:1.
209. See e.g. Isa. 13:1; 15:1; 17:1; 19:1; 21:1, 11, 13; 23:1; Nah. 1:1; Hab. 1:1; Mal. 1:1.

There are a number of forms of prophetic speech. Giese identifies oracles of salvation, announcement of judgment and apocalyptic.[210] However, while apocalyptic may have affinities with prophecy, there appear to be sufficient differences for it to be treated separately.[211] This section will consider the other two: oracles of judgment and oracles of salvation.

Oracles of judgment

The *judgment speech* frequently includes the messenger formula, an accusation, or reason for impending judgment, and a threat:

> Now then, hear the word of the LORD. You say,
>
> 'Do not prophesy against Israel [accusation],
> and stop preaching against the house of Isaac.'
>
> Therefore this is what the LORD says [messenger formula]:
>
> 'Your wife will become a prostitute in the city [threat/judgment],
> and your sons and daughters will fall by the sword.
> Your land will be measured and divided up,
> and you yourself will die in a pagan country.
> And Israel will certainly go into exile,
> away from their native land.'
> (Amos 7:16–17)[212]

This form may be addressed to an individual, as here, or to the nation as a whole.[213]

Another form of judgment announcement is the *woe oracle*. These oracles begin with the Hebrew interjection *hôy*, which is often rendered 'woe (to)', though may be better translated as 'Alas!' or 'Ah!' These oracles also include the reasons for, and threat of, coming judgment,[214] and may include the messenger

210. Giese, 'Literary Forms', in Sandy and Giese, *Cracking OT Codes*, pp. 18–19.

211. See below, pp. 194–198.

212. See also e.g. 1 Kgs 20:42; 21:17–19; 2 Kgs 1:3–4; 21:11–15; Jer. 11:9–11, 21–23; 14:14–16; 25:8–11; 29:30–32; Ezek. 5:5–12; 25:12–14; Amos 1:3 – 2:16. The oath formula replaces the message formula in e.g. Jer. 51:13–14; Amos 4:1–3.

213. According to Westermann, the judgment against the individual speech (JI) was the earlier form, and this was developed into judgments against the nation (JN) (Westermann, *Basic Forms*).

214. E.g. Isa. 10:1–4, 5–11; 28:1–4; 29:1–4; 30:1–3; 31:1–3; Mic. 2:1–4.

(e.g. Ezek. 13:1–16; 34:2–10; Mic. 2:1–4), or oath (Isa. 5:8–10;[215] Amos 6:4–8), formula. Sometimes they appear as a series of 'woes' (e.g. Isa. 5:8–25; Hab. 2:6–19). Woe oracles may also be linked with the funeral lament, indicating the prophet's sorrow at the prospect of divine judgment.[216]

Judgment speeches and woe oracles feature in the *oracles against the nations*, found in several prophetic books.[217] It has been suggested that these might have developed from war oracles, spoken against military enemies,[218] and might have been incorporated into worship as part of the celebration of Yahweh's victory. However, there is little in the oracles themselves to suggest such a setting. And it is significant that, in those oracles, offences against Israel are not as prominent as a military or cultic setting might suggest. A key reason for divine judgment is hubris: the pride of those who exalt themselves against God and who usurp a glory that belongs to him alone.[219]

Some judgment oracles have the appearance of legal or judicial texts. In the *covenant lawsuit* God brings charges against the nation because of its failure to meet its covenant obligations (e.g. Isa. 1:2–3; Jer. 2:4–13; Hos. 4:1–3; Mic. 6:1–8).[220]

---

215. Isa. 5:9 appears to include an abbreviated oath form (see Oswalt, *Isaiah 1–39*, p. 155).

216. See e.g. Butler, 'Announcements of Judgment', in Sandy and Giese, *Cracking OT Codes*, p. 163; Waldemar Janzen, *Mourning Cry and Woe Oracle* (Berlin: de Gruyter, 1972).

217. Isa. 13 – 23; Jer. 46 – 51; Ezek. 25 – 32; Amos 1 – 2; Zeph. 2; Obadiah; Nahum.

218. See e.g. Duane L. Christensen, *Transformations of the War Oracle in Old Testament Prophecy* (Missoula: Scholars Press, 1975); J. H. Hayes, 'The Usage of Oracles Against Foreign Nations in Ancient Israel', *JBL* 87 (1968), pp. 81–92. However, see John Barton, *Amos's Oracles Against the Nations* (Cambridge: Cambridge University Press, 1980), pp. 8–15; R. E. Clements, *Prophecy and Tradition* (Oxford: Blackwell, 1975), pp. 58–65.

219. Clements, *Prophecy and Tradition*, p. 65; Routledge, *OT Theology*, pp. 316–317.

220. See e.g. Leslie C. Allen, *The Books of Joel, Obadiah, Jonah and Micah*, NICOT (London: Hodder & Stoughton, 1976), pp. 363–367; Richard M. Davidson, 'The Divine Covenant Lawsuit Motif in Canonical Perspective', *Journal of the Adventist Theological Society* 21.1 (2010), pp. 45–84; Herbert B. Huffmon, 'The Covenant Lawsuit in the Prophets', *JBL* 78 (1959), pp. 285–295; Hetty Lalleman - de Winkel, *Jeremiah in Prophetic Tradition: An Examination of the Book of Jeremiah in the Light of Israel's Prophetic Traditions* (Leuven: Peeters, 2000), pp. 171–172; James L. Mays, *Micah*, OTL (London: SCM Press, 1976), pp. 128–136; Kirsten Nielsen, *Yahweh as Prosecutor and Judge: An Investigation of the Prophetic Lawsuit (Rîb-Pattern)*, JSOTSup 9 (Sheffield: JSOT Press, 1978).

There is debate about whether this type of oracle has a legal setting.[221] It does, though, reflect a particular kind of 'controversy' (*rîb*) between God and Israel. The suggested structure ('*rîb*-pattern') includes a call to listen (Isa. 1:2a; Jer. 2:4; Hos. 4:1a; Mic. 6:1–2), possibly invoking heaven and earth as witnesses; an accusation (Isa. 1:2b–3; Hos. 4:1b–2; Mic. 6:3–8), maybe set against the background of God's faithfulness, and the threat of judgment (Hos. 4:3). In other 'courtroom texts' God demonstrates the truth of his claim to be God, based on his lordship over history, and the worthlessness of the gods of the nations (Isa. 41:21–24; 43:8–13; 44:6–8; 45:20–25).

Though perhaps not strictly an announcement of judgment, the *admonition* or *call to repentance* is a prophetic challenge to the people to change their ways. In this case the admonition, often preceded by the messenger formula (or its equivalent), is followed by the motivation for the called-for change, which may be a threat or a promise.[222]

Oracles of salvation

Westermann divides the most frequently occurring type of salvation oracle into two categories. The proclamation of deliverance, which is a feature of the historical books (e.g. 1 Sam. 1:17–20; 1 Kgs 17:12–16; 2 Kgs 2:19–22; 4:11–17), follows a fixed pattern: 'distress; cry for help (lament); the cry is heard; deliverance'.[223] In the classical prophetic literature this is accompanied by a further promise of future blessing, which, after the exile, may also include the restoration of the nation.[224] Westermann also notes oracles in which a proclamation of salvation for God's people is accompanied by proclamation of judgment on their enemies.[225] Subcategories of salvation oracles in the classical prophets

221. Huffmon suggests that it may have origins in international law, and particularly Hittite suzerain–vassal treaties ('Covenant Lawsuit', pp. 291–292); however, see Michael De Roche, 'Yahweh's *Rîb* Against Israel: A Reassessment of the So-Called "Prophetic Lawsuit" in the Preexilic Prophets', *JBL* 102.4 (1983), pp. 563–574; Dwight R. Daniels, 'Is There a "Prophetic Lawsuit" Genre?', *ZAW* 99.3 (1987), pp. 339–360.

222. E.g. Isa. 1:10–17, 18–20; Jer. 3:12–13; 4:1–4; 13:15–17; Joel 2:12–14; Amos 5:4–5, 14–15.

223. Westermann, *Prophetic Oracles*, p. 16.

224. Ibid., pp. 16, 34.

225. Westermann includes these as Group 2. He notes that 'strictly speaking groups 3 and 4 cannot be included among the prophetic oracles of salvation' (ibid., p. 17), and, therefore, they have been omitted from this discussion. Examples of this twofold oracle include Isa. 14:3–4a, 22–23, 24–27; Jer. 30:4–22; Joel 2:18–20; 3:18–21; Zech. 9:13–16; see further ibid., pp. 195–223.

include the *promise of salvation*, which offers reassurance to the people, encouraging them to 'fear not' in the light of the coming deliverance.[226] The *proclamation of salvation* frequently responds to a lament or complaint, and again offers the hope of future blessing.[227] Non-Israelite nations appear to be included in some oracles of salvation.[228]

Wisdom literature[229]

'Wisdom' in the OT is wide ranging. As well as intelligence, discernment, insight and understanding,[230] it also includes technical and artistic skill,[231] and political acumen.[232] The relationship between instructor and student is often described in terms of the relationship between parent and child (e.g. Gen. 45:8; 2 Kgs 2:12; Prov. 1:8; Eccl. 12:12), suggesting that teaching may, at first, have been focused within the family.[233] Parents and elders, who had learned from their

---

226. Ibid., p. 42; see also VanGemeren, 'Oracles of Salvation', in Sandy and Giese, *Cracking OT Codes*, pp. 143–144; Aune terms this 'oracle of assurance' (*Prophecy*, pp. 94–95). These oracles include Isa. 41:8–13, 14–16; 43:1–7; 44:1–5; 51:7–8, 12–16; 54:4–6; Jer. 1:17–19; 30:10–11; 42:9–12; 46:27–28.
227. E.g. Isa. 2:2–4; 9:2–7; 11:1–9; 19:19–25; 41:17–20; 42:14–17; 43:16–21; 45:14–17; 49:7–12, 14–26; 51:9 – 52:3; Jer. 28:2–4; 31:31–34; Ezek. 37:1–15; Hos. 2:14–23; 11:8–9, 10–11; Amos 9:8–15; Mic. 2:12–13; 4:6–8; Zeph. 3:18b–20; Zech. 9:11–12; 10:8–12.
228. E.g. Isa. 2:2–4; 19:19–25; see above, p. 20, n. 63.
229. For bibliography, see Further reading, p. 387. See also e.g. Arnold, *Introduction*, pp. 275–290; Ted A. Hildebrandt, 'Proverb', in Sandy and Giese, *Cracking OT Codes*, pp. 232–254; Andrew E. Hill, 'Non-Proverbial Wisdom', in Sandy and Giese, *Cracking Old Testament Codes*, pp. 255–280; Osborne, *Hermeneutical Spiral*, pp. 242–257; Routledge, *OT Theology*, pp. 215–224, 248–249.
230. E.g. Gen. 41:39; 1 Kgs 4:29; 2 Chr. 2:12; Prov. 5:1; 10:13; Dan. 5:11, 14.
231. E.g. Exod. 28:3; 31:2–5; 35:25–26; Isa. 10:13; Jer. 9:17; Ezek. 27:8–9.
232. The OT includes references to 'wise men' in Egypt (1 Kgs 4:30; Isa. 19:11; cf. Gen. 41:8; Exod. 7:11), Edom (Jer. 49:7; Obad. 8), Babylon (Jer. 50:35; 51:57; Dan. 2:12) and Persia (Esth. 1:13).
233. See e.g. Ronald E. Clements, *Wisdom in Theology* (Carlisle: Paternoster, 1992), pp. 126–150. There appear to have been schools in Mesopotamia and Egypt from the third millennium BC, but the situation in Israel is less clear; see e.g. David M. Carr, *Writing on the Tablet of the Heart: Origins of Scripture and Literature* (Oxford:

experiences of life, offered advice and guidance to the next generation, possibly in the form of short, easy to remember, sayings. Rather than setting out conduct in legal terms, this guidance gives warnings about the personal and social consequences of taking the wrong path and points to the rewards of doing what is right (which includes seeking after wisdom).[234] As elsewhere in the ANE, wise counsellors helped to guide Israel's national affairs (e.g. 2 Sam. 16:23), and by Jeremiah's time there appears to have been a distinct group of sages, who worked alongside priests and prophets (Jer. 18:18).

Wisdom literature as a genre

As we have seen, OT wisdom literature includes, primarily, the books of Job, Proverbs, Ecclesiastes and possibly the Song of Songs,[235] as well as some psalms.[236] We have noted several key aspects of this literature, including its emphasis on practical advice for successful living.[237] There is, though, some debate about whether 'wisdom literature' should be categorized as a *genre*; or whether it is better viewed as a collection of texts that share a similar purpose and perspective on life.[238]

These books have some generic elements in common. Wisdom literature is so called because of its emphasis on 'wisdom', and well over half of all OT occurrences of words from the Hebrew root *ḥkm* are in these three books, particularly Proverbs and Ecclesiastes.[239] Proverbs and Ecclesiastes also share a number of literary forms.[240] Job shares fewer generic characteristics, though it includes proverbial (Job 8:11–12) and numerical (Job 5:19–21; 13:20–21; 33:14–15) sayings, as well as reflective passages similar to those found in Proverbs

---

(*Footnote 233 cont.*) Oxford University Press, 2005); G. I. Davies, 'Were There Schools in Ancient Israel', in Day, Gordon and Williamson, *Wisdom in Ancient Israel*, pp. 199–211; Stuart Weeks, *Early Israelite Wisdom* (Oxford: Oxford University Press, 1994), pp. 132–156; Gerald H. Wilson, 'Education in the OT', in *NIDOTTE* 4:559–564.

234. See Kidner, *Wisdom*, p. 11; Routledge, *OT Theology*, pp. 248–249.
235. Childs argues that ascribing of the Song of Songs to Solomon (1:1) indicates that it is to be understood as wisdom literature (*Introduction*, pp. 574–579).
236. And, usually, the apocryphal books of Sirach and the Wisdom of Solomon.
237. See above, pp. 124–125.
238. For further discussion, see e.g. Alastair Hunter, *Wisdom Literature* (London: SCM Press, 2006), pp. 3–26.
239. See e.g. Lucas, *Psalms and Wisdom*, p. 79; cf. Hunter, *Wisdom Literature*, p. 21.
240. See below, pp. 190–194.

and Ecclesiastes.[241] Another common feature is the relative scarcity of references to Israel's salvation history and covenant faith.[242] Answers to life's problems are, more often, linked with general revelation, and are found by careful observation of, and reflection on, human behaviour and the natural world.

Job and Ecclesiastes are also linked in that they present a tension with the moral law of cause and effect, sometimes thought to underlie wisdom teaching. The idea that wisdom teaching includes maxims for a successful life is particularly evident in Proverbs. The divine wisdom that orders creation results in a view of the world that is ordered, predictable and fair, and people reap what they sow, a principle sometimes referred to as the 'law of retribution'.[243] Proverbs does not portray a purely mechanistic view of the world. It admits that human wisdom is limited (Prov. 20:24; 30:2–9), and the contrast between fearing God and the lure of wealth (e.g. Prov. 15:16) contains the implicit recognition that doing right may not always bring prosperity. Nevertheless, that is not developed. It is in the books of Job and Ecclesiastes that the law of retribution and the idea that human wisdom can make sense of the world are questioned, and this further reinforces the view that Job should be included within the wisdom genre.

Types of wisdom literature

There are several suggested types of wisdom texts. These are sometimes categorized as proverbial and non-proverbial forms of wisdom,[244] with the latter including riddles, allegories and fables, hymns, dialogue, confession or

---

241. See e.g. Katharine Dell, *'Get Wisdom, Get Insight': An Introduction to Israel's Wisdom Literature* (London: Darton, Longman & Todd, 2000), pp. 39–42; Hunter, *Wisdom Literature*, pp. 21–23.

242. However, see J. A. Grant, 'Wisdom and Covenant', in *DOTWPW*, pp. 858–863; David A. Hubbard, 'The Wisdom Movement and Israel's Covenant Faith', *TynBul* 17 (1966), pp. 3–33.

243. This is expressed negatively in Job 4:8: 'those who plough evil and . . . sow trouble reap it'.

244. E.g. Sandy and Giese, *Cracking OT Codes*, pp. 18–19, 21, 233–280. Others list 'proverbs' as one of several categories; e.g. James L. Crenshaw, *Urgent Advice and Probing Questions: Collected Writings on Old Testament Wisdom* (Macon: Mercer University Press, 1995), pp. 48–56; Hunter, *Wisdom Literature*, pp. 32–35; Osborne, *Hermeneutical Spiral*, pp. 247–250; Thomas Smothers, 'Biblical Wisdom in Its Ancient Middle Eastern Context', in H. Wayne Ballard Jr. and W. Dennis Tucker Jr. (eds.), *An Introduction to Wisdom Literature and the Psalms: Festschrift Marvin E. Tate* (Macon: Mercer University Press, 2000), pp. 167–180.

autobiographical narrative/reflection, lists (*onomastica*) and 'didactic poetry and narrative'.[245] However, although the OT refers to different kinds of wisdom literature, it rarely gives clear examples of what they look like. As a result, categorization of texts is based, primarily, on what appear to be shared formal features.[246]

Proverbial wisdom

An important category of wisdom text is the *proverb* (*māšāl*).[247] Proverbs are succinct sayings, offering valuable insights, based on experience and observations of life. They sometimes use metaphor or simile, and are designed to be memorable.[248] There are several proverbial forms, though little general agreement about precise classification. McKane argues for two basic forms: instruction and wisdom sentence.[249] Others have extended the number of categories.[250]

One recognizable form of instruction is the admonition. Here a command is followed by an explanation, often introduced by 'for' or 'because' (*kî*):

---

245. Crenshaw, *Urgent Advice*, pp. 57–76 (the Crenshaw reference is to the whole list of categories, including the last); see also Hill, 'Non-Proverbial Wisdom', in Sandy and Giese, *Cracking OT Codes*, pp. 257–268.

246. See Hunter, *Wisdom Literature*, p. 32.

247. The NRSV translates *māšāl* as 'proverb' (e.g. Deut. 28:37; 1 Sam. 10:12; 24:13; Job 13:12; Ps. 49:4; Prov. 1:1, 6; Eccl. 12:9; Ezek. 12:22), 'byword' (e.g. Pss 44:14; 69:11; Jer. 24:9; Ezek. 14:8; cf. Joel 2:17) and 'taunt' (Isa. 14:4; Hab. 2:6). The term is also translated 'parable' (Ps. 78:2) and 'allegory' (Ezek. 17:2; 20:49; 24:3). *Māšāl* suggests a comparison, which is present in many proverbs and also in parables or allegories; see K.-M. Beyse, '*māšāl*', in *TDOT* 9:58–67; Crenshaw, *Urgent Advice*, pp. 48–56; Gerald Wilson, '*mšl*', in *NIDOTTE* 2:1134–1136.

248. The OT records several sayings, described as 'proverbs', outside the traditional 'wisdom texts' (1 Sam. 10:12; 24:14; Ezek. 12:22–23; 18:2–3).

249. William McKane, *Proverbs*, OTL (London: SCM Press, 1970); see also Lucas, *Psalms and Wisdom*, pp. 92–93.

250. Crenshaw notes the following: sentence, instruction, exhortation or admonition, numerical, comparison and antithetical (*Urgent Advice*, p. 49). Osborne's list is similar (*Hermeneutical Spiral*, p. 247). Hildebrandt identifies as many as eleven different kinds of proverb ('Proverbs', in Sandy and Giese, *Cracking OT Codes*, p. 240); see also T. Hildebrandt, 'Proverb, Genre of', in *DOTWPW*, pp. 528–539. Tucker separates 'additional sayings', which includes numerical, 'better . . . than' and 'blessed' sayings, from 'proverbs' ('Literary Forms', in Ballard and Tucker, *Introduction to Wisdom Literature*, pp. 156–158).

My son, do not forget my teaching,
  but keep my commands in your heart,
for [*kî*] they will prolong your life many years
  and bring you prosperity.
(Prov. 3:1–2)[251]

Wisdom sentences often occur in parallel couplets. This includes synonymous parallelism:

Pride goes before destruction,
  a haughty spirit before a fall.
(Prov. 16:18)

Like a gold ring in a pig's snout
  is a beautiful woman who shows no discretion.
(Prov. 11:22)

Another form of proverb is the numerical saying, which frequently uses the x / x + 1 pairing:

There are three things that are too amazing for me,
  four that I do not understand:
the way of an eagle in the sky,
  the way of a snake on a rock,
the way of a ship on the high seas,
  and the way of a man with a maiden.
(Prov. 30:18–19)[252]

Proverbs frequently include, too, antithetic parallelism, contrasting what is right with what is wrong:

A cheerful heart is good medicine,
  but a crushed spirit dries up the bones.
(Prov. 17:22)

---

251. See also e.g. Prov. 3:11–12; 4:20–22, 23; Eccl. 5:2; 7:9, 10; 10:20; 11:1, 2.

252. This 'three/four' parallelism is common (see also Prov. 30:15b–16, 21–23, 29–31; Sir. 26.5–6), though other pairings occur (e.g. Job 5:19–22; 33:14–15; Prov. 6:16–19; Sir. 25.7–11; 26.28; 50.25–26). Other numerical sayings include Job 13:20–21; Prov. 30:7–9, 24–28; Eccl. 11:2; Sir. 25.1–2.

Words from a wise man's mouth are gracious,
but a fool is consumed by his own lips.
(Eccl. 10:12)

A particular category of antithetic parallelism is the 'better . . . than' saying:

Better a poor man whose walk is blameless
than a rich man whose ways are perverse.
(Prov. 28:6)[253]

Synonymous and antithetic parallelism may feature, too, in sayings that emphasize that those who follow the right course are 'blessed' or 'happy' (*'ašrê*):

Blessed is the man who finds wisdom,
the man who gains understanding.
(Prov. 3:13)

He who despises his neighbour sins,
but blessed is he who is kind to the needy.
(Prov. 14:21)[254]

Non-proverbial wisdom

Judges 14:10–18 is the only clear example of a *riddle* (*ḥîdâ*), though there are several references to the form,[255] possibly indicating its popularity.[256] Riddles appear to be based on the possibility of ambiguity in language, and the term may refer to something unclear or obscure (e.g. Num. 12:8) or deliberately misleading (Dan. 8:23). Some suggest a link between riddles and numerical proverbs.[257]

Closely associated with the riddle, is the *allegory* or *fable* (e.g. Ezek. 17:2). This narrative form uses images drawn from the natural world, often animals or plants, as metaphors for aspects of human life. OT wisdom literature includes

---

253. See also e.g. Prov. 12:9; 15:16–17; 16:8; 17:1, 12; 19:1; 27:5; Eccl. 4:6, 13; 6:9; 7:2, 5; Sir. 10.27; 19.24; 41.15.
254. See also e.g. Job 5:17; Pss 1:1; 40:4; Prov. 3:18; 8:32, 34; 16:20; 20:7; 28:14; 29:18; Eccl. 10:17.
255. See e.g. Num. 12:8; 1 Kgs 10:1 (= 2 Chr. 9:1) ('hard questions'); Pss 49:4; 78:2 ('dark sayings', NRSV); Prov. 1:6; Ezek. 17:2; Hab. 2:6; Dan. 8:23 ('intrigue'). See also V. Hamp, '*ḥîdâ*', in *TDOT* 4:320–323; Gerald Wilson, '*ḥîdâ*', in *NIDOTTE* 2:107–108.
256. So Crenshaw, *Urgent Advice*, p. 57.
257. Ibid., p. 58; Osborne, *Hermeneutical Spiral*, p. 248.

two such allegories. Proverbs 5:15–17 appears to encourage marital faithfulness. Ecclesiastes 12:1–6 uses vivid images to describe old age and eventual death, and urges the young to make the most of life while they can.[258]

Wisdom literature also includes *hymns* (Job 5:9–16; 9:5–13; 12:13–25; 26:5–14; Prov. 1:20–33; 8).[259] Their main themes include extolling the virtue of wisdom and praising God, particularly as creator and redeemer. Several psalms, which share stylistic features or key themes with wisdom texts,[260] are categorized as 'wisdom psalms'. The criteria are, though, subjective, and there is wide disagreement as to which psalms should be included in this category.[261] Later writings note a link between wisdom and *tôrâ*,[262] and this may be reflected in Psalm 1 (and possibly Ps. 119). The *Sitz im Leben* of wisdom psalms is also unclear. They may have a worship setting, reflecting the post-exilic emphasis on exposition of the Law as a central feature of worship. Or they may originate in a more instructional setting, such as the home or school.

As noted already, the book of Job is similar to Egyptian and Babylonian texts that take the form of a *dialogue* or *dispute* between its characters.[263] Crenshaw relates this to 'imagined speech', where a statement is imagined and then refuted.[264] Questions designed to have rhetorical effect, and which feature prominently in Job and Ecclesiastes, may also suggest an imagined dialogue.[265]

---

258. See also e.g. Judg. 9:8–15; 2 Kgs 14:9; Ezek. 17:3–10; 19:1–9, 10–14.
259. See also J. A. Grant, 'Wisdom Poems', in *DOTWPW*, pp. 891–894. Hymns are also present in non-canonical wisdom texts; e.g. Wis. 6.12–20; 7.22b – 8.21; Sir. 1.1–10; 24.1–22; 39.12–35.
260. E.g. 'happy/blessed' and 'better . . . than' sayings, the contrast between righteous and wicked, and references to 'wisdom'.
261. Murphy lists Pss 1, 32, 34, 37, 49, 112, 128 as wisdom psalms, though notes that others have wisdom influences; see Roland E. Murphy, 'A Consideration of the Classification, "Wisdom Psalms"', in *Congress Volume: Bonn 1962*, VTSup 9 (Leiden: Brill, 1963), pp. 156–167. Collins includes Pss 1; 14; 37; 73; 91; 112; 119; 128 (*Introduction*, p. 486); see also Crenshaw, *Urgent Advice*, pp. 65–67; Grant, 'Wisdom Poems', in *DOTWPW*, pp. 893–894; LaSor, Hubbard and Bush, *OT Survey*, p. 440; Tucker, 'Psalms 1', in *DOTWPW*, p. 585.
262. Sir. 24.1–22 extols wisdom, which, in vv. 23–29, is identified with God's Law.
263. See above, pp. 126–127.
264. Crenshaw, *Urgent Advice*, pp. 69–70; see also Osborne, *Hermeneutical Spiral*, p. 249. See e.g. Prov. 1:11–14, 22–33; 7:14–20; 9:16–17; 22:13.
265. See e.g. Tucker, 'Literary Forms', in Ballard and Tucker, *Introduction to Wisdom Literature*, pp. 160–161. Questions, which might suggest an imagined dialogue, appear in e.g. Eccl. 1:3; 3:9; 4:11; 6:8.

Because wisdom literature is related to experience of the world, it is no surprise that it may contain *autobiographical confessions* or *reflections*.[266] This is clearly evident in Ecclesiastes (e.g. 1:12 – 2:26), though it is present, too, in Psalms (e.g. 37:35–36), Proverbs (e.g. 4:3–9; 24:30–34) and (maybe) Job (e.g. 4:8; 15:17).

Von Rad has drawn attention to similarities between the Egyptian *Onomasticon of Amenemope* and Job 38.[267] The *Onomasticon* is a compilation of thematic lists relating to different aspects of life, including the wonders of nature. Similarities between this and the content of the questions posed to Job, as well as closely related material in Psalm 148 and Sirach 43, have led to the suggestion that this form was common in Israel, too.[268]

There are several kinds of didactic poem or narrative.[269] Childs notes the 'summary-appraisal' form, which also occurs in prophetic texts.[270] As the name implies, this offers a summary and evaluation of what precedes (e.g. Job 5:27; 8:13; Prov. 1:19; Eccl. 4:8). 'Problem passages' reflect on the prosperity of the wicked and encourage the faithful to trust God's final justice (e.g. Pss 37; 73). In didactic narratives the writer describes a scene in considerable detail, in order to bring it to life and make the message more compelling (e.g. Prov. 7:6–23).

Apocalyptic[271]

What is apocalyptic?

Jewish apocalyptic literature is widely held to include the canonical book of Daniel, as well as a number of non-canonical texts. Prior to the 1970s this

---

266. See Crenshaw, *Urgent Advice*, pp. 70–71; Tucker, 'Literary Forms', in Ballard and Tucker, *Introduction to Wisdom Literature*, pp. 161–163.
267. Gerhard von Rad, 'Job xxxviii and Ancient Egyptian Wisdom', in James L. Crenshaw (ed.), *Studies in Ancient Israelite Wisdom* (New York: Ktav, 1976), pp. 267–280.
268. Crenshaw sees evidence of this form in Job 28; 36:27 – 37:13; 38:4 – 39:30; 40:15 – 41:34; Sir. 43; Wis. 7.17–20, 22–23; 14.25–26 (*Urgent Advice*, p. 72).
269. Ibid., pp. 73–75.
270. Childs, *Assyrian Crisis*, pp. 128–136.
271. See e.g. Arnold, *Introduction*, pp. 355–369; Richard Bauckham, 'The Rise of Apocalyptic', *Them* 3.2 (1978), pp. 10–23; John J. Collins, 'Introduction: Towards the Morphology of a Genre', in John J. Collins (ed.), *Semeia 14: Apocalypse: The Morphology of a Genre* (Missoula: Scholars Press, 1979), pp. 1–20; *The Apocalyptic Imagination: An Introduction to Jewish Apocalyptic Literature*, 2nd ed. (Grand Rapids: Eerdmans, 1998), esp. pp. 1–42; W. J. Dumbrell, 'Apocalyptic Literature', in *NIDOTTE* 4:394–399;

literature was generally defined by content. However, not all so-called 'apocalypses' share the same features, and some of those features are evident in other literature.[272] This raised the question of what the distinctive characteristics of apocalyptic are. A more recent, frequently quoted, statement defines apocalyptic as

> a genre of revelatory literature with a narrative framework, in which a revelation is mediated by an otherworldly being to a human recipient, disclosing a transcendent reality which is both temporal, insofar as it envisages eschatological salvation, and spatial, insofar as it involves another supernatural world.[273]

While this has been widely accepted as a working definition, some want to include other elements, particularly in relation to the purpose of apocalyptic texts. It is widely recognized that apocalyptic arises out of crises within the life of the nation, and many such writings appeared during the difficult national and political circumstances from the late third century BC. Israel's prophets had looked forward to the rebirth, restoration and renewal of the nation after the exile. Those expectations, though, remained unfulfilled: instead of the establishment of God's kingdom, the people suffered under a succession of pagan rulers, culminating in Antiochus Epiphanes, who opposed the Jewish faith and way of life. In the normal course of historical and political events there seemed

---

B. C. Gregory, 'Wisdom and Apocalyptic', in *DOTWPW*, pp. 847–853; Paul D. Hanson, *The Dawn of Apocalyptic: The Historical and Sociological Roots of Jewish Apocalyptic Eschatology*, rev. ed. (Philadelphia: Fortress, 1979); *Old Testament Apocalyptic* (Nashville: Clarendon, 1987); T. J. Johnson, 'Apocalypticism, Apocalyptic Literature', in *DOTPr*, pp. 36–43; George W. E. Nickelsburg, 'The Study of Apocalypticism from H. H. Rowley to the Society of Biblical Literature', in *Society of Biblical Literature Seminar Papers* 33 (Atlanta: Scholars Press, 1994), pp. 715–732; Osborne, *Hermeneutical Spiral*, pp. 275–290; John Oswalt, 'Recent Studies in Old Testament Apocalyptic', in Baker and Arnold, *Face of OT Studies*, pp. 369–370; Rogerson and Davies, *OT World*, pp. 198–208; H. H. Rowley, *The Relevance of Apocalyptic* (New York: Association, 1964); D. S. Russell, *The Method and Message of Jewish Apocalyptic*, OTL (London: SCM Press, 1964); *Apocalyptic Ancient and Modern* (London: SCM Press, 1978); D. Brent Sandy and Martin G. Abegg Jr., 'Apocalyptic', in Sandy and Giese, *Cracking OT Codes*, pp. 177–196.

272. Collins criticizes older scholarship 'because of its tendency to assume that the setting of one or two well-known apocalypses is representative of the whole genre' (*Apocalyptic Imagination*, p. 37).
273. Collins, 'Morphology of a Genre', in Collins, *Apocalypse*, p. 9.

to be little hope for the nation, but apocalyptic writers did not want to abandon God's promises, and so they looked forward to a day when God would defeat the powers of darkness and bring the present evil age to an end. Apocalyptic literature, therefore, also includes encouragement for those who are suffering,[274] and the call to persevere and remain faithful in the light of promised future deliverance.[275]

The origins of apocalyptic

There is also debate about the origins of apocalyptic. One view is that it grew out of earlier prophetic literature.[276] The book of Ezekiel appears to be an important influence. This stresses the transcendence of God and humankind's individual accountability. It contains, too, some of the elaborate imagery and symbolism that were features of later apocalyptic. There is also a reference to a final battle (Ezek. 38 – 39) and the triumph of good over evil, which is another apocalyptic theme. In Zechariah revelation comes through visions, and future hope is expressed in terms of a coming golden age, the appearance of God's chosen messianic leader and the final destruction of evil. Isaiah 24 – 27 points to God's victory over the powers that oppose him and oppress his people. Other prophets refer to the Day of the Lord when God will bring to an end the pride and power of the nations and establish his own kingdom. It is possible that the increased use of mythological imagery in post-exilic prophetic texts, maybe to emphasize supernatural control over history, also opened the way for apocalyptic.[277] However, while it seems likely that these and other prophetic texts influenced apocalyptic, key differences between prophecy and apocalyptic[278] indicate that there were other factors too.

---

274. Hellholm notes that apocalyptic literature is '*intended for a group in crisis with the purpose of exhortation and/or consolation by means of divine authority*' (David Hellholm, 'The Problem of Apocalyptic Genre and the Apocalypse of John', *Semeia* 36 [1986], pp. 13–64 [27] [italics his]). See also Osborne, *Hermeneutical Spiral*, p. 276.
275. See e.g. Johnson, *Apocalypticism*, in *DOTPr*, pp. 40–41.
276. Prior to the 1970s this view was expressed by Rowley and Russell; the link between prophecy and apocalyptic is also emphasized by Hanson (see refs. above); see also Bauckham, 'Rise of Apocalyptic', pp. 10–13, 17–18; Collins, *Apocalyptic Imagination*, pp. 23–25; Oswalt, 'OT Apocalyptic', in *Face of OT Studies*, pp. 374–378.
277. See e.g. John J. Collins, 'What Is Apocalyptic Literature', in John J. Collins (ed.), *The Oxford Handbook of Apocalyptic Literature* (New York: Oxford University Press, 2014), pp. 1–16 (8–9); Oswalt, 'OT Apocalyptic', in *Face of OT Studies*, pp. 374–378.
278. See below.

The idea that apocalyptic developed from prophecy has been challenged by von Rad. He argues that their different views of history are too far apart and claims, instead, that apocalyptic has its origins in wisdom literature.[279] This view received little support, initially; however, several scholars now recognize a link between these genres. One possible influence is Mesopotamian *mantic* wisdom,[280] in which 'diviners' foretold the future by interpreting dreams and other omens, including signs in the stars. Johnson also suggests that more study needs to be done on the possible relationship between apocalyptic and more distinctively Jewish wisdom literature.[281] There is the possibility, too, of Persian and Hellenistic influences.[282] It would seem, though, that any such influences have been absorbed into what is a distinctively Jewish genre. It is arguable that the influence of prophecy remains a key element,[283] and apocalyptic is sometimes viewed as a category within prophecy.[284] However, Jewish wisdom literature as well as non-Jewish influences and the historical context in which it arose may all have contributed to the distinctive features of apocalyptic.

Features of apocalyptic

Despite possible links, apocalyptic has several features that distinguish it from prophecy. One is their different view of history. Prophets envisaged the coming of God's kingdom within history; apocalyptic often appears pessimistic about the present world order and looks for deliverance in a new order, beyond history. This leads to different understandings of 'eschatology': apocalyptic eschatology focuses on that radically new world order; prophetic eschatology looks for a coming age that is different from, but also continuous with, the present age.[285] Linked with that, prophets were preachers with a contemporary message; they

---

279. Gerhard von Rad, *Old Testament Theology*, 2 vols. (Edinburgh: Oliver & Boyd, 1962–5), 2:301–308.
280. See e.g. Bauckham, 'Rise of Apocalyptic', pp. 13–15; Collins, *Apocalyptic Imagination*, pp. 26–29; B. A. Mastin, 'Daniel and Wisdom', in Day, Gordon and Williamson, *Wisdom in Ancient Israel*, pp. 161–169; Gregory, 'Wisdom and Apocalyptic', in *DOTWPW*, pp. 850–851; Rogerson and Davies, *OT World*, pp. 200–202.
281. Johnson, 'Apocalypticism', in *DOTPr*, pp. 42–43.
282. See e.g. Collins, *Apocalyptic Imagination*, pp. 29–37.
283. E.g. Bauckham, 'Rise of Apocalyptic', pp. 17–18.
284. See e.g. Giese, 'Literary Forms', in Sandy and Giese, *Cracking OT Codes*, p. 22.
285. See e.g. Routledge, *OT Theology*, pp. 272–273; see also Collins, *Apocalyptic Imagination*, pp. 11–12; Dumbrell, 'Apocalyptic', in *NIDOTTE* 4:395–396; Johnson, 'Apocalypticism', in *DOTPr*, pp. 37–38.

wanted to influence and shape the nation's history according to God's will. Prophetic literature, therefore, expresses a strong moral and ethical interest, and when it looks to the future, it is often to stress God's judgment on sin and to call the people to repent before it is too late. Apocalyptic is less interested in the present, and emphasizes the future vindication of God's people. The call to repentance in the prophetic writings admits a level of contingency in God's future plans. Apocalyptic, on the other hand, seems to take a more determinative view of history, in which God's plans are being worked out through the ages according to a fixed scheme. This emphasizes God's control and ultimate victory, even in the face of fierce persecution and seemingly impossible odds. As Russell notes, 'tyrants might rule, but it was only by the permissive will of God. The rise and fall of empires were in the control of one in whose hands lay the final victory and in whose kingdom they would have a glorious part.'[286] This focus on the future frequently results in a dualism between the present evil age and God's coming reign of righteousness.

Other features of apocalyptic include messages encoded in elaborate symbolism and imagery. This can make exegesis difficult, since the significance of particular imagery, which might have been clear to the original writers and their audience, is unfamiliar to us. Apocalyptic texts are also, often, pseudonymous; they bear the name of a significant figure from Israel's past, probably to give the text greater credibility. They may employ pseudo-prediction (*vaticinium ex eventu*), that is, prophecy given after the events described, often between the time of the pseudonymous author and the actual time of writing.

There has been an increased interest in apocalyptic literature in recent years. It is of interest in OT studies primarily in relation to the book of Daniel. Most scholars argue that Daniel was written in the second century BC, and that it bears many of the hallmarks of other apocalyptic writings dating from the same period, including pseudonymity and pseudo-prediction. Those conclusions may not, though, be inevitable. This will be considered further when we look at that book in more detail.

286. Russell, *Apocalyptic*, p. 29.

5. INTERPRETING THE OLD TESTAMENT

A key aim of OT study, in my view, must be to gain an understanding of the text that will facilitate its interpretation and so provide a basis for its application to the belief and praxis of the church. This chapter focuses particularly on approaches to the interpretation of the OT.[1]

The 'meaning' of a text

The interpretation of a text and its meaning are clearly very closely related. There is, though, debate about what 'meaning' signifies in this context.[2] Those

---

1. Biblical interpretation falls under the wider category of *hermeneutics*. For a more detailed discussion of hermeneutics see e.g. John Barton (ed.), *The Cambridge Companion to Biblical Interpretation* (Cambridge: Cambridge University Press, 1998); *Reading the OT*; Brown, *Scripture as Communication*; Duncan S. Ferguson, *Biblical Hermeneutics: An Introduction* (Atlanta: John Knox, 1986); John Goldingay, *Models for Interpretation of Scripture* (Carlisle: Paternoster; Grand Rapids: Eerdmans, 1995); Stanley E. Porter and Beth M. Stovell (eds.), *Biblical Hermeneutics: Five Views* (Downers Grove: InterVarsity Press, 2012); Osborne, *Hermeneutical Spiral*; Anthony C. Thiselton, *Hermeneutics: An Introduction* (Grand Rapids: Eerdmans, 2009); *Thiselton on Hermeneutics: The Collected Works and New Essays of Anthony Thiselton* (Aldershot: Ashgate, 2006); *New Horizons in Hermeneutics: The Theory and Practice of Transforming Biblical Reading* (Grand Rapids: Zondervan, 1992).
2. See e.g. Osborne, *Hermeneutical Spiral*, pp. 465–499; Thiselton, *Hermeneutics*, pp. 1–5.

who view Scripture as the inspired and authoritative Word of God may think in terms of divine revelation: a text means what God intends it to mean. And as such, texts have, in theory at least, a single meaning. That meaning has been identified, traditionally, with the author's intention. Though it is also recognized that there may be a fuller meaning (*sensus plenior*), which is intended by God, but not fully appreciated by the human author.[3] More recent literary approaches attach little or no significance to the author's intention. They focus, instead, on the interaction between text and reader. The result is a more subjective understanding of a text's meaning, which opens the possibility of several different, but equally valid, interpretations.

Approaches to the interpretation of the Old Testament

As noted already, there are three main elements in the transmission of a text (see Figure 5.1).[4]

Figure 5.1

When we focus on the author, we also look at what is frequently referred to as 'the world behind the text', that is, the world in which the text came to be written. Key issues here are discussions of the text's origins: its date, authorship, historical and literary context, and how it came to be in the form we have it in our OT. Significant, too, is the author's intention in writing. Historical-critical approaches, and also social-scientific criticism, focus on the world behind the text.

Some more recent approaches focus primarily on the text. We have already considered narrative texts, which present their own world, in which characters exist and interact with one another. Some make a clear distinction between this 'world of the text' and the world behind the text, and so take an ahistorical view of OT narrative. It may be history-like, but it is not history in the sense of what really happened. I have argued for a closer correlation between those two worlds;

3. See below, pp. 223–227.
4. See above, pp. 165–166. Intervening categories include implied author, narrator, narratee and implied reader. These three, though, are the main categories relevant to the present discussion.

however, because of the poetic devices employed by the narrator and the more imaginative content of ancient historiography, the two are not identical. Other approaches with a primary focus on the text include structuralism, rhetorical criticism and what is sometimes termed 'canonical criticism'.

Important, too, is the reader, who comes to the text from his or her own world. Thiselton, following Gadamer, describes the worlds of the reader and of the world of the text in terms of two horizons. For understanding to take place, there needs to be engagement between those two worlds, leading to a 'fusion of horizons',[5] which in turn results in the reader's own world being changed. The world of the reader is conditioned by background, theological tradition, culture and world view. Some of that conditioning may be unconscious, though the reader also may seek, deliberately, to interpret the text from a particular ideological perspective. Approaches that put the primary focus on the reader include reader-response criticism, which is closely related to ideological readings.

The world behind the text

Historical-critical methods

Behind these methods of enquiry is the assumption that the more we know about the background, original setting and development of a text, the more we are able to understand its meaning. We have already looked at the main historical criticisms: source, form and redaction criticism.[6]

Social-scientific criticism[7]

This is a relatively recent approach and is often linked with other new approaches to the text. It does, though, focus on the world behind the text and so it is

---

5. Gadamer's term is *Horizontverschmelzung*; see Anthony C. Thiselton, *The Two Horizons: New Testament Hermeneutics and Philosophical Description* (Grand Rapids: Eerdmans; Exeter: Paternoster, 1980); *New Horizons*, p. 8; Hans-Georg Gadamer, *Truth and Method*, 2nd rev. ed. (London: Sheed & Ward, 1989), pp. 302–307.
6. See above, pp. 51–62.
7. The classic work in this field is Gottwald, *Tribes of Yahweh*; see also e.g. David J. Chalcraft (ed.), *Social-Scientific Old Testament Criticism*, Sheffield Readers (Sheffield: Sheffield Academic Press, 1997); Norman K. Gottwald, 'Social Matrix and Canonical Shape', *ThTo* 42.3 (1985), pp. 307–321; 'Sociological Criticism of the Old Testament', *ChrCent* 99 (1982), pp. 474–477; *The Politics of Ancient Israel*, LAI (Louisville: Westminster John Knox, 2001); *Hebrew Bible*, pp. 26–29; Paula McNutt, *Reconstructing the Society of Ancient Israel*, LAI (Louisville: Westminster John Knox,

appropriate to note it here. Social-scientific criticism looks at the developing faith of Israel in the light of the nation's changing social and political structures, and recognizes that what may appear to be religious movements have underlying sociological factors. Gottwald sets out what he calls 'the guiding question for social science approaches to the Bible' as 'What social structures, processes, and codes are explicit or implicit in the biblical literature, in the scattered social data it contains, in the overtly political history it recounts or touches on, and in the religious beliefs and practices it attests?'[8]

This approach has been applied to Israel's 'conquest' of Canaan, which is described in terms of social movements within and around Canaan.[9] Cook has also applied social-scientific methods to his discussion of the development of biblical Yahwism.[10] Traditions, which go back to the Sinaitic covenant, were preserved by particular social groups, notably by 'the people of the land'. In Cook's view these are rural property owners who argued for land-rights and opposed the centralization of Israel's institutions in Jerusalem. The emergence of these traditions at various points in Israel's history corresponds to the social prominence of those groups. Social factors may be seen to be dominant, too, in the institution of the monarchy in Israel.[11]

This approach provides useful insights into the life of Israel, and the forces and tensions at work within Israelite society. There is need, though, for caution. By representing key movements in Israel's history as the result of sociological processes, the religious aspect may be minimized, thus reducing God to a sociological construct. It shares, too, the key limitation of all 'behind the text' readings: how much we can really know about that world, and how much rests on speculation.

(*Footnote 7 cont.*) 1999); Dale P. Martin, 'Social-Scientific Criticism', in McKenzie and Haynes, *To Each Its Own Meaning* (1999), pp. 125–141; V. H. Matthews, 'Social-Scientific Approaches', in *DOTP*, pp. 787–793; Leo G. Perdue, *The Collapse of History: Reconstructing Old Testament Theology*, OBT (Minneapolis: Fortress, 1994), pp. 69–109; Redditt, *Introduction to the Prophets*, pp. 41–42.

8. Gottwald, 'Social Matrix', p. 307.
9. See above, pp. 90–93.
10. Cook, *Social Roots*.
11. See e.g. Finkelstein, 'Emergence of the Monarchy'; James W. Flanagan, 'Chiefs in Israel', *JSOT* 20 (1981), pp. 47–73; Norman K. Gottwald, 'The Participation in Free Agrarians in the Introduction of Monarchy to Ancient Israel: An Application of H. A. Landsberger's Framework for the Analysis of Peasant Movements', *Semeia* 37 (1986), pp. 77–106.

Focus on the text

While historical criticism analyses the diachronic development of the text, more recent approaches are synchronic, focusing on the text in its final form. They also tend to view the text from a literary perspective, and this invites interaction with non-biblical literary criticism, and the use of tools and methods developed within the more general literary field. As noted already, this approach includes narrative criticism, structuralism, rhetorical criticism and canonical criticism. Another recent method, intertextuality, emphasizes connections between texts. Scholarly approaches to intertexuality range from applying traditional diachronic methods, to focusing primarily on the reader.[12] However, because it involves looking at relationships within the text, it will also be considered here.

Structuralism[13]

Structuralism is an older literary approach. It is closely associated with semiotics, which looks at how meaning is communicated through the use of 'signs'. Human beings make use of a variety of actions, words and gestures in their relationships with one another. It is significant, too, that those things are meaningful only within a particular culture. Certain gestures in one culture may mean something completely different, and may even be offensive, in another. Similarly, the meaning of words and sentences is also a function of culture: so, for example, the word 'chat' means one thing in English and something very different in French.

Ferdinand de Saussure, a key figure in structuralism, argues that in linguistics signs have two aspects: the 'signifier', the sound or spelling of the word, and

---

12. For a recent summary, see e.g. Geoffrey D. Miller, 'Intertextuality in Old Testament Research', *CurBR* 9.3 (2011), pp. 283–309.
13. See e.g. Peter Barry, *Beginning Theory: An Introduction to Literary and Cultural Theory*, 2nd ed. (Manchester: Manchester University Press, 2002), pp. 39–60; Barton, *Reading*, pp. 104–139, 180–197; Gottwald, *Hebrew Bible*, pp. 24–26; Longman, 'Literary Approaches', in Baker and Arnold, *Face of OT Studies*, pp. 102–105; *Literary Approaches*, pp. 27–35; Osborne, *Hermeneutical Spiral*, pp. 470–474; Daniel Patte, *What Is Structural Exegesis?* (Philadelphia: Fortress, 1976); 'Structural Criticism', in McKenzie and Haynes, *To Each Its Own Meaning* (1999), pp. 183–200; Vern S. Poythress, 'Structuralism and Biblical Studies', *JETS* 21.3 (1978), pp. 221–237 (these last three texts focus primarily on NT texts); Redditt, *Introduction to the Prophets*, pp. 43–44; Thiselton, *Hermeneutics*, pp. 195–201.

the 'signified', the concept attached to it.[14] He notes, too, that there is no natural or inherent link between the signifier and the signified. So, for example, words denoting a particular object or concept vary from language to language, and some idiomatic expressions, even when translated, make little sense outside the culture that gave rise to them. Consequently, correspondences between signifiers and signified cannot be defined categorically, but only by noting relationships with, and, more particularly, by differentiating them from, other terms and concepts within the system. So something is a 'table' because it is not a chair or a door, and so on. Written text thus functions as a kind of code that is meaningful within a particular cultural system, and to extract the meaning from the text it is necessary to understand the literary structures of that system.

According to this approach, meaning does not depend on the intention of the writer, but is inherent within the text itself, and within the literary conventions that it assumes, and a writer may not move outside the conventions that allow meaning to be communicated. As Barton observes, 'for a structuralist, the meaning of a text is a function of the type of literature that it is, and the sorts of significance that the words composing it are capable of bearing'.[15] And the goal of a structuralist approach to a text is to discover the conventions that allow it to have meaning. This has affinities with other approaches, such as rhetorical and narrative criticism, which focus on literary conventions that are assumed within the text, and that have an impact on interpretation.

An important text in the development of structuralism is Vladimir Propp's *The Morphology of the Folktale*, which influenced key figures including Claude Lévi-Strauss and Roland Barthes. Several biblical scholars have also applied the structural model of A. J. Greimas to biblical texts.[16]

---

14. Ferdinand de Saussure, *Course in General Linguistics*, trans. Roy Harris (Paris: Carus, 1972); see also e.g. John Coker, 'Jacques Derrida', in Robert C. Solomon and David L. Sherman (eds.), *The Blackwell Guide to Continental Philosophy* (Oxford: Blackwell, 2003), pp. 265–284 (268–270).
15. Barton, *Reading*, p. 114.
16. See Routledge, 'Narrative Substructure'; see also e.g. Rollin G. Grams, 'Narrative Dynamics in Isaiah's and Matthew's Mission Theology', *Transformation* 21.4 (2004), pp. 238–255; Richard Hayes, *The Faith of Jesus Christ – An Investigation of the Narrative Substructure of Galatians 3:1–4:11*, SBLDS 56 (Chico: Scholars Press, 1983); Longman, *Literary Approaches*, pp. 35–37; Daniel Patte, *The Religious Dimensions of Biblical Texts: Greimas' Structural Semiotics and Biblical Exegesis*, SemeiaSt (Atlanta: Scholars Press, 1990); Mark W. G. Stibbe, '"Return to Sender": A Structuralist Approach to John's Gospel', in John Ashton (ed.), *The Interpretation of John*, 2nd ed., Studies in New

Structuralism attempts to offer an objective 'scientific' method of analysing texts. However, later exponents recognized that identifying structures within the text is subjective, allowing different readers to arrive at different interpretations. Thus it is necessary, too, to consider interaction between the text and the reader, who is thus significant in the interpretative process. This reader-centred aspect is significant in post-structural criticisms.

Rhetorical criticism[17]

As a specifically designated focus of OT study, 'rhetorical criticism' owes its beginnings to James Muilenburg.[18] He noted the importance of close reading of biblical texts, with particular focus on the literary devices that were used to communicate their message. He labelled this approach 'rhetorical criticism', though the focus was on the more general literary character of the text, and includes, largely, what has already been considered under narrative criticism. Since Muilenburg, attempts to distinguish rhetorical criticism from narrative and other literary criticisms focus on the significance of the term 'rhetorical'.

In its classical understanding, as articulated, for example, by Aristotle,[19] rhetoric is about the art of persuasion, and there has been an increasing tendency in rhetorical criticism to focus on that aspect of a biblical text. The rhetorical critic is concerned, according to Barton, with 'the persuasive structuring of arguments'.[20] The way texts are constructed and the literary devices employed

---

Testament Interpretation (London: T&T Clark, 1997), pp. 261–278; Ellen J. van Wolde, *A Semiotic Analysis of Genesis 2–3: A Semiotic Theory and Method of Analysis Applied to the Story of the Garden of Eden* (Assen: Van Gorcum, 1989).

17. See e.g. J. D. Barker, 'Rhetorical Criticism', in *DOTPr*, pp. 676–684; Barton, *Reading*, pp. 199–204; Yehoshua Gitay, 'Rhetorical Criticism', in McKenzie and Haynes, *To Each Its Own Meaning* (1993), pp. 135–149; David M. Howard Jr., 'Rhetorical Criticism in Old Testament Studies', *BBR* 4 (1992), pp. 87–104; P. Overland, 'Rhetorical Criticism', in *DOTWPW*, pp. 655–663; Redditt, *Introduction to the Prophets*, pp. 38–40; Phyllis Trible, *Rhetorical Criticism: Context, Method, and the Book of Jonah* (Minneapolis: Augsburg Fortress, 1994); Patricia K. Tull, 'Rhetorical Criticism and Intertextuality', in McKenzie and Haynes, *To Each Its Own Meaning* (1999), pp. 156–179; Steve Walton, 'Rhetorical Criticism: An Introduction', *Them* 21.2 (1996), pp. 4–9.
18. James Muilenburg, 'Form Criticism and Beyond', *JBL* 88.1 (1969), pp. 1–18.
19. Aristotle, *Rhetoric*.
20. Barton, *Reading*, p. 204.

are still important, but the primary focus is on how those things contribute to the persuasive character of the text.[21] In one sense, anything that contributes to the effective communication of a text is 'rhetorical', in so far as it encourages the hearer or reader to take note of what is being said; hence the overlap with narrative criticism. The narrator may also portray characters or situations in a way that makes them more, or less, sympathetic to the reader.[22] However there is value in looking more specifically at the way texts are intended not only to communicate or evoke sympathy, but also to change the mind of those who receive the message.

Rhetoric may be analysed in a variety of contexts,[23] though it is, perhaps, more usually associated with the prophetic books. An important task of the prophets was to reverse the decline in the moral and spiritual life of the nation, and call the nation back to their covenant faith and obligations. And that required persuasion. In Isaiah 1:18–20 God appeals to the people:

> 'Come now, let us reason together,' says the Lord.
> 'Though your sins are like scarlet,
>   they shall be as white as snow;
> though they are red as crimson,
>   they shall be like wool.
> If you are willing and obedient,
>   you will eat the best from the land;
> but if you resist and rebel,
>   you will be devoured by the sword.'
> For the mouth of the Lord has spoken.[24]

This passage uses several rhetorical devices. It presents God as one who is interested: who wants to talk and listen. It invites the listener to consider the difference that turning to God brings. Sin results in a stain that is 'red as crimson', but that stain can be expunged and can become pure white. The passage points to the benefits and reward associated with obedience to God: 'you will eat the best of the land'. But alongside the carrot is the stick, and we see, too, a dire warning for disobedience. The inclusio 'says the Lord' and 'the

21. The term 'rhetorical criticism' is still used with its wider meaning by some scholars.
22. See Sternberg, *Poetics*, pp. 441–481, 482–515.
23. See e.g. Overland, 'Rhetorical Criticism', in *DOTWPW*, pp. 657–661.
24. Gitay includes this in his discussion of Isa. 1:2–20 ('Rhetorical Criticism', in McKenzie and Haynes, *To Each Its Own Meaning* [1993], pp. 138–141).

mouth of the Lord has spoken' adds divine authority to the case being made. By appealing in this way, the prophet seeks to persuade his audience to change their minds.

There is a clear rhetorical structure in Amos 1:3 – 2:16. The prophet begins by denouncing the sin of nations surrounding Israel. And his Israelite audience, we may assume, would have agreed, wholeheartedly, with the divine verdict. The judgment on Judah (2:4–5), which Israel would also have gladly endorsed, is significant in that it moves from general wickedness to the particular sin of disobeying God's law. At that point, having brought the people to a place where they agree that those who sin, including those who disregard God's law, should suffer the consequences, Amos rounds on Israel (2:6–16). The repeated structure 'for three sins . . . and for four' places Israel (and Judah) among the sinful kingdoms: Israel, too, has disobeyed God so also deserves to be punished.[25]

Some see a link between rhetorical criticism, viewed as the way words are used to achieve a particular goal, and *speech-act theory*, which features in linguistic theory more generally.[26] Speech-act theory has been summarized as 'how to do things with words'.[27] It recognizes that when words are spoken, they have an effect, and looks at how they are used to achieve particular results. This theory notes three 'acts'. First, the 'locutionary act' (or 'speech act') is the act of saying something. Second, the 'illocutionary act' is the act that is intended to result from what is said. This focuses on the content of the speech act. Language intended 'to do something' is generally divided into five categories: (1) making an assertion about something ('assertives'); (2) giving direction to the hearer to do something ('directives'); (3) making a commitment to a particular course of action ('commissives'); (4) expressing feelings or thoughts about something, such as giving thanks or offering congratulations ('expressives'); (5) and making a declaration that brings about change, such as a judge pronouncing a person guilty, or a dignitary naming a ship ('declaratives'). Third, the 'perlocutionary act' is the act that actually results from what is said, whether intentional

---

25. Nathan employs a similar rhetorical strategy when confronting David over his sin with Bathsheba (2 Sam. 12:1–7).

26. E.g. Barker, 'Rhetorical Criticism', in *DOTPr*, pp. 681–682. For a more cautionary approach, see Richard S. Briggs, *Words in Action: Speech Act Theory and Biblical Interpretation* (Edinburgh: T&T Clark International, 2001), pp. 95–97.

27. This expression comes from the title of the book recording a series of lectures by Austin in 1955, which first discussed speech-act theory; see J. L. Austin, *How to Do Things with Words*, 2nd ed. (Oxford: Oxford University Press, 1975).

or otherwise.[28] Several scholars recognize the value of this approach for OT studies.[29]

'Canonical criticism'[30]

Two key figures are associated with the emphasis on the canon of Scripture: James Sanders and Brevard Childs. Their approaches have a number of points in common. Both focus attention on the canonical text. Both reflect concerns

---

28. For further discussion of speech-act theory in relation to biblical studies, see e.g. Jim W. Adams, *The Performative Nature and Function of Isaiah 40–55* (London: T&T Clark, 2006), esp. pp. 1–8; Richard S. Briggs, 'Speech-Act Theory', in Firth and Grant, *Words and the Word*, pp. 75–110; 'Getting Involved: Speech Acts and Biblical Interpretation', *Anvil* 20.1 (2003), pp. 25–34; *Words in Action: Speech Act Theory and Biblical Interpretation* (Edinburgh: T&T Clark International, 2001); Brevard S. Childs, 'Speech Act Theory and Biblical Interpretation', *SJT* 58 (2005), pp. 375–392; Walter Houston, 'What Did the Prophets Think They Were Doing? Speech Acts and Prophetic Discourse in the Old Testament', in Robert P. Gordon (ed.), *The Place Is Too Small for Us: The Israelite Prophets in Recent Scholarship*, SBTS 5 (Winona Lake: Eisenbrauns, 1995), pp. 133–153; Thiselton, *Thiselton on Hermeneutics*, pp. 51–149; Hugh C. White (ed.), *Semeia 41: Speech Act Theory and Biblical Criticism* (Decatur: Scholars Press, 1988); see also Nicholas Wolterstorff, *Divine Discourse: Philosophical Reflections on the Claim that God Speaks* (Cambridge: Cambridge University Press, 1995).
29. See e.g. Karl Möller, *A Prophet in Debate: The Rhetoric of Persuasion in the Book of Amos* (Sheffield: Sheffield Academic Press, 2003), pp. 33–36; Robson, *Word and Spirit*, pp. 11–12.
30. See e.g. John Barton, 'Canon and Old Testament Interpretation', in *Collected Essays*, pp. 31–42; 'Canonical Approaches Ancient and Modern', in ibid., pp. 43–52; *Reading*, pp. 77–103; Dale A. Brueggemann, 'Brevard Childs Canon Criticism: An Example of Post-Critical Naiveté', *JETS* 32.3 (1989), pp. 311–326; Mary C. Callaway, 'Canonical Criticism', in McKenzie and Haynes, *To Each Its Own Meaning* (1999), pp. 142–155; Childs, *Introduction*, esp. pp. 69–83; *Biblical Theology*, pp. 70–106; *OT Theology*, pp. 6–18; R. A. Harrisville and W. Sundberg, *The Bible in Modern Culture: Baruch Spinoza to Brevard Childs*, 2nd ed. (Grand Rapids: Eerdmans, 2002); Iain Provan, 'Canons to the Left of Him: Brevard Childs, His Critics and the Future of Old Testament Theology', *SJT* 50.1 (1977), pp. 1–38; Redditt, *Introduction to the Prophets*, pp. 40–41; James A. Sanders, *Canon and Community: A Guide to Canonical Criticism* (Eugene: Wipf & Stock, 1984); Chen Xun, *Theological Exegesis in the Canonical Context: Brevard Springs Childs's Methodology of Biblical Theology* (New York: Peter Lang, 2010), esp. pp. 57–110.

that the diachronic approach of historical-critical methods does not do justice to the authoritative role of that text within the believing community – while also recognizing the value of the insights derived from historical criticism and seeking to build on, rather than dismiss, it.[31] And, in the way they frame their alternative approaches, both seek to recover the significance of the biblical text for the church. In other respects, though, there are significant differences.

Sanders coined the term 'canonical criticism' to describe his approach.[32] He points to two key features of canonical literature: stability and adaptability,[33] and suggests that from the sixth century BC to the first century AD, the formative period for the OT canon, those emphases ran side by side: 'the idea of the living Word of God ever dynamically new and fresh, and the idea of traditions which were becoming stabilized into certain forms but were generation after generation in need of being adapted to and heard afresh in new historical contexts'.[34] A key focus of Sanders's approach is to explore the way texts and traditions were adapted in order to give them contemporary relevance to the believing community.[35]

Whereas Sanders focuses on the process by which the canon was developed, Childs emphasizes the significance of the final form of the text. He rejects the term 'canonical criticism' in favour of 'canonical approach', arguing that his intention is not to add just one more critical technique, but to establish 'a stance from which the Bible can be read as sacred scripture'.[36] Childs does not dismiss the insights of historical criticism. He recognizes that the biblical text has developed over time, with earlier material selected, arranged and expanded by those who passed it on, and he sees value in noting the way that development has taken place. However, only the final form of the text, which has been

---

31. Childs describes his approach as 'post-critical' (*Introduction*, pp. 16, 127); this may, in part, be prompted by the criticism that his approach was reverting to a pre-critical position.
32. James A. Sanders, *Torah and Canon*, 2nd ed. (Eugene: Wipf & Stock, 2005), p. vii.
33. James A. Sanders, 'Text and Canon: Concepts and Method', *JBL* 98.1 (1979), pp. 5–29 (13).
34. Ibid., p. 21.
35. According to Sanders, 'study of text and canon today focuses increasing attention upon the intra-biblical hermeneutics at every stage in biblical antiquity – how the biblical authors and thinkers themselves contemporized and adapted and reshaped the traditions they received and how those traditions functioned for them when called upon' (ibid., pp. 28–29).
36. Childs, *Introduction*, p. 82.

accepted as normative by the believing community, 'bears witness to the full history of revelation';[37] and thus that final form should be the focus for exegesis and interpretation. Childs allows for the presence of multiple sources and of editorial layers, but the primary consideration is the way these things function within the canon.

When it comes to exegesis, Childs notes historical-critical data relating to the development and canonical shaping of the text, including how parts of the text might have functioned in an earlier context. That, though, is subordinated to the way it functions within its new, canonical setting. An example of this is the prophecy of Hosea, which, Childs argues, went through three redactional stages.[38] The first stage was Hosea's original prophecy, addressed primarily to the northern kingdom of Israel. Stage two was the selection and arrangement of those oracles. The inclusion of several references to Judah, which appear not to have been part of Hosea's original preaching, suggests that redaction took place in the south, and that the prophet's message of judgment was extended and reapplied to Judah. Childs further suggests a third stage in which Yahweh's relationship with Judah is presented positively, in contrast to that with Israel, and introduces a message of hope. Taken as a canonical whole the book is addressed to both Israel and Judah; and while it threatens judgment, that judgment is inextricably linked with the hope of salvation.

Canonical approaches focus, primarily, on the text. However, the final canonical form of the text is rooted in the historical encounter between God and his people, and Childs distances himself from other final-form approaches, which separate the text from its historical setting. He asserts that

> by shaping Israel's traditions into the form of a normative scripture the biblical idiom no longer functions for the community of faith as a free-floating metaphor, but as the divine imperative and promise to a historically conditioned people of God whose legacy the Christian church confesses to share.[39]

The canonical approach has been criticized from all sides. One inherent weakness is debate over the development of the OT canon and what now constitutes the canonical text. Another is that the process of divine inspiration is associated with the believing community, rather than with the OT writers. Nevertheless, this approach has value in that, while not dismissing the usefulness

37. Ibid., p. 76.
38. Ibid., pp. 377–382.
39. Ibid., p. 77.

of historical criticism, it focuses on the text as a canonical whole and seeks to retain the authority of that canonical text as Scripture, which was, and continues to be, normative for the people of God.

Intertextuality[40]

Intertextuality, as the name implies, focuses on the interrelationships between texts. It is frequently applied to the use of the OT by NT writers,[41] though it is used, too, to compare texts within the same Testament. In the latter case, though, there is a question about the relative dating of the texts. Miller notes that this is answered in two ways.[42] For some, the issue is not relevant; if there

---

40. See e.g. John Barton, 'Déjà Lu: Intertextuality, Method or Theory?', in Katharine Dell and Will Kynes (eds.), *Reading Job Intertextually* (London: Bloomsbury, 2013), pp. 1–16; Danna Nolan Fewell, *Reading Between Texts: Intertextuality and the Hebrew Bible* (Philadelphia: Westminster John Knox, 1996); P. E. Koptak, 'Intertextuality', in *DOTWPW*, pp. 325–332; G. D. Miller, 'Intertextuality'; Steve Moyise, 'Intertextuality and Biblical Studies: A Review', *VE* 23.2 (2002), pp. 418–431; Tull, 'Rhetorical Criticism and Intertextuality', in McKenzie and Haynes, *To Each Its Own Meaning* (1999), pp. 164–167. For discussion of intertextuality in relation to specific OT texts, see (as a small example), Katharine Dell and Will Kynes (eds.), *Reading Ecclesiastes Intertextually* (London: Bloomsbury, 2014); *Reading Job Intertextually*; Greg A. King, 'The Message of Zephaniah: An Urgent Echo', *AUSS* 32.2 (1996), pp. 211–222; Hava Shalom-Guy, 'Three-Way Intertextuality: Some Reflections of Abimelech's Death at Thebez in Biblical Narrative', *JSOT* 34.4 (2010), pp. 419–432; Michael R. Stead, *The Intertextuality of Zechariah 1–8* (London: T&T Clark International, 2009); Gary E. Yates, 'Intertextuality and the Portrayal of Jeremiah the Prophet', *BSac* 170 (2013), pp. 283–300.
41. See Moyise, 'Intertextuality and Biblical Studies'; see also e.g. Brian J. Abasciano, *Paul's Use of the Old Testament in Romans 9:10–18: An Intertextual and Theological Exegesis* (London: T&T Clark International, 2011); Richard B. Hays, *Echoes of Scripture in the Letters of Paul*, new ed. (New Haven: Yale University Press, 1993); Sylvia C. Keesmaat, *Paul and His Story: (Re)Interpreting the Exodus Tradition* (Sheffield: Sheffield Academic Press, 1999); Steve Moyise (ed.), *The Old Testament in the New Testament: Essays in Honor of J. L. North* (Sheffield: Sheffield Academic Press, 2000); Jon Paulien, 'Dreading the Whirlwind: Intertextuality and the Use of the Old Testament in Revelation', *AUSS* 39.1 (2001), pp. 5–22. See also Richard B. Hays, Stefan Alkier and Leroy A. Huizenga (eds.), *Reading the Bible Intertextually* (Waco: Baylor University Press, 2009).
42. G. D. Miller, 'Intertextuality', pp. 286–287.

is a link, then that may be explored regardless of which text may have been written first. For others, intertextual allusions are deliberate acts of the author or editor, and texts alluded to must, therefore, be earlier. The view that is adopted will, in part, be determined by the significance attached to authorial intention.[43] In my view the author's intention should not be quickly dismissed. However, the acceptance, by the believing community, of the OT as a canonical whole may also be taken to imply the acceptance, too, of the web of intertextual relationships contained within it. It seems possible, too, that though a text might have been written down later, the underlying tradition might have been known earlier. Consequently, when looking at intertextuality, there needs to be some caution about assuming the need for a direct historical relationship.

Intertextual relationships take various forms. The clearest instances are where words or phrases from one text appear in another. This is generally significant only where those expressions are relatively uncommon, or are used in a distinctive way.[44] So, for example, we have noted that the occurrence of the relatively uncommon expression 'go forth' in Genesis 12:1 and 22:2 suggests a link between the texts. Genesis 6:1–8 picks up the theme of 'good and evil' evident in the earlier part of the book (Gen. 2:9; 3:5). And there appears to be a further link in the occurrence of the words 'saw', 'good' and 'took'. In Genesis 3:6, when Eve '*saw* that [the fruit of the] tree was *good* [*ṭōb*] . . . she *took*'; in Genesis 6:2 the sons of God '*saw* that [the daughters of men] were *fair* [*ṭōb*] and they *took*' (NRSV). This suggests a link between Genesis 6:1–8 and the episode in the Garden.[45]

Correspondences in content or in the form or structure of texts, even where the language may not be the same, may also be evidence of intertextuality.[46] The description of Abishag as 'very beautiful' (1 Kgs 1:4) echoes the similar description of Bathsheba (2 Sam. 11:2) even though different words for 'beautiful' are used. There may be an intended correspondence between the parting of the Red Sea and the drying up of the Jordan – events that mark the beginning and end of Israel's journey to the Promised Land. It also would have provided

43. For discussion of the significance of the author's intention, see below, pp. 220–227.

44. For a suggested hierarchy when seeking to determine the significance of intertextual links, see Jeffery M. Leonard, 'Identifying Inner-Biblical Allusions: Psalm 78 as a Test Case', *JBL* 127.2 (2008), pp. 241–265 (245–257).

45. See Routledge, 'My Spirit', pp. 243–244.

46. See G. D. Miller, 'Intertextuality', pp. 295–298; cf. Alter's discussion of 'type-scenes' (*Art of Biblical Narrative*, pp. 47–62).

encouragement both for Joshua, as he took over the mantle of leadership from Moses, and also for the people.[47]

Intertexuality is sometimes used as an interpretative tool in its own right. However, as the examples above indicate, it is perhaps most useful when used in conjunction with other approaches, particulary narrative and rhetorical criticism.

Discourse analysis[48]

Discourse analysis focuses on spoken and written communication, though when applied to biblical hermeneutics the primary emphasis is on the latter. It looks at the respective parts played in the act of communication by the writer, the text and the reader. As such, it is a very broad field, and there are areas of overlap with other approaches, including narrative and rhetorical criticism, speech-act theory and intertextuality. It has been included at this point because the text is central to the approach. Though it also contains elements from writer- and reader-centred approaches.

It is difficult to define discourse analysis precisely. A key element, though, as its name suggests, is that meaning is found by looking at a whole discourse,[49] rather than at the smaller textual elements that have often been the subject of textual and linguistic study. A commonly noted feature of discourse analysis is

---

47. See also below, pp. 258–259.

48. For a general introduction to discourse analysis, see e.g. Brian Paltridge, *Discourse Analysis: An Introduction*, 2nd ed. (London: Bloomsbury Academic, 2012). On the role of discourse analysis in biblical hermeneutics see e.g. Walter R. Bodine, *Discourse Analysis of Biblical Literature: What It Is and What It Offers*, SemeiaSt (Atlanta: Society of Biblical Literature, 1995); Jack Collins, 'Discourse Analysis and the Interpretation of Genesis 2:4–7', *WTJ* 61 (1999), pp. 269–276; Vern S. Poythress, 'Analysing a Biblical Text: What Are We After?', *SJT* 32.4 (1979), pp. 319–331; Jeffrey T. Reed, 'Discourse Analysis as New Testament Hermeneutic: A Retrospective and Prospective Appraisal', *JETS* 39.2 (1996), pp. 223–240; David Toshio Tsumura, *The First Book of Samuel*, NICOT (Grand Rapids: Eerdmans, 2007), pp. 49–55; Terence R. Wardlaw Jr., 'Discourse Analysis', in Firth and Grant, *Words and the Word*, pp. 266–317.

49. In this context a 'discourse' is what is generally taken to be a complete spoken or written unit: 'texts are what hearers and readers treat as texts' (Gillian Brown and George Yule, *Discourse Analysis*, Cambridge Textbooks in Linguistics [Cambridge: Cambridge University Press, 1983], p. 199; see also Reed, 'Discourse Analysis', p. 225; Wardlaw, 'Discourse Analysis', in Firth and Grant, *Words and the Word*, p. 268).

that it looks at units 'beyond the level of the sentence'.[50] The meaning of words and phrases is linked to the wider context in which they appear, and that requires study of the larger textual unit. Important, too, is the way the discourse is structured, including the order in which the material is presented, and the use of poetic and rhetorical devices. Because language is socially and culturally conditioned, discourse analysis considers, too, why particular words and phrases have been chosen. This, in turn, involves looking at the text's historical and social context, and at what the writer might have intended to convey, by particular language choices. However, because communication is two-way, it involves, too, looking at the reception of the text by its readers. *Critical discourse analysis* looks, further, at how language in discourse not only reflects, but also influences social and cultural perceptions and ideologies.[51]

From this brief description it is clear that discourse analysis is very wide ranging in its scope. As such, it may appear unwieldy; however, it recognizes that the various ways of looking at biblical texts are not discrete, and seeks to offer an integrated approach, in which no single aspect takes priority over the others. It allows study of the text, but with due regard to its historical and social context and also its contemporary significance. It might be argued that much of this might, anyway, have been included in the detailed exegesis of a text. Discourse analysis serves to formalize that wider approach, and that can be welcome where there is a tendency towards narrowing the hermeneutical focus. It also offers something new by emphasizing the role of linguistics in approaches to exegesis, though this also involves the use of more specialist terminology that might make the approach less widely accessible.

Focus on the reader

Reader-response criticism[52]

As we have seen, post-structural approaches move the locus of meaning away from the text. In reader-response criticism, meaning is created in the interaction

---

50. Paltridge, *Discourse Analysis*, p. 2; cf. Reed, 'Discourse Analysis', p. 231.

51. Paltridge, *Discourse Analysis*, pp. 187–203; Reed, 'Discourse Analysis', pp. 237–238; Wardlaw, 'Discourse Analysis', in Firth and Grant, *Words and the Word*, pp. 276–278.

52. See e.g. Barton, *Reading*, pp. 209–217; David J. A. Clines, 'Methods in Old Testament Study', in John Rogerson, John Barton, David J. A. Clines and Paul Joyce, *Beginning Old Testament Study* (London: SPCK; Danvers: Chalice, 1998), pp. 25–48 (41–42); 'A World Established on Water (Psalm 24): Reader-Response, Deconstruction and Bespoke Interpretation', in *Interested Parties*, pp. 172–186; Longman, 'Literary Approaches', in Baker and Arnold, *Face of OT Studies*, pp. 105–107; *Literary*

between text and reader. In one form of this approach the reader completes the meaning of the text, by filling in gaps.[53] In such cases, though, the range of possibilities, and so the range of interpretations, is controlled by the narrative.[54]

Another approach puts greater emphasis on the reader, and the text is a vehicle through which the reader creates meaning. That may allow a text to mean whatever the reader wants it to mean. In general, though, it is recognized that there are conventions governing legitimate interpretations. Clines, for example, suggests that while there is no right interpretation, 'there may be bad ones'.[55] The key to separating the acceptable from the unacceptable, and thereby avoiding an interpretative free-for-all, lies with the idea of 'interpretative communities', a term coined by Stanley Fish.[56] Most scholars look to peers to validate a position. Fish widens that scope. Because interpretation is influenced by socio-culturally conditioned norms, religious background and ideological emphases, those things must feature in defining an interpretative community. And that community, made up of those who share the reader's sociological, cultural and religious outlook, validates the interpretation.

A significant feature of reader-response criticism is pluralism: the possibility of different, but all equally valid, interpretations. Gunn and Fewell note different interpretations of Genesis 4,[57] each influenced by the interpreter's sociocultural and religious context. Martin Luther focuses on the significance of procreation and uses the text to attack the celibacy of the Roman Catholic priesthood. John Calvin emphasizes different aspects of the story, including that Cain's murder of Abel was linked to Adam's sin, thereby pointing to the doctrine of original sin. Although not included in Gunn and Fewell's analysis, Calvin, like Luther, also uses the text to attack the Roman Catholic Church, and likens Cain's offering to

---

Approaches, pp. 38–41; Edgar V. McKnight, 'Reader Response Criticism', in McKenzie and Haynes, *To Each Its Own Meaning* (1999), pp. 230–252; Osborne, *Hermeneutical Spiral*, pp. 478–482; Redditt, *Introduction to the Prophets*, pp. 46–49.

53. See e.g. Wolfgang Iser, *The Implied Reader: Patterns of Communication in Prose Fiction from Bunyan to Beckett* (Baltimore: Johns Hopkins University Press, 1974); *Prospecting: From Reader Response to Literary Anthropology* (Baltimore: Johns Hopkins University Press, 1993), pp. 3–70.
54. See Iser, *Prospecting*, p. 33.
55. Clines, 'World Established on Water', p. 184.
56. See Stanley Fish, *Is There a Text in This Class: The Authority of Interpretative Communities* (Cambridge, Mass.: Harvard University Press, 1980).
57. Gunn and Fewell, *Narrative*, pp. 12–27.

hypocritical external ritual, without inward dedication.[58] Readings by Allan Boesak and Itumeleng Mosala are set within the context of South African apartheid, though their interpretations are very different. Boesak takes a more traditional approach. Cain is the oppressor who kills his brother. However, there is hope of forgiveness and the birth of Seth opens up the possibility of a new start. Mosala turns the story around. As part of J, the passage supports the ideology of monarchy, which led to the formation of large estates by the king and his nobles, thus contradicting the principle that each family would have a stake in the land. In Mosala's view Abel represents the rise of these landed classes, and Cain, who is deprived of his land and forced to become a wanderer, is the real victim in the story. This way of reading the text, which challenges the ideology of the writer, is sometimes referred to as 'resistant reading' or 'reading against the grain'.[59]

Clearly, not all such interpretations can be 'correct' in any absolute sense. However, any interpretation that is validated by an interpretative community may be considered legitimate. Reader-response criticism thus raises questions about the authority of Scripture, particularly in relation to its normative role. However, it does keep us alert to the fact that no interpreter is neutral. All come from a particular background, with expectations, assumptions, questions and preconceptions, and all need to be aware of how those things might influence exegesis and interpretation.

Deconstruction[60]

Post-structural approaches proceed from the premise that a text has no inherent meaning. It means something only when read, and that meaning will depend on the reader and what the reader brings to the text. Deconstruction takes this further, and theorizes that 'every text always and necessarily undermines or contradicts the philosophy on which its own plausibility rests'.[61]

---

58. See J. Calvin, *Genesis*, Geneva Commentaries (London: Banner of Truth Trust, 1965), p. 196.
59. See Clines, 'God in the Pentateuch', in *Interested Parties*, pp. 206–207.
60. See e.g. Barry, *Beginning Theory*, pp. 61–80; Barton, *Reading*, pp. 220–236; Clines, 'Methods in OT Study', in Rogerson et al., *Beginning OT Study*, pp. 42–43; Coker, 'Jacques Derrida', in Solomon and Sherman, *Continental Philosophy*, pp. 265–284; Longman, 'Literary Approaches', in Baker and Arnold, *Face of OT Studies*, pp. 107–110; *Literary Approaches*, pp. 41–45; Osborne, *Hermeneutical Spiral*, pp. 482–489.
61. Barton, *Readings*, p. 224.

Clines uses the example of Genesis 9:6 – 'Whoever sheds the blood of man, by man shall his blood be shed'. This is a strong warning against murder; however, Clines argues, by expressing the penalty in the same terms as the crime, 'the command allows what it also prohibits'.[62] However, deconstruction goes beyond particular examples and posits that such contradictions lie within every text, and that the medium of writing is therefore inadequate to convey meaning.

Deconstruction is widely associated with Jacques Derrida.[63] He uses Saussure's terms of signifier and signified, though disagrees with his conclusions. Because the correspondence between signifier and signified depends on its relationships with other correspondences within the system, and each of those correspondences also depends on relationships with others, and so on, the 'meaning' of a sign, in theory at least, must be deferred until all such relationships have been considered. Derrida notes, too, that there is 'slippage' in the correspondence between signifier and signified. The same signifier may, for example, have more than one signified; so 'door' may correspond to a physical opening, an opportunity, or a barrier that closes off an opportunity. Signifiers, therefore, need to be qualified. But that introduces more signifiers, more deferred meaning and more potential for slippage. This, then, contributes to conclusions about the severe limitations of the written text as a medium for communication.[64]

Deconstruction tends to be essentially negative. It challenges the view that we can infer definitive meaning from a text, and so undermines traditional interpretations of biblical passages, and the theology that derives from them. According to Clines, deconstruction 'relativizes the authority attributed to biblical texts, and makes it evident that much of the power that is felt to lie in texts is really the power of the community that supports them and sanctions them'.[65] Deconstruction thus encourages readers to approach the text with some cynicism, both towards the text itself, and towards structures that may look to those texts for their validation. One outcome of this approach is the emphasis on ideological readings of the text.

---

62. Clines, 'Methods in OT Study', in Rogerson et al., *Beginning OT Study*, p. 43.
63. This discussion seeks to give only the gist of the debate in order to indicate where aspects of the discussion that influence biblical studies have come from.
64. Ironically, by using the medium of the written text to demonstrate the inadequacy of the written text this discussion itself deconstructs.
65. Clines, 'Methods in OT Study', in Rogerson et al., *Beginning OT Study*, p. 43.

Ideological readings[66]

Texts are written and read from a particular ideological perspective. Generally, the ideological standpoints of the OT writers reflect the values and norms of their context, which will, in turn, reflect the world view of those with power and influence. One consequence of this might be that the voices of those without power and of those on the margins of society are not heard. So, for example, in a patriarchal society, this might exclude the voices of women. The text also, understandably, reflects the values of Israel, over against, for example, the Egyptians, who suffered as a result of the plagues, or the Canaanites, who were dispossessed during the conquest. In such cases ideological readings include a critique of the standpoint of the writers and speak up in favour of those who are ignored. This may appear to raise problems for the view that Scripture is divinely inspired, and therefore may be assumed to reflect God's perspective. However, as noted already, inspiration does not override the writers' cultural and theological world view, and that may also include ideological perspectives. Indeed, it could be argued that if texts are to be applied to a contemporary Christian setting, ideological elements need to be identified and taken into account.

Sometimes the critique of the ideology reflected in the OT text will be related to the ideological perspective that the reader brings to it. Such perspectives include feminist, political, liberation, postcolonial and queer readings.[67] We have

66. See e.g. Clines, *Interested Parties*, pp. 9–25; David Jobling and Tina Pippin, *Ideological Criticism of Biblical Texts*, Semeia 59 (Atlanta: Scholars Press, 1992); Redditt, *Introduction to the Prophets*, pp. 49–50; Johanna Stiebert, *The Exile and the Prophet's Wife: Historic Events and Marginal Perspectives* (Collegeville: Michael Glazier, 2005), pp. 65–83; 'Ideological Criticism', in The Bible and Culture Collective, *The Postmodern Bible* (New Haven: Yale University Press, 1995), pp. 272–308.

67. Stiebert, *Prophet's Wife*, pp. 67–68. See further e.g. Barry, *Beginning Theory*, pp. 121–202; E. B. Farisani, 'Black Biblical Hermeneutics and Ideologically Aware Reading of Texts', *Scriptura* 105 (2010), pp. 507–518; D. N. Fewell, 'Reading the Bible Ideologically: Feminist Criticism', in McKenzie and Haynes, *To Each Its Own Meaning* (1999), pp. 268–282; Norman K. Gottwald (ed.), *The Bible and Liberation: Political and Social Hermeneutics* (Maryknoll: Orbis, 1983); Teresa J. Hornsby and Ken Stone (eds.), *Bible Trouble: Queer Readings at the Boundaries of Biblical Scholarship*, SemeiaSt 67 (Atlanta: Society of Biblical Literature, 2011); Alastair G. Hunter and Philip R. Davies (eds.), *Sense and Sensitivity: Essays on Reading the Bible in Memory of Robert Carroll* (London: Sheffield Academic Press, 2002); Lazare S. Rukundwa, 'Postcolonial Theory as a Hermeneutical Tool for Biblical Reading', *HTS* 64.1 (2008), pp. 339–351.

already noted two political readings of Genesis 4. In his essay 'A Reader-Response Approach to Prophetic Conflict',[68] Francisco Garcia-Treto, because of his ethnic background and cultural allegiance, describes himself as a Hispanic American, and places himself within that interpretative community. The relative powerlessness of that community leads to a political reading of texts, which focuses not on doctrinal issues, but on the relationship between the powerful and the powerless, and God's response to each.

There are a significant number of feminist readings of biblical texts. According to Clines and Exum, 'the starting point of feminist criticism is . . . not the given texts but the issues and concerns of feminism as a world view and as a political enterprise'.[69] Trible notes the role of this kind of approach: 'as a critique of culture and faith in the light of misogyny, feminism is a prophetic movement, examining the status quo, pronouncing judgment, and calling for repentance'.[70] This approach may be applied to the biblical text in different ways. It may analyse texts to emphasize their male orientation, and their suppression of the role and voice of women. It may seek to listen for women's voices within the male-centred text, and so to uncover texts that challenge patriarchal structures. More negatively, by emphasising the way texts marginalize and devalue women, it may seek to subvert the text and expose the Bible as just another tool of male-dominated oppression.

We might mention, briefly, two examples. Alice Bach discusses the 'test for an unfaithful wife' in Numbers 5:11–31.[71] This is particularly one-sided. A husband may subject his wife to this investigation with no basis for suspicion other than feelings of jealousy; it leaves him free from guilt whether his suspicions are confirmed or not, and, significantly, there is no similar test for a husband. The main purpose of the ritual, according to Bach, is to keep women in their place. Though it does give women, who might otherwise be at the mercy of their husbands, some recourse in the face of unjust accusation.

Danna Fewell notes that in Genesis 35:18 a dying Rachel names her child Ben-Oni (son of my trouble). Jacob, however, renames him Benjamin. Fewell

---

68. Francisco Garcia-Treto, 'A Reader-Response Approach to Prophetic Conflict', in J. Cheryl Exum and David J. A. Clines (eds.), *The New Literary Criticism and the Hebrew Bible*, JSOTSup 143 (Sheffield: Sheffield Academic Press, 1993), pp. 114–124.
69. Exum and Clines, *New Literary Criticism*, p. 17.
70. Phyllis Trible, *Texts of Terror: Literary-Feminist Readings of Biblical Narratives*, OBT (Philadelphia: Fortress, 1984), p. 3.
71. A. Bach, 'Good to the Last Drop', in Exum and Clines, *New Literary Criticism*, pp. 26–54.

takes this as an example of the way women's experiences are 'inscribed or reinscribed by men. Women's sufferings, joys and concerns have been "written over", altered, and even negated in subservience to what has been of significance to men.'[72] Again this reflects patriarchal ideology. However, the fact that we know Rachel's dying wish does at least show that her voice has not been written out of the text altogether.

Meaning and the author's intention[73]

Within traditional evangelical scholarship the author's intention has been a crucial factor in determining the meaning of a text.[74] By contrast, literary approaches argue that, even if it could be determined, authorial intention is not relevant for interpretation.[75] More significant is the interaction between the

72. Fewell, 'Feminist Criticism', in McKenzie and Haynes, *To Each Its Own Meaning* (1999), p. 270.
73. See e.g. Hirsch, *Validity in Interpretation*, pp. 1–23; Osborne, *Hermeneutical Spiral*, pp. 24, 468, 495–498; Philip B. Payne, 'The Fallacy of Equating Meaning with the Human Author's Intention', *JETS* 20 (1977), pp. 243–252; Routledge, 'Guest or Gatecrasher', pp. 20–24; John H. Sailhamer, *The Meaning of the Pentateuch: Revelation, Composition, and Interpretation* (Downers Grove: InterVarsity Press, 2009), pp. 68–99; D. Christopher Spinks, *The Bible and the Crisis of Meaning: Debates on the Theological Interpretation of Scripture* (London: T&T Clark, 2007), pp. 69–111; Robert H. Stein, 'The Benefits of an Author-Oriented Approach to Hermeneutics', *JETS* 44.3 (2001), pp. 451–466; Sternberg, *Poetics*, pp. 6–16; Peter A. Sutcliffe, *Is There an Author in This Text: Discovering the Otherness of the Text* (Eugene: Wipf & Stock, 2014), esp. pp. 46–70; Thiselton, *Hermeneutics*, pp. 24–31; Karel Van der Toorn, *Scribal Culture and the Making of the Hebrew Bible* (Cambridge, Mass.: Harvard University Press, 2007); Kevin J. Vanhoozer, 'Intention/Intentional Fallacy', in Kevin J. Vanhoozer et al. (eds.), *DTIB*, pp. 327–330; *Is There a Meaning?*, pp. 43–97, 201–280.
74. E.g. Tremper Longman III, *Making Sense of the Old Testament: Three Crucial Questions* (Grand Rapids: Baker, 1998), pp. 25–28; T. Norton Sterret and Richard L. Schultz, *How to Understand Your Bible*, 3rd ed. (Downers Grove: InterVarsity Press, 2010), pp. 84–89.
75. Whether extrinsic facts about the author can be intrinsically related to the meaning of the text is discussed in W. K. Wimsatt and M. Beardsley, 'The Intentional Fallacy', in W. K. Wimsatt, *The Verbal Icon: Studies in the Meaning of Poetry* (Lexington: University of Kentucky Press, 1954), pp. 3–20. A key text in questioning the role of

text and the reader, which allows a text to have several equally valid meanings. This raises questions about the text's authority. At best, its authority is limited to a particular interpretative group; at worst, it has no real authority at all. For those who regard Scripture as authoritative and normative for faith and practice that raises serious concerns. And that has, in turn, resulted in a renewed emphasis on the role of the author in interpretation.

A crucial issue here is the view of text as *communication*. When thoughts and ideas are committed to writing, it is because there is something to communicate. And, while the meaning of the written word depends on conventions of speech and language, an awareness of those conventions, alone, is not sufficient to determine meaning. If a person receives an invitation to dinner, at what time should he or she arrive? Some eat dinner in the middle of the day; some, in the evening. Unless the person receiving the message has some knowledge of the intention of its originator, the message is unclear: the text fails to communicate.

When we come to the biblical text, it is reasonable to suggest that the 'author', by which term we mean the originator of the text and the redactors through whose hands the text may have passed, had an intention in writing. That is true for any author; it may certainly be assumed in the case of those responsible for the OT text, which, among any other purposes it might have served, clearly had an important role in teaching. If that is the case, there are two further questions. Can we know that intention? And, how might that knowledge help to determine the text's meaning?

Can we know the author's intention?

There are several problems associated with discovering the author's intention. Our knowledge of the background of particular texts is often limited. Even where we may be able to ascertain the wider historical context, the more specific details of where and how the text relates to that context are rarely clear. It is difficult, if not impossible, to identify a text's author, or the redactional stages the text may have gone through before reaching its final form. And even if an author can be identified, we cannot know beyond doubt what was intended. Nevertheless, some understanding of the historical context, where that

---

the author is Roland Barthes' paper 'The Death of the Author' (1968), reproduced in Roland Barthes, *Image Music Text* (London: Fontana, 1977), pp. 142–148. Ricoeur further argues that once written, a text takes on a meaning of its own, independent of the author or first audience; see Paul Ricoeur, *Interpretation Theory Discourse and the Surplus of Meaning* (Fort Worth: Christian University Press, 1976), p. 92.

information is available, together with a careful reading of the text, can often give us important clues about its purpose and intention.

Because what we can glean about authorial intention comes, primarily, through the text, it is more appropriate in this context to talk about the *implied* rather than the *actual* author. However, the implied author is a construct of the actual author; Sternberg describes them as 'two faces of the same entity'.[76] There may be a conceptual distinction, but communication will take place only if there is a significant correlation between them. In some texts the author may choose to hide his or her persona behind that of the implied author. That seems less likely in the case of the biblical text; but even if it were so, it would be counter-productive if the author also hid what he or she intended to convey. It seems reasonable to conclude, therefore, that the intention of the implied author, inferred from the text, corresponds in large measure to the intention of the author.[77]

So, for example, in the case of Isaiah 1 – 39 external data helps to determine the historical context: the rise of the power of Assyria, which led to a political crisis for much of the ANE, including Israel and Judah. There are several passages that focus on the response to that crisis; in particular by urging dependence on God, rather than other things. In the face of a Syro-Ephraimite coalition, set up to oppose Assyrian expansion, Ahaz is urged to trust God, and not to place confidence in Assyria (7:1–9). Later, when the Assyrian threat had increased, Judah is criticized for trusting in alliances with other nations (e.g. 30:1–5; 31:1–3) and in military preparations and weaponry (22:1–14). This suggests that a key intention of the text is to urge faith in God alone.

An example of a more problematic text is the book of Jonah. This seems to criticize Jonah for his unwillingness to allow divine mercy to extend to the Ninevites. However, it may also raise questions about God's justice, in forgiving a nation (Assyria) that was responsible for the destruction of Israel.[78] This indicates that the intention of a text cannot always be determined beyond doubt. Though it is usually possible to narrow it down to a relatively small range of likely possibilities.

Does the author's intention matter?

This second question is also crucial. Even if we were able to determine the author's intention, would that define, categorically, the meaning of the text?

---

76. Sternberg, *Poetics*, p. 69.

77. Vanhoozer, *Is There a Meaning?*, pp. 238–240.

78. See below, pp. 322–323.

Hirsch answers that question forcefully in the affirmative. He maintains that 'to banish the original author as the determiner of meaning was to reject the only compelling normative principle that could lend validity to an interpretation'.[79] Vanhoozer also supports the view that the author's intention is crucial. If text is to be viewed as communication, there must be correlation between what the writer meant and what the reader understands: the text, according to Vanhoozer, is 'a communicative act of a communicative agent fixed by writing' and 'the proper ground for textual meaning is found in the communicative activity . . . of the author'.[80]

Even in a narrative approach, which focuses attention on the text, there is an implicit recognition of authorial intent. Close reading looks at the structure and language of a text. For that process to have value, we must assume intentionality: that the characterization, plot and employment of poetic devices is purposeful. Where a text appears to combine sources, such as when Joseph is sold into slavery or the introductions to David, a synchronic approach to the text asks why those sources have been combined in that way. And that, again, assumes intentionality.

The question of whether the author's intention is always the final arbiter of meaning will be considered in the next section. However, whether or not there are other factors to be considered, the author's intention, and related to that, the way the text would have been understood by its first audience, remain important elements in ascertaining meaning. To ignore those things as a matter of methodological dogma is to leave out an important piece of the interpretative jigsaw.

Sensus plenior *and typology*

Since we are dealing here with divine revelation as well as human communication, the meaning of the text is, ultimately, what God intends us to understand by it. Within our understanding of the idea of inspiration, which sees God working with the agenda and concerns of the Bible's human writers,[81] that divine intention will, in general, be closely linked to authorial intention. There are occasions, though, where a text may appear to have a fuller meaning (*sensus plenior*) that the author was not aware of at the time; for example, in OT passages that appear to find their fulfilment in Christ. Before discussing this in more detail, it is important to distinguish it from typology.

79. Hirsch, *Validity*, p. 5.

80. Vanhoozer, *Is There a Meaning?*, p. 225.

81. See above, pp. 13–15.

Typology

In the past, typology was closely associated with allegory, and involved finding a Christian, and usually a Christological, significance to OT texts. We have noted already the way the *Epistle of Barnabas* reinterprets the OT food laws.[82] That letter also has an interesting way of linking circumcision with the sacrifice of Christ.[83] It is noted that 'Abraham circumcised eighteen and three hundred' men.[84] Eighteen in Greek is represented by the letters IH, which are the first letters of the name Jesus (Gk *ΙΗΣΟΥΣ*), and 300 is represented by T, which is the shape of a cross.

Another well-known application of this approach is to link the scarlet cord, let down by Rahab to ensure that she and her household were spared when Jericho was captured (Josh. 2:17–18), with salvation through Christ's blood.[85]

More recently, there has been a renewed interest in typology.[86] One reason for this is the recognition that it might have played an important part in the interpretation of the OT by writers of the NT.[87] This approach, though, has a different understanding of what constitutes typology. It recognizes God's consistent activity in history, and especially in the history of his people in the Old and New Testaments.[88] However, it focuses on more general correspondences

---

82. See above, p. 7.
83. *Barnabas* 9; see Staniforth, *Early Christian Writings*, p. 206.
84. Gen. 14:14 refers to 318 trained men born in Abraham's household, and Gen. 17:23 indicates that 'every male in his household' was circumcised.
85. *The First Epistle of Clement to the Corinthians* 12; see Staniforth, *Early Christian Writings*, pp. 28–29.
86. See especially the discussion in David L. Baker, *Two Testaments, One Bible: The Theological Relationship Between the Old and New Testaments*, 3rd ed. (Nottingham: Apollos, 2010), pp. 169–189; 'Typology and the Christian Use of the Old Testament', *SJT* 29 (1976), pp. 137–157; G. von Rad, 'Typological Interpretation of the Old Testament', in Westermann, *Essays*, pp. 17–39; Wolff, 'Hermeneutics of the OT', in Westermann, *Essays*, pp. 160–199; W. Eichrodt, 'Is Typological Exegesis an Appropriate Method?', in Westermann, *Essays*, pp. 224–245; Leonhard Goppelt, *Typos: The Typological Interpretation of the Old Testament in the New* (Grand Rapids: Eerdmans, 1981); Christopher R. Seitz, *Figured Out: Typology and Providence in Christian Scripture* (Louisville: Westminster John Knox, 2001). For a further brief overview, see Osborne, *Hermeneutical Spiral*, pp. 328–329; Routledge, *OT Theology*, pp. 43–47.
87. According to Goppelt, 'typology is the method of interpreting Scripture that is predominant in the NT and characteristic of it' (Goppelt, *Typos*, p. 198).
88. D. L. Baker, 'Typology', p. 153; *Two Testaments*, p. 180.

between patterns and structures rather than on specific details (such as Rahab's scarlet cord). Thus the faith of Abraham is 'typical' of the faith that God asks of all believers; there are things in the story of Moses that parallel the ministry of Jesus; the redemption of Israel from Egypt, which includes the death of the Passover Lamb, corresponds to the redemption we have through Christ's death as our Passover sacrifice, and its continued remembrance in the Passover corresponds to the Christian celebration of the Lord's Supper; and elements of the OT sacrificial system also correspond to Christ's sacrifice. There is also a negative correspondence between Adam, through whom sin came into the world, and Christ, who brings righteousness and forgiveness.[89] This idea of more general correspondences has led, also, to a comparison of narrative patterns: thus there are correspondences between the story of Israel and the story of the church, and correspondences between the ministry of Jesus and the narrative of Israel.[90]

Because typological correspondences are noted by looking back, they should not, generally, be seen as part of the intention of the original text. It does, though, play a significant part in biblical theology, which seeks to relate texts and their theology to one another. The recognition that 'every part of the bible is an expression of the consistent activity of the one God',[91] allows us to search for, and expect to find, correspondences between different parts of the OT, and between the OT and the NT. Typology also plays a part in preaching from the OT; noting patterns that are 'typical' of God's dealings with his people and that may then be applied to the life and practice of the church.

Sensus plenior

Unlike typology, *sensus plenior* assumes that, although the human author was unaware of it, the fuller sense is part of the text's original meaning.[92]

---

89. For further discussion, see e.g. Goppelt, *Typos*.
90. This includes a substantial and growing interest in the significance of exodus typology, both in the application of exodus traditions to the return from exile, especially in Isa. 40 – 55, and in links with NT texts; see below, p. 10, n. 30.
91. D. L. Baker, 'Typology', p. 155.
92. An important discussion of this is Raymond E. Brown, *The Sensus Plenior of Sacred Scripture* (Eugene: Wipf & Stock, 1955); 'The History and Development of the Theory of a Sensus Plenior', *CBQ* 15 (1953), pp. 141–162; 'The *Sensus Plenior* in the Last Ten Years', *CBQ* 25 (1963), pp. 262–285; see also William Sanford LaSor, 'Prophecy, Inspiration, and *Sensus Plenior*', *TynBul* 29 (1978), pp. 49–60; Douglas J. Moo, 'The Problem of Sensus Plenior', in D. A. Carson and John D. Woodbridge

That meaning is discerned from additional revelation within the wider context of the canon of Scripture. It may be better to see some instances as examples of typology,[93] though sometimes the idea of *sensus plenior* may be required.

One frequently noted example is Genesis 3:15: 'I will put enmity between you and the woman, and between your offspring and hers; he will strike your head, and you will strike his heel' (NRSV). This is part of the serpent's punishment, and it could simply refer to the ongoing hostility between human beings and snakes. That, though, seems rather trivial. Another possibility is that it refers to the ongoing struggle between human beings and the ever-present temptation to sin. That fits the context better, though on its own it may appear to be more suited to a punishment for human beings. The contrast between 'head' and 'heel' may, further, suggest that the ongoing struggle will end decisively in favour of human beings. That much can be determined from the text, and that may be sufficient. The additional element, that the final victory will be won through one particular offspring, Jesus Christ, is evident only after reading the NT. Prophecies that point to a coming deliverer may also be seen to be fulfilled in Christ, though, again, the precise details are available only through the NT, and would have been unknown to the author. In all such cases, though, the *sensus plenior* represents a development of the meaning determined by a grammatical and historical analysis of the text, and which is closely associated with authorial intention.

(*Footnote 92 cont.*) (eds.), *Hermeneutics, Authority, and Canon* (Eugene: Wipf & Stock, 1986), pp. 175–211; Douglas A. Oss, 'Canon as Context: The Function of Sensus Plenior in Evangelical Hermeneutics', *GTJ* 9.1 (1988), pp. 105–127; Jack R. Riggs, 'The "Fuller Meaning" of Scripture: A Hermeneutical Question for Evangelicals', *GTJ* 7.2 (1986), pp. 213–227; Vanhoozer, *Is There a Meaning?*, pp. 263–265.

93. Vanhoozer suggests Isa. 53 as a possible example of *sensus plenior* (*Is There a Meaning?*, pp. 264–265). However, the link between the Servant and Christ could be seen as typological: the NT writers recognized that what God was doing through the Servant in the OT corresponded to, and was intensified in, what took place through the ministry of Jesus. James Hamilton argues for a typological interpretation of Isa. 7:14, which is sometimes taken as a prophetic reference to Jesus' virgin birth; see James M. Hamilton Jr., 'The Virgin Will Conceive: Typological Fulfillment in Matthew 1:18–23', in Daniel M. Gurtner and John Nolland (eds.), *Built upon the Rock: Studies in the Gospel of Matthew* (Grand Rapids: Eerdmans, 2008), pp. 228–247. See also Moo, 'Problem of Sensus Plenior', in Carson and Woodbridge, *Hermeneutics*, pp. 195–198.

To accommodate the idea of *sensus plenior* it is necessary to see the meaning of a text in the light of the whole canon of Scripture.[94] However, because any fuller meaning is a development of the meaning of the text within its immediate context, it remains necessary to explore that meaning first. This will include looking at the theological as well as the historical and narrative context of the text, and setting out, in so far as it is possible, what the author (still taking that term in its widest sense) intended, and what the text would have meant to its original audience. It can then be compared with other texts in order to discern any fuller meaning.

A crucial part of this is whether the fuller sense is consistent with the text. With Genesis 3:15 that might be shown to be the case. In another frequently quoted example, Hosea 11:1b ('out of Egypt I called my son'), it seems less likely. Hosea, here, is clearly referring to Israel and the exodus, but it is later applied to the return from Egypt of the infant Jesus (Matt. 2:15). LaSor takes this as another instance of *sensus plenior*, explaining how the exodus is part of the plan of God, which culminates in the coming of Jesus.[95] However this interpretation of the link between the texts seems forced, and it seems better to understand Matthew's reference as typological. In his life and ministry Jesus fulfils the narrative of Israel, and so presents himself as the ideal Israel.[96]

---

94. See e.g. LaSor, 'Prophecy, Inspiration, and *Sensus Plenior*', pp. 59–60; Moo, 'Problem of Sensus Plenior', in Carson and Woodbridge, *Hermeneutics*, pp. 204–209; Oss, 'Canon as Context'; Vanhoozer, *Is There a Meaning?*, p. 265. See also the discussion above of the canonical approach to the text, pp. 208–211.
95. LaSor, 'Prophecy, Inspiration, and *Sensus Plenior*', pp. 57–58; see also Riggs, 'The "Fuller Meaning" of Scripture', pp. 219–220; John Sailhamer, 'Hosea 11:1 and Matthew 2:15', *WTJ* 63 (2001), pp. 87–96; *Meaning of the Pentateuch*, pp. 510–521; cf. James M. Hamilton Jr., 'John Sailhamer's *The Meaning of the Pentateuch*: A Review Essay', *SBJT* 14.2 (2010), pp. 62–76 (69); 'The Virgin Will Conceive', in Gurtner and Nolland, *Built upon the Rock*, p. 241; Dan McCartney and Peter Enns, 'Matthew and Hosea: A Response to John Sailhamer', *WTJ* 63 (2001), pp. 97–105.
96. See e.g. R. T. France, *The Gospel of Matthew*, NICNT (Grand Rapids: Eerdmans, 2007), pp. 80–81. N. T. Wright suggests that in the ministry of Jesus we see 'the history of Israel in miniature', including an exodus, evident in Matt. 2:15 (*The New Testament and the People of God* [Minneapolis: Fortress; London: SPCK, 1992], p. 402).

6. THE PENTATEUCH

Introduction to the Pentateuch

Date, authorship and composition[1]

The Pentateuch comprises the first five books of the OT. It is also referred to as Torah or Law, and includes substantial legal sections, relating to the social, personal and religious well-being of the nation. These legal sections, comprising the second part of Exodus, Leviticus, parts of Numbers and Deuteronomy, are set within a narrative framework, which tells the story from the creation of the world to the point where the people are ready to enter and take possession of the land. We have noted, too, possible links with other ANE literature, including creation and flood narratives. And the text also includes poetry, national history and biography.

The narrative sections of the Pentateuch, seen by some as the work of J, which then might have been combined with E after the fall of the northern kingdom,[2] continues into the books that follow. Some scholars have noted the close connection between the Pentateuch and the book of Joshua, and refer to those six books as the 'Hexateuch'.[3] Joshua includes the account of the

1. For bibliography on the composition of the Pentateuch, see above, p. 52, n. 115.
2. E.g. Arnold, *Introduction*, pp. 55–57.
3. For further discussion, see below, pp. 258–259.

conquest, and without it the story of the promises to the patriarchs might be considered incomplete.[4]

Others see the narrative extending beyond the conquest to the fall of Jerusalem and the Babylonian exile, and so link the Pentateuch with Joshua, Judges, Samuel and Kings. So, for example, Blenkinsopp, following Rendtorff, notes a parallel between Exodus 1:6–8 – 'Now Joseph and all his brothers and all that generation died . . . Then a new king, who did not know about Joseph, came to power in Egypt' – and Judges 2:8–10 – 'Joshua son of Nun, the servant of the LORD, died . . . After that whole generation had been gathered to their fathers, another generation grew up, who knew neither the LORD nor what he had done for Israel.'[5] These introduce key phases in the story, and their similarity suggests continuity in the narrative. These first nine books of the OT are sometimes referred to as the 'Enneateuch' or, more commonly, the 'Primary History' or 'Primary Narrative'.[6]

Another view sees a closer link between Deuteronomy and the books that follow (the so-called 'Deuteronomistic History') than with the rest of the Pentateuch, and refer to Genesis–Numbers as a 'tetrateuch'.[7] In the Hebrew text Exodus, Leviticus and Numbers each begin with the conjunction 'and', suggesting that they form, with Genesis, a continuous narrative.[8]

---

4. E.g. Gerhard von Rad, *The Problem of the Hexateuch and Other Essays*, trans. E. W. Trueman Dicken (London: SCM Press, 1984); see also Pekka Pitkänen, 'Reading Genesis–Joshua as a Unified Document from an Early Date: A Settler Colonial Perspective', *BTB* 45.1 (2015), pp. 3–31.
5. Blenkinsopp, *Pentateuch*, pp. 36–37; see also Ska, *Reading the Pentateuch*, p. 6. In each case, too, the resulting oppression meant the people 'cried out' (Exod. 2:23; cf. e.g. Judg. 3:9, 15; 6:6) and that in turn prompts divine deliverance.
6. See e.g. Arnold, *Introduction*, p. 60; W. Brueggemann, *Introduction*, pp. 35–36; Thomas B. Dozeman, Thomas Römer and Konrad Schmid (eds.), *Pentateuch, Hexateuch, or Enneateuch? Identifying Literary Works in Genesis Through Kings* (Atlanta: Society of Biblical Literature, 2011); Ska, *Reading the Pentateuch*, pp. 3–9; see also Blenkinsopp, *Pentateuch*, pp. 34–37.
7. This is the view of Martin Noth, who sees Deuteronomy as a theological introduction to the Deuteronomistic History. For further discussion, see below, pp. 253–257. See also Victor P. Hamilton, *Exodus: An Exegetical Commentary* (Grand Rapids: Baker Academic, 2011), p. 3.
8. The LXX omits the conjunction in Exod. 1:1, though the Hebrew text is more likely. See further e.g. Graham Davies, 'The Transition from Genesis to Exodus', in Katherine J. Dell, Graham Davies and Yee Von Koh (eds.), *Genesis, Isaiah and Psalms:*

The traditional view associates authorship of the Pentateuch with Moses, in the twelfth, or possibly fifteenth century, BC, depending on the date of the exodus.[9] The Pentateuch does not claim Mosaic authorship. However, there are references to Moses' receiving revelation from God, particularly relating to the laws in Deuteronomy (Deut. 1:1; 4:44; 31:24; 32:45). The OT also refers, frequently, to the 'law of Moses' (e.g. Josh. 8:31–32; 1 Kgs 2:3; 2 Chr. 30:16; Neh. 8:1). Sirach refers to 'the book of the covenant . . . the law that Moses commanded' (Sir. 24.23), and the NT refers to Mosaic legislation (e.g. Matt. 19:7; Mark 7:10; John 1:17). Josephus and *Baba Batra* both link the first five books of the OT specifically with Moses.[10] There is general recognition that some sections might have been written later;[11] and that the transmission of the material and its editing into its present form is complex. Nevertheless, many conservative scholars regard the Pentateuch, or at least the traditions that lie behind it, as essentially Mosaic.[12]

Wellhausen's 'documentary hypothesis' and its later modifications have raised questions regarding this traditional view, and many recent scholars recognize the presence of several sources, which might have been brought together, finally, only after the exile.[13] In its original form, and in some of the revisions, the Documentary Hypothesis emphasizes the centrality of written sources. It seems possible, though, that some of the traditions that contributed to the final form of the Pentateuch were passed on orally.[14] It is argued, too, that some of these sources may go back to the exodus period. So, for example, similarities between the structure of Deuteronomy and twelfth century BC Hittite treaties suggest an early, possibly Mosaic, date for material in

---

A Festschrift to Honour Professor John Emerton on His Eightieth Birthday, VTSup 135 (Leiden: Brill, 2010), pp. 59–78 (60–61); Peter Enns, *Exodus*, NIVAC (Grand Rapids: Zondervan, 2000), pp. 60–61; Hamilton, *Exodus*, p. 3.

9. See above, pp. 85–88.

10. Josephus, *Ag. Ap.* 1.38–40 (see above, p. 26). According to the Talmud, Moses wrote the Pentateuch, though possibly not the last eight verses, which were written by Joshua (*b. B. Bat.* 15a).

11. See above, p. 53.

12. See e.g. LaSor, Hubbard and Bush, *OT Survey*, pp. 10; Longman and Dillard, *Introduction*, p. 42.

13. See e.g. LaSor, Hubbard and Bush, *OT Survey*, p. 9.

14. For a wider discussion of the relationship between oral and written material, see e.g. D. M. Carr, *Writing*.

Deuteronomy.[15] Thus the influence of Moses on the Pentateuch cannot be simply dismissed.

However, if, as seems probable, the Pentateuch reached its final form in the exilic period, that interpretative context is also important.[16] The exile appears to have been a formative time in the development of Israel's theology. The destruction of Jerusalem and the temple, and exile from the land, led to a re-evaluation of the nation's relationship with God, and a clearer exposition of ideas that might have been present in earlier traditions, but that took the crisis of exile to bring them to the fore.

Other approaches, while not denying the presence of multiple sources, focus on the text in its final form, and how it functions coherently within its canonical setting. Here questions focus, primarily, not on the sources themselves, but on the way the sources have been combined into the final version of the text. This, though, does not necessarily remove the need for, and may need to run alongside, historical-critical discussion.[17]

The theme of the Pentateuch

The story of the Pentateuch covers the creation of the world to the death of Moses. That story may be the result of a prolonged process of editing and combining a variety of oral and written material. In the light of that, can we expect to see a single coherent theme being worked out through all five books?

Martin Noth identified several key themes reflected in the Pentateuch: stories of the exodus and conquest, the promise to the patriarchs, wilderness wanderings and the giving of the law at Sinai.[18] However, in his view these stories arose

---

15. On Hittite suzerain–vassal treaties see above, pp. 121–123. See also e.g. Craigie, *Deuteronomy*, pp. 22–24.
16. E.g. Rainer Albertz, *Israel in Exile: The History and Literature of the Sixth Century B.C.E.*, Studies in Biblical Literature 3 (Atlanta: Society of Biblical Literature, 2003), pp. 246–271; W. Brueggemann, *Introduction*, pp. 41–42; Clines, *Theme*, pp. 103–126; LaSor, Hubbard and Bush, *OT Survey*, p. 118; Wenham notes this and other historical contexts (*Pentateuch*, pp. 187–195).
17. See e.g. Ska, *Reading the Pentateuch*, pp. 161–164.
18. Martin Noth, *A History of Pentateuchal Traditions*, trans. B. W. Anderson (Englewood Cliffs: Prentice-Hall, 1972); see also e.g. Douglas A. Knight, *Rediscovering the Traditions of Israel*, 3rd ed., SBLSBL 16 (Atlanta: Society of Biblical Literature, 2006), pp. 109–130; Robert Polzin, 'Martin Noth's *A History of Pentateuchal Traditions*', *BASOR* 221 (1976), pp. 113–120; Wenham, *Pentateuch*, pp. 145–147.

and were expanded in different contexts and, initially, had no connection with each other. It was only later that they were brought together. Von Rad focuses on the Hexateuch,[19] and points to short historical credal statements that summarize its contents (e.g. Deut. 26:5b–9; see also Deut. 6:20–24; Josh. 24:2b–13). These, he argues, were expanded in the tenth century BC by the Yahwist, who added most of the 'primeval history' (Gen. 1 – 11) and references to the giving of the Law at Sinai, while maintaining the basic framework. The addition of the Priestly material complemented the Yahwistic, setting out the legal traditions in more detail, and also nuancing the promises to the patriarchs by including God's commitment to the special relationship with his people (e.g. Gen. 17:7), which was fulfilled at Sinai.[20]

Noth and von Rad argue from a historical-critical perspective and note the way key themes in the Pentateuch were developed. By contrast, David Clines takes a synchronic approach and considers the theme of the Pentateuch in its final form.[21] That theme, he argues, is the 'partial fulfilment – which implies also the partial non-fulfilment – of the promises to or blessing of the patriarchs'.[22] This promise has three main elements: Abraham's posterity, the relationship between God and his people, and the land. These form the main emphases of Genesis 12 – 50, Exodus–Leviticus and Numbers–Deuteronomy respectively. Genesis 1 – 11 is the preface to the overall theme.[23] It emphasizes that though human sin destroys what God has made, and threatens uncreation, in the form of the flood,[24] God's grace continues to save human beings from the full consequences of their sin. Acts of divine judgment in the primeval history are followed by mitigation. So Adam and Eve are expelled from the Garden of Eden, but not before God has clothed them (3:21); Cain becomes a wanderer, but is given a mark of divine protection (4:15); despite the global destruction of the flood, Noah his family and representatives of every living

---

19. Von Rad, *Problem of the Hexateuch*; see also e.g. Clines, *Theme*, pp. 87–89; D. A. Knight, *Traditions of Israel*, pp. 77–109; Wenham, *Pentateuch*, pp. 147–149.
20. According to von Rad, the earliest promises to the patriarchs were posterity and the land; the promise that God would be the God of Abraham and his descendants (Gen. 17:7) is from P; see Gerhard von Rad, *Genesis*, rev. ed. OTL (London: SCM Press, 1972), p. 200.
21. Clines, *Theme*; see also Wenham, *Pentateuch*, pp. 150–158.
22. Clines, *Theme*, p. 30.
23. Ibid., pp. 66–86.
24. For discussion of Gen. 6:1–8 as an introduction to the flood narrative, see Routledge, 'My Spirit'.

creature are saved in the ark. And the judgment at Babel is followed by the call of Abraham and the promises to the patriarchs.[25]

In this formulation the primeval history serves primarily as a preface to the theme of the Pentateuch, rather than featuring as an essential part of it. Clines includes the reaffirmation of God's intention for human beings, set out in Genesis 1. However, promises relating to Israel seem tangential to that cosmic purpose. In my view it is better to extend Clines's argument, and see a missiological focus tying both parts of the Pentateuch together.

The call of Abraham (12:1–3) is generally recognized as programmatic, and an important element in that call and, subsequently, in the Abrahamic covenant, is God's commitment to the nations. In direct contrast to the judgment that fell on 'the families [*mišpāḥâ*] of Noah's sons' (Gen. 10:32, NRSV) at Babel, through Abraham 'all the families [*mišpāḥâ*] of the earth shall be blessed' (Gen. 12:3, NRSV; cf. 28:14). That divine blessing, which embraces the whole world, and thus links back to the creation narratives, will be made available through Abraham and his offspring (Gen. 22:18; 26:4; 28:14). The fulfilment of the promises to the patriarchs plays an essential part in the divine purpose, but it is not the primary theme. The call of Abraham and the establishment of the people of Israel may be seen, rather, as a means to an end: God chose, blessed, entered into a unique relationship with, and brought them into their own land so that they might embody, in microcosm, God's purpose for the whole of creation,[26] and thereby become the channel of divine blessing to the world.[27]

We see this, further, in Exodus 19:5–6. Israel is singled out as God's 'treasured possession', to enjoy an intimacy with him that other nations do not yet know. That relationship is embodied in the Sinaitic covenant, and the divine promise 'I will take you as my own people, and I will be your God' (Exod. 6:7). This 'covenant formula', which is repeated in a similar form on numerous occasions

---

25. Clines, *Theme*, pp. 85–86; see also LaSor, Hubbard and Bush, *OT Survey*, pp. 3–6; von Rad, *Genesis*, pp. 152–154. Von Rad suggests that the primeval history leaves the question of God's continuing grace open; but the narrator then provides the answer in the patriarchal narratives that follow.

26. See e.g. Routledge, 'Mission and Covenant', in Grams et al., *Bible and Mission*; see also e.g. James C. Okoye, *Israel and the Nations: A Mission Theology of the Old Testament* (Maryknoll: Orbis, 2006), esp. pp. 31–32.

27. Wenham emphasizes the theme of blessing, and notes the importance of the promises for humankind (*Pentateuch*, pp. 153–157); see also Terence E. Fretheim, 'The Reclamation of Creation: Redemption and Law in Exodus', *Int* 45 (1991), pp. 354–365.

throughout the OT,[28] is in continuance with the commitment to Abraham and his descendants: 'I will be their God' (Gen. 17:8).[29] However, the goal of that special relationship is that Israel will minister as a 'kingdom of priests'. The priest in Israel was an intermediary, representing the people before God, and God before the people.[30] Israel, similarly, was called to be an intermediary, between God and the 'whole earth', which also belongs to him.[31]

The ongoing role of Israel in relation to the whole created order may be seen, further, in the construction of the tabernacle (Exod. 35:4 – 40:38). Language describing the completion of the tabernacle echoes the description of the completion of God's work in creation.[32] This suggests that the tabernacle, and later the temple, were intended to reflect the divine order of creation.[33]

God's interest in the whole world, and his ongoing commitment to what he has made, are further reflected in the unfolding narrative of Genesis 1 – 11. God created the world, and has given human beings a unique place within it (Gen. 1 – 3). However, human sin has disrupted God's very good creation,

---

28. Jer. 7:23; 11:4; 24:7; 30:22; 31:33; 32:38; Ezek. 11:20; 36:28; 37:27; Zech. 13:9; see also Hos. 1:9; 2:23.
29. For further discussion, see Rolf Rendtorff, *The Covenant Formula: An Exegetical and Theological Investigation*, OTS (Edinburgh: T&T Clark, 1998).
30. See Routledge, *OT Theology*, pp. 171, 172.
31. The NIV translation 'Although the whole earth is mine' (Exod. 19:5) is typical, indicating the particularity of Israel's election. However, 'although' translates the Hebrew *kî*, which is more usually translated 'because'; God chose Israel '*because* the whole earth is [his]', suggesting that Israel's election has a universal purpose. See Terence E. Fretheim, '"Because the Whole Earth Is Mine": Theme and Narrative in Exodus', *Int* 50.3 (1996), pp. 229–239.
32. See e.g. Fretheim, *God and World*, pp. 128–129; Okoye, *Israel and the Nations*, pp. 31–32; Walton, *Lost World*, esp. pp. 72–92. There is also a link between the institution of the Sabbath and the construction of the temple. Sabbath regulations immediately follow the first set of instructions for building the tabernacle (Exod. 31:12–17) and immediately precede the second set (Exod. 35:1–3). Childs suggests that observing the Sabbath and building the tabernacle 'are two sides of the same reality' and 'both testify to God's rule over his creation' (Brevard S. Childs, *Exodus*, OTL [London: SCM Press, 1974], pp. 541–542).
33. See e.g. Beale, *The Temple and the Church's Mission*, pp. 32–36; Clements, *God and Temple*; Fretheim, *God and World*, p. 128; Routledge, 'Mission and Covenant', in Grams et al., *Bible and Mission*, pp. 19–20.

resulting both in a universal fall (Gen. 3),[34] and in the flood, which is depicted as a return to the watery chaos of Genesis 1:2.[35] The subsiding of the flood-waters represents re-creation, and in that new world order Noah, like Adam, received a divine commission to 'Be fruitful and increase in number and fill the earth' (Gen. 9:1; cf. 1:28).[36] We see here, too, God's renewed promise to maintain the order of creation (Gen. 8:22), and that continuing commitment to the world and its inhabitants is further embodied in the Noahic covenant, which includes every living creature.[37] The flood has not removed human sin, and at Babel we see continued rebellion against God, which, again, cannot go unpunished (11:1–9). However, God's commitment to his world remains, and divine judgment is followed by the genealogy of Shem (11:10–26), which links the primeval history to the patriarchs, and introduces the promise of restoration through Abraham and his offspring, the key theme of the rest of the Pentateuch.

Genesis[38]

Structure and outline

Genesis is generally divided into two parts: chapters 1–11, the primeval history,

---

34. See Routledge, 'Cursing and Chaos', in Moo and Routledge, *Earth Endures*; Routledge, *OT Theology*, pp. 154–156; however, see Bimson, 'Reconsidering a "Cosmic Fall"'.
35. There appears to be a close relationship between Gen. 3:6 and 6:2, which are preludes to the fall and flood respectively (above, p. 212), and between the cursing of the ground, as a result of the fall, and the return to chaos represented by the flood (Routledge, 'Cursing and Chaos', in Moo and Routledge, *Earth Endures*).
36. See further Turner, *Announcements*, pp. 21–49.
37. The Noahic, Abrahamic and Sinaitic covenants each, therefore, have missiological trajectories; see Routledge, 'Mission and Covenant', in Grams et al., *Bible and Mission*.
38. Commentaries on Genesis include Blenkinsopp, *Creation, Uncreation, Re-Creation*; Walter Brueggemann, *Genesis*, IBC (Louisville: John Knox, 1982); Victor P. Hamilton, *Genesis 1–17*; *Genesis 18–50*, NICOT (Grand Rapids: Eerdmans, 1995); John E. Hartley, *Genesis*, NIBCOT (Peabody: Hendrickson; Carlisle: Paternoster, 2000); Derek Kidner, *Genesis*, TOTC (Leicester: Inter-Varsity Press, 1967); Longman, *How to Read Genesis*; James McKeown, *Genesis*, THOTC (Grand Rapids: Eerdmans, 2008); Nahum M. Sarna, *Genesis*, JPSTC (Philadelphia: Jewish Publication

and chapters 12–50, which contain the stories of the patriarchs.[39] The book may be further divided by what has become known as the '*toledot* formula'.[40] The Hebrew term *toledot*, which is translated 'generations' or 'descendants' (NRSV) or this is the 'account' of (NIV), occurs frequently in Genesis,[41] and appears to set out the general direction of the narrative. Generally, the *toledot* formula introduces the section that follows. However, its occurrence in Genesis 2:4a ('the *tôlĕdôt* of the heavens and the earth') appears to refer back to the previous account of creation, and forms an inclusio with Genesis 1:1.[42]

This formula is generally taken to divide Genesis into ten sections. Of these, five are in Genesis 1 – 11: the heavens and the earth (1:1 – 2:4a or, possibly, 2:4 – 4:26), Adam (5:1 – 6:8), Noah (6:9 – 9:29), Noah's sons (10:1 – 11:9), Shem (11:10–26). And five are in Genesis 12 – 50: Terah (11:27 – 25:11), Ishmael (25:12–18), Isaac (25:19 – 35:29), Esau (36:1–43),[43] Jacob (37:2 – 50:26). Because *toledot* indicates 'descendants', the focus of each section is, primarily, on the family of the person named in the formula, rather than on the person himself. So Abraham is the main figure in the *toledot* of Terah; the *toledot* of Isaac focuses on Jacob; and the principal character in the *toledot* of Jacob is Joseph. The use of the formula appears to narrow the focus from the cosmos to a single family, and that narrowing may continue in the recurrence of the formula in Numbers 3:1.

(*Footnote 38 cont.*) Society, 1989); Speiser, *Genesis*; Laurence A. Turner, *Genesis: Readings* (Sheffield: Phoenix, 2009); von Rad, *Genesis*; John H. Walton, *Genesis*, NIVAC (Grand Rapids: Zondervan, 2001); Gordon J. Wenham, *Genesis 1–15*, WBC 1 (Waco: Word, 1987); *Genesis 16–50*, WBC 2 (Dallas: Word, 1994); Claus Westermann, *Genesis*, 3 vols., CC (Minneapolis: Fortress, 1994–2002).

39. The patriarchal narratives proper are often taken to begin with the genealogy of Terah (Gen. 11:26).

40. For a summary of views of this formula, as well as his own contribution to the debate, see Matthew A. Thomas, *These Are the Generations: Identity, Covenant and the 'Toledot' Formula* (New York: T&T Clark, 2011); see also e.g. Blenkinsopp, *Pentateuch*, pp. 58–71, 99–108; LaSor, Hubbard and Bush, *OT Survey*, pp. 16–17; Hill and Walton, *Survey*, pp. 78–79.

41. When referred to generally, this term has not been transliterated because it appears in several forms. It occurs eleven times in Genesis: 2:4 (*tôlĕdôt*); 5:1; 6:9; 10:1; 11:10, 27; 25:19 (*tôlĕdōt*); 25:12 (*tōlĕdōt*); 36:1, 9; 37:2 (*tōlĕdôt*); and in Num. 3:1; Ruth 4:18.

42. See e.g. McKeown, *Genesis*, p. 29; Turner, *Genesis*, pp. 16–18; von Rad, *Genesis*, p. 63; Westermann, *Genesis*, 1:81; however, see also e.g. Hamilton, *Genesis 1–17*, pp. 150–151; Walton, *Genesis*, p. 39; Wenham, *Genesis 1–15*, p. 49.

43. There are two references to the *toledot* of Esau (Gen. 36:1, 9).

Main themes

Genesis 1 – 11

The Hebrew name of the book is taken from its opening word, *bĕrēʾšît*, which is often translated 'in the beginning'. This is reflected in the LXX title 'Genesis', from the Greek meaning 'origin'.

The first part of the book, sometimes referred to as the 'primeval history', deals with the creation of the world, and offers a theological explanation for the way things are. It is set out as narrative, and so is sometimes regarded as historiography. However, the nature of the narrative seems different from that of Genesis 12 onwards. The emphasis in the primeval history seems to be on global issues. These include the sovereignty of God as the Creator, the significance of human beings, created as male and female, and their place within creation. They include, too, the fundamental issues that affect the lives of all human beings, including sin, death, marriage, conflict within families and between nations, human development and the origin of different languages, as well as the introduction to key peoples and places. There is some development of more complex characters, notably Eve and Cain, though most are relatively flat, and interaction between them appears little more than functional. Thus, while the events recorded in Genesis 1 – 11 may have some historical basis, the main issue is their theological significance.[44]

The opening chapters of Genesis give two complementary creation accounts. The first (1:1 – 2:4a) emphasizes God's transcendence, creating all things with his word (1:3, 6, 9, 11, 14, 20, 24, 26). The term *bārāʾ* (to create) appears in the OT only with God as subject, and occurs here in relation to 'the heavens and the earth' (1:1; 2:4a) and human beings (1:27).[45] Another significant term is *bādal* (to separate). Creation takes place as a series of separations: light from darkness (1:4, 18), the waters under the dome of the heavens from the water above it (1:6–7) and day from night (1:14). There also appears to be a correspondence between the first three and the last three days of creation (see Table 6.1, overleaf).

The pinnacle of God's work is the creation of human beings. They alone are made in the image of God (1:26);[46] and after their creation God's assessment of his work changes from 'good' to 'very good' (1:31).

---

44. See further Routledge, *OT Theology*, pp. 124–158.

45. The only other occurrence of *bārāʾ* in these verses is in relation to 'the great sea monsters' (1:21, NRSV). That may be significant. ANE creation myths portray primeval deities as sea monsters. Gen. 1:21 emphasizes that they are merely part of God's creation.

46. For discussion of what it means for human beings to be made 'in the image of God', see Routledge, *OT Theology*, pp. 139–141.

Table 6.1

Day 1: Light, including day and night	Day 4: Sun, moon and stars
Day 2: Sky (and the waters under the earth)	Day 5: Birds and fish
Day 3: Earth and plants	Day 6: Animals, insects, human beings

The second creation account (2:4b–25) emphasizes God's immanence. He forms (*yāṣar*) Adam, as a potter forms clay, and breathes into him the 'breath of life' (2:7); he plants a garden (2:8) and places Adam in it (2:15); he is concerned that Adam is alone and provides a companion for him (2:18).

As in other ANE accounts, the flood forms an important division in human history. One aspect of this, which has already been noted, is the new beginning through Noah. Another is the significant reduction in age of the characters. This is a feature of other ANE flood stories, where the ages of the antediluvians is very much higher than in the biblical account.[47] Prior to the flood the average age is around 900 years (Gen. 5), with Methuselah dying in the year of the flood at the age of 969. The ages of those born after the flood are much lower: starting in the 400s and dropping to the 100s.[48] There have been several attempts to explain the high ages of those born before the flood, including some using complicated mathematical formulae, though none is entirely convincing.[49]

Genesis 12 – 50

Following the judgment at the Tower of Babel, the genealogy of Terah (11:27) and the call of Abraham (12:1–3) signal the way back. These chapters focus, particularly, on the ancestors of the nation: Abraham, Isaac and Jacob, whose name was changed to Israel, and on Jacob's sons, who became the patriarchs of the tribes of Israel. The theme of covenant, which was introduced in connection with Noah (6:18; 9:9–17), is developed in relation to Abraham and his descendants (15; 17), and with it the continuity of God's promises (26:24; 28:13). The story of Joseph features prominently in the latter part of the book. This describes God's providence in ensuring the survival of his people during a time of famine (45:5–7; 50:20). The presence of the people of Israel in Egypt also sets the scene for the rest of the Pentateuch, which focuses on the exodus (cf. 50:24).

---

47. See above, p. 106, n. 160.
48. E.g. Abraham (175), Jacob (147), Moses (120), Joshua (110). David died aged 70 (2 Sam. 5:4) 'at a good old age having enjoyed long life' (1 Chr. 29:28); cf. Ps. 90:10, which may reflect on David's age.
49. For an overview, see Wenham, *Genesis 1–15*, pp. 130–134.

The patriarchal narratives emphasize the worship of one God. The deity most frequently associated with the patriarchs is *'ēl šadday* ('God almighty'; e.g. 17:1; 28:3; 43:14; 48:3; cf. Exod. 6:3), though other names compounded with *'ēl* are also mentioned, including *'ēl 'elyôn* ('God Most High', Gen. 14:22), *'ēl rŏ'î* ('God who sees me', 16:13), *'ēl 'ôlām* ('Eternal God', 21:33) and *'ēl bêt-'ēl* ('God of Bethel', 31:13). Some suggest that these *'ēl*-deities were originally separate Canaanite gods, who were worshipped by Israel's ancestors and eventually replaced by Yahweh.[50] When the stories of the patriarchs were retold, they were fused into a single god, who was then identified with Yahweh. However, it is reasonable to argue that the narrative of Genesis 12 – 50 rests on reliable tradition,[51] and accurately reflects patriarchal religion. This includes the recognition of one God, who was primarily associated with Abraham's family, rather than a specific place, and who committed himself to successive generations.

Exodus[52]

Structure and outline

The book of Exodus does not have a clear inner structure, and the material is generally divided by content. One possibility is to divide the material, broadly,

---

50. See e.g. F. M. Cross, *Canaanite Myth and Hebrew Epic: Essays in the History and the Religion of Israel* (Cambridge, Mass.: Harvard University Press, 1973), pp. 3–75; John Day, *Yahweh and the Gods and Goddesses of Canaan*, JSOTSup 265 (Sheffield: Sheffield Academic Press, 2000), pp. 13–41; Routledge, *OT Theology*, pp. 85–94; Mark S. Smith, *The Early History of God: Yahweh and Other Deities in Ancient Israel*, 2nd ed. (Grand Rapids: Eerdmans, 2002), pp. 19–43; Gordon J. Wenham, 'The Religion of the Patriarchs', in Alan R. Millard and Donald J. Wiseman (eds.), *Essays on the Patriarchal Narratives* (Leicester: Inter-Varsity Press, 1980), pp. 157–188.
51. For discussion of the historicity of the patriarchal narratives, see above, pp. 69–70, esp. n. 17; see also Wenham, *Genesis 16–50*, pp. xx–xxx.
52. Commentaries on Exodus include James K. Bruckner, *Exodus*, NIBCOT (Peabody: Hendrickson; Carlisle: Paternoster, 2008); Childs, *Exodus*; R. Alan Cole, *Exodus*, TOTC (Leicester: Inter-Varsity Press, 1983); Thomas B. Dozeman, *Exodus*, ECC (Grand Rapids: Eerdmans, 2009); John Durham, *Exodus*, WBC 3 (Waco: Word, 1987); Enns, *Exodus*; Terence E. Fretheim, *Exodus*, IBC (Louisville: Westminster John Knox, 1991); Hamilton, *Exodus*; William H. C. Propp, *Exodus 1–18*, AB 2 (New York: Doubleday, 1999); *Exodus 19–40*, AB 2A (New York: Doubleday, 2006); Nahum M. Sarna, *Exodus*, JPSTC (Philadelphia: Jewish Publication Society, 1991).

into three sections, corresponding to Israel's location: in Egypt (1:1 – 15:21), in the wilderness on the way to Sinai (15:22 – 18:26) and at Sinai (19:1 – 40:38). These sections can be further subdivided to give more detail.

Outline

- Israel in Egypt (1:1 – 15:21)
  - Call of Moses (1:1 – 4:31)
  - Moses and Pharaoh (5:1 – 7:13)
  - The plagues (7:14 – 12:30)
  - The tenth plague, Passover and exodus (12:1 – 15:21)
- Israel's journey to Sinai (15:22 – 18:26)
- Israel at Sinai (19:1 – 40:38)
  - Theophany, Law and Covenant (19:1 – 24:18)
  - Instructions for building the tabernacle (25:1 – 31:18)
  - The golden calf: sin and covenant renewal (32:1 – 34:35)
  - Building the tabernacle (35:1 – 40:38)

Main themes

A key theme of the Pentateuch is the restoration of humankind through Abraham and his offspring. The book of Genesis ends with the family of Jacob, now renamed Israel, moving to Egypt as guests of Pharaoh. The book of Exodus continues that story. It begins with a list of the sons of Israel who went down into Egypt, recalling Genesis 46:8. And, in language reminiscent of the commission given to the first human beings as part of the creation narrative (Gen. 1:28; cf. 9:1),[53] it notes Israel's numerical growth (Exod. 1:7). This also sets the scene for the oppression that forms the background to the first part of the book. Continuity with Genesis is further indicated by the conjunction 'and', which starts the book.

Exodus also includes the account of the birth and call of Moses, the central figure in the rest of the Pentateuch. Exodus 2:3–10 describes how, in order to preserve his life, Moses' mother put him in a basket, which was then placed on the river, where he was found and raised by Pharaoh's daughter. The Mesopotamian birth legend of Sargon I, the founder of the Akkadian Empire, tells a similar story;[54] and some have suggested that the biblical account is a variant of

53. See e.g. Enns, *Exodus*, p. 41; Fretheim, *Exodus*, p. 25.
54. This describes how Sargon, for his own protection, was also placed in a basket by his mother, high priestess of the goddess Inanna, and 'abandoned' to the river, where he was found and adopted by Aqqi, the 'drawer of water'; see e.g. *COS* 1:133; Matthews and Benjamin, *OT Parallels*, pp. 89–90; Arnold and Beyer, *Readings*, pp. 75–76.

it, and therefore not historical.[55] It is possible, though, that this was a common way of abandoning infants in the ancient world. Where the river was shallow a basket would be clearly visible, and there would be a number of people coming to the river to bathe, to wash clothes, to collect water, and so on. If so, it was something that Moses' mother might very well have done in an attempt to keep him safe, and there is no need, therefore, to suggest dependence on other stories.

Another key theme in Exodus is Israel's redemption from slavery in Egypt. This focuses, particularly, on the first Passover, in which the firstborn in Egyptian households died, while the blood of the Passover lamb, smeared on the door frames of their houses, protected the Israelites. This has ongoing significance. The exodus is paradigmatic for expressions of redemption in the OT,[56] and, in particular, the hope of return following the Babylonian exile is viewed as a second exodus. And Passover and second exodus imagery are also evident in the NT.[57]

Significant, too, is the election of Israel (e.g. Exod. 19:5–6), which is widely regarded as marking the birth of the nation. This is associated with the covenant at Sinai, and the giving of the Law, themes that are also found in the rest of the Pentateuch. A key expression associated with Israel's covenant faith is found in Exodus 34:6–7 – 'the LORD, the LORD, the compassionate and gracious God, slow to anger, abounding in love and faithfulness, maintaining love to thousands, and forgiving wickedness, rebellion and sin', and variations of this statement appear in a number of OT passages.[58] This occurs after the incident of the

---

55. For further discussion, see e.g. Blenkinsopp, *Pentateuch*, pp. 146–148; Tremper Longman III, *Fictional Akkadian Autobiography: A Generic and Comparative Study* (Winona Lake: Eisenbrauns, 1991), pp. 53–60, 70–72, 215–216; Kenton L. Sparks, 'Genre Criticism', in Thomas B. Dozeman (ed.), *Methods for Exodus* (New York: Cambridge University Press, 2010), pp. 55–94 (84–85).
56. See e.g. Michael Fishbane, 'The "Exodus" Motif/The Paradigm of Historical Renewal', in Michael Fishbane (ed.), *Text and Texture: A Literary Reading of Selected Texts* (Oxford: One World, 1998), pp. 121–140; Christopher J. H. Wright, *The Mission of God: Unlocking the Bible's Grand Narrative* (Nottingham: Inter-Varsity Press; Downers Grove: InterVarsity Press, 2006), pp. 265–288 (275).
57. See above, p. 10, n. 30; see also e.g. Sylvia C. Keesmaat, 'Exodus and the Intertextual Transformation of Tradition in Romans 8.14–30', *JSNT* 54 (1994), pp. 29–56; *Paul and His Story*; Robin Routledge, 'Passover and Last Supper', *TynBul* 53.2 (2002), pp. 203–221; William J. Webb, *Returning Home: New Covenant and Second Exodus as the Context for 2 Corinthians 6:14–7:1*, JSNTSup 85 (Sheffield: JSOT Press, 1993).
58. Pss 86:15; 103:8; 145:8; Neh. 9:17; Joel 2:13; Jon. 4:2; see also Num. 14:18.

'golden calf', and is presented as an affirmation of God's renewed commitment to his people, despite their sin.[59] The traditional literary-critical view sees Exodus 34:1–10 (J) and Exodus 20:1–17 (E) as parallel accounts. This would make Exodus 34:1–10 the earlier of the two. However, in the final canonical account it is presented as the renewal of the covenant.[60] Moberly notes differences between Exodus 34:6–7 and Exodus 20:5b–6. After Israel's sin, grace now precedes judgment, there is a new emphasis on God's willingness to forgive, and, importantly, divine love is not presented as being conditional on obedience.[61] In that way the fulfilment of God's purpose though Israel is ensured.

Leviticus[62]

Structure and outline

Leviticus follows on from Exodus. There is a brief summary statement at the end of Exodus (40:34–38), marking a break in the narrative. Nevertheless, the conjunction 'and' at the start of the book, as well as the subject matter,

59. See Routledge, 'Mission and Covenant', in Grams et al., *Bible and Mission*, pp. 10–13.
60. Childs, *Exodus*, pp. 604–607.
61. R. W. L. Moberly, *At the Mountain of God: Story and Theology in Exodus 32–34*, JSOTSup (Sheffield: JSOT Press, 1983), pp. 86–88.
62. Commentaries on Leviticus include W. H. Bellinger Jr., *Leviticus, Numbers*, NIBCOT/UBC (Peabody: Hendrickson, 2001); Samuel E. Balentine, *Leviticus*, IBC (Louisville: John Knox, 2002); Philip J. Budd, *Leviticus*, NCB (London: Marshall Pickering; Grand Rapids: Eerdmans, 1996); Mary Douglas, *Leviticus as Literature* (Oxford: Oxford University Press, 1999); Erhard S. Gerstenberger, *Leviticus*, OTL (Louisville: Westminster John Knox, 1996); John E. Hartley, *Leviticus*, WBC 4 (Dallas: Word, 1992); Nobuyoshi Kiuchi, *Leviticus*, AOTC (Nottingham: Apollos; Downers Grove: InterVarsity Press, 2007); Baruch A. Levine, *Leviticus*, JPSTC (Philadelphia: Jewish Publication Society, 1989); Jacob Milgrom, *Leviticus: A Book of Ritual and Ethics*, CC (Minneapolis: Fortress, 2004); *Leviticus 1–16*, AB 3 (New York: Doubleday, 1991); *Leviticus 17–22*, AB 3A (New York: Doubleday, 2000); *Leviticus 23–27*, AB 3B (New York: Doubleday, 2001); Gordon J. Wenham, *Leviticus*, NICOT (Grand Rapids: Eerdmans, 1979); Rolf Rendtorff and Robert A. Kugler (eds.), *The Book of Leviticus: Composition and Reception*, VTSup 93 (Leiden: Brill, 2003); Jay Sklar, *Leviticus*, TOTC (Downers Grove: IVP Academic, 2014).

points to essential continuity with what has gone before. The legal material in Leviticus is generally assigned to P (as part of the extensive section of legal material running from Exod. 25 to Num. 10).

The second part of the book (chs. 17 – 26), sometimes referred to as the 'Holiness Code' (H),[63] is widely taken to form a subsection within the P material. One distinctive feature of this section is the frequent occurrence of the expression 'I am the LORD (your God)'.[64] Some scholars also note the extension of the idea of holiness beyond ritual, which is characteristic of P, to wider ethical behaviour.[65] This is also evident in Deuteronomy, and links have been noted between H and Deuteronomy, including blessings and curses (Lev. 26:3–45).[66] The older view is that H is based on an earlier code, which was then incorporated into P, to provide that ethical dimension.[67] More recently, H has been viewed as a later 'corrective' to the priestly emphasis on ritual purity.[68] Averbeck suggests that, rather than implying alternative sources and ideologies, the difference in emphasis is, primarily, one of sociological perspective: Leviticus 1 – 16 is written from the perspective of the priests, while Leviticus 17 – 26 (27) is written from the perspective of the community.[69]

Leviticus seems to be structured according to content. The instructions for the Day of Atonement (ch. 16) form a logical centre.[70] It belongs to the section

---

63. The view that Lev. 17 – 26 formed a separate section of Leviticus is suggested by Klostermann (1877). See further e.g. Budd, *Leviticus*, pp. 14–19; Jan Joosten, *People & Land in the Holiness Code: An Exegetical Study of the Ideational Framework of the Law in Leviticus 17–26*, VTSup 67 (Leiden: Brill, 1996), pp. 1–27.
64. The expression 'I am the LORD your God' occurs twenty times in H (e.g. 18:2, 4, 30; 19:3, 4, 10, 25, 31; 20:7; 23:22; 24:22; 25:17; 26:1; cf. 26:44), and only twice more in Exod. 25 – Num. 10 (Lev. 11:44; Num. 10:10). The shorter expression 'I am the LORD' occurs a further twenty-six times in H (e.g. 18:5, 6; 19:12, 14, 16, 28, 30, 32; 20:8; 21:12; 22:2, 3, 8; 26:2, 45), and only a handful of times in the rest of Exod. 25 – Num. 10.
65. E.g. Collins, *Introduction*, p. 155; Milgrom, *Leviticus*, p. 215.
66. See e.g. Jeffrey Stackert, *Rewriting the Torah: Literary Revision in Deuteronomy and the Holiness Legislation*, FAT 52 (Tübingen: Mohr Siebeck, 2007).
67. E.g. Budd, *Leviticus*, pp. 17–18.
68. See e.g. Israel Knohl, *The Sanctuary of Silence: The Priestly Torah and the Holiness School* (Minneapolis: Augsburg Fortress, 1995; repr. Winona Lake: Eisenbrauns, 2007); *Leviticus*, pp. 175–183.
69. R. E. Averbeck, 'Tabernacle', in *DOTP*, pp. 807–827 (820).
70. See Hartley, *Leviticus*, pp. xxxiv–xxxv.

of the book dealing with ritual purity, but its focus on confessing and dealing with the sin of the nation opens the way for the greater emphasis in chapters 17–26 on the ethical dimension of purity.

Outline[71]

- Instructions about sacrifices (1:1 – 7:38)
- Institution of the Aaronic priesthood (8:1 – 10:20)
- Regulations relating to ritual uncleanness (11:1 – 15:33)
- The Day of Atonement (16:1–34)
- Instructions for holy living (17:1 – 26:46)
- Redemption of offerings promised to God (27:1–34)

Main themes

Leviticus comes from the name of the book in the LXX, and reflects the fact that it includes a great deal of material relating to the priests, who were from the tribe of Levi. It was probably not, though, as some have suggested, primarily a manual for priests.[72] Much of its content is addressed to the people as a whole. And even where the priests are addressed, the instructions are general, and do not include the details that might be expected in such a manual.[73] The book's Hebrew name is taken from its opening word *wayyiqrā'* (and he [the LORD] called). This reflects the fact that the instructions contained within Leviticus have divine authority.[74]

A key theme of the book is holiness. The main emphasis is on the holiness of the people. This continues the theme of the Pentateuch. The people who have been called by God to fulfil his purpose must conduct themselves appropriately, both in worship, and in their everyday lives. Sin, which remains an ongoing problem for the people, must be dealt with, so that God's presence among his people may be maintained. And this forms the basis of the

71. For an alternative structure, centred on ch. 19, see Mary Douglas, 'The Forbidden Animals in Leviticus', *JSOT* 59 (1993), pp. 3–23 (9–12).
72. The Talmud refers to Leviticus as 'instructions for the priests' (*tôrat kōhănîm*), and Milgrom refers to it as a 'priestly manual' (e.g. *Leviticus*, p. 333); see also W. Brueggemann, *Introduction*, p. 90.
73. E.g. LaSor, Hubbard and Bush, *OT Survey*, pp. 81–82; Wenham, *Leviticus*, p. 3. Levine suggests that *tôrat kōhănîm* may be interpreted 'instruction of/by the priests' to the people (cf. Jer. 18:18; Mal. 2:6–7), which also widens its scope (*Leviticus*, pp. xi–xii).
74. E.g. LaSor, Hubbard and Bush, *OT Survey*, p. 81.

regulations relating to sacrifice.[75] Other forms of uncleanness also have an impact on the life of the community, and they, too, must be taken seriously.

One of the factors in distinguishing clean from unclean in Leviticus appears to be related to what is whole or complete.[76] That could, in turn, be seen to relate to what is normal: to what the world was meant to be. One aspect of this is to identify God with order rather than disorder. The fall in Genesis 3 brought chaos into God's very good world. And separation from these things may relate to the Pentateuchal theme of the restoration of order to creation.

The holiness of the people is focused, primarily, on the character and self-revelation of God. This is summed up in the divine imperative 'Be holy because I, the LORD your God, am holy' (Lev. 19:2; see also 11:44–45; 20:26; 1 Pet. 1:16). It is evident, too, in the frequent reminders, particularly in Leviticus 17 – 26, that 'I am the LORD'. Because Israel is called into a relationship with a holy God, the people, and especially those with religious oversight of the nation, must reflect that in the holiness of their own lives.

Numbers[77]

Structure and outline

According to source critics, Numbers 1:1 – 10:28, in which Israel is still at Mount Sinai, continues the substantial block of P material that runs from Exodus 25.

---

75. For further discussion of sacrifice, see also Routledge, *OT Theology*, pp. 188–204; 'Sacrifice, Prayer and Forgiveness'.
76. See e.g. Mary Douglas, *Purity and Danger: An Analysis of Concepts of Pollution and Taboo* (London: Routledge & Kegan Paul, 1966), pp. 51–57; see also Bandstra, *Reading the OT*, pp. 152–153; Walter Brueggemann, *Deuteronomy*, AbOTC (Nashville: Abingdon, 2001), pp. 158–159; Joe M. Sprinkle, 'The Rationale of the Laws of Clean and Unclean in the Old Testament', *JETS* 43.4 (2000), pp. 637–657 (649–650); Wenham, *Leviticus*, pp. 23–25. For other, possibly overlapping, suggestions, see Sprinkle, 'Clean and Unclean', pp. 646–654. See also Walter J. Houston, 'Towards an Integrated Reading of the Dietary Laws of Leviticus', in Rendtorff and Kugler, *Leviticus*, pp. 142–161.
77. Commentaries on Numbers include Timothy R. Ashley, *Numbers*, NICOT (Grand Rapids: Eerdmans, 1993); Bellinger, *Leviticus, Numbers*; Budd, *Numbers*; Davies, *Numbers*; Martin Noth, *Numbers*, OTL (London: SCM Press, 1968); Jacob Milgrom, *Numbers*, JPSTC (Philadelphia: Jewish Publication Society, 1990); Dennis T. Olsen, *Numbers*, IBC (Louisville: John Knox, 1996); Wenham, *Numbers*.

The rest of the book includes elements of J and E, though with signs of priestly editing.[78] It is, nevertheless, presented as a continuous narrative without clear structural breaks. This makes any suggested outline tentative. One suggested structure is based on Israel's location at various points in the narrative.[79]

Outline

- At Sinai (1:1 – 10:10)
- The journey to the plains of Moab (10:11 – 22:1)
  - From Sinai to Kadesh (10:11 – 12:16)
  - At Kadesh (13:1 – 20:13)
  - From Kadesh to the plains of Moab (20:14 – 22:1)
- On the plains of Moab (22:2 – 36:13)

Olsen takes, instead, the two censuses described in the book (1:1–46; 26:1–51),[80] as key dividing points in the narrative.[81] The following is based on his outline:

- The fall of the generation that left Egypt (1:1 – 25:18)
  - Preparation for the journey (1:1 – 10:36)
  - Rebellion in the desert (11:1 – 25:18)
- The rise of a new generation to enter the Promised Land (26:1 – 36:13)
  - Second census: a new generation of people and leaders (26:1 – 27:23)
  - Offerings and vows (for a new generation) (28:1 – 30:16)
  - Preparation for conquest and division of the land (31:1 – 36:13)

Main themes

In the opening chapters of Numbers Israel is still at Sinai, and there is a continuation of legal material, particularly relating to the consecration and duties of the Levites, whose role appears to have been to assist the priests, the descendants of Aaron. Included, too, is the first census (1:1–46), and the organization of the Israelite camp, around the Tent of Meeting (2:1–34).[82] Wenham notes

78. E.g. Collins, *Introduction*, pp. 158–160.

79. E.g. Ashley, *Numbers*, pp. 2–3; Wenham, *Numbers*, p. 54; see also Davies, *Numbers*, pp. lxx–lxxiv.

80. These censuses give the book its Greek title *Arithmoi*, and hence 'Numbers'.

81. Olsen, *Numbers*; see also Longman and Dillard, *Introduction*, pp. 96–97.

82. Exod. 33:7 refers to an earlier 'tent of meeting', pitched outside the camp. The term was transferred to the tabernacle, suggesting it incorporated the characteristics of the former structure. Some suggest that the 'tent of meeting' belongs to an earlier

that this arrangement reflected the way the Egyptian camp was likely to have been organized, around the royal tent.[83] This emphasizes the idea of Yahweh as Israel's king.[84]

A theme of Israel's journey through the desert is persistent complaining[85] and rebellion. This culminates in the people's unwillingness to enter Canaan (13:25 – 14:12), and the consequence that the generation who left Egypt, with the exception of Caleb, would die without seeing the Promised Land (14:20–24). This necessitated a further extended period of desert wandering. A second census (26:2) signals the rise of a new generation, who may now go on to enter the land. In a post-exilic setting the fallen generation might be identified with those who provoked divine judgment and exile from the land. Joshua and Caleb then represent the faithful remnant, and the new generation points to the hope of eventual return.[86]

The population figures recorded in Numbers have been the cause of some debate. In each of the censuses the number of those able to fight in the army exceeds 600,000. That indicates a total population, including women and children, in excess of 2 million, which seems very unlikely.[87] One possibility is that the term translated 'thousand' (*'elep*) could refer to a 'clan' or 'tent-group'. According to Olsen, the 'forty-six thousand five hundred' attributed to Reuben (Num. 1:21) might be translated, instead, 'forty-six "tent-groups," with a total of five hundred people'.[88] Another suggestion is that the figures relate to a later time, though it is unlikely that numbers were ever that high in the OT period.[89] It may be that the high numbers are intended to be taken at face value in the narrative, not necessarily as a literal historical record, but to represent the fulfilment of the promise to Abraham of innumerable descendants.[90]

---

tradition (maybe E), and was merged with the tabernacle by P. See further e.g. Routledge, *OT Theology*, p. 177, n. 5.

83. Wenham, *Numbers*, pp. 66–67, 175.
84. Yahweh's kingship appears to be affirmed also in Num. 23:21. See too Eichrodt, *OT Theology*, 1:108, 194.
85. Terms from the Hebrew root *lûn* ('to complain, murmur'; NIV 'grumble') are found in 14:2, 27, 29, 36; 16:11, 41 (17:6); 17:5 (20), 10 (25). Another verb, *'ānan*, appears in 11:1.
86. See W. Brueggemann, *Introduction*, pp. 100–101.
87. See above, p. 92, n. 104; see also e.g. LaSor, Hubbard and Bush, *OT Survey*, pp. 103–106; Olsen, *Numbers*, pp. 13–17; Wenham, *Pentateuch*, p. 106; *Numbers*, pp. 60–66.
88. Olsen, *Numbers*, p. 13.
89. LaSor, Hubbard and Bush, *OT Survey*, p. 105; Wenham, *Numbers*, p. 62.
90. See e.g. LaSor, Hubbard and Bush, *OT Survey*, pp. 105–106; Olsen, *Numbers*, pp. 13–14; Wenham, *Pentateuch*, p. 106.

Deuteronomy[91]

Date and composition

Deuteronomy is associated with the Law Book found in the temple at the end of the seventh century BC (2 Kgs 22:8). Many consider that it was written not long before its discovery, to encourage Josiah's reforms, particularly in relation to the centralization of worship in the Jerusalem temple.[92] This dating is important for the traditional formulation of the Documentary Hypothesis.

Others argue for a much earlier date, maybe even going back to the time of Moses. McConville, for example, suggests that Deuteronomy 12, which is usually linked to Josiah's centralization, could reflect a time just before Israel entered the Promised Land,[93] though he stops short of claiming Mosaic authorship.[94]

---

91. Commentaries on Deuteronomy include Stephen L. Cook, *Deuteronomy: A Literary and Theological Commentary* (Macon: Smyth & Helwys, 2015); Duane L. Christenson, *Deuteronomy*, 2 vols., WBC 6A–B (Nashville: Nelson, 2001, 2002); Craigie, *Deuteronomy*; Jack Lundbom, *Deuteronomy* (Grand Rapids: Eerdmans, 2013); McConville, *Deuteronomy*; A. D. H. Mayes, *Deuteronomy*, NCB (Grand Rapids: Eerdmans, 1996); Patrick D. Miller, *Deuteronomy*, IBC (Louisville: Westminster John Knox, 1990); Richard D. Nelson, *Deuteronomy*, OTL (Louisville: Westminster John Knox, 2002); Rofé, *Deuteronomy*; Thompson, *Deuteronomy*; Jeffrey H. Tigay, *Deuteronomy*, JPSTC (Philadelphia: Jewish Publication Society, 1996); Gerhard von Rad, *Deuteronomy*, OTL (London: SCM Press, 1966); Moshe Weinfeld, *Deuteronomy 1–11*, AB 5 (New York: Doubleday, 1991); Christopher J. H. Wright, *Deuteronomy*, NIBCOT (Peabody: Hendrickson, 1996); see also David G. Firth and Philip S. Johnston (eds.), *Interpreting Deuteronomy: Issues and Approaches* (Nottingham: Apollos, 2012); McConville, *Law and Theology*; Peter T. Vogt, *Deuteronomic Theology and the Significance of the Torah: A Reappraisal* (Winona Lake: Eisenbrauns, 2006).
92. E.g. Collins, *Introduction*, pp. 166–168; Bernard M. Levinson, 'The Hermeneutics of Tradition in Deuteronomy: A Reply to J. G. McConville', *JBL* 119.2 (2000), pp. 269–286; 'Esarhaddon's Succession Treaty as the Source for the Canon Formula in Deuteronomy 13:1'; Mayes, *Deuteronomy*, pp. 85–103; Weinfeld, *Deuteronomy* (though Weinfeld suggests that it followed rather than prompted Josiah's reform).
93. McConville, *Law and Theology*, pp. 155–156.
94. McConville, *Deuteronomy*, p. 39. Those who favour a date around the time of Moses, maybe with editorial additions, include Craigie, *Deuteronomy*, pp. 24–29; Hill and Walton, *Survey*, pp. 164–165; Kitchen, *Reliability*, pp. 289–304; LaSor, Hubbard and Bush, *OT Survey*, pp. 114–117; Wenham, 'Date of Deuteronomy 1'; 'Date of Deuteronomy 2'.

Parallels with second millennium BC treaties reinforce arguments for an early date.[95]

Other historical settings have also been suggested.[96] One places it nearer to the time of Hezekiah, who, like Josiah, is recorded as removing the 'high places' (2 Kgs 18:4). Though no Law Book is mentioned in connection with Hezekiah's reform, his actions conform to the requirements set out in Deuteronomy; suggesting that those aspects of the tradition might have been known. Several links have been noted between Deuteronomy and Hosea;[97] and it has been suggested that Deuteronomy may have a link with the north,[98] and was compiled prior to the fall of Samaria, or by northerners, who fled to Judah at that time, thus implying a date in the late eighth or early seventh century BC.

There seems little doubt that Deuteronomy (or a substantial part of it) gave impetus to Josiah's reforms, and the description of him as one who 'turned to the LORD . . . with all his heart and with all his soul and with all his strength, in accordance with all the Law of Moses' (2 Kgs 23:25) appears to be a deliberate allusion to Deuteronomy 6:5. However, the possibility of an earlier date for Deuteronomy suggests that it might not have been written expressly for that purpose.[99]

There is also debate about the process of Deuteronomy's composition. Those who accept Mosaic authorship generally view the book as a unity, with minor editorial elements. Arguments for its unity have been strengthened by links between the structure of Deuteronomy and ANE treaties. Those who assign

---

95. Arguments for the later date claim support from similarities with Assyrian treaties; see above, pp. 121–122.

96. For an overview, see e.g. Christopher B. Ansberry and Jerry Hwang, 'No Covenant Before the Exile: The Deuteronomic Torah and Israel's Covenant Theology', in Christopher M. Hays and Christopher B. Ansberry (eds.), *Evangelical Faith and the Challenge of Historical Criticism* (London: SPCK, 2013), pp. 74–94; Thompson, *Deuteronomy*, pp. 47–68.

97. See e.g. Ansberry and Hwang, 'No Covenant', in Hays and Ansberry, *Evangelical Faith*, p. 77; Mayes, *Deuteronomy*, pp. 103–104; von Rad, *Deuteronomy*, p. 26; James Robson, 'The Literary Composition of Deuteronomy', in Firth and Johnston, *Interpreting Deuteronomy*, pp. 19–59 (48–49); Weinfeld, *Deuteronomy*, pp. 366–370; R. R. Wilson, *Prophecy and Society*, p. 227.

98. See e.g. Lundbom, *Deuteronomy*, pp. 10–11; R. R. Wilson, *Prophecy and Society*, pp. 156–225.

99. See Robson, 'Literary Composition', in Firth and Johnston, *Interpreting Deuteronomy*, pp. 40–43.

the book to a later period often see a longer process of transmission, with several editorial layers. The central legal section (12 – 26) has affinities with Exodus 21 – 23. This may then have been given its own introduction and conclusion (5 – 11; 27 – 31), with much of the rest added when the text was edited to form the introduction to the so-called 'Deuteronomistic History'.[100]

We have noted, already, that the 'law of the king' (Deut. 17:14–20) raises some issues. It is unlikely that the similarity between 17:14 and 1 Samuel 8:5, and between the potential royal abuses noted in 17:16–17 and the activities of Solomon, are accidental. The traditional view maintains that this is prophetic, and that Moses foresaw both the monarchy and the problems associated with it. If so, the request for a king and Solomon's failings may be couched in language that deliberately echoes Moses' words. Alternatively, the wording in Deuteronomy may be editorial, post-dating the time of Samuel and Solomon. A post-Mosaic date for some of the content of Deuteronomy does not, though, necessarily require its fundamental separation from Moses. As Thompson suggests, 'there is something to be said for the view that, while Moses himself provided Israel with the heart of Deuteronomy, it became necessary in new situations to re-present the words of Moses and to show their relevance to the new day'.[101] The theology of Deuteronomy is not something essentially new;[102] traditions such as those relating to the power and role of the king, and to the purity of worship, may well go back to Moses. However, their particular expression may be the work of later editors, who have adapted it to fit the needs of their own situation.

Structure and outline

An important feature of the structure of Deuteronomy is its similarity, particularly, to second millennium BC Hittite suzerain–vassal treaties.[103] Within that broad structure the book is made up, primarily, of three sermons delivered by Moses to the people as they prepare to cross over to begin their new life in the Promised Land. Its setting, in Moab, east of the Jordan (1:1–5) suggests continuity with Numbers (cf. Num. 36:13).

---

100. However, see below, pp. 253–257.

101. Thompson, *Deuteronomy*, pp. 67–68; see also Ansberry and Hwang, 'No Covenant', in Hays and Ansberry, *Evangelical Faith*, pp. 83–89. Robson, too, usefully distinguishes between Mosaic *authorship* and Mosaic *origin* ('Literary Composition', in Firth and Johnston, *Interpreting Deuteronomy*, pp. 20, 57–58).

102. However, Bernard M. Levinson, *Deuteronomy and the Hermeneutics of Legal Innovation* (Oxford: Oxford University Press, 1997), does regard Deuteronomy as innovative.

103. See above, pp. 121–123.

Outline

- Introduction to Moses' first sermon (1:1–5)
- Moses' first sermon (1:6 – 4:40)
  - – The story so far: the journey from Horeb to Moab (1:6 – 3:29)
  - – The challenge to obedience (4:1–40)
- Cities of refuge east of the Jordan (4:41–43)
- Introduction to Moses' second sermon (4:44–49)
- Moses' second sermon (5:1 – 28:68)
  - – The demands of the covenant (5:1 – 11:32)
  - – Detailed covenant stipulations (12:1 – 26:19)
  - – Charge to the people: blessings and curses (27:1 – 28:68)
- Moses' third sermon (29:1 – 30:20)
- Epilogue
  - – Joshua appointed to succeed Moses (31:1–23)
  - – The book of the Law deposited in the Ark (31:24–29)
  - – The Song of Moses (31:30 – 32:43)
  - – Moses' final charge, blessing and death (32:48 – 34:12)

Main themes

The name 'Deuteronomy' comes from the LXX version of 17:18, which translates the 'copy of this law' that the king is required to make as *to deuteronomion touto* (this second law). Deuteronomy does not, though, present new material. Rather, it reviews the legal requirements of Israel's covenant relationship with God that is also found in Exodus–Numbers, including the Ten Commandments (Deut. 5:1–21; cf. Exod. 20:1–17). The Hebrew title derives from the book's opening, *'ēlleh haddĕbārîm* (these are the words).

The genre of Deuteronomy is mixed. While its broad structure links it to ANE legal texts such as suzerain–vassal treaties and law codes, it is set out as a series of speeches, and so also includes rhetoric and exhortation; and its purpose seems to be not only to review the requirements of the covenant relationship between God and Israel, but also to encourage the people to play their part in maintaining it (cf. Deut. 31:10–13). The presentation of these speeches as the last words of Moses, who will not accompany the people into the Promised Land, and the description of his death suggest that there is also a significant biographical element in the book.

A central theme in Deuteronomy is the promise of the land. The people are on the borders of Canaan, and there are frequent references to the land that God has given them to possess (e.g. 1:8, 21, 39; 5:31; 9:1–3; 10:11; 26:1). Possession of the land is also related to the themes of law and covenant. God has entered into a relationship with Israel, and as the people prepare to enter the land that relationship needs to be maintained. Obedience to God's requirements will result in blessing and continued possession of the land (e.g. 4:1; 5:32–33; 6:18; 8:1; 11:18–21; 12:28; 16:20; 28:1–14); while disobedience will result is disaster, and eventual expulsion (e.g. 4:25–27; 28:15–68). There appears to be an implicit threat, too, in references to God's driving out the nations because of their sinfulness (e.g. 9:4–5; 18:9–13). This would have had particular resonance during the exile. Deuteronomy offers a stark choice between obedience and disobedience leading, respectively, to 'a blessing' and 'life and prosperity' or 'a curse' and 'death and destruction' (e.g. 11:26–28; 30:15–20). I will have more to say about these 'two ways' when discussing the 'Deuteronomistic History'.

Because of the importance of continued obedience there is an emphasis on teaching the next, and subsequent, generations (e.g. 4:9–10; 6:2, 7; 11:18–21). The key feasts of Passover, Unleavened Bread and Tabernacles are also continuing reminders of what God has done. And the provision to read the law every seven years (31:10–13) further ensures that all generations remain aware of their responsibility. This emphasis, and whether or not it was heeded, forms an important basis for the continuing history of Israel.

7. THE FORMER PROPHETS

The Deuteronomistic History[1]

The term 'Deuteronomistic History' (sometimes written as DtrH or DH) is

---

1. For an overview of the main areas of discussion, see e.g. Antony F. Campbell and Mark A. O'Brien, *Unfolding the Deuteronomistic History: Origins, Upgrades, Present Text* (Minneapolis: Augsburg Fortress, 2000), pp. 1–37; Robert P. Gordon, *1 & 2 Samuel*, OTG (Sheffield: Sheffield Academic Press, 1984), pp. 14–22; J. Gordon McConville, *Grace in the End: A Study in Deuteronomic Theology*, SOTBT (Grand Rapids: Zondervan, 1993); Richard D. Nelson, *The Historical Books*, IBT (Nashville: Abingdon, 1998), pp. 67–78; Brian Neil Peterson, *The Authors of the Deuteronomistic History: Locating a Tradition in Ancient Israel* (Minneapolis: Fortress, 2014), pp. 1–23; S. L. Richter, 'Deuteronomistic History', in *DOTHB*, pp. 219–230; Thomas Römer, *The So-Called Deuteronomistic History: A Sociological, Historical and Literary Introduction* (London: T&T Clark, 2005), pp. 3–43; Philip Satterthwaite and Gordon McConville, *Exploring the Old Testament*, vol. 3: *The Histories* (London: SPCK, 2007), pp. 199–219. For more detailed discussion, see Mignon R. Jacobs and Raymond F. Person Jr. (eds.), *Israelite Prophecy and the Deuteronomistic History: Portrait, Reality, and the Formation of a History* (Atlanta: Society of Biblical Literature, 2013); G. N. Knoppers, 'Rethinking the Relationship Between Deuteronomy and the Deuteronomistic History: The Case of Kings', *CBQ* 63 (2001), pp. 393–415; Steven L. McKenzie and M. Patrick Graham (eds.), *The History*

attributed to Martin Noth.[2] It is generally seen to comprise the historical books Joshua, Judges, Samuel and Kings. According to Noth, an edition of Deuteronomy, comprising chapters 5–30, was expanded to form the theological introduction to this history (thereby arguing in favour of regarding Genesis–Numbers as a Tetrateuch). Noth viewed the DH as a unified history of Israel, from conquest to exile, composed by a single author, the Deuteronomist (Dtr), some time after Jehoiachin's release from prison (2 Kgs 25:27–30). Its purpose, based on the Deuteronomic principle that obedience leads to blessing and disobedience leads to disaster and eventual expulsion from the land, was to demonstrate divine activity in Israel's history, and to explain that the exile was God's just punishment for the nation's apostasy, which had continued despite all previous warnings and judgments.

Von Rad offered an early challenge to Noth's view that the DH focused solely on judgment. He agreed that the exile represents deserved retribution: 'God's word is the key to the history of salvation. God has given his commandments, and he has threatened severe judgments as the consequence of disobedience. Those judgments have occurred.'[3] However, alongside the threat of judgment is God's long-suffering, based on his promises to David. When the sin of the people deserved an earlier and more complete judgment, God held back (e.g. 1 Kgs 11:13; 2 Kgs 8:18–19). The 'postscript' (2 Kgs 25:27–30) also offers hope of the eventual restoration of David's line.[4]

(*Footnote 1 cont.*) *of Israel's Traditions: The Heritage of Martin Noth*, JSOTSup 182 (Sheffield: JSOT Press, 1994); K. L. Noll, 'Deuteronomistic History or Deuteronomic Debate? (A Thought Experiment)', *JSOT* 31.3 (2007), pp. 311–345; Mark A. O'Brien, *The Deuteronomistic History Hypothesis: A Reassessment* (Göttingen: Vandenhoeck & Ruprecht, 1989); Albert de Pury and Raymond F. Person Jr., *The Deuteronomic School: History, Social Setting, and Literature* (Atlanta: Society of Biblical Literature, 2002); Albert de Pury, Thomas Römer and Jean-Daniel Macchi (eds.), *Israel Constructs Its History: Deuteronomistic Historiography in Recent Research*, JSOTSup 306 (Sheffield: Sheffield Academic Press, 2000); Raymond F. Person Jr. (ed.), 'In Conversation with Thomas Römer, *The So-Called Deuteronomistic History: A Sociological, Historical and Literary Introduction* (London: T&T Clark, 2005)', *JHS* 9.17 (2009), pp. 1–49; Linda S. Shearing and Stephen L. McKenzie (eds.), *Those Elusive Deuteronomists: 'Pandeuteronomism and Scholarship in the Nineties'* (Sheffield: Sheffield Academic Press, 1999).

2. Martin Noth, *The Deuteronomistic History*, JSOTSup 15 (Sheffield: JSOT Press, 1981); this was first published in German in 1943.
3. Von Rad, *God at Work in Israel*, p. 146.
4. Von Rad, *OT Theology*, 1:343.

A significant modification of Noth's original theory is the suggestion of a double redaction: the first at the time of Josiah, and the second during the exile.[5] Cross identified two redactors: Dtr[1] and Dtr[2]. Dtr[1] emphasizes two parallel, contrasting themes: judgment, linked to the sin of Jeroboam,[6] and grace, based on the faithfulness of the Davidic line.[7] This contrast reaches a climax with Josiah, who 'walked in all the ways of his father David' (2 Kgs 22:2), cleansed the temple and destroyed Jeroboam's altar at Bethel (2 Kgs 23:15). The first redaction thus ends positively; it presents Josiah's reforms as being in accordance with Deuteronomic requirements, and his reign as an example of the blessings that accompany obedience. A further redaction then took place after the exile. Dtr[2] recognizes that the days of blessing are past, and emphasizes the judgment that follows disobedience.

Another view, put forward by Göttingen scholars Smend, Dietrich and Veijola, agrees with Noth and places the first redaction, DtrG (or DtrH), in the early post-exilic period, but then identifies further redactions: DtrP, which emphasizes the fulfilment of prophecy, and DtrN, which focuses on the importance of obedience to the law.[8]

Brueggemann notes that these and further developments broadly follow Noth's view that the DH has an underlying interpretative intention.[9] It might be asked, however, as the number of potential redactions grows and the text is considered to be increasingly diverse, is it any longer possible to speak in a meaningful way of a Deuteronomistic History?

---

5. See e.g. Cross, *Canaanite Myth*, pp. 274–289; Richard D. Nelson, *The Double Redaction of the Deuteronomistic History*, JSOTSup 18 (Sheffield: JSOT Press, 1981); 'The Double Redaction of the Deuteronomistic History: The Case Is Still Compelling', *JSOT* 29.3 (2005), pp. 319–337; though see also J. Gordon McConville, 'Narrative and Meaning in the Books of Kings', *Bib* 70.1 (1989), pp. 31–49.
6. E.g. 1 Kgs 16:2, 26; 22:52; 2 Kgs 3:3; 10:29; 13:2.
7. E.g. 1 Kgs 15:11; 2 Kgs 18:3; 22:2; cf. 1 Kgs 15:3.
8. See e.g. Longman and Dillard, *Introduction*, pp. 156–158; Richter, 'Deuteronomistic History', in *DOTHB*, pp. 224–227 (224–225); Römer, *So-Called Deuteronomistic History*, pp. 29–43 (29–30); Satterthwaite and McConville, *Histories*, pp. 204–208 (205–206). See also Walter Dietrich, 'The Layer Model of the Deuteronomistic History and the Book of Samuel', in Cynthia Edenburg and Juha Pakkala (eds.), *Is Samuel Among the Deuteronomists? Current Views on the Place of Samuel in a Deuteronomistic History* (Atlanta: Society of Biblical Literature, 2013), pp. 39–65. For an outline of additional views, see Peterson, *Authors of the Deuteronomistic History*, pp. 12–20.
9. W. Brueggemann, *Introduction*, p. 133.

A further issue is the relationship between Deuteronomy and the DH. As we have seen, Deuteronomy acts as a bridge between the Pentateuch and Joshua–Kings. However, canonically, it remains part of the Pentateuch, while Joshua, though closely related to what goes before, is separated from it.[10] We have noted, too, that the historical books have links with other parts of the Pentateuch, not just Deuteronomy.[11] This raises further questions about the use of the term 'Deuteronomistic History'.

Concerns about the idea of the DH as suggested by Noth do not necessarily mean dismissing all of the insights provided by the discussion. The final form of Joshua–Kings dates from after Jehoiachin's release from prison, and, while no doubt incorporating older, and sometimes diverse, traditions, as well as different theological emphases, it is presented as a single narrative.[12] And aspects of the narrative reflect the Deuteronomic principle that obedience leads to blessing, success and life while disobedience leads to defeat, exile and death. Thus, in the conquest narrative, obedience leads to an unlikely victory at Jericho (Josh. 6:2–21), while disobedience leads to an equally unlikely defeat at Ai (Josh. 7:1–5). The book of Judges includes a repeating cycle (e.g. Judg. 2:11–19): disobedience, usually in the form of idolatry, is followed by defeat and oppression, which is, in turn, followed by deliverance through a divinely appointed judge, often after the Israelites 'cried out to the LORD' (Judg. 3:9, 15; 6:6; 10:10). There is a period of peace, during the lifetime of the judge,[13] after which the people revert to their old ways, and the cycle starts again. The success of the kings of Israel and Judah is judged not by civic or military achievements, but by whether or not they did right in the eyes of the Lord, and their actions are frequently compared with those of Jeroboam or David – though that might reflect a more particular criticism of Israel's rejection of the Davidic monarchy. The defeat and exile of the northern kingdom are attributed to their rejection of the Lord's 'decrees and the covenant he had made with their fathers and the warnings he had given them' (2 Kgs 17:15), and that is further linked with their persistence in the ways of Jeroboam (2 Kgs 17:22–23). In this context the reforms of Josiah are presented as being in fulfilment of the requirements of Deuteronomy, and

---

10. Childs, *Introduction*, pp. 232–236.

11. See above, p. 229; see also Satterthwaite and McConville, *Histories*, p. 216.

12. For arguments in favour of Joshua–Kings as a unified work, see e.g. Paul R. House, *1, 2 Kings*, NAC 8 (Nashville: B&H, 1995), pp. 29–39; Burke O. Long, *1 Kings with an Introduction to Historical Literature*, FOTL 9 (Grand Rapids: Eerdmans, 1984), pp. 16–21.

13. This is not specifically attributed to obedience, though it may be implied in that, after the death of the judge, they returned to their corrupt ways (Judg. 2:19).

that offers a glimmer of hope to Judah. Though Judah, too, continued in disobedience, particularly under Manasseh, whose sins are held directly responsible for the Babylonian exile (2 Kgs 21:10–15; 24:3–4).

There is no need to separate the positive and negative elements here. Certainly, the final outcome is negative. However, just as the judgments that follow disobedience serve as warnings, the occasions where blessing follows obedience offer a promise of hope. That hope receives further expression in the promises made to David, and in the release of Jehoiachin, which suggests that judgment is not God's final word.[14]

It is important to note, however, that while the Deuteronomic principle may be present in Joshua–Kings, it is not necessarily the only, or even the dominant, theme, and so cannot be seen to determine the purpose and direction of the whole work. The theme has been woven into the narrative, indicating that it was significant, but other important themes, such as God's promises to David, are also in evidence.

Joshua[15]

Date and composition

The book of Joshua has clear links with Deuteronomy.[16] Joshua is presented as the successor to Moses, and the command given to him 'to obey all the law my

14. McConville, *Grace in the End*, p. 67. For discussion of the tension between judgment and hope, see Nathan Lovell, 'The Shape of Hope in the Book of Kings: The Resolution of Davidic Blessing and Mosaic Curse', *JESOT* 3.1 (2014), pp. 3–27.
15. Commentaries on Joshua include Robert G. Boling and G. Ernest Wright, *Joshua*, AB 6 (New York: Doubleday, 1982); Trent C. Butler, *Joshua*, WBC 7 (Waco: Word, 1988); J. Gordon Harris, 'Joshua', in J. Harris, C. Brown and M. Moore, *Joshua, Judges, Ruth*, NIBCOT/UBC (Peabody: Hendrickson, 2000), pp. 1–119; Jerome F. D. Creach, *Joshua*, IBC (Louisville: John Knox, 2003); David G. Firth, *The Message of Joshua*, BST (Nottingham: Inter-Varsity Press, 2015); L. Daniel Hawk, *Joshua*, Berit Olam (Collegeville: Liturgical Press, 2000); Hess, *Joshua*; Robert L. Hubbard Jr., *Joshua*, NIVAC (Grand Rapids: Zondervan, 2009); J. Gordon McConville and Stephen Williams, *Joshua*, THOTC (Grand Rapids: Eerdmans, 2010); Richard D. Nelson, *Joshua*, OTL (Louisville: Westminster John Knox, 1997); Pitkänen, *Joshua*; Martin H. Woudstra, *Joshua*, NICOT (Grand Rapids: Eerdmans, 1981).
16. See e.g. Gordon J. Wenham, 'The Deuteronomic Theology of the Book of Joshua', *JBL* 90.2 (1971), pp. 140–148.

servant Moses gave you; do not turn from it to the right or to the left' (Josh. 1:7; cf. 23:6) echoes Deuteronomy (Deut. 5:32; 17:11, 20; 28:14). The book continues the theme of war carried out by, and on behalf of, Yahweh, which is also an important motif in Deuteronomy. As noted already, Israel's experiences at Jericho and Ai reflect Deuteronomy's 'two ways'; and Joshua repeats Moses' threat that if they serve other gods, Israel will 'perish from the good land' they have received (Josh. 23:15–16; cf. Deut. 11:16–17; see also Deut. 4:25–26; 30:17–18). Joshua sets up an altar on Mount Ebal in accordance with Moses' instructions (Josh. 8:30–35; cf. Deut. 27:2–8). The return of the eastern Jordanian tribes (Josh. 22:4) is described using the same language as Deuteronomy 3:20. This includes the idea of God-given 'rest' from their enemies (see also Josh. 21:44; 23:1; cf. Deut. 12:10; 25:19). And the commission to keep the Lord's commandments and to love and serve him with all their heart and soul (Josh. 22:5) further reflects Moses' commission to all the Israelites (Deut. 10:12; 11:13).

These close ties with Deuteronomy have been taken to support Joshua's place within the DH. However, links with other Pentateuchal material also support the view of Joshua as part of the Hexateuch. There is evidence of priestly material, particularly in chapters 13–22.[17] Eleazar, the priest, who is barely mentioned in Deuteronomy, is involved alongside Joshua in the allocation of the land (14:1–5; 19:51; 21:1–2; cf. Num. 34:17), and the formulaic nature of those passages is also characteristic of P. The Hebrew terms *maṭṭeh* (tribe) and *gôrāl* (lot) appear together in this connection in both Joshua (e.g. 14:1–2; 15:1; 17:1; 18:11; 19:1; 21:4) and Numbers (26:55; 33:54; 34:13; 36:3), but not in Deuteronomy.[18] There appears to be priestly language in 22:9–34, which is linked to Numbers 32, and gives prominence to Eleazar's son, Phinehas (22:13).[19]

It has been noted, further, that the account of crossing the Jordan and the celebration of the Passover at Gilgal (3:1 – 5:12), has parallels with the celebration of the Passover in Egypt and crossing the Red Sea (Exod. 12 – 14).[20] God's words to Joshua 'Today I will begin to exalt you in the eyes of all Israel, so that they may know that I am with you as I was with Moses' (3:7) suggests a

---

17. See e.g. John E. Petersen, 'Priestly Materials in Joshua 13–22: A Return to the Hexateuch?', *HAR* 4 (1980), pp. 131–146; Donald G. Schley, *Shiloh: A Biblical City in Tradition and History*, JSOTSup 63 (Sheffield: JSOT Press, 1989), pp. 101–110.
18. *Maṭṭeh* appears throughout Exodus–Numbers; the usual word for 'tribe' in Deuteronomy is *šēbeṭ*.
19. E.g. Nelson, *Joshua*, p. 247; Pitkänen, *Joshua*, pp. 357–358, 363–380.
20. See e.g. Collins, *Introduction*, pp. 198–199; Pitkänen, *Joshua*, p. 110.

connection between the crossings, which is made explicit in 4:23. The chiastic arrangement *Passover–crossing / crossing–Passover* provides an inclusio, marking the beginning and end of Israel's journey. Both passages describe the crossing 'on dry ground' (*bayyabāšâ*) (4:22; Exod. 14:16, 22, 29), and both emphasize the importance of circumcision prior to taking part in the Passover celebrations (5:1–8; Exod. 12:48).

Much current discussion views Joshua as part, either of the DH or of a Hexateuch. It is not necessary, though, to make such a stark choice.[21] Points of contact with Exodus and Numbers as well as Deuteronomy, raise questions about Joshua's place in the DH. But it is going too far to see Joshua as the final instalment of the narrative beginning in Genesis. Despite questions about the DH, there appear to be Deuteronomic influences in the rest of the Former Prophets, including the eventual fulfilment of the threat of exile from the land; thus the story continues beyond Joshua. We have noted, too, links between the Former Prophets and other parts of the Pentateuch.[22] It may be better, therefore, to view Joshua as unique: it represents a partial fulfilment of what is promised in the Pentateuch, and is also a bridge between the Pentateuch and the rest of the Former Prophets.

The possibility of both Deuteronomistic and Priestly editing of Joshua suggests a post-exilic date. However, debate about the date of Deuteronomy and of P may allow that it was written much earlier. It has also been suggested that the priestly material in Joshua may not be directly related to the Pentateuchal source.[23] Hess argues that some material in Joshua is best explained by tracing its origin to the second millennium BC;[24] and while that may not preclude a later date of composition, it does require that the compilers made use of earlier, maybe eye-witness, traditions. The frequent references to situations described in Joshua that remain 'to this day' (e.g. 4:9; 5:9; 7:26; 8:28–29; 10:27),[25]

---

21. See e.g. Arnold, *Introduction*, p. 189.
22. See above, p. 229.
23. See e.g. Collins, *Introduction*, pp. 198–200; Nelson, *Joshua*, p. 9; Pitkänen, *Joshua*, p. 57.
24. Hess, *Joshua*, pp. 26–31; see also Richard S. Hess, 'West Semitic Texts and the Book of Joshua', *BBR* 7 (1997), pp. 63–76; Pitkänen, *Joshua*, p. 380. Strange, at the other extreme, suggests a second century BC date, though this seems unlikely; see J. Strange, 'Joshua: A Hasmonean Manifesto?', in A. Lemaire and B. Otzen (eds.), *History and Tradition of Early Israel: Studies Presented to Eduard Nielsen*, VTSup 50 (Leiden: Brill, 1993), pp. 136–141.
25. See Brevard S. Childs, 'A Study of the Formula "Until This Day"', *JBL* 82.3 (1963), pp. 279–292.

indicate that these were written after the events they describe, though suggest, too, that the writer is reporting historical facts that readers could check for themselves.

Structure and outline

The opening verses of Joshua suggest continuity with what has gone before, and, with the death of Moses and the commissioning of Joshua as Israel's new leader, they also point to a new phase in the nation's history. The book focuses, primarily, on the conquest of Canaan and on Israel's possession of the land promised to the patriarchs. The narrative can be divided, broadly, into three parts: battles for the land (1 – 12), division of the land (13 – 22) and Joshua's final exhortation and renewal of the covenant (23 – 24).[26]

Outline

- Battles for the land (1:1 – 12:24)
  - Preparations for conquest (1:1 – 5:15)
    - Joshua's commissioning and charge to the people (1:1–18)
    - Spies sent to Jericho (2:1–24)
    - Crossing the Jordan; circumcision and Passover at Gilgal (3:1 – 5:12)
    - Joshua's vision (5:13–15)
  - Conquest (6:1 – 12:24)
    - Defeat of Jericho and Ai (6:1 – 8:29)
    - Renewal of the covenant (8:30–35)
    - Alliance with Gibeon and victory over a southern coalition (9:1 – 10:43)
    - Victory over northern kings (11:1–15)
    - Summary of victories (11:16 – 12:24)
- Division of the land (13:1 – 22:34)
  - Introduction and allocation of land east of the Jordan (13:1–33)
  - Allocation of land west of the Jordan (14:1 – 19:51)
  - Cities of refuge and cities allocated to Levites (20:1 – 21:45)
  - Return of eastern Jordanian tribes; affirmation of unity (22:1–34)
- Joshua's final exhortation and renewal of the covenant (23:1 – 24:33)

---

26. Differences between the MT and LXX texts of Joshua do not significantly affect its interpretation. See further e.g. Hess, *Joshua*, pp. 17–20; Leonard Greenspoon, 'The Book of Joshua – Part 1: Texts and Versions', *CBR* 3.2 (2005), pp. 229–261; Nelson, *Joshua*, pp. 22–24.

Main themes

A key theme is the fulfilment of the promise of the land. Joshua will lead the people across the Jordan to take possession of the land God 'swore to their forefathers to give them' (Josh. 1:6; 21:43–44; cf. 5:6; 14:9). The territory allocated to the tribes is described as their 'inheritance' (*naḥălâ*) (e.g. 11:23; 13:6–8; 14:13; 24:28). This emphasizes that the land belongs to God, and the people receive it from him.

There is also an emphasis on the unity of Israel. Although the land is divided among the tribes, there is still a strong sense that Israel is one people. So the tribes that settled east of the Jordan were expected to cross the Jordan and help their 'brothers' (1:14–15). There are numerous references, too, to 'all Israel' being involved in the various stages in the conquest (e.g. 3:7; 7:24–25; 8:33; 10:29–39, 43; 23:2).[27] The sin of one man, Achan, affects the whole nation (7:11–12), and the rest of Israel feels similarly threatened when they, mistakenly, interpret the altar set up by the Transjordan tribes as an act of idolatry (22:20).

One of the more difficult ideas associated with the 'holy war',[28] envisaged by Deuteronomy and Joshua, is the wholesale destruction of the Canaanites. This is linked with the Hebrew term *ḥērem*,[29] which is sometimes referred to as the 'ban', and is generally taken to refer to the spoils of war, which, because Yahweh has given the victory, belong to him.[30] They are God's

---

27. See also e.g. Younger, *Ancient Conquest Accounts*, pp. 247–249.
28. There is debate about the use of the expression 'holy war' in this context. Von Rad sees such warfare as essentially cultic; see Gerhard von Rad, *Holy War* (Grand Rapids: Eerdmans, 1991). However, the expression and the cultic nature of warfare have been questioned; see e.g. Peter C. Craigie, *The Problem of War in the Old Testament* (Grand Rapids: Eerdmans, 1978); Gwilym H. Jones, '"Holy War" or "Yahweh War"', *VT* 25.3 (1975), pp. 642–658.
29. The noun *ḥērem* appears in 6:17–18; 7:1, 11–15 (cf. Deut. 7:26; 13:17 [18]); the associated verb *ḥāram* appears in e.g. 2:10; 6:21; 10:1, 28–40; 11:11–12. See further e.g. A. C. Emery, '*ḥērem*', in *DOTP*, pp. 383–387; N. Lohfink, '*ḥāram*', in *TDOT* 5:180–199; Jackie A. Naudé, '*ḥrm*', in *NIDOTTE* 2:276–277.
30. See further e.g. Creach, *Joshua*, pp. 7–9; Hess, *Joshua*, pp. 42–46; Nelson, *Joshua*, pp. 19–20; Pitkänen, *Joshua*, pp. 161–162. The term is frequently associated with genocide; though applying modern definitions to ancient practices is problematic. See e.g. Markus Zehnder, 'The Annihilation of the Canaanites: Reassessing the Brutality of the Biblical Witnesses', in Markus Zehnder and Hallvard Hagelia (eds.), *Encountering Violence in the Bible* (Sheffield: Sheffield Phoenix, 2013), pp. 263–290.

'portion', and their complete destruction, which removes them from human use, indicates their total dedication to God. Niditch also relates *ḥērem* to divine justice,[31] which is linked to the sin of the Canaanites, which might lead Israel astray.

Although the idea of *ḥērem* causes problems for believers today, it appears to have been part of ancient warfare, and the Mesha Stele includes a statement with similar content and language: 'Kemosh said to me: "Go, take Nebo from Israel!" . . . I took it, and I killed [its] whole population . . . for I had put it to the ban for Ashtar Kemosh.'[32] It appears, too, that even where there is a call for total annihilation of an enemy, there is the possibility of some being spared. This is especially evident in the case of Rahab. The city of Jericho and everything in it is declared to be *ḥērem*, except for Rahab and her family, because she showed allegiance to Israel's God by sheltering Israelite spies (6:17). Conversely, Achan, an Israelite, does come under the ban because of his disobedience (6:18; 7:1). Earl takes this further. He sees references to *ḥērem* as symbolic. In his view it would never have been applied historically, but rather functions rhetorically, to emphasize the need for exclusive allegiance to Yahweh. The contrast between Rahab, an outsider who acts faithfully and so is not put under *ḥērem*, and Achan, an Israelite who acts unfaithfully and is put under *ḥērem*, emphasizes that the people of God are identified, primarily, by their faithfulness to Yahweh.[33] However, though Earl's assessment of the rhetorical impact of the narrative may be correct, it seems less likely that the accounts are unhistorical, particularly in view of elements that suggest the opposite.

---

31. Susan Niditch, *War in the Hebrew Bible: A Study in the Ethics of Violence* (New York: Oxford University Press, 1993), pp. 28–77.

32. *COS* 2:23 (lines 14–17); see e.g. Hess, *Joshua*, p. 43; Niditch, *War*, pp. 31–32; Pitkänen, *Joshua*, p. 162; Younger, *Ancient Conquest Accounts*, pp. 235–236.

33. Douglas S. Earl, 'Holy War and *ḥrm*: A Biblical Theology of *ḥrm*', in Heath A. Thomas, Jeremy Evans and Paul Copan (eds.), *Holy War in the Bible: Christian Morality and an Old Testament Problem* (Downers Grove: InterVarsity Press, 2013), pp. 152–175; see also Douglas S. Earl, *The Joshua Delusion? Rethinking Genocide in the Bible* (Eugene: Cascade, 2010), pp. 94–112. However, see Christopher J. H. Wright, 'Response to Douglas Earl', in Thomas, Evans and Copan, *Holy War*, pp. 139–148. See also David G. Firth, 'Models of Inclusion and Exclusion in Joshua' (forthcoming).

Judges[34]

Composition, structure and outline

The opening of the book (1:1 – 3:6) is in two parts (1:1 – 2:5; 2:6 – 3:6). Both follow on from the death of Joshua and emphasize the importance of taking possession of the land, and thus express continuity with the narrative of Joshua. These 'introductions' are complementary. The first focuses on the tribes' continuing problems as they seek to claim the territory allocated to them. The second offers a theological explanation of those problems in terms of the worship of Canaanite gods, and includes the cycle that recurs throughout much of the book: *idolatry – oppression – appeal to God – deliverance by a judge – peace during the judge's lifetime – further idolatry.*

The book also appears to have two 'conclusions' (17:1 – 18:31; 19:1 – 21:25). The second picks up the theme of the first introduction, of the tribes going to war, though this time against one of their own (20:18; cf. 1:1–2). The first focuses on idolatry, and seems to reflect the theme of the second introduction. This has led to the view that these sections form a chiastic inclusio around the central section of the book.[35] These chapters also share a common theme, indicated by the inclusio 'In those days Israel had no king; everyone did as he saw fit' (17:6; 21:25; cf. 18:1; 19:1).[36] This appears to present the monarchy in a favourable light, and, against the background of national failure, may be intended to highlight the importance of a righteous king, such as Josiah.[37]

---

34. Commentaries on Judges include Daniel I. Block, *Judges, Ruth*, NAC 6 (Nashville: B&H, 1999); Robert G. Boling, *Judges*, AB 6 (New York: Doubleday, 1975); Trent Butler, *Judges*, WBC 8 (Nashville: Nelson, 2000); Cundall, 'Judges', in Cundall and Morris, *Judges and Ruth*; Cheryl A. Brown, 'Judges', in Harris, Brown and Moore, *Joshua, Judges, Ruth*, pp. 121–289; J. Clinton McCann, *Judges*, IBC (Louisville: Westminster John Knox, 2002); Victor H. Matthews, *Judges & Ruth*, NCBC (Cambridge: Cambridge University Press, 2004); Susan Niditch, *Judges*, OTL (Louisville: Westminster John Knox, 2008); Tammi J. Schneider, *Judges*, Berit Olam (Collegeville: Liturgical Press, 2000); J. Alberto Soggin, *Judges*, OTL (London: SCM Press, 1981); Barry Webb, *Judges*, NICOT (Grand Rapids: Eerdmans, 2012); K. Lawson Younger, *Judges, Ruth*, NIVAC (Grand Rapids: Zondervan, 2002). For a detailed analysis of recent scholarly work, see Webb, *Judges*, pp. 35–53.
35. See e.g. Younger, *Judges, Ruth*, pp. 30–33; cf. Webb, *Judges*, pp. 32–35.
36. See Philip Satterthwaite, '"No King in Israel": Narrative Criticism and Judges 17–21', *TynBul* 44.1 (1993), pp. 75–88.
37. See e.g. Matthews, *Judges & Ruth*, p. 10.

The central section is made up of stories about Israel's judges. These vary in length and style, and show signs of having been compiled by a later editor.[38] Some of the traditions may be old, though there is little information either to date the stories[39] or to indicate when the book appeared in its final form. The account of the first judge, Othniel (3:7–11), which follows, closely, the cycle set out in 2:6 – 3:6, may be programmatic, and the stories of Ehud, Deborah and Barak, Gideon, Jephthah and Samson follow a similar pattern. These are categorized as 'major' or 'cyclical' judges. Other judges, described as 'minor' or 'non-cyclical', receive only brief mention.

While Judges in its final form shows signs of editing, the editorial process is not clear. One suggestion is that one version of the book comprised 2:6 – 16:31, and that 1:1 – 2:5 and 17:1 – 21:25 were the result of later editing.[40]

Outline

- Introduction (1:1 – 3:6)
  - Attempt to occupy the land: war against Canaanites (1:1 – 2:5)
  - Israel's idolatry: introduction to a recurring theme (2:6 – 3:6)
- Israel's judges (3:7 – 16:31)
- Conclusion: anarchy because 'there was no king' (17:1 – 21:25)
  - Domestic difficulties: war against the Benjamites (17:1 – 18:31)
  - Micah and the Danites: ingrained idolatry (19:1 – 21:25)

Main themes

'Judges' translates the Hebrew *šōpĕṭîm*, which relates to the book's main characters (e.g. 2:16–19). In the wider OT, words from the same root are associated

38. Expressions such as 'to this day' (1:21, 26; 6:24; 10:4; 15:19 [NRSV]; 18:12) and 'in those days' (17:6; 18:1; 19:1; 20:27–28; 21:25) indicate later editing. See also e.g. Matthews, *Judges & Ruth*, pp. 6–7; Satterthwaite and McConville, *Histories*, p. 96; Younger, *Judges, Ruth*, p. 23.
39. See above, pp. 91–94. For suggested chronologies, see Kitchen, *Reliability*, pp. 204–210; Satterthwaite and McConville, *Histories*, pp. 101–102. Any such scheme, though, remains speculative.
40. E.g. A. D. H. Mayes, *Judges*, OTG (Sheffield: JSOT Press, 1985), pp. 10–36; see also Satterthwaite and McConville, *Histories*, pp. 96–99. Mayes suggests that the central section was edited, with the cyclical accounts, except for Othniel, forming the nucleus. Othniel was included as an 'ideal', and stories of the minor judges were also added later. For more detailed discussion of theories of compilation, see e.g. Boling, *Judges*, pp. 29–38; Niditch, *Judges*, pp. 8–13; Webb, *Judges*, pp. 20–32.

with ruling and decision-making, which may include exercising a judicial function.[41] In Judges the primary role of Israel's judges appears to be to bring deliverance, though they also governed the people, and thus had wider responsibility for society's moral and spiritual well-being. This is evident with Deborah (4:4–5; cf. 11:27). Nevertheless, as Block notes, the title of the book may be misleading.[42] The main focus, even in the case of Deborah, is on deliverance, and chapters 1 and 17–21 contain no references to 'judges'.

As already noted, the book of Judges reflects the Deuteronomic principle that obedience leads to blessing, and disobedience leads to disaster and defeat. Here, though, while there is some respite, the overwhelming emphasis is negative. The book appears to offer an explanation of why the Israelites failed to take full possession of the land. So, for example, 2:6–10 repeats the account of the death of Joshua in Joshua 24:28–31, but goes on to highlight the apostasy that followed,[43] an apostasy evident, primarily, in worshipping Canaanite gods and adopting Canaanite practices.[44] However, despite Israel's repeated unfaithfulness, God continues to show grace, and so appoints 'deliverers', through whom God's ultimate purposes for the people are maintained. The final chapters point to the institution of the monarchy as an antidote to anarchy.

Another significant theme in the book of Judges is the importance of leadership. The slide into idolatry and apostasy began after the death of Joshua and 'the elders who outlived him' (2:7). And chapters 3–16 suggest that, with the right leadership, that slide may be halted. The description of Othniel, as a 'deliverer', appointed by God and enabled by the Spirit of God to 'judge' Israel, may be a pattern for the ideal judge. The Spirit is mentioned specifically in relation only to three other judges, Gideon, Jephthah and Samson, who are far from exemplary. But that may be the point. If Othniel is the pattern, it may be assumed that other judges are similarly equipped. The questionable character of Gideon, Jephthah and Samson may raise doubts about that assumption, but the narrator wants to make it clear that they too, despite their flaws, are part of

---

41. E.g. Exod. 18:13–16, 26; Deut. 1:16; 16:18–20; 1 Sam. 7:15–17; 2 Sam. 15:4; 1 Kgs 3:9. See also Niditch, *Judges*, pp. 1–3; H. Niehr, '*šāpaṭ*', in *TDOT* 15:411–431; Richard Schultz, '*špṭ*', in *NIDOTTE* 4:213–220.
42. Block, *Judges, Ruth*, pp. 21–25.
43. There may be irony in the additional comment 'to take possession of the land' (2:6), in view of the following narrative, which indicates Israel's failure to do so.
44. Block describes this as 'the Canaanization of Israel' (*Judges, Ruth*, p. 71, and *passim*); see also Satterthwaite and McConville, *Histories*, p. 94.

God's purpose. The closing chapters point, further, to the role of the king in providing stability and order.[45]

It seems apparent, too, that in Judges the nation is politically fragmented. Whereas in Joshua there is an emphasis on 'all Israel' working together, here that is less evident. Judges were, probably, local leaders, who led only a few tribes. There is tension between the tribes (e.g. 8:1; 12:1), and even civil war (12:4–6; 20:14–35). It seems likely that intertribal conflict also contributed to the failure of the nation to take possession of the land.

1 and 2 Samuel[46]

Text, composition, structure and outline

Samuel, like Kings, was originally a single book. It was divided into two sections, probably because of its size. This division occurs in the LXX, where the four books of Samuel and Kings appear as 1, 2, 3 and 4 Kingdoms. The MT title 'Samuel' reflects the role of one of its central characters.[47]

There are issues relating to the text of Samuel. The LXX is substantially longer than the MT, and while it was thought that the LXX expanded the MT, the discovery

45. See e.g. Webb, *Judges*, pp. 420, 426–427; see also Robert H. O'Connell, *The Rhetoric of the Book of Judges* (Leiden: Brill, 1996). However, see Niditch, *Judges*, pp. 13, 181–182. McCann argues that since the final editing of Judges took place after the failure of the Davidic monarchy, the book cannot be taken simply as Davidic propaganda; apostasy will cause all institutions to fail (*Judges*, pp. 10–12).
46. Commentaries on 1 and 2 Samuel include Alter, *David Story*; A. A. Anderson, *2 Samuel*, WBC 11 (Dallas: Word, 1989); Bill T. Arnold, *1 & 2 Samuel*, NIVAC (Grand Rapids: Zondervan, 2003); A. Graeme Auld, *I & II Samuel*, OTL (Louisville: Westminster John Knox, 2011); Joyce Baldwin, *1 and 2 Samuel*, TOTC (Leicester: Inter-Varsity Press, 1988); Robert D. Bergen, *1, 2 Samuel*, NAC 7 (Nashville: B&H, 1996); Walter Brueggemann, *First and Second Samuel*, IBC (Louisville: John Knox, 1990); Mary J. Evans, *1 and 2 Samuel*, NIBCOT (Peabody: Hendrickson, 2000); Firth, *1 & 2 Samuel*; Robert P. Gordon, *I & II Samuel: A Commentary* (Carlisle: Paternoster, 1986); Ralph W. Klein, *1 Samuel*, WBC 10 (Waco: Texas, 1983); P. Kyle McCarter Jr., *I Samuel*, AB 8 (New York: Doubleday, 1980); *II Samuel*, AB 9 (New York: Doubleday, 1984); Tsumura, *1 Samuel*.
47. According to *Baba Batra*, the book was written predominantly by Samuel (*b. B. Bat.* 14b). This seems unlikely, though some of it may have links with Samuel (cf. 1 Chr. 29:29–30).

of texts at Qumran, which confirm some LXX readings, indicate that it may preserve an earlier Hebrew text. Thus differences may be the result of copyists' errors in the MT.[48] There is also an apparent inconsistency relating to the defeat of Goliath. In 1 Samuel 17 this is attributed to David, though 2 Samuel 21:19 names Elhanan. It has been suggested that David has been given the credit for the exploits of a lesser figure;[49] or that Elhanan is the throne name of David,[50] though it is unclear why this title suddenly appears here. In the parallel text of 1 Chronicles 20:5 Elhanan is reported to have killed Lahmi, Goliath's *brother*. This is sometimes taken to be a later correction, but it may be that 1 Chronicles 20:5 preserves the correct text, and the MT text includes a copyist error.[51] These discrepancies, though, affect only a small part of the text, and while this emphasizes the importance of comparing versions, we should not dismiss the MT too quickly.[52]

Even among those who view Samuel as part of the DH, it is widely recognized that it shows signs of only light Deuteronomistic editing, and includes 'relatively little Deuteronomic language'.[53] There are Deuteronomic elements,

---

48. See e.g. the note on 1 Sam. 14:41, p. 50 above.
49. E.g. Baruch Halpern, *David's Secret Demons: Messiah, Murderer, Traitor, King* (Grand Rapids: Eerdmans, 2001), pp. 7–8; *First Historians*, p. 65.
50. E.g. Baldwin, *1 and 2 Samuel*, p. 286; LaSor, Hubbard and Bush, *OT Survey*, p. 771, n. 46; see also A. M. Honeyman, 'The Evidence for Regnal Names Among the Hebrews', *JBL* 67 (1948), pp. 13–25 (23–24).
51. E.g. Firth, *1 & 2 Samuel*, pp. 508–509; Provan, Long and Longman, *Biblical History*, pp. 224–225; see also Arnold, *1 & 2 Samuel*, pp. 622–624, though Arnold is less concerned about the presence of an inconsistency.
52. See e.g. Baldwin, *1 and 2 Samuel*, pp. 37–44; Bergen, *1, 2 Samuel*, pp. 25–27; Firth, *1 & 2 Samuel*, pp. 39–40; McCarter, *1 Samuel*, pp. 5–11; see also Gordon, *1 & 2 Samuel*, pp. 12–13.
53. Collins, *Introduction*, p. 228; see also e.g. Gordon, *1 & 2 Samuel*, pp. 18–20; *I & II Samuel*, p. 21; McCarter, *1 Samuel*, pp. 14–17. Dietrich suggests that only 120 out of 1,506 verses in Samuel (i.e. 8%) may be assigned to one of the three Deuteronomic redactions ('Layer Model', in Edenburg and Pakkala, *Is Samuel Among the Deuteronomists?*, pp. 45–46, 51). On suggested Deuteronomic language see also Weinfeld, *Deuteronomy*, pp. 320–365; however, cf. Firth, *1 & 2 Samuel*, pp. 24–26. For a recent summary of views on Samuel's place in the DH, see Cynthia Edenburg and Juha Pakkala, 'Is Samuel Among the Deuteronomists', in *Is Samuel Among the Deuteronomists?*, pp. 1–15. The apparent intractability of the debate is indicated by the wide range of views expressed by contributors to that volume.

especially in 1 Samuel 12 and 2 Samuel 7, though these are not necessarily the result of Deuteronomistic editing. And there are also links to other parts of the Pentateuch; for example, the promise that David will have an heir, 'from your own body' (2 Sam. 7:12), closely corresponds to the similar promise made to Abraham (Gen. 15:4).[54]

There are several suggested sources for Samuel.[55] One view identifies two sources: pro- and anti-monarchic.[56] However, while differing in emphasis, these may relate to the nature of the monarchy rather than to the monarchy itself.[57] A different approach, following Rost, recognizes three sources.[58] 'The Ark narrative' (1 Sam. 4:1b – 7:2) focuses on the Ark of the Covenant, and how it came to move from Shiloh and, eventually, to Jerusalem. Emphasis on the Ark, together with the absence of any reference to Samuel, suggests that this narrative might have circulated separately. Rost included the account of the return of the Ark to Jerusalem (2 Sam. 6) in that narrative, though that seems less likely.[59] According

54. For discussion of links between Abraham and David, see e.g. Ronald E. Clements, *Abraham and David*, SBT 2.5 (London: SCM Press, 1967); Robin Routledge, 'Psalm 110, Melchizedek and David: Blessing (the Descendants of) Abraham', *Baptistic Theologies* 1.2 (2009), pp. 1–16; *OT Theology*, pp. 235–236.
55. See e.g. Arnold, *Introduction*, p. 216; *1 & 2 Samuel*, pp. 25–28; Bergen, *1, 2 Samuel*, pp. 19–22; Baldwin, *1 and 2 Samuel*, pp. 20–32; W. Brueggemann, *Introduction*, pp. 163–175; Childs, *Introduction*, pp. 268–271; Walter Dietrich, *The Early Monarchy in Israel: The Tenth Century B.C.E.* (Atlanta: Society of Biblical Literature, 2007), pp. 227–262; Firth, *1 & 2 Samuel*, pp. 26–30; Gordon, *I & II Samuel*, pp. 24–26, 38–44; LaSor, Hubbard and Bush, *OT Survey*, pp. 166–167; Longman and Dillard, *Introduction*, pp. 153–158; McCarter, *1 Samuel*, pp. 23–30; Satterthwaite and McConville, *Histories*, pp. 137–139; Tsumura, *1 Samuel*, pp. 11–15.
56. For proponents of the DH, these may correspond, respectively, to Cross's first and second redactions (see e.g. Collins, *Introduction*, p. 228), or to DtrH and DtrN (see Dietrich, 'Layer Model', in Edenburg and Pakkala, *Is Samuel Among the Deuteronomists?*, p. 44).
57. See above, p. 171.
58. Rost, *Succession*.
59. E.g. Gordon, *I & II Samuel*, pp. 24–25; Terence Kleven, 'Hebrew Style in 2 Samuel 6', *JETS* 35.3 (1992), pp. 299–314 (302–303); see also Patrick D. Miller Jr. and J. J. M. Roberts, *The Hand of the Lord: A Reassessment of the 'Ark Narrative' of 1 Samuel* (Baltimore: Johns Hopkins University Press, 1977); John Van Seters, *In Search of History: Historiography in the Ancient World and the Origins of Biblical History* (New Haven: Yale University Press, 1997), pp. 346–353.

to Rost, a second source, 'the story of David's rise' (1 Sam. 16 – 2 Sam. 5), emphasizes the legitimacy of David's reign, following Saul's death.[60] Rost's third source, the 'succession narrative' (2 Sam. 9 – 20; 1 Kgs 1 – 2), explains how Solomon came to succeed David. Carlson questions this, and, following the Deuteronomic principle, divides the text, instead, into 'David under the blessing' (2 Sam. 2 – 5) and 'David under the curse' (2 Sam. 9 – 24).[61] Other suggested sources include stories of Samuel's youth, linked with Shiloh (1 Sam. 1 – 3), pro- and anti-monarchical accounts of the appointment and reign of Saul (1 Sam. 8 – 15) and 2 Samuel 21 – 24, which appears to be an appendix, with its own internal structure.[62] There is little firm evidence that all of these existed as independent literary traditions.[63] And because material from possible sources has been worked into a cohesive narrative,[64] it is important, theories of sources and redaction notwithstanding, to read the text in its final form.[65] It is reasonable to assume,

---

60. Firth argues that the 'accession narrative' (1 Sam. 27 – 2 Sam. 1), rather than being part of a separate source, has affinities with other passages across the alleged sources and serves as a climax to the Samuel narrative; see David G. Firth, 'The Accession Narrative (1 Samuel 27 – 2 Samuel 1)', *TynBul* 58.1 (2007), pp. 61–81. See also Robert P. Gordon, 'David's Rise and Saul's Demise: Narrative Analogy in 1 Samuel 24–26', *TynBul* 31 (1980), pp. 37–64.
61. D. A. Carlson, *David the Chosen King: A Traditio-Historical Approach to the Second Book of Samuel* (Stockholm: Almqvist & Wiksell, 1964); see also Childs, *Introduction*, pp. 270–271, 275–277; D. A. Knight, *Traditions of Israel*, pp. 245–253.
62. These chapters are arranged chiastically: *a* Famine (21:1–14); *b* Exploits of David's men (21:15–22); *c* David's song of thanksgiving (22:1–51); *c'* David's oracle (23:1–7); *b'* Exploits of David's men (23:8–39); *a'* Plague (24:1–25); there is also similar language following the famine/plague (21:14; 24:25).
63. See especially Gordon's discussion, *I & II Samuel*, pp. 22–46.
64. E.g. David G. Firth, '"Play It Again Sam": The Poetics of Narrative Repetition in 1 Samuel 1–7', *TynBul* 56.1 (2005), pp. 1–17; 'Accession Narrative'; *1 & 2 Samuel*, pp. 26–30. See also Childs, *Introduction*, pp. 271–278.
65. Literary treatments of the books of Samuel include Alter, *David Story*; David M. Gunn, *The Story of King David: Genre and Interpretation*, JSOTSup 6 (Sheffield: JSOT Press, 1978); *The Fate of King Saul: An Interpretation of a Biblical Story*, JSOTSup 14 (Sheffield: JSOT Press, 1980); David Jobling, *1 Samuel*, Berit Olam (Collegeville: Liturgical Press, 1998); J. P. Fokkelmann, *Narrative Art and Poetry in the Books of Samuel*, 4 vols. (Assen: Van Gorcum, 1981–93); Robert Polzin, *Samuel and the Deuteronomist: A Literary Study of the Deuteronomistic History*, pt. 2: *1 Samuel*

too, that these texts, as with the wider record of Israel's early history, are broadly historical.[66]

Outline

- Samuel's rise (1 Sam. 1:1 – 7:17)
  - Birth, call and ministry of Samuel (1:1 – 4:1a)
  - The Ark Narrative (4:1b – 7:2)
    - The Ark captured; the demise of Eli's house (4:1b–22)
    - The Ark with the Philistines (5:1–12)
    - The Ark returned to Israel (6:1 – 7:2)
  - Samuel leads the people: repentance and victory (7:3–17)
- The institution of the monarchy: Saul as king (1 Sam. 8:1 – 15:35)
- David comes to prominence; Saul's hostility (1 Sam. 16:1 – 26:23)
- The 'accession narrative' (1 Sam. 27:1 – 2 Sam. 1:27)
  - David among the Philistines (1 Sam. 27:1–12)
  - Saul and the witch of Endor (1 Sam. 28:1–25)
  - David leaves the Philistines; victory over the Amalekites (1 Sam. 29:1 – 30:31)
  - Saul's death; David's lament (1 Sam. 31:1–13 – 2 Sam. 1:27)
- David anointed king (2 Sam. 2:1 – 5:5)
- David's reign (2 Sam. 5:6 – 20:26)
  - David's reign consolidated (5:6 – 8:18)
  - David and Mephibosheth (9:1–13)
  - Victory over the Ammonites and Arameans (10:1–19)
  - David and Bathsheba (11:1 – 12:25)
  - Victory over the Ammonites (12:26–31)
  - David and Absalom (13:1 – 19:43)
  - Sheba's rebellion (20:1–26)
- Appendix: stories from David's reign (2 Sam. 21:1 – 24:25)

(*Footnote 65 cont.*) (Bloomington: University of Indiana Press, 1989); *David and the Deuteronomist: A Literary Study of the Deuteronomistic History*, pt. 3: *2 Samuel* (Bloomington: University of Indiana Press, 1993); see also Tsumura, *1 Samuel*, pp. 19–23.

66. See e.g. Arnold, *Introduction*, pp. 217–219; Bergen, *1, 2 Samuel*, pp. 28–32; LaSor, Hubbard and Bush, *OT Survey*, p. 167; V. P. Long, *Art of Biblical History*, pp. 201–223; Satterthwaite and McConville, *Histories*, pp. 141–143; see also above, pp. 70 (n. 17), 96–97.

Main themes

There are elements in the books of Samuel that reflect the Deuteronomic principle that obedience leads to blessing and disobedience leads to disaster. These 'two ways' are illustrated in the early chapters in the contrast between Samuel and the sons of Eli, whom Samuel eventually replaced. There may be a parallel in the similar contrast between Saul and David. Samuel's statement 'If you are returning to the LORD with all your hearts' (1 Sam. 7:3), echoes Deuteronomy 30:2 (see also Deut. 4:29–30), and the people's right response (1 Sam. 7:4) results in victory. The principle is evident in Samuel's recollection of Israel's salvation history (1 Sam. 12:8–11), and verses 14–15 are further reminiscent of covenantal blessings and curses.[67] This principle is evident, too, in the story of David. The early part of his reign is marked by blessing and success. This is summarized in 2 Samuel 5:12;[68] and results in the Lord giving him 'rest from all his enemies around him' (2 Sam. 7:1; cf. Deut. 12:10; Josh 23:1). However, following his adultery with Bathsheba and murder of Uriah (2 Sam. 11), he faces trouble, largely from within his own family (2 Sam. 12:11). The theme recurs in 2 Samuel 21 – 24, where sin results in national disaster.

The similarity between the people's request to 'appoint a king . . . like all the other nations' (1 Sam. 8:5) and Deuteronomy 17:14 appears deliberate. The request, as it is foreseen in Deuteronomy, is not necessarily wrong, and the words might have been chosen by the people to legitimate their request.[69] Or this may be ironic. Though the request may be in line with Deuteronomy, the nature of kingship as implemented, initially, through Saul is anything but! Saul's visit to the medium at Endor (1 Sam. 28:7–24) is also contrary to Deuteronomy 18:10–11.

As already suggested, a key issue in the institution of the monarchy is the relationship between the appointed king and Israel's divine king.[70] Where that relationship is maintained, and the human king does not usurp divine authority, the monarchy may be seen as part of God's purpose, and not something that he merely tolerates. Indeed, in Hannah's song (1 Sam. 2:10) and words of the man of God to Eli (1 Sam. 2:35) the narrative has prepared

67. E.g. Gordon, *I & II Samuel*, p. 129. Although implied, there is no specific reference here to blessings.
68. E.g. Childs, *Introduction*, p. 276.
69. Firth, *1 & 2 Samuel*, p. 116.
70. See the discussion above, p. 171.

for the coming of an anointed king.[71] The kingly ideal appears to be fulfilled in David, who was chosen by God as 'a man after his own heart' (1 Sam. 13:14). God, further, committed himself to David's house, and promised him a continuing dynasty (2 Sam. 7:11b–16). Although that passage does not refer, specifically, to a covenant (*bĕrît*),[72] it contains covenantal language, and is widely held to mark the foundation of the Davidic covenant.[73] It appears to allow for the failure of individual kings (v. 14), and thus includes conditional as well as unconditional elements. This provides a basis for, though does not guarantee, the permanence of the monarchy, and may also look to an eventual messianic fulfilment.

Another important theme is the Ark. This symbolizes the presence of God among his people;[74] and its eventual movement to Jerusalem gives divine authentication to the city and to David's kingship. Significantly, because the Ark represents God, human beings may not manipulate it. Thus taking it into battle does not assure victory, and it is God, not David, who chooses when it may be installed in Jerusalem. And, even when 'captured' by the Philistines, the Ark continues to symbolize God's holy presence.

Hannah's song introduces the further theme of exalting and bringing low (1 Sam. 2:4–8; cf. 2 Sam. 22:28). This is seen in the contrasting fortunes of Eli's sons and Samuel (e.g. 1 Sam. 2:22–26; 3:10–14; cf. 3:19 – 4:1a), and of Saul and his house and David (1 Sam. 16:1; 18:12; 2 Sam. 3:1). A similar theme is evident in the stories of David and Goliath (1 Sam. 17:41–51) and David and Nabal (1 Sam. 25:39). An important aspect of this is that exaltation and vindication come, ultimately, from God (cf. 2 Sam. 5:10).

---

71. In Childs's view Hannah's song is significant in the canonical shaping of the text (*Introduction*, pp. 272–273).

72. Some see this as an indication that the promise was only viewed as a covenant at a later date; see e.g. David G. Firth, 'Speech Acts and Covenant in 2 Samuel 7:1–17', in Jamie A. Grant and Alistair I. Wilson (eds.), *God of Covenant: Biblical, Theological and Contemporary Perspectives* (Leicester: Apollos, 2005), pp. 79–99; *1 & 2 Samuel*, pp. 382, 387; Steven L. McKenzie, *Covenant* (St. Louis: Chalice, 2000), pp. 65–81.

73. For more on the Davidic covenant, see e.g. Leslie C. Allen, *A Theological Approach to the Old Testament: Major Themes and New Testament Connections* (Eugene: Cascade, 2014), pp. 102–112; Michael A. Grisanti, 'The Davidic Covenant', *TMSJ* 10.2 (1999), pp. 233–250; Routledge, *OT Theology*, pp. 233–236.

74. See e.g. Routledge, *OT Theology*, pp. 177–178.

1 and 2 Kings[75]

Composition, structure and outline

Kings, which, like Samuel, is a single book in the Hebrew Bible, continues the history of Israel and Judah from the end of David's reign to Jehoiachin's release from prison, in around 560 BC.[76] It makes no reference to the return from Babylon, suggesting that the book as a whole dates from the middle of the sixth century BC.

It appears, though, to incorporate material from a number of earlier sources.[77] Three are named: the annals of Solomon (1 Kgs 11:41), the annals of the kings of Israel (e.g. 1 Kgs 14:19; 15:31; 16:5) and the annals of the kings of Judah (e.g. 1 Kgs 14:29; 15:7; 22:45). These may have been official court records, though little is known about them.[78] The stories of Elijah and Elisha may also have circulated separately. Other suggested sources include a Prophetic Record, which emphasizes the relationship between prophets and kings, material relating to Solomon, and a 'Hezekian King List', which includes regnal details of the kings

---

75. Commentaries on 1 and 2 Kings include Lissa M. Wray Beal, *1 & 2 Kings*, AOTC (Nottingham: Apollos; Downers Grove: InterVarsity Press, 2014); Walter Brueggemann, *1 & 2 Kings*, SHBC 8 (Macon: Smith & Helwys, 2000); Mordechai Cogan, *I Kings*, AB 10 (New York: Doubleday, 2001); Mordechai Cogan and Hayim Tadmor, *II Kings*, AB 11 (New York: Doubleday, 1988); Simon J. DeVries, *1 Kings*, 2nd ed., WBC 12 (Nashville: Nelson, 2004); T. R. Hobbs, *2 Kings*, WBC 13 (Waco: Word, 1985); House, *1, 2 Kings*; Burke O. Long, *1 Kings*; *2 Kings*, FOTL 10 (Grand Rapids: Eerdmans, 1991); Richard Nelson, *First and Second Kings*, IBC (Louisville: John Knox, 1987); Iain W. Provan, *1 & 2 Kings*, NIBCOT (Peabody: Hendrickson; Carlisle: Paternoster, 1985); Marvin A. Sweeney, *I & II Kings*, OTL (Louisville: Westminster John Knox, 2007). See also André Lemaire and Baruch Halpern (eds.), *The Books of Kings: Sources, Composition, Historiography and Reception* (Leiden: Brill, 2010).
76. According to 2 Kgs 25:27, Jehoiachin was released thirty-seven years after his capture (in 597 BC).
77. The expression 'to this day' appears several times (1 Kgs 8:8, NRSV; 9:13, 21, NRSV; 10:12, NRSV; 12:19; 2 Kgs 2:22; 8:22; 14:7; 16:6; 17:34, 41); see Childs, 'A Study of the Formula "Until This Day"'. Some are not applicable in the sixth century BC (e.g. 1 Kgs 8:8; 9:21); they may have been part of older sources that reflect the situation at the time those sources were written.
78. See e.g. Cogan, *I Kings*, pp. 89–91; House, *1, 2 Kings*, pp. 31–32.

of Judah.[79] Sweeney refers to several earlier 'editions' of Kings, including a Josianic edition, a Hezekian edition, which contrasts the fall of the northern kingdom with Judah's survival under Hezekiah, a northern 'Jehu edition', which presents Jehu as a source of hope for the north, and a Solomonic edition.[80] Regular variations in the formulae at the beginning and end of each king's reign may also suggest different sources. These include, generally, the ruler's name, the regnal year of the king of the other kingdom, the length of reign, the city from which he reigned and an evaluation of his reign. In the case of Judah the name of the king's mother is also given, and, often, his age at accession. Others argue that, despite the use of different, and possibly disparate, sources, Kings (and indeed Joshua–Kings as a whole) should be viewed as a cohesive, unified work.[81]

Further questions relate to the text's chronological accuracy.[82] One issue is internal inconsistencies.[83] Some are small and may be accounted for by different methods of counting regnal years in Israel and Judah. Larger differences may be due to the possibility that some kings had a period of co-regency,[84] or maybe

---

79. See e.g. Campbell and O'Brien, *Unfolding the Deuteronomic History*, pp. 323–470; Satterthwaite and McConville, *Histories*, pp. 184–188; see also Steven L. McKenzie, 'The Books of Kings in the Deuteronomistic History', in McKenzie and Graham, *History of Israel's Traditions*, pp. 281–305.
80. E.g. Sweeney, *I & II Kings*, pp. 3–33.
81. House, *1, 2 Kings*, pp. 29–39; B. O. Long, *1 Kings*, pp. 16–21; Satterthwaite and McConville, *Histories*, p. 188. See also McKenzie, 'Books of Kings', in McKenzie and Graham, *History of Israel's Traditions*; William Schniedewind, 'The Problem with Kings: Recent Study of the Deuteronomistic History', *RSR* 22.1 (1996), pp. 22–27.
82. E.g. Beal, *1 & 2 Kings*, pp. 41–45; Hobbs, *2 Kings*, pp. xxxviii–xliv; Provan, Long and Longman, *Biblical History*, pp. 242–246; Satterthwaite and McConville, *Histories*, pp. 191–192; Thiele, *Mysterious Numbers*, pp. 33–42. For a comparison of regnal years, see Hill and Walton, *Survey*, pp. 289–290.
83. E.g. 2 Kgs 1:17; cf. 3:1; 8:25; cf. 9:29; 15:30; cf. 17:1. According to 2 Kgs 16:2 Ahaz began to reign when he was 20 and reigned for 16 years; Hezekiah came to the throne aged 25 (2 Kgs 18:2), suggesting that he was born when Ahaz was 11.
84. See e.g. Thiele, *Mysterious Numbers*; see also Kitchen, *Reliability*, pp. 26–32. Another factor may be *non-accession* or *accession year dating*, whereby the king's first regnal year was reckoned either from the year in which he became king or from the next New Year after his accession. For suggested dates, see below, p. 278.

to textual corruption.[85] There are also differences relating to external events.[86] While here, too, there may be some plausible explanations, it is important, also, to note that chronological precision may not have been as important for the writer of Kings as it is for modern historiographers. Thus Hobbs suggests that there is 'a greater stress upon what happens and the general characterization of what happens, rather than on the precise location of an event in a larger time frame'.[87]

The narrative of Kings moves between Israel and Judah, and backwards and forwards chronologically (e.g. 1 Kgs 15:16–17; cf. vv. 27–28; 22:2, 29; cf. v. 41). Within that framework the accounts of Elijah and Elisha describe the prophets' relationship with particular kings, but also include other stories. And Elijah and Elisha also appear at other points in the narrative. This makes it less than straightforward to set out an outline, without significant simplification. The following is a general outline, noting some highlights.

Outline

- The united kingdom (1 Kgs 1:1 – 11:43)
  - David's succession (1:1 – 2:46)
  - Solomon's reign (3:1 – 11:43)
    - The glory of Solomon's kingdom (3:1 – 10:29)
    - Solomon's decline: idolatry, rebellion, death (11:1–43)
- Division of the kingdom: Jeroboam (Israel), Rehoboam (Judah) (1 Kgs 12:1 – 14:31)
- Israel and Judah as separate kingdoms (1 Kgs 15:1 – 2 Kgs 17:41)
  - Ahab: the increase of Baal worship (1 Kgs 16:29 – 22:40)
  - Elijah (17:1 – 19:21; 21:17–29; 2 Kgs 1:2–18)
  - Elisha succeeds Elijah (2 Kgs 2:1–18)
  - Elisha (2 Kgs 3:1 – 8:15; 9:1; 13:14–21)
  - Hoshea: fall of Samaria; exile of the northern kingdom (2 Kgs 17:1–41)

85. Sweeney suggests greater inaccuracies in the MT and emphasizes the priority of the LXX and other versions (*I & II Kings*, pp. 43–44), though his calculations are hard to follow. Thiele's chronological construction allows greater weight to be placed on the MT.

86. E.g. the fall of Samaria (around 722/721 BC) was in Hezekiah's sixth year (2 Kgs 18:10), and Sennacherib's invasion of Judah (701 BC) was in his fourteenth year (2 Kgs 18:13).

87. Hobbs, *2 Kings*, pp. xxxix–xli (xli).

- The kingdom of Judah (2 Kgs 18:1 – 25:26)
  - Hezekiah (18:1 – 20:21)
    - Reforms (18:1–12)
    - Invasion and deliverance (18:13 – 20:11)
    - Babylonian envoys: exile foretold (20:12–21)
  - Manasseh: increase in wickedness (21:1–18)
  - Josiah: significant religious reforms (22:1 – 23:30)
  - Jehoahaz and Jehoiakim (23:31 – 24:7)
  - Jehoiachin: first deportations to Babylon (24:8–17)
  - Zedekiah: fall of Jerusalem; exile of Judah (24:18 – 25:26)
- Epilogue: Jehoiachin released from prison (25:27–30)

Main themes

A key theme of Kings is the evaluation of the kings of Israel and Judah, and the impact of their conduct on the destiny of their respective nations. According to Noth, the purpose of the DH was to explain the Babylonian exile in terms of the two ways set out in Deuteronomy. In my view that remains a major aim of Joshua–Kings, and in particular of Kings, which is the climax to this section of the OT. There also appear to be several related subthemes.

The picture of Israel's kings is overwhelmingly negative. After the division of the kingdom, Jeroboam's decision to set up altars at Dan and Bethel and to install golden calves there is seen to parallel Israel's sin with the golden calf in the desert (1 Kgs 12:28; cf. Exod. 32:4).[88] And Israel's kings are accused of following in the ways of Jeroboam,[89] and, like him, of provoking the Lord to anger.[90] This intensifies under the Omrides, and particularly Ahab, who 'did more to provoke the Lord, the God of Israel, to anger than did all the kings of Israel before him' (1 Kgs 16:33). Jehu's annihilation of Ahab's house and of the worship of Baal appears to offer some hope, but he, too, falls back into the ways of Jeroboam (2 Kgs 10:29, 31). This persistent sin of idolatry is linked with the fall of the northern kingdom (1 Kgs 14:15–16; 2 Kgs 17:21–23).

---

88. Jeroboam's reported words 'Here are your gods, O Israel, who brought you up out of Egypt' (1 Kgs 12:28) are the same as those spoken by Aaron. Jeroboam might have openly advocated idolatry; though that would be counter-productive to his purpose of winning over those who might otherwise go to worship in Jerusalem (cf. Hill and Walton, *Survey*, pp. 298–299). It may be that the narrator, wanting to emphasize the long-term significance of Jeroboam's actions, has put the words into his mouth.
89. E.g. 1 Kgs 15:26, 34; 16:19, 26; 2 Kgs 3:3; 10:29; 13:2; 14:24; 15:9, 18, 24, 28.
90. E.g. 1 Kgs 14:9; 15:30; 16:2, 26; 2 Kgs 17:17; 23:19.

The kings of Judah fare a little better. Several are commended for doing 'what was right in the eyes of the LORD';[91] with Asa, Hezekiah and Josiah even being compared with David (1 Kgs 15:11; 2 Kgs 18:3; 22:2.). Even when kings of Judah did evil in God's eyes, divine judgment was deferred for the sake of David (1 Kgs 15:4; 2 Kgs 8:19; cf. 19:34; 20:6), emphasizing God's commitment to the Davidic covenant.[92] We have seen, already, the significance of Josiah within the DH. There appears, too, to be a deliberate contrast between Israel's defeat by Assyria and Judah's deliverance from Assyria under Hezekiah. However, that is quickly undermined by Hezekiah's pride, which led to the threat of a Babylonian captivity (2 Kgs 20:12–19), and Manasseh's sin, which echoes Ahab's (2 Kgs 21:2–3), and makes the exile inevitable (2 Kgs 21:10–15; 24:3).[93]

An important Deuteronomic theme is proper worship. This includes warnings against worship of other gods.[94] That remains a key element in Kings.[95] Idolatry is the chief sin of the northern kings. And in the south there is frequent reference to kings' failure to remove 'high places'.[96] Some of these might at one time have been Canaanite shrines, which were taken over as local Israelite sanctuaries, but became associated with idolatry. They were to be destroyed and replaced with worship at a central sanctuary (Deut. 12:2–14); however, only Hezekiah and Josiah made serious attempts to destroy them (2 Kgs 18:4; 23:4–20).[97] That central sanctuary, which God will choose as a place for his name (e.g. Deut. 12:5; 14:23; 16:2; 26:2), is identified with the Jerusalem temple (1 Kgs 3:2; 5:3, 5; 8:17, 20, 43), further highlighting Jeroboam's sin.[98]

---

91. 1 Kgs 15:11; 22:43; 2 Kgs 12:2; 15:3, 34; 18:3; 22:2.

92. See above, p. 272, n. 73; see also e.g. Beal, *1 & 2 Kings*, pp. 48–50; House, *1, 2 Kings*, pp. 79–81; Satterthwaite and McConville, *Histories*, pp. 179–180.

93. After Hezekiah every king, except Josiah, is described as doing 'evil in the eyes of the LORD' (2 Kgs 21:20; 23:32, 37; 24:9, 19).

94. E.g. Deut. 6:14; 7:4; 8:19; 11:16, 26–28; 30:17–18.

95. See e.g. House, *1, 2 Kings*, pp. 74–75.

96. 1 Kgs 15:14; 22:43b; 2 Kgs 12:3; 14:4; 15:4.

97. Kings often uses Deuteronomic language in relation to these shrines and the practices associated with them; e.g. 1 Kgs 14:23; 2 Kgs 16:4; 17:10; cf. Deut. 12:2; 1 Kgs 14:24; 2 Kgs 16:3; 21:2, 11; cf. Deut. 7:25–26; 18:9, 12; 20:18; 2 Kgs 16:3; 17:17; 21:6; 23:10; cf. Deut. 18:10. See Beal, *1 & 2 Kings*, pp. 46–47.

98. God's presence in the temple is confirmed in 1 Kgs 8:10–11, in language reminiscent of Exod. 40:34–35.

Table 7.1[99]

Kings of Judah				Kings of Israel			
	Kitchen	*Thiele*	*Miller and Hayes*		*Kitchen*	*Thiele*	*Miller and Hayes*
Rehoboam	930–914	930–913	924–907	Jeroboam (ND)	930–910	930–909	924–903
Abijam	914–911	913–910	907–906	Nadab	910–909	909–908	903–902
Asa	911–870	910–869	905–874	Baasha (ND)	909–886	908–886	902–886
				Elah	886–885	886–885	886–885
				Zimri (ND)	885	885	–
				Omri (ND)	885–874	885–874	885–873
Jehoshaphat (CR)	870–848	869–848	874–850	Ahab	874–853	874–853	873–851
Joram/Jehoram (CR)	848–842	848–841	850–843	Ahaziah	853–852	853–852	851–849
Ahaziah	842–841	841	843	Joram	852–841	852–841	849–843
Athaliah	841–835	841–835	843–837	Jehu (ND)	841–813	841–814	843–816
Joash	835–795	835–796	837–?	Jehoahaz	813–805	814–798	816–800
Amaziah	795–775	796–767	?–?	Joash	805–790	798–782	800–785
Azariah/Uzziah (CR)	775–735	767–740	?–?	Jeroboam II (CR)	790–749	782–753	785–745
				Zechariah	749	753	745
				Shallum (ND)	749	752	745
				Menahem (ND)	748–738	752–742	745–736
				Pekahiah	738–736	742–740	736–735
Jotham (CR)	735–730	740–732	?–742	Pekah (ND)	736–731	740–732	735–732
Ahaz (CR)	730–715	732–715	742–727	Hoshea (ND)	731–722	732–723	732–723
Hezekiah (CR)	715–686	715–686	727–698				
Manasseh (CR)	686–642	686–642	697–642				
Amon	642–640	642–640	642–640				
Josiah	640–609	640–609	639–609				
Jehoahaz	609	609	609				
Eliakim/Jehoiakim	609–598	609–598	608–598				
Jehoiachin	598	598–597	598–597				
Zedekiah	597–586	597–586	597–586				

CR *denotes a possible period of co-regency, where a king reigned with his father; periods of overlap are not included.*
ND *indicates a change of royal house or a usurper to the throne.*

99. This list gives the dates according to Kitchen (*Reliability*, pp. 30–32), as simplified by Satterthwaite and McConville (*Histories*, pp. 155–170), Thiele (*Mysterious Numbers*, pp. 10–12) and the standard list by Miller and Hayes (*History*, pp. 220–221). In general I am inclined towards Kitchen and/or Thiele, though prefer 587 BC as the date of the fall of Jerusalem (see above, p. 102, n. 147). See also Hill and Walton, *Survey*, pp. 232–233.

A further key theme of Kings is the importance of prophets and prophecy.[100] Kings are challenged and held to account by prophets, something most clearly evident in the confrontations between Elijah and Ahab. And there is a significant emphasis, too, on the announcement and subsequent fulfilment of the prophetic word. Thus an unnamed man of God prophesies the destruction of Jeroboam's altar at Bethel by Josiah (1 Kgs 13:2–3; cf. 2 Kgs 23:15–20); Ahijah announces the end of Jeroboam's dynasty (1 Kgs 14:7–14; cf. 15:29); Jehu declares the end of Baasha's house (1 Kgs 16:1–4; cf. v. 12); and Elijah signals the deaths of Ahab and Jezebel (1 Kgs 21:20b–24; cf. 2 Kgs 9:36; 10:17). The fulfilment of prophecy also highlights God's control over history. He directs the rise and fall of the kings of Israel and Judah, and uses other nations for the eventual fulfilment of his purposes (see Table 7.1 for a list of the kings of Judah and Israel, and their dates).[101]

---

100. See e.g. Beal, *1 & 2 Kings*, pp. 50–53; Satterthwaite and McConville, *Histories*, pp. 177–179.
101. See Beal, *1 & 2 Kings*, pp. 53–55.

8. THE LATTER PROPHETS

Isaiah[1]

Date, authorship and composition

Its opening verse attributes the book to Isaiah, son of Amoz, who prophesied during the reigns of Uzziah, Jotham, Ahaz and Hezekiah of Judah. Chapter 6,

---

1. Commentaries on Isaiah include Klaus Baltzer, *Deutero-Isaiah*, Hermeneia (Philadelphia: Fortress, 2001); Joseph Blenkinsopp, *Isaiah*, 3 vols., AB 19–19B (New York: Doubleday, 2000–2003); Walter Brueggemann, *Isaiah*, 2 vols., Westminster Bible Companion (Louisville: Westminster John Knox, 1998); Childs, *Isaiah*; Clements, *Isaiah 1–39*; John Goldingay, *Isaiah*, NIBCOT (Carlisle: Paternoster, 2001); Paul D. Hanson, *Isaiah 40–66*, IBC (Louisville: Westminster John Knox, 1995); Otto Kaiser, *Isaiah 1–12*, 2nd ed. (London: SCM Press; Philadelphia: Westminster, 1983); *Isaiah 13–39*; John L. McKenzie, *Second Isaiah*, AB 20 (New York: Doubleday, 1968); Alec Motyer, *The Book of Isaiah* (Leicester: Inter-Varsity Press, 1993); *Isaiah*, TOTC (Leicester: Inter-Varsity Press, 1999); John N. Oswalt, *Isaiah*, NIVAC (Grand Rapids: Zondervan, 2003); *Isaiah 1–39*; *The Book of Isaiah 40–66*, NICOT (Grand Rapids: Eerdmans, 1997); Shalom M. Paul, *Isaiah 40–66*, ECC (Grand Rapids: Eerdmans, 2012); Seitz, *Isaiah 1–39*; Gary V. Smith, *Isaiah 1–39*, NAC 15A (Nashville: B&H, 2007); *Isaiah 40–66*, NAC 15B (Nashville: B&H, 2009); John D. W. Watts, *Isaiah 1–33*, rev. ed., WBC 24 (Nashville: Nelson, 2005); *Isaiah 34–66*, rev. ed., WBC 25

which appears to describe the prophet's call, suggests that his ministry began at the end of Uzziah's reign (c. 740 BC). The last datable event in the prophet's life is the siege of Jerusalem by the Assyrians (701 BC). This indicates a ministry of at least forty years. There is, though, little information about the prophet himself. He was married, with at least two children (7:3; 8:3). According to Jewish tradition, Amoz was the brother of Amaziah of Judah,[2] making Isaiah Joash's grandson. That cannot be substantiated, though Isaiah appears to have had relatively easy access to the king and the royal court. According to another tradition, Isaiah was martyred during the reign of Manasseh, by being sawn in two (cf. Heb. 11:37).[3]

Isaiah 1 – 39 (also referred to as First- or Proto-Isaiah) broadly covers the life and ministry of the eighth-century prophet. The rest of the book appears to relate to two further distinct historical settings. Isaiah 40 – 55 (Second- or Deutero-Isaiah), is set during the Babylonian exile. It affirms God's power and continuing love for a dejected people, and gives them hope of a glorious return. In the final section, Isaiah 56 – 66 (Third- or Trito-Isaiah), the people appear to be back in Judah, facing problems associated with the return from exile, including the need for right worship and right living.[4]

The traditional view is that Isaiah, in the eighth century BC, was responsible for the whole book, and that sections relating to the exile and return are predictive. That is not impossible. However, prophets were also preachers, who engaged directly with their community and delivered a contemporary message.

(Nashville: Nelson, 2005); Claus Westermann, *Isaiah 40–66*, OTL (London: SCM Press, 1969). For discussion of the book of Isaiah in the NT and the church, see e.g. Steve Moyise and Marten J. J. Menken (eds.), *Isaiah in the New Testament* (London: T&T Clark, 2005); John F. A. Sawyer, *The Fifth Gospel: Isaiah in the History of Christianity* (Cambridge: Cambridge University Press, 1996).

2. *b. Meg.* 10b.
3. *The Ascension of Isaiah* 11.41. This Christian composition, dated between the first and third centuries AD, is based on other traditions. Isaiah's martyrdom probably belongs to a Jewish tradition (cf. *b. Yebam.* 49b).
4. LaSor, Hubbard and Bush suggest that issues described in Isa. 57:9–11 and 59:1–8 may indicate a time before the exile (*OT Survey*, p. 284); see also Motyer, *Isaiah* (1993), p. 26. Others date all of Isa. 40 – 66 to the exilic period; see Lena-Sofia Tiemeyer, 'Continuity and Discontinuity in Isaiah 40–66. History of Research', in Lena-Sofia Tiemeyer and Hans M. Barstad (eds.), *Continuity and Discontinuity: Chronological and Thematic Development in Isaiah 40–66* (Göttingen: Vandenhoeck & Ruprecht, 2014), pp. 13–55 (14–16).

When they spoke about the future it was to warn, challenge or comfort the present generation. It would be unusual, therefore, for a message that related to exiles in Babylon to be delivered well over a century in advance. As Goldingay observes, while God *could have* revealed this word in the eighth century, it is not clear why he *would have* done so.[5] The view that the book can be divided into three sections, with separate authors – Isaiah (sometimes referred to as Isaiah of Jerusalem) in the eighth century BC, Deutero-Isaiah, an anonymous prophet who ministered to the exiles, and Trito-Isaiah, who prophesied after the return to Judah – goes back to an influential commentary by Duhm, published in 1892.[6] Most recent scholars accept a version of that view, with a minority continuing to argue for single authorship.[7]

It is unclear how the book came to be in its present form. One suggestion is that the sections of the book circulated independently and were put together, to fill up a single scroll, maybe because of common themes, but with little concern for the coherence of the final composition.[8]

More recently there has been a greater emphasis on the unity of the book. A common view is that the book is a redactional unity: the various sections did not exist independently, but each built on earlier material. Isaiah appears to have had a group of disciples who wrote down at least some of his words (Isa. 8:16; 30:8), and it is possible that they passed on his teaching to subsequent

---

5. John Goldingay, *God's Prophet, God's Servant: A Study in Jeremiah and Isaiah 40–55* (Exeter: Paternoster, 1984), pp. 11–12. It is sometimes claimed that proponents of a multiple-author view deny predictive prophecy (e.g. Oswald T. Allis, *The Unity of Isaiah* [London: Tyndale, 1951], esp. pp. 1–21; Oswalt, *Isaiah 1–39*, p. 41). That may be justified; however, the current debate relates, primarily, to the nature and relevance of prophecy.
6. Bernard Duhm, *Das Buch Jesaia: Übersetzt und erklärt* (Göttingen: Vandenhoeck & Ruprecht, 1892). By then Isaiah was already viewed in two parts. For discussion of the historical development of the theory, see Childs, *Introduction*, pp. 316–325; H. G. M. Williamson, 'Isaiah', in *DOTPr*, pp. 364–378 (366–371).
7. For a summary of arguments, see e.g. LaSor, Hubbard and Bush, *OT Survey*, pp. 281–288; Longman and Dillard, *Introduction*, pp. 303–311; Oswalt, *Isaiah 1–39*, pp. 23–29; *Isaiah*, pp. 33–41; cf. R. N. Whybray, *The Second Isaiah*, OTG (Sheffield: Sheffield Academic Press, 1983), pp. 2–4.
8. Whybray suggests the link was a common 'devotion to Jerusalem and its religious traditions' (*Second Isaiah*, p. 5; see also Collins, *Introduction*, p. 327). He argues though that the addition of 40 – 66 to 1 – 39 was not accidental, nor was it to produce a coherent work. It was, rather, to 'brighten up' the earlier prophecy and invest the later work with greater authority.

generations, who then edited, expanded and reapplied it to their own situation.[9] Thus Goldingay suggests that in the case of Deutero-Isaiah the later prophet may have seen himself taking up the mantle of Isaiah of Jerusalem and 'bringing to his day the message that Isaiah would have brought had he still been alive'.[10] Childs sees the final text as the result of redaction; however, rather than identifying different and sometimes competing theological agendas, he emphasizes the importance of viewing the canonical text as a coherent whole.[11] He and others note several intertextual and thematic links between Isaiah 1 – 39 and the later sections, emphasizing the overall continuity of the message.[12] In Childs's view a key aspect of this is the idea of prophecy and fulfilment: what God announced in Isaiah 1 – 39, 'the former things' (41:2b; 42:9; 43:9; 46:9; 48:3), is fulfilled in Isaiah 40 – 55.[13] Others suggest that some, or all, of Isaiah 40 – 55 formed a separate exilic corpus,[14] which has intertextual links with

---

9. For further discussion, see e.g. R. E. Clements, 'Beyond Tradition History': Deutero-Isaianic Development of First Isaiah's Themes', *JSOT* 31 (1985), pp. 95–113; 'The Unity of Isaiah', *Int* 36 (1982), pp. 117–129; Jacob Stromberg, *An Introduction to the Study of Isaiah* (London: T&T Clark, 2011); H. G. M. Williamson, *The Book Called Isaiah: Deutero-Isaiah's Role in Composition and Redaction* (Oxford: Clarendon, 1994); 'Recent Issues in the Study of Isaiah', in Firth and Williamson, *Interpreting Isaiah*, pp. 21–39. On Isaiah 40 – 66 see Tiemeyer and Barstad, *Continuity and Discontinuity*.
10. Goldingay, *God's Prophet*, pp. 11–12.
11. Childs, *Isaiah*, p. 4; *Introduction*, pp. 325–334.
12. Childs notes intertextual links in e.g. Isa. 40:5 (6:3); 40:9–10 (35:4); 41:25 (13:17) (ibid., pp. 299, 301, 322). Further key themes include first/last and darkness/light; see Hugh G. M. Williamson, 'First and Last in Isaiah', in Heather A. McKay and David J. A. Clines (eds.), *Of Prophets' Visions and the Wisdom of Sages: Essays in Honour of R. Norman Whybray on His Seventieth Birthday*, JSOTSup 162 (Sheffield: JSOT Press, 1993), pp. 95–108; see also Bernard Gosse, 'Isaiah 8:23b and the Three Great Parts of the Book of Isaiah', *JSOT* 70 (1996), pp. 57–62. Clements notes the theme of deafness and blindness, which appears in 6:9–10, and recurs in 42:16, 18–19; 43:8; 44:18 ('Beyond Tradition History', pp. 101–104).
13. Childs, *Introduction*, p. 329. So in 13:17 God promises to 'stir up' the Medes; and in 41:25 he announces that he has 'stirred up' Cyrus.
14. Albertz, *Israel in Exile*, pp. 377–379; Tiemeyer, 'Continuity and Discontinuity', in Tiemeyer and Barstad, *Continuity and Discontinuity*, pp. 18–21; Williamson, 'Recent Issues', in Firth and Williamson, *Interpreting Isaiah*, pp. 27–28; see also Ulrich Berges, 'The Book of Isaiah as Isaiah's Book: The Latest Developments in the Research of the Prophets', *OTE* 23.3 (2010), pp. 549–573.

other parts of the OT,[15] and did not only develop the teaching of the earlier prophet. This material was combined with Isaiah 1 – 39 after the exile to form a unified message of deliverance, and the rest of the book was built up through further redactions.[16]

There are four passages in Deutero-Isaiah that are widely taken to relate to the Servant of the Lord:[17] 42:1–4 (frequently extended to v. 9); 49:1–6; 50:4–9; 52:13 – 53:12.[18] Some view these as distinct from the material around them;[19] though it is now common to view them within their canonical context.[20] Debate about the identity of the Servant continues, and commentators suggest a range of possibilities. The Servant's relationship to law (*tôrâ*, 42:4), his prophetic role (49:2; 50:4; cf. 61:1–3), which has points of contact with Jeremiah's ministry,[21] and the proximity of the Servant passages to second-exodus imagery

---

15. Thus the reference to 'comfort' (Isa. 40:1) may counter the lack of comfort reflected in Lam. 1:2, 9, 16, 17, 21; see also Isa. 51:15 (cf. Jer. 31:35); Isa. 52:11 (cf. Lam. 4:15); see Berges, 'Book of Isaiah', pp. 565–567.
16. For discussion of 56 – 66, see e.g. Childs, *Isaiah*, pp. 439–449; Smith, *Isaiah 40–66*, pp. 55–70; see also Paul V. Niskanen, *Isaiah 56–66*, Berit Olam (Collegeville: Liturgical Press, 2014); P. A. Smith, *Rhetoric and Redaction in Trito-Isaiah: The Structure, Growth and Authorship of Isaiah 40–66*, VTSup 62 (Leiden: Brill, 1995).
17. These are often referred to as 'Servant Songs', though that description is misleading.
18. See e.g. Childs, *Introduction*, pp. 334–336; J. Goldingay, 'Servant of Yahweh', in *DOTPr*, pp. 700–707; Gordon P. Hugenberger, 'The Servant of the Lord in the "Servant Songs" of Isaiah', in Philip E. Satterthwaite, Richard S. Hess and Gordon J. Wenham (eds.), *The LORD's Anointed: Interpretation of Old Testament Messianic Texts* (Carlisle: Paternoster, 1995), pp. 105–140; Routledge, *OT Theology*, pp. 291–296; Peter Wilcox and David Paton-Williams, 'The Servant Songs in Deutero-Isaiah', *JSOT* 42 (1988), pp. 79–102; see also Lindblom, *Prophecy*, pp. 267–270; Sigmund Mowinckel, *He That Cometh: The Messiah Concept in the Old Testament and Later Judaism* (Oxford: Blackwell, 1956), pp. 187–257; Christopher R. North, *The Suffering Servant in Deutero-Isaiah*, 2nd ed. (Oxford: Oxford University Press, 1956); H. H. Rowley, *The Servant of the Lord and Other Essays on the Old Testament* (Oxford: Blackwell, 1965), pp. 1–88; Whybray, *The Second Isaiah*, pp. 65–78; H. G. M. Williamson, *Variations on a Theme: King, Messiah and Servant in the Book of Isaiah*, Didsbury Lectures (Carlisle: Paternoster, 1998), pp. 133–166.
19. See e.g. Mowinckel, *He That Cometh*; Westermann, *Isaiah 40–66*, p. 92.
20. An influential text in this context is Tryggve N. D. Mettinger, *A Farewell to the Servant Songs: A Critical Examination of an Exegetical Axiom* (Lund: Gleerup, 1983).
21. E.g. 49:1b; Westermann notes several links between Jeremiah and Isa. 50:4–9 (*Isaiah 40–66*, pp. 227–228).

(42:15–16; 49:8–12; 52:7–12) suggest links with Moses. Many Christians see this figure fulfilled, ultimately, in Christ.

Some also argue that chapters 1–39 also went through a redactional process. The location of the prophet's call in chapter 6 is unusual, and this has led some to the view that chapters 6–8, sometimes called the 'Isaiah memoir' (Ger. *Denkschrift*), set against the background of the Syro-Ephraimite war, is the original core of the book. Other prophecies were then added: some during the prophet's lifetime; some during a major redaction in Josiah's reign.[22] Other material, including 'apocalyptic' elements (e.g. chs. 24–27), may be later still.[23] More recently that view, including the idea of a *Denkschrift*, has been challenged.[24] It is also possible that most of Isaiah 1 – 39 comprises authentic prophecies that were written down by Isaiah's immediate disciples, though the material may have been shaped by a final editor, to set these chapters within the context of a unified whole.

The earliest MT version of Isaiah is the Leningrad Codex (AD 1009). A number of much earlier Hebrew manuscripts, some of which contain substantial sections of text, have been discovered among the Dead Sea Scrolls. A largely complete text, 1QIsa[a] (or 1QIsa), also referred to as the 'Great Isaiah Scroll', is dated around 100 BC. Another significant text, 1QIsa[b] (dated around 50 BC), includes some three-quarters of the book.[25] This generally agrees with the MT, and so emphasizes the general accuracy of that text. 1QIsa[a] includes a number of variations,[26] and may represent a stream of transmission separate from the

---

22. See above, pp. 60–61.
23. See e.g. Clements, *Isaiah 1–39*, pp. 3–8. Paul argues that ch. 35 (and possibly 34) may be attributed to Deutero-Isaiah (*Isaiah 40–66*, pp. 4–5).
24. H. G. M. Williamson, 'The Isaiah Memoir Reconsidered', Ethel Wood Lecture, 1996; 'Recent Issues in the Study of Isaiah', in Firth and Williamson, *Interpreting Isaiah*, p. 33; Childs, *Isaiah*, pp. 42–44.
25. See further Emmanuel Tov, 'The Text of Isaiah at Qumran', in *Hebrew Bible, Greek Bible, and Qumran* (Tübingen: Mohr Siebeck, 2008), pp. 42–56; Eugene Ulrich, 'An Index to the Contents of the Isaiah Manuscripts from the Judean Desert', in Craig C. Broyles and Craig A. Evans (eds.), *Writing and Reading the Scroll of Isaiah: Studies in an Interpretative Tradition*, VTSup 70 (Leiden: Brill, 1997), pp. 477–480; Peter W. Flint, 'The Isaiah Scrolls from the Judean Desert', in Broyles and Evans, *Writing and Reading*, pp. 481–489; Dwight Swanson, 'The Text of Isaiah at Qumran' in Firth and Williamson, *Interpreting Isaiah*, pp. 191–212; 'Dead Sea Scrolls', in *DOTWPW*, pp. 88–99.
26. E.g. Oswalt, *Isaiah 1–39*, pp. 29–31; Ulrich, 'Sharper Focus', pp. 2–4.

MT.[27] While, in general, the MT remains the preferred text, 1QIsa[a] has sometimes confirmed a variant reading (e.g. Isa. 14:4; 21:8; 33:8; 53:11). However, while there may be several minor variations, the number of significant differences is relatively small.[28]

Structure and outline

As we have noted, it is generally agreed that the book of Isaiah can be divided into two or more sections. Isaiah 39 records the visit of envoys from Babylon, which, at the time, would have been a relatively minor province, under Assyrian control. That visit prompts a prophecy of coming exile (39:5–7), and in the following chapter the setting changes to one where that prophecy has been fulfilled. The division between chapters 55 and 56, though widely accepted, is less obvious. Some suggest that 56 – 66 has a concentric structure, beginning and ending with emphasis on the nations.[29]

However, regardless of these divisions, or of how the material came to be in its present form, it appears that the book as a whole is intentionally associated with Isaiah, son of Amoz. Thus Childs suggests that historical detail in 40 – 66 is left deliberately vague, to allow these chapters to be linked with the earlier message.[30] He notes, further, that 'no new prophet is called in Isaiah 40, but rather the word of God through Isaiah continues to work to fulfil the promise'.[31]

Outline

- Judah's sin: judgment and redemption (1:1 – 12:6)
- Oracles against the nations (13:1 – 23:18)
- Eschatological judgment and salvation (24:1 – 27:13)
- Judgment and future hope under a righteous king (28:1 – 35:10)
- Deliverance from Assyria; threat of exile in Babylon (36:1 – 39:8)
- God as redeemer: the promise of return from exile (40:1 – 55:13)
  - The only God will fulfil his purpose through Cyrus (40:1 – 48:22)
  - The compassionate God will save Zion through his Servant (49:1 – 55:13)
- Living in preparation for God's coming worldwide salvation (56:1 – 66:24)

---

27. Swanson, 'Text of Isaiah', in Firth and Williamson, *Interpreting Isaiah*, p. 198.
28. Oswalt, *Isaiah 1–39*, p. 31; Swanson, 'Text of Isaiah', in Firth and Williamson, *Interpreting Isaiah*, p. 198; however, see Ulrich, 'Sharper Focus', p. 9.
29. E.g. Goldingay, *Isaiah*, p. 14; Oswalt, *Isaiah 40–55*, p. 465.
30. Childs, *Introduction*, pp. 325–327.
31. Childs, *Isaiah*, pp. 302–303 (302).

Main themes

The book of Isaiah contains a number of key theological themes.[32] Some of these run through the whole book. Others relate more specifically to a pre- or post-exilic setting, and so appear more in one section than another. Several are picked up by the NT, making Isaiah one of its most quoted, or alluded to, books of the OT.[33]

Central to the book is Isaiah's vision of God. He is 'high and exalted' (6:1); he sits enthroned above the circle of the earth (40:22); he is the Creator (e.g. 40:26, 28; 42:5; 45:7; 65:17); and he directs international affairs, including using Assyria to punish Israel (10:5–6) and Cyrus to bring deliverance from Babylon (e.g. 44:28; 46:11). God has a unique claim to deity (e.g. 40:18, 25; 44:8; 45:5–6; 46:5, 9), over against the gods of Babylon, who are presented as no more than worthless idols (e.g. 40:19–20; 44:12–17; 46:1–2);[34] and this is affirmed by his control over historical events (e.g. 41:21–23; 43:8–13; 44:6–8; 45:20–25). A key aspect of this is God's power to deliver his people from exile – a deliverance that is seen as a second and better exodus.[35]

---

32. See also John Goldingay, 'The Theology of Isaiah', in Firth and Williamson, *Interpreting Isaiah*, pp. 168–190; *The Theology of Isaiah* (Downers Grove: IVP Academic, 2014); John N. Oswalt, *The Holy One of Israel: Studies in the Book of Isaiah* (Cambridge: James Clarke, 2014). See also above, pp. 180–183.
33. See e.g. Moyise and Menken, *Isaiah in the NT*; Rikk E. Watts, 'Isaiah in the New Testament', in Firth and Williamson, *Interpreting Isaiah*, pp. 213–233; Jan Fekkes, *Isaiah and Prophetic Traditions in the Book of Revelation: Visionary Antecedents and Their Development*, JSNTSup 93 (Sheffield: Sheffield Academic Press, 1994). See too material relating to second-exodus imagery (below, n. 35).
34. Biblical monotheism, which asserts that there is only one God and no other gods exist, appears to be set out in Isa. 40 – 55; see e.g. Routledge, *OT Theology*, pp. 94–101 (99–101). However, cf. Nathan MacDonald, 'Monotheism and Isaiah', in Firth and Williamson, *Interpreting Isaiah*, pp. 43–61. Bauckham notes links between the monotheism of 40 – 55 and the NT portrayal of Christ; see Richard Bauckham, *God Crucified: Monotheism and Christology in the New Testament* (Carlisle: Paternoster, 1998).
35. See e.g. Bernard W. Anderson, 'Exodus Typology in Second Isaiah', in B. W. Anderson and Walter Harrelson (eds.), *Israel's Prophetic Heritage: Essays in Honor of James Muilenburg* (New York: Harper, 1962), pp. 177–195; 'Exodus and Covenant in Second Isaiah and Prophetic Tradition', in Frank Moore Cross et al. (eds.), *Magnalia Dei, the Mighty Acts of God: Essays on the Bible and Archaeology in Memory of G. Ernest Wright* (New York: Doubleday, 1976), pp. 339–360; Pao, *Acts and the Isaianic New Exodus*; Rikk E. Watts, 'Consolation or Confrontation: Isaiah 40–55 and the Delay of the New Exodus', *TynBul* 41.1 (1990), pp. 31–59; *Isaiah's New Exodus*.

A favourite title for God in all three sections of the book is 'the Holy One of Israel'.[36] This is related to the prophet's call, particularly the hymn of the seraphim (6:3):

> Holy, holy, holy is the LORD Almighty;
> the whole earth is full of his glory.

God's holiness is closely linked with his glory. Holiness is an inward characteristic of God; glory may be viewed as the outward revelation of that holiness.[37] Isaiah was confronted with a holy God whose glory already filled the earth, and the divine purpose implicit throughout the book is that the nations will increasingly recognize that fact (e.g. 35:2; 40:5; 60:1–3; 66:18).[38]

God's holiness contrasts with the sinfulness of humankind (e.g. 6:5; cf. 1:4; 5:18–24; 30:12–13). Sin takes a variety of forms in the book of Isaiah,[39] but it is commonly viewed as rebellion;[40] and the book begins and ends with that theme (1:2; 66:24).[41] One aspect of this is the pride that seeks to usurp the glory that belongs to God alone, and that results in the proud being cast down (2:11–17; 10:12–19; 13:11; 14:12–15; 23:9; 42:8; 48:11). Another is the temptation to put confidence in human resources, including alliances (e.g. 30:1–2; 31:1) and military preparations (22:8b–11), rather than placing trust in God alone (e.g. 7:9b; 25:9; 26:3–4; 28:16; 30:15; 40:31; 42:17; 50:10). And this points to a related key theme of the book: faith in God.[42]

---

36. This title occurs twenty-five times in Isaiah (1:4b; 5:19b, 24b; 10:20b; 12:6b; 17:7; 29:19; 30:11, 12, 15; 31:1b; 37:23b; 41:14b, 16, 20b; 43:3, 14; 45:11; 47:4; 48:17; 49:7; 54:5; 55:5b; 60:9b, 14b; cf. 10:17; 29:23b; 40:25; 43:15), and only six in the rest of the OT (2 Kgs 19:22b; Pss 71:22b; 78:41b; 89:18; Jer. 50:29b; 51:5b).
37. See Routledge, *OT Theology*, pp. 105–106; see also Goldingay, 'Theology of Isaiah', in Firth and Williamson, *Interpreting Isaiah*, pp. 171–174.
38. See Routledge, 'Narrative Substructure', pp. 194–195; *OT Theology*, pp. 49–50, 313–314.
39. E.g. above, pp. 180–183.
40. A significant Hebrew verb here is *pāšaʿ* (to rebel); e.g. 1:2, 28; 43:27; 46:8; 48:8; 53:12; 59:13; 66:24; see Oswalt, *Isaiah 1–39*, pp. 38–39; Routledge, 'Narrative Substructure', p. 188.
41. Oswalt, *Isaiah 1–39*, p. 38.
42. For further discussion, see e.g. David Bostock, *A Portrayal of Trust: The Theme of Faith in the Hezekiah Narratives* (Carlisle: Paternoster, 2006); Philip S. Johnston, 'Faith in Isaiah', in Firth and Williamson, *Interpreting Isaiah*, pp. 104–121; Oswalt, *Isaiah*, pp. 46–49.

Closely associated with the call to faith is the idea of the remnant (e.g. 7:3; 10:20–23): those few from within the nation who put their trust in God and so make up the redeemed community in the coming kingdom.[43] This is a significant development, in that the future people of God are no longer identified with Israel as a whole, but with a small minority, characterized not by their ethnicity but by their faith.[44]

Oswalt also notes the importance of servanthood.[45] God's people are called to serve him, but have failed because of their sin. The cleansing received by the prophet at his call offers a solution: 'sinful Israel can become servant Israel when the experience of Isaiah becomes the experience of the nation'.[46] Despite continued failure, God's purpose is to purify and restore (a remnant of) his people, and that is made possible through the Servant of the Lord. He demonstrates ideal servanthood, and through his ministry and sacrifice the nation may become what it was meant to be. This includes being the channel through which God's glory is revealed to the nations (e.g. 60:1–3).[47]

The emphasis on the nations is also an important theme in Isaiah.[48] Chapters 56–66 begin and end with non-Israelites worshipping God. Chapters 1–39 also suggest that nations who turn to Yahweh may also experience the blessings of salvation alongside Israel (2:2–4; 19:19–25; 25:6–8). There are several passages in Deutero-Isaiah, too, that indicate the inclusion of non-Israelite nations (e.g. 45:22), and the ministry of the Servant also appears to extend to the nations (42:4, 6; 49:6).[49]

---

43. See Gerhard F. Hasel, *The Remnant: The History and Theology of the Remnant Idea from Genesis to Isaiah*, 3rd ed. (Berrien Springs: Andrews University Press, 1980); see also e.g. R. E. Clements, '*šā'ar*', in *TDOT* 14:272–286; Craig Evans, 'Isa. 6:9–13 in the Context of Isaiah's Theology', *JETS* 29.2 (1986), pp. 139–146; Sang Hoon Park, '*š'r*', in *NIDOTTE* 4:11–17; Routledge, *OT Theology*, pp. 266–267.
44. See further Routledge, 'Replacement or Fulfillment', pp. 144–146.
45. Oswalt, *Isaiah 1–39*, pp. 54–60.
46. Ibid., pp. 174–175.
47. See also Routledge, 'Narrative Substructure'.
48. E.g. Richard L. Schultz, 'Nationalism and Universalism in Isaiah', in Firth and Williamson, *Interpreting Isaiah*, pp. 122–144; Williamson, *Variations*, pp. 113–166.
49. There is debate as to the extent of this inclusion. Some argue that Deutero-Isaiah is nationalistic and only Israel may experience salvation; e.g. H. M. Orlinsky, '"A Light of Nations" (*'ôr gôyim*) – "A Covenant of People" (*bĕrît 'ām*)', in H. M. Orlinsky and N. H. Snaith, *Studies in the Second Part of the Book of Isaiah*, VTSup 14 (Leiden: Brill, 1967), pp. 97–117; N. H. Snaith, 'The Servant of the Lord in Deutero-Isaiah', in H. H. Rowley

The nations also feature in the emphasis on Zion/Jerusalem, which, following the exile, will be rebuilt and glorified (e.g. 44:26–28; 60; 62), and will become a place of pilgrimage for all peoples (e.g. 2:2–4; 66:20). Traditions associated with Sinai, including giving the Law, and what appears to be a covenant meal shared with Israel's elders (Exod. 24:9–11), are transferred to Zion (2:2–4; 24:23; 25:6–8; see also 4:5),[50] where they are also extended to include other nations. Isaiah begins, though, by highlighting the city's corruption (1:21–23). As with the nation as a whole, to be what it was made to be, Zion must be restored and renewed (e.g. 1:25–27; 4:2–4; 33:5).

Zion is the place where God may be found, and in the future consummation the Lord's 'holy mountain' appears to represent the whole kingdom (11:6–9). There are passages in 1 – 39 that may be taken to suggest that the prophet regarded Jerusalem as inviolable: God would always step in to protect it (e.g. 17:12–14; 29:5–8; 31:4–5), and that view might have been prevalent among the false prophets confronted by Jeremiah.[51] That, though, seems unlikely in view of the prophet's constant call to faith. Thus during the Assyrian crisis, God promises to save the city for the sake of David (37:35), but it comes, also, in response to Hezekiah's faith.

A further important theme in the book of Isaiah is the Messiah (anointed one).[52] The term, itself, does not appear in the OT in its later, technical sense;

(*Footnote 49 cont.*) (ed.), *Studies in Old Testament Prophecy: Presented to Professor Theodore H. Robinson* (Edinburgh: T&T Clark, 1950), pp. 187–200. Others suggest that the nations may experience salvation but in subjection to Israel; e.g. Michael A. Grisanti, 'Israel's Mission to the Nations in Isaiah 40–55: An Update', *TMSJ* 9.1 (1998), pp. 39–61; D. W. van Winkle, 'The Relationship of the Nations to Yahweh and to Israel in Isaiah XL–LV', *VT* 35.4 (1985), pp. 446–458; 'Proselytes in Isaiah XL–LV? A Study of Isaiah XLIV 1–5', *VT* 47.3 (1997), pp. 341–359. In my view it can be argued that Isaiah anticipates the inclusion of the non-Israelite nations alongside Israel as equals (Routledge, *OT Theology*, pp. 330–333; 'Narrative Substructure'; 'Mission and Covenant', in Grams et al., *Bible and Mission*). See also Oswalt, 'The Nations in Isaiah: Friend or Foe; Servant or Partner', in *Holy One of Israel*, pp. 94–105.

50. See e.g. McConville, 'Jerusalem in the OT', in Walker, *Jerusalem Past and Present*, p. 25; Routledge, *OT Theology*, pp. 276, 329; see also Jon D. Levenson, *Sinai and Zion: An Entry into the Jewish Bible*, New Voices in Biblical Studies (Minneapolis: Winston, 1985), pp. 89–96.

51. See below, p. 298.

52. On the Messiah see Routledge, *OT Theology*, pp. 280–298 (283–289); see also J. Becker, *Messianic Expectation in the Old Testament* (Edinburgh: T&T Clark, 1980); Bright,

nevertheless, we see, in Isaiah a clear expectation of a future Davidic ruler associated with the era of salvation. Key passages here are 9:2–7 and 11:1–9.[53] The first refers to the birth of a child, who will be called 'Wonderful Counsellor, Mighty God, Everlasting Father, Prince of Peace' (9:6). This has, traditionally, been taken to describe characteristics of the child; and 'Mighty God', and maybe also 'Everlasting Father', suggest deity. However, the Messiah was not generally regarded as divine, and it may be better to understand these names as theophoric, referring to God rather than to the child: 'a wonderful counsellor is the mighty God; the everlasting father is a prince of peace'.[54] The second passage notes the characteristics of the messianic king (11:1–5), and also describes, figuratively, the peace and harmony associated with the coming kingdom (11:6–9; cf. 65:25). There are a number of parallels between the descriptions of the Messiah, here, and the Servant in 42:1–6, suggesting a possible link between them.[55] Common

---

Covenant and Promise; Ronald E. Clements, 'The Messianic Hope in the Old Testament', *JSOT* 43 (1989), pp. 3–19; D. G. Firth, 'Messiah', in *DOTPr*, pp. 537–544; Joseph A. Fitzmyer, *The One Who Is to Come* (Grand Rapids: Eerdmans, 2007); Walter C. Kaiser Jr., *The Messiah in the Old Testament, Studies in Old Testament Biblical Theology* (Grand Rapids: Zondervan, 1995); LaSor, Hubbard and Bush, *OT Survey*, pp. 688–694; Mowinckel, *He That Cometh*; Stanley E. Porter (ed.), *The Messiah in the Old and New Testaments* (Grand Rapids: Eerdmans, 2007); Satterthwaite, Hess and Wenham, *Lord's Anointed*; Paul D. Wegner, *An Examination of Kingship and Messianic Expectation in Isaiah 1–35* (New York: Edwin Mellin, 1992); Williamson, *Variations*, pp. 30–72.

53. These passages are debated, though it seems reasonable to associate them with the eighth-century prophet.

54. For further discussion, see John Goldingay, 'The Compound Name in Isaiah 9:5 (6)', *CBQ* 61 (1999), pp. 239–244; McConville, *Prophets*, p. 36; Paul D. Wegner, 'A Re-Examination of Isaiah IX 1–6', *VT* 42.1 (1992), pp. 103–112; 'What's New in Isaiah 9:1–7?', in Firth and Williamson, *Interpreting Isaiah*, pp. 237–249 (244–245); Williamson, *Variations*, pp. 43–44.

55. Richard L. Schultz, 'The King in the Book of Isaiah', in Satterthwaite, Hess and Wenham, *Lord's Anointed*, pp. 141–165. According to Rowley, the link between Servant and Messiah is not evident before the NT period (Rowley, *Servant*, pp. 61–88; see also Russell, *Method and Message*, pp. 334–340). However, Hugenberger links the Servant with the Prophet like Moses ('Servant', in Satterthwaite, Hess and Wenham, *Lord's Anointed*, pp. 119–140), who is sometimes viewed as messianic. Isa. 55:3–4 describes David as 'a witness to the peoples'; this reflects Israel's failed calling, now embodied in the ministry of the Servant (Childs, *Isaiah*, pp. 435–437; Oswalt, *Isaiah 40–66*, pp. 439–440). There is a probable link, too, between Servant passages and Isa. 61:1–3.

features include endowment with the Spirit (11:2; 42:1) and righteousness (11:4–5; 42:6), and the key task of establishing justice (11:3–4; 42:1, 4).

The Immanuel prophecy (7:14) is sometimes seen as messianic, particularly in view of its quotation in Matthew 1:23. However, to be a 'sign' to Ahaz, it must have had significance at the time, and it is better to understand the reference in Matthew 1:23 as typological.[56] The child born in Isaiah's day will point to God's presence and the hope of deliverance. In the coming days the pattern of God's promise of hope will be repeated and intensified in another child, who will also be called Immanuel and who will, indeed, be God, present among his people.[57]

Jeremiah[58]

Date, authorship and composition

According to the superscription (1:1–3), Jeremiah was called in the thirteenth

---

56. On 'typology' see above, pp. 224–225, 227.
57. See also Hamilton, 'The Virgin Will Conceive', in Daniel and Nolland, *Built Upon the Rock*; see also e.g. R. E. Clements, 'The Immanuel Prophecy of Isaiah 7:10–17 and Its Messianic Interpretation', in *Old Testament Prophecy: From Oracles to Canon* (Louisville: Westminster John Knox, 1996), pp. 65–77; W. McKane, 'The Interpretation of Isaiah VII 14–25', *VT* 17 (1967), pp. 208–219; M. Tsevat et al., '*bětûlâ*', *TDOT* 2:338–356; John H. Walton, '*bětûlâ*'; '*ʿalûmîm*', *NIDOTTE* 1:781–784; 3:415–419; Paul D. Wegner, 'How Many Virgin Births Are in the Bible? (Isaiah 7:14): A Prophetic Pattern Approach', *JETS* 54.3 (2011), pp. 467–484; Gordon J. Wenham, '*Betulah*: "A Girl of Marriageable Age"', *VT* 22 (1972), pp. 326–348; Williamson, *Variations*, pp. 73–112; Herbert Martin Wolf, 'A Solution to the Immanuel Prophecy in Isaiah 7:14–8:22', *JBL* 91 (1972), pp. 449–456.
58. Commentaries on Jeremiah include Leslie C. Allen, *Jeremiah*, OTL (Louisville: Westminster John Knox, 2008); John Bright, *Jeremiah*, AB 21 (New York: Doubleday, 1965); W. Brueggemann, *Exile and Homecoming*; Robert P. Carroll, *Jeremiah*, OTL (London: SCM Press, 1986); R. E. Clements, *Jeremiah*, IBC (Louisville: Westminster John Knox, 1989); Peter C. Craigie, Page H. Kelley and Joel F. Drinkard Jr., *Jeremiah 1–25*, WBC 26 (Dallas: Word, 1991); J. Andrew Dearman, *Jeremiah and Lamentations*, NIVAC (Grand Rapids: Zondervan, 2002); Terence E. Fretheim, *Jeremiah*, SHBC 15 (Macon: Smyth & Helwys, 2002); R. K. Harrison, *Jeremiah and Lamentations*, TOTC (London: Inter-Varsity Press, 1973); William L. Holladay, *Jeremiah*, 2 vols., Hermeneia (Philadelphia: Fortress, 1986, 1989); F. B. Huey Jr.,

year of Josiah's reign (around 627 BC),[59] and prophesied during the subsequent reigns of Jehoiakim and Zedekiah. This was a period of great political change, which saw the end of the Assyrian Empire, the re-emergence of Egypt and the rise of Babylon as the new international superpower. It saw, too, the fall of Jerusalem and the exile of the nation. Following Jerusalem's capture, Jeremiah was taken, against his will, to Egypt (43:4–7), and it seems likely that he died there.

The book gives a number of insights into the life and personal struggles of Jeremiah.[60] He was from a priestly family, based in Anathoth, a few miles from Jerusalem. This was the home of Abiathar. He had been one of David's priests, but supported Adonijah's claim to the throne and was banished by Solomon, thus ending the prominence of Eli's priestly line (1 Kgs 2:26–27). Jeremiah might have been descended from Abiathar and therefore from Eli, thus adding poignancy to his references to Shiloh (7:12, 14; 26:6, 9) and to the Ark of the Covenant (3:16).

Jeremiah's call appears to have come during Josiah's reforms, five or six years before the discovery of the Book of the Law, yet he makes little comment on

---

Jeremiah, Lamentations, NAC 16 (Nashville: B&H, 1993); Gerald L. Keown, Pamela J. Scalise and Thomas G. Smothers, *Jeremiah 26–52*, WBC 27 (Dallas: Word, 1995); Hetty Lalleman, *Jeremiah and Lamentations*, TOTC (Nottingham: Inter-Varsity Press, 2013); Tremper Longman III, *Jeremiah, Lamentations*, NIBCOT (Peabody: Hendrickson, 2008); Jack R. Lundbom, *Jeremiah*, 3 vols., AB 21A–21C (New York: Doubleday, 1999–2004); *Jeremiah Among the Prophets* (Cambridge: James Clarke, 2013); J. G. McConville, *Judgment and Promise: An Interpretation of the Book of Jeremiah* (Leicester: Apollos, 1993); William McKane, *Jeremiah*, 2 vols., ICC (Edinburgh: T&T Clark, 1986, 1996); Louis Stulman, *Jeremiah*, AbOTC (Nashville: Abingdon, 2005); J. A. Thompson, *Jeremiah*, NICOT (Grand Rapids: Eerdmans, 1980); Christopher J. H. Wright, *The Message of Jeremiah*, BST (Nottingham: Inter-Varsity Press, 2014).

59. See the list of Judah's monarchs, and possible dates, above, p. 278.

60. Some question the historical accuracy of the information. Carroll regards it as largely editorial; see e.g. Robert P. Carroll, *From Chaos to Covenant: Uses of Prophecy in the Book of Jeremiah* (London: SCM Press, 1981); *Jeremiah*; *Jeremiah*, OTG (Sheffield: Sheffield Academic Press, 1989), pp. 9–16. Holladay (*Jeremiah* 1) and Lundbom (*Jeremiah* 1) take it as broadly historical. Brueggemann argues that historical material has been unintentionally filtered by later editors; see Walter Brueggemann, 'The Book of Jeremiah: Portrait of the Prophet', in Mays and Achtemeier, *Interpreting the Prophets*, pp. 13–29; *The Theology of the Book of Jeremiah* (Cambridge: Cambridge University Press, 2007), pp. 27–28.

them. Most of his prophetic activity was during the reigns of Jehoiakim and Zedekiah. In Arnold's view this was because Jeremiah was largely optimistic about Josiah's reforms and needed to speak out only when the king's untimely death brought them to an end.[61] Alternatively, Jeremiah might have had concerns about the superficiality of the reforms (e.g. 3:10),[62] and was reluctant to support them, but nor did he want to undermine what they might achieve.[63] Another suggestion is that 627 BC is the year Jeremiah was born (cf. 1:5),[64] and his ministry began after Josiah's death, though that seems unlikely.[65]

While the historical setting of the book is fairly clear, questions remain about how much may be attributed to Jeremiah himself. Chapter 36 gives an insight into the way the book may have grown. In Jehoiakim's fourth year (605 BC) Jeremiah's words were dictated to Baruch and written on a scroll. It is likely that this was made up of the oracles recorded in chapters 1–25 (cf. 25:1–3). When Jehoiakim destroyed this scroll, Jeremiah dictated a second version, with the addition of 'many similar words' (36:32b). This suggests that a substantial part of Jeremiah's message was recorded during his lifetime, and also points to the significant role of Baruch.

Commentators generally note three kinds of material in the book: (1) poetic oracles, which are generally attributed to Jeremiah; (2) narrative sections, which give biographical details about Jeremiah, which may be the work of Baruch, though some see signs of Deuteronomistic editing; and (3) prose sermons, which are commonly attributed to Deuteronomistic redactors.[66] According to

---

61. Arnold, *Introduction*, p. 328.

62. E.g. Lalleman, *Jeremiah and Lamentations*, p. 23; Thompson, *Jeremiah*, pp. 60–62.

63. Jer. 22:15b–16 indicates that Jeremiah had great respect for Josiah. And the family of Shaphan, Josiah's secretary during the reforms (2 Kgs 22), protected Jeremiah (e.g. Jer. 26:24; 39:14), suggesting that Jeremiah had not opposed him.

64. Holladay, *Jeremiah* 1.

65. See e.g. Longman and Dillard, pp. 325–326; Thompson, *Jeremiah*, pp. 50–56.

66. The suggestion that only poetic oracles were by Jeremiah was put forward by Duhm. Mowinckel divided the remaining material into biographical narrative and prose sermons, and designated the three types A, B and C. For a summary of views, see e.g. Carroll, *Jeremiah* (1989), pp. 31–40; Ronald E. Clements, 'Prophets, Editors and Tradition', in Gordon, *The Place Is Too Small for Us*, pp. 443–452; James L. Crenshaw, 'A Living Tradition: The Book of Jeremiah in Recent Research', in Mays and Achtemeier, *Interpreting the Prophets*, pp. 100–112; Gordon McConville, *Exploring the Old Testament*, vol. 4: *The Prophets* (London: SPCK, 2002), pp. 47–51; Carolyn J. Sharp, *Prophecy and Ideology in Jeremiah: Struggles for Authority in the Deutero-Jeremianic*

Allen, the prose sermons are 'a version of Jeremiah's message, written for a later generation';[67] though some suggest that they may reflect little of Jeremiah's actual message.[68] Others go further and argue that the whole book is the product of redaction, and that the poetic sections, too, have been manipulated to reflect Deuteronomic theology.[69]

There are similarities between Jeremiah and the books of Kings (e.g. 2 Kgs 25; cf. Jer. 52:4–34).[70] Parts of the prophet's message also reflect Deuteronomic language and theology (e.g. 3:1 [cf. Deut. 24:1]; 21:8 [cf. Deut. 30:15]).[71] Though that may be due to Jeremiah's familiarity with Deuteronomy, which took on renewed significance during the period of his ministry. It is unlikely that a Deuteronomistic editor, intent on promoting Josiah's reforms, would portray Jeremiah as offering little or no support for them. Similarly, the (Deuteronomistic) editors of Kings take no notice of Jeremiah, and when Josiah's assistants seek prophetic assistance, they consult Huldah (2 Kgs 22:14).[72]

Prose, OTS (London: T&T Clark, 2003), pp. 1–39. See also Lalleman, *Jeremiah in Prophetic Tradition*, pp. 19–48; *Jeremiah*, pp. 28–37; McConville, *Judgment and Promise*, pp. 12–23.

67. Allen, *Jeremiah*, pp. 7–11 (9); see also John Bright, 'The Date of the Prose Sermons of Jeremiah', *JBL* 70.1 (1951), pp. 15–35.
68. See e.g. E. W. Nicholson, *Preaching to the Exiles: A Study of the Prose Tradition in the Book of Jeremiah* (Oxford: Basil Blackwell, 1970). Nicholson sees links to Jeremiah's message and ministry; but argues that the prose sermons were developed specifically to meet the needs of the Babylonian exiles. See further Holladay, *Jeremiah* 2:10–95; Louis Stulman, *The Prose Sermons of the Book of Jeremiah: A Redescription of the Correspondence with Deuteronomistic Literature in Light of Recent Text-Critical Research*, SBLDS 83 (Atlanta: Scholars Press, 1986).
69. See e.g. Carroll, *Jeremiah* (1986), pp. 38–50; W. Thiel, *Die deuteronomistische Redaktion von Jeremia 1–25*, WMANT 41 (Neukirchen-Vlyn: Neukirchener Verlag, 1973); McKane, *Jeremiah* 1:l–lxxxiii. McKane argues for a 'rolling corpus', whereby sections of text, maybe, in the case of poetry, going back to Jeremiah, have given rise to prose commentary, and those additions, in turn, have been expanded by later redactors; so e.g. 7:29b–34 is an expansion based on 7:29a (1:lxiii).
70. See also Nicholson, *Preaching to the Exiles*, pp. 38–71.
71. See e.g. J. Philip Hyatt, 'Jeremiah and Deuteronomy', *JNES* 1.2 (1942), pp. 156–173; see also Holladay, *Jeremiah* 2:53–63.
72. See e.g. McConville, *Prophets*, pp. 49–50. McConville also notes consistent theological differences between Jeremiah and the DH (*Judgment and Promise*, pp. 15–22).

The compositional history of the book of Jeremiah is complex. It is probable that it was built up over a lengthy period of time, extending beyond the lifetime of the prophet. A further complication is that the LXX version is around one-eighth shorter than the MT, and some of the material is ordered differently.[73] At one time it was thought that the LXX was an abbreviated version of the proto-MT, though discoveries at Qumran suggest that the LXX and MT reflect different editions of the Hebrew text.[74] It is often argued that the shorter text is earlier, and that this was later expanded and rearranged,[75] though a good case can be made, too, for the priority of the longer text.[76] The respective histories of the editions are not known; however, some prose sermons appear in the shorter edition, indicating that, even if it was the earlier text, by the time it was written some redaction had already taken place. Both editions appear to have been accepted as authentic, though the MT came to be given priority, and many commentators follow the MT, while noting key points of divergence in the LXX.

Notwithstanding these complications, it does not seem unreasonable to attribute most, if not all, of the prophetic content of the book to Jeremiah himself: either as his actual words or, in the case of some prose sermons, as an adaptation of his words by editors, possibly including Baruch, who sought to preserve the essence of his message.

Commentators also consider possible earlier influences on Jeremiah. One, in particular, is the prophecy of Hosea.[77] Both prophets use the picture of

---

73. In the LXX the oracles against the nations (Jer. 46 – 51) follow 25:13a, and are in a different order.

74. 4QJer[a] and 4QJer[c] are close to the MT; whereas 4QJer[b] is closer to the LXX. See Emmanuel Tov, 'The Literary History of the Book of Jeremiah in Light of Its Textual History', in *The Greek & Hebrew Bible: Collected Essays on the Septuagint*, VTSup 72 (Leiden: Brill, 1999), pp. 363–384; *Textual Criticism*, pp. 286–294.

75. See e.g. J. Gerald Janzen, *Studies in the Text of Jeremiah*, HSM 6 (Cambridge, Mass.: Harvard University Press, 1973).

76. E.g. Jack R. Lundbom, 'Haplography in the Hebrew *Vorlage* of LXX Jeremiah', in *Writing Up Jeremiah: The Prophet and the Book* (Eugene: Wipf & Stock, 2013), pp. 19–45; 'The Text of Jeremiah', in *Jeremiah Closer Up: The Prophet and the Book*, HBM (Sheffield: Sheffield Phoenix, 2010), pp. 1–9; Christopher R. Seitz, 'The Prophet Moses and the Canonical Shape of Jeremiah', *ZAW* 101.1 (1989), pp. 3–27.

77. See e.g. Thompson, *Jeremiah*, pp. 81–85; Lalleman, *Jeremiah in Prophetic Tradition*, pp. 225–232; McConville, *Judgment and Promise*, pp. 152–163. Holladay notes connections with Hosea (*Jeremiah* 2:44–45) as well as with other prophetic traditions

Israel as God's unfaithful wife, who has committed adultery by following other gods (2:2–3, 20; 3:1, 6–10, 14, 20; Hos. 1:2; 2:2–13). Both look at the days spent in the desert after leaving Egypt as an ideal time in that relationship (2:2–3; Hos. 2:14–15) and look forward to a new relationship with God that will recapture that early faithfulness (31:2; Hos. 2:14–15), and both describe that new relationship in terms of a new and better covenant (31:31–34; Hos. 2:16–23). Both prophets also use the picture of father and son to describe God's relationship with Israel (31:9; Hos. 11:1–4).

Structure and outline

The book of Jeremiah comprises a series of collections that have been put together over a long period of time. Some material has dates,[78] but is not arranged chronologically. Some commentators see a general pattern of judgment followed by salvation, in accordance with the prophet's commission 'to destroy and overthrow, to build and to plant' (1:10).[79] There is, though, little agreement on how to divide up the book. The following is one suggestion, based on the MT.

Outline

- Prologue: Jeremiah's call (1:1–19)
- Call to repentance and threat of judgment (2:1 – 6:30)
- Corruption of worship; Jeremiah's laments (7:1 – 10:25)
- Broken covenant; Jeremiah's inner conflict ('confessions') (11:1 – 20:18)
- Prophecies concerning Judah's leaders (21:1 – 24:10)
  - Kings (21:1 – 23:8)
  - Prophets (23:9 – 24:10)

(2:45–52). R. R. Wilson places Jeremiah and Hosea within a northern 'Ephraimite tradition', based on the Mosaic covenant; see Wilson, *Prophecy and Society*, pp. 135–252 (225–252). Though Cook questions whether this tradition was associated primarily with the north; see Cook, *Social Roots*, pp. 18–19; see also McConville, *Judgment and Promise*, pp. 163–171.

78. See e.g. LaSor, Hubbard and Bush, *OT Survey*, pp. 353–355; Longman and Dillard, *Introduction*, p. 341.

79. E.g. Allen, *Jeremiah*, pp. 12–14; Childs, *Introduction*, pp. 350–352. Elements of hope appear in e.g. 3:14–18; 12:14–17; 16:14–15; 23:5–8; 24:5–7; 27:22; 29:10–14, as well as in the so-called 'book of consolation' (30 – 33). It is also implicit in the oracles against the nations (46 – 51) and in Jehoiachin's release from prison (52:31–34).

- Judgment on the nations (25:1–38)
- Babylonian captivity anticipated; conflict with false prophets (26:1 – 29:32)
- 'Book of consolation' (30:1 – 33:26)
- Rejection of God's message and God's messenger (34:1 – 38:28)
- The last days of Judah (39:1 – 45:5)
- Oracles against the nations (46:1 – 51:64)
- Epilogue (52:1–34)

Main themes

In common with other classical prophets, Jeremiah emphasizes the failure of the nation, led by kings and prophets, to fulfil their covenant obligations. In Jeremiah 2:4–13 God brings a covenant lawsuit against his people;[80] and elsewhere coming judgment is viewed as the inevitable consequence of their failure to listen to, and obey, his word (e.g. Jer. 11:7–8; 13:8–11; 22:8–9; 40:2–3). Alongside the message of judgment, though, are glimpses of hope, emphasizing God's commitment to his people (e.g. 29:11) and promising restoration (e.g. 3:14–18; 23:5–8).[81] This culminates in the 'book of consolation', which includes the promise of a new covenant made with a renewed people (31:31–34; see also 24:7; 32:38–39).[82]

Jeremiah's message challenges false confidence in the temple (e.g. 7:1–15; 26:1–6). This was where, in the heart of Jerusalem, God had his throne, and because of that, and also because of his relationship with David, the city's founder, it was believed that God would protect Jerusalem from all attackers.[83] That had happened in Isaiah's day, and now, under threat from Babylon, the people expected the same. However, that earlier deliverance had come in response to faith and repentance; something lacking in Jeremiah's day. As a result, just as God had not spared Shiloh in the past, the temple, too, would become desolate (7:12–14; 26:6).

Jeremiah also calls the people to repent; to turn from their evil ways (e.g. 18:11; 23:22; 25:5; 26:3) and back to the Lord (e.g. 3:12, 14, 22; 4:1).[84] However,

---

80. See above, pp. 185–186.
81. See above, n. 79.
82. See above, p. 182.
83. For further discussion of what is sometimes termed 'Zion tradition', see e.g. McConville, 'Jerusalem in the OT', in Walker, *Jerusalem Past and Present*, esp. pp. 37–40; Routledge, *OT Theology*, pp. 268–269, 276–277.
84. 'Return' translates the frequently occurring Hebrew term *šûb*. For further discussion of the significance of this term in Jeremiah, see Lalleman, *Jeremiah and Lamentations*, pp. 37–40.

it seems that, because of the people's intransigence, there came a point in his ministry when judgment, in the form of exile, became inevitable, to the extent that the prophet was forbidden to intercede for the nation (11:14). Hope of restoration and renewal remains, but lies beyond the coming judgment.

False hope was encouraged by those who 'prophesy lies' (5:31; see also e.g. 6:13–14; 14:14–15; 23:25–26; 27:14–16; 29:8–9). 'Lies' translates the Hebrew term *šeqer*, which may also be rendered 'deceit' or 'falsehood'.[85] In particular, prophets were deceiving the people about the extent of their sin and the seriousness of its consequences:

> They dress the wound of my people
> as though it were not serious.
> 'Peace, peace,' they say,
> when there is no peace.
> (6:14; 8:11)

A characteristic of false prophets is God has not sent them (14:15; 23:21, 32), and consequently they prophesy by Baal (2:8; 23:13), or out of their own imagination (14:14; 23:16, 26). By contrast, Jeremiah receives his message from God, through access to the divine council (23:18, 22).[86] No doubt exacerbated by the actions of Judah's leaders (e.g. 5:31; 6:13; 8:8, 10; 23:14), falsehood is also characteristic of the nation as a whole. The people's relationship with God is a pretence (3:10). They trust in lies (28:15) and in the delusion of idolatry (3:23; 10:14; 13:25; 51:17), and there is also deceit and dishonesty in relationships within society (e.g. 5:2; 9:3–6).

Jeremiah also refers to the Davidic Messiah. This is not a major theme; maybe because Judah's priests and prophets had misrepresented God's promises to David. Nevertheless, there are references to the Branch, who will come from David's line, and will preside over a secure kingdom of justice and righteousness (23:5; 33:15); a hope that stands in sharp contrast to the failure of the last kings of Judah (cf. 22:11–30).

The Davidic covenant is also a basis for hope (33:21, 26), and its surety is linked with God's commitment to his 'covenant with day and night and the fixed

---

85. Jeremiah contains 37 of the 113 occurrences of *šeqer* in the OT. For further discussion, see e.g. W. Brueggemann, *Theology of the Book of Jeremiah*, pp. 66–70; Lalleman, *Jeremiah and Lamentations*, pp. 47–50; Thomas W. Overholt, *The Threat of Falsehood: A Study in the Theology of the Book of Jeremiah*, SBT 16 (London: SCM Press, 1970).

86. See above, p. 180, n. 195.

laws of heaven and earth' (33:25; cf. 33:20). This appears to allude to Genesis 8:22, which promises renewed stability in the created order after the flood, an event that represented a (partial) return to the pre-creation chaos of Genesis 1:2. For Jeremiah, the exile, which is the result of sin, also represents the reversal of creation (4:23–26) and a return to a world that is *tōhû wābōhû* (4:23; cf. Gen. 1:2).[87] However, God's commitment, both to creation and to his people, offers the hope of restoration and renewal.[88]

A significant element in the book of Jeremiah is what it reveals about the heart of the prophet. Although he challenged the people's sin, he was concerned for them, and felt pain over their plight (8:21 – 9:1; see also 4:19–22; 13:17; 14:17–18). In several communal laments, reminiscent of those found in the Psalms,[89] Jeremiah cries out on behalf of the nation (e.g. 14:2–9, 19–22). Jeremiah's 'confessions',[90] which take the form of individual laments, reveal an inner struggle with his calling. He complains about hostility and rejection (11:19; 15:10; 18:18, 20; 20:10), and calls on God to deliver him and judge his enemies (11:20; 12:3; 15:15; 17:18; 18:21–23). He complains that God has deceived him (15:18; 20:7), and that by remaining faithful to his calling (15:16; 17:16) he has endured hardship, while the wicked prosper (12:1–2). And yet he knows that he has no choice but to persevere with what seems a thankless ministry (20:9).

Ezekiel[91]

Date, authorship and composition

According to 1:2, Ezekiel received his call in Babylon,[92] around 593 BC (the 'fifth year of the exile of King Jehoiachin'). He is described as a priest (1:3), and that

---

87. See above, p. 117.

88. Routledge, 'Cursing and Chaos', in Moo and Routledge, *Earth Endures*, pp. 83–87.

89. On psalms of lament see above, pp. 154–155.

90. Jer. 11:18–23; 12:1–6; 15:10–21; 17:14–18; 18:18–23; 20:7–18. For further discussion, see e.g. Walter Baumgartner, *Jeremiah's Poems of Lament* (Sheffield: Almond, 1987); Collins, *Introduction*, pp. 363–365; A. R. Diamond, *The Confessions of Jeremiah in Context: Scenes of Prophetic Drama* (Sheffield: JSOT Press, 1987); Lalleman, *Jeremiah and Lamentations*, pp. 51–54; Jack R. Lundbom, 'The Confessions of Jeremiah', in *Jeremiah Closer Up*, pp. 75–103.

91. Commentaries on Ezekiel include Leslie C. Allen, *Ezekiel*, 2 vols., WBC 28, 29 (Dallas: Word, 1986, 1990); Joseph Blenkinsopp, *Ezekiel*, IBC (Louisville: John Knox, 1990); Daniel I. Block, *Ezekiel*, 2 vols., NICOT (Grand Rapids: Eerdmans,

accounts for his particular concern for the purity of the temple and its worship. Ezekiel was among the first wave of those taken into captivity (597 BC), indicating that he had some prominence in the community, and that seems to have continued among the exiles (8:1; 14:1; 20:1).

Ezekiel's visionary experiences and extreme behaviour (e.g. 3:1–3, 24–27 [cf. 33:22]; 4:4–15; 5:1–4; 24:15–18) have sometimes been associated with psychological phenomena.[93] Certainly, Ezekiel's behaviour is stranger than most. However, as Taylor notes, 'for a prophet a certain degree of "abnormality" was

---

1997, 1998); LaMar Eugene Cooper, *Ezekiel*, NAC 17 (Nashville: B&H, 1994); Peter C. Craigie, *Ezekiel*, DSB (Edinburgh: St. Andrew; Louisville: John Knox, 1983); Iain M. Duguid, *Ezekiel*, NIVAC (Grand Rapids: Zondervan, 1999); Walther Eichrodt, *Ezekiel*, OTL (London: SCM Press, 1970); Moshe Greenberg, *Ezekiel 1–37*, 2 vols., AB 22, 22A (New York: Doubleday, 1983, 1997); Paul M. Joyce, *Ezekiel* (London: T&T Clark, 2007); John B. Taylor, *Ezekiel*, TOTC (Leicester: Inter-Varsity Press, 1969); Steven Tuell, *Ezekiel*, NIBCOT/UBC (Peabody: Hendrickson, 2009); Walther Zimmerli, *Ezekiel*, 2 vols., Hermeneia (Philadelphia: Fortress, 1979, 1983). See also Daniel I. Block, *By the Chebar River: Historical, Literary, and Theological Studies in Ezekiel* (Eugene: Cascade, 2013); *Beyond the River Chebar: Studies in Kingship and Eschatology in the Book of Ezekiel* (Eugene: Cascade, 2013); Michael A. Lyons, *An Introduction to the Study of Ezekiel* (London: Bloomsbury T&T Clark, 2015); Henry McKeating, *Ezekiel*, OTG (Sheffield: Sheffield Academic Press, 1993).

92. The detailed description of events in Jerusalem (8 – 11) and some oracles, especially in 1 – 24, being directed against Jerusalem, have led to the view that some of Ezekiel's ministry was in Judah. Blenkinsopp suggests that knowledge of Pelatiah's death (11:13) may not be consistent with an exclusively Babylonian location, and allows the possibility of some ministry in Judah (*Ezekiel*, p. 27). That knowledge, though, may be attributed to divine revelation.

93. For further discussion, see e.g. Edwin C. Broome Jr., 'Ezekiel's Abnormal Personality', *JBL* 66 (1946), pp. 277–292; Stephen Garfinkel, 'Another Model for Ezekiel's Abnormalities', *JANES* 19 (1989), pp. 39–50; David J. Halperin, *Seeking Ezekiel: Text and Psychology* (University Park: Pennsylvania State University Press, 1993); John J. Schmitt, 'Psychoanalyzing Ezekiel', in J. Harold Ellens and Wayne G. Rollins (eds.), *Psychology and the Bible: A New Way to Read the Scriptures*, vol. 2: *From Genesis to Apocalyptic Vision* (Westport: Praeger, 2004), pp. 185–201; David Jobling, 'An Adequate Psychological Approach to the Book of Ezekiel', in Ellens and Rollins, *Psychology and the Bible*, pp. 203–213; David G. Garber Jr., 'Traumatizing Ezekiel, the Exilic Prophet', in Ellens and Rollins, *Psychology and the Bible*, pp. 215–235.

normal'.[94] It is important to emphasize, too, that the text views this as prophetic symbolism, and, in fact, Ezekiel demonstrates a remarkable degree of control in carrying out God's instructions, in order to communicate his message effectively to his audience.

The first serious question about the authorship and unity of the book came in 1924, when Hölscher claimed that only one-seventh of the book (around 170 verses) was original to Ezekiel; the rest, made up largely of the prose sections, was added in the fifth century BC. Torrey went further, viewing the whole book as a literary invention from the third century BC.[95]

More recent scholarship, though, attributes most of the text to Ezekiel or his followers. In his influential commentary Zimmerli points to an original, pre-canonical text, which has then been developed by a 'school' of disciples.[96] He views the additional material as commentary on the primary text. Childs agrees that there has been some redaction, which he suggests is closely in line with the original message. In his view this is part of the canonical shaping of the book, and, against Zimmerli, maintains that the whole text should be regarded as primary.[97] Allen suggests that some redactional material sets the prophecies in historical context, and may be attributed to Ezekiel himself. Other material is a literary expansion of the oracles, and some of that, too, may be the work of Ezekiel.[98] Also, because it is unclear which material is from Ezekiel, and which is from redactors, it seems possible that most, if not all, of the text may be attributed to the prophet himself.[99] If there was a final shaping of the book, it is likely to have been during the exilic period, since there is no indication that a return to Jerusalem has taken place.[100]

---

94. Taylor, *Ezekiel*, p. 26. For criticism of the psychoanalytical approach, see also Block, *Ezekiel*, 1:10–12; Zimmerli, *Ezekiel*, 1:17–18.
95. For a summary of discussion of authorship, see e.g. Childs, *Introduction*, pp. 357–360; McKeating, *Ezekiel*, pp. 30–61; Zimmerli, *Ezekiel*, 1:3–8.
96. Zimmerli, *Ezekiel*, 1:68–74. However, see R. E. Clements, 'The Ezekiel Tradition: Prophecy in a Time of Crisis', in Richard Coggins, Anthony Phillips and Michael Knibb (eds.), *Israel's Prophetic Tradition: Essays in Honour of Peter Ackroyd* (Cambridge: Cambridge University Press, 1982), pp. 119–136.
97. Childs, *Introduction*, pp. 360–361.
98. Allen, *Ezekiel*, 1:xxv; 2:xxv–xxvii.
99. E.g. Block, *Ezekiel*, 1:17–23; Greenberg, *Ezekiel 1–37*, 1:26–27; Taylor, *Ezekiel*, pp. 13–20.
100. Zimmerli suggests that 40 – 48 may have been added just before the return from exile (*Ezekiel*, 2:553).

Commentators have noted links between Ezekiel and other traditions. One such is the Holiness Code (H).[101] Some suggest that Ezekiel was its author, though it seems more likely that Ezekiel and any subsequent redactors were aware of, and were influenced by, material that formed the basis of H.[102] There may also be influences from other parts of the Priestly writings, from Deuteronomy and from earlier prophetic traditions, including Jeremiah.[103]

There is an issue with the text of Ezekiel. There are several differences between the MT and the LXX, which is around 4% to 5% shorter. Some have taken this to suggest that there were two editions of the underlying Hebrew text;[104] though many of the differences may be due to issues of transmission.[105] Greenberg criticizes the tendency among some scholars to assume that the shorter text must be original and who then try to reconstruct the MT on the basis of it.[106] It cannot be assumed, either, that the MT is always correct; nevertheless, as the only complete Hebrew text we have,[107] it seems reasonable to give it general priority, while recognizing the importance of other ancient versions, including the LXX.

Structure and outline

The book of Ezekiel is organized around a detailed, historical (though non-chronological), framework (see Table 8.1, overleaf).

---

101. See above, p. 243.
102. See e.g. Zimmerli, *Ezekiel*, 1:46–52; see also Michael A. Lyons, 'Transformation of Law: Ezekiel's Use of the Holiness Code (Leviticus 17–26)', in William A. Tooman and Michael A. Lyons (eds.), *Transforming Visions: Transformations of Text, Tradition, and Theology in Ezekiel*, Princeton Theological Monograph Series 127 (Eugene: Wipf & Stock, 2010), pp. 1–32.
103. Keith W. Carley, *Ezekiel Among the Prophets: A Study of Ezekiel's Place in Prophetic Tradition*, SBT 2.31 (London: SCM Press, 1975); McKeating, *Ezekiel*, pp. 92–98; Zimmerli, *Ezekiel*, 1:41–46.
104. See e.g. Emmanuel Tov, 'Recensional Differences Between the Masoretic Text and the Septuagint of Ezekiel', in *Greek and Hebrew Bible*, pp. 397–410.
105. One possibility is that words and ideas might have been misunderstood by later copyists; see e.g. Block, *Ezekiel*, 1:41–42; Taylor, *Ezekiel*, pp. 47–48. See also Lawrence Boadt, 'Textual Problems in Ezekiel and Poetic Analysis of Paired Words', *JBL* 97.4 (1978), pp. 489–499.
106. Moshe Greenberg, 'The Use of the Ancient Versions for Interpreting the Hebrew Text: A Sampling from Ezekiel ii 1 – iii 11', in *Congress Volume: Göttingen 1977*, VTSup 29 (Leiden: Brill, 1978), pp. 131–148.
107. Ibid., p. 147.

Table 8.1

		Day	*Month*	*Year*	
1:1	Ezekiel's call	5	4	30	
1:2–3	Ezekiel's call	5	(4)	5	July 593
8:1	Vision of idolatry in the temple	5	6	6	September 592
20:1	Visit by elders	10	5	7	August 591
24:1	Revelation of the siege of Jerusalem	10	10	9	January 588
26:1	Oracle against Tyre	1		11	587/586
29:1	Oracle against Egypt	12	10	10	January 587
29:17	Egypt will fall to Babylon	1	1	27	April 571
30:20	Revelation of Pharaoh's defeat	7	1	11	April 587
31:1	Oracle to Pharaoh	1	3	11	June 587
32:1	Lament over Pharaoh	1	12	12	March 585
32:17	Lament over Egypt	15	(12)	12	March 585
33:21	News of the fall of Jerusalem received	5	10	12	January 585
40:1	Vision of the new temple	10	1	25	April 573

Apart from 1:1, these all date from the year Jehoiachin was taken into exile (597 BC). The 'thirtieth year' in 1:1, which appears to parallel the fifth year of Jehoiachin's exile (1:2), is problematic, though probably refers to the prophet's age at his call.[108] If 30 was the minimum age for service as a priest (Num. 4:30; 1 Chr. 23:3), this might have particular significance for Ezekiel.

The book falls into three sections. Chapters 1–24 are set before the fall of Jerusalem and focus on divine judgment. This section includes Ezekiel's call to be a watchman (3:16–21), and also describes God's glory leaving the temple (10 – 11). The second section, chapters 25–32, is made up of oracles against the nations, and offers reassurance of God's power to eventually restore his people. The final section, chapters 33–48, relates to the aftermath of the fall of Jerusalem. Ezekiel's call to be a watchman is repeated (33:7–9), the glory of God returns to a renewed temple (43:1–12), and the people are given hope of a new beginning in a restored land.

Outline

- Judgment on Jerusalem (1:1 – 24:27)
  - Ezekiel's call (1:1 – 3:15)
  - Messages of judgment (3:16 – 7:27)
  - Idolatry in the temple: God's glory departs (8:1 – 11:25)
  - Messages of judgment (12:1 – 24:27)

108. See Allen, *Ezekiel*, 1:20–21; Zimmerli, *Ezekiel*, 1:113–114.

- Oracles against the nations (25:1 – 32:32)
- Jerusalem's fall and future (33:1 – 48:35)
  - Challenge and promise (33:1 – 37:28)
  - Gog and Magog: future security (38:1 – 39:29)
  - New temple; new Jerusalem: God's glory returns (40:1 – 48:35)

Main themes

One of Ezekiel's key tasks was to support and encourage the exilic community through what was a traumatic time in the nation's history. However, as a priest he was aware of the sinfulness of the people and their leaders, and while he gives a message of hope and of new beginnings, he is also clear about the national failure that has led to the exile.

A significant theme for Ezekiel is God's glory, which is closely linked with the divine presence. When the tabernacle and later the temple were consecrated, they were filled with 'the glory of the LORD' (Exod. 40:34–35; 1 Kgs 8:11), signifying his presence among his people. Ezekiel was made aware of God's glory in his inaugural vision (1:28; 3:12, 23), and in his later vision of the temple, which recalls the earlier event (10:15–22), 'the glory of the LORD' is again central (8:4; 9:3; 10:4, 18–19; 11:22–23).[109] God's glory, and thus his presence, is depicted as leaving the temple because of the corruption there, and the similarity of language suggests that God is present, instead, among the exiles. However, the glory that left the temple, and which Ezekiel saw by the Kebar River, will return to fill the new temple (43:1–5) and restore God's presence among his people (43:9; 48:35b). God's glory is also revealed in his judgment on the nations (28:22; 39:21).

Closely associated with God's glory, is his holiness.[110] In line with his priestly background Ezekiel presents Israel's sin as profaning what is holy, and being or becoming unclean.[111] This is primarily linked with disregarding God's ordinances, especially with regard to the Sabbath,[112] and idolatry;[113] though

---

109. 'The glory of the God of Israel' (8:4; 9:3; 11:22) parallels 'the glory of the LORD' in 11:22–23.

110. See above, p. 288. In his judgment on Sidon, God displays both his holiness and his glory (28:22).

111. The terms *ḥālal* (to profane) and *ṭāmē'* (to be/become unclean, defile) occur around twenty and thirty times respectively.

112. E.g. 5:11; 14:11; 20:13, 16, 18–21, 24; 22:8; 23:38–39; 44:7.

113. E.g. 20:7, 18, 31; 22:3–4; 23:7, 30; 36:18; 37:23.

disobedience and moral failure are also noted.[114] The nation's leaders are implicated in this (34:2–6). Priests do not distinguish between what is holy and what is not (22:26; cf. 44:23); false prophets (13:1–23; 22:28) and elders (11:1–3) mislead the people. In keeping with this idea of sin as uncleanness, restoration is described in terms of cleansing.[115]

The people are also charged with profaning or defiling God's (holy) name (20:39; 36:20–23; cf. 39:7; 43:7–9). This is particularly seen in relation to the exile. The defeat of those who are known as God's people brings God's name into disrepute. In the past he bore with their sins for the sake of his name (20:8–9, 14, 22), but he has now allowed the exile as a step towards their rehabilitation. God's continued concern for the holiness of his name will, though, also result in the people's ultimate restoration and renewal.

Related to God's concern for his name,[116] a further key feature of Ezekiel's prophecy is that the objects of divine action in judgment or salvation will 'know that I am the Lord'. This 'recognition formula' occurs over fifty times in the book,[117] and emphasizes that God will act decisively in the lives of his people and of the surrounding nations to fulfil his sovereign purposes.

As indicated, the promise of future restoration and renewal is also an important element in the book. Though the people feel that hope has gone, they will be brought back from exile (37:1–14). The divided kingdoms will be reunified under the Davidic Messiah (37:22–25; see also 34:23–24).[118] And the people will be renewed, and enabled to obey God's laws (36:26–27). The appearance of the covenant formula 'you will be my people, and I will be your God' (36:28) sets

114. E.g. 11:6; 20:18, 43; 22:3, 11–13, 29; 36:17–18.

115. The verb *ṭāhēr*, which relates to ritual cleansing/purification, is used in e.g. 24:13; 36:25, 33; 37:23; 43:26; see also 22:15, 17–22.

116. See e.g. Alex Luc, 'A Theology of Ezekiel: God's Name and Israel's History', *JETS* 26.2 (1983), pp. 137–143.

117. E.g. 7:27; 13:14; 16:62; 20:20; 29:6; 33:29; 37:6, 13; 38:23; 39:28. This is over two-thirds of the total number of occurrences in the OT. The similar expression 'know that I am the Sovereign Lord', which is unique to Ezekiel, occurs a further five times (e.g., 13:9b). See e.g. Dexter Callender Jr., 'The Recognition Formula and Ezekiel's Conception of God', in Paul M. Joyce and Dalit Rom-Shiloni (eds.), *The God Ezekiel Creates*, LBS (London: Bloomsbury T&T Clark, 2015), pp. 71–86; Zimmerli, *Ezekiel*, 1:36–40.

118. The future Davidic ruler is described as a 'prince' (*nāśî'*) in 34:24; 37:25 (though cf. 37:24, where he is referred to as 'king' [*melek*]). The ruler in 44 – 48 is also a *nāśî'*, and this, too, may refer to the Messiah.

the promise of renewal within a covenantal framework, which appears to parallel Jeremiah's promise of the New Covenant.[119] Also, in language that echoes Hosea 2:18, Ezekiel refers to a future 'covenant of peace' (34:25; 37:26). The restored temple points to the restoration of pure worship in the coming kingdom. And the allocation of land to the twelve tribes, recalling the original settlement in Canaan, promises a new beginning. A new start may be indicated, too, in allusions to the garden of Eden. Ezekiel 28:13–14 identifies the mountain of God with Eden,[120] and the river that flows from the temple (47:1–12; cf. Ps. 46:4) may also recall the river that flows from Eden (Gen. 2:10).[121] This new beginning will also be marked by new security in the land, with the removal of all threats to God's people, symbolized by the armies of Gog (chs. 38 – 39).[122]

Another key idea for Ezekiel is individual responsibility.[123] This was also noted by Jeremiah, though is developed further by Ezekiel (18:1–32; see also 3:17–21; 14:12–23; 33:1–20). The proverb 'The fathers have eaten sour grapes, and the children's teeth are set on edge' (Jer. 31:29; Ezek. 18:2–3) appears to

---

119. See Daniel I. Block, 'Prophet of the Spirit: The Use of *rwḥ* in the Book of Ezekiel', *JETS* 32.1 (1989), pp. 27–49 (39); 'The View from the Top: The Holy Spirit in the Prophets', in Firth and Wegner, *Presence*, pp. 175–207 (196–197); Routledge, 'Spirit and the Future', in Firth and Wegner, *Presence*, pp. 357–358.

120. The downfall of the king of Tyre appears to be described in mythological language relating to the expulsion of Adam from Eden. Some also see a priestly allusion. For further discussion, see e.g. Gregory K. Beale, 'Eden, the Temple, and the Church's Mission in the New Creation', *JETS* 48.1 (2005), pp. 5–31; Block, *Ezekiel*, 2:99–120; Donald E. Gowan, *When Man Becomes God: Humanism and Hubris in the Old Testament* (Eugene: Pickwick, 1975), pp. 69–91; Norman C. Habel, 'Ezekiel 28 and the Fall of the First Man', *CTM* 38 (1967), pp. 516–524; Carol A. Newsom, 'A Maker of Metaphors: Ezekiel's Oracle Against Tyre', in Gordon, *The Place Is Too Small*, pp. 191–204.

121. See e.g. Beale, 'Eden', pp. 8–10; Martha Himmelfarb, *Between Temple and Torah*, Texts and Studies in Ancient Judaism 151 (Tübingen: Mohr Siebeck, 2013), pp. 11–15; Jon Douglas Levenson, *Theology of the Program of Restoration of Ezekiel 40–48*, HSM 10 (Missoula: Scholars Press, 1976), pp. 25–53.

122. Some take this to refer to an eschatological battle between God and Antichrist prior to the messianic kingdom, anticipated in Ezek. 40 – 48 (e.g. Cooper, *Ezekiel*, p. 240). In my view it is better to see this as figurative, indicating the removal of future threats.

123. See also e.g. Collins, *Introduction*, pp. 383–385; Barnabas Lindars, 'Ezekiel and Individual Responsibility', *VT* 15.4 (1965), pp. 452–467; Herbert G. May, 'Individual Responsibility and Retribution', *HUCA* 32 (1961), pp. 107–120; cf. Deut. 24:16.

have been used to evade responsibility for the exile, which was the fault of previous generations, and particularly of Manasseh (cf. 2 Kgs 21:10–15; 24:3–4), and to question God's justice (Ezek. 18:25). Ezekiel, like Jeremiah, emphasizes that 'The soul who sins is the one who will die' (Ezek. 18:4; cf. Jer. 31:30). Conversely, righteousness brings personal salvation (18:19; cf. 14:12–20); there is hope for the individual, and in the light of that Ezekiel urges the people to make the right choices (18:31–32).

The Twelve (Minor Prophets)

The designation 'minor prophets' relates more to their size, than to their significance. It seems likely that they were brought together to fill a scroll and, maybe, to prevent some of the shorter texts from being lost.[124] Nevertheless, early descriptions of the canon count them as one book.[125] Also, some of the shorter books with only a single subject, such as Obadiah and Nahum, appear limited in scope and significance, and some argue that they fit better as part of a wider collection, rather than as prophetic books in their own right. This has led to the conclusion that the 'book of the twelve' should be read as a redactional unity, in which editors have assembled texts by different writers.[126] However, in the cases of Isaiah, Jeremiah and Ezekiel there is some agreement that those

124. E.g. *b. B. Bat.* 14b.

125. See above, p. 23, n. 5.

126. See e.g. Rainer Albertz, James D. Nogalski and Jakob Wöhrle (eds.), *Perspectives on the Formation of the Book of the Twelve: Methodological Foundations – Redactional Processes – Historical Insights*, BZAW 433 (Berlin: de Gruyter, 2013); R. J. Coggins, 'The Minor Prophets – One Book or Twelve?', in Stanley E. Porter, Paul Joyce and David E. Orton (eds.), *Crossing the Boundaries: Essays in Biblical Interpretation in Honour of Michael D. Goulder* (Leiden: Brill, 1994), pp. 57–68; T. Collins, *The Mantle of Elijah: The Redaction Criticism of the Prophetic Books* (Sheffield: Sheffield Academic Press, 1993), pp. 59–87; Collins, *Introduction*, pp. 440–441; Paul R. House, *The Unity of the Twelve* (Sheffield: Sheffield Academic Press, 1990); Joy Philip Kakkanattu, *God's Enduring Love in the Book of Hosea*, FAT 2.14 (Tübingen, Mohr Siebeck, 2006), pp. 181–183; James D. Nogalski, *Literary Precursors to the Book of the Twelve*, BZAW 217 (Berlin: de Gruyter, 1993); James D. Nogalski and Marvin A. Sweeney (eds.), *Reading and Hearing the Book of the Twelve* (Atlanta: Society of Biblical Literature, 2000); Paul L. Redditt and Aaron Schart (eds.), *Thematic Threads in the Book of the Twelve*, BZAW 325 (Berlin: Walter de Gruyter, 2003).

who edited the material were developing and reapplying the prophet's message. In the case of the 'twelve' there is no such unifying element, and any theory of its composition as a single book is a matter of speculation.[127]

One common theme, the Day of the Lord, is present in most of the books, and the expectation of a new order in Malachi 4:5–6 provides a fitting conclusion to the collection. The references to Moses and Elijah may also serve to link Malachi and the Minor Prophets with other parts of the canon.[128] Hosea has also been placed first in the collection,[129] even though, chronologically, Amos was earlier. Joel appears to have been placed next to Amos because of similar language (e.g. 3:16 [cf. Amos 1:2]; 3:18 [cf. Amos 9:13]). Obadiah's position after Amos might have been influenced by the reference to Edom in Amos 9:12. This suggests a possible thematic structure of the twelve books,[130] though that is very different from arguing that they have a more developed compositional unity.[131] While recognizing the possibility of an overall canonical structure, the following discussion treats the Minor Prophets as twelve distinct texts.

Hosea[132]

Date, authorship and composition

Hosea prophesied in the northern kingdom from around the middle of the eighth century BC. While there is no reference to the fall of the northern

---

127. See David L. Petersen, *The Prophetic Literature: An Introduction* (Louisville: Westminster John Knox, 2002), pp. 169–170.

128. Collins, *Introduction*, pp. 440–441; Petersen, *Prophetic Literature*, p. 212.

129. In the Talmud this is based on its translation of Hos. 1:2, 'God *first* spoke to Hosea' (*b. B. Bat.* 14b).

130. House argues for a threefold structure: Hosea–Micah focuses on sin; Nahum–Zephaniah sets out the consequences of sin; and Haggai–Malachi points to restoration (*Unity*, pp. 63–109). He does not, though, explain how the 'book' came to be compiled into its present form.

131. Their different ordering in the LXX may suggest a different structural agenda; see John Barton, *Joel and Obadiah*, OTL (Louisville: Westminster John Knox, 2001), pp. 116–117.

132. Commentaries on Hosea include Elizabeth Achtemeier, *Minor Prophets I*, NIBCOT/UBC (Peabody: Hendrickson, 1999); Francis I. Andersen and David Noel Freedman, *Hosea*, AB 24 (New York: Doubleday, 1980); J. Andrew Dearman, *Hosea*, NICOT (Grand Rapids: Eerdmans, 2010); Duane A. Garrett, *Hosea, Joel*, NAC 19a (Nashville:

kingdom to Assyria (722/721 BC), it is anticipated, suggesting that material in the book may run up to around 725 BC. The reference to God's punishing the house of Jehu (1:4) points to a start date for the book's content of just before the death of Jeroboam II, around 755–750 BC. This makes Hosea a later contemporary of Amos, in the north, and his ministry might also have overlapped with the early preaching of Isaiah.

There is some agreement that the book, though primarily from Hosea, received its final canonical shape in Judah after the fall of Samaria.[133] Several passages refer to Judah. Some indict both Israel (or Ephraim) and Judah (e.g. 5:5, 13–14; 6:4; 12:2) and are likely to be part of Hosea's own preaching. Others (e.g. 1:7, 11; 4:15) are regarded as editorial,[134] as is the reference to the Davidic king (3:5). The opening verse, which focuses on kings of Judah, also appears to be a later addition. As noted earlier, Hosea has several points of contact with Deuteronomy.[135] This suggests either that Hosea knew Deuteronomy, or that those responsible for the compilation and transmission of the book might have been forerunners of the later Deuteronomic movement.[136]

There are a great many textual problems in Hosea. This may be partly due to variations in dialect between Israel, where it originated, and Judah, where it was compiled. The primary text remains the consonantal MT, though this sometimes needs to be repointed.

Structure and outline

Hosea is frequently divided into three sections. Chapters 1–3 focus on Hosea's family life, which becomes a metaphor for God's relationship with Israel.

(*Footnote 132 cont.*) B&H, 1997); David Allan Hubbard, *Hosea*, TOTC (Leicester: Inter-Varsity Press, 1989); G. A. F. Knight, *Hosea*, TBC (London: SCM Press, 1960); James Limburg, *Hosea–Micah*, IBC (Louisville: Westminster John Knox, 1988); A. A. Macintosh, *Hosea*, ICC (Edinburgh: T&T Clark, 1997); James Luther Mays, *Hosea*, OTL (London: SCM Press, 1969); Daniel J. Simundson, *Hosea, Joel, Amos, Obadiah, Jonah, Micah*, AbOTC (Nashville: Abingdon, 2005); Gary V. Smith, *Hosea, Amos, Micah*, NIVAC (Grand Rapids: Zondervan, 2001); Douglas Stuart, *Hosea–Jonah*, WBC 31 (Waco: Word, 1987); Hans Walter Wolff, *Hosea*, Hermeneia (Philadelphia: Fortress, 1974); Ehud Ben Zvi, *Hosea*, FOTL 21A.1 (Grand Rapids: Eerdmans, 2005).

133. E.g. Childs, *Introduction*, pp. 377–380; Collins, *Introduction*, p. 323.

134. However, as Stuart observes, if some references to Judah are authentic, why not all of them? (*Hosea–Jonah*, pp. 14–15).

135. Above, p. 249.

136. E.g. Wolff, *Hosea*, p. xxxi.

Chapters 4–14 can be divided into two sets of oracles relating to Israel (and Judah). Wolff suggests that each section has a parallel structure, moving 'from accusation to threat, and then to the proclamation of salvation'.[137]

Outline

- Hosea's marriage: Israel as God's unfaithful wife (1:1 – 3:5)
- Oracles relating to sinful Israel (4:1 – 11:11)
  - Challenge to the people and leaders (4:1 – 7:16)
  - Corruption of true worship (8:1 – 11:11)
- Past ingratitude; future hope (11:12 – 14:9) [12:1 – 14:10][138]

Main themes

Hosea appears to come closer to the NT than any other OT book in depicting the heart-felt love of God for his people, and his gracious commitment, despite their waywardness and sin, to their ultimate well-being. This is seen in the repeated movement from accusation and threat of judgment to the promise of salvation. It is also seen in the two models of the intimate relationship between God and Israel: Israel as God's bride (1 – 3), and Israel as God's son (11:1–4).

Hosea, like Jeremiah, regards the Sinaitic covenant as a marriage bond between Yahweh and Israel.[139] And both idealize the early days of that relationship in the desert (2:15; Jer. 2:2). For Hosea, things began to go wrong in Canaan, and he refers specifically to Achan's sin after the capture of Jericho (2:15; cf. Josh. 7:1–26). The real issue for Hosea, though, was the increasing worship of Baal, which seems to have included the assimilation of Canaanite ideas and cultic practices into the worship of Yahweh. By Hosea's day the worship of Baal and associated Canaanite gods, described collectively as 'Baals', was widespread, and if Yahweh was worshipped at all it was as one of these Baals. Hosea sees such false worship as spiritual adultery against Yahweh. And this is the subject of the prophetic symbolism in chapters 1–3.

There is some debate about the status of Hosea's wife, described in 1:2 as *'ēšet zĕnûnîm* (literally, 'wife of harlotries'), prior to their marriage. Some suggest that

---

137. Ibid., p. xxxi.
138. English and Hebrew chapter divisions vary: 2:1 = 1:10 (Heb.); 11:12 = 12:1 (Heb.); 13:16 = 14:1 (Heb.).
139. There is no reason to doubt the authenticity of Hosea's references to the covenant between God and Israel. For further discussion of the date of the covenant concept in Israel, see above, pp. 121–123. See also John Day, 'Pre-Deuteronomic Allusions to the Covenant in Hosea and Psalm LXXVIII', *VT* 36.1 (1986), pp. 1–12.

she was a shrine prostitute:[140] a woman whose profession characterized the spiritual adultery into which Israel has fallen. Others argue that she was a woman of known promiscuous tendencies.[141] Another suggestion is that the term simply refers to any woman from what has become an adulterous nation,[142] or perhaps one who has submitted to Israel's current (heathen) bridal rites.[143] Another possibility may be that this description is retrospective. Hosea discovered Gomer's unfaithfulness only later,[144] possibly after the birth of their second or third child.[145] This fits better with Hosea's idealized picture of the beginning of the Yahweh–Israel relationship. Chapter 2 then applies the acted parable to the relationship between God and Israel. Israel's adultery will result in punishment and a breakdown in the marriage, but God's commitment to his people will seek after his bride and open the way for the relationship to be restored. He will lead her back into the desert, the place of new beginnings (2:14), and will transform past failure into hope for the future (2:15). He will establish a new covenant (2:16–20) and reverse the judgment implied in the names of Hosea's children (2:22–23). Hosea then acts out that promise of forgiveness, hope and continued love, as he seeks after and takes back his adulterous wife (3:1–3).[146]

Hosea also uses the picture of God as Israel's father (11:1–4). And here, again, we have an insight into God's feelings for his wayward people. We see something of the pain of the father, who has done everything for his son, even teaching him to walk, but who is ultimately rejected. This, too, opens the way for judgment (11:5–7), but the nature of the relationship and the character of God also emphasize the hope of eventual restoration (11:8–11).

A key element in that relationship is the Hebrew term *ḥesed*,[147] which the NIV translates as 'love' (2:19; 4:1; 6:4; 12:6), 'unfailing love' (10:12) and 'mercy' (6:6).

---

140. E.g. Mays, *Hosea*, pp. 25–26.
141. E.g. E. Achtemeier, *Minor Prophets I*, p. 5; Dearman, *Hosea*, pp. 365–366; Limburg, *Hosea–Micah*, p. 2; Smith, *Hosea, Amos, Micah*, pp. 27–28.
142. E.g. Stuart, *Hosea–Jonah*, p. 12; see also Wolff, *Hosea*, pp. 13–14.
143. Wolff, *Hosea*, pp. 14–15.
144. E.g. D. H. Hubbard, *Hosea*, pp. 54–55; G. A. F. Knight, *Hosea*, pp. 27–29.
145. Only the first of Gomer's children is specifically referred to as Hosea's (1:3); see G. A. F. Knight, *Hosea*, pp. 44–46.
146. Viewing this as a different woman (e.g. Stuart, *Hosea–Jonah*, pp. 65–66) seems to miss the point of the symbolism.
147. See further Robin Routledge, '*Ḥesed* as Obligation: A Re-examination', *TynBul* 46.1 (1995), pp. 188–191; *OT Theology*, pp. 108–110; see also e.g. Gordon R. Clark, *The Word Ḥesed in the Hebrew Bible*, JSOTSup 157 (Sheffield: Sheffield Academic Press, 1993).

Ḥesed includes the ideas of kindness and mercy, but also of loyalty and obligation. In the OT it occurs primarily within relationships based on a covenant. It expresses God's loving commitment to his people, and their right response in terms of love and obedience towards God, and right relationships within society. This was, though, all too fleeting (6:4). This inward commitment contrasts with the mechanistic approach to sacrifice characteristic of Baal-worship (6:6),[148] and will be at the heart of the new covenant relationship between God and his people (2:19). Other key terms in Hosea include faithfulness and righteousness. These, too, are relational, and both are closely related to *ḥesed*.[149]

Joel[150]

Date, authorship and composition

The position of Joel in the canon, between the eighth century BC prophecies of Hosea and Amos, has led to an assumption that it has a similar date. The text, though, gives no clear indication of its historical context. There are some clues.[151] Israel has been 'scattered ... among the nations' (3:2). This suggests a date after the fall of Jerusalem, though it may possibly refer to deportations by the Assyrians.[152] References to the temple (e.g. 1:13–14, 16; 2:17) indicate a time after, or not long before, its restoration around 515 BC. Wolff argues that the city walls had also been completed (cf. 2:7, 9), implying a date after

148. See Routledge, 'Sacrifice, Prayer and Forgiveness'.
149. See Routledge, '*Ḥesed* as Obligation'.
150. Commentaries on Joel include E. Achtemeier, *Minor Prophets I*; Allen, *Joel, Obadiah, Jonah, Micah*; David W. Baker, *Joel, Obadiah, Malachi*, NIVAC (Grand Rapids: Zondervan, 2006); Barton, *Joel and Obadiah*; James L. Crenshaw, *Joel*, AB 24C (New York: Doubleday, 1995); Garrett, *Hosea, Joel*; David Allan Hubbard, *Joel and Amos*, TOTC (Leicester: Inter-Varsity Press, 1989); Limburg, *Hosea–Micah*; Simundson, *Hosea, Joel, Amos, Obadiah, Jonah, Micah*; Stuart, *Hosea–Jonah*; Wolff, *Joel and Amos*. See also Elie Assis, *The Book of Joel: A Prophet Between Calamity and Hope* (London: Bloomsbury, 2013); Rex Mason, *Zephaniah, Habakkuk, Joel*, OTG (Sheffield: JSOT Press, 1994); Willem S. Prinsloo, *The Theology of the Book of Joel*, BZAW 163 (Berlin: de Gruyter, 1985).
151. See e.g. Allen, *Joel, Obadiah, Jonah, Micah*, pp. 19–24; Longman and Dillard, *Introduction*, pp. 411–414.
152. E.g. Stuart, *Hosea–Jonah*, pp. 225–226.

445 BC.[153] Though Allen notes that substantial sections of the wall remained before then, and prefers a date in the late sixth century BC.[154] Thus, while a post-exilic date seems likely, precisely when, in the century or so after the return, is not clear.

There is also some debate about the unity of the text. Some argue that the first part of the book, 1:1 – 2:27, is a prophecy relating to the effects and aftermath of a literal locust swarm; while the second part, 2:28 – 3:21,[155] is an eschatological reinterpretation by a later writer.[156] It has also been suggested that 3:4–8 does not fit with its immediate context. Nevertheless, several commentators accept the text as the work of a single prophet, though maybe with minor editorial elements.[157]

A significant feature of Joel's prophecy is its use of earlier traditions. According to Wolff, there are three main areas: the Day of the Lord (e.g. 1:15; 2:1, 11; cf. Zeph. 1 – 2; Isa. 13; Ezek. 30; Obadiah; Mal. 3 – 4), oracles against the nations (3:2–16; cf. Jer. 46; 49 – 51; Ezek. 29 – 32; 35) and references to the enemy from the north (2:20; cf. Jer. 4 – 6; Ezek. 38 – 39). In addition, there are several sentences and phrases that appear to have been quoted directly (e.g. 2:32 [cf. Obad. 17]; 3:16 [cf. Amos 1:2]; 3:18 [cf. Amos 9:13]).[158] This, though, is not simply recycling material, but reapplying important traditions to the new situation that confronts Joel and the nation.

---

153. Wolff, *Joel and Amos*, pp. 4–6 (4). Wolff argues for a date in the first half of the fourth century BC. See also Barton, *Joel & Obadiah*, pp. 14–18 (17).

154. Allen, *Joel, Obadiah, Jonah, Micah*, p. 24.

155. In the Hebrew text 2:28–32 (EVV) is numbered 3:1–5; and 3:1–21 (EVV) becomes 4:1–21.

156. This view was developed by Duhm. For recent expressions, see e.g. Barton, *Joel & Obadiah*, pp. 5–14 (13–14); Blenkinsopp, *History of Prophecy*, pp. 229–230; Childs, *Introduction*, pp. 389–392. Childs argues that the book is a redactional unity.

157. E.g. Allen, *Joel, Obadiah, Jonah, Micah*; D. A. Hubbard, *Joel and Amos*, pp. 31–34; Stuart, *Hosea–Jonah*, pp. 226–227; Wolff, *Joel and Amos*.

158. Wolff, *Joel and Amos*, pp. 10–11; see also D. A. Hubbard, *Joel and Amos*, p. 24. For further discussion of intrabiblical allusions and quotations, see e.g. Michael Fishbane, *Biblical Interpretation in Ancient Israel* (Oxford: Clarendon, 1985), esp. pp. 345–347; Richard L. Schultz, *The Search for Quotation: Verbal Parallels in the Prophets*, JSOTSup 180 (Sheffield: Sheffield Academic Press, 1999); John Strazicich, *Joel's Use of Scripture and Scripture's Use of Joel: Appropriation and Resignification in Second Temple Judaism and Early Christianity* (Leiden: Koninklijke Brill, 2007), pp. 35–162.

Structure and outline

Commentators note the close structure of the book. Those who argue for a prophecy in the aftermath of a locust swarm followed by its eschatological reinterpretation divide the book at 2:27. Taking a more unified view of the text, a better division is at 2:17, which ends the lament and opens the way for the promise of deliverance, which continues from 2:18.

Within this broad structure 1:2–12 corresponds with 2:1–11, 1:13–20 with 2:12–17, 2:18–27 with 3:1–12, and 2:28–32 with 3:13–21. Similarly across the two parts the call to repentance (2:12–17) results in a promise of deliverance (2:18–27), the day of darkness (2:1–11) becomes a day of blessing and salvation (2:28–32), and the scarcity of food (1:2–20) is balanced with the promise of abundant provision (3:17–21).

Outline

- Introduction (1:1)
- Locust swarm and the Day of the Lord (1:2 – 2:17)
  - The locust swarm (1:2–20)
  - The Day of the Lord (2:1–17)
- Promise of deliverance (2:18 – 3:21)
  - Present and future blessings (2:18–32) [2:18 – 3:5]
  - Judgment on the nations; deliverance for Judah (3:1–21) [4:1–21]

Main themes

The key emphasis of the book of Joel is the promise of future hope following the threat of judgment, and subsequent repentance. After describing the destruction of what appears to be a literal locust swarm (1:2–12), the corresponding passage (2:1–11) reconfigures this in vivid, poetic language, and links it with divine judgment associated with the Day of the Lord. The common expectation was that this was the occasion when God would break into world history, defeat his enemies, establish his kingdom and exalt his people. Joel, like Amos and Zephaniah, challenges that view: judgment on that day will also include God's people.[159] However, after the call to repent and return to the Lord (2:12–17; cf. 1:13–20), Joel reverses the expectation again. The Day of the Lord will indeed bring deliverance to God's people and judgment on their enemies (2:28–32; 3:13–16). Joel 2:18–27 also has the character of covenant renewal. The term itself does not appear, but there are aspects of the covenant formula in 2:27.

---

159. See above, p. 182.

The future blessings promised to God's people include the pouring out of the Spirit on 'all people' (2:28–29; cf. Acts 2:17–18). In the wider OT the Spirit is associated with inspired individuals, including prophets and kings. In the coming era of salvation, though, the Spirit will be available to all. This suggests that all of God's people may know his renewing and enabling power (cf. Ezek. 36:26–28). The link with divine revelation may also indicate a new intimacy with God, paralleling the promise associated with Jeremiah's new covenant, in which all people will have direct access to God (Jer. 31:34).[160]

Amos[161]

Date, authorship and composition

Amos was from Tekoa, in Judah, though his ministry was in the northern kingdom, mainly focused around the sanctuary at Bethel. He asserts that he was 'neither a prophet nor a prophet's son' (7:14), indicating, probably, that he was not part of a formal prophetic group and so owed no allegiance to the religious establishment. According to 1:1, he prophesied during the reigns of Jeroboam II and Uzziah. There is also a reference to an earthquake (cf. Zech. 14:5). Internal evidence, therefore, points to a date for Amos' ministry of 765–745 BC.[162]

The date of the book is more difficult to determine. Wolff suggests several stages of compilation.[163] Amos' original oracles, comprising largely chapters

---

160. See Routledge, 'Spirit and the Future', in Firth and Wegner, *Presence*, pp. 354–356; see also Erika Moore, 'Joel's Promise of the Spirit', in ibid., pp. 245–256.

161. Commentaries on Amos include E. Achtemeier, *Minor Prophets I*; Francis I. Andersen and David Noel Freedman, *Amos*, AB 24A (New York: Doubleday, 1989); Duane A. Garrett, *Amos: A Handbook on the Hebrew Text* (Waco: Baylor University Press, 2008); D. A. Hubbard, *Joel and Amos*; Jörg Jeremias, *Amos*, OTL (Louisville: Westminster John Knox, 1998); Limburg, *Hosea–Micah*; James L. Mays, *Amos*, OTL (London: SCM Press, 1969); Shalom M. Paul, *Amos*, Hermeneia (Philadelphia: Fortress, 1991); Simundson, *Hosea, Joel, Amos, Obadiah, Jonah, Micah*; Billy K. Smith, 'Amos', in Billy K. Smith and Frank S. Page, *Amos, Obadiah, Jonah*, NAC 19b (Nashville: B&H, 1995), pp. 23–170; G. Smith, *Hosea, Amos, Micah*; Wolff, *Joel and Amos*; Stuart, *Hosea–Jonah*. See also M. Daniel Carroll R., *Amos – The Prophet and His Oracles* (Louisville: Westminster John Knox, 2002); Möller, *Prophet In Debate*.

162. See e.g. D. A. Hubbard, *Joel and Amos*, pp. 89–90; Jeremias, *Amos*, pp. 1–2; Wolff, *Joel and Amos*, pp. 89–90.

163. Wolff, *Joel and Amos*, pp. 106–113; see also Jeremias, *Amos*, pp. 5–9; Mays, *Amos*, pp. 12–14.

3–6, were written down, and other material, including most of 1:3 – 2:16, 7:1–8, 8:1–2 and 9:1–4, were added. An early Amos 'school' was then responsible for 1:1 and 7:9–17. These strata belong to the eighth century BC and go back, essentially, to Amos himself. A Josianic redaction then added the (positive) view of Zion/Jerusalem (1:2), material against Bethel (3:14; 4:4; 5:5–6; cf. 2 Kgs 23:15) and a number of hymnic elements (4:13; 5:8–9; 9:5–6). Oracles against Tyre (1:9–10), Edom (1:11–12) and Judah (2:4–5) and the expansion of the oracle against Israel (2:10–12) are from a later Deuteronomistic redaction. Finally, 9:11–15 is a post-exilic promise of hope.

Much of this, though, rests on circular comparisons with what are deemed 'genuine' oracles, or assumptions about when particular material might have originated, and the evidence is not compelling.[164] Some material, such as the third-person insertions, is clearly editorial. But it is by no means improbable that the rest may go back to Amos, and even that Amos might have been involved in the editorial process.[165] This may suggest that the book was compiled within a few years of Amos' ministry.

Structure and outline

After the introduction (1:1–2) the book is generally divided into three or four sections.[166] Oracles against the nations (1:3 – 2:16) appear to form a single rhetorical unit, and include Israel (and Judah) among the nations under God's judgment. This is followed by further judgment on Israel. Three oracles are introduced by 'Hear this word' (3:1; 4:1; 5:1),[167] and two by 'Woe to' (5:18; 6:1).

---

164. Thus 1:2 is deemed editorial because its language and ideas are not used elsewhere by Amos (Wolff, *Joel and Amos*, pp. 124–125); but that argument is circular. Oracles in 1:9–12, 2:4–5 have a slightly different pattern from others in 1:3 – 2:16 (ibid., pp. 139–140). But it seems more likely that a redactor would keep the same formula; and thus any variation is by Amos himself. Passages relating to the destruction of Bethel are dated during Josiah's reign (2 Kgs 23:15), and this has been linked to popular traditions about Amos (v. 17) (ibid., p. 111); but Amos could have prophesied Bethel's destruction. See e.g. Longman and Dillard, *Introduction*, pp. 426–428; D. A. Hubbard, *Joel and Amos*, pp. 96–102; McConville, *Prophets*, pp. 165–166.

165. E.g. Andersen and Freedman, *Amos*, pp. 74–75.

166. However, see James Limburg, 'Sevenfold Structures in the Book of Amos', *JBL* 106.2 (1987), pp. 217–222.

167. Boyle argues that 3:1 – 4:13 follow the pattern of a 'covenant lawsuit'; see Marjorie O'Rourke Boyle, 'The Covenant Lawsuit of the Prophet Amos: III 1 – IV 13', *VT* 21.3 (1971), pp. 338–362; see above, pp. 185–186.

Judgment continues in five visions (7:1 – 9:10), before the final message of hope.

Outline

- Introduction (1:1–2)
- Oracles against the nations, including Judah and Israel (1:3 – 2:16)
- Oracles against Israel (3:1 – 6:14)
  - 'Hear this word' (3:1 – 5:17)
  - 'Woe to . . .' (5:18 – 6:14)
- Visions (7:1 – 9:10)
- Promise of restoration (9:11–15)

Main themes

As we have noted, Amos challenges the social and religious sin of the nation.[168] This was compounded by national complacency. The people assumed that, as God's elect, they would be spared the judgment that was coming on the rest of the world. This false confidence might have been linked to the general prosperity during Jeroboam's reign, which could have been interpreted as a sign of divine favour. Amos flatly rejects such misplaced confidence. Israel has, indeed, been chosen by God, but that makes the people more, not less, accountable (3:2). There is no specific reference to God's covenant with Israel in Amos. However, it is implicit in references to 'my people' (e.g. 7:8, 15; 8:2), which forms a key part of the covenant formula, and to the exodus (2:10; 3:1–2; 9:7).[169] Israel's failure, particularly to maintain justice and righteousness (e.g. 2:6–7; 5:7, 12, 24; 6:12) is thus, essentially, a breach of their covenant relationship with God.[170] And this might provide the basis for a covenant lawsuit. Ultimately, though, God's commitment to his people will result in their restoration (9:11–15).

Israel's unique status is challenged at the start and towards the end of the book. They may be God's people, but God has an interest, too, in other nations.

---

168. See above, pp. 180–183.

169. See e.g. E. Achtemeier, *Minor Prophets I*, pp. 167–169; D. A. Hubbard, *Joel and Amos*, pp. 111–113; Frank H. Seilhamer, 'The Role of Covenant in the Mission and Message of Amos', in Howard N. Bream, Ralph D. Heim and Carey A. Moore (eds.), *A Light unto My Path: Old Testament Studies in Honor of Jacob M. Myers* (Philadelphia: Temple University Press, 1974), pp. 435–451; however, see Joseph Jensen, *Ethical Dimensions of the Prophets* (Collegeville: Liturgical Press, 2006), pp. 70–71.

170. As with Hosea (above, p. 311, n. 139), there is no reason God's relationship with Israel might not be viewed as a covenant in the eighth century BC.

In 1:3 – 2:3 Israel's neighbours are held accountable to God for their misdeeds,[171] and in this context Israel and Judah are just two more sinful nations (cf. 9:8), under the judgment of the God of the whole earth. Consequently, the Day of the Lord, to which they look forward, will provide no comfort (5:18–20). In 9:7 the exodus, an event crucial to Israel's self-understanding as the people of God, is compared with the migrations of the Syrians and Philistines. This is intended to challenge Israel's complacency.[172] But it also indicates God's involvement in the history of other nations, and that may provide the basis for their accountability in 1:3 – 2:3.[173]

Obadiah[174]

Obadiah's twenty-one verses make it the shortest OT book. It is directed against Edom, the nation descended from Esau (Gen. 36), and therefore viewed as having a 'brotherly' relationship with Israel and Judah (10, 12; cf. Num. 20:14; Amos 1:11). However, there was also a history of animosity between the two

---

171. See e.g. Barton, *Amos's Oracles*; see also Routledge, *OT Theology*, pp. 247–248. For discussion of a possible link between these nations and David's empire (cf. 9:11), see Christensen, *Transformations*, pp. 71–72; John Mauchline, 'Implicit Signs of a Persistent Belief in the Davidic Empire', *VT* 20.3 (1970), pp. 287–303; John Priest, 'The Covenant of Brothers', *JBL* 84.4 (1965), pp. 400–406.
172. See Gary V. Smith, 'Continuity and Discontinuity in Amos' Use of Tradition', *JETS* 34.1 (1991), pp. 33–42 (39–40).
173. See e.g. Walter Brueggemann, *Texts That Linger: Words That Explode* (Minneapolis: Fortress, 2000), pp. 89–103; Routledge, *OT Theology*, pp. 317–318; 'Exodus', in Fox, *Reverberations*, pp. 197–198; 'Creation and Covenant: God's Direct Relationship with the Non-Israelite Nations in the Old Testament' (forthcoming).
174. Commentaries on Obadiah include E. Achtemeier, *Minor Prophets I*; Allen, *Joel, Obadiah, Jonah, Micah*; David W. Baker, 'Obadiah', in David W. Baker, T. Desmond Alexander and Bruce K. Waltke, *Obadiah, Jonah and Micah*, TOTC (Leicester: Inter-Varsity Press, 1988), pp. 17–44; *Joel, Obadiah, Malachi*; Barton, *Joel and Obadiah*; Limburg, *Hosea–Micah*; Paul R. Raabe, *Obadiah*, AB 24D (New York: Doubleday, 1996); Simundson, *Hosea, Joel, Amos, Obadiah, Jonah, Micah*; B. Smith, 'Obadiah', in Smith and Page, *Amos, Obadiah, Jonah*, pp. 171–202; Stuart, *Hosea–Jonah*; Hans Walter Wolff, *Obadiah and Jonah*, CC (Minneapolis: Fortress, 1986); Ehud Ben Zvi, *A Historical-Critical Study of the Book of Obadiah*, BZAW 242 (Berlin: de Gruyter, 1996).

peoples (e.g. Num. 20:14–21; 1 Sam. 14:47; 2 Sam. 8:11–12; 2 Kgs 8:20–22), and other prophets also announce judgment on Edom (e.g. Isa. 34:5–17; Jer. 49:7–22; Ezek. 25:12–14; Joel 3:19; Amos 1:11–12). The particular occasion for Obadiah's prophecy is thought to be Edom's role in the fall of Jerusalem (11–14; see also Ps. 137:7; Lam. 4:21–22).[175] Some argue that there is no evidence for Edom's direct involvement,[176] though Collins notes that there must have been some basis for the resentment felt towards Edom in connection with that event.[177] This suggests a date for the prophecy of shortly after 587 BC. We have no information about Obadiah himself, but it may be that he was an eyewitness of the destruction of Jerusalem.

Obadiah has affinities with other prophetic books. Its position immediately after Amos in the Hebrew text may be because of the reference to Edom in Amos 9:12. There are close similarities between 1–9 and Jeremiah 49:7–16, though it is difficult to determine the direction of dependence or if both depend on a third source.[178] And 15, 17 appear to be used in Joel 3:4; 2:32.

After a brief introduction to the prophet and his subject (1), the book contains oracles pronouncing divine judgment on Edom because of crimes against Judah (2–14, 15b).[179] It then extends that judgment to other nations, and promises that God's people will again occupy the land (15a, 16–21). Because this latter section has an eschatological aspect some argue that it is by a different writer. However, the book as it stands holds together as a unity. Edom has gloated over Judah's distress, something all the more blameworthy for a 'brother' (10, 12). At the hands of Edom and other nations Judah has experienced a day of disaster (11–14). However, in the future those nations will face the 'day of the LORD'; a day of reckoning, when what they have done to Judah and Jerusalem will come back on to their own heads (15). In that day the tables will be turned and God's people will be restored and vindicated.

175. Wolff, *Obadiah and Jonah*, pp. 18–19.

176. E.g. J. R. Bartlett, 'Edom and the Fall of Jerusalem, 587 BC', *PEQ* 114 (1982), pp. 13–24; see also Barton, *Joel and Obadiah*, pp. 120–122; Ben Zvi, *Obadiah*, pp. 236–239.

177. Collins, *Introduction*, p. 392.

178. See e.g. Allen, *Joel, Obadiah, Jonah, Micah*, pp. 131–133.

179. It is possible that the two parts of 15 have been transposed; e.g. ibid., p. 159, n. 16; Barton, *Joel and Obadiah*, p. 118; however, see D. W. Baker, 'Obadiah', in Baker, Alexander and Waltke, *Obadiah, Jonah and Micah*, pp. 24–25.

Jonah[180]

Date, authorship, purpose and composition

According to 2 Kings 14:25, Jonah son of Amittai prophesied in Israel during the reign of Jeroboam II. The book itself, though, is anonymous, and many argue that, although it mentions the historical figure, the narrative itself is not historical.[181] There are apparent inaccuracies.[182] And the subject matter, including the 'great fish' that swallowed Jonah (1:17) and the plant that sprang up overnight and disappeared just as quickly (4:6–7), seems the stuff of story rather than history. This does not require that the story is

---

180. Commentaries on Jonah include E. Achtemeier, *Minor Prophets I*; T. Desmond Alexander, 'Jonah', in Baker, Alexander and Waltke, *Obadiah, Jonah and Micah*, pp. 45–131; Allen, *Joel, Obadiah, Jonah, Micah*; James Bruckner, *Jonah, Nahum, Habakkuk, Zephaniah*, NIVAC (Grand Rapids: Zondervan, 2004); Terence E. Fretheim, *The Message of Jonah: A Theological Commentary* (Minneapolis: Augsburg, 1977); James Limburg, *Jonah*, OTL (Louisville: Westminster John Knox, 1993); *Hosea–Micah*; Frank S. Page, 'Jonah', in Smith and Page, *Amos, Obadiah, Jonah*, pp. 203–283; Jack M. Sasson, *Jonah*, AB 24B (New York: Doubleday, 1995); Uriel Simon, *Jonah*, JPSBC (Philadelphia: Jewish Publication Society, 1999); Simundson, *Hosea, Joel, Amos, Obadiah, Jonah, Micah*; Stuart, *Hosea–Jonah*. See also Thomas M. Bolin, *Freedom Beyond Forgiveness: The Book of Jonah Re-examined*, JSOTS 236 (Sheffield: Sheffield Academic Press, 1997); John Day, 'Problems in the Interpretation of the Book of Jonah', in A. S. van der Woude (ed.), *In Quest of the Past: Studies in Israelite Religion, Literature and Prophetism* (Leiden: Brill, 1990), pp. 32–47; Katharine J. Dell, 'Reinventing the Wheel: The Shaping of the Book of Jonah', in John Barton and David J. Reimer (eds.), *After the Exile: Essays in Honour of Rex Mason* (Macon: Mercer University Press, 1996), pp. 85–101; Jonathan Magonet, *Form and Meaning: Studies in Literary Techniques in the Book of Jonah* (Sheffield: Almond, 1983); Trible, *Rhetorical Criticism*; Ehud Ben Zvi, *Signs of Jonah: Reading and Rereading in Ancient Yehud*, JSOTSup (Sheffield: Sheffield Academic Press, 2003).

181. See e.g. Allen, *Joel, Obadiah, Jonah, Micah*, pp. 175–181, 186; Collins, *Introduction*, pp. 437–440; Fretheim, *Jonah*, pp. 61–72; McConville, *Prophets*, pp. 185–186. Limburg describes it as a 'didactic story' (*Jonah*, pp. 22–28).

182. Nineveh was not capital of Assyria during Jeroboam's reign, 'king of Nineveh' (3:6) is not an accurate term and the city's size (3:3) is exaggerated. Christensen suggests that 'Nineveh' may contain wordplay on the terms for 'fish' and 'Jonah'; see Duane Christensen, *Nahum*, AB 24F (New Haven: Yale University Press, 2009), p. 3.

unhistorical,[183] but nor is there anything to suggest that it may not be a parable, intended to convey a theological message.[184] Its interpretation does not turn, ultimately, on its historicity.[185]

The frequent use of two divine names, the Lord (Yahweh) and God (*'ĕlōhîm*), led some in the past to consider the presence of multiple sources, as in Pentateuchal criticism. In current scholarship, however, the only serious discussion relates to 2:2–9. Some commentators argue, on grounds of structure and content, that it is not part of the original text.[186] Others, though, argue for its inclusion.[187] In my view it is reasonable, with Allen, to view this as a hymn chosen by the narrator to express the prophet's thanks for having been saved from drowning.[188]

The purpose of the book is also unclear.[189] Some have viewed it as possibly a satirical tract against the rigid exclusivism of Ezra and Nehemiah, though there is nothing to relate it, directly, to that. It may offer an explanation for unfulfilled prophecy, but that does not appear to be its primary purpose. Another suggestion is the questioning of divine justice.[190] Jonah is opposed to the

---

183. Several commentators continue to argue in favour of historicity; see e.g. Alexander, 'Jonah', in Baker, Alexander and Waltke, *Obadiah, Jonah and Micah*, pp. 69–77; Page, 'Jonah', in Smith and Page, *Amos, Obadiah, Jonah*, pp. 209–219; Stuart, *Hosea–Jonah*, pp. 440–442.

184. In his reference to Jonah in Matt. 12:39–41 Jesus may be reflecting his audience's traditional understanding, rather than commenting on the historicity, of the source.

185. See e.g. LaSor, Hubbard and Bush, *OT Survey*, pp. 382–386; Longman and Dillard, *Introduction*, pp. 444–445.

186. E.g. Day, 'Problems', in van der Woude, *In Quest of the Past*, pp. 40–42; Trible, *Rhetorical Criticism*, pp. 157–173.

187. E.g. Allen, *Joel, Obadiah, Jonah, Micah*, pp. 181–185; Alexander, 'Jonah', in Baker, Alexander and Waltke, *Obadiah, Jonah and Micah*, pp. 63–69; Duane L. Christensen, 'The Song of Jonah: A Metrical Analysis', *JBL* 104 (1985), pp. 217–231; Limburg, *Jonah*, pp. 31–33; Sasson, *Jonah*, pp. 16–20.

188. Allen, *Joel, Obadiah, Jonah, Micah*, p. 184.

189. See e.g. Alexander, 'Jonah', in Baker, Alexander and Waltke, *Obadiah, Jonah, Micah*, pp. 81–91; Allen, *Joel, Obadiah, Jonah, Micah*, pp. 189–191; Ronald E. Clements, 'The Purpose of the Book of Jonah', *Congress Volume, Edinburgh* 1974, VTSup 28 (Leiden: Brill, 1975), pp. 16–28; G. M. Landes, 'The Kerygma of the Book of Jonah', *Int* 21 (1967), pp. 3–31; John H. Walton, 'The Object Lesson of Jonah 4:5–7 and the Purpose of the Book of Jonah', *BBR* 2 (1992), pp. 47–57.

190. E.g. Terence E. Fretheim, 'Jonah and Theodicy', *ZAW* 90 (1978), pp. 227–237.

forgiveness of the Ninevites, not primarily because they are foreigners, but because they deserve divine retribution, and Assyria's historical treatment of Israel would only have added to the sense of injustice. Nevertheless, God is concerned even about the people of Nineveh, and when there is true repentance they, too, may be forgiven. It is significant, in this context, that Jonah 4:2 restates a credal formula relating to Israel's orthodox faith (cf. Exod. 34:6–7), which includes the covenant term *ḥesed* and reapplies it to God's dealings with a non-Israelite nation.[191]

The lack of clarity with regard to the book's purpose makes it difficult to determine its setting and date. A common view is that it was written in the fifth or fourth century BC.[192]

Structure and outline

The book of Jonah appears to have a closely worked structure, both in the book as a whole, and within smaller sections.[193] The two main sections are introduced in the same way: 'the word of the LORD came to Jonah . . . "Go to the great city of Nineveh"' (1:1–2; 3:1–2), though with different outcomes.

Outline

- Jonah's first call (1:1 – 2:10) [1:1 – 2:11]
  - Jonah's call: disobedience (1:1–3)
  - Jonah's flight: sailors pay homage to the Lord (1:4–16)
  - Jonah's rescue (1:17) [2:1]
  - Jonah's prayer (praise); God's response (2:1–10) [2:2–11]
- Jonah's second call (3:1 – 4:11)
  - Jonah's call: obedience (3:1–3)
  - Jonah in Nineveh; Nineveh's repentance (3:4–10)
  - Jonah's anger (4:1)
    Jonah's prayer (complaint); God's response (4:2–11)

Main themes

We see, in Jonah, the sovereignty of God. Even though Jonah tries to evade responsibility, God, through various means, turns him around and brings him

191. See further Routledge, 'Mission and Covenant', in Grams et al., *Bible and Mission*, pp. 10–15; *OT Theology*, pp. 320–321; 'Creation and Covenant'.
192. See e.g. Allen, *Joel, Obadiah, Jonah, Micah*, pp. 185–191. References to Jonah in Tob. 14.4, 8 (fourth century BC) are tenuous.
193. See e.g. Allen, *Joel, Obadiah, Jonah, Micah*, pp. 197–200; Trible, *Rhetorical Criticism*.

to where he was called to be. The book also emphasizes God's interest in a non-Israelite nation. The use of the two divine names Yahweh and Elohim may reflect concern both for his covenant people and for the world he has created.[194] And we see, too, the significance of repentance. This is not, though, a missionary text: Jonah preaches only judgment. Nevertheless, there is an outworking of Jeremiah 18:7–8, that even where judgment has been announced, it can be averted by true contrition.[195]

Micah[196]

Date, authorship and composition

According to 1:1, Micah prophesied during the reigns of Jotham, Ahaz and Hezekiah (cf. Jer. 26:18–19 [Mic. 3:12]). Although some of the prophecy relates to Samaria, Micah, like Isaiah, of whom he would have been a contemporary, primarily addresses Judah and Jerusalem.

Although much of the text is ascribed to Micah, some commentators argue that the prophet's message, found predominantly in chapters 1–3, was supplemented and reapplied at the time of the Babylonian invasion, and again to the

194. The sailors first refer to Jonah's 'god' (*'ĕlōhîm*) (1:6). They acknowledge Yahweh (1:14–16) only after Jonah's explanation (1:9). While Jonah's dealings are generally with Yahweh, to the Ninevites he is 'God'. In 4:7–9 he is, again, 'God' even in his conversation with Jonah, maybe emphasizing the concern for the world that Jonah questions. That, though, cannot be divorced from God's relationship with Israel, and so he reappears as Yahweh in 4:10. See further Limburg, *Jonah*, pp. 45–46.

195. For discussion of God's 'relenting', see e.g. Routledge, *OT Theology*, pp. 251–254.

196. Commentaries on Micah include E. Achtemeier, *Minor Prophets I*; Allen, *Joel, Obadiah, Jonah, Micah*; Francis I. Andersen and David Noel Freedman, *Micah*, AB 24E (New York: Doubleday, 2000); Kenneth L. Barker, 'Micah', in Kenneth L. Barker and Waylon Bailey, *Micah, Nahum, Habakkuk, Zephaniah*, NAC 20 (Nashville: B&H, 1998); Limburg, *Hosea–Micah*; Mays, *Micah*; Simundson, *Hosea, Joel, Amos, Obadiah, Jonah, Micah*; G. Smith, *Hosea, Amos, Micah*; Ralph L. Smith, *Micah–Malachi*, WBC 32 (Waco: Word, 1984); Bruce K. Waltke, 'Micah', in Baker, Alexander and Waltke, *Obadiah, Jonah and Micah*, pp. 133–207; *Micah* (Grand Rapids: Eerdmans, 2007); Hans Walter Wolff, *Micah*, CC (Minneapolis: Augsburg Fortress, 1990); Ehud Ben Zvi, *Micah*, FOTL 21B (Grand Rapids: Eerdmans, 2000).

post-exilic community.[197] Achtemeier dates the final form of the book to sometime after 515 BC.[198] However, there is no consensus about the process of composition. Some commentators assume that hopeful elements would undermine the prophets' message of judgment, and so must be editorial. But in the attempt to persuade the people to turn back to God it seems reasonable to suppose prophets would offer hope beyond judgment.[199] According to Allen, the only passages that must be later than Micah are 4:6–8 and 7:8–20,[200] with the latter reflecting the book's liturgical use.[201] Waltke argues that these, too, could have originated with Micah in the eighth century BC.[202]

Micah also appears to have influenced Jeremiah (e.g. 3:5 [cf. Jer. 6:14]; 4:9–10a [cf. Jer. 4:31]; 7:5–6 [cf. Jer. 9:4–5; 12:6]). There is a very close correspondence, too, between 4:1–3 and Isaiah 2:2–4. There is debate about which is original or whether both draw from a common source. Another suggestion is that the material has been added to both books by a later redactor, though traditions attached to Jerusalem were probably already known in the eighth century BC.[203] While it is impossible to be certain, several scholars suggest that the text might have originated with Micah.[204]

Structure and outline

Whatever the conclusion with regard to the origin of its content, it seems clear that the book is the result of editing. Commentators are, though, divided as to its overall structure. Chapters 1–3 comprise, primarily, oracles of judgment, though this is broken by 2:12–13, which offers hope. Also, 1:2, 3:1 and 6:1 begin

---

197. See e.g. Rex Mason, *Micah, Nahum, Obadiah*, OTG (Sheffield: Sheffield Academic Press, 1991), pp. 43–54; Mays, *Micah*, pp. 21–33; Wolff, *Micah*, pp. 17–26.
198. E. Achtemeier, *Minor Prophets I*, p. 290.
199. E.g. Allen, *Joel, Obadiah, Jonah, Micah*, p. 251.
200. Ibid., pp. 241–253; see also Smith, *Micah–Malachi*, p. 6.
201. See also E. Achtemeier, *Minor Prophets I*, p. 287; Limburg, *Hosea–Micah*, p. 162.
202. Waltke, 'Micah', in Baker, Alexander and Waltke, *Obadiah, Jonah and Micah*, pp. 145–149; *Micah*, pp. 8–13.
203. See Allen, *Joel, Obadiah, Jonah, Micah*, pp. 243–244; Routledge, *OT Theology*, pp. 276–277. However, cf. Mason, *Micah, Nahum, Obadiah*, p. 49; Mays, *Micah*, pp. 95–96. Childs suggests that the book was put into its present shape by a similar group to those who edited the Isaiah corpus (*Introduction*, pp. 434–436).
204. E.g. Andersen and Freedman, *Micah*, p. 423; Waltke, 'Micah', in Baker, Alexander and Waltke, *Obadiah, Jonah and Micah*, pp. 170–175; see also Oswalt, *Isaiah 1–39*, pp. 115–116.

with the imperative 'hear' or 'listen' (Heb. *šimʿû*). This suggests a threefold structure, 1 – 2, 3 – 5, 6 –7, each incorporating alternating oracles of judgment and hope.[205]

Outline

- Heading (1:1)
- Judgment and hope (1:2 – 2:13)
  - – Judgment on Judah and Samaria (1:2 – 2:11)
  - – God will gather his scattered people (2:12–13)
- Judgment and hope (3:1 – 5:15)
  - – Indictment and punishment; Jerusalem destroyed (3:1–12)
  - – Deliverance and hope; Jerusalem exalted (4:1 – 5:15) [4:1 – 5:14]
- Judgment and hope (6:1 – 7:20)
  - – Judgment; God's case against Israel (6:1 – 7:7)
  - – Israel's future hope (7:8–20)

Main themes

Although the term 'covenant' does not appear in Micah, the relationship between God and his people, and obligations that result from it, is at the heart of the oracles of judgment and the promise of future hope. We have noted that 6:1–8 is in the form of a 'covenant lawsuit',[206] and the key covenant term *ḥesed* appears several times (6:8; 7:18, 20). References to 'my people' coming up out of Egypt and the incident with Balaam and Balak (6:3–5) recall the exodus, as does the idea of Israel as God's 'inheritance' (*naḥălâ*; 7:14, 18; cf. Deut. 4:20; 9:26, 29; 32:8–9), and also, maybe, the 'rest' that the people are not experiencing because of sin (2:10; cf. Deut. 12:9), something that may be reflected, too, in the reference to apportioning of the land 'by lot' (2:5; cf. Num. 26:55; 33:44; Josh. 14:2).

For Micah, as with other prophets, social and religious sin cannot be separated. He challenges leaders who have failed to maintain justice (3:1, 9), and calls for a right relationship with God that results in right relationships within the community of God's people (6:8). In place of leaders who lead God's people astray, in the future God himself will lead his flock (2:13; 4:7). And there is the

---

205. E.g. Allen, *Joel, Obadiah, Jonah, Micah*, pp. 257–261; Limburg, *Hosea–Micah*, pp. 159–162; Waltke, 'Micah', in Baker, Alexander and Waltke, *Obadiah, Jonah and Micah*, pp. 144–145, 150. Some include ch. 3 in the first section (e.g. Anderson and Freedman, *Micah*, p. 7; Mason, *Micah, Nahum, Obadiah*, pp. 13–15); Mays suggests a twofold structure (*Micah*, pp. 22–23).

206. See above, pp. 185–186.

well-known promise, too, of a ruler from Bethlehem (5:2–4). This was the city of David's birth, and so points to the Davidic Messiah,[207] who, in a further allusion to David, will also shepherd God's flock and bring security and peace (cf. Isa. 9:6–7; 11:6–9).

For Micah, Israel's God is also 'the Lord of all the earth' (4:13), and the judgment coming on God's people is set in the context of the coming world-judgment (1:2; cf. 5:15). The alternating themes of judgment and hope, as well as the nature of that judgment (e.g. 1:7; 5:10–14), indicate that God's aim for his people is their restoration. Judgment on the nations is part of that. Many nations will surround Jerusalem (4:11), maybe reflecting the Assyrian invasion of 701 BC, but those nations will be defeated (4:13), and Jerusalem will be delivered and exalted (cf. 4:6–8). The main emphasis of 4:1–4 seems to be the security and vindication of God's people: just as 'many nations' attacked Jerusalem so, in the coming days, 'many nations' will recognize its priority. Though there is also the suggestion that the nations may have a place in that coming kingdom.

Nahum[208]

Nahum focuses on God's judgment on Nineveh, and has, therefore, something in common with Jonah. Some readers find this pouring out of unmitigated divine wrath disturbing. It does, though, offer hope and comfort to God's people,[209] by signalling the end of Assyria's cruel oppression (e.g. 1:7–8, 12–13, 15). And

207. For more on the Davidic Messiah, see above, p. 290, n. 52.

208. Commentaries on Nahum include Elizabeth Achtemeier, *Nahum–Malachi*, IBC (Atlanta: John Knox, 1986); Wayne Bailey, 'Nahum', in Barker and Bailey, *Micah, Nahum, Habakkuk, Zephaniah*, pp. 137–243; David W. Baker, *Nahum, Habakkuk, Zephaniah*, TOTC (Leicester: Inter-Varsity Press, 1988); Bruckner, *Jonah, Nahum, Habakkuk, Zephaniah*; Christensen, *Nahum*; John Goldingay, 'Nahum, Habakkuk, Zephaniah', in J. Goldingay and P. Scalise, *Minor Prophets II*, NIBCOT/UBC (Peabody: Hendrickson, 2009), pp. 1–134; Tremper Longman III, 'Nahum', in Thomas Edward McComiskey (ed.), *The Minor Prophets* (Grand Rapids: Baker Academic, 2009), pp. 765–829; Julia M. O'Brien, *Nahum, Habakkuk, Zephaniah, Haggai, Zechariah, Malachi*, AbOTC (Nashville: Abingdon, 2004); J. J. M. Roberts, *Nahum, Habakkuk and Zephaniah*, OTL (Louisville: Westminster John Knox, 1991); Robertson, *Nahum, Habakkuk and Zephaniah*; Smith, *Micah–Malachi*. See also Mason, *Micah, Nahum, Obadiah*; Klaas Spronk, *Nahum* (Kampen: Pharos, 1997).

209. The name 'Nahum' means 'comfort'.

within the Twelve it is balanced by Jonah's message, that even Nineveh may be the object of God's *ḥesed*.[210] The absence of any criticism of Israel is, similarly, balanced by the message of other prophets within the Twelve, including Amos, Hosea and Habakkuk.

Nothing is known of the prophet, himself. The description 'Elkoshite' (1:1), suggests that he is from Elkosh, whose location is unknown, but might have been in Judah.[211]

The material is likely to have been edited into its current form. Its description as a 'book' (1:1), suggests that it circulated as written text, rather than as a collection of spoken oracles. It is generally dated between the fall of Thebes (3:8–10), in around 663 BC, and the fall of Nineveh in 612 BC, probably towards the end of that period.

It is widely recognized that 1:2–8, which takes the form of a hymn of praise, includes a partial acrostic.[212] Nine of the first eleven letters of the Hebrew alphabet appear in order in the MT, and some amend the text in an attempt to locate the missing letters.[213] Longman prefers to read it as an incomplete acrostic, signifying the chaos and cosmic upheaval that accompany divine judgment.[214]

Outline

- Heading (1:1)
- Psalm of praise to God (1:2–8)
- Judgment on Assyria, salvation for Judah (1:9 – 2:2) [1:9 – 2:3]
- Assyria defeated and humiliated (2:3–13) [2:4–14]
- 'Woe' oracle against Nineveh (3:1–19)

---

210. Christensen describes it as a literary complement to Jonah (*Nahum*, p. 2), and suggests that both offer Midrashic reflections on Exod. 34:6–7 (ibid., pp. 17–18).

211. See e.g. D. W. Baker, *Nahum, Habakkuk and Zephaniah*, p. 19; Christensen, *Nahum*, pp. 159–161; Roberts, *Nahum, Habakkuk, Zephaniah*; Robertson, *Nahum, Habakkuk, Zephaniah*, pp. 56–57; Smith, *Micah–Malachi*, p. 63.

212. See e.g. Bailey, 'Nahum', in Barker and Bailey, *Micah, Nahum, Habakkuk, Zephaniah*, pp. 164–165; Duane L. Christensen, 'The Acrostic of Nahum Reconsidered', *ZAW* 87.1 (1975), pp. 17–30; 'The Acrostic of Nahum Once Again: A Prosodic Analysis of Nahum 1:1–10', *ZAW* 99.3 (1987), pp. 409–415; Longman, 'Nahum', in McComiskey, *Minor Prophets*, pp. 773–775. For a more complicated literary, poetic and numerical analysis of the whole book, see Christensen, *Nahum*.

213. E.g. Roberts, *Nahum, Habakkuk, Zephaniah*, pp. 42–45.

214. Longman, 'Nahum', in McComiskey, *Minor Prophets*, p. 775; see also Thomas Renz, 'A Perfectly Broken Acrostic In Nahum 1?', *JHS* 9 (2009), pp. 1–26.

Habakkuk[215]

Date, authorship and composition

Habakkuk is not mentioned elsewhere in the OT, though does appear in the apocryphal *Bel and the Dragon* (33–39). His oracle is not dated, though the mention of 'Babylonians' or 'Chaldeans' (*kaśdîm*, 1:6) indicates a setting during the Neo-Babylonian Empire (626–539 BC). Their rapid advance (1:5–11) suggests a time after the fall of Nineveh (612 BC), though attacks on Judah are still future. This suggests a date near the end of the seventh century BC.

The book comprises complaints by Habakkuk (1:2–4, 12–17), each followed by God's response (1:5–11; 2:2–5), a series of 'woe' oracles (2:6–20) and a prayer (3:1–19), reminiscent of some psalms.[216] Habakkuk may have been associated with the temple,[217] and his words are set in the context of worship, though a temple connection is not certain. Chapter 3 is not present in a commentary on Habakkuk found at Qumran (1QpHab), leading to the suggestion that it may be a later addition. Most commentators, though, accept the structural unity of the book.

Outline

- Heading (1:1)
- Habakkuk's complaints and God's responses (1:2 – 2:5)
  - Habakkuk's first complaint (1:2–4)
  - God's response: the rise of Babylon (1:5–11)
  - Habakkuk's second complaint (1:12–17)
  - God's response (2:1–5)
- Woes against Babylon (2:6–20)
- Habakkuk's prayer of confidence in God (3:1–19)

---

215. For commentaries on Habakkuk, see on Nahum (above, n. 208); others include Francis I. Andersen, *Habakkuk*, AB 25 (New York: Doubleday, 2001); Wayne Bailey, 'Habakkuk', in Barker and Bailey, *Micah, Nahum, Habakkuk, Zephaniah*, pp. 245–378. See also Grace Ko, *Theodicy in Habakkuk* (Milton Keynes: Paternoster, 2014); Mason, *Zephaniah, Habakkuk, Joel*; Marvin A. Sweeney, 'Structure, Genre, and Intent in the Book of Habakkuk', *VT* 41.1 (1991), pp. 63–83.

216. 'Prayer' (*tĕpillâ*) appears in the titles of Pss 17; 86; 90; 102. 'Shigionoth' appears in the singular in Ps. 7:1.

217. E.g. Lindblom, *Prophecy*, p. 254; Sweeney, 'Structure', p. 70; R. R. Wilson, *Prophecy and Society*, p. 278.

Main themes

Habakkuk's complaints focus on how a holy God can tolerate wickedness (1:3, 13). In the first he questions God's apparent inaction. There is debate about the identity of the 'wicked' in 1:4. The usual interpretation is that these are from within Judah, and God's response is to bring judgment through Babylon. This leads to Habakkuk's second concern: that God is using a more wicked nation to punish Judah. God's response is that Babylon, too, will be judged, and that is further emphasized in the series of woes. Some identify the wicked in 1:4 with the Assyrians, though that would not lead to the concern expressed in 1:13. Sweeney suggests that it refers to Babylon, and God's response (1:5–11) is not a resolution of the problem, but rather a further statement of it.[218] However, identifying the wicked with Babylon (or Assyria) requires identifying Judah, as a whole, as 'righteous', and that seems unlikely in the light of Habakkuk's emphasis on divine holiness. The reference to paralysis of the law (1:4) also suggests an internal problem.

Part of the answer to Habakkuk's concern regarding divine justice is that, ultimately, the wicked will be punished, while 'the righteous will live by his faith [or faithfulness]' (2:4b, NIV mg.). There is possible ambiguity over the antecedent of 'his'.[219] The text may refer to God's faithfulness (the LXX reads 'my' instead of 'his').[220] However, it is more natural to relate it to the righteous, whose faithfulness to God will ensure that they enjoy life in the coming days. Faithfulness is sometimes viewed as trust in God,[221] in contrast to arrogant self-reliance (2:4a), and so is close in meaning to 'faith' (cf. Paul's use of 2:4 in Rom. 1:17). Habakkuk's prayer goes on to recognize God's glory and majesty, and expresses his trust in God even in the midst of difficulties.

Zephaniah[222]

Date, authorship and composition

According to 1:1, Zephaniah was the great-great grandson of Hezekiah. The

---

218. R. R. Wilson, *Prophecy and Society*, pp. 73–74.

219. See D. W. Baker, *Nahum, Habakkuk, Zephaniah*, pp. 60–61; McConville, *Prophets*, pp. 216–217.

220. Roberts relates this, instead, to the reliability of the vision (*Nahum, Habakkuk, Zephaniah*, pp. 105–112).

221. E.g. E. Achtemeier, *Micah–Malachi*, pp. 46–46; Robertson, *Nahum, Habakkuk, Zephaniah*, pp. 175–183.

222. For commentaries on Zephaniah, see on Nahum (above, n. 208); see also Wayne

text does not say, explicitly, that this is the king of Judah, though if not, why include the extended genealogy? The heading also places Zephaniah during the reign of Josiah, making him a contemporary of Nahum, Jeremiah and Habakkuk. Zephaniah is sometimes identified with a priest of the same name, who was killed by Nebuchadnezzar in 587 BC (2 Kgs 25:18–21).[223]

His ministry is usually placed before Josiah's reforms, since 1:4–9 notes idolatrous practices that the reforms sought to address. Some suggest that he might have been part of the group that influenced the changes.[224] However, there is a question about how thoroughgoing Josiah's reforms were,[225] and the reference to a 'remnant of Baal' (1:4b) may suggest that his attempts to eradicate Baal worship were less than successful. That allows the possibility of a date later in Josiah's reign, and some place him during the reign of Jehoiakim.[226] It used to be thought that a Scythian invasion (*c.*627 BC) prompted Zephaniah's expectation that Jerusalem would soon fall. More recently that has been questioned,[227] and those who argue for a later date suggest that attacks by Babylon provide a more likely scenario.[228] It is not always necessary, though, to relate prophetic messages of judgment to particular historical threats.

Commentators differ as to how much of the book to attribute to Zephaniah. Most critical scholars see evidence of post-exilic editing.[229] This includes some

---

Bailey, 'Zephaniah', in Barker and Bailey, *Micah, Nahum, Habakkuk, Zephaniah*, pp. 379–500; Adele Berlin, *Zephaniah*, AB 25A (New York: Doubleday, 1994). See also William L. Holladay, 'Reading Zephaniah with a Concordance: Suggestions for a Redaction History', *JBL* 120.4 (2001), pp. 671–684; Paul R. House, *Zephaniah: A Prophetic Drama*, JSOTSup 69 (Sheffield: JSOT Press, 1988); Ehud Ben Zvi, *A Historical-Critical Study of the Book of Zephaniah*, BZAW 198 (Berlin: de Gruyter, 1991).

223. E.g. Donald L. Williams, 'The Date of Zephaniah', *JBL* 82.1 (1963), pp. 77–88 (86–88).

224. E.g. E. Achtemeier, *Nahum–Malachi*, p. 62.

225. Above, p. 294; R. R. Wilson, *Prophecy and Society*, p. 281; see also Duane L. Christensen, 'Zephaniah 2:4–15: A Theological Basis for Josiah's Program of Political Expansion', *CBQ* 46 (1984), pp. 669–682.

226. See e.g. J. Philip Hyatt, 'The Date and Background of Zephaniah', *JNES* 7.1 (1948), pp. 25–29; Williams, 'Date'.

227. See e.g. Smith, *Micah–Malachi*, pp. 122–123; Williams, 'Date', pp. 79–81.

228. Smith suggests Assyria (*Micah–Malachi*, pp. 122–123), though that seems unlikely.

229. E.g. Childs, *Introduction*, p. 459. Ben Zvi sees the book as a post-monarchic composition reflecting little of Zephaniah's original message (*Zephaniah*).

elements of hope and more developed eschatological ideas,[230] though, as already noted, arguments of what may or may not be primary are often circular. References to a remnant (2:7, 9; 3:13) may suggest a date after the Babylonian exile, though the prospect of God's people being reduced to a remnant might have already been apparent in the eighth century BC (e.g. Isa. 10:20–23). Others consider that most of the text reflects Zephaniah's message.[231]

There are a number of points of contact with other OT books, including Jeremiah.[232] The direction of influence is not certain, though since many think that Zephaniah prophesied before Josiah's reforms while Jeremiah preached after them, it is a common view that Jeremiah used material from Zephaniah.

Outline

- Heading (1:1)
- The Day of the Lord (1:2 – 3:20)
  - Judgment on the world (1:2 – 2:15)
    - Reversal of creation (1:2–3)
    - Judgment on Judah and Jerusalem and all humankind (1:4–18)
    - Call for repentance (2:1–3)
    - Oracles against the nations (2:4–15)
  - Judgment and salvation for Jerusalem and the world (3:1–13)
  - Song of joy and promise of restoration (3:14–20)

Main themes

The major emphasis in the book of Zephaniah is the coming Day of the Lord. This is referred to in 1:7 – 2:3 and 3:8–13, though other material is closely related to it. As with Joel and Amos, that day will include judgment on the religious and social sin of God's people. However, while the prophet's primary interest is in Judah and Jerusalem, God's dealings with his people are set within the context of his dealings with the whole world, which is also subject to his judgment (e.g. 1:2–3,[233] 14–18; 2:4–15; 3:8).

---

230. E.g. Mason, *Zephaniah, Habakkuk, Joel*, pp. 44–54.

231. E.g. D. W. Baker, *Nahum, Habakkuk, Zephaniah*, pp. 86–88; Robertson, *Nahum, Habakkuk, Zephaniah*, pp. 38–40. House (*Zephaniah*) views the text as a literary unity, in the form of a dramatic dialogue between God and the prophet.

232. See Holladay, 'Reading Zephaniah'. Examples include houses being filled with deceit (*mirmâ*) (Zeph. 1:9; cf. Jer. 5:27), and future disaster as a 'loud crash' (Zeph. 1:10b) or 'terrible destruction' (Jer. 4:6), both translating the Hebrew *šeber gādôl*.

233. See above, p. 117.

As with Joel, however, if the people repent, the Day of the Lord also offers hope. A remnant of Israel will be brought home, Jerusalem will be restored and the people will know God's presence among them as their king (3:14–20). This will include judgment on Judah's enemies (e.g. 2:7, 9; 3:19). Though there is, too, the prospect of salvation for the nations (3:9–13), including what appears to be the reversal of the judgment at Babel (v. 9).[234]

Haggai[235]

Date, authorship and composition

Haggai, like Zechariah and Malachi, is set after the return from exile, and, particularly, in the period prior to the completion of the temple. The book comprises

---

234. See e.g. Phillip Michael Sherman, *Babel's Tower Translated: Genesis 11 and Ancient Jewish Interpretation* (Leiden: Koninklijke Brill, 2013), pp. 72–75; see also Berlin, *Zephaniah*, pp. 14, 133; D. W. Baker, *Nahum, Habakkuk, Zephaniah*, p. 115; Peter C. Craigie, *Twelve Prophets*, vol. 2, DSB (Edinburgh: St Andrew; Louisville: Westminster John Knox, 1985), p. 128.

235. Commentaries on Haggai include E. Achtemeier, *Nahum–Malachi*; Joyce G. Baldwin, *Haggai, Zechariah, Malachi*, TOTC (Leicester: Inter-Varsity Press, 1972); Mark J. Boda, *Haggai, Zechariah*, NIVAC (Grand Rapids: Zondervan, 2009); John Goldingay, 'Haggai', in Goldingay and Scalise, *Minor Prophets II*, pp. 135–178; Andrew Hill, *Haggai, Zechariah and Malachi*, TOTC (Nottingham: Inter-Varsity Press, 2012); Rex Mason, *The Books of Haggai, Zechariah and Malachi*, CBC (Cambridge: Cambridge University Press, 1977); Eugene H. Merrill, *Haggai, Zechariah, Malachi* (Chicago: Moody, 1994); Carol L. Meyers and Eric M. Meyers, *Haggai and Zechariah 1–8*, AB 25B (New York: Doubleday, 1987); O'Brien, *Nahum, Habakkuk, Zephaniah, Haggai, Zechariah, Malachi*; David L. Petersen, *Haggai & Zechariah 1–8*, OTL (Philadelphia: Westminster, 1984); Anthony R. Petterson, *Haggai, Zechariah, Malachi*, AOTC (Nottingham: Apollos, 2015); Paul L. Redditt, *Haggai, Zechariah, Malachi*, NCB (Grand Rapids: Eerdmans, 1995); Smith, *Micah–Malachi*; Richard A. Taylor, 'Haggai', in Richard A. Taylor and E. Ray Clendenen, *Haggai, Malachi*, NAC 21A (Nashville: B&H, 2004), pp. 23–201; Peter A. Verhoef, *The Books of Haggai and Malachi*, NICOT (Grand Rapids: Eerdmans, 1987). See also R. J. Coggins, *Haggai, Zechariah, Malachi*, OTG (Sheffield: Sheffield Academic Press, 1987); Janet E. Tollington, *Tradition and Innovation in Haggai and Zechariah 1–8*, JSOTSup 150 (Sheffield: Sheffield Academic Press, 1993).

four oracles, attributed to Haggai,[236] within a narrative framework that dates them to a five-month period in 520 BC, 'the second year of King Darius' (1:1).[237] Haggai's role is noted in Ezra 5:1, 6:14, though nothing is known about the prophet himself.[238]

Most commentators attribute the narrative sections to an editor. In an influential study Beuken argues that the editor shared the same religious and cultural background as the Chronicler, and that Zechariah 1 – 8 was composed in the same setting.[239] This suggests that the final form of the book is to be dated maybe a century after Haggai.[240] While there is some agreement regarding the link with Zechariah 1 – 8, several scholars argue that the material was compiled much closer to the time of the oracles, possibly by Zechariah.[241]

Outline

- Call to rebuild the temple: first oracle and response (1:1–15)
- Second oracle: the glory of the rebuilt temple (2:1–9)
- Third oracle: warning against unclean offerings; promise of blessing (2:10–19)
- Fourth oracle: God's choice of Zerubbabel (2:20–23)

---

236. Some suggest that 2:10–14 and 15–19 are unrelated, and were combined by an editor (e.g. Childs, *Introduction*, pp. 467–469); however, see e.g. Petersen, *Haggai & Zechariah 1–8*, pp. 87–88; Verhoef, *Haggai and Malachi*, pp. 112–114.
237. 'The first day of the sixth month' (1:1) = 29 August; 'the twenty-first day of the seventh month' (2:1) = 21 September; 'the twenty-fourth day of the ninth month' (2:10, 20) = 18 December.
238. For discussion of various views, see e.g. Smith, *Micah–Malachi*, pp. 146–147; Verhoef, *Haggai and Malachi*, pp. 3–8.
239. W. A. M. Beuken, *Haggai-Sacharja 1–8: Studien zur Überlieferungsgeschichte der frühnachexilischen Prophetie*, SSN 10 (Assen: Van Gorcum, 1967); however, cf. R. A. Mason, 'The Purpose of the "Editorial Framework" of Haggai', *VT* 27.4 (1977), pp. 413–421.
240. On the date of Chronicles see below, pp. 381–382.
241. E.g. Meyers and Meyers, *Haggai and Zechariah 1–8*, pp. xliv–xlviii; Tollington, *Tradition and Innovation*, pp. 23, 34, 47. See also Baldwin, *Haggai, Zechariah, Malachi*, pp. 29–30; Petterson, *Haggai, Zechariah and Malachi*, pp. 44–45; Taylor, 'Haggai', in Taylor and Clendenen, *Haggai, Malachi*, pp. 49–54.

Main themes

A key concern of Haggai is the rebuilding of the temple. The work began shortly after the return from exile, but stopped because of opposition (Ezra 4:24). Encouraged by Haggai and Zechariah, the work resumed in 520 BC (1:14–15; cf. Ezra 5:1–2), and included a ceremony to mark the laying of the foundation (2:18).[242] While the temple does not, in itself, guarantee blessing, it represents God's presence among his people, and building the temple indicates the people's willingness to put God at the centre of their life together, rather than focus on individual concerns (cf. 1:4).

It has been argued that, for Haggai, the rebuilding of the temple and the choice of Zerubbabel (cf. 2:20–23) marked the fulfilment of God's purposes for his people.[243] If so, Zerubbabel's subsequent disappearance from the scene suggests that Haggai was mistaken. In that case, though, it is difficult to see how he would retain his prophetic credibility.[244] It seems better to assign an eschatological, and maybe messianic, dimension to the prophecy, and to view the choice of Zerubbabel, who belonged to the Davidic house, as indicative of God's wider plan to restore the Davidic dynasty.[245]

Zechariah[246]

Date, authorship and composition

'Zechariah' could be translated 'God remembers', and is an appropriate name

242. This appears to conflict with Ezra 3:10–13, which some, then, regard as unhistorical. However, both are possible. The previous work had stopped, and it would not seem inappropriate to mark this new phase with a further ceremony. See Verhoef, *Haggai and Malachi*, pp. 129–130.
243. E.g. Hanson, *Dawn of Apocalyptic*, pp. 247–249.
244. However, see Robert P. Carroll, *When Prophecy Failed: Reactions and Responses to Failure in the Old Testament Prophetic Traditions* (London: SCM Press, 1979), esp. pp. 157–183; Collins, *Introduction*, pp. 419–420; Meyers and Meyers, *Haggai and Zechariah 1–8*, p. 84.
245. E.g. Taylor, 'Haggai', in Taylor and Clendenen, *Haggai, Malachi*, pp. 198–201; Verhoef, *Haggai and Malachi*, pp. 146–150.
246. For commentaries on Zechariah, see on Haggai (above, n. 235); see also George L. Klein, *Zechariah*, NAC 21B (Nashville: B&H, 2008); Carol L. Meyers and Eric M. Meyers, *Zechariah 9–14*, AB 25C (New York: Doubleday, 1993); David L. Petersen, *Zechariah 9–14 & Malachi* (Louisville: Westminster John Knox, 1995); Pamela J. Scalise, 'Zechariah', in Goldingay and Scalise, *Minor Prophets II*, pp. 179–316.

for a prophet ministering at a time when God's people are seeking to rebuild their lives. He prophesied at the same time as Haggai, just before the completion of the second temple, and appears to have been from a priestly family (Neh. 12:16), though little else is known about him.

The book is usually divided into two main parts: 1 – 8 and 9 – 14. The first, sometimes referred to as Proto-Zechariah, contains material dated in the second and fourth years of Darius (1:1, 7; 7:1), that is, 520–518 BC. Despite evidence of editing,[247] much of the content may be attributed to Zechariah. As noted above, these chapters are frequently associated with Haggai. The second part, Deutero-Zechariah, has a markedly different style and structure. It is sometimes further divided into 9 – 11 and 12 – 14, and is usually attributed to other writers.[248] Some, though, continue to attribute the whole book to Zechariah.[249] Suggested dates for this material range from the eight to second centuries BC,[250] though most recent scholars place it in the late sixth or early fifth century BC.[251]

---

247. E.g. Boda, *Haggai, Zechariah,* pp. 39–41; Childs, *Introduction*, pp. 474–475; Peterson, *Haggai & Zechariah 1–8*, pp. 120–125; Redditt, *Haggai, Zechariah, Malachi*, pp. 38–43.

248. E.g. E. Achtemeier, *Nahum–Malachi*, p. 107; Petersen, *Zechariah 9–14 & Malachi*, pp. 23–29; Redditt, *Haggai, Zechariah, Malachi*, pp. 37–38.

249. E.g. Byron G. Curtis, *Up the Steep and Stony Road: The Book of Zechariah in Social-Location Trajectory Analysis* (Atlanta: Society of Biblical Literature, 2006), pp. 231–276; Hill, *Haggai, Zechariah, Malachi*, pp. 24–25; G. L. Klein, *Zechariah*, pp. 22–34; Petterson, *Haggai, Zechariah and Malachi*, pp. 92–96. Baldwin, following Lamarche, sees a chiastic structure in chs. 9 – 14, suggesting a single author. She notes a corresponding structure in chs. 1 – 8, and concludes that Zechariah may have written both (*Haggai, Zechariah, Malachi*, pp. 74–81); cf. Hill, *Haggai, Zechariah, Malachi*, pp. 69–70; G. L. Klein, *Zechariah*, pp. 44–45. Others are more cautious; see e.g. Childs, *Introduction*, p. 483; Smith, *Micah–Malachi*, pp. 171, 246–248.

250. Matt. 27:9 attributes words from Zech. 11:12 to Jeremiah, leading to the view that Jeremiah wrote Zech. 9 – 11. Chs. 12–14 were later also assigned to Jeremiah. References to both northern and southern kingdoms (e.g. 9:10, 13) and to Egypt and Assyria (10:11) may suggest the eighth century BC. For Stade, the reference to Greece (9:13) indicates a fourth century BC date, and Treves placed the material in the Maccabean era; see Marco Treves, 'Conjectures Concerning the Date and Authorship of Zechariah ix–xiv', *VT* 13.2 (1963), pp. 196–207.

251. E.g. E. Achtemeier, *Nahum–Malachi*, p. 146; Meyers and Meyers, *Haggai and Zechariah 1–8*, pp. 26–28; Petersen, *Zechariah 9–14 & Malachi*, pp. 3–5; Redditt, *Haggai, Zechariah, Malachi*, pp. 94–100 (99–100); see also Andrew E. Hill, 'Dating Second Zechariah: A Linguistic Reexamination', *HAR* 6 (1982), pp. 105–134.

A significant factor in the discussion of Zechariah 9 – 14 is the expression 'An Oracle / The word of the LORD' (*maśśāʾ dĕbar yhwh*), which occurs only in 9:1; 12:1; and Malachi 1:1. This has led to the suggestion that Zechariah 9 – 11, 12 – 14 and Malachi 1 – 4 were independent oracles, which were compiled into a single, anonymous, collection, and added to the rest of the Minor Prophets, maybe to make their number up to twelve. At some point the third was separated,[252] and the others were linked with Zechariah, though the reasons and process are unclear.

Chapters 9–14, and especially 12–14, are sometimes described as apocalyptic.[253] However, while they have some of the characteristics of apocalyptic, including the vision of a new world order, Collins notes, too, that 'major defining characteristics . . . are lacking'.[254] Hill describes it as 'proto-apocalyptic',[255] though it appears still to have much in common with prophecy.[256]

There are also points of contact between Proto- and Deutero-Zechariah. These include the following:[257] the protection of Jerusalem (2:5; 9:8; 12:6; 14:11); cleansing from sin (3:9; 13:1); the fertility of the age to come (8:12; 9:17; 14:8); divine judgment on the nations (1:18–21; 14:3–5), and their eventual conversion (8:20–23; 14:16); the gathering of the exiles (8:7–8; 10:9–10); God's presence among his people (2:10; 8:3; 9:14; 14:3–5, 9); and the coming of a messiah who does not rely on outward strength (4:6; 9:9–10).[258] God's ongoing commitment to his people is affirmed in restatements of the covenant formula (8:8; 13:9). Childs also notes that second-exodus language in 1 – 8 (2:6–7 [cf. Isa. 48:20; Jer. 50:8]; 4:7 [cf. Isa. 40:4]) has been reapplied to future redemption,[259] and this

---

252. See e.g. Childs, *Introduction*, pp. 491–492; Hill and Walton, *Survey*, pp. 534, 544; LaSor, Hubbard and Bush, *OT Survey*, pp. 414–415; Petersen, *Zechariah 9–14 & Malachi*, pp. 2–3. However, see Childs, *Introduction*, pp. 491–492.
253. E.g. G. L. Klein, *Zechariah*, pp. 41–44; Merrill, *Haggai, Zechariah, Malachi*, pp. 67–71.
254. Collins, *Apocalyptic Imagination*, p. 24; see also Petterson, *Haggai, Zechariah, Malachi*, pp. 97–98.
255. Hill, *Haggai, Zechariah, Malachi*, pp. 113–115; cf. Smith, *Micah–Malachi*, pp. 173–175. See also Hanson, *Dawn of Apocalyptic*, pp. 334–400. This suggests, though, that apocalyptic developed primarily from prophecy; cf. above, pp. 196–197.
256. E.g. Petersen, *Zechariah 9–14 & Malachi*, pp. 23–24.
257. See Childs, *Introduction*, pp. 482–485; see also Baldwin, *Haggai, Zechariah, Malachi*, pp. 68–70; McConville, *Prophets*, p. 244; Mason, *Haggai, Zechariah and Malachi*, pp. 78–79; Petterson, *Haggai, Zechariah, Malachi*, p. 96.
258. Zerubbabel appears to be a symbol of messianic hope; see the discussion below.
259. Childs, *Introduction*, pp. 478–479. Childs sees this as the work of a redactor, though there is no reason why it may not be part of Zechariah's original message.

development continues in 9 – 14.[260] Consequently, Childs argues, the book should be seen as a redactional whole; with each part viewed in the light of the other.[261]

Outline

- Part one (1:1 – 8:23)
  - Introduction: call to return to the Lord (1:1–6)
  - Eight visions and oracles (1:7 – 6:8)
  - Joshua (and Zerubbabel) crowned (6:9–15)
  - Rebuke, judgment and future blessing (7:1 – 8:19)
  - Conclusion: conversion of the nations (8:20–23)
- Part two (9:1 – 11:17)
  - The Lord returns to Jerusalem (9:1–17)
    - Judgment on Israel's oppressors (9:1–8)
    - Zion's coming king (9:9–10)
    - Return of the people (9:11–17)
  - The Lord's care for his people (10:1 – 11:3)
  - Prophetic sign act: a rejected and a worthless shepherd (11:4–17)
- Part three (12:1 – 14:21)
  - Defeat of the nations gathered against Judah (12:1–9)
  - Repentance and cleansing (12:10 – 13:6)
  - The shepherd struck, the sheep scattered (13:7–9)
  - The Lord comes and reigns (14:1–21)

Main themes

Several key themes have been noted already, when discussing points of continuity between chapters 1–8 and 9–14. This section will highlight some of them.

The book of Zechariah emphasizes the 'now and not yet' aspects of salvation. In fulfilment of Jeremiah's prophecy God has acted to restore his people (1:12; cf. Jer. 25:11–12). The return from exile has taken place, and the first part of the book emphasizes the key roles, among the returnees, of Joshua, the high priest (3:1–9; 6:11), and of Zerubbabel (4:6–10). However, there

260. Ibid., p. 483. Use of older prophetic material is another common feature of Proto- and Deutero-Zechariah; see e.g. Mason, *Haggai, Zechariah and Malachi*, pp. 79–82. Further examples in 1 – 8 include: 1:12 (cf. Jer. 25:11–12); 3:8; 6:12 (cf. Jer. 23:5; 33:15).

261. Childs, *Introduction*, pp. 482–485; see also Baldwin, *Haggai, Zechariah, Malachi*, p. 70.

are also references to 'the Branch' (*ṣemaḥ*; 3:8; 6:12–13). This term refers to the coming Davidic king (Jer. 23:5; 33:15), and here it probably refers to Zerubbabel. The word for 'crown', in 6:11, is plural, suggesting that the Branch is crowned alongside Joshua. Thus Zerubbabel becomes a symbol of future, messianic, hope.[262] We have seen, too, that the second-exodus theme, which would, initially, have referred to the return from exile, is reapplied to point to a redemption that is yet future. In 9 – 14 this hope is developed, and focuses both on the arrival of God's chosen king (9:9–10) and on the coming of the Lord himself (9:14; 14:3) to fight for his people and establish his kingdom (cf. 14:9).[263] The messianic king may also be identified with the Shepherd, who is rejected by the people (11:7–14; cf. 13:7–9), and also with the 'one they have pierced' (12:10).[264]

Another important theme is God's universal reign. He will judge the nations that have oppressed his people in the past (e.g. 1:18–21; 9:1–8), and, in language that recalls Zion tradition,[265] the book also points to his future victory over the nations that gather to fight against Jerusalem (12:1–9; 14:1–5). The ultimate goal, though, is the conversion of the nations, who will recognize God's presence among his people (2:11; 8:20–23), and, with Israel, will come to worship him (14:9, 16).

Cleansing is also important. The cleansing of Joshua (3:1–5) appears to symbolize the cleansing of the nation (3:9), whose sin is highlighted in the remaining visions, and cleansing from sin will also be a feature of the coming kingdom (13:1). This will include judgment on unfaithful national leaders (e.g. 11:4–5, 17; 13:2–6), and the establishment of a worshipping community based on obedience and true worship (14:17–21). Some associate cleansing in the coming age with the 'one they have pierced' (12:10), and see links, too, with the Servant (Isa. 52:13 – 53:12), whose suffering is also vicarious.[266]

---

262. See further Wolter H. Rose, *Zemah and Zerubbabel: Messianic Expectations in the Early Postexilic Period*, JSOTSup 304 (Sheffield: Sheffield Academic Press, 2000).

263. For discussion of the relationship between God as king and the Messiah as king, see e.g. Routledge, *OT Theology*, pp. 287–289.

264. For further discussion, see commentaries. This has traditionally been seen as pointing forward to Christ (e.g. Matt. 26:31; John 19:37; Rev. 1:7). The references, though, may be better understood typologically: the rejection of God's appointed leader typifies, and is intensified in, the rejection of Christ

265. See above, p. 298, n. 83.

266. E.g. Petterson, *Haggai, Zechariah, Malachi*, pp. 263–264, 280–284; however, cf. Petersen, *Zechariah 9–14 & Malachi*, p. 121.

Malachi[267]

Date, authorship and composition

The title of the book is based on the Hebrew term *mal'ākî* (1:1). This could be translated 'my messenger' (as in 3:1), though it is frequently taken as the proper name 'Malachi'.[268] Whichever is the case, it provides little information about the book's author.

The reference to a 'governor' (1:8) places the book in the Persian period. And some time after the completion of the temple. The problems addressed are reminiscent of those faced by Ezra and Nehemiah, including foreign marriages (2:11; cf. Ezra 9 – 10), and some date the book before their reforms. However, those reforms might not have been wholly successful (cf. Neh. 13:23–28), and Malachi could be dated later.[269]

There is general agreement about the unity of the text.[270] There appear to be two appendices (4:4; 4:5–6), which refer to Moses and Elijah. These tie the book (and the Twelve as a whole) to the Torah and Former Prophets, and so may be editorial.[271] However, there is little reason to doubt that the rest of the text may be attributed to Malachi.

Structure and outline

The book consists, primarily, of a series of six 'disputations' or 'diatribes',[272] which include a claim made by God, one or more questions from the supposed

---

267. For commentaries on Malachi, see on Haggai (above, n. 235) and Zechariah (above, n. 246); see also D. W. Baker, *Joel, Obadiah, Malachi*; E. Ray Clendenen, 'Micah', in Taylor and Clendenen, *Haggai, Malachi*, pp. 203–464; Andrew E. Hill, *Malachi*, AB 25D (New York: Doubleday, 1998); Pamela J. Scalise, 'Malachi', in Goldingay and Scalise, *Minor Prophets II*, pp. 317–366.
268. Childs argues that it is unlikely that the prophet would be identified with the eschatological messenger of 3:1 (*Introduction*, pp. 492–494); see also Petterson, *Haggai, Zechariah, Malachi*, pp. 306–307.
269. Hill suggests shortly after 500 BC (*Malachi*, pp. 83–84; *Haggai, Zechariah, Malachi*, p. 279); Verhoef places the book between Nehemiah's first and second visit (*Haggai and Malachi*, pp. 156–160). McConville notes a wider range: 516–330 BC (*Prophets*, pp. 259–260); see also D. W. Baker, *Joel, Obadiah, Malachi*, pp. 207–210; Petterson, *Haggai, Zechariah, Malachi*, pp. 307–308.
270. However, see Redditt, *Haggai, Zechariah, Malachi*, pp. 152–155.
271. E.g. Hill, *Haggai, Zechariah, Malachi*, pp. 361–362; however, cf. Petterson, pp. 308–309.
272. See Petersen, *Zechariah 9–14 & Malachi*, pp. 30–34.

audience, followed by answers and further statements in support of the claim. While such disputations do not require a legal setting, it has been suggested that the book may be viewed as a court case, beginning with an initial indictment, and leading to a final verdict.[273]

Outline

- Introduction (1:1)
- First disputation: God's love for Israel (1:2–5)
- Second disputation: priests do not fulfil their responsibilities (1:6 – 2:9)
- Third disputation: breaking faith in marriage and divorce (2:10–16)
- Fourth disputation: questioning God's justice (2:17 – 3:5)
- Fifth disputation: returning to God; giving the full tithe (3:6–12)
- Sixth disputation: speaking against God (3:13 – 4:3) [3:13–21]
- Appendix 1: remember the law of Moses (4:4) [3:22]
- Appendix 2: the coming of Elijah (4:5–6) [3:23–24]

Main themes

Commentators note Malachi's substantial use of Deuteronomic language.[274] This suggests a significant covenantal emphasis. The term *bĕrît* occurs six times, referring to the expected conduct of priests and Levites (2:4–5, 8), what most commentators take to be the Sinaitic covenant (2:10; 3:1) and the relationship between husband and wife (2:14). The idea of covenant faithfulness, though, permeates Malachi's whole message.[275]

The book begins with an affirmation of divine love (1:2; cf. Deut. 4:37; 7:6–8), but that love is not acknowledged, and the people have not responded appropriately. This is evident in their unwillingness to bring unblemished, and therefore costly, sacrifices (1:6–14), in withholding tithes and offerings (3:6–12; cf. Deut. 26:12–15) and, more generally, in questioning the value of serving God (3:14). They have broken faith with God in their marriages to 'the daughter of a foreign god' (2:11b), probably a reference to taking wives who worship

273. E. Achtemeier, *Nahum–Malachi*, p. 172; see also Hill, *Haggai, Zechariah, Malachi*, pp. 329, 341. Petersen suggests a pedagogical setting (*Zechariah 9–14 & Malachi*, p. 32).

274. E.g. Hill, *Malachi*, p. 42; Smith, *Micah–Malachi*, p. 300; see also e.g. Coggins, *Haggai, Zechariah, Malachi*, pp. 48–50; McConville, *Prophets*, p. 265; Gordon P. Hugenberger, *Marriage as a Covenant: Biblical Law and Ethics as Developed from Malachi* (Eugene: Wipf & Stock, 2014), pp. 48–50.

275. Hugenberger, *Marriage as a Covenant*, p. 50; Stephen L. McKenzie and Howard N. Wallace, 'Covenant Themes in Malachi', *CBQ* 45 (1983), pp. 549–563.

other gods (cf. Neh. 13:27). They have also broken faith with their previous partners by divorcing them (2:14). The general view is that they have divorced Israelite wives in order to make way for those foreign marriages, though Collins takes this as a criticism of Ezra and Nehemiah's insistence that those in mixed marriages separate from their non-Israelite spouses.[276]

Malachi also admonishes priests and Levites, because they are not living up to their calling (2:1–9).[277] There is a further reference to a 'covenant with Levi' (2:4–6) in Jeremiah 33:21 (cf. Neh. 13:29). There is no specific reference to the establishment of this covenant; though, following Israel's sin with the golden calf, the Levites were 'set apart' because of their faithfulness (Exod. 32:26–29; Deut. 10:8; 33:8–11).

Malachi also refers to the future. God will come to his temple (3:1; cf. Ezek. 10; 43:1–5; Hag. 2:1–9). Like other prophets, he points to the judgment associated with the Day of the Lord (3:1–2; 4:1, 5). However, the people remain God's 'treasured possession' (*sĕgullâ*, 3:17; cf. Exod. 19:5; Deut. 7:6; 14:2; 26:18; Ps. 135:4), and he will refine the people (Mal. 3:2–5; 4:1–3), so that they offer true worship (3:3–4). There may be the suggestion, too, that other nations can be included in that eschatological hope (1:11; cf. 1:14; 3:12).[278]

---

276. See John J. Collins, 'Marriage, Divorce, and Family in Second Temple Judaism', in Leo G. Perdue, Joseph Blenkinsopp, John J. Collins and Carol Meyers, *Families in Ancient Israel* (Louisville: Westminster John Knox, 1997), pp. 104–162; *Introduction*, pp. 433–435.

277. Their role in giving true instruction echoes the blessing of Levi in Deut. 33:9, rather than P material, which appears to make a sharper distinction between priests and Levites.

278. E.g. J. G. Baldwin, 'Malachi 1:11 and the Worship of the Nations in the Old Testament', *TynBul* 23 (1972), pp. 117–124; cf. Petterson, *Haggai, Zechariah, Malachi*, pp. 333–335; Smith, *Micah–Malachi*, pp. 312–316; Verhoef, *Haggai and Malachi*, pp. 222–232.

9. THE WRITINGS

Psalms[1]

Composition and structure

The Hebrew title of the book is *tĕhillîm* (praises); 'psalms' comes from the Greek *psalmoi*. It contains 150 psalms, divided into five books (1 – 41, 42 –72, 73 – 89,

1. Commentaries on the Psalms include Allen, *Psalms 101–150*; A. A. Anderson, *Psalms*, 2 vols., NCB (London: Oliphants, 1972); Craig C. Broyles, *Psalms*, NIBCOT/UBC (Peabody: Hendrickson; Carlisle: Paternoster, 1999); Peter C. Craigie, *Psalms 1–50*, WBC 19 (Waco: Word, 1983); Mitchell Dahood, *Psalms*, 3 vols., AB 16–17A (New York: Doubleday, 1965–70); Erhard Gerstenberger, *Psalms, Part 1, with an Introduction to Cultic Poetry*, FOTL 14 (Grand Rapids: Eerdmans, 1988); *Psalms, Part 2, and Lamentations*, FOTL 15 (Grand Rapids: Eerdmans, 2001); Goldingay, *Psalms*; Geoffrey W. Grogan, *Psalms*, THOTC (Grand Rapids: Eerdmans, 2008); Kidner, *Psalms*; Hans-Joachim Kraus, *Psalms*, 2 vols., CC (Minneapolis: Fortress, 1993); James L. Mays, *Psalms*, IBC (Louisville: Westminster John Knox, 1994); Marvin E. Tate, *Psalms 51–100*, WBC 20 (Dallas: Word, 1990); Artur Weiser, *Psalms*, OTL (London: SCM Press, 1962); Gerald H. Wilson, *Psalms*, vol. 1, NIVAC (Grand Rapids: Zondervan, 2002). See also William P. Brown (ed.), *The Oxford Handbook of the Psalms* (Oxford: Oxford University Press, 2014); Day, *Psalms*; Peter W. Flint and

90 – 106, 107 – 150), each ending with a doxology (41:13; 72:18–19; 89:52; 106:48; 150). The possible parallel with the five books of the Torah may indicate the significance of the Psalms in teaching.[2]

'Psalm' generally translates *mizmôr*, which appears in many titles, and may indicate accompaniment by musical instruments; 'song' (*šîr*) may be similar. 'Prayer' (*tĕpillâ*) may indicate a lament. There are also several untranslated terms. A *šiggāyôn* may also be a lament; a *maśkîl* may be a psalm for instruction; a *miktām* may be linked with atonement. Some terms suggest musical directions. 'According to *šĕmînît* [eighth]' may suggest an eight-stringed instrument, though the meaning of other terms, including *selâ*, which appears in many psalms, is unclear.

The book is generally associated with David. The expression 'of David' (*lĕdāwid*) in many psalm titles,[3] has traditionally been taken to imply authorship. Other ascriptions include Asaph (50; 73 – 83) and the Sons of Korah (42; 44 – 49; 84; 85; 87; 88).[4] However, the headings are not generally regarded as integral to the text. They offer insight into the history of interpretation and

---

(*Footnote 1 cont.*) Patrick D. Miller (eds.), *The Book of Psalms: Composition and Reception*, VTSup 99, FOTL 4 (Leiden: Koninklijke Brill, 2005); Johnston and Firth, *Interpreting the Psalms*; Hans-Joachim Kraus, *Theology of the Psalms*, CC (Minneapolis: Fortress, 1992); J. Clinton McCann Jr., *A Theological Introduction to the Book of Psalms: The Psalms as Torah* (Nashville: Abingdon, 1993); J. Clinton McCann Jr. (ed.), *The Shape and Shaping of the Psalter*, JSOTSup 159 (Sheffield: JSOT Press, 1993).

2. Goldingay, *Psalms*, 1:23; see also e.g. David G. Firth, 'The Teaching of the Psalms', in Johnston and Firth, *Interpreting the Psalms*, pp. 159–174; J. Clinton McCann Jr., 'The Psalms as Instruction', *Int* 46.2 (1992), pp. 117–128; *Theological Introduction*; James Luther Mays, 'The Place of the Torah Psalms in the Psalter', *JBL* 106.1 (1987), pp. 3–12; Gordon J. Wenham, 'The Ethics of the Psalms', in Johnston and Firth, *Interpreting the Psalms*, pp. 175–194; *Psalms as Torah: Reading Biblical Songs Ethically* (Grand Rapids: Baker Academic: 2012).
3. Pss 3 – 32; 34 – 41; 51 – 65; 68 – 70; 86; 101; 103; 108 – 110; 122; 124; 131; 133; 138 – 145.
4. For further discussion, see e.g. Martin J. Buss, 'The Psalms of Asaph and Korah', *JBL* 82.4 (1963), pp. 382–392; Michael D. Goulder, *The Psalms of the Sons of Korah*, JSOTSup 20 (Sheffield: JSOT Press, 1982); *The Psalms of Asaph and the Pentateuch*, JSOTSup 102 (Sheffield: Sheffield Academic Press, 1996); J. M. Miller, 'The Korahites of Southern Judah', *CBQ* 32 (1970), pp. 58–68. In 1 Chr. 16:7–36 Asaph is linked also with Ps. 96 and parts of 105 and 106. Psalms appear, also, to be associated with other court musicians: Jeduthun (39; 62; 77), Heman (88) and Ethan (89); see e.g. 1 Chr. 15:16–17; 16:41–42.

should not be dismissed, but attributions of authorship and setting are not definitive.[5] The preposition *lĕ* also has other meanings, including 'to', 'for', 'belonging to' and 'about', and headings may indicate, instead, the collection that a psalm belonged to.

The psalter appears to have been made up of smaller collections. The statement in 72:20 'this concludes the prayers of David son of Jesse' suggests that Davidic psalms in Books 1 and 2 formed collections separate from those in Books 3 – 5. Asaph and Korah psalms, and 'songs of ascents' (120 – 134) may indicate other collections. Psalms 42 – 83 are often referred to collectively as the 'Elohistic Psalter', because the divine name Elohim occurs around five times more frequently than Yahweh, whereas the reverse is true in the rest of the book,[6] apparently as the result of editing.[7]

There is speculation about the growth of the psalter.[8] It may be that collections circulated separately and were combined over a period of time. The Elohistic Psalter, made up primarily of David, Asaph and Korah psalms, might have been edited in the north. This was later combined with an earlier (unedited) collection of David psalms, with Psalm 2 added as an introduction to this larger collection. Psalms 84 – 89, sometimes viewed as an appendix to the Elohistic Psalter, might also have been added at this point. Texts from Qumran indicate few variations in this section of the psalter, suggesting that it was accepted in its present form by the second century BC.[9] The process by which Psalms 90 – 150 were added is less clear. Material from Qumran suggests that their order was not fixed before the first century AD, though from that time the MT version appears to have increased in prominence. At some point Psalm 1 was included as an introduction to the whole collection. Finally, the completed text was divided into five books.

---

5. Some argue that titles are significant (e.g. Kidner, *Psalms*, 1:16, 32–46), whereas others attach little significance to them (e.g. Childs, *Introduction*, p. 509); see also Dillard and Longman, *Introduction*, pp. 240–244.
6. See e.g. Day, *Psalms*, pp. 113–114.
7. Elohim replaces Yahweh in Ps. 68:1, 7–8, which quote Num. 10:35, Judg. 5:4–5 respectively, and in 53:2, 4, 6, which duplicate 14:2, 4, 6.
8. See e.g. Anderson, *Psalms*, 1:24–28; Jerome F. D. Creach, *Yahweh as Refuge and the Editing of the Hebrew Psalter*, JSOTSup 217 (Sheffield: Sheffield Academic Press, 1996); J. W. Rogerson and J. W. McKay, *Psalms 101–150*, CBC (Cambridge: Cambridge University Press, 1977), pp. 3–6; Klaus Seybold, *Introducing the Psalms* (London: T&T Clark, 1990), pp. 14–22.
9. See e.g. Dwight D. Swanson, 'Qumran and the Psalms', in Johnston and Firth, *Interpreting the Psalms*, pp. 247–261.

Gerald Wilson has made a significant contribution to discussion of the editorial shaping of the psalter.[10] He notes the presence of 'royal psalms' at key 'seams' of the first three books (2; 72; 89), and argues that those books focus on the Davidic covenant: 'its introduction in divine grace (Ps. 2), its transmission to David's successors with hope (Ps. 72), and its collapse in the destruction and despair of the Exile (Ps. 89)'.[11] Following this crisis, Book 4 transfers focus from the Davidic king to Yahweh, whose continuing reign is affirmed in Psalms 93; 95 – 99. Book 5 then calls for trust in God, and ends with praise. This hope is generally focused on God himself, though Wilson also accepts some messianic significance. Despite criticism,[12] Wilson's focus on the macrostructure of the book marks an important move forward.

As we have noted, Psalms are frequently associated with the cult.[13] Mowinckel, in particular, links their setting with Israel's festivals,[14] thus challenging the traditional view that some psalms are linked with episodes in David's life.[15] If so, headings might then have been added because content suggested possible links with David. However, there is also the possibility that real-life situations prompted songs, which then found their way into the hymnbook. Such may be the case with the hymn celebrating David's victory in 2 Samuel

---

10. Gerald Henry Wilson, *The Editing of the Hebrew Psalter*, SBLDS 76 (Chico: Scholars Press, 1985); 'The Use of Royal Psalms at the "Seams" of the Hebrew Psalter', *JSOT* 35 (1986), pp. 85–94; 'The Shape of the Book of Psalms', *Int* 46.2 (1992), pp. 129–142; 'The Structure of the Psalter', in Johnston and Firth, *Interpreting the Psalms*, pp. 229–246; 'King, Messiah, and the Reign of God: Revisiting the Royal Psalms and the Shape of the Psalter', in Flint and Miller, *Book of Psalms*, pp. 392–406.
11. G. H. Wilson, 'Shape', p. 134.
12. E.g. Longman and Dillard, *Introduction*, pp. 253–254; David C. Mitchell, 'Lord Remember David: G. H. Wilson and the Message of the Psalter', *VT* 56 (2006), pp. 526–548; Robert E. Wallace, 'Gerald Wilson and the Characterization of David in Book 5 of the Psalter', in Nancy L. De Claissé-Walford (ed.), *The Shape and Shaping of the Book of Psalms: The Current State of Scholarship* (Atlanta: Society of Biblical Literature, 2014), pp. 193–207; Norman Whybray, *Reading the Psalms as a Book* (Sheffield: Sheffield Academic Press, 1996), pp. 19–22.
13. See e.g. D. J. A. Clines, 'Psalm Research Since 1955: I. The Psalms and the Cult', *TynBul* 18 (1967), pp. 103–126; Jerome F. D. Creach, 'The Psalms and the Cult', in Johnston and Firth, *Interpreting the Psalms*, pp. 119–137.
14. Mowinckel, *Psalms in Israel's Worship.*
15. Pss 3; 18 (= 2 Sam. 22:1–51); 34; 51; 52; 54; 56; 57; 59; 60; 63; 142.

22:1–51 (= Ps. 18). Psalm 68 may celebrate bringing the Ark to Jerusalem, and this may then have been used at a regular worship event (cf. Ps. 132).

Mowinckel focuses attention on an annual Enthronement/New Year festival,[16] which, he argues, formed part of the Feast of Tabernacles. He associated this, particularly, with Psalms 47; 93; 96 – 99. These include the affirmation *Yhwh mālāk*,[17] usually translated 'the LORD reigns' or 'the LORD is king'. Mowinckel translates it instead, 'the LORD has become king', and argues that these psalms 'salute Yahweh as the king, who has just ascended his royal throne to wield his royal power'.[18] There was such a festival in Babylon, linked with Marduk's victory over chaos, though evidence for its existence in Israel is tenuous.[19] Weiser also links the Psalms with an annual celebration, but sees this, instead, as a covenant renewal festival.[20] Some psalms may be understood in that context (e.g. 50; 78; 81), and others focus on the exodus (see below). But it is difficult to see this as the setting for the majority of psalms. And there remains the lack of clear biblical evidence for such a festival. A third suggestion, by Kraus, is that the annual festival celebrated God's choice of Zion and David.[21] This is particularly linked with 'Royal Psalms' and 'Hymns of Zion' (46; 48; 76; 84; 87; 122). Again, though, the evidence is scant.

Main themes

A primary focus of the book of Psalms is the relationship between God and his people. This includes recognizing who God is. The one on whom his people rely is the 'Maker of heaven and earth' (e.g. 115:15; 121:2; 146:6), who has subdued the primeval waters (e.g. 65:6–8; 74:12–17; 89:9–13; 93:2–4; 104:5–9). He is Israel's only God (e.g. 81:9–10), who is superior to other gods (e.g. 95:3; 97:7; cf. 96:5; 115:3–7; 135:15–18). We have noted the emphasis on divine kingship. And God is portrayed, too, as his people's shepherd (e.g. 23:1; 28:9; 80:1; 100:3) and their rock or fortress (e.g. 18:2; 31:1–3; 62:2, 6; 71:3;

---

16. Mowinckel, *Psalms in Israel's Worship*, 1:106–192; see also Day, *Psalms*, pp. 67–87; J. J. M. Roberts, 'Mowinckel's Enthronement Festival: A Review', in Flint and Miller, *Psalms*, pp. 97–115.
17. Ps. 47:7 reads, 'God [*'ĕlōhîm*] is the King'.
18. Mowinckel, *Psalms in Israel's Worship*, 1:106–192 (106).
19. The post-biblical Jewish New Year was celebrated at the same time as the Feast of Trumpets (Lev. 23:24); cf. Ps. 47:5. In Zech. 14:16 nations worship God as king at the Feast of Tabernacles.
20. Weiser, *Psalms*, pp. 23–52.
21. Kraus, *Psalms*, 1:78.

94:22), giving refuge and displaying care and tenderness (e.g. 17:8; 36:7; 57:1; 61:4; 91:4).

Several psalms recount the events of the exodus (e.g. 78:11–55; 81:10; 105:26–45; 114; 135:8–12; 136:10–22), and there are references, too, to the Sinaitic covenant, emphasizing the need to obey God's law (e.g. 25:10; 50:16; 78:10, 37; 103:18; see also 1:2; 19:7–11; 37:31; 40:8; 105:44–45; 119). God's covenant love, *ḥesed*, also features prominently, emphasizing his faithful commitment to his people (36:5; 100:5; 106:45; 107:8, 21, 31; 117:2; 136), as the basis for the people's confidence (e.g. 52:8; 90:14; 143:8; 147:11), deliverance (e.g. 6:4; 17:7; 31:16; 33:18–19; 85:7; 130:7) and forgiveness (e.g. 25:6–7; 51:1–2; 86:5, 15; 103:8).

There is emphasis, too, on God's presence among his people. This focuses, primarily, on the sanctuary (e.g. 11:4; 27:4–6; 63:2; 80:1; 99:1; 100:2, 4), and is a significant element in the prominence given to Zion (46:7, 11; 48:3; 76:2; 84).[22]

The close relationship between God and the Davidic monarchy is also reflected in the idea of kingship in the Psalms. The Davidic king is God's 'anointed' (e.g. 2:2; 18:50; 89:20), and God is committed to preserving the royal line, though also calls for obedience (89:30–37; 132:11–12). This emphasizes the unique relationship between the king and God, but also that the king rules as God's representative. Psalm 72 sets out the model for the ideal king, who rules justly over God's people (vv. 2–4, 12–14). And, as we have noted, some of the psalms focusing on the Davidic king were reapplied and given a messianic significance.

Job[23]

Date, authorship and composition

The book of Job is made up of a prose prologue (1:1 – 2:13) and epilogue (42:7–17), which form the framework for the much larger section of poetic

22. For further references to God's presence, see e.g. 16:11; 21:6; 31:20; 41:12; 51:11; 89:15; 102:28; 139:7.

23. Commentaries on Job include Robert L. Alden, *Job*, NAC (Nashville: B&H, 1993); Francis I. Andersen, *Job*, TOTC (Leicester: Inter-Varsity Press, 1976); Clines, *Job*; Robert Gordis, *The Book of God and Man: A Study of Job* (Chicago: Chicago University Press, 1966); Norman C. Habel, *Job*, OTL (Philadelphia: Westminster, 1985); Hartley, *Job*; J. Gerald Janzen, *Job*, IBC (Atlanta: John Knox, 1985); Tremper Longman III, *Job*, BCOTWP (Grand Rapids: Baker Academic, 2012);

speeches (3:1 – 42:6). There seems to be general agreement that the prose sections belong together, and reflect an old story about Job,[24] maybe the same figure mentioned in Ezekiel 14:14, 20. The speeches, though, make little sense without the narrative, and the narrative assumes the kind of dialogue recorded in the speeches (e.g. 42:7–8). This suggests that both are by the same author, who retells the original story and incorporates the poetic material within it.[25]

There is debate about the place of some of the material in the poetic section, particularly the Elihu speeches (32 – 37) and the 'hymn to wisdom' (28).[26] While Job's friends Bildad, Eliphaz and Zophar are mentioned in the prologue and epilogue, Elihu appears unannounced and there is no response to his contribution, which appears to add little to the discussion. Some see this section, therefore, as a late addition. Others view Elihu as an arbiter (cf. 31:35),[27] whose speeches summarize what has been said and prepare for God's reply.[28] The delay between Job's last speech and the divine response also serves to build suspense, and, as tension rises, Elihu may even provide a comic interlude.[29]

The calm tone of chapter 28 appears to distinguish it from Job's speeches in chapters 27 and 29. It might have existed as a separate poem, and has been inserted here, though it may be the work of the same author. It should probably

---

Marvin H. Pope, *Job*, AB 15 (New York: Doubleday, 1965); H. H. Rowley, *Job*, NCB (London: Oliphants, 1970); N. H. Tur Sinai, *The Book of Job: A New Commentary* (Jerusalem: Kiryat Sepher, 1957); John H. Walton, *Job*, NIVAC (Grand Rapids: Zondervan, 2012); Gerald H. Wilson, *Job*, NIBCOT (Peabody: Hendrickson, 2007); Lindsay Wilson, *Job*, THOTC (Grand Rapids: Eerdmans, 2015). See also John H. Eaton, *Job*, OTG (Sheffield: JSOT Press, 1970); Lucas, *Psalms and Wisdom*, pp. 117–144. For more on wisdom literature, see above, pp. 124–128, 187–194.

24. E.g. Nahum M. Sarna, 'Epic Substratum in the Prose of Job', *JBL* 76 (1957), pp. 13–25.
25. E.g. Hartley, *Job*, pp. 21–24.
26. There is debate, too, over Yahweh's second speech (40:6 – 41:34); e.g. Rowley, *Job*, p. 15. Most scholars, though, accept both speeches as original.
27. E.g. Andersen, *Job*, p. 51; Habel, *Job*, pp. 36–37; L. Wilson, *Job*, p. 15.
28. E.g. Robert V. McCabe, 'Elihu's Contribution to the Thought of the Book of Job', *Detroit Baptist Seminary Journal* 2 (1997), pp. 47–80; Lindsay Wilson, 'The Role of the Elihu Speeches in the Book of Job', *RTR* 55.2 (1996), pp. 81–92.
29. J. W. Whedbee, 'The Comedy of Job', *Semeia* 7 (1977), pp. 1–39.

be read as an interlude by the narrator, contrasting the true way of wisdom with the speeches of Job and his friends.[30]

There is debate, too, around the third cycle of speeches (22 – 27). Bildad's speech is short, and there is nothing from Zophar. Some reconfigure the text to extend Bildad's speech, and attribute other material to Zophar.[31] Though the differences in pattern may be intentional, and several commentators interpret the text as it stands.[32]

Details about Job suggest a patriarchal setting.[33] His wealth is measured in livestock (1:3; cf. Gen. 12:16), he offers sacrifices as family head (1:5), and his age, well over 140 (42:16),[34] also fits with that era. The date of writing, though, is debated. The Talmud attributes it to Moses,[35] though most commentators suggest a date between the eighth and second centuries BC. Points of contact with other OT books, including Psalms, Proverbs and Isaiah 40 – 55,[36] may help with dating,[37] though any conclusion is uncertain. The author, too, is unknown, though may have been among the sages of the day.

The text of Job is corrupt in places, and includes a large number of rare words, making it one of the most obscure texts in the OT. While generally close to the MT, the LXX is shorter, and shows some variations. A Targum from Qumran (11QTgJob), whose language dates to the second or first century BC,[38] also generally agrees with the MT, though supports some of the LXX variants.

---

30. See further Daniel J. Estes, 'Job 28 in Its Literary Context', *JESOT* 2.2 (2013), pp. 151–164; see also e.g. Andersen, *Job*, p. 53; Habel, *Job*, pp. 391–392. Some, however, see it as part of Job's speech; e.g. Childs, *Introduction*, pp. 542–543; Janzen, *Job*, pp. 187–189; Alison Lo, *Job 28 as Rhetoric: An Analysis of Job 28 in the Context of Job 22–31*, VTSup 97 (Leiden: Koninklijke Brill, 2003).
31. Bildad's speech is often extended by adding 26:5–14; Hartley adds, instead, 27:13–23 (cf. Longman and Dillard, *Introduction*, p. 228). There is little agreement over what to assign to Zophar. See e.g. Habel, *Job*, pp. 37–38; Lucas, *Psalms and Wisdom*, pp. 124–125.
32. E.g. Andersen, *Job*, pp. 53–54, 216; Janzen, *Job*, pp. 171–172.
33. E.g. Habel, *Job*, pp. 39–40; Sarna, 'Epic Substratum', p. 14.
34. The 'twofold' restoration (42:10) may suggest that Job was 70 when the further 140 years were added.
35. *b. B. Bat.* 15a.
36. See e.g. Hartley, *Job*, pp. 11–13.
37. Hartley supports the view that Job pre-dates Isa. 40 – 55 (ibid., p. 19). Its date may thus depend on conclusions about the date and authorship of Isaiah.
38. See e.g. Stephen A. Kaufman, 'The Job Targum from Qumran', *JAOS* 93.3 (1973), pp. 317–327.

Outline

- Prologue: Job's affliction (1:1 – 2:13)
- Job's lament (3:1–26)
- First cycle of speeches (4:1 – 14:22)
- Second cycle of speeches (15:1 – 21:34)
- Third cycle of speeches (22:1 – 27:23)
- Interlude: hymn in praise of wisdom (28:1–28)
- Job's final speech (29:1 – 31:40)
- Elihu's speeches (32:1 – 37:24)
- Yahweh and Job (38:1 – 42:6)
  - First speeches (38:1 – 40:5)
  - Second speeches (40:6 – 42:6)
- Epilogue (42:7–17)

Main themes

One theme, raised by the Satan's[39] accusation in 1:9–11, is the possibility of serving God without expectation of reward. Job passes this test (2:10), and the rest of the book is set in the context of seeking to understand what is happening, while maintaining faith in God.

This then leads to the main theme, the problem of innocent suffering. Job is introduced as one who is upright, pious and wealthy (e.g. 1:1–5), but who, following scenes in the heavenly court, where God holds him up as an example and gives (the) Satan permission to 'test' his faith, loses wealth, family and health. The book, whose characters remain ignorant of the real reason for Job's suffering, then addresses the question, Why does this happen to one who is 'blameless and upright'? Job's friends reflect the orthodox law of retribution, which is summed up in 4:8 – 'those who sow trouble reap it'. By contrast, God blesses the righteous (e.g. 8:20–22), and despite his protestations, Job must confess his sin in order to be restored (11:13–20). The second and third cycles of speeches build on the first, and Elihu adds little more, though he does develop the idea, noted in 5:17–18, that suffering may serve as a means of turning people from sin (33:29–30; 36:8–16). This, too, though, assumes that Job is guilty; whereas the prologue emphasizes his innocence. Finally, Job's 'comforters' are criticized, and Job is vindicated, though not before he is rebuked for his presumption in questioning God's justice. The book thus challenges the

---

39. 'The Satan' (*haśśāṭān*), with the definite article, is a title rather than a name, probably meaning 'adversary'. By the time of 1 Chr. 21:1 'Satan' (*śāṭān*) had become a proper name. See Routledge, *OT Theology*, pp. 120–122; see also above, pp. 19–20.

traditional understanding of wisdom, represented by Job's friends, and also Job's own questions about God's justice. Instead, it gives a picture of a God who is greater than human understanding, whose ways are inscrutable and who will, finally, vindicate those who trust him.[40]

Proverbs[41]

Date, authorship and composition

Like Psalms, Proverbs is a collection of collections. Three of these are associated with Solomon (1:1; 10:1; 25:1). However, 1:1 may be part of an introduction, not just to chapters 1–9, but to the complete collection, indicating Solomon's general link with the book as a whole.

There may, thus, be only two Solomonic collections, with the first beginning at 10:1.[42] There are two collections associated with 'the wise'. The first (22:17 – 24:22), which refers to thirty sayings (22:20), has, as we have seen, points of contact with the Egyptian *Wisdom of Amenemope*.[43] Other sections are associated

---

40. Without a clearly developed theology of the afterlife, vindication must come in this life; see above, p. 19.
41. Commentaries on Proverbs include Richard J. Clifford, *Proverbs*, OTL (Louisville: Westminster John Knox, 1999); Fox, *Proverbs*; Duane A. Garrett, *Proverbs, Ecclesiastes, Song of Songs*, NAC 14 (Nashville: B&H, 1993); Derek Kidner, *Proverbs*, TOTC (London: Inter-Varsity Press, 1964); Paul E. Koptak, *Proverbs*, NIVAC (Grand Rapids: Zondervan, 2003); Tremper Longman III, *Proverbs*, BCOTWP (Grand Rapids: Baker Academic, 2006); McKane, *Proverbs*; Roland E. Murphy, 'Proverbs', in Roland E. Murphy and Elizabeth Huwiler, *Proverbs, Ecclesiastes and Song of Songs*, NIBCOT/UBC (Peabody: Hendrickson, 1999), pp. 219–290; Murphy, *Proverbs*; Leo G. Perdue, *Proverbs*, IBC (Louisville: John Knox, 2000); Waltke, *Proverbs*; Christine R. Yoder, *Proverbs*, AbOTC (Nashville: Abingdon, 2009). See also Longman, *How to Read Proverbs*. For more on wisdom literature, see above, pp. 124–128, 187–194.
42. E.g. Childs, *Introduction*; Kidner, *Proverbs*, p. 22; Longman, *Proverbs*, pp. 24–25. Kitchen argues that 1 – 24 is a unity, written by Solomon in the tenth century BC; see K. A. Kitchen, 'Proverbs and Wisdom Books of the Ancient Near East: The Factual History of a Literary Form', *TynBul* 28 (1977), pp. 69–114. See also e.g. Garrett, *Proverbs, Ecclesiastes, Song of Songs*, pp. 39–46; Waltke *Proverbs*, 1:9–37.
43. See above, p. 125.

with Agur (30:1–33) and King Lemuel (31:1–9). These are non-Israelites, though we know nothing else about them. The numerical sayings in 30:15–33 are sometimes separated from Agur's oracle. And the final section (31:10–31), written as an acrostic, extolling the virtues of a noble wife, probably forms an anonymous conclusion to the book.[44]

Some scholars argue that the association of Solomon with Proverbs is merely traditional,[45] and that he is responsible for little, if any, of its content.[46] However, those sections attributed to Solomon (10:1 – 22:16; 25:1 – 29:27) are widely regarded as pre-exilic, and though he may not have written all, or even most, of the material, Solomon could well have initiated the collections, and have made contributions to them. Its links with Egypt suggest that the thirty sayings of the wise (22:17 – 24:22) may also be pre-exilic, and also, possibly, part of a Solomonic collection.

The process of compilation of the book is not clear. One possibility is that an initial collection associated with Solomon (10:1 – 22:16), maybe with the sayings of the wise appended, was in existence at the time of Hezekiah, and was enlarged by adding 25:1 – 29:27 during his reign. Chapters 1–9 and 30–31 might have been added during a post-exilic redaction, between the sixth and fourth centuries BC,[47] though much of the material in 1 – 9 may also be pre-exilic.[48]

Outline

- Introduction (1:1–7)
- Discourse on wisdom (1:8 – 9:18)
  - A parent's advice (1:8 – 7:27)
  - The call of wisdom (8:1–36)
  - Wisdom and Folly (9:1–18)
- Proverbs of Solomon (10:1 – 22:16)

---

44. The order of the text is different in the LXX after 24:22. Based on the MT numbering, the order is 30:1–14; 24:23–34; 30:15–33; 31:1–9; 25:1 – 29:27; 31:10–31. This separates the numerical sayings and the acrostic on the noble wife from the sections attributed to Agur and Lemuel respectively.
45. See e.g. 1 Kgs 4:29–34.
46. E.g. Collins, *Introduction*, p. 508; Yoder, *Proverbs*, p. xxii.
47. E.g. Clifford, *Proverbs*, pp. 3–4; Yoder, *Proverbs*, p. xxiii.
48. LaSor, Hubbard and Bush suggest that the collection's final editing was in the fifth century BC, but note that much of the content is earlier (*OT Survey*, p. 470); see also Lucas, *Psalms and Wisdom*, pp. 104–105.

- Thirty sayings of the wise (22:17 – 24:22)
- More sayings of the wise (24:23–34)
- More proverbs of Solomon, collected by Hezekiah (25:1 – 29:27)
- Sayings of Agur (30:1–14)
- Numerical sayings (30:15–33)
- Sayings of King Lemuel (31:1–9)
- Acrostic on a noble wife (31:10–31)

Main themes

We have already noted some important aspects of the role of Proverbs, when looking at wisdom literature, including its emphasis on the principle of moral cause and effect.

Another key feature is the depiction of wisdom as a virtuous woman, who invites the young and easily led to seek her, follow her ways and so find life (1:20–33; 8:1 – 9:6; cf. 3:13–20; 4:5–9). She is contrasted with the adulteress,[49] whose intention is to lead the weak and gullible astray (e.g. 2:16–19; 5:3–6; 6:23–29; 7:1–27), and also with Folly (9:13–18). There are echoes of this portrayal of wisdom in the description of the 'ideal wife' (31:10–31). Both are more valuable 'than rubies' (31:10; cf. 3:15; 8:11), both are worth finding (31:10; cf. 3:13; 4:22; 8:17, 35) and both are associated with the fear of the Lord (31:30; cf. 9:10).[50]

As noted above, wisdom is also associated with creation (3:19–20; 8:22–31),[51] and there are points of contact between wisdom in 8:22–31 and the Logos in John 1:1–3. The part played by wisdom in creation is indicated by *'āmôn* (Prov. 8:30),[52] translated 'craftsman' (NIV) or 'master worker' (NRSV). This suggests active involvement, though another possibility 'little child'

---

49. The woman in 2:16 and 7:5 is described as 'strange' (*zārâ*), which parallels 'foreign' (*nokrî*). The text gives no indication that this is a foreigner; it seems more likely that the reference is to one who operates outside the bounds of generally accepted behaviour (e.g. Longman, *Proverbs*, p. 164), or maybe to 'the other woman' (Garrett, *Proverbs, Ecclesiastes, Song of Songs*, p. 91). There may also be an allusion to the spiritual adultery associated with worshipping foreign gods.
50. E.g. Clifford, *Proverbs*, pp. 54, 273–274; Ellen F. Davis, *Proverbs, Ecclesiastes, Song of Songs*, Westminster Bible Companion (Louisville: Westminster John Knox, 2000), pp. 151–152; Lucas, *Psalms and Wisdom*, p. 104.
51. Above, p. 124.
52. See Waltke's discussion (*Proverbs*, 2:417–420).

(NRSV mg.), points to a more passive role. The portrayal of wisdom in these passages has raised questions as to whether this is a 'personification', in which personal characteristics are attributed to divine wisdom only as a literary device,[53] or a 'hypostasis', viewing wisdom as a separate divine being. Later wisdom texts, probably under Greek influence, do present Wisdom (Sophia) as a hypostasis (e.g. Wis. 7.22b – 8.1; cf. Sir. 24). In Proverbs, though, it is better to take this as a personification.

As noted already, proverbial wisdom is often linked with observations of, and reflections on, the world, and is thus based more on general than on special revelation.[54] And there are few direct references to Israel's covenant faith. Wisdom in the OT does, though, have an important theological dimension, and in Proverbs it is closely linked with the 'fear of the LORD' (1:7; 8:13; 9:10; 15:33; cf. Deut. 10:12–13, 20).[55] Wisdom comes from God, and while aspects of it may be more generally available, true wisdom is found in relationship with God.

Proverbs also includes some stock characters. There are frequent references to the 'fool', particularly contrasting him with the wise.[56] The 'mocker' (NRSV 'scoffer') is also contrasted with those who are wise (e.g. 9:8, 12; 13:1; 14:6; 15:12; 29:8). Particular characteristics include arrogance (21:24), unteachability (9:7–8; 13:1; 14:6; 15:12), quarrelling and divisiveness (22:10; 29:8). The 'sluggard' is a comic figure, whose laziness results in his ruin (6:6–11; 24:30–34; see also e.g. 20:4; 21:25; 26:13–15).

There are several other significant themes. As might be expected from a collection of proverbs, there is an emphasis on the right use of words. In contrast to the wicked, the words of the wise are worth hearing (e.g. 10:11, 20). Words should be used carefully,[57] and appropriately (15:23; 25:11); they should be gentle and pleasant (15:1; 16:21, 24; 25:15), but should not avoid giving rebuke where necessary (25:12; 27:5). Other themes include the value of friendship,[58] the importance of family (12:4; 18:22; 19:14), and the responsibility of parents, particularly in the context of discipline (e.g.

---

53. See e.g. Koptak, 'Personification', in *DOTWPW*, pp. 516–519; Roland E. Murphy, 'The Personification of Wisdom', in Day, Gordon and Williamson, *Wisdom in Ancient Israel*, pp. 222–233.
54. Above, pp. 124, 189.
55. See also 2:5; 10:27; 14:27; 15:16; 16:6; 19:23; 22:4; 23:17; 31:30.
56. E.g. 1:7; 10:8, 14; 12:15–16, 23; 15:5; 16:22; 18:2; 24:7.
57. E.g. 10:19; 12:18; 13:3; 16:23; 18:13; 21:23; 29:20.
58. E.g. 14:20; 17:17; 18:24; 19:4, 6–7; 27:6, 9.

13:24; 19:18; 22:15; 23:13–14; 29:15, 17) and instruction (e.g. 22:6; cf. 1:8; 2:1; 3:1; 6:20).[59]

The *mĕgillôt* (scrolls)

The books of Ruth, Song of Songs, Ecclesiastes, Lamentations and Esther are collectively known as the *mĕgillôt*. They were read at the five Jewish festivals of Weeks (Pentecost), Passover, Tabernacles, the ninth day of Ab (commemorating the destruction of the temple) and Purim, respectively.[60]

Ruth[61]

Its opening verse sets the book of Ruth during the time of the Judges (1:1). The writer, though, is looking back, suggesting a date no earlier than the monarchy.[62]

---

59. As noted earlier, wisdom teaching probably began in the family (see above, pp. 187–188).
60. See e.g. B. C. Gregory, 'Megilloth and Festivals', in *DOTWPW*, pp. 457–464; Timothy J. Stone, *The Compilational History of the Megilloth*, FAT 2.59 (Tübingen: Mohr Siebeck, 2013): Barry G. Webb, *Five Festal Garments: Christian Reflections on the Song of Songs, Ruth, Lamentations, Ecclesiastes, Esther*, NSBT 10 (Leicester: Apollos, 2000).
61. Commentaries on Ruth include Block, *Judges, Ruth*; Frederic Bush, *Ruth/Esther*, WBC 9 (Dallas: Word, 1996); Edward F. Campbell Jr., *Ruth*, AB 7 (New York: Doubleday, 1975); Tamara Cohn Eskenazi and Tikva Frymer-Kensky, *Ruth*, JPSBC (Philadelphia: Jewish Publication Society, 2011); Robert L. Hubbard Jr., *The Book of Ruth*, NICOT (Grand Rapids: Eerdmans, 1988); André Lacocque, *Ruth*, CC (Minneapolis: Augsburg Fortress, 2004); Todd Linafelt, *Ruth*, Berit Olam (Collegeville: Liturgical Press, 1999); Matthews, *Judges & Ruth*; Michael S. Moore, 'Ruth', in Harris, Brown and Moore, *Joshua, Judges, Ruth*, pp. 291–373; Leon Morris, 'Ruth', in Cundall and Morris, *Judges, Ruth*, pp. 217–318; Kirsten Nielsen, *Ruth*, OTL (Louisville: Westminster John Knox, 1997); Katharine Doob Sakenfeld, *Ruth*, IBC (Louisville: Westminster John Knox, 1999); Younger, *Judges, Ruth*. See also Murray D. Gow, *The Book of Ruth: Its Structure, Theme and Purpose* (Leicester: Apollos, 1992); Phyllis Trible, 'Two Women in a Man's World: A Reading of the Book of Ruth', *Sound* 59.3 (1976), pp. 251–279; rev. and expanded as 'A Human Comedy', in *God and the Rhetoric of Sexuality*, OBT (Philadelphia: Fortress, 1978), pp. 166–199.
62. This makes its traditional attribution to Samuel (*b. B. Bat.* 15a) unlikely.

The book gives no indication of its author, though, because it gives a predominantly female perspective, and the main drivers of the narrative are Naomi and Ruth,[63] many suggest a woman writer.[64] In the past the book was regarded as post-exilic, challenging the exclusivism of Ezra and Nehemiah.[65] More recent commentators favour a pre-exilic date.[66] However, evidence for either is inconclusive.[67]

The book is generally regarded as a unity up to 4:17a. Several scholars regard the naming of the child (4:17b), and the genealogy linking Ruth to David (4:18–22), which it introduces, as secondary.[68] Others, though, have put forward a good case for viewing this section as integral to the book and its purpose.[69]

The presence of the genealogy suggests a purpose linked with David. This may be to honour or legitimize him and his heirs, both by pointing to the quality of his ancestry and by connecting it to the patriarchs (4:11–12).[70] To that end, the main characters epitomize love and loyalty that go beyond the requirements of the law. Ruth is particularly commended for her 'kindness' (*ḥesed*) to Naomi (3:10; cf. 1:8),[71] which is greater than the normal duties of a daughter-in-law,

---

63. E.g. Trible, 'Two Women', esp. pp. 278–279; see also Richard Bauckham, *Is the Bible Male? The Book of Ruth and Biblical Narrative* (Cambridge: Grove, 1966).
64. E.g. Adrien J. Bledstein, 'Female Companionships', in Athalya Brenner (ed.), *A Feminist Companion to Ruth* (Sheffield: Sheffield Academic Press, 1993), pp. 116–133; Campbell, *Ruth*, pp. 21–23; Irmtraud Fischer, 'The Book of Ruth: A Feminist Commentary to the Torah', in Athalya Brenner (ed.), *Ruth and Esther*, FCB (Sheffield: Sheffield Academic Press, 1999), pp. 24–49 (33–34); Gottwald, *Hebrew Bible*, pp. 555–557; R. L. Hubbard, *Ruth*, p. 24; Lacocque, *Ruth*, p. 13; Sakenfeld, *Ruth*, p. 5.
65. E.g. Lacocque, *Ruth*, p. 2.
66. E.g. Campbell, *Ruth*, pp. 23–27; R. L. Hubbard, *Ruth*, pp. 30–35; Nielsen, *Ruth*, p. 27.
67. See e.g. surveys of evidence by Bush (*Ruth/Esther*, pp. 18–30), R. L. Hubbard (*Ruth*, pp. 24–35) and Satterthwaite and McConville, *Histories*, pp. 226–227.
68. E.g. Childs, *Introduction*, p. 566; John Gray, *Joshua, Judges and Ruth*, NCB (London: Oliphants, 1967), pp. 298–301.
69. E.g. Bush, *Ruth/Esther*, pp. 10–16; R. L. Hubbard, *Ruth*, pp. 11–23; Lacocque, *Ruth*, p. 13 (though Lacocque considers it to be fictitious); Nielsen, *Ruth*, p. 27. Though secondary, for Childs it is part of the book's canonical shaping.
70. See e.g. Bush, *Ruth/Esther*, pp. 48–53 (53); R. L. Hubbard, *Ruth*, pp. 35–42 (39–42); Nielsen, *Ruth*, p. 27. There may be a link between the narratives of Ruth and Tamar (Gen. 38); see e.g. Nielsen, *Ruth*, pp. 13–17.
71. For further discussion of *ḥesed*, see above, pp. 312–313.

and contrasts with Naomi's other daughter-in-law, Orpah (1:14).[72] Boaz, too, shows willingness to go beyond what may be legally expected of him,[73] in accepting the responsibility of 'kinsman-redeemer' (*gō'ēl*) even though he is not the closest relative (3:12),[74] an action that contrasts with that of the one who may be expected to fulfil the role (4:6). The book also emphasizes the Lord's hand behind all that takes place (e.g. 1:6, 21; 2:20; 4:13–15). This includes Naomi's hardship, but ultimately results in blessing, both to Naomi and, through David, to Israel.

Outline

- Prologue: Naomi's bereavement and emptiness (1:1–22)
  - Bereavement in Moab (1:1–6)
  - Return to Bethlehem with Ruth (1:7–22)
- Ruth meets Boaz (2:1–23)
- Naomi's plan for Ruth to marry Boaz (3:1–18)
- Boaz marries Ruth (4:1–12)
- Epilogue: Joy and blessing (4:13–22)
  - A child for Naomi (4:13–16b)
  - Genealogy of David (4:17b–22)

---

72. Orpah behaved correctly, and also showed *ḥesed* to Naomi (1:8); however, her 'reasonable' behaviour is limited, thus highlighting Ruth's greater commitment.
73. Though the construction is ambiguous, 2:20 probably refers to *ḥesed* shown by Boaz (cf. 2 Sam. 2:5); see e.g. Bush, *Ruth/Esther*, pp. 134–136; R. L. Hubbard, *Ruth*, p. 186; Basil A. Rebera, 'Yahweh or Boaz? Ruth 2:20 Reconsidered', *BT* 36 (1985), pp. 317–327. It has been suggested that the ambiguity is deliberate: in experiencing Boaz's *ḥesed*, Ruth also experiences the wider kindness shown by God to Israel; see C. John Collins, 'Ambiguity and Theology in Ruth: Ruth 1:21 and 2:20', *Presb.* 19.2 (1993), pp. 97–102 (99–101); Linafelt, *Ruth*, pp. 41–42.
74. Where someone needed to sell land, in order to keep it within the family, the nearest relative (*gō'ēl*) was expected to redeem the purchase (Lev. 25:25). The law of levirate marriage, by which the brother of a childless husband was expected to marry his widow to preserve his name (Deut. 25:5–6; cf. Gen. 38:6–11) is not usually linked with the responsibility of the *gō'ēl*. Here, though, the two appear to have been combined (see also 4:7–8; cf. Deut. 25:7–10). This may further indicate that Boaz does more than the law requires. For further discussion of the legalities, see e.g. Bush, *Ruth/Esther*, pp. 211–215; R. L. Hubbard, *Ruth*, pp. 48–63; Satterthwaite and McConville, *Histories*, pp. 227–228.

Song of Songs[75]

The title comes from its opening verse: 'Solomon's Song of Songs'. 'Song of songs', like the term 'holy of holies', expresses a superlative: 'the best song'. It is linked with Solomon but, as with psalm titles, the preposition *lĕ* does not necessarily imply authorship. Childs suggests that the reference to Solomon is, primarily, to categorize the book as wisdom literature.[76] Others see Solomon if not as the author, then as one of the main protagonists, though that raises the question of how the book should be interpreted.[77]

The Song is widely thought to be post-exilic, with dates ranging from the fourth to the second century BC.[78] Comparisons with Egyptian love poetry suggest that some elements are much older.[79] It is possible that material may go back to Solomon's time,[80] though maybe with later editorial

---

75. Commentaries on the Song of Songs/Solomon include Dianne Bergant, *The Song of Songs*, Berit Olam (Collegeville: Liturgical Press, 2001); G. Lloyd Carr, *The Song of Solomon*, TOTC (Leicester: Inter-Varsity Press, 1984); Davis, *Proverbs, Ecclesiastes, Song of Songs*; Iain M. Duguid, *The Song of Songs*, TOTC (Nottingham: Inter-Varsity Press, 2015); Daniel J. Estes, 'The Song of Songs', in Daniel C. Fredericks and Daniel J. Estes, *Ecclesiastes & the Song of Songs*, AOTC (Nottingham: Apollos; Downer's Grove: InterVarsity Press, 2010), pp. 265–444; J. Cheryl Exum, *Song of Songs*, OTL (Louisville: Westminster John Knox, 2005); Duane A. Garrett, 'Song of Songs', in Duane A. Garrett and Paul House, *Song of Songs, Lamentations*, WBC 23B (Nashville: Nelson, 2004), pp. 1–265; *Proverbs, Ecclesiastes, Song of Songs*; Richard S. Hess, *Song of Songs*, BCOTWP (Grand Rapids: Baker Academic, 2005); Elizabeth Huwiler, 'Song of Songs', in Murphy and Huwiler, *Proverbs, Ecclesiastes, Song of Songs*; Robert W. Jenson, *Song of Songs*, IBC (Louisville: John Knox, 2005); Longman, *Song of Songs*; Roland E. Murphy, *The Song of Songs*, Hermeneia (Minneapolis: Fortress, 1990); Marvin H. Pope, *Song of Songs*, AB 7C (New York: Doubleday, 1977); Iain Provan, *Ecclesiastes, Song of Songs*, NIVAC (Grand Rapids: Zondervan, 2001).
76. Childs, *Introduction*, pp. 573–575.
77. Pope's lengthy section on this indicates the wide variety of interpretations (*Song of Songs*, pp. 89–229). See also J. Paul Tanner, 'The History of Interpretation of the Song of Songs', *BSac* 154 (1997), pp. 23–46.
78. E.g. Davis, *Proverbs, Ecclesiastes, Song of Songs*, p. 231; Exum, *Song of Songs*, p. 66.
79. E.g. Fox, *Song of Songs*, pp. 186–193. Though Fox nevertheless argues for a post-exilic date.
80. E.g. Garrett, *Proverbs, Ecclesiastes, Song of Songs*, pp. 348–352; 'Song of Songs', in Garrett and House, *Song of Songs, Lamentation*, pp. 16–22.

revision.[81] The evidence is inconclusive,[82] but on balance a post-exilic date for the final composition of the book seems more likely.[83]

Jewish and Christian interpreters have, traditionally, understood the book allegorically, referring to God's love for Israel, or Christ's love for the church. That, though, is very unlikely to have been its original intention.

The Song has three voices: a girl, described as a Shulammite (6:13), who has the largest part,[84] her shepherd-lover (cf. 1:7–8), who may be identified with Solomon, and a chorus, addressed as the 'daughters of Jerusalem' (e.g. 2:7; 3:5; 5:16; 8:4). It is sometimes viewed as a drama, about either the two lovers, or the two lovers and Solomon, whose intention to bring the girl into his harem threatens their relationship. However there is not the clear narrative plot or development of characters that would indicate drama, and it seems better to see the book as a collection of poems.[85] However, the consistency of the background and characters, and an identifiable overall structure, suggest that the components form a coherent literary unity,[86] offering snapshots of the lovers' relationship.

The book celebrates human love, both emotional and physical.[87] Some maintain that there is no indication that the couple are married,[88] though 3:6 – 5:1 may indicate a wedding, which is anticipated in earlier expressions of

81. E.g. Carr, *Song of Solomon*, pp. 17–19, 37–44; Estes, 'Song of Songs', in Fredericks and Estes, *Ecclesiastes & Song of Songs*, pp. 271–273; Fox, *Song of Songs*, pp. 222–224; G. Schwab, 'Song of Songs I: Book of', in *DOTPW*, pp. 737–750 (739).

82. E.g. Exum, *Song of Songs*, pp. 66–67; Hess, *Song of Songs*, pp. 17–19; Longman, *Song of Songs*, p. 19.

83. E.g. Duguid, *Song of Songs*, pp. 19–23; Provan, *Ecclesiastes, Song of Solomon*, pp. 236–237.

84. This leads some to suggest that the author was a woman; see e.g. Davis, *Proverbs, Ecclesiastes, Song of Songs*, p. 239; André Lacocque, *Romance, She Wrote: A Hermeneutical Essay on Song of Songs* (Eugene: Wipf & Stock, 2006), p. 19; see also Exum, *Song of Songs*, pp. 65–66.

85. This may be a secondary inference of the title: a song made up of songs; see e.g. Estes, 'Song of Songs', in Fredericks and Estes, *Ecclesiastes & Song of Songs*, p. 290; Garrett, 'Song of Songs', in Garrett and House, *Song of Songs, Lamentations*, p. 26.

86. E.g. Carr, *Song of Solomon*, pp. 44–49; Estes, 'Song of Songs', in Fredericks and Estes, *Ecclesiastes & Song of Songs*, pp. 289–291; Garrett, 'Song of Songs', in Garrett and House, *Song of Songs, Lamentations*, pp. 25–35.

87. A feature of the Song is the metaphorical description of parts of the body, often referred to using the Arabic term *wasf*.

88. E.g. Collins, *Hebrew Bible*, p. 502; Lacocque, *Romance*, pp. 7–8, 161; Trible, *God and the Rhetoric of Sexuality*, p. 162.

love.[89] And within its wider OT context the Song cannot be taken as licence for sexual relations outside marriage. As a wisdom text, the book may, also, be intended to provide instruction. Though it does not mention God, possible links with Genesis 2 – 3,[90] suggest that the Song points to the restoration of God's intention for love between a man and a woman lost after the fall.

There are several suggestions for the structure and outline of the book. The repeated calls to the daughters of Jerusalem, 'Do not arouse or awaken love until it so desires' (2:7b; 3:5b; 8:4b) mark some of the breaks. Some commentators also suggest a chiastic structure.[91] One approach is to divide the text into six cycles.[92]

Outline

- Title (1:1)
- First cycle: passion and anticipation (1:2 – 2:7)
- Second cycle: a springtime meeting; a lover lost and found (2:8 – 3:5)
- Third cycle: the lovers' wedding and consummation (3:6 – 5:1)
- Fourth cycle: a lover lost and found (5:2 – 6:3)
- Fifth cycle: passion and anticipation (6:4 – 8:4)
- Sixth cycle: love and contentment (8:5–14)

Ecclesiastes[93]

Date, authorship and composition

'Ecclesiastes' is based on the Greek translation of the Hebrew *qōhelet* (1:1). This is from *qāhal* (to assemble), and indicates 'one who assembles', which in the OT

---

89. Duguid, *Song of Songs*, pp. 40–42; Estes, 'Song of Songs', in Fredericks and Estes, *Ecclesiastes & Song of Songs*, pp. 293–296; Garrett, 'Song of Songs', in Garrett and House, *Song of Songs, Lamentations*, pp. 102–104.

90. See e.g. Richard M. Davidson, 'Theology of Sexuality in the Song of Songs: Return to Eden', *AUSS* 27.1 (1989), pp. 1–19; Davis, *Proverbs, Ecclesiastes, Song of Songs*, pp. 231–232; Duguid, *Song of Songs*, pp. 39–40; Estes, 'Song of Songs', in Fredericks and Estes, *Ecclesiastes & Song of Songs*, pp. 298–299; Francis Landy, 'The Song of Songs and the Garden of Eden', *JBL* 98 (1979), pp. 513–528; Trible, *God and the Rhetoric of Sexuality*, pp. 145–165.

91. E.g. Carr, *Song of Songs*, pp. 44–49; Garrett, 'Song of Songs', in Garrett and House, *Song of Songs, Lamentations*, pp. 30–35.

92. E.g. Duguid, *Song of Songs*, p. 53; Hess, *Song of Songs*, p. 31.

93. Commentaries on Ecclesiastes include Craig G. Bartholomew, *Ecclesiastes*, BCOTWP (Grand Rapids: Baker Academic, 2009); William P. Brown, *Ecclesiastes*, IBC (Louisville:

is generally used in relation to assembling people (e.g. Exod. 35:1; Num. 1:18; 1 Kgs 8:1; 12:21). One of the aims of gathering a congregation may be to preach or teach (e.g. 12:9), possibly giving rise to the translation 'Preacher' or 'Teacher'. It is, though, not strictly accurate, and many commentators leave the term untranslated.

On the basis of the opening, 'son of David, king of Jerusalem' (1:1; cf. 1:12), Qohelet has been, traditionally, identified with Solomon, whose life and achievements seem, also, to be reflected in 2:1–11; nevertheless, there is a wide consensus that Solomon is not the author. It is unclear why Solomon would not be named, and the language is usually dated between the late fifth and third century BC.[94] There are also internal inconsistencies.[95] According to 1:12, Qohelet's kingship is in the past, but there is no indication that Solomon left office before his death.

(*Footnote 93 cont.*) Westminster John Knox, 2000); James L. Crenshaw, *Ecclesiastes*, NICOT (Philadelphia: Westminster, 1987); Davis, *Proverbs, Ecclesiastes, Song of Songs*; Michael A. Eaton, *Ecclesiastes*, TOTC (Leicester: Inter-Varsity Press; Downers Grove: InterVarsity Press, 1983); Peter Enns, *Ecclesiastes*, THOTC (Grand Rapids: Eerdmans, 2011); Michael V. Fox, *Ecclesiastes*, JPSBC (Philadelphia: Jewish Publication Society, 2004); Daniel C. Fredericks, 'Ecclesiastes', in Fredericks and Estes, *Ecclesiastes & the Song of Songs*, pp. 16–263; Garrett, *Proverbs, Ecclesiastes, Song of Songs*; Elizabeth Huwiler, 'Ecclesiastes', in Murphy and Huwiler, *Proverbs, Ecclesiastes and Song of Songs*, pp. 157–218; Tremper Longman III, *The Book of Ecclesiastes*, NICOT (Grand Rapids: Eerdmans, 1998); Murphy, *Ecclesiastes*; Provan, *Ecclesiastes, Song of Solomon*; Choon-Leong Seow, *Ecclesiastes*, AB 18C (New York: Doubleday, 1997). See also Michael V. Fox, *Qoheleth and His Contradictions*, BLS 18 (Sheffield: Almond, 1989). For more on wisdom literature, see above, pp. 124–128, 187–194. See also Eric S. Christianson, *A Time to Tell: Narrative Strategies in Ecclesiastes*, JSOTSup 280 (Sheffield: Sheffield Academic Press, 1998); Michael V. Fox, *A Time to Tear Down and a Time to Build up* (Grand Rapids: Eerdmans, 1999).

94. Seow places it in the Persian period, in the late fifth or early fourth century BC; see C. L. Seow, 'Linguistic Evidence and the Dating of Qohelet', *JBL* 115.4 (1996), pp. 643–666; *Ecclesiastes*, pp. 12–21. Others place it in the Greek period, in the fourth/third century BC; e.g. Brown, *Ecclesiastes*, pp. 7–8; Fox, *Ecclesiastes*, p. xiv; Murphy, *Ecclesiastes*, pp. xxii, xxvii. Longman suggests that the language is not sufficient to determine the date (*Ecclesiastes*, pp. 11–15); see also Bartholomew, *Ecclesiastes*, pp. 48–54. Fredericks argues for a pre-exilic date, and allows the possibility of identifying Solomon with Qohelet (Fredericks, 'Ecclesiastes', in Fredericks and Estes, *Ecclesiastes & the Song of Songs*, pp. 31–36, 58–61).

95. See e.g. Bartholomew, *Ecclesiastes*, pp. 46–48; Longman, *Ecclesiastes*, pp. 4–8.

And it seems strange for only Jerusalem's second king to refer to 'anyone who has ruled over Jerusalem before me' (1:16; cf. 2:9).[96]

It seems more likely that the writer adopts the persona of Solomon, at least in the first two chapters, in order to give Solomon's perspective.[97] The writer reflects on the ephemerality and futility of human existence from the standpoint of one who has wealth, great achievements and superlative wisdom, to emphasize that none of those things can give life meaning. The allusions to Solomon may also help to place Ecclesiastes within the wisdom genre, though, like Job, it points to the limitations of wisdom. Childs suggests that the link with Solomon may also be to emphasize that this challenge to conventional wisdom teaching is 'not to be regarded as the personal idiosyncrasy of a nameless teacher'.[98]

As we have noted, some of the issues raised in Ecclesiastes are also evident in other ANE literature.[99] There is, though, no suggestion of dependence. While some date the book in the Greek period, there is no evidence that it has been influenced by Greek philosophy, though it may share some of the same concerns.[100]

The book is generally thought to comprise, primarily, Qohelet's teaching, but with some editorial material,[101] including an epilogue (12:9–14), the inclusio '"Meaningless! Meaningless!" says the Teacher. "Everything is meaningless"' (1:2; 12:8) and 7:27. Because Qoheleth seems to introduce himself in 1:12–18, 1:3–11 is sometimes seen as a prologue. There are also apparent contradictions.[102] In the past that was taken to indicate further editors,[103] though more recently other explanations have been suggested. Qohelet may be arguing with an

---

96. It seems unlikely that this would be intended to include Jebusite kings before David.

97. Allusions to Solomon end after ch. 2. Some suggest that in subsequent chapters Qohelet speaks as a sage (e.g. Fox, *Ecclesiastes*, p. x; Murphy, *Ecclesiastes*, pp. xx–xxi).

98. Childs, *Introduction*, p. 584.

99. See above, pp. 126–128.

100. E.g. Fox, *Qoheleth*, p. 16; *Ecclesiastes*, pp. xi–xii; Murphy, *Ecclesiastes*, pp. xli–xlv; see also Crenshaw, *Ecclesiastes*, p. 51.

101. E.g. Crenshaw, *Ecclesiastes*, pp. 39–49; Longman, *Ecclesiastes*, pp. 7–9, 15–21; Murphy, *Ecclesiastes*, p. 33; see also Michael V. Fox, 'Frame-Narrative and Composition in the Book of Qohelet', *HUCA* 48 (1977), pp. 83–106.

102. E.g. 1:17–18 (cf. 7:11); 2:11 (cf. 5:18); 4:2 (cf. 9:4–6); 8:12–13 (cf. v. 14) (see also 3:16–17). See Crenshaw, *Ecclesiastes*, pp. 46–47; Fox, *Qoheleth*.

103. See the discussion by Crenshaw, *Ecclesiastes*, pp. 46–47.

unnamed adversary or with conventional wisdom teaching. Or, more likely, he may recognize that a single viewpoint cannot do justice to the complexity of the issues.[104]

Structure and outline

There is some agreement on the overall structure of the book (see below). Beyond that, though, commentators note the difficulties in discerning any clear pattern. There are several key phrases or ideas, such as 'meaningless, a chasing after the wind' (1:14b; 2:11b, 17b, 26b; 4:4, 16; 6:9) and the encouragement to enjoy life (2:24; 3:12–13, 22; 5:18–20; 8:15; 9:7–10; 11:7–10), that may serve to divide the text.[105] However, there are no common themes linking the sections.

Outline[106]

- Superscription (1:1)
- Inclusio (1:2)
- Prologue (1:3–11)
- Qohelet's teaching (1:12 – 12:7)
- Inclusio (12:8)
- Epilogue (12:9–14)

Main themes

A key term in Ecclesiastes is *hebel*,[107] which is translated 'meaningless' (NIV) or 'vanity' (NRSV, AV). The term may be translated 'breath', referring to something fleeting or transient, and some prefer to understand it that way in Ecclesiastes: the key concern of the writer is not the meaninglessness or futility of life, but

---

104. See e.g. Fox, *Qoheleth*, pp. 19–28; Lucas, *Psalms and Wisdom*, pp. 149–151. Crenshaw notes Hertzberg's 'zwar-aber' (true-but) analysis (*Ecclesiastes*, p. 46); see also Lucas, *Psalms and Wisdom*, pp. 151–152. However, see Fredericks, 'Ecclesiastes', in Fredericks and Estes, *Ecclesiastes & the Song of Songs*, p. 48.

105. For suggested outlines, see e.g. Crenshaw, *Ecclesiastes*, pp. 34–49; Lucas, *Psalms and Wisdom*, pp. 152–155.

106. There are variations on this theme. Longman takes 1:1–11 as the prologue and 12:8–14 as the epilogue (*Ecclesiastes*, pp. 20, 21). Some take only 1:1–3 as the prologue (e.g. Lucas, *Psalms and Wisdom*, p. 152). Crenshaw sees two epilogues, 12:9-11 and 12:12–14 (*Ecclesiastes*, pp. 48, 189–192).

107. The term occurs thirty-eight times in Ecclesiastes, around half of the total number in the OT.

its transience or ephemerality.[108] And taken this way, many of the apparent contradictions in the text may be resolved. It seems strange, though, to complain about the transience of injustice (8:14). Elsewhere in the OT the term appears to have a generally negative connotation,[109] and it seems reasonable to take it the same way in Ecclesiastes.[110]

Longman argues that while Qoheleth is cynical, the epilogist is more positive.[111] Qohelet's outlook on life, though, is not one of total cynicism. He challenges the view that conventional wisdom, or anything else generally thought of as desirable, can give life meaning, and a significant part of that is his focus on death, which, in the absence of a clear theology of after-life,[112] brings everything, good and bad, wise and foolish, animal and human, to the same end (e.g. 2:15–16; 3:19; 9:1–2). Nevertheless, even though God's ways are incomprehensible (e.g. 5:2; 11:5), Qohelet continues to believe in him (e.g. 5:1–7; cf. 12:13), and to trust in his final justice (e.g. 3:17; cf. 12:14). And though wisdom has its limitations, it is still better than folly (2:13). The possibility that life can be enjoyed, despite its apparent meaninglessness, also suggests a less cynical outlook. His overall emphasis appears to be not to look for meaning in places where it cannot be found, but, instead, in the uncertainty and apparent futility of life, to go on trusting God, whose ways we cannot ultimately fathom, and make the most of the life he gives.

---

108. E.g. Daniel C. Fredericks, *Coping with Transience: Ecclesiastes on Brevity of Life* (Sheffield: JSOT Press, 1993), esp. pp. 11–32; 'Ecclesiastes', in Fredericks and Estes, *Ecclesiastes & the Song of Songs*, pp. 46–54; Leo G. Perdue, *Wisdom & Creation: The Theology of Wisdom Literature* (Eugene: Wipf & Stock, 1994), pp. 206–208.

109. The term is parallel to 'lie' in Ps. 62:9 and to what is false or deceptive in Prov. 31:30; Jer. 16:19; Zech. 10:2. See Christianson, *Time to Tell*, pp. 79–91 (79–81); Longman, *Ecclesiastes*, pp. 61–65.

110. Suggestions include 'meaningless' (Longman, *Ecclesiastes*, pp. 61–65); 'absurd', in the sense of unreasonable (Fox, *Qoheleth*, pp. 29–51; *Time to Tear Down*, pp. 79–91; see also Enns, *Ecclesiastes*, p. 9, n. 20); 'enigmatic' (Bartholomew, *Ecclesiastes*, pp. 93–94).

111. Longman, *Ecclesiastes*, pp. 29–39.

112. See above, p. 19.

Lamentations[113]

Lamentations is made up of five laments describing the horror of the destruction of Jerusalem by the Babylonians in 587 BC. It appears to be a first-hand account and has been traditionally linked with Jeremiah.[114] Jeremiah is associated with national lament (e.g. 2 Chr. 35:25) and there are similarities in language;[115] though there are also differences, which, for some, make Jeremianic authorship unlikely.[116] Some of the language, including references to the city and people being 'unclean', may suggest a priestly background.[117] Few, though, question the literary unity of the book. And there is general agreement, too, that it was written in the sixth century BC, maybe shortly after the events described.[118] There is some discussion about the identity of the man in

---

113. Commentaries on Lamentations include Dianne Bergant, *Lamentations*, AbOTC (Nashville: Abingdon, 2003); Berlin, *Lamentations*; Dearman, *Jeremiah and Lamentations*; F. W. Dobbs-Allsopp, *Lamentations*, IBC (Louisville: Westminster John Knox, 2002); Harrison, *Jeremiah and Lamentations*; Delbert R. Hillers, *Lamentations*, 2nd ed., AB 7 (New York: Doubleday, 1992); Paul R. House, 'Lamentations', in Garrett and House, *Song of Songs, Lamentations*, pp. 269–473; Huey, *Jeremiah, Lamentations*; Lalleman, *Jeremiah and Lamentations*; Longman, *Jeremiah, Lamentations*; Robin Parry, *Lamentations*, THOTC (Grand Rapids: Eerdmans, 2010); Iain Provan, *Lamentations*, NCB (London: Marshall Pickering; Grand Rapids: Eerdmans, 1991); Christopher J. H. Wright, *The Message of Lamentations*, BST (Nottingham: Inter-Varsity Press, 2015).
114. *Baba Batra* (*b. B. Batra* 15b) and *Tg. Lam.* associate it with Jeremiah; the LXX includes a title attributing it to Jeremiah, and that is reflected in the Vulgate.
115. E.g. 1:16; 3:48–49 (Jer. 9:1, 18; 14:17); 2:15 (Jer. 18:16); 2:22 (Jer. 6:25); 4:11 (Jer. 21:14).
116. E.g. Lalleman, *Jeremiah and Lamentations*, pp. 320–322 (322). However, see Huey, *Jeremiah, Lamentations*, pp. 442–443. Others are agnostic (e.g. Parry, *Lamentations*, pp. 3–5). Berlin suggests that Jeremiah may be the implied author (*Lamentations*, pp. 30–32).
117. E.g. Lalleman, *Jeremiah and Lamentations*, p. 322. The term, *ṭāmē'* (unclean) occurs in 4:15; the related term *niddâ* (impurity) occurs in 1:8, 17.
118. The possible dependence of Isa. 40 – 55 on Lamentations points to a date no later than 538 BC; see e.g. Berlin, *Lamentations*, p. 34; Claus Westermann, *Lamentations: Issues and Interpretation* (Minneapolis: Fortress, 1994), pp. 97–105; cf. Todd Linafelt, *Surviving Lamentations: Catastrophe, Lament, and Protest in the Afterlife of a Biblical Book* (Chicago: University of Chicago Press, 2000), pp. 52–79.

chapter 3. He is probably to be seen as representative of those who suffered during the Babylonian invasion, and may correspond to the female figure of Zion in chapters 1–2.[119]

Chapters 1–4 are written as alphabetic acrostics.[120] Chapter 5 is not, though it also has twenty-two verses. The reason for the structure is not clear. If the purpose of the acrostics is to indicate the completeness of Judah's suffering, the prayer in chapter 5 may stand in contrast, leaving open the possibility of future salvation.

The main emphasis of the book is the horror associated with the destruction of Jerusalem. There is, though, the recognition that this is God's doing. He is in control, and all things, good and bad, come from him (3:37–38; cf. Job 2:10). The defeat of Judah is the result of sin (e.g. 1:5, 7, 18–22; 3:42; 5:16). Continued presence in the land was conditional on obedience (e.g. Deut. 28); now disobedience has brought divine judgment (2:17). However, while punishment is justified, the intensity of the suffering leads the poet to question its severity (e.g. 2:20; 5:7–22) and God's apparent unwillingness to forgive (3:42), and to want revenge on Judah's enemies (e.g. 1:21–22; 3:64–66).

There is, though, hope for a desolate people, based on God's faithfulness and *ḥesed* (3:21–23, 32; cf. Exod. 34:6). God will not abandon them for ever (3:31–33; 4:22); he will restore them and, finally, will bring judgment on their enemies too (4:21–22). In the light of that hope the book invites trust (e.g. 3:24–26) and repentance (3:40–42), and calls for God's help (5:21).

Outline

- The Daughter of Zion mourns (1:1–22)
- The Lord's judgment on the city (2:1–22)
- Suffering and hope (3:1–66)
- Continued suffering (4:1–22)
- A prayer for relief and restoration (5:1–22)

It has been argued that it may be linked with the rebuilding of the temple, around 520 BC, though that seems unlikely; see e.g. Berlin, *Lamentations*, pp. 35–36; F. W. Dobbs-Allsopp, 'Linguistic Evidence for the date of Lamentations', *JANES* 29 (1998), pp. 1–36 (9, n. 47); *Lamentations*, pp. 10–12; Longman and Dillard, *Introduction*, pp. 347–348.

119. See e.g. Berlin, *Lamentations*, pp. 84–85; Dobbs-Allsopp, *Lamentations*, pp. 105–110; Lalleman, *Jeremiah and Lamentations*, pp. 350–352.

120. See above, pp. 151–152.

Esther[121]

Text and composition

The book of Esther has been transmitted in a number of variant forms. The LXX version differs substantially from the MT, particularly with the inclusion of six 'additions to the book of Esther',[122] which some religious traditions include within the canon. There is also evidence of another Greek text, the Alpha- or A-text (AT), which appears to be based on a different Hebrew text from the LXX or MT, together with additions from the LXX.[123] The Hebrew text underlying the AT is thought to be close to the earliest Hebrew version of the story, and this was edited and expanded into the version found in the MT.

---

121. Commentaries on Esther include Joyce G. Baldwin, *Esther*, TOTC (Leicester: Inter-Varsity Press; Downers Grove: InterVarsity Press, 1984); Timothy K. Beal, *Esther*, Berit Olam (Collegeville: Liturgical Press, 1999); Carol M. Bechtel, *Esther*, IBC (Louisville: Westminster John Knox, 2002); Adele Berlin, *Esther*, JPSBC (Philadelphia: Jewish Publication Society, 2001); Mervin Breneman, *Ezra, Nehemiah, Esther*, NAC 10 (Nashville: B&H, 1993); Bush, *Ruth/Esther*; D. J. Clines, *Ezra, Nehemiah, Esther*, NCB (Grand Rapids: Eerdmans, 1996); Linda M. Day, *Esther*, AbOTC (Nashville: Abingdon, 2005); Karen H. Jobes, *Esther*, NIVAC (Grand Rapids: Zondervan, 1999); T. Laniak, 'Esther', in L. Allen and T. Laniak, *Ezra, Nehemiah, Esther*, NIBCOT/UBC (Peabody: Hendrickson, 2003), pp. 167–274; Jon D. Levenson, *Esther*, OTL (Louisville: Westminster John Knox, 1997); Carey A. Moore, *Esther*, AB 7B (New York: Doubleday, 1971); *Daniel, Esther, and Jeremiah: The Additions*, AB 44 (New York: Doubleday, 1977); Debra Reid, *Esther*, TOTC (Nottingham: IVP, 2008). See also Brenner, *Ruth and Esther*.
122. These are listed as A–F. A (before 1:1) describes Mordecai's dream of deliverance; B (after 3:13) gives the text of Artaxerxes' (*sic*) decree to destroy the Jews; C (after 4:17) contains Mordecai's and Esther's prayers; D (after C) describes how God changed the king's attitude towards Esther after she had fainted; E (after 8:12) gives the text of Artaxerxes' decree to allow the Jews to defend themselves; F (after 10:3) interprets Mordecai's dream (A) in the light of what has transpired. They appear in context in the Apocrypha section of the NRSV. See further e.g. Levenson, *Esther*, pp. 28–32; Moore, *Additions*, pp. 153–254.
123. See David J. A. Clines, *The Esther Scroll: The Story of the Story*, JSOTSup 30 (Sheffield: JSOT Press, 1984), pp. 71–92, 215–247; Michael V. Fox, *The Redaction of the Books of Esther: On Reading Composite Texts* (Atlanta: Scholars Press, 1991), pp. 10–95; see also Bush, *Ruth/Esther*, pp. 281–292.

The Hebrew text underlying the AT is different from the MT in several ways. It appears to end with chapter 8, suggesting that chapters 9–10 are part of the later MT redaction.[124] The MT also adds references to the immutable laws of the Medes and Persians (1:19; 8:8) and the way of ensuring the survival of the Jews despite them, something that also presents the killing of the Jews' enemies as self-defence. Significantly, too, the MT also introduces specific references to the 'lot' (*pûr*), which determined when these events would take place (3:7; 9:24), and thus explains the origin of Purim. It also appears to have removed all references to God. This final version of the text is widely recognized as a skilfully composed literary unity.

Date, authorship and historicity

Esther is set during the time of Ahasuerus, better known as Xerxes I (486–465 BC). Views on when it was written vary, but the suggestions of most commentators fall between the late fifth and third centuries BC.[125] The author/editor is unknown.

There is some debate about the book's historicity. Some commentators note historical inaccuracies and conclude that it is a work of fiction.[126] Others defend its essential historicity,[127] while, maybe, allowing narrative latitude.[128] Much of the book reflects, accurately, life in the Persian Empire under Ahasuerus. And many of the so-called 'inaccuracies' can be explained. However, the key issue is its genre,[129] and the book of Esther has the hallmarks of a carefully

---

124. Some suggest that chs. 1 – 8 are built from two sources: a Mordecai scroll and an Esther scroll (see Clines, *Esther Scroll*, pp. 115–138), though the evidence is not compelling; see e.g. Fox, *Redaction*, pp. 97–99.

125. See e.g. Berlin, *Esther*, pp. xli–xliii; Bush, *Ruth/Esther*, p. 297; Michael V. Fox, *Character and Ideology in the Book of Esther*, 2nd ed. (Eugene: Wipf & Stock, 2010), pp. 139–140; Levenson, *Esther*, p. 26; Reid, *Esther*, pp. 21–22.

126. E.g. Fox, *Character and Ideology*, pp. 131–140; Levenson, *Esther*, pp. 23–26; Moore, *Esther*, pp. xxxiv–xlvi.

127. E.g. Baldwin, *Esther*, pp. 16–24; see also Robert Gordis, 'Religion, Wisdom and History in the Book of Esther – a New Solution to an Ancient Crux', *JBL* 100.3 (1981), pp. 359–388 (382–388); William H. Shea, 'Esther and History', *AUSS* 14 (1976), pp. 227–248; J. Stafford Wright, 'The Historicity of Esther', in J. Barton Payne (ed.), *New Perspectives of the Old Testament* (Waco: Word, 1970), pp. 37–47.

128. E.g. Jobes, *Esther*, pp. 30–37.

129. See e.g. Bush, *Ruth/Esther*, pp. 297–309; Fox, *Character and Ideology*, pp. 141–152; Reid, *Esther*, pp. 30–34.

constructed narrative, which depends on coincidences, and uses exaggeration, irony and reversals of fortune to satirize the Persian court and, despite the seriousness of the topic, to produce comedic, even farcical, effects.[130] It seems better, therefore, to see it as a novel with a historical setting, rather than as historiography.[131]

Outline

- Setting the scene (1:1 – 2:23)
  - Vashti deposed (1:1–22)
  - Esther becomes queen; Mordecai uncovers a plot (2:1–23)
- Haman plans to destroy the Jews: the first edict (3:1–15)
- Mordecai asks Esther to help (4:1–17)
- Esther finds favour with Ahasuerus: her first banquet (5:1–8)
- Haman humiliated; Mordecai honoured (5:9 – 6:14)
- Esther's second banquet: Haman's downfall (7:1–10)
- A second edict on behalf of the Jews (8:1–17)
- The Jews defeat their enemies; institution of Purim (9:1–32)
- Mordecai honoured by Ahasuerus and among the Jews (10:1–3)

Main themes

The addition of chapters 9–10 suggest that a main purpose of the MT is to explain and legitimate the feast of Purim, the only OT festival not based on the Torah.

The book also echoes other OT passages.[132] Esther, like Joseph, is raised to prominence in a foreign court and is thus able to save her people from disaster. The deliverance of the Jews from their enemies, and the institution of a festival in celebration may also suggest the exodus narrative,[133] though in Esther the

130. We have noted the use of irony in Esther (above, p. 167). Berlin emphasizes the comedic element, describing the story as farce (*Esther*, xvi–xxiii); see also Adele Berlin, 'The Book of Esther and Ancient Storytelling', *JBL* 120.1 (2001), pp. 3–14; Kathleen M. O'Connor, 'Humour, Turnabouts and Survival in the Book of Esther', in Athalya Brenner (ed.), *Are We Amused? Humour and Women in the Biblical Worlds* (London: T&T Clark, 2003), pp. 52–64.

131. According to Levenson, 'Esther is best seen as a historical novella . . . This is not to say that the book is false, only that its truth . . . is relative to its genre' (*Esther*, p. 25).

132. See e.g. Berlin, *Esther*, pp. xxxvii–xxxix; Day, *Esther*, pp. 18–19.

133. Links with Passover may also be suggested by the reference to casting the *pûr* 'in the first month' (3:7, 12).

threat is not directly from the state. The conflict between Mordecai and Haman appears, intentionally, to recall the conflict between Saul and Agag in 1 Samuel 15. Mordecai, like Saul, is a Benjamite, descended from Kish (2:5), while Haman is an Agagite, suggesting descent from Agag. In this continuation of their fight Mordecai succeeds in bringing about the death of his enemy, something that Saul failed to do.

Even though God is not mentioned by name, divine sovereignty is central to the book. It may be that the writer wants to emphasize that God's hidden power underlies all of human history.[134] Haman represents those who put their trust in *pûr*, which may also be translated 'chance' or 'fate'.[135] Ultimately, though, it is God, whether named or unnamed, who controls human destiny, and throughout the book faithful Jews will see his sovereign hand, working behind the scenes, to ensure their deliverance. Significant, too, in the fulfilment of that hidden purpose, is the role of God's people (e.g. 4:14).

Daniel[136]

Date, authorship and composition

Although often regarded as prophecy, the Hebrew Bible includes Daniel among the Writings. This may be because it reached its final form after the prophetic canon had been closed. Alternatively, it might have been viewed from the outset

---

134. Gordis suggests that the book avoids references to God or to Jewish religious custom because it is written from the perspective of a Gentile Persian chronicler ('Religion, Wisdom and History', esp. pp. 375–378); see also Baldwin, *Esther*, pp. 35–36.

135. E.g. ibid, pp. 37–38.

136. Commentaries on Daniel include Baldwin, *Daniel*; John J. Collins, *Daniel*, Hermeneia (Minneapolis: Fortress, 1993); *Daniel: With an Introduction to Prophetic Literature*, FOTL 20 (Grand Rapids: Eerdmans, 1984); Goldingay, *Daniel*; Louis F. Hartman and Alexander A. Di Lella, *Daniel*, AB 23 (New York: Doubleday, 1978); Tremper Longman III, *Daniel*, NIVAC (Grand Rapids: Zondervan, 1999); Lucas, *Daniel*; Stephen R. Miller, *Daniel*, NAC 18 (Nashville: B&H, 1994); William B. Nelson, *Daniel*, UBC (Grand Rapids: Baker, 2012); Newsom, *Daniel*; Porteous, *Daniel*; D. S. Russell, *Daniel*, DSB (Edinburgh: St Andrew, 1981); W. Sibley Towner, *Daniel*, IBC (Atlanta: John Knox, 1984). See also John J. Collins and Peter W. Flint (eds.), *The Book of Daniel: Composition and Reception*, 2 vols., VTSup 83, FOTL 1 (Leiden: Koninklijke Brill, 2001); P. R. Davies, *Daniel*, OTG (Sheffield: JSOT Press, 1985); Wiseman, *Problems*. See above, pp. 194–198.

as different from other prophetic literature. As we have noted, it has some characteristics of apocalyptic,[137] which may have links to wisdom as well as prophecy. And Daniel, himself, is viewed among the 'wise men of Babylon' (2:12–13; 5:7–12).

In terms of its content Daniel divides into two parts. Chapters 1–6, written in the third person, describe the experiences of Daniel and his companions in the royal court during the reigns of Nebuchadnezzar, Belshazzar, Darius and Cyrus. Chapters 7–12 relate Daniel's dreams and visions about the future. These describe the rise and fall of world empires, and appear to focus on the time of Antiochus IV, in the second century BC.[138]

The traditional view, that the book was written in the sixth century BC, has been questioned, because of apparent historical inaccuracies in the court narratives. This might indicate that they were written later, by someone with limited knowledge of the period. By contrast, chapter 11 contains accurate detail, including the suppression of Judaism following Antiochus' abortive Egyptian campaign (167 BC). The lack of reference to the rededication of the temple (164 BC) suggests a date between 167 BC and 165 BC, and implies that Daniel, like other apocalyptic writing, includes pseudonymity and pseudo-prediction.

Several conservative scholars continue to maintain both the historical integrity of chapters 1–6, which show signs of a Babylonian origin, and the view that the dreams and visions in chapters 8–12 are genuine prophecy.[139] A text of Daniel from Qumran (4QDan^{c}) is thought to date from the end of the second century BC, and it is unlikely to have acquired the status necessary to be accepted and preserved by the Qumran community if it was written as recently as 165 BC.[140] There is also the question of why Daniel, who is known only from this book, would be chosen as a pseudonymous author.[141]

---

137. See above, p. 198.
138. See above, pp. 103–104.
139. E.g. Baldwin, *Daniel*, pp. 19–29; A. R. Millard, 'Daniel 1–6 and History', *EvQ* 49.2 (1977), pp. 67–73; S. R. Miller, *Daniel*, pp. 22–43; Wiseman, 'Some Historical Problems', in Wiseman, *Problems*.
140. E.g. Harrison, *Introduction*, p. 1127.
141. Some identify Daniel with Dan'el in Ezek. 14:14, 20; 28:3 (e.g. S. R. Miller, *Daniel*, pp. 41–43). This figure is usually identified with Danel in the Ugaritic 'Tale of Aqhat'. It seems unlikely that Daniel would have acquired a sufficient reputation during Ezekiel's ministry to allow him to be compared with Noah and Job. But if that were so, it would indicate only that the stories may have some historical basis, while also giving credibility to the use of 'Daniel' as a pseudonym.

The evidence is inconclusive, and neither view is without merit or difficulties. Accepting a second-century BC date was seen, in the past, as a denial of predictive prophecy and a challenge to the integrity of Scripture. Today the demarcation is less stark. Daniel in the sixth century BC could have forecast events up to four hundred years later, but why? We understand, too, that ancient historiography is not preoccupied with historical detail, and also that pseudonymity and pseudo-prediction were recognized literary forms and would not have been seen as deceptive.[142] Rather, presenting past events as prophecy emphasizes God's final control over them. It seems reasonable to conclude that both views are viable, and that supporting an early date is not naive, while accepting a later date does not necessarily challenge the inspiration and authority of Scripture.[143]

Although the book is frequently considered a unity, composed in the sixth or second century BC, recent scholarship suggests a process of composition. The court stories (1 – 6) are generally thought to have originated within the Persian Diaspora.[144] A text from Qumran, *The Prayer of Nabonidus*,[145] is very similar to the story about Nebuchadnezzar's madness in Daniel 4, and thus may support a Mesopotamian background,[146] though it may also indicate that the Daniel passage developed from a legendary account originally related to Nabonidus.[147] The visions (7 – 12) may have been added, possibly in the second century BC, though they may be earlier. The final compilation may have been by those described as 'wise' (11:33; 12:3, 10).

Another factor here, however, is that Daniel is written in two languages: Hebrew (1:1 – 2:4a; 8:1 – 12:13) and Aramaic (2:4b – 7:28),[148] and this suggests

---

142. E.g. Bruce M. Metzger, 'Literary Forgeries and Canonical Pseudepigrapha', *JBL* 91.1 (1972), pp. 3–24 (21–22).

143. Goldingay, *Daniel*, pp. xxxix–xl, 320–322; Lucas, *Daniel*, pp. 308–309 (309); see also LaSor, Hubbard and Bush, *OT Survey*, p. 576; Longman, *Daniel*, pp. 22–23.

144. See e.g. Davies, *Daniel*, p. 48; W. Lee Humphreys, 'A Life-Style for Diaspora: A Study of the Tales of Esther and Daniel', *JBL* 92.2 (1973), pp. 211–223; Newsom, *Daniel*, pp. 21–23; see also articles by Karel van der Toorn and Shalom Paul, in Collins and Flint, *Daniel*, 1:37–68.

145. *COS* 1:89.

146. E.g. Baldwin, *Daniel*, pp. 36–37; Newsom, *Daniel*, p. 9.

147. However, see Baldwin, *Daniel*, pp. 116–118.

148. The language in the Aramaic sections is thought to suggest a later date; however, see e.g. K. A. Kitchen, 'The Aramaic of Daniel', in Wiseman, *Problems*, pp. 31–79; Lucas, *Daniel*, pp. 307–308.

a different division of the book. One possibility is that chapters 2–6 were originally written in Aramaic, the common language of the day, maybe to reflect their international character. Chapter 1 may also have been in Aramaic, but was translated into Hebrew when the visions were added. Of these, chapters 8–12 would have been in Hebrew, maybe because it suited the genre better, or, possibly, to reflect increasing Jewish nationalism. Chapter 7 might then have been written in, or translated into, Aramaic because of its ties to chapter 2.[149]

Structure and outline

The natural division of the book is into two parts (1 – 6; 7 – 12). However, taking account of the different languages, it is possible to see chapters 2–7 as a chiastic unit (see below),[150] with chapter 1 forming an introduction to the whole book, and chapters 8–12 focusing on the oppression of the Jews under Antiochus IV, and their final deliverance.

Outline

- Introduction: Daniel and his companions taken to Babylon (1:1–21)
- God's sovereignty over world empires (2:1 – 7:28)
  - Nebuchadnezzar's dream of four kingdoms (2:1–49) *a*
  - Shadrach, Meshach and Abednego rescued (3:1–30) *b*
  - Revelation and execution of judgment on Nebuchadnezzar (4:1–37) *c*
  - Revelation and execution of judgment on Belshazzar (5:1–31) *c′*
  - Daniel rescued (6:1–28) *b′*
  - Daniel's vision of four kingdoms (7:1–28) *a′*
- Oppression and vindication of God's people (8:1 – 12:13)
  - Persian and Greek empires; the rise of an oppressor (8:1–27)
  - Daniel's prayer; the vision of seventy 'sevens' (9:1–27)
  - A heavenly messenger previews history up to Antiochus' demise (10:1 – 11:45)
  - Future refining; those who persevere will be rewarded (12:1–13)

---

149. See e.g. Rainer Albertz, 'The Social Setting of the Aramaic and Hebrew Book of Daniel', in Collins and Flint, *Daniel*, 1:171–204; Lucas, *Daniel*, p. 315; McConville, *Prophets*, p. 115; Newsom, *Daniel*, pp. 8–9.
150. This outline is based on Baldwin, *Daniel*, p. 75.

Main themes

A key theme of the book is God's authority in human affairs: 'that the living may know that the Most High is sovereign over the kingdoms of men' (4:17b; cf. 4:25b, 32b; 5:21b).[151] We see this in the way God preserves his servants in the Babylonian court, and in his dealings with Nebuchadnezzar and Belshazzar. It is seen, too, in Daniel's visions, which emphasize God's control over the rise and fall of empires and his ultimate vindication of his people. If the book was compiled in the second century BC, it would serve to encourage those who were suffering under the regime of Antiochus Epiphanes that God would, ultimately, bring their oppression to an end.

As well as emphasizing God's sovereignty over human kingdoms, the book also points to the final inbreaking of God's kingdom. In chapters 2 and 7 successive world empires are brought to an end by the coming of God's kingdom. The four empires are often identified as Babylon, Medo-Persia, Greece (Macedonia) and Rome, and this fits with the view that God's kingdom has come in the person of Jesus. However, it seems natural to identify the small horn in 8:9, which can be related to Antiochus Epiphanes, with the little horn in 7:8. The deliverance of God's people in 12:1 also seems to follow the demise of Antiochus. This gives the sequence Babylon, Media, Persia, Greece. However, confidence in God's control over history, his ultimate victory over every power that rises up against him and the vindication of his people may be reapplied to any oppressive situation faced by God's people.[152]

The beasts come out of the sea (7:3), and their ultimate demise may reflect God's victory over chaos at creation, further emphasizing the wider application of the imagery. There may be echoes of several ANE myths in Daniel 7.[153] In particular, the description of the Ancient of Days is similar to that of El in the Baal myth, and the 'one like a son of man', like Baal, rides on the clouds.[154] This

---

151. See Routledge, *OT Theology*, pp. 300–302.

152. So 2 Esd. 12.11–12 interprets the fourth beast as Rome, though the text suggests that this is an innovative view. Some imagery is taken up in Revelation; and some use Daniel's visions as a blueprint for the end times.

153. E.g. John H. Walton, 'The *Anzu* Myth as Relevant Background for Daniel 7?', in Collins and Flint, *Daniel*, 1:69–89.

154. See above, p. 115. On the 'Son of Man' see Routledge, *OT Theology*, pp. 289–291. Comparison with the Baal myth may suggest that the 'son of man' rides into God's presence and receives sovereign authority after defeating the beast from the sea.

expression also links the figure with God (Deut. 33:26; Pss 18:9–11; 68:4; 104:3), and it is perhaps best to see the 'son of man' as the heavenly representative of God's people (cf. 7:18, 22).[155]

In Daniel, too, we see that God ordains the detailed events of history (e.g. 9:24–27). However, this is not rigid determinism. The delay of the heavenly messenger (10:13) suggests contingency in human history, due to conflict in the heavenly realm. Though that, too, is under God's control. Just as world empires fulfil only their allotted span, so interference from their heavenly representatives is also limited.

Ezra-Nehemiah[156]

Date, authorship and composition

Although printed separately, the books of Ezra and Nehemiah were traditionally viewed as a single work,[157] and it is generally agreed that the combined text should be treated as a unity. Until recently it was also a common view that the writer of Ezra-Nehemiah also wrote Chronicles.[158] Ezra-Nehemiah begins where Chronicles ends, and repeats the final verses (1:1–3; cf. 2 Chr. 36:22–23); the apocryphal text 1 Esdras includes material from the last two chapters of Chronicles as well as from Ezra without a break (1 Esdras 1.1 – 2.8), and there

155. Jesus relates the 'son of man' in Dan. 7 to himself (Matt. 26:64). However, as a heavenly figure this is distinct from the earthly, Davidic Messiah. The term 'messiah' does occur in Dan. 9:25–26; though probably not in the later, technical sense; see above, p. 290, n. 52.

156. Commentaries on Ezra-Nehemiah include Leslie C. Allen, 'Ezra-Nehemiah', in Allen and Laniak, *Ezra, Nehemiah, Esther*, pp. 1–166; Joseph Blenkinsopp, *Ezra-Nehemiah*, OTL (Philadelphia: Westminster, 1988); Breneman, *Ezra, Nehemiah, Esther*; Gordon F. Davies, *Ezra & Nehemiah*, Berit Olam (Collegeville: Liturgical Press, 1999); F. Charles Fensham, *The Books of Ezra and Nehemiah*, NICOT (Grand Rapids: Eerdmans, 1982); Derek Kidner, *Ezra and Nehemiah*, TOTC (Leicester: Inter-Varsity Press, 1979); Mark A. Throntveit, *Ezra-Nehemiah*, IBC (Louisville: John Knox, 1992); H. G. M. Williamson, *Ezra, Nehemiah*, WBC 16 (Waco: Word, 1985).

157. See e.g. Williamson, *Ezra, Nehemiah*, p. xxi. Significantly, the MT combines summary material for both books and places it after Nehemiah, and further identifies Neh. 3:32 as the middle verse.

158. This was also the traditional Jewish view (*b. B. Bat.* 15a).

are also theological and linguistic similarities. However, it is now widely recognized that similarities are outweighed by differences, and many scholars regard them as separate books.[159]

Ezra-Nehemiah is a composite text, which includes a wide range of source material. These include a substantial first-person narration by Nehemiah, the so-called 'Nehemiah Memoir', comprising Nehemiah 1 – 7 and parts of 12:27–43 and 13:4–31. Williamson suggests that this might have included a report to the king on the success of his first visit to Jerusalem, which he later edited, maybe in the light of criticism received.[160] Another account highlights the role of Ezra. This 'Ezra Memoir' is generally thought to comprise Ezra 7 – 10 (7:27 – 9:15 is written in the first person) and Nehemiah 7:73b – 8:18.[161] This last section appears to refer to a later period in Ezra's ministry,[162] though some suggest that it is out of chronological sequence and took place not long after Ezra arrived in Jerusalem.[163] Other sources, some of which may have been part of these 'memoirs', include royal communications, letters, inventories and lists of returning exiles. Some of the text, primarily communication to and from the Persian king, is in Aramaic (Ezra 4:8 – 6:18; 7:12–26), the official language of the day. The final text may have been composed in three stages:[164] the compilation of the primary sources; the composition of the Ezra and Nehemiah memoirs, together with additional material; and the inclusion of Ezra 1 – 6 by a later redactor, as an introduction to the whole.[165] The writer

---

159. An influential article in this debate has been Sara Japhet, 'The Supposed Common Authorship of Chronicles and Ezra-Nehemiah Investigated Anew', *VT* 18.3 (1968), pp. 330–371. See also Allen, 'Ezra-Nehemiah', in Allen and Laniak, *Ezra, Nehemiah, Esther*, p. 9; H. G. M. Williamson, 'The Composition of Ezra i–vi', *JTS* NS 34.1 (1983), pp. 1–30. However, see Blenkinsopp, *Ezra-Nehemiah*, pp. 47–54; Fensham, *Ezra and Nehemiah*, pp. 2–4.

160. Williamson, *Ezra, Nehemiah*, pp. xxiv–xxviii.

161. Ibid., pp. xxviii–xxxii. However, see Lester L. Grabbe, *Ezra-Nehemiah* (London: Routledge, 1998), p. 130.

162. E.g. Breneman, *Ezra, Nehemiah, Esther*, pp. 38–41; Kidner, *Ezra and Nehemiah*, pp. 150–152.

163. This is generally placed after Ezra 8, or after Ezra 10. See e.g. Allen, 'Ezra-Nehemiah', in Allen and Laniak, *Ezra, Nehemiah, Esther*, p. 125; Williamson, *Ezra-Nehemiah*, pp. 283–286.

164. Williamson, *Ezra, Nehemiah*, pp. xxxiii–xxxv; see also Throntveit, *Ezra-Nehemiah*, pp. 9–10.

165. See Williamson, 'Composition of Ezra i–vi'.

is unknown, though it has been suggested that he might have been part of a Levitical group.[166]

Since much of the material comes from shortly after the events described, there seems little reason to doubt the book's essential historicity.[167] However, it is also narrative, which, in its canonical form, has a literary structure and purpose. Eskenazi suggests a single narrative, focusing on the rebuilding of God's house, which includes temple, people and city. The plot is introduced in Ezra 1:1–4, and brought to a successful conclusion in Nehemiah 8 – 13.[168] It may be better, though, to see three related narratives, focusing on building the temple (Ezra 1 – 6), the community (Ezra 7 – 10) and the city (Neh. 1 – 7). When Ezra's reading of the Law (Neh. 8) took place is not clear. However, in its present position it brings those themes together, and introduces the climax of the book. As part of a unit focusing on covenant renewal (Neh. 8 – 10), it emphasizes the importance of obedience prior to the resettlement of the city,[169] and it views the people's response as the combined achievement of both Ezra and Nehemiah.[170]

Ezra 1 – 6 covers the time from the edict of Cyrus (538 BC), which opened the way for Jewish exiles to return to Jerusalem, to the completion of the temple (516 BC). The rest of the book is set much later. It is generally agreed that Nehemiah came to Jerusalem in 445 BC, the 'twentieth year' (1:1) of Artaxerxes I (465–424 BC). After twelve years he went back to Persia, and returned a few years later (Neh. 13:6–7). There is debate about when Ezra was in Jerusalem.

---

166. E.g. Kyung-jin Min, *The Levitical Authorship of Ezra-Nehemiah*, JSOTSup 409 (London: T&T Clark, 2004).
167. There is considerable debate on this issue. See the discussion in commentaries; see also e.g. Miller and Hayes, *History*, pp. 437–475; Provan, Long and Longman, *Biblical History*, pp. 278–303; H. G. M. Williamson, 'Exile and After: Historical Study', in Baker and Arnold, *Face of OT Studies*, pp. 236–265. See too essays in Philip R. Davies et al. (eds.), *Second Temple Studies,* JSOTSup, 4 vols. (Sheffield: Sheffield Academic Press; London: Bloomsbury T&T Clark, 1991–2012).
168. See e.g. Tamara Cohn Eskenazi, *In an Age of Prose: A Literary Approach to Ezra-Nehemiah*, SBLMS (Atlanta: Scholars Press, 1988); 'The Structure of Ezra-Nehemiah and the Integrity of the Book', *JBL* 107.4 (1988), pp. 641–656. See however, David J. A. Clines, 'The Force of the Text: A Response to Tamara C. Eskenazi's "Ezra-Nehemiah: From Text To Actuality"', in J. Cheryl Exum (ed.), *Signs and Wonders: Biblical Texts in Literary Focus*, SemeiaSt (Atlanta: Scholars Press, 1989), pp. 199–215.
169. Allen, 'Ezra-Nehemiah', in Allen and Laniak, *Ezra, Nehemiah, Esther*, p. 125.
170. E.g. Childs, *Introduction*, p. 635.

According to Ezra 7:8, he arrived in the seventh year of Artaxerxes (458 BC), thirteen years before Nehemiah. But there are few other signs that they knew each other, and it is not clear why Ezra waited until Nehemiah arrived before reading the law (Neh. 8).[171] This has led some to suggest that Ezra arrived much later, in the seventh year of Artaxerxes *II* (404–358 BC).[172] However, the traditional order is generally preferred.[173] This allows that Ezra 7 – Nehemiah 13, and possibly the whole book, might have been written by 400 BC.[174]

Outline

- The return from exile: building the temple (Ezra 1:1 – 6:22)
  - The edict of Cyrus; preparations to return (1:1–11)
  - Lists of returning exiles (2:1–70)
  - Rebuilding the altar and temple; celebration of Passover (3:1 – 6:22)
- Ezra's mission: building the community (7:1 – 10:44)
  - Ezra's royal commission (7:1–28)
  - List of returnees (8:1–14)
  - Preparation for service in the temple; sacrifices (8:15–36)
  - Problem of mixed marriages; Ezra's reform (9:1 – 10:44)
- Nehemiah's mission: building the city (Neh. 1:1 – 7:73a)
  - Nehemiah's concern; royal assent (1:1 – 2:10)
  - The wall of Jerusalem rebuilt (3:1 – 7:3)
  - List of returnees (7:4–73a)
- Covenant renewal; resettlement of the city, dedication of walls (8:1 – 12:47)
- Nehemiah's later reforms (13:1–31)

---

171. For discussion of the chronological relationship between Ezra and Nehemiah, see e.g. Fensham, *Ezra and Nehemiah*, pp. 6–9; Kidner, *Ezra and Nehemiah*, pp. 146–158; Williamson, *Ezra, Nehemiah*, pp. xxxix–xliv; see also n. 172, below.
172. See e.g. J. A. Emerton, 'Did Ezra Go to Jerusalem in 428 B.C.?', *JTS* NS 17.1 (1966), pp. 1–19; H. H. Rowley, 'The Chronological Order of Ezra and Nehemiah', in *Servant of the Lord*, pp. 131–159. Several scholars see the reference to Nehemiah in Neh. 8:10, as an addition (e.g. Allen, 'Ezra-Nehemiah', in Allen and Laniak, *Ezra, Nehemiah, Esther*, pp. 129–130; Blenkinsopp, *Ezra-Nehemiah*, p. 284; Williamson, *Ezra, Nehemiah*, p. 279).
173. E.g. Allen, 'Ezra-Nehemiah', in Allen and Laniak, *Ezra, Nehemiah, Esther*, pp. 7–8; Fensham, *Ezra and Nehemiah*, p. 218; Kidner, *Ezra and Nehemiah*, pp. 148–150; Williamson, *Ezra, Nehemiah*, p. xliv.
174. E.g. Allen, 'Ezra-Nehemiah', in Allen and Laniak, *Ezra, Nehemiah, Esther*, p. 10; Breneman, *Ezra, Nehemiah, Esther*, p. 42. Williamson suggests that Ezra 1 – 6 was added around 300 BC (*Ezra, Nehemiah*, pp. xxxv–xxxvi).

Main themes

An important theme in Ezra-Nehemiah is divine control over secular powers, in favour of his people. So 'the LORD moved the heart of Cyrus' to issue his edict (Ezra 1:1) and put it into the heart of Artaxerxes to commission Ezra (Ezra 7:27). Artaxerxes sent Nehemiah, following the latter's prayer (Neh. 1:4 – 2:9).

Another significant element is continuity. The return from exile is viewed as the fulfilment of Jeremiah's prophecy (Ezra 1:1).[175] The rebuilding of the temple and the city, celebration of the Passover, the centrality of the Law, and the family histories of those returning link this new phase in the life of God's people with what has gone before. The prayer in Nehemiah 9:5b–37 further sets the current situation of the returnees within the full sweep of God's dealings with his people from the time of Abraham.

This is linked, too, with the emphasis on the religious purity of the community, including refusing help to rebuild the temple (Ezra 4:1–3), addressing the issue of mixed marriages (Ezra 9 – 10; Neh. 13:23–27) and calling for a renewed obedience to the Law (e.g. Neh. 7:73b – 9:38). This relates, primarily, to avoiding things that might lead to the distinctiveness of Israel's faith and worship being compromised.[176]

While it is clear that Ezra and Nehemiah play a significant role in the book, the various lists indicate the part played by a range of people, and emphasize the importance of community. This is exemplified in the way individual groups worked together to complete the city walls.

Finally, there is a sense that the new beginning is only partially successful. Nehemiah 9:36–37 notes that the people are still ruled over by others, and rather than end with a celebration (Neh. 12:27–47), the narrator notes that problems addressed earlier have resurfaced (Neh. 13). This is not a purely pessimistic conclusion, though it does indicate that God's people need to look to him for more and better things to come.

---

175. The reference to Cyrus' heart being 'moved' (*'ûr*) also recalls Isa. 13:17, 41:2, 25, where the same verb is used.

176. Thus Isa. 56 – 66, which reflects a similar historical context, suggests that foreigners who accept Israel's faith and laws may be accepted (see above, p. 289).

Chronicles[177]

Date, authorship and composition

The Hebrew title of Chronicles is *dibrê hayyāmîm* (literally, 'words/events of the days'), which is generally translated 'annals' (e.g. 1 Kgs 14:19; 15:7; 2 Kgs 1:18; Neh. 12:23; 1 Chr. 27:4). As noted already, it was traditionally thought to have the same author as Ezra-Nehemiah, though many commentators now view it as a separate work.[178]

Chronicles comprises several different kinds of text, including genealogies, lists, speeches or sermons as well as historiography, and this has contributed to the debate about its unity. In particular, 1 Chronicles 1 – 9 and 23 – 27 are often viewed as secondary.[179] However, there are good reasons for viewing the text

---

177. Commentaries on Chronicles include Roddy Braun, *1 Chronicles*, WBC 14 (Waco: Word, 1986); Raymond B. Dillard, *2 Chronicles*, WBC 15 (Waco: Word, 1987); Andrew E. Hill, *1 & 2 Chronicles*, NIVAC (Grand Rapids: Zondervan, 2003); Sara Japhet, *I & II Chronicles*, OTL (London: Westminster John Knox, 1993); Louis C. Jonker, *1 & 2 Chronicles*, UBC (Grand Rapids: Baker, 2013); Ralph W. Klein, *1, 2 Chronicles*, Hermeneia, 2 vols. (Minneapolis: Fortress, 2006, 2012); Gary N. Knoppers, *1 Chronicles*, AB 12, 12A, 2 vols. (New York: Doubleday, 2004); Steven L. McKenzie, *I & II Chronicles*, AbOTC (Nashville: Abingdon, 2004); Jacob M. Myers, *II Chronicles*, AB 13 (New York: Doubleday, 1995); Martin J. Selman, *1, 2 Chronicles*, TOTC, 2 vols. (Leicester: Inter-Varsity Press, 1994); J. A. Thompson, *1, 2 Chronicles*, NAC 9 (Nashville: B&H, 1994); Steven S. Tuell, *First and Second Chronicles*, IBC (Louisville: John Knox, 2001); H. G. M Williamson, *1 and 2 Chronicles*, NCB (London: Marshall, Morgan & Scott; Grand Rapids: Eerdmans, 1982). See also Gwilym H. Jones, *1 & 2 Chronicles*, OTG (Sheffield: JSOT Press, 1993); Simon J. De Vries, *1 and 2 Chronicles*, FOTL 11 (Grand Rapids: Eerdmans, 1989).
178. See above, pp. 376–377; see also e.g. Braun, *1 Chronicles*, pp. xx–xxi; Jones, *1 & 2 Chronicles*, pp. 86–92; R. W. Klein, *1, 2 Chronicles*, 1:6–10; Selman, *1, 2 Chronicles*, pp. 65–69.
179. See e.g. Braun, *I Chronicles*, pp. xix–xx, 11–12, 231. Cross has suggested that 1 Chr. 10 – 2 Chr. 34 were part of an earlier edition that was later expanded; see Frank Moore Cross, 'A Reconstruction of the Judean Restoration', *JBL* 94.1 (1975), pp. 4–18 (11–14); see also Tuell, *First and Second Chronicles*, pp. 11–12. Some accept most of 1 Chr. 1 – 9 as original, with secondary additions, particularly, in 1 Chr. 23 – 27; see e.g. De Vries, *1 & 2 Chronicles*, pp. 12–13; H. G. M. Williamson, 'The Origins of the Twenty-Four Priestly Courses: A Study of 1 Chronicles xxiii–xxvii', in J. A. Emerton (ed.), *Studies in the Historical Books of the Old Testament*, VTSup50 (Leiden: Brill, 1979), pp. 251–268.

as 'one work, composed essentially by a single author'.[180] The identity of that author is unknown. He is generally referred to as 'the Chronicler', and it is possible that he was a Levite, or from a pro-levitical circle.[181]

The view of the composition of the book affects when it is dated. The earliest date is after the completion of the second temple in 515 BC. At least two generations after Zerubbabel are referred to in 1 Chronicles 3:19–21,[182] indicating a date for the book of no earlier than 450 BC. And some suggest that material in 1 Chronicles 23 – 27 may be later still.[183] Most date the final composition of the book between the middle of the fifth and end of the third centuries BC.[184] However, if 1 Chronicles 1 – 9 and 23 – 27 were added later, much of the rest might have been written shortly after the completion of the temple.

Chronicles depends on several sources, including the Primary History and, in particular, the books of Samuel and Kings.[185] The careful use of sources suggests an interest in history.[186] However, while all history writing in the OT is concerned with the meaning of events, from the way the Chronicler adapts material, and from what he chooses to include and to omit, it is particularly evident that his main purpose is theological.

Outline

- From Adam to the return from exile (1 Chr. 1:1 – 9:44)
- David and Solomon (1 Chr. 10:1 – 2 Chr. 9:31)
  - Transfer of kingship from Saul to David (1 Chr. 10:1 – 12:40)
  - David's reign (1 Chr. 13:1 – 29:30)
    - Worship in Jerusalem; bringing the Ark (13:1 – 16:43)
    - God's promise to David (17:1–27)

---

180. Japhet, *I & II Chronicles*, pp. 5–7 (7); see also e.g. Selman, *1, 2 Chronicles*, pp. 72–75.
181. See e.g. Jones, *1 & 2 Chronicles*, pp. 94–96; R. W. Klein, *1, 2 Chronicles*, 1:16–17; Williamson, 'Origins' in Emerton, *Studies*, pp. 265–268.
182. The text after v. 21a is unclear; see commentaries.
183. See e.g. Williamson, 'Origins' in Emerton, *Studies*.
184. See e.g. Braun, *1 Chronicles*, pp. xxviii–xxix; Japhet, *I & II Chronicles*, pp. 24–28; Jones, *1 & 2 Chronicles*, pp. 92–94; R. W. Klein, *1, 2 Chronicles*, 1:13–16; Selman, *1, 2 Chronicles*, pp. 69–71.
185. See e.g. Japhet, *I & II Chronicles*, pp. 14–23; Jones, *1 & 2 Chronicles*, pp. 65–85; R. W. Klein, *1, 2 Chronicles*, 1:30–44.
186. For further discussion of the historicity of Chronicles, see e.g. M. Patrick Graham, Kenneth G. Hoglund and Steven L. McKenzie, *The Chronicler as Historian*, JSOTSup 238 (Sheffield: Sheffield Academic Press, 1997).

- David's wars (18:1 – 20:8)
- Preparations for the temple; enthronement of Solomon (21:1 – 29:30)
- Solomon's reign; building the temple (2 Chr. 1:1 – 9:31)

• From the division of the kingdom to the edict of Cyrus (2 Chr. 10:1 – 36:23)

Main themes

A key feature of Chronicles is its focus on the Davidic monarchy,[187] and in particular on David and Solomon. Through these two kings, whose work is frequently viewed as a unity,[188] the temple and its institutions, which formed the foundation of the life of God's people, were established. These kings are presented more positively than in Samuel–Kings. David's adultery with Bathsheba and murder of Uriah are not mentioned, though shortcomings relating to the building of the temple are noted (e.g. 1 Chr. 21:1 – 22:1; 22:8; 28:3). Solomon's failings are not mentioned; instead, he is presented as a man of peace (1 Chr. 22:9). Among the other Davidic kings, Hezekiah and Josiah are given particular prominence. Both are described as following in the ways of their 'father David' (2 Chr. 29:2; 34:2–3), and their main roles relate to removing pagan shrines and restoring the temple and its worship (29:3 – 31:19; 34:1 – 35:19).[189]

The emphasis on the Davidic monarchy means that the Chronicler says little about the history of the northern kingdom, which he appears to regard as illegitimate. He does, nevertheless, emphasize the unity of the nation, and frequently refers to 'all Israel'. As in the 'primary history', before the kingdoms divided, this expression usually refers to the whole nation (e.g. 1 Chr. 11:1, 10; 29:21–23; cf. 1 Sam. 3:20; 1 Kgs 1:20; 4:1; 11:42). In Kings and Chronicles it

---

187. This theme is not present in Ezra-Nehemiah, and is an important factor in the argument that the books have different authors.
188. E.g. Japhet, *I & II Chronicles*, p. 48; H. G. M. Williamson, 'Eschatology in Chronicles', *TynBul* 28 (1977), pp. 115–154 (132, 140–141).
189. According to Johnstone, a significant issue in Chronicles is 'guilt' (*ma'al*; the corresponding verb is *mā'al*), which needs to be atoned for through sacrifice and is provided for through the temple and its institutions; see William Johnstone, *Chronicles and Exodus: An Analogy and Its Application*, JSOTSup 275 (Sheffield: Sheffield Academic Press, 1998), pp. 90–127. There is no *ma'al* associated with David and Solomon because of their idealized role in establishing the means of atonement (pp. 117–118).

then refers to the northern tribes (e.g. 1 Kgs 12:20; 15:33; 1 Chr. 13:4, 15). The Chronicler also relates it to the south (e.g. 2 Chr. 11:31; 12:1; 24:25; 28:23; 29:24). And families from the north and the south are included in the genealogies in 1 Chronicles 1 – 9. Thus, while the Davidic monarchy, and its association with the temple and its institutions, may carry the hope of the nation, that hope includes all Israelites. This also means that those who return from exile have continuity, not only with pre-exilic Judah, but also with the nation whose ancestry goes back to Jacob and beyond.

With the focus on God's covenant with David,[190] the exodus and Sinaitic covenant is not prominent. Japhet takes this to suggest that Israel's election is not tied to a particular historical event, but goes back to the creation, and that the time in Egypt and, by analogy, the exile, does not disrupt Israel's association with the land.[191] However, there are references to the exodus (e.g. 1 Chr. 17:21–22; 2 Chr. 6:5; 7:22), the Sinaitic covenant (2 Chr. 5:10; 34:31–32) and the Law (1 Chr. 22:13 [cf. Josh. 1:7]; 2 Chr. 34:14–21), as well as to the celebration of Passover (2 Chr. 30; 35), all of which are significant for the narrative.

Chronicles emphasizes God's continued involvement in his people's history. This includes judgment on sin, and reward for faithfulness (e.g. 1 Chr. 28:9). Retribution is often immediate (e.g. 1 Chr. 21:1–16; 2 Chr. 12:5; 16:7–9; 20:37; 21:12–19),[192] but there is also provision for repentance (e.g. 2 Chr. 7:14) and the possibility of a new start. Thus in the case of Manasseh sin resulted in his imprisonment in Assyria, and that led to repentance and subsequent forgiveness and restoration (2 Chr. 33:10–13; cf. 2 Kgs 21:1–18). Important in this is God's ongoing covenant commitment (*ḥesed*) to the Davidic house (e.g. 1 Chr. 17:13; 2 Chr. 1:8; 6:14, 42; 20:21).

This possibility of divine intervention in times of crisis, linked to David, provides a basis for future hope. Although Chronicles ends with the positive prospect of rebuilding the temple, there is the suggestion that all is not yet as it should be. The Chronicler appears to envisage a time of peace, corresponding

---

190. God's promises to David are specifically described as a 'covenant' in 2 Chr. 7:18; 13:5; 21:7.

191. Sara Japhet, *The Ideology of the Book of Chronicles and Its Place in Biblical Thought* (Frankfurt: Peter Lang, 1989); *I & II Chronicles*, pp. 44–47; however, see Johnstone, *Chronicles and Exodus*, pp. 115–127; R. W. Klein, *1, 2 Chronicles*, 1:44, n. 307.

192. For discussion of 'immediate retribution', see e.g. Dillard, *2 Chronicles*, pp. 76–81; Japhet, *Ideology*, pp. 150–198; Brian E. Kelley, *Retribution and Eschatology in Chronicles*, JSOTSup 211 (Sheffield: Sheffield Academic Press, 1996); Selman, *1, 2 Chronicles*, pp. 61–63.

to the era of David and Solomon, which will include all the tribes of Israel, and he is thus looking for a more complete, eschatological, fulfilment of God's promises.[193] The repeated promise of a perpetual Davidic-Solomonic dynasty (e.g. 1 Chr. 22:10; 28:6–7) suggests that this hope may also be messianic.[194]

---

193. E.g. Kelly, *Retribution and Eschatology*, pp. 135–185; Williamson, 'Eschatology', p. 154.
194. E.g. Satterthwaite and McConville, *Histories*, pp. 280–281.

FURTHER READING

Old Testament canon

Chapman, Stephen B., 'The Canon Debate: What It Is and Why It Matters', *Journal of Theological Interpretation* 4.2 (2010), pp. 273–294.

Childs, Brevard S., *Introduction to the Old Testament as Scripture* (Philadelphia: Fortress, 1979), pp. 41–68.

Evans, Craig A. and Emmanuel Tov (eds.), *Exploring the Origins of the Bible: Canon Formation in Historical, Literary, and Theological Perspective* (Grand Rapids: Baker Academic, 2008).

Kaiser, Walter C. Jr., *The Old Testament Documents: Are They Reliable and Relevant?* (Downers Grove: InterVarsity Press; Leicester: Inter-Varsity Press, 2001), pp. 29–39.

McDonald, Lee Martin, *The Origin of the Bible: A Guide for the Perplexed* (London: Continuum, 2011).

Merrill, Eugene H. 'The Canonicity of the Old Testament', in Eugene H. Merrill, Mark F. Rooker and Michael A. Grisanti, *The World and the Word: An Introduction to the Old Testament* (Nashville: B&H, 2011), pp. 93–107.

Vasholz, Robert I., 'Canon', in *NIDOTTE* 4:460–4.

Historicity of the Old Testament

Davies, P. R., *In Search of Ancient Israel*, JSOTSup 148 (Sheffield: JSOT Press, 1992).

—— 'Whose History? Whose Israel? Whose Bible? Biblical Histories, Ancient and Modern', in L. E. Grabbe (ed.), *Can a 'History of Israel' Be Written?*, JSOTSup 245 (Sheffield: Sheffield Academic Press, 1996), pp. 104–122.

Dever, William G., *What Did the Biblical Writers Know and When Did They Know It? What Archaeology Can Tell Us About the Reality of Ancient Israel* (Grand Rapids: Eerdmans, 2001).

—— *Who Were the Early Israelites and Where Did They Come From?* (Grand Rapids: Eerdmans, 2003).

Finkelstein, Israel, and Neil Asher Silberman, *The Bible Unearthed: Archaeology's New Vision of Ancient Israel and the History of Its Ancient Texts* (New York: Touchstone, 2001).

Finkelstein, Israel, Amihai Mazar and Brian B. Schmidt, *The Quest for the Historical Israel: Debating Archaeology and the History of Early Israel* (Atlanta: Society of Biblical Literature, 2007).

Miller, J. Maxwell, and John H. Hayes, *A History of Ancient Israel and Judah* (London: SCM Press, 1986).

Redford, Donald B., *Egypt, Canaan, and Israel in Ancient Times* (Princeton: Princeton University Press, 1992).

Shanks, Hershel (ed.), *The Rise of Ancient Israel* (Washington: BAS, 1992).

—— *Ancient Israel: A Short History from Abraham to the Destruction of the Temple* (Washington: BAS, 1989).

Thompson, T. L., *The Bible in History: How Writers Create a Past* (London: Pimlico, 2000).

Wisdom teaching in the Old Testament

Anderson, Bernard W., *The Living World of the Old Testament*, 4th ed. (Harlow: Longman, 1988), pp. 568–575.

Arnold, Bill T., *Introduction to the Old Testament* (Cambridge: Cambridge University Press, 2014), pp. 275–291.

Clifford, Richard J., (ed.), *Wisdom Literature in Mesopotamia and Israel* (Atlanta: Society of Biblical Literature, 2007).

Crenshaw, James L., *Old Testament Wisdom: An Introduction*, 3rd ed. (Philadelphia: Westminster John Knox, 2010), pp. 1–21, 251–272.

—— *Urgent Advice and Probing Questions: Collected Writings on Old Testament Wisdom* (Macon: Mercer University Press, 1995).

Day, John, Robert P. Gordon and H. G. M. Williamson (eds.), *Wisdom in Ancient Israel* (Cambridge: Cambridge University Press, 1995).

Dell, Katharine, *'Get Wisdom, Get Insight': An Introduction to Israel's Wisdom Literature* (London: Darton, Longman & Todd, 2000).

Gammie, John G., and Leo G. Perdue, *The Sage in Israel and the Ancient Near East* (Winona Lake: Eisenbrauns, 1990).

Hess, Richard S., 'Wisdom Sources', in *DOTWPW*, pp. 894–901.

Hill, Andrew E., and John H. Walton, *A Survey of the Old Testament*, 3rd ed. (Grand Rapids: Zondervan, 2009), pp. 379–383.

Hubbard, David A., 'The Wisdom Movement and Israel's Covenant Faith', *TynBul* 17 (1966), pp. 3–33.

Hunter, Alastair, *Wisdom Literature* (London: SCM Press, 2006).

Kidner, Derek, *An Introduction to Wisdom Literature: The Wisdom of Proverbs, Job and Ecclesiastes* (Leicester: Inter-Varsity Press; Downers Grove: InterVarsity Press, 1985).

Lambert, W. G., *Babylonian Wisdom Literature* (Oxford: Oxford University Press, 1960).

LaSor, William Sanford, David Allan Hubbard and Frederic William Bush, *Old Testament Survey: The Message, Form, and Background of the Old Testament*, 2nd ed. (Grand Rapids: Eerdmans, 1996), pp. 447–459.

Lucas, Ernest, *Exploring the Old Testament*, vol. 3: *The Psalms and Wisdom Literature* (London: SPCK, 2003), pp. 79–90.

Murphy, Roland E., 'Wisdom in the OT', in *ABD* 6:920–931.

—— *The Tree of Life: An Exploration of Biblical Wisdom Literature*, 3rd ed. (Grand Rapids: Eerdmans, 2002).

Perdue, Leo G., *Wisdom & Creation: The Theology of Wisdom Literature* (Eugene: Wipf & Stock, 1994).

Rogerson, John, and Philip Davies, *The Old Testament World*, rev. and expanded ed. (London: T&T Clark, 2005), pp. 184–188.

Routledge, Robin, *Old Testament Theology: A Thematic Approach* (Nottingham: Apollos; Downers Grove: IVP Academic, 2008), pp. 215–224.

Rad, Gerhard von, *Wisdom in Israel* (Nashville: Abingdon, 1972).

Smothers, Thomas, 'Biblical Wisdom in Its Ancient Middle Eastern Context', in H. Wayne Ballard Jr. and W. Dennis Tucker Jr. (eds.), *An Introduction to Wisdom Literature and the Psalms: Festschrift Marvin E. Tate* (Macon: Mercer University Press, 2000), pp. 167–180.

Troxel, Ronald L., Kelvin G. Friebel and Dennis R. Magary (eds.), *Seeking out the Wisdom of the Ancients: Essays Offered to Honor Michael V. Fox on the Occasion of His Sixty-Fifth Birthday* (Winona Lake: Eisenbrauns, 2005).

Waltke, Bruce K., and David Diewert, 'Wisdom Literature', in David W. Baker and Bill T. Arnold (eds.), *The Face of Old Testament Studies: A Survey of Contemporary Approaches* (Grand Rapids: Baker; Leicester: Apollos, 1999), pp. 295–328.

Walton, John H., *Ancient Israelite Literature in Its Cultural Context: A Survey of Parallels Between Biblical and Ancient Near East Texts* (Grand Rapids: Zondervan, 1989), pp. 169–197.

Walton, John H., *Ancient Near Eastern Thought: Introducing the Conceptual World of the Hebrew Bible* (Grand Rapids: Baker Academic, 2006), pp. 74–78, 302–311.

Walton, John H., Victor H. Matthews and John W. Chavalas, *IVP Bible Background Commentary* (Downers Grove: InterVarsity Press, 2000), pp. 492–494.

Wilson, Gerald H., 'Wisdom', in *NIDOTTE* 4:1276–1285.

BIBLIOGRAPHY

Achtemeier, Elizabeth, *Nahum–Malachi*, IBC (Atlanta: John Knox, 1986).

—— *Minor Prophets I*, NIBCOT/UBC (Peabody: Hendrickson, 1999).

Achtemeier, Paul J., *Inspiration and Authority: The Nature and Function of Christian Scripture* (Peabody: Hendrickson, 1999; Grand Rapids: Baker Academic, 2010).

Aharoni, Yohanan, *The Land of the Bible: A Historical Geography*, rev. and enlarged ed. (Philadelphia: Westminster, 1979).

Albertz, Rainer, *A History of Israelite Religion in the Old Testament Period*, 2 vols. (London: SCM Press; Louisville: Westminster John Knox, 1994).

—— *Israel in Exile: The History and Literature of the Sixth Century B.C.E.*, Studies in Biblical Literature 3 (Atlanta: Society of Biblical Literature, 2003).

Allen, Leslie C., *The Books of Joel, Obadiah, Jonah and Micah*, NICOT (London: Hodder & Stoughton, 1976).

—— *Psalms 101–150*, WBC 21 (Waco: Word, 1983).

—— *Ezekiel*, 2 vols., WBC 28, 29 (Dallas: Word, 1986, 1990).

—— *Jeremiah*, OTL (Louisville: Westminster John Knox, 2008).

Allen L., and T. Laniak, *Ezra, Nehemiah, Esther*, NIBCOT/UBC (Peabody: Hendrickson, 2003).

Alt, Albrecht, *Essays on Old Testament History and Religion* (Oxford: Blackwell, 1966).

Alter, Robert, *The David Story: A Translation with Commentary of 1 and 2 Samuel* (New York: Norton, 1999).

—— *The Art of Biblical Narrative*, rev. ed. (New York: Basic, 2011).

—— *The Art of Biblical Poetry*, rev. ed. (New York: Basic, 2011).

Amit, Yairah, *Reading Biblical Narrative: Literary Criticism and the Hebrew Bible* (Minneapolis: Fortress, 2001).

Andersen, Francis I., *Job*, TOTC (Leicester: Inter-Varsity Press, 1976).

Andersen, Francis I., and David Noel Freedman, *Amos*, AB 24A (New York: Doubleday, 1989).

—— *Micah*, AB 24E (New York: Doubleday, 2000).

Anderson, Bernard W., *The Living World of the Old Testament*, 4th ed. (Harlow: Longman, 1988).

—— *From Creation to New Creation: Old Testament Perspectives*, OBT (Minneapolis: Fortress, 1994).

Arnold, Bill T., *1 & 2 Samuel*, NIVAC (Grand Rapids: Zondervan, 2003).

—— *Who Were the Babylonians?* (Atlanta: Society of Biblical Literature, 2004).

—— *Introduction to the Old Testament* (Cambridge: Cambridge University Press, 2014).

Arnold, Bill T., and Bryan E. Beyer (eds.), *Readings from the Ancient Near East: Primary Sources for Old Testament Study* (Grand Rapids: Baker Academic, 2002).

Ashley, Timothy R., *Numbers*, NICOT (Grand Rapids: Eerdmans, 1993).

Aune, David E., *Prophecy in Early Christianity and the Ancient Mediterranean World* (Grand Rapids: Eerdmans, 1983).

Baker, David L., 'Typology and the Christian Use of the Old Testament', *SJT* 29 (1976), pp. 137–157.

—— *Two Testaments, One Bible: The Theological Relationship Between the Old and New Testaments*, 3rd ed. (Nottingham: Apollos, 2010).

Baker, David W., *Nahum, Habakkuk, Zephaniah*, TOTC (Leicester: Inter-Varsity Press, 1988).

—— *Joel, Obadiah, Malachi*, NIVAC (Grand Rapids: Zondervan, 2006).

Baker, David W., and Bill T. Arnold (eds.), *The Face of Old Testament Studies: A Survey of Contemporary Approaches* (Grand Rapids: Baker; Leicester: Apollos, 1999).

Baker, David W., T. Desmond Alexander and Bruce K. Waltke, *Obadiah, Jonah and Micah*, TOTC (Leicester: Inter-Varsity Press, 1988).

Baldwin, Joyce G., *Haggai, Zechariah, Malachi*, TOTC (Leicester: Inter-Varsity Press, 1972).

—— *Daniel*, TOTC (Leicester: Inter-Varsity Press, 1978).

—— *Esther*, TOTC (Leicester: Inter-Varsity Press; Downers Grove: InterVarsity Press, 1984).

—— *1 and 2 Samuel*, TOTC (Leicester: Inter-Varsity Press, 1988).

Ballard, H. Wayne Jr., and W. Dennis Tucker Jr. (eds.), *An Introduction to Wisdom Literature and the Psalms: Festschrift Marvin E. Tate* (Macon: Mercer University Press, 2000).

Bar-Efrat, Shimon, *Narrative Art in the Bible*, JSOTSup 70 (Sheffield: JSOT Press, 2000).

Barker, Kenneth L., and Waylon Bailey, *Micah, Nahum, Habakkuk, Zephaniah*, NAC 20 (Nashville: B&H, 1998).

Barry, Peter, *Beginning Theory: An Introduction to Literary and Cultural Theory*, 2nd ed. (Manchester: Manchester University Press, 2002).
Bartholomew, Craig G., *Ecclesiastes*, BCOTWP (Grand Rapids: Baker Academic, 2009).
Barton, John, *Amos's Oracles Against the Nations* (Cambridge: Cambridge University Press, 1980).
—— *Reading the Old Testament: Method in Biblical Study*, 2nd ed. (Louisville: Westminster John Knox, 1996).
—— *Joel and Obadiah*, OTL (Louisville: Westminster John Knox, 2001).
—— *The Old Testament: Canon, Literature and Theology: Collected Essays* (Aldershot: Ashgate, 2007).
—— *Oracles of God: Perceptions of Ancient Prophecy in Israel After the Exile* (London: Darton, Longman & Todd, 2007).
Bauckham, Richard, 'The Rise of Apocalyptic', *Them* 3.2 (1978), pp. 10–23.
Beal, Lissa M. Wray, *1 & 2 Kings*, AOTC (Nottingham: Apollos; Downers Grove: InterVarsity Press, 2014).
Beale, G. K., *The Temple and the Church's Mission: A Biblical Theology of the Dwelling Place of God* (Leicester: Apollos; Downers Grove: InterVarsity Press, 2004).
—— *The Erosion of Inerrancy in Evangelicalism: Responding to New Challenges to Biblical Authority* (Wheaton: Crossway, 2008).
Beckwith, Roger, *The Old Testament Canon of the New Testament Church and Its Background in Early Judaism* (London: SPCK, 1985).
Bellinger, W. H. Jr., *Leviticus, Numbers*, NIBCOT/UBC (Peabody: Hendrickson, 2001).
Bergen, Robert D., *1, 2 Samuel*, NAC 7 (Nashville: B&H, 1996).
Berges, Ulrich, 'The Book of Isaiah as Isaiah's Book: The Latest Developments in the Research of the Prophets', *OTE* 23.3 (2010), pp. 549–573.
Berlin, Adele, *Poetics and Interpretation of Biblical Narrative* (Sheffield: Almond, 1983; Winona Lake: Eisenbrauns, 1994).
—— *Zephaniah*, AB 25A (New York: Doubleday, 1994).
—— *Esther*, JPSBC (Philadelphia: Jewish Publication Society, 2001).
—— *Lamentations*, OTL (Louisville: Westminster John Knox, 2002).
—— *The Dynamics of Biblical Parallelism*, rev. and expanded ed. (Grand Rapids: Eerdmans, 2008).
Bimson, John J., 'Reconsidering a "Cosmic Fall"', *Science & Christian Belief* 18.1 (2006), pp. 63–81.
Blenkinsopp, Joseph, *Ezra-Nehemiah*, OTL (Philadelphia: Westminster, 1988).
—— *Ezekiel*, IBC (Louisville: John Knox, 1990).
—— *A History of Prophecy in Israel*, rev. and enlarged ed. (Louisville: Westminster John Knox, 1996).
—— *The Pentateuch: An Introduction to the First Five Books of the Bible*, ABRL (New Haven: Yale University Press, 2000).

—— 'The Midianite–Kenite Hypothesis Revisited and the Origins of Judah', *JSOT* 33.2 (2008), pp. 131–153.

—— *Creation, Uncreation, Re-Creation: A Discursive Commentary on Genesis 1–11* (London: T&T Clark International, 2011).

Block, Daniel I., *Ezekiel*, 2 vols., NICOT (Grand Rapids: Eerdmans, 1997, 1998).

—— *Judges, Ruth*, NAC 6 (Nashville: B&H, 1999).

Boadt, Lawrence, *Reading the Old Testament: An Introduction* (Mahwah: Paulist Press, 1984).

Boda, Mark J., *Haggai, Zechariah*, NIVAC (Grand Rapids: Zondervan, 2009).

Boer, Roland (ed.), *Bakhtin and Genre Theory in Old Testament Studies* (Atlanta: Society of Biblical Literature, 2007).

Boling, Robert G., *Judges*, AB 6 (New York: Doubleday, 1975).

Braun, Roddy, *1 Chronicles*, WBC 14 (Waco: Word, 1986).

Breneman, Mervin, *Ezra, Nehemiah, Esther*, NAC 10 (Nashville: B&H, 1993).

Brenner, Athalya (ed.), *Ruth and Esther*, FCB (Sheffield: Sheffield Academic Press, 1999).

Bright, John, *Covenant and Promise: The Prophetic Understanding of the Future in Ancient Israel* (Philadelphia: Westminster, 1976).

—— *History of Israel*, 4th ed. (Louisville: Westminster John Knox, 2000).

Brotzman, Ellis R., *Old Testament Textual Criticism: A Practical Introduction* (Grand Rapids: Baker Academic, 1994).

Brown, William P., *Ecclesiastes*, IBC (Louisville: Westminster John Knox, 2000).

Broyles, Craig C., and Craig A. Evans (eds.), *Writing and Reading the Scroll of Isaiah: Studies in an Interpretative Tradition*, VTSup 70 (Leiden: Brill, 1997).

Bruce, F. F., *The Canon of Scripture* (Glasgow: Chapter House, 1988).

Bruckner, James, *Jonah, Nahum, Habakkuk, Zephaniah*, NIVAC (Grand Rapids: Zondervan, 2004).

Brueggemann, Walter, *The Message of the Psalms: A Theological Commentary* (Minneapolis: Augsburg, 1984).

—— *Old Testament Theology: Testimony, Dispute, Advocacy* (Minneapolis: Augsburg Fortress, 1997).

—— *Jeremiah: Exile and Homecoming* (Grand Rapids: Eerdmans, 1998).

—— *The Theology of the Book of Jeremiah* (Cambridge: Cambridge University Press, 2007).

—— *An Introduction to the Old Testament: The Canon and Christian Imagination*, 2nd ed. (Louisville: Westminster John Knox, 2012).

Budd, Philip J., *Numbers*, WBC 5 (Waco: Word, 1984).

—— *Leviticus*, NCB (London: Marshall Pickering; Grand Rapids: Eerdmans, 1996).

Bush, Frederic, *Ruth/Esther*, WBC 9 (Dallas: Word, 1996).

Campbell, Antony F., and Mark A. O'Brien, *Sources of the Pentateuch: Texts, Introductions, Annotations* (Minneapolis: Augsburg Fortress, 1993).

—— *Unfolding the Deuteronomistic History: Origins, Upgrades, Present Text* (Minneapolis: Augsburg Fortress, 2000).

Campbell, Edward F. Jr., *Ruth*, AB 7 (New York: Doubleday, 1975).

Carr, David M., *Writing on the Tablet of the Heart: Origins of Scripture and Literature* (Oxford: Oxford University Press, 2005).

Carr, G. Lloyd, *The Song of Solomon*, TOTC (Leicester: Inter-Varsity Press, 1984).

Carroll, Robert P., *Jeremiah*, OTL (London: SCM Press, 1986).

—— *Jeremiah*, OTG (Sheffield: Sheffield Academic Press, 1989).

Carson, D. A., and John D. Woodbridge (eds.), *Hermeneutics, Authority, and Canon* (Eugene: Wipf & Stock, 1986).

Chapman, Stephen B., *The Law and the Prophets: A Study in Old Testament Canon Formation* (Tübingen: Mohr Siebeck, 2000).

—— 'The Old Testament Canon and Its Authority for the Christian Church', *ExAud* 19 (2003), pp. 125–148.

—— 'What Are We Reading? Canonicity and the Old Testament', *WW* 24.4 (2009), pp. 334–347.

Chavalas, Mark W. (ed.), *The Ancient Near East: Historical Sources in Translation* (Oxford: Blackwell, 2006).

Childs, Brevard S., 'A Study of the Formula "Until This Day"', *JBL* 82.3 (1963), pp. 279–292.

—— *Isaiah and the Assyrian Crisis*, SBT 2.3 (London: SCM Press, 1967).

—— *Exodus*, OTL (London: SCM Press, 1974).

—— *Introduction to the Old Testament as Scripture* (London: SCM Press; Minneapolis: Fortress, 1979).

—— *Biblical Theology of the Old and New Testaments: Theological Reflection on the Christian Bible* (London: SCM Press, 1992).

—— *Isaiah*, OTL (Louisville: Westminster John Knox, 2001).

Christensen, Duane L., *Transformations of the War Oracle in Old Testament Prophecy* (Missoula: Scholars Press, 1975).

—— *Nahum*, AB 24F (New Haven: Yale University Press, 2009).

Christianson, Eric S., *A Time to Tell: Narrative Strategies in Ecclesiastes*, JSOTSup 280 (Sheffield: Sheffield Academic Press, 1998).

Clements, R. E., *God and Temple* (Oxford: Basil Blackwell, 1965).

—— *Prophecy and Tradition* (Oxford: Blackwell, 1975).

—— *A Century of Old Testament Study* (London: Lutterworth, 1976).

—— *Isaiah 1–39*, NCB (London: Marshall, Morgan & Scott; Grand Rapids: Eerdmans, 1980).

—— *Isaiah and the Deliverance of Jerusalem*, JSOTSup 13 (Sheffield: JSOT Press, 1984).

—— 'Beyond Tradition History': Deutero-Isaianic Development of First Isaiah's Themes', *JSOT* 31 (1985), pp. 95–113.

Clifford, Richard J., *Proverbs*, OTL (Louisville: Westminster John Knox, 1999).

—— (ed.), *Wisdom Literature in Mesopotamia and Israel* (Atlanta: Society of Biblical Literature, 2007).

Clines, David J. A., *Interested Parties: The Ideology of Writers and Readers of the Hebrew Bible* (London: Bloomsbury, 1995).

—— *Ezra, Nehemiah, Esther*, NCB (Grand Rapids: Eerdmans, 1996).

—— *The Theme of the Pentateuch*, 2nd ed. (Sheffield: Sheffield Academic Press, 1997).

—— *Job*, 3 vols., WBC 17–18B (Dallas: Word, 1989; Nashville: Nelson, 2006, 2011).

Clines, David J. A., Stephen E. Fowl and Stanley E. Porter (eds.), *The Bible in Three Dimensions: Essays in Celebration of Forty Years of Biblical Studies in the University of Sheffield* (Sheffield: JSOT Press, 1990).

Cogan, Mordechai, *I Kings*, AB 10 (New York: Doubleday, 2001).

Coggins, R. J., *Haggai, Zechariah, Malachi*, OTG (Sheffield: Sheffield Academic Press, 1987).

Collins, John J., *The Apocalyptic Imagination: An Introduction to Jewish Apocalyptic Literature*, 2nd ed. (Grand Rapids: Eerdmans, 1998).

—— *Introduction to the Hebrew Bible*, 2nd ed. (Minneapolis: Fortress, 2014).

—— (ed.), *Semeia 14: Apocalypse: The Morphology of a Genre* (Missoula: Scholars Press, 1979).

Collins, John J., and Peter W. Flint (eds.), *The Book of Daniel: Composition and Reception*, 2 vols., VTSup 83, FOTL 1 (Leiden: Koninklijke Brill, 2001).

Coogan, Michael (ed.), *The Oxford History of the Biblical World* (Oxford: Oxford University Press, 1998).

Cook, Stephen L., *The Social Roots of Biblical Yahwism*, SBLSBL 8 (Leiden: Brill, 2004).

Cooper, LaMar Eugene, *Ezekiel*, NAC 17 (Nashville: B&H, 1994).

Craigie, Peter C., *The Book of Deuteronomy*, NICOT (Grand Rapids: Eerdmans; London: Hodder & Stoughton, 1976).

Crenshaw, James L., *Ecclesiastes*, NICOT (Philadelphia: Westminster, 1987).

—— *Urgent Advice and Probing Questions: Collected Writings on Old Testament Wisdom* (Macon: Mercer University Press, 1995).

—— *Old Testament Wisdom: An Introduction*, 3rd ed. (Philadelphia: Westminster John Knox, 2010).

Cross, F. M., *Canaanite Myth and Hebrew Epic: Essays in the History and the Religion of Israel* (Cambridge, Mass.: Harvard University Press, 1973).

Cross, Frank Moore, and Shemaryahu Talmon (eds.), *Qumran and the History of the Biblical Text* (Cambridge, Mass.: Harvard University Press, 1975).

Cundall, Arthur E., and Leon Morris, *Judges and Ruth*, TOTC (Leicester: Inter-Varsity Press, 1968).

Dalley, Stephanie, *Myths from Mesopotamia: Creation, The Flood, Gilgamesh, and Others*, rev. ed. (Oxford: Oxford University Press, 2000).

Davies, Eryl W., *Numbers*, NCB (London: Marshall Pickering; Grand Rapids: Eerdmans, 1995).
Davis, Ellen F., *Proverbs, Ecclesiastes, Song of Songs*, Westminster Bible Companion (Louisville: Westminster John Knox, 2000).
Day, John (ed.), *God's Conflict with the Dragon and the Sea: Echoes of a Canaanite Myth in the Old Testament*, University of Cambridge Oriental Publications 35 (Cambridge: Cambridge University Press, 1985).
—— *Psalms*, OTG (Sheffield: Sheffield Academic Press, 1992).
—— *In Search of Pre-Exilic Israel* (London: T&T Clark International, 2004).
Day, John, Robert P. Gordon and H. G. M. Williamson (eds.), *Wisdom in Ancient Israel* (Cambridge: Cambridge University Press, 1995).
Day, Linda M., *Esther*, AbOTC (Nashville: Abingdon, 2005).
Dearman, J. Andrew, *Jeremiah and Lamentations*, NIVAC (Grand Rapids: Zondervan, 2002).
—— *Hosea*, NICOT (Grand Rapids: Eerdmans, 2010).
Dell, Katharine, *'Get Wisdom, Get Insight': An Introduction to Israel's Wisdom Literature* (London: Darton, Longman & Todd, 2000).
Dempster, Stephen, 'Canons on the Right and Canons on the Left: Finding a Resolution in the Canon Debate', *JETS* 52.1 (2009), pp. 47–77.
Dever, William G., *What Did the Biblical Writers Know and When Did They Know It? What Archaeology Can Tell Us About the Reality of Ancient Israel* (Grand Rapids: Eerdmans, 2001).
—— *Who Were the Early Israelites and Where Did They Come From?* (Grand Rapids: Eerdmans, 2003).
Dillard, Raymond B., *2 Chronicles*, WBC 15 (Waco: Word, 1987).
Dines, Jennifer, *The Septuagint* (New York: Continuum, 2004).
Dobbs-Allsopp, F. W., *Lamentations*, IBC (Louisville: Westminster John Knox, 2002).
Drews, Robert, *The End of the Bronze Age: Changes in Warfare and the Catastrophe CA. 1200 B.C.* (Princeton: Princeton University Press, 1993).
Duguid, Iain M., *The Song of Songs*, TOTC (Nottingham: Inter-Varsity Press, 2015).
Edenburg, Cynthia, and Juha Pakkala (eds.), *Is Samuel Among the Deuteronomists? Current Views on the Place of Samuel in a Deuteronomistic History* (Atlanta: Society of Biblical Literature, 2013).
Eichrodt, Walther, *Theology of the Old Testament*, 2 vols. (London: SCM Press, 1961–7).
Ellens, J. Harold, and Wayne G. Rollins (eds.), *Psychology and the Bible: A New Way to Read the Scriptures*, vol, 2: *From Genesis to Apocalyptic Vision* (Westport: Praeger, 2004).
Ellis, E. Earle, *The Old Testament in Early Christianity: Canon and Interpretation in the Light of Modern Research*, WUNT 54 (Tübingen: Mohr, 1991).
Emerton, J. A. (ed.), *Studies in the Historical Books of the Old Testament*, VTSup50 (Leiden: Brill, 1979).
Enns, Peter, *Exodus*, NIVAC (Grand Rapids: Zondervan, 2000).

—— *Inspiration and Incarnation: Evangelicals and the Problem of the Old Testament* (Grand Rapids: Baker, 2005).

—— *Ecclesiastes*, THOTC (Grand Rapids: Eerdmans, 2011).

Erickson, Millard J., *Christian Theology*, 3rd ed. (Grand Rapids: Baker, 2013).

Eslinger, Lyle, 'Viewpoints and Points of View in 1 Samuel 8 – 12', *JSOT* 26 (1983), pp. 61–76.

Evans, Craig A., and Emmanuel Tov (eds.), *Exploring the Origins of the Bible: Canon Formation in Historical, Literary, and Theological Perspective* (Grand Rapids: Baker Academic, 2008).

Exum, J. Cheryl, *Song of Songs*, OTL (Louisville: Westminster John Knox, 2005).

Exum, J. Cheryl, and David J. A. Clines (eds.), *The New Literary Criticism and the Hebrew Bible*, JSOTSup 143 (Sheffield: Sheffield Academic Press, 1993).

Fensham, F. Charles, *The Books of Ezra and Nehemiah*, NICOT (Grand Rapids: Eerdmans, 1982).

Finkelstein, Israel, 'The Emergence of the Monarchy in Israel: The Environmental and Socio-Economic Aspects', *JSOT* 44 (1989), pp. 43–74.

Finkelstein, Israel, and Neil Asher Silberman, *The Bible Unearthed: Archaeology's New Vision of Ancient Israel and the History of Its Ancient Texts* (New York: Touchstone, 2001).

Finkelstein, Israel, Amihai Mazar and Brian B. Schmidt, *The Quest for the Historical Israel: Debating Archaeology and the History of Early Israel* (Atlanta: Society of Biblical Literature, 2007).

Firth, David G., 'The Accession Narrative (1 Samuel 27 – 2 Samuel 1)', *TynBul* 58.1 (2007), pp. 61–81.

—— *1 & 2 Samuel*, AOTC (Nottingham: Apollos; Downers Grove: InterVarsity Press, 2009).

Firth, David G., and Jamie A. Grant (eds.), *Words and the Word: Explorations in Biblical Interpretation and Literary Theory* (Nottingham: Apollos, 2008).

Firth, David G., and Philip S. Johnston (eds.), *Interpreting Deuteronomy: Issues and Approaches* (Nottingham: Apollos, 2012).

Firth, David G., and Paul D. Wegner (eds.), *Presence, Power and Promise: The Role of the Spirit of God in the Old Testament* (Nottingham: Apollos; Downers Grove: InterVarsity Press, 2011).

Firth, David G., and H. G. M. Williamson (eds.), *Interpreting Isaiah: Issues and Approaches* (Nottingham: Apollos; Downers Grove: IVP Academic, 2009).

Fisher, Loren R., 'From Chaos to Cosmos', *Enc* 26.2 (1965), pp. 183–197.

Flint, Peter W., and Patrick D. Miller (eds.), *The Book of Psalms: Composition and Reception*, VTSup 99, FOTL 4 (Leiden: Koninklijke Brill, 2005).

Fokkelmann, J. P., *Reading Biblical Narrative: An Introductory Guide* (Louisville: Westminster John Knox; Leiderdorp: Deo, 1999).

—— *Reading Biblical Poetry: An Introductory Guide* (Philadelphia: Westminster John Knox, 2001).

Follis, Elaine R. (ed.), *Directions in Hebrew Biblical Poetry* (Sheffield: Sheffield Academic Press, 1987).

Fox, Michael V., *The Song of Songs and the Ancient Egyptian Love Songs* (Madison: University of Wisconsin Press, 1985).

—— *Qoheleth and His Contradictions*, BLS 18 (Sheffield: Almond, 1989).

—— *A Time to Tear Down and a Time to Build Up* (Grand Rapids: Eerdmans, 1999).

—— *Proverbs*, 2 vols., AB 18A–B (New Haven: Yale University Press, 2000, 2009).

—— *Ecclesiastes*, JPSBC (Philadelphia: Jewish Publication Society, 2004).

—— *Character and Ideology in the Book of Esther*, 2nd ed. (Eugene: Wipf & Stock, 2010).

Freedman, David Noel, 'Pottery, Poetry, and Prophecy: An Essay on Biblical Poetry', *JBL* 96.1 (1977), pp. 5–26.

Fretheim, T. E., *The Message of Jonah: A Theological Commentary* (Minneapolis: Augsburg, 1977).

—— *Exodus*, IBC (Louisville: Westminster John Knox, 1991).

—— *God and World in the Old Testament: A Relational Theology of Creation* (Nashville: Abingdon, 2005).

Frymer-Kensky, Tikva, 'The Atrahasis Epic and Its Significance for Our Understanding of Genesis 1 – 9', *BA* 40.4 (1977), pp. 147–155.

Garrett, Duane A., *Proverbs, Ecclesiastes, Song of Songs*, NAC 14 (Nashville: B&H, 1993).

—— *Hosea, Joel*, NAC 19a (Nashville: B&H, 1997).

Garrett, Duane A., and Paul House, *Song of Songs, Lamentations*, WBC 23B (Nashville: Nelson, 2004).

Geisler, Norman L. (ed.), *Inerrancy* (Grand Rapids: Zondervan, 1980).

Gillingham, Susan E., *The Poems and Psalms of the Hebrew Bible* (Oxford: Oxford University Press, 1994).

—— (ed.), *Jewish & Christian Approaches to the Psalms: Conflict & Convergence* (Oxford: Oxford University Press, 2013).

Gnuse, Robert, *Misunderstood Stories: Theological Commentary on Genesis 1–11* (Eugene: Cascade, 2014).

Goldingay, John E., *God's Prophet, God's Servant: A Study in Jeremiah and Isaiah 40–55* (Exeter: Paternoster, 1984).

—— *Daniel*, WBC 30 (Dallas: Word, 1987).

—— *Old Testament Theology 1: Israel's Gospel* (Downers Grove: InterVarsity Press; Milton Keynes: Paternoster, 2003).

—— *Psalms*, BCOTWP, 3 vols. (Grand Rapids: Baker Academic, 2006–8).

—— *An Introduction to the Old Testament: Exploring Text, Approaches & Issues* (Downers Grove: IVP Academic, 2015).

Goldingay, J., and P. Scalise, *Minor Prophets II*, NIBCOT/UBC (Peabody: Hendrickson, 2009).

Goodman, Martin (ed.), *The Apocrypha*, Oxford Bible Commentaries (Oxford: Oxford University Press, 2001).

Goppelt, Leonhard, *Typos: The Typological Interpretation of the Old Testament in the New* (Grand Rapids: Eerdmans, 1981).

Gordon, Robert P., *1 & 2 Samuel*, OTG (Sheffield: Sheffield Academic Press, 1984).

—— *I & II Samuel: A Commentary* (Carlisle: Paternoster, 1986).

—— (ed.), *The Place Is Too Small for Us: The Israelite Prophets in Recent Scholarship*, SBTS 5 (Winona Lake: Eisenbrauns, 1995).

Gottwald, Norman K., 'Social Matrix and Canonical Shape', *ThTo* 42.3 (1985), pp. 307–321.

—— *The Hebrew Bible: A Sociological Introduction* (Philadelphia: Fortress, 1987).

—— *The Tribes of Yahweh: A Sociology of the Religion of Liberated Israel, 1220–1050 BCE* (Maryknoll: Orbis, 1979; Sheffield: Sheffield Academic Press, 1999).

Grabbe, Lester L., *A History of the Jews and Judaism in the Second Temple Period: 2. The Early Hellenistic Period (335–175 BCE)* (London: T&T Clark, 2008).

Grams, Rollin G., I. Howard Marshall, Peter F. Penner and Robin Routledge (eds.), *Bible and Mission: A Conversation Between Biblical Studies and Missiology* (Schwarzenfeld: Neufeld, 2008).

Greenberg, Moshe, 'The Use of the Ancient Versions for Interpreting the Hebrew Text: A Sampling from Ezekiel ii 1 – iii 11', in *Congress Volume: Göttingen 1977*, VTSup 29 (Leiden: Brill, 1978), pp. 131–148.

—— *Ezekiel 1–37*, 2 vols., AB 22, 22A (New York: Doubleday, 1983, 1997).

Greidanus, Sidney, *Preaching Christ from the Old Testament: A Contemporary Hermeneutical Method* (Grand Rapids: Eerdmans, 1999).

Grudem, Wayne, *Systematic Theology: An Introduction to Biblical Doctrine* (Grand Rapids: Zondervan; Leicester: Inter-Varsity Press, 1994).

Gunkel, Hermann, *An Introduction to the Psalms*, trans. James D. Nogalski (Macon: Mercer, 1998).

Gunn, David M., and Danna Nolan Fewell, *Narrative in the Hebrew Bible*, Oxford Bible Series (Oxford: Oxford University Press, 1993).

Gurtner, Daniel M., and John Nolland (eds.), *Built upon the Rock: Studies in the Gospel of Matthew* (Grand Rapids: Eerdmans, 2008).

Habel, Norman C., *Job*, OTL (Philadelphia: Westminster, 1985).

Hafemann, Scott J., and Paul R. House (eds.), *Central Themes in Biblical Theology: Mapping Unity in Diversity* (Nottingham: Apollos; Grand Rapids: Baker, 2007).

Hallo, William W., *The World's Oldest Literature: Studies in Sumerian Belle-Lettres* (Leiden: Brill, 2010).

Hallo, William W., and William Kelly Simpson, *The Ancient Near East: A History*, 2nd ed. (Orlando: Harcourt Brace, 1991).

Halpern, Baruch, *The First Historians: The Hebrew Bible and History* (University Park: Pennsylvania State University Press, 1996).

Hamilton, Victor P., *The Book of Genesis: Chapters 1–17*, NICOT (Grand Rapids: Eerdmans, 1990).
—— *Exodus: An Exegetical Commentary* (Grand Rapids: Baker Academic, 2011).
Hanson, Paul D., *The Dawn of Apocalyptic: The Historical and Sociological Roots of Jewish Apocalyptic Eschatology*, rev. ed. (Philadelphia: Fortress, 1979).
Harris, J., C. Brown and M. Moore, *Joshua, Judges, Ruth*, NIBCOT/UBC (Peabody: Hendrickson, 2000).
Harrison, R. K., *Introduction to the Old Testament* (London: Inter-Varsity Press, 1977).
Hartley, John E., *The Book of Job*, NICOT (Grand Rapids: Eerdmans, 1988).
—— *Leviticus*, WBC 4 (Dallas: Word, 1992).
Hayes, John H., *Interpreting Israelite History, Prophecy, and Law* (Eugene: Cascade, 2013).
Hayes, John Haralson, and Carl R. Holladay, *Biblical Exegesis: A Beginner's Handbook*, 3rd ed. (Louisville: Westminster John Knox, 2007).
Hays, Christopher M., and Christopher B. Ansberry (eds.), *Evangelical Faith and the Challenge of Historical Criticism* (London: SPCK, 2013).
Hess, Richard S., *Joshua*, TOTC (Leicester: Inter-Varsity Press, 1996).
Hess, Richard S., Philip E. Satterthwaite and Gordon J. Wenham (eds.), *He Swore an Oath* (Cambridge: Tyndale House, 1993).
Hill, Andrew, *Malachi*, AB 25D (New York: Doubleday, 1998).
—— *Haggai, Zechariah and Malachi*, TOTC (Nottingham: Inter-Varsity Press, 2012).
Hill, Andrew E., and John H. Walton, *A Survey of the Old Testament*, 3rd ed. (Grand Rapids: Zondervan, 2009).
Hirsch, E. D., *Validity in Interpretation* (New Haven: Yale University Press, 1967).
Hobbs, T. R., *2 Kings*, WBC 13 (Waco: Word, 1985).
Hoffmeier, James K., *Ancient Israel in Sinai: The Evidence for the Authenticity of the Wilderness Traditions* (Oxford: Oxford University Press, 2005).
Holladay, William L., *Jeremiah*, 2 vols., Hermeneia (Philadelphia: Fortress, 1986, 1989).
—— 'Reading Zephaniah with a Concordance: Suggestions for a Redaction History', *JBL* 120.4 (2001), pp. 671–684.
House, Paul R., *Zephaniah: A Prophetic Drama*, JSOTSup 69 (Sheffield: JSOT Press, 1988).
—— *The Unity of the Twelve* (Sheffield: Sheffield Academic Press, 1990).
—— *1, 2 Kings*, NAC 8 (Nashville: B&H, 1995).
Hubbard, David Allan, 'The Wisdom Movement and Israel's Covenant Faith', *TynBul* 17 (1966), pp. 3–33.
—— *Hosea*, TOTC (Leicester: Inter-Varsity Press, 1989).
—— *Joel and Amos*, TOTC (Leicester: Inter-Varsity Press, 1989).
Hubbard, Robert L. Jr., *The Book of Ruth*, NICOT (Grand Rapids: Eerdmans, 1988).
Huey, F. B. Jr., *Jeremiah, Lamentations*, NAC 16 (Nashville: B&H, 1993).
Huffmon, Herbert B., 'The Covenant Lawsuit in the Prophets', *JBL* 78 (1959), pp. 285–295.

Hugenberger, Gordon P., *Marriage as a Covenant: Biblical Law and Ethics as Developed from Malachi* (Eugene: Wipf & Stock, 2014).

Hunter, Alastair, *Wisdom Literature* (London: SCM Press, 2006).

Janzen, J. Gerald, *Job*, IBC (Atlanta: John Knox, 1985).

Japhet, Sara, *I & II Chronicles*, OTL (Louisville: Westminster John Knox, 1993).

Jeremias, Jörg, *Amos*, OTL (Louisville: Westminster John Knox, 1998).

Jobes, Karen H., *Esther*, NIVAC (Grand Rapids: Zondervan, 1999).

Johnston, Gordon H., 'Genesis 1 and the Ancient Egyptian Creation Myths', *BSac* 165 (2008), pp. 178–194.

Johnston, Philip S., and David G. Firth, *Interpreting the Psalms: Issues and Approaches* (Leicester: Apollos; Downers Grove: IVP Academic, 2005).

Johnstone, William, *Chronicles and Exodus: An Analogy and Its Application*, JSOTSup 275 (Sheffield: Sheffield Academic Press, 1998).

Jones, Gwilym H., *1 & 2 Chronicles*, OTG (Sheffield: JSOT Press, 1993).

Kaiser, Otto, *Isaiah 13–39*, OTL (London: SCM Press, 1974).

Kelley, Brian E., *Retribution and Eschatology in Chronicles*, JSOTSup 211 (Sheffield: Sheffield Academic Press, 1996).

Kidner, Derek, *Proverbs*, TOTC (London: Inter-Varsity Press, 1964).

—— *Psalms*, 2 vols., TOTC (London: Inter-Varsity Press, 1975).

—— *Ezra and Nehemiah*, TOTC (Leicester: Inter-Varsity Press, 1979).

—— *An Introduction to Wisdom Literature: The Wisdom of Proverbs, Job and Ecclesiastes* (Leicester: Inter-Varsity Press; Downers Grove: InterVarsity Press, 1985).

Killebrew, Ann E., *Biblical Peoples and Ethnicity: An Archaeological Study of Egyptians, Canaanites, Philistines, and Early Israelites, 1300–1100 B.C.E.* (Atlanta: Society of Biblical Literature, 2005).

Killebrew, Ann E., and Gunnar Lehmann (eds.), *The Philistines and Other 'Sea Peoples' in Text and Archaeology* (Atlanta: Society of Biblical Literature, 2013).

Kitchen, K. A., *On the Reliability of the Old Testament* (Grand Rapids: Eerdmans, 2003).

Klein, George L., *Zechariah*, NAC 21B (Nashville: B&H, 2008).

Klein, Ralph W., *1, 2 Chronicles*, Hermeneia, 2 vols. (Minneapolis: Fortress, 2006, 2012).

Knight, Douglas A., *Rediscovering the Traditions of Israel*, 3rd ed., Studies in Biblical Literature 16 (Atlanta: Society of Biblical Literature, 2006).

Knight, G. A. F., *Hosea*, TBC (London: SCM Press, 1960).

Kraus, Hans-Joachim, *Psalms*, 2 vols., CC (Minneapolis: Fortress, 1993).

Kugel, James L., *The Idea of Biblical Poetry: Parallelism and Its History* (New York: Yale University Press, 1981).

Lacocque, André, *Ruth*, CC (Minneapolis: Augsburg Fortress, 2004).

—— *Romance, She Wrote: A Hermeneutical Essay on Song of Songs* (Eugene: Wipf & Stock, 2006).

Lalleman, Hetty, *Jeremiah and Lamentations*, TOTC (Nottingham: Inter-Varsity Press, 2013).

Lalleman-de Winkel, Hetty, *Jeremiah in Prophetic Tradition: An Examination of the Book of Jeremiah in the Light of Israel's Prophetic Traditions* (Leuven: Peeters, 2000).

Lambert, W. G., *Babylonian Wisdom Literature* (Oxford: Oxford University Press, 1960).

LaSor, William Sanford, 'Prophecy, Inspiration, and *Sensus Plenior*', *TynBul* 29 (1978), pp. 49–60.

LaSor, William Sanford, David Allan Hubbard and Frederic William Bush, *Old Testament Survey: The Message, Form, and Background of the Old Testament*, 2nd ed. (Grand Rapids: Eerdmans, 1996).

Law, David R., *The Historical-Critical Method: A Guide for the Perplexed* (London: T&T Clark International, 2012).

Levenson, Jon D., *Creation and the Persistence of Evil: The Jewish Drama of Divine Omnipotence* (Princeton: Princeton University Press, 1988).

—— *Esther*, OTL (Louisville: Westminster John Knox, 1997).

Lim, Timothy H., *The Formation of the Jewish Canon* (New Haven: Yale University Press, 2013).

Limburg, James, *Hosea–Micah*, IBC (Louisville: Westminster John Knox, 1988).

—— *Jonah*, OTL (Louisville: Westminster John Knox, 1993).

Linafelt, Todd, *Ruth*, Berit Olam (Collegeville: Liturgical Press, 1999).

Lindblom, Johannes, *Prophecy in Ancient Israel* (Oxford: Blackwell, 1962).

Liverani, Mario, *The Ancient Near East: History, Society and Economy* (Abingdon: Routledge, 2014).

Long, Burke O., *1 Kings with an Introduction to Historical Literature*, FOTL 9 (Grand Rapids: Eerdmans, 1984).

Long, V. Philips, *The Art of Biblical History* (Grand Rapids: Zondervan, 1994).

—— (ed.), *Israel's Past in Present Research: Essays on Ancient Israelite Historiography*, SBTS 7 (Winona Lake: Eisenbrauns, 1999).

Longman III, Tremper, 'A Critique of Two Recent Metrical Systems', *Bib* 63 (1982), pp. 230–254.

—— 'Form Criticism, Recent Developments in Genre Theory and the Evangelical', *WTJ* 47 (1985), pp. 46–47.

—— *Literary Approaches to Biblical Interpretation* (Grand Rapids: Zondervan, 1987).

—— *How to Read the Psalms* (Downers Grove: InterVarsity Press, 1988).

—— *The Book of Ecclesiastes*, NICOT (Grand Rapids: Eerdmans, 1998).

—— *Daniel*, NIVAC (Grand Rapids: Zondervan, 1999).

—— *Song of Songs*, NICOT (Grand Rapids: Eerdmans, 2001).

—— *How to Read Proverbs* (Downers Grove: InterVarsity Press, 2002).

—— *How to Read Genesis* (Downers Grove: InterVarsity Press; Milton Keynes: Paternoster, 2005).

—— *Proverbs*, BCOTWP (Grand Rapids: Baker Academic, 2006).

Longman III, Tremper, and Raymond B. Dillard, *An Introduction to the Old Testament*, 2nd ed. (Nottingham: Apollos, 2007).

Lucas, Ernest C., 'Covenant, Treaty and Prophecy', *Them* 8.1 (1982), pp. 19–23.

—— *Daniel*, AOTC 20 (Leicester: Apollos; Downers Grove: InterVarsity Press, 2002).

—— *Exploring the Old Testament*, vol. 3: *The Psalms and Wisdom Literature* (London: SPCK, 2003).

Lundbom, Jack R., *Jeremiah*, 3 vols., AB 21A–21C (New York: Doubleday, 1999–2004).

—— *Jeremiah Closer Up: The Prophet and the Book*, HBM (Sheffield: Sheffield Phoenix, 2010).

—— *Deuteronomy* (Grand Rapids: Eerdmans, 2013).

McCann, J. Clinton, *A Theological Introduction to the Book of Psalms: The Psalms as Torah* (Nashville: Abingdon, 1993).

—— *Judges*, IBC (Louisville: Westminster John Knox, 2002).

McCarter, P. Kyle Jr., *I Samuel*, AB 8 (New York: Doubleday, 1980).

McComiskey, Thomas Edward (ed.), *The Minor Prophets* (Grand Rapids: Baker Academic, 2009).

McConville, J. G., *Law and Theology in Deuteronomy*, JSOTSup 33 (Sheffield: JSOT Press, 1984).

—— *Grace in the End: A Study in Deuteronomic Theology*, SOTBT (Grand Rapids: Zondervan, 1993).

—— *Deuteronomy*, AOTC 5 (Leicester: Apollos; Downers Grove: InterVarsity Press, 2002).

—— *Exploring the Old Testament*, vol. 4: *The Prophets* (London: SPCK, 2002).

McDonald, Lee Martin, *The Biblical Canon: Its Origin, Transmission and Authority* (Grand Rapids: Baker Academic, 2007).

McKane, William, *Proverbs*, OTL (London: SCM Press, 1970).

—— *Jeremiah*, 2 vols., ICC (Edinburgh: T&T Clark, 1986, 1996).

McKeating, Henry, *Ezekiel*, OTG (Sheffield: Sheffield Academic Press, 1993).

McKenzie, Steven L., and Stephen R. Haynes (eds.), *To Each Its Own Meaning: An Introduction to Biblical Criticisms and Their Application* (London: Geoffrey Chapman, 1993; rev. and expanded ed. Louisville: Westminster John Knox, 1999).

McKeown, James, *Genesis*, THOTC (Grand Rapids: Eerdmans, 2008).

Mason, Rex, *The Books of Haggai, Zechariah and Malachi*, CBC (Cambridge: Cambridge University Press, 1977).

—— *Zephaniah, Habakkuk, Joel*, OTG (Sheffield: JSOT Press, 1994).

Matthews, Victor H., *Judges & Ruth*, NCBC (Cambridge: Cambridge University Press, 2004).

Matthews, Victor H., and Don C. Benjamin, *Old Testament Parallels: Laws and Stories from the Ancient Near East*, 3rd ed. (Mahwah: Paulist Press, 2006).

Matthews, Victor H., and James C. Moyer, *The Old Testament: Text and Context*, 3rd ed. (Grand Rapids: Baker Academic, 2012).

Mayes, A. D. H., *Deuteronomy*, NCB (Grand Rapids: Eerdmans, 1996).

Mays, James Luther, *Amos*, OTL (London: SCM Press, 1969).
—— *Hosea*, OTL (London: SCM Press, 1969).
—— *Micah*, OTL (London: SCM Press, 1976).
Mays, James Luther, and Paul J. Achtemeier (eds.), *Interpreting the Prophets* (Philadelphia: Fortress, 1987).
Mays, James Luther, David L. Petersen and Kent Harold Richards (eds.), *Old Testament Interpretation Past, Present, and Future: Essays in Honour of Gene M. Tucker* (Nashville: Abingdon, 1995).
Merrill, Eugene H., *Haggai, Zechariah, Malachi* (Chicago: Moody, 1994).
Merrill, Eugene H., Mark F. Rooker and Michael A. Grisanti, *The World and the Word: An Introduction to the Old Testament* (Nashville: B&H, 2011).
Metzger, Bruce M., 'Important Early Translations of the Bible', *BSac* 150 (1993), pp. 35–49.
Meyers, Carol L., and Eric M. Meyers, *Haggai and Zechariah 1–8*, AB 25B (New York: Doubleday, 1987).
Mieroop, Marc Van De, *A History of the Ancient Near East: Ca. 3000–323 BC*, 2nd ed. (Oxford: Blackwell, 2007).
—— *A History of Ancient Egypt* (Chichester: Wiley-Blackwell, 2011).
Milgrom, Jacob, *Leviticus: A Book of Ritual and Ethics*, CC (Minneapolis: Fortress, 2004).
Miller, Cynthia L., 'A Linguistic Approach to Ellipsis in Biblical Poetry (or, What to Do When Exegesis of What Is There Depends on What Isn't), *BBR* 13.2 (2003), pp. 251–270.
Miller, Geoffrey D., 'Intertextuality in Old Testament Research', *CurBR* 9.3 (2011), pp. 283–309.
Miller, J. Maxwell, and John H. Hayes, *A History of Ancient Israel and Judah* (London: SCM Press, 1986).
Miller, Stephen R., *Daniel*, NAC 18 (Nashville: B&H, 1994).
Miscall, Peter D., *The Workings of Old Testament Narrative*, SemeiaSt (Philadelphia: Fortress; Chico: Scholars Press, 1983).
Mitchell, T. C., *The Bible in the British Museum: Interpreting the Evidence*, new ed. (Mahwah: Paulist Press, 2004).
Möller, Karl, *A Prophet in Debate: The Rhetoric of Persuasion in the Book of Amos* (Sheffield: Sheffield Academic Press, 2003).
Moo, Jonathan, and Robin Routledge (eds.), *As Long as the Earth Endures: Biblical and Theological Perspectives on Creation and the Environment* (Nottingham: Apollos, 2014).
Moore, Carey A., *Esther*, AB 7B (New York: Doubleday, 1971).
—— *Daniel, Esther, and Jeremiah: The Additions*, AB44 (New York: Doubleday, 1977).
Moore, Megan Bishop, and Brad E. Kelle, *Biblical History and Israel's Past: The Changing Study of the Bible and History* (Grand Rapids: Eerdmans, 2011).
Motyer, Alec, *The Book of Isaiah* (Leicester: Inter-Varsity Press, 1993).

Mowinckel, Sigmund, *He That Cometh: The Messiah Concept in the Old Testament and Later Judaism* (Oxford: Blackwell, 1956).

—— *The Psalms in Israel's Worship*, 2 vols. (Oxford: Blackwell, 1962).

Moyise, Steve, 'Intertextuality and Biblical Studies: A Review', *VE* 23.2 (2002), pp. 418–431.

Murphy, Roland, *Ecclesiastes*, WBC 23A (Dallas: Word, 1992).

—— *Proverbs*, WBC 22 (Nashville: Thomas Nelson, 1998).

Murphy, Roland E., and Elizabeth Huwiler, *Proverbs, Ecclesiastes and Song of Songs*, NIBCOT/UBC (Peabody: Hendrickson, 1999).

Na'aman, Nadav, 'The Exodus Story: Between Historical Memory and Historiographical Composition', *JANER* 11 (2011), pp. 39–69.

Nelson, Richard D., *Joshua*, OTL (Louisville: Westminster John Knox, 1997).

Newman, Robert C., 'The Council of Jamnia and the Old Testament Canon', *WTJ* 38.4 (1976), pp. 319–348.

Newsom, Carol A., with Brennan W. Breed, *Daniel*, OTL (Louisville: Westminster John Knox, 2014).

Nicholson, E. W., *Preaching to the Exiles: A Study of the Prose Tradition in the Book of Jeremiah* (Oxford: Basil Blackwell, 1970).

Niditch, Susan, *War in the Hebrew Bible: A Study in the Ethics of Violence* (New York: Oxford University Press, 1993).

—— *Judges*, OTL (Louisville: Westminster John Knox, 2008).

Nielsen, Kirsten, *Ruth*, OTL (Louisville: Westminster John Knox, 1997).

Nissen, Hans J., *The Early History of the Ancient Near East: 9000–2000 B. C.* (Chicago: University of Chicago Press, 1988).

Noll, K. L., *Canaan and Israel in Antiquity: A Textbook on History and Religion*, 2nd ed. (London: T&T Clark, 2013).

O'Brien, Julia M., *Nahum, Habakkuk, Zephaniah, Haggai, Zechariah, Malachi*, AbOTC (Nashville: Abingdon, 2004).

O'Connor, M., *Hebrew Verse Structure* (Winona Lake: Eisenbrauns, 1980).

Oeste, Gordon K., *Legitimacy, Illegitimacy and the Right to Rule: Windows on Abimelech's Rise and Demise in Judges 9* (London: T&T Clark, 2011).

Okoye, James C., *Israel and the Nations: A Mission Theology of the Old Testament* (Maryknoll: Orbis, 2006).

Olsen, Dennis T., *Numbers*, IBC (Louisville: John Knox, 1996).

Osborne, Grant R., *The Hermeneutical Spiral: A Comprehensive Introduction to Biblical Interpretation*, 2nd ed. (Downers Grove: InterVarsity Press, 2006).

Oss, Douglas A., 'Canon as Context: The Function of Sensus Plenior in Evangelical Hermeneutics', *GTJ* 9.1 (1988), pp. 105–127.

Oswalt, John, *The Book of Isaiah 1–39*, NICOT (Grand Rapids: Eerdmans, 1986).

—— *The Book of Isaiah 40–66*, NICOT (Grand Rapids: Eerdmans, 1997).

—— *Isaiah*, NIVAC (Grand Rapids: Zondervan, 2003).
—— *The Holy One of Israel: Studies in the Book of Isaiah* (Cambridge: James Clarke, 2014).
Paltridge, Brian, *Discourse Analysis: An Introduction*, 2nd ed. (London: Bloomsbury Academic, 2012).
Pao, David W., *Acts and the Isaianic New Exodus*, BSL (Grand Rapids: Baker Academic, 2002).
Parry, Robin, *Lamentations*, THOTC (Grand Rapids: Eerdmans, 2010).
Paul, Shalom M., *Isaiah 40–66*, ECC (Grand Rapids: Eerdmans, 2012).
Perdue, Leo G., *Wisdom & Creation: The Theology of Wisdom Literature* (Eugene: Wipf & Stock, 1994).
Petersen, David L., *The Roles of Israel's Prophets*, JSOTSup 17 (Sheffield: JSOT Press, 1981).
—— *Haggai & Zechariah 1–8*, OTL (Philadelphia: Westminster, 1984).
—— *Zechariah 9–14 & Malachi* (Louisville: Westminster John Knox, 1995).
—— *The Prophetic Literature: An Introduction* (Louisville: Westminster John Knox, 2002).
Petersen, David L., and Kent Harold Richards, *Interpreting Hebrew Poetry*, GBS: OT Series (Philadelphia: Fortress, 1992).
Peterson, Brian Neil, *The Authors of the Deuteronomistic History: Locating a Tradition in Ancient Israel* (Minneapolis: Fortress, 2014).
Petterson, Anthony R., *Haggai, Zechariah, Malachi*, AOTC (Nottingham: Apollos, 2015).
Pitkänen, Pekka M. A., *Joshua*, AOTC 6 (Nottingham: Apollos; Downers Grove: InterVarsity Press, 2010).
Pollock, Susan, *Ancient Mesopotamia* (Cambridge: Cambridge University Press, 1999).
Porteous, Norman W., *Daniel*, OTL (London: SCM Press; Philadelphia: Westminster, 1965).
Provan, Iain, *Ecclesiastes, Song of Songs*, NIVAC (Grand Rapids: Zondervan, 2001).
Provan, Iain, V. Philips Long and Tremper Longman III, *A Biblical History of Israel* (Louisville: Westminster John Knox, 2003).
Rad, Gerhard von, *Old Testament Theology*, 2 vols. (Edinburgh: Oliver & Boyd, 1962–5).
—— *Deuteronomy*, OTL (London: SCM Press, 1966).
—— *Genesis*, rev. ed., OTL (London: SCM Press, 1972).
—— *God at Work in Israel* (Nashville: Abingdon, 1980).
—— *The Problem of the Hexateuch and Other Essays*, trans. E. W. Trueman Dicken (London: SCM Press, 1984).
Rainey, Anson, 'Shasu or Habiru: Who Were the Early Israelites', *BAR* 34.6 (2008), pp. 51–55.
Redditt, Paul L., *Haggai, Zechariah, Malachi*, NCB (Grand Rapids: Eerdmans, 1995).
—— *Introduction to the Prophets* (Grand Rapids: Eerdmans, 2008).
Redford, Donald B., *Egypt, Canaan, and Israel in Ancient Times* (Princeton: Princeton University Press, 1992).

Reed, Jeffrey T., 'Discourse Analysis as New Testament Hermeneutic: A Retrospective and Prospective Appraisal', *JETS* 39.2 (1996), pp. 223–240.

Reid, Debra, *Esther*, TOTC (Nottingham: Inter-Varsity Press, 2008).

Rendtorff, Rolf, 'Old Testament Theology, Tanakh Theology, or Biblical Theology. Reflections in an Ecumenical Context', *Bib* 73.2 (1992), pp. 441–451.

—— *The Canonical Hebrew Bible: A Theology of the Old Testament* (Leiden: Deo, 2005).

Rendtorff, Rolf, and Robert A. Kugler (eds.), *The Book of Leviticus: Composition and Reception*, VTSup 93 (Leiden: Brill, 2003).

Riggs, Jack R., 'The "Fuller Meaning" of Scripture: A Hermeneutical Question for Evangelicals', *GTJ* 7.2 (1986), pp. 213–227.

Roberts, J. J. M., *Nahum, Habakkuk and Zephaniah*, OTL (Louisville: Westminster John Knox, 1991).

Robertson, O. Palmer, *The Books of Nahum, Habakkuk and Zephaniah*, NICOT (Grand Rapids: Eerdmans, 1991).

Robson, James, *Word and Spirit in Ezekiel*, LBS (London: T&T Clark International, 2006).

Rofé, Alexander, *Deuteronomy: Issues and Interpretation* (Edinburgh: T&T Clark, 2002).

Rogerson, John, *Chronicles of the Bible Lands: A History of the Holy Land* (London: Angus, 2003).

Rogerson, John, John Barton, David J. A. Clines and Paul Joyce, *Beginning Old Testament Study* (London: SPCK; Danvers: Chalice, 1998).

Rogerson, John, and Philip Davies, *The Old Testament World*, rev. and expanded ed. (London: T&T Clark, 2005).

Römer, Thomas, *The So-Called Deuteronomistic History: A Sociological, Historical and Literary Introduction* (London: T&T Clark, 2005).

Rost, Leonhard, *The Succession to the Throne of David* (Sheffield: Almond, 1982).

Routledge, Robin, '*Ḥesed* as Obligation: A Re-examination', *TynBul* 46.1 (1995), pp. 188–191.

—— 'Guest or Gatecrasher: Questioning Assumptions in a Narrative Approach to the Old Testament', *JEBS* 3.3 (2003), pp. 17–28.

—— 'Is There a Narrative Substructure Underlying the Book of Isaiah', *TynBul* 55.2 (2004), pp. 183–204.

—— *Old Testament Theology: A Thematic Approach* (Nottingham: Apollos; Downers Grove: IVP Academic, 2008).

—— 'Sacrifice, Prayer and Forgiveness', *EJT* 18.1 (2009), pp. 17–28.

—— 'Did God Create Chaos? Unresolved Tension In Genesis 1:1–2', *TynBul* 61.1 (2010), pp. 69–88.

—— '"My Spirit" in Genesis 6:1–4', *JPT* 20 (2011), pp. 232–251.

—— 'Replacement or Fulfillment: Re-applying Old Testament Designations of Israel to the Church', *STR* 4.2 (2013), pp. 137–154.

Rowley, H. H., *The Servant of the Lord and Other Essays on the Old Testament* (Oxford: Blackwell, 1965).

—— *Job*, NCB (London: Oliphants, 1970).

Russell, D. S., *The Method and Message of Jewish Apocalyptic*, OTL (London: SCM Press, 1964).

—— *The Jews from Alexander to Herod*, new ed. (Oxford: Oxford University Press, 1973).

—— *Apocalyptic Ancient and Modern* (London: SCM Press, 1978).

Sailhamer, John H., *The Meaning of the Pentateuch: Revelation, Composition, and Interpretation* (Downers Grove: InterVarsity Press, 2009).

Sakenfeld, Katharine Doob, *Ruth*, IBC (Louisville: Westminster John Knox, 1999).

Sanderson, James A., 'Text and Canon: Concepts and Method', *JBL* 98.1 (1979), pp. 5–29.

Sandy, D. Brent, and Ronald L. Giese (eds.), *Cracking Old Testament Codes: A Guide to Interpreting the Literary Genres of the Old Testament* (Nashville: B&H, 1995).

Sarna, Nahum M., 'Epic Substratum in the Prose of Job', *JBL* 76 (1957), pp. 13–25.

Sasson, Jack M., *Jonah*, AB 24B (New York: Doubleday, 1995).

Satterthwaite, Philip E., Richard S. Hess and Gordon J. Wenham (eds.), *The LORD's Anointed: Interpretation of Old Testament Messianic Texts* (Carlisle: Paternoster, 1995).

Satterthwaite, Philip, and Gordon McConville, *Exploring the Old Testament*, vol. 3: *The Histories* (London: SPCK, 2007).

Seitz, Christopher R., *Isaiah 1–39*, IBC (Louisville: John Knox, 1993).

Selman, Martin J., *1, 2 Chronicles*, TOTC, 2 vols. (Leicester: Inter-Varsity Press, 1994).

Seow, Choon-Leong, *Ecclesiastes*, AB 18C (New York: Doubleday, 1997).

Shanks, Hershel (ed.), *Ancient Israel: A Short History from Abraham to the Destruction of the Temple* (Washington: BAS, 1989).

Shaw, Ian (ed.), *The Oxford History of Ancient Egypt*, new ed. (Oxford: Oxford University Press, 2003).

Simundson, Daniel J., *Hosea, Joel, Amos, Obadiah, Jonah, Micah*, AbOTC (Nashville: Abingdon, 2005).

Ska, Jean-Louis, *Reading the Pentateuch*, trans. Pasquale Dominique (Winona Lake: Eisenbrauns, 2006).

Smith, Billy K., and Frank S. Page, *Amos, Obadiah, Jonah*, NAC 19b (Nashville: B&H, 1995).

Smith, Gary V., *Hosea, Amos, Micah*, NIVAC (Grand Rapids: Zondervan, 2001).

—— *Isaiah 40–66*, NAC 15B (Nashville: B&H, 2009).

Smith, Ralph L., *Micah–Malachi*, WBC 32 (Waco: Word, 1984).

Smothers, Thomas, 'Biblical Wisdom in Its Ancient Middle Eastern Context', in H. Wayne Ballard Jr. and W. Dennis Tucker Jr. (eds.), *An Introduction to Wisdom Literature and the Psalms: Festschrift Marvin E. Tate* (Macon: Mercer University Press, 2000).

Solomon, Robert C., and David L. Sherman (eds.), *The Blackwell Guide to Continental Philosophy* (Oxford: Blackwell, 2003).

Speiser, E. A., *Genesis*, AB 1 (New York: Doubleday, 1964).

Sternberg, Meir, *The Poetics of Biblical Narrative: Ideological Literature and the Drama of Reading* (Bloomington: Indiana University Press, 1987).

Stiebert, Johanna, *The Exile and the Prophet's Wife: Historic Events and Marginal Perspectives* (Collegeville: Michael Glazier, 2005).

Stiebing, William H. Jr., *Uncovering the Past: A History of Archaeology* (Oxford: Oxford University Press, 1993).

Stuart, Douglas, *Hosea–Jonah*, WBC 31 (Waco: Word, 1987).

Sundberg, Albert C., *The Old Testament of the Early Church*, HTS 20 (Cambridge, Mass.: Harvard University Press; London: Oxford University Press, 1964).

Sweeney, Marvin A., 'Structure, Genre, and Intent in the Book of Habakkuk', *VT* 41.1 (1991), pp. 63–83.

—— *I & II Kings*, OTL (Louisville: Westminster John Knox, 2007).

Sweeney, Marvin A., and Ehud Ben Zvi (eds.), *The Changing Face of Form Criticism for the Twenty-First Century* (Grand Rapids: Eerdmans, 2003).

Taylor, Richard A., and E. Ray Clendenen, *Haggai, Malachi*, NAC 21A (Nashville: B&H, 2004).

Thiele, Edwin R., *Mysterious Numbers of the Hebrew Kings*, 3rd ed. (Grand Rapids: Zondervan, 1983).

Thiselton, Anthony C., *New Horizons in Hermeneutics: The Theory and Practice of Transforming Biblical Reading* (Grand Rapids: Zondervan, 1992).

—— *Thiselton on Hermeneutics: The Collected Works and New Essays of Anthony Thiselton* (Aldershot: Ashgate, 2006).

—— *Hermeneutics: An Introduction* (Grand Rapids: Eerdmans, 2009).

Thompson, John A., *Deuteronomy*, TOTC (Leicester: Inter-Varsity Press, 1974).

—— *Jeremiah*, NICOT (Grand Rapids: Eerdmans, 1980).

Throntveit, Mark A., *Ezra-Nehemiah*, IBC (Louisville: John Knox, 1992).

Tiemeyer, Lena-Sofia and Hans M. Barstad (eds.), *Continuity and Discontinuity: Chronological and Thematic Development in Isaiah 40–66* (Göttingen: Vandenhoeck & Ruprecht, 2014).

Tollington, Janet E., *Tradition and Innovation in Haggai and Zechariah 1–8*, JSOTSup 150 (Sheffield: Sheffield Academic Press, 1993).

Tolmie, Francois, *Narratology and Biblical Narratives: A Practical Guide* (Eugene: Wipf & Stock, 2012).

Tov, Emmanuel, *Textual Criticism of the Hebrew Bible*, 3rd ed. (Minneapolis: Fortress, 2012).

Trible, Phyllis, 'Two Women in a Man's World: A Reading of the Book of Ruth', *Sound* 59.3 (1976), pp. 251–279.

—— *God and the Rhetoric of Sexuality*, OBT (Philadelphia: Fortress, 1978).

—— *Rhetorical Criticism: Context, Method, and the Book of Jonah* (Minneapolis: Augsburg Fortress, 1994).

Troxel, Ronald L., Kelvin G. Friebel and Dennis R. Magary (eds.), *Seeking out the Wisdom of the Ancients: Essays Offered to Honor Michael V. Fox on the Occasion of His Sixty-Fifth Birthday* (Winona Lake: Eisenbrauns, 2005).

Tsumura, David T., *Creation and Destruction: A Reappraisal of the Chaoskampf Theory in the Old Testament* (Winona Lake: Eisenbrauns, 2005).

—— *The First Book of Samuel*, NICOT (Grand Rapids: Eerdmans, 2007).

Tucker, Gene M., *Form Criticism of the Old Testament* (Philadelphia: Fortress, 1971).

Tuell, Steven S., *First and Second Chronicles*, IBC (Louisville: John Knox, 2001).

Turner, Lawrence A., *Announcements of Plot in Genesis*, JSOTSup 96 (Sheffield: Sheffield Academic Press, 1990).

—— *Genesis: Readings* (Sheffield: Phoenix, 2009).

Ulrich, Eugene, 'The Non-Attestation of a Tripartite Canon in 4QMMT', *CBQ* 65 (2003) pp. 202–214.

—— 'Our Sharper Focus on the Bible and Theology Thanks to the Dead Sea Scrolls', *CBQ* 66 (2004), pp. 1–24.

VanderKam, James C., 'Questions of Canon Viewed Through the Dead Sea Scrolls', *BBR* 11.2 (2001), pp. 269–292.

—— *The Dead Sea Scrolls and the Bible* (Grand Rapids: Eerdmans, 2012).

Vanhoozer, Kevin J., *Is There a Meaning in This Text? The Bible, the Reader, and the Morality of Literary Knowledge* (Leicester: Apollos, 1998).

Verhoef, Pieter A., *The Books of Haggai and Malachi*, NICOT (Grand Rapids: Eerdmans, 1987).

Walker, P. W. L. (ed.), *Jerusalem Past and Present in the Purposes of God* (Cambridge: Tyndale House, 1992).

Walsh, Jerome T., *Old Testament Narrative: A Guide to Interpretation* (Louisville: Westminster John Knox, 2010).

Waltke, Bruce K., *The Book of Proverbs*, 2 vols., NICOT (Grand Rapids: Eerdmans, 2004, 2005).

—— *Micah* (Grand Rapids: Eerdmans, 2007).

Walton, John H., *Ancient Israelite Literature in Its Cultural Context: A Survey of Parallels Between Biblical and Ancient Near East Texts* (Grand Rapids: Zondervan, 1989).

—— *Genesis*, NIVAC (Grand Rapids: Zondervan, 2001).

—— *Ancient Near Eastern Thought: Introducing the Conceptual World of the Hebrew Bible* (Grand Rapids: Baker Academic, 2006).

—— *The Lost World of Genesis One: Ancient Cosmology and the Origins Debate* (Downers Grove: InterVarsity Press, 2009).

Watson, Rebecca S., *Chaos Uncreated: A Reassessment of the Theme of 'Chaos' in the Hebrew Bible*, BZAW 341 (Berlin: de Gruyter, 2005).

Watson, Wilfred G. E., *Classical Hebrew Poetry: A Guide to Its Techniques*, JSOTSup 26 (Sheffield: Sheffield Academic Press, 1984).

Watts, Rikki E., *Isaiah's New Exodus in Mark*, BSL (Grand Rapids: Baker Academic, 1997).

Webb, Barry, *Judges*, NICOT (Grand Rapids: Eerdmans, 2012).

Wegner, Paul D., *A Student's Guide to Textual Criticism of the Bible: Its History, Methods and Results* (Downers Grove: IVP Academic, 2006).

Weinfeld, Moshe, *Deuteronomy and the Deuteronomic School* (Oxford: Oxford University Press, 1972).

Weiser, Artur, *Psalms*, OTL (London: SCM Press, 1962).

Wenham, Gordon J., *Leviticus*, NICOT (Grand Rapids: Eerdmans, 1979).

—— *Numbers*, TOTC (Leicester: Inter-Varsity Press; Downers Grove: InterVarsity Press, 1981).

—— 'The Date of Deuteronomy: Linch-pin of Old Testament Criticism. Part One', *Them* 10.3 (1985), pp. 15–20.

—— 'The Date of Deuteronomy: Linch-pin of Old Testament Criticism. Part Two', *Them* 11.1 (1985), pp. 15–18.

—— *Genesis 1–15*, WBC 1 (Waco: Word, 1987).

—— *Genesis 16–50*, WBC 2 (Dallas: Word, 1994).

—— *Exploring the Old Testament*, vol. 1: *The Pentateuch* (London: SPCK, 2003).

Westermann, Claus, *Isaiah 40–66*, OTL (London: SCM Press, 1969).

—— *Praise and Lament in the Psalms* (Atlanta: John Knox, 1981).

—— *Basic Forms of Prophetic Speech* (Cambridge: Lutterworth; Louisville: Westminster John Knox, 1991).

—— *Prophetic Oracles of Salvation in the Old Testament* (Louisville: Westminster John Knox, 1991).

—— *Genesis*, 3 vols., CC (Minneapolis: Fortress, 1994–2002).

—— (ed.), *Essays on Old Testament Interpretation* (London: SCM Press, 1963).

Whybray, R. N., *The Second Isaiah*, OTG (Sheffield: Sheffield Academic Press, 1983).

Wilkinson, Toby, *The Rise and Fall of Ancient Egypt: The History of a Civilisation from 3000 BC to Cleopatra* (London: Bloomsbury, 2010).

Williams, Donald L., 'The Date of Zephaniah', *JBL* 82.1 (1963), pp. 77–88.

Williamson, H. G. M., 'Eschatology in Chronicles', *TynBul* 28 (1977), pp. 115–154.

—— *Ezra, Nehemiah*, WBC 16 (Waco: Word, 1985).

—— *Variations on a Theme: King, Messiah and Servant in the Book of Isaiah*, Didsbury Lectures (Carlisle: Paternoster, 1998).

Wilson, Gerald Henry, 'The Shape of the Book of Psalms', *Int* 46.2 (1992), pp. 129–142.

Wilson, Lindsay, *Job*, THOTC (Grand Rapids: Eerdmans, 2015).

Wilson, Robert R., *Prophecy and Society in Ancient Israel* (Philadelphia: Fortress, 1980).

Wiseman, D. J. (ed.), *Notes on Some Problems in the Book of Daniel* (London: Tyndale, 1965).

Wolff, Hans Walter, *Hosea*, Hermeneia (Philadelphia: Fortress, 1974).

—— *Joel and Amos*, Hermeneia (Philadelphia: Fortress, 1977).

—— *Obadiah and Jonah*, CC (Minneapolis: Fortress, 1986).

Wood, Leon J., *A Survey of Israel's History*, rev. ed. (Grand Rapids: Zondervan, 1986).

Woude, A. S. van der (ed.), *In Quest of the Past: Studies in Israelite Religion, Literature and Prophetism* (Leiden: Brill, 1990).

Würthwein, Ernst, *The Text of the Old Testament: An Introduction to the Biblia Hebraica*, 2nd ed. (Grand Rapids: Eerdmans, 1995).

Yoder, Christine R., *Proverbs*, AbOTC (Nashville: Abingdon, 2009).

Younger, K. Lawson Jr., *Ancient Conquest Accounts: A Study in Ancient Near Eastern and Biblical History Writing*, JSOTSup 98 (Sheffield: JSOT Press, 1990).

—— *Judges, Ruth*, NIVAC (Grand Rapids: Zondervan, 2002).

Zimmerli, Walther, *Ezekiel*, 2 vols., Hermeneia (Philadelphia: Fortress, 1979, 1983).

Zvi, Ehud Ben, *A Historical-Critical Study of the Book of Zephaniah*, BZAW 198 (Berlin: de Gruyter, 1991).

—— *A Historical-Critical Study of the Book of Obadiah*, BZAW 242 (Berlin: de Gruyter, 1996).

INDEX OF MODERN AUTHORS

INDEX OF SUBJECTS

INDEX OF SCRIPTURE REFERENCES

(Please note this list is not exhaustive.)

OLD TESTAMENT

Genesis

Lamentations

Ezekiel